Aristotelian Metaphysics

Aristotelian Metaphysics

Essays in Honour of David Charles

Edited by
DAVID BRONSTEIN
THOMAS KJELLER JOHANSEN
MICHAIL PERAMATZIS

Great Clarendon Street, Oxford, OX2 6DP,
United Kingdom

Oxford University Press is a department of the University of Oxford.
It furthers the University's objective of excellence in research, scholarship,
and education by publishing worldwide. Oxford is a registered trade mark of
Oxford University Press in the UK and in certain other countries

© Oxford University Press 2024

The moral rights of the authors have been asserted

All rights reserved. No part of this publication may be reproduced, stored in
a retrieval system, or transmitted, in any form or by any means, without the
prior permission in writing of Oxford University Press, or as expressly permitted
by law, by licence or under terms agreed with the appropriate reprographics
rights organization. Enquiries concerning reproduction outside the scope of the
above should be sent to the Rights Department, Oxford University Press, at the
address above

You must not circulate this work in any other form
and you must impose this same condition on any acquirer

Published in the United States of America by Oxford University Press
198 Madison Avenue, New York, NY 10016, United States of America

British Library Cataloguing in Publication Data
Data available

Library of Congress Control Number: 2023923357

ISBN 978–0–19–890867–8

DOI: 10.1093/oso/9780198908678.001.0001

Printed and bound by
CPI Group (UK) Ltd, Croydon, CR0 4YY

Links to third party websites are provided by Oxford in good faith and
for information only. Oxford disclaims any responsibility for the materials
contained in any third party website referenced in this work.

To David

Table of Contents

Abbreviations of Aristotle's Texts	ix
List of Contributors	xi
List of Figures	xv
Introduction *David Bronstein, Thomas Kjeller Johansen, and Michail Peramatzis*	xvii
List of David Charles' Publications	xxix

PART I. DEFINITION, MEANING, AND LANGUAGE

1. A Puzzle in Aristotle's Theory of Definition *David Bronstein*	3
2. Antisthenes on Definition: *Metaphysics* H.3 *Marko Malink*	30
3. Focality, Analogy, and the Articulation of Concepts *S. G. Williams*	49
4. David Charles on Wittgenstein, Aristotle, and Artisans *Paul Snowdon*	79

PART II. CATEGORIES, SUBSTANCE, AND ESSENCE

5. Plato's Butcher: Realism and Platonic Classification *Verity Harte*	97
6. Non-substance Individuals in Aristotle's *Categories* *Jennifer Whiting*	120
7. Essential Predication in Aristotle's *Categories*: A Defence *Christof Rapp*	143
8. Aristotle on How Essence Grounds Necessity *Michail Peramatzis*	168

PART III. FORM, MATTER, AND TELEOLOGY

9. Predicative Hylomorphism in *Metaphysics* Z *Mary Louise Gill*	201

viii TABLE OF CONTENTS

10. Aristotelian Matter and 'the Underlier'   227
    Lindsay Judson

11. Matter-Involving Form and Hypothetical Necessity in
    Aristotle's *De Anima*   248
    T. K. Johansen

12. Life, Agency, and Value   270
    James G. Lennox

PART IV. MODALITY, CHANGE, AND SPACE

13. Reflections on Aristotle's Modal Ontology   297
    Kei Chiba

14. How Aristotle Understands Change: A Reading of *Physics* 3.1–3   320
    Frank A. Lewis

15. Aristotle: Processes and Continuants   345
    Ursula Coope

16. Why Is Space Discontinuous? *De Lineis Insecabilibus* 968b5–22   362
    Vassilis Karasmanis

Index Locorum   377
General Index   385

Abbreviations of Aristotle's Texts

APo.	*Posterior Analytics*
APr.	*Prior Analytics*
Cat.	*Categories*
DA	*De Anima*
DC	*De Caelo*
De Int.	*De Interpretatione*
EE	*Eudemian Ethics*
GA	*Generation of Animals*
GC	*On Generation and Corruption*
HA	*History of Animals*
Met.	*Metaphysics*
Meteor.	*Meteorology*
NE	*Nicomachean Ethics*
PA	*Parts of Animals*
Phys.	*Physics*
Pol.	*Politics*
SE	*Sophistical Refutations*
Top.	*Topics*

List of Contributors

David Bronstein is Associate Professor and Senior Research Fellow in the Institute for Ethics and Society at the University of Notre Dame Australia, Sydney, and Australian Research Council Future Fellow (2023–6). He previously held positions at the University of New South Wales, Georgetown University, Boston University, and the University of Oxford. He is the author of *Aristotle on Knowledge and Learning: The* Posterior Analytics (OUP 2016) and several articles on Plato and Aristotle.

Kei Chiba received his D.Phil. in Philosophy from the University of Oxford. He is Emeritus Professor at Hokkaido University and is currently living together with thirty-five students as a master of a Christian dormitory. He is the author of several articles on Aristotle and *Philosophy of Faithfulness: Intellectus ante fidem* (Hokkaido UP 2018), which carries out a semantic analysis of the Apostle Paul's Romans and develops Paul's philosophy of mind from an Aristotelian perspective.

Ursula Coope is Professor of Ancient Philosophy at Oxford University and a Professorial Fellow of Keble College. She is the author of *Time for Aristotle* (OUP 2005) and of *Freedom and Responsibility in Neoplatonist Thought* (OUP 2020). From 2016 to 2022, she was Co-editor of *Phronesis*. She is also the co-editor (with Barbara Sattler) of *Ancient Ethics and the Natural World* (CUP 2021).

Mary Louise Gill is David Benedict Professor of Classics and Philosophy at Brown University. She specializes in the method, natural philosophy, and metaphysics of Plato and Aristotle, and is the author of *Aristotle on Substance: The Paradox of Unity* (Princeton UP 1989), an Introduction and co-translation of *Plato: Parmenides* (Hackett 1996), and *Philosophos: Plato's Missing Dialogue* (OUP 2012). She has also co-edited three collections of papers on Aristotle and ancient philosophy.

Verity Harte is George A. Saden Professor of Philosophy and Classics at Yale University. She is the author of *Plato on Parts and Wholes: The Metaphysics of Structure* (OUP 2002) and editor of *Aristotle and the Stoics Reading Plato* (with M. M. McCabe, R. W. Sharples and Anne Sheppard) (ICS, London 2011), of *Politeia in Greek and Roman Philosophy* (with Melissa Lane) (CUP 2013), and of *Rereading Ancient Philosophy: Old Chestnuts and Sacred Cows* (with Raphael Woolf) (CUP 2017).

Thomas Kjeller Johansen is Professor of Philosophy at the University of Oslo. He was previously Professor of Ancient Philosophy at Oxford and Tutorial Fellow at Brasenose College. He is the author of *Aristotle on the Sense-Organs* (CUP 1997), *Plato's Natural Philosophy* (CUP 2004), and *The Powers of Aristotle's Soul* (OUP 2012).

Lindsay Judson is Professor of Ancient Philosophy at the University of Oxford and an Official Student (Tutorial Fellow) of Christ Church, Oxford. He works mainly on Aristotle and Plato and is the General Editor of the *Clarendon Aristotle Series* and of *Oxford Aristotle*

xii   LIST OF CONTRIBUTORS

Studies. His recent publications include *Aristotle:* Metaphysics Λ: *A Translation and Commentary* (OUP 2019), 'What Is Aristotle's Metaphysics About?', *Phronesis* 2023, 'The Meno', in Gail Fine (ed.), *The Oxford Handbook of Plato*, 2nd edition (OUP 2019), and 'Aristotle and Crossing the Boundaries between the Sciences', *Archiv für Geschichte der Philosophie* 2019.

Vassilis Karasmanis (D.Phil. Oxford) is Emeritus Professor of Philosophy at the National Technical University of Athens, Greece. He specializes in Ancient Philosophy and Ancient Science (mainly mathematics). He has published four books and is the editor of nine volumes, two of which are co-edited and published by Oxford University Press. He has also published fifty-two articles in various philosophical journals or collected volumes. Since 2013 he has been an elected member of the International Federation of Philosophical Societies (FISP).

James G. Lennox is Professor Emeritus of History and Philosophy of Science, University of Pittsburgh. He has published widely on the history and philosophy of biology with a special focus on Aristotle, Charles Darwin, and evolutionary biology. His books include *Aristotle: On the Parts of Animals I–IV*, a translation and commentary in Oxford's Clarendon Aristotle Series (OUP 2001), *Aristotle's Philosophy of Biology* in the Cambridge Studies in Philosophy and Biology Series (CUP 2001), *Aristotle on Inquiry* (CUP 2021), as well as many co-edited volumes, including *Philosophical Issues in Aristotle's Biology* (CUP 1987), *Self-motion from Aristotle to Newton* (Princeton UP 1994), and *Concepts and Their Role in Knowledge: Reflections on Objectivist Epistemology* (Pittsburgh UP 2013).

Frank A. Lewis is Professor Emeritus of Philosophy at the University of Southern California. He taught previously at the University of Arizona and at UCLA; has held visiting positions at Stanford and UCLA; and has twice held fellowships from the American Council of Learned Societies. He is the author of *Substance and Predication in Aristotle* (CUP 1991) and *How Aristotle Gets By in* Metaphysics Zeta (OUP 2013), and with Robert Bolton co-edited *Form, Matter, and Mixture in Aristotle* (Blackwell 1996).

Marko Malink is Professor of Philosophy and Classics at New York University. Previously he held positions at Humboldt University Berlin and the University of Chicago. He has published on ancient philosophy, especially Aristotle's logic and metaphysics, as well as the history of logic, especially Leibniz and the algebraic tradition in logic.

Michail Peramatzis is an Associate Professor at the Philosophy Faculty, University of Oxford, and the Hinton Clarendon Tutorial Fellow in Philosophy at Worcester College. He works on Aristotle's and Plato's theoretical philosophies but also has interests in logic, epistemology, metaphysics, and the philosophy of science. He is the author of *Priority in Aristotle's Metaphysics* (OUP 2011) and many articles on Aristotle and Plato.

Christof Rapp has been Professor of Ancient Philosophy at Ludwig-Maximilians-Universität, Munich, since 2009. From 1993 to 2000, he was Assistant Professor at the University of Tübingen. From 2001 to 2009, he held the Chair of Ancient and Contemporary Philosophy at Humboldt-Universität in Berlin. He has also held visiting positions in Berkeley (2000), Oxford (2008), and Paris (2014). He has authored numerous books and articles on ancient philosophy.

The late **Paul Snowdon** was Grote Professor of the Philosophy of Mind and Logic at University College London from 2001 until his retirement in 2015. From 1971 to 2001 he was tutorial fellow and university lecturer at Exeter College, University of Oxford. He was the author of *Persons, Animals, Ourselves* (OUP 2014) and co-editor of a collection, *Animalism*, with Stephan Blatti (OUP 2016). A collection of his essays on perception is in production from OUP.

Jennifer Whiting is Distinguished Professor of Philosophy at the University of Pittsburgh. She has also taught at Harvard, Cornell, and the University of Toronto. OUP has published two collections of her work on Aristotle: *Living Together: Essays on Aristotle's Ethics* and *Body and Soul: Essays on Aristotle's Hylomorphism*.

S. G. Williams is Emeritus Fellow in Philosophy at Worcester College, Oxford. He is the author of papers in the philosophy of language, metaphysics, and the philosophy of action; and he is the co-editor (with Sabina Lovibond) of *Identity, Truth, and Value: Essays for David Wiggins* (Wiley-Blackwell 1999). He is currently writing a book on homonymy and metaphysics which draws on Aristotelian notions of focality and analogy.

List of Figures

1.1.	First division tree	15
1.2.	Second division tree	15
1.3.	Third division tree	16
1.4.	Fourth division tree	19
1.5.	Fifth division tree	20
1.6.	Sixth division tree	23
1.7.	Seventh division tree	24
1.8.	Eighth division tree	25
5.1.	Three shapes	104

Introduction

David Bronstein, Thomas Kjeller Johansen, and Michail Peramatzis

The aim of the present collection of essays is twofold. First, it seeks to re-examine central themes in Aristotle's metaphysics, understood broadly to include areas such as psychology, biology, and mathematics that develop these themes. Our second aim is to honour and celebrate Professor David Charles' work, which admirably combines historical, textual, and exegetical study with philosophical rigour, precision, and engagement with contemporary debates. Charles' work covers a remarkable scope in Aristotelian studies, from logic and philosophy of language to ethics and natural science. He has also made significant contributions to systematic philosophy on topics such as supervenience, concept possession, and the nature of processes and events. The present collection focuses on a thread that unites the different strands in Charles' writings: Aristotelian metaphysics. Charles has done important work on all the topics covered in this collection, including definition, meaning, essence, substance, hylomorphism, teleology, modality, and change. Moreover, the contributors reflect the wide influence his work has had on colleagues and students alike.

David Charles' first book, *Aristotle's Philosophy of Action* (1984), introduced to a broad philosophical audience topics such as Aristotle's account of the nature of action, the role of desire and belief in explaining action, and the relation between desire and belief, on the one hand, and the physical processes that cause bodily movements, on the other. His *Aristotle on Meaning and Essence* (2000) examined central topics in Aristotle's philosophy of language, theory of science, and metaphysics, offering interpretations of works including *De Interpretatione*, *Posterior Analytics*, *De Anima*, and *Metaphysics* in dialogue with theories of meaning and essence defended by philosophers such as Hilary Putnam. His most recent book, *The Undivided Self: Aristotle and the 'Mind–Body' Problem* (2021), on Aristotle's psychology, argues for a novel interpretation of Aristotle's theory of the soul, and shows its implications for contemporary discussions of the mind–body problem. All three books, and Charles' many published essays, have had an enormous impact on Aristotle scholarship and beyond. He has deservedly been called 'one of the greatest systematizers of Aristotle's philosophy of the past four decades'.[1]

Aristotelian metaphysics is both a central theme of David Charles' work and a topic of great historical and philosophical interest. Aristotle was the first to

---

[1] Reece 2022.

introduce the discipline of metaphysics. He does not view metaphysical inquiry as merely ancillary to science. Nor does he think that it consists simply in clarifying and disabusing us of conceptual confusions. It is distinctive of Aristotelian metaphysics that it has a 'real-world' subject-matter: being itself as such. Moreover, Aristotle identifies what we call 'metaphysics' with wisdom and first philosophy: that is, the primary or basic philosophical subdiscipline. Such a science seeks not to catalogue the different types of existent but to discover and give an account of the fundamental principles and causes of being for every type of existent. Further, it inquires into the features that all types of existent have necessarily and, more importantly, insofar as they are simply existents and not in virtue of being any specific kind of existent or having any characteristics that are peculiar to only some existents.

This distinctive feature of Aristotelian metaphysics is not only a matter of historical interest. It has been revived in contemporary discussions, with different versions of it forming what is aptly called 'neo-Aristotelian' metaphysics. Examples of its proponents include thinkers such as Kit Fine, Kathrin Koslicki, E. J. Lowe, Michael Rea, Peter Simons, and David Wiggins, among many others.[2] The present collection aims to add to this recent resurgence of interest in Aristotelian metaphysics. We hope that it will open and encourage a dialogue between historically oriented thinkers and systematic metaphysicians. This is congenial to David Charles' own view of the inseparability of historical scholarship from contemporary philosophy in an approach he calls 'philosophical scholarship'. In his words, this approach 'aims to represent Aristotle's discussion as focused, where appropriate, on questions which also interest contemporary theorists, and to assess the philosophical significance of his answers by comparing them with solutions put forward today' (1984, ix).

Part I: Definition, Meaning, and Language

In 'A Puzzle in Aristotle's Theory of Definition' David Bronstein focuses on a central theme in David Charles' work on Aristotelian scientific definition: his emphasis on two requirements Aristotle imposes on definition.

Unity: a definition must be unified and not describe an accidental conjunction of essential features.

Explanatory priority: a definition must describe essential features that are explanatorily prior to other necessary (but non-essential) features of the *definiendum*. On this basis, a definition can serve as a starting-point for explanations of such features.

---

[2] For recent collections of essays on neo-Aristotelian metaphysics, see Tahko 2012, Feser 2013, Groff and Greco 2013, and Novotný and Novák 2014.

Bronstein diagnoses a tension between these two requirements. Definable items have many disparate necessary features that the essential features described in a definition ought to be able to explain. Given this plurality of *explananda* it seems inevitable that the definition itself will consist of many terms that pick out a corresponding plurality of essential features. But if this is correct, how are these many essential features unified? Bronstein argues that the tension between the two requirements on definition is evident in Aristotle's discussion of definition by division in *Posterior Analytics* 2.13. Bronstein contends that in this text Aristotle operates with two different and incompatible conceptions of definition, and that this is a result of the difficulty he faces in combining the two requirements on definition.

The nature and structure of definition is also the theme of Marko Malink's 'Antisthenes on Definition: *Metaphysics* H.3'. In *Metaphysics* H.3, Aristotle discusses a difficulty raised by Antisthenes and his followers that aims to undermine the possibility of definition. Aristotle suggests that because of this difficulty the Antistheneans maintained that it is impossible to define what a thing is, though we can specify what a thing is like or what sort of thing it is. While this passage is one of the major sources on the thought of Antisthenes, it has proved difficult to understand. Most importantly, it is not clear what the difficulty raised by the Antistheneans was, and why Aristotle chose to address it in his discussion of hylomorphism in *Metaphysics* H.3. Malink seeks to understand the Antisthenean difficulty by considering the context of Aristotle's discussion of it in *Metaphysics* H.3. In Malink's view, the difficulty derives from an argument according to which any attempt at defining what a thing is leads to an infinite regress of definitions. Malink argues that the Antisthenean argument is based on a compositional model of definition, in which the definition of a thing must mention the constituents of which the thing is composed.

While Aristotle emphasized that definitions, and the things they define, must be strict unities, he also recognized the existence and importance of concepts that are not strictly unified, and he introduced theoretical machinery for treating such concepts. In his 'Focality, Analogy, and the Articulation of Concepts', Stephen Williams studies key aspects of this theoretical machinery from a contemporary perspective. Unlike Plato, Aristotle thought that some of our most important philosophical concepts, such as *being*, *goodness*, and *justice*, were non-unitary. He also detected subtly linked fragmentation within such concepts, and employed analogy and focality to provide the links between the fragments. For he thought that, while there is no strict unity in such concepts, the links provided by analogy and focality indicate whether and when we have a satisfactory, if second-best, sort of unity. Williams advocates a revival of this Aristotelian approach. Using the concepts of knowledge and identity, among others, as case studies, he argues that analogy and focality are tools that can help us uncover and articulate important non-unitary or fragmented philosophical concepts. Williams argues powerfully that this Aristotelian method of conceptual articulation can counter the dismal narrative of the failures of the programme of conceptual analysis in twentieth-century analytic philosophy.

Aristotle sometimes discusses the theme of conceptual unity using examples of practitioners, such as the master craftsperson. Such practitioners, unlike experienced manual labourers, grasp their concepts in a universal and explanatory fashion, even if they are not as epistemically privileged as the scientist or the metaphysician (*Metaphysics* A.1). In 'David Charles on Wittgenstein, Aristotle, and Artisans', Paul Snowdon critically reflects on some ideas that David Charles has formulated in a comparison between Wittgenstein's and Aristotle's views of the unlikely trio of concepts, understanding, and manual workers.[3] Snowdon's main disagreement with Charles is whether the master craftsperson is a clearcut model of realist thinking, as Charles contends. Charles' Aristotle holds that the master craftsperson's grasp of concepts such as 'elm wood' consists (*inter alia*) in understanding part of the nature of the kind *elm wood* as such and that this explanatory grasp richly informs their various craft practices. Snowdon, however, argues that the master craftsperson's practices are compatible with, and thus fail to undermine, Wittgenstein's anti-realist account of language learning and concept mastery.

Part II: Categories, Substance, and Essence

The question of realism is also central to Verity Harte's 'Plato's Butcher: Realism and Platonic Classification'. She examines Plato's approach to classification in the *Phaedrus* and especially the *Philebus*, an approach that is cognate with Aristotelian definition by division into genus and differentia. Contemporary philosophers speak of 'carving nature at the joints', a turn of phrase that picks up, often intentionally, an image from Plato's *Phaedrus* and signals a theorist's commitment to a strong form of realism. While more moderate forms of realism have been developed as interpretations of Aristotle's view, including by David Charles, Plato is widely considered to be the father of strong forms of realism. Indeed, such views are standardly called 'Platonist' realism. Harte studies both the *Phaedrus* passage (265c–266c) and a related passage in Plato's *Philebus* (16c–18d) and seeks to challenge any particularly strong reading of Plato's realism. While she accepts that his classificatory system is presented as being constrained by and tracking reality, she argues that it is also sensitive to the structure of any relevant craft-expertise or skill (*technē*). In her view, this approach can help us understand the picture of reality that underlies Plato's classificatory system and the difficulties, also

---

[3] We were saddened by the news of Paul Snowdon's death during the late stages of preparing the present collection in 2022.

encountered and discussed by Aristotle, in understanding the ontological status of any kind (*genos*) we may attempt to classify.

Reality, for Aristotle, is populated not only by kinds but also by other types of existent. Among them, particular objects such as Socrates (this human) or Bucephalus (this horse)—what are traditionally called 'substances' (*ousiai*)—are metaphysically basic or primary in that other types of existent depend on them and not vice versa. An interesting case of a type of dependent, non-substance entity are non-substance individuals, which are introduced and discussed in Aristotle's work *Categories*. This is the topic of Jennifer Whiting's 'Non-substance Individuals in Aristotle's *Categories*'. There has been much debate about the *Categories*' conception of non-substance individuals. Some commentators (e.g., J. L. Ackrill and Robert Heinaman) argue that such individuals are peculiar to the individual substances to which they belong, so that Socrates' pallor, even if it is qualitatively indistinguishable from that of his identical twin, is numerically distinct from that of his twin. Others (e.g., G. E. L. Owen and Michael Frede) argue that Aristotle allows such individuals to belong to numerically distinct substances. Each side claims to have solid textual evidence in its favour. Whiting defends a hybrid reading, in which different categories admit different conceptions of non-substance individuals, so that one cannot (as Heinaman does) appeal to the fact that non-substance individuals in the category of acting (*poiein*) are action tokens rather than types to support taking non-substance individuals in *all* categories to be peculiar to the individual substances to which they belong. This hybrid account, Whiting argues, does justice to the textual arguments on both sides. It also has important advantages when we turn to other works in Aristotle's corpus. For it provides a conception of what is 'individual and one in number' (*atomon kai hen arithmō(i)*) that does not require spatiotemporal unity (which would make it impossible to understand how an *immaterial* substance such as Aristotle's god could be individual and one in number).

Aristotle's account in the *Categories* of the relation between substances and other types of existent is also Christof Rapp's focus in his 'Essential Predication in Aristotle's *Categories*: A Defence'. Rapp argues that the *Categories* is mostly about classification and is thus a far cry from the *Metaphysics*' much more ambitious project of first philosophy, which aims to identify the first principles and causes of everything. Because of this difference between the two treatises, it is unclear whether we should expect the *Categories* to be defending any genuinely metaphysical position at all, especially if we want to reserve the characterization 'metaphysical' for the kind of project pursued in the *Metaphysics*. Against this background, interpreters have come to doubt whether we should saddle a modest, mostly classificatory project like the *Categories* with the 'heavy metaphysical baggage' or the 'ontologically loaded' notion of essential predication. Rapp, by contrast, argues that the *Categories* does demarcate a type of essential predication—even though, in his view, the essentialism we find in the *Categories* is very different from the metaphysical theory of the *Metaphysics*. Rapp defends the traditional essentialist reading of the *Categories* against a recent heterodox interpretation (advanced by Paolo Crivelli) by offering a careful codification of Aristotle's uses of the key expressions 'said of' (*legesthai kata*, *legesthai* plus genitive) and 'predicated of' (*katēgoreisthai*).

A distinctive commitment of Aristotle's essentialism is that essences are metaphysically basic relative not only to particular substances but also to the substance-kinds that particular substances are essentially the members of. Moreover, they are prior to the characteristic necessary features of particular substances and their kinds. In 'Aristotle on How Essence Grounds Necessity', Michail Peramatzis discusses this issue by engaging with two important themes in Aristotle's theoretical philosophy, both of which are central to David Charles' work. The first is the relation between our knowledge or practice of explaining and that of defining, as well as the correlate underlying bond between cause and essence. The second is Aristotle's view of essence and necessity. Charles summarizes this view as follows: 'the essence is the one cause of all the kind's necessary properties' (2000, 203). Peramatzis argues that Aristotle does not conceive of necessity as primitive or basic. Rather, Aristotle maintains that necessary features of (types of) things are grounded in things' essences. In Aristotle's view, modality quite generally is grounded in essence, while the converse is not the case. After sketching the main aspects of this view, Peramatzis discusses whether and, if so, how Aristotle's essentialism can sustain this claim of asymmetry of essence over necessity. He argues that to underwrite this asymmetry we have to adopt a strong interpretation of Aristotle's thesis that essence (the 'what-it-is') and cause (the 'why-it-is') are the same. Essence and cause are the same or interdependent in that any essence intrinsically involves not only a thin, formal but also a robust, efficient, final, or material type of cause. Conversely, too, at least in the central cases an Aristotelian cause is sensitive to the nature of the relevant item caused (the *explanandum*) in that it determines (at least partly) that item's identity.

Part III: Form, Matter, and Teleology

It is plausible to think that, in Aristotle's view, the metaphysical primacy of essence cannot be addressed simply on the basis of speculative or 'armchair' metaphysical theorizing. Rather, it requires engagement with heavier-duty scientific inquiry. A starting-point for such engagement would be to study Aristotle's hylomorphism, a view that underlies most, if not all, of his scientific projects. Mary Louise Gill's 'Predicative Hylomorphism in *Metaphysics* Z' takes on this task. She contends that the central books of the *Metaphysics* explore two versions of hylomorphism, and that Aristotle settles on the second version. This version of hylomorphism enables him to make progress in answering a fundamental metaphysical question: what entities succeed as primary substances, the things that are most real? Aristotle asks the same question in the *Categories*, and there his answer is clear: individual physical objects, such as Socrates and Bucephalus, are primary substances because they are the basic underlying *subjects*. When he returns to the question about primary substance in the *Metaphysics*, having analysed physical objects into matter and form to explain their generation and destruction in the *Physics*, physical objects are no longer primary, given their composition from matter and form. As Gill reads the first and second stages of the investigation in the *Metaphysics* (Z.3–16 and Z.17–H.5), Aristotle employs what she calls the Predicative Model of hylomorphism, in which matter relates to form in a hylomorphic compound much as a physical object relates to its non-substance properties. In this model, a hylomorphic compound is posterior to its matter and form and is defined with reference to them. The third stage of the investigation, initially broached in Z.12 and developed in H.6 and Θ in terms of potentiality and actuality, employs a different model of hylomorphism, which she calls the Genus-Differentia Model. In it the relation between matter and form resembles the relation between an ordinary genus and differentia specified in the definition of human as 'biped animal'. In her view this new model allows Aristotle to argue that hylomorphic compounds are primary substances definable with reference to their form alone, a conclusion consistent with the simpler scheme in the *Categories*.

While form, for Aristotle, is metaphysically basic, it is not the only item that carries out important explanatory work in his hylomorphism. Lindsay Judson's 'Aristotelian Matter and "the Underlier"' turns to another hylomorphic player—matter—and its role in explaining change. This chapter owes much to David Charles' discussions of Aristotelian matter. It considers two related questions, arising from *Physics* 1.7, *On Generation and Corruption* 1.3, and *Metaphysics* Θ.7–8, and offers different answers from those proposed by Charles.

(1) What is the status of the claim that what underlies (*to hupokeimenon*) persists through the change?

(2) In Aristotle's understanding of matter as potentiality, is the potentiality to become *F* always grounded in some (other) matter, or is this potentiality in certain cases (say, those involving substantial generation) the explanatory bedrock?

On the first question, Judson agrees with Charles that Aristotle thinks that the claim is true even in the case of substantial generation, and that it is not, in his view, an empirical truth. The issue is whether persisting through change is definitional of what underlies (Charles' view) or not (Judson's view). On Judson's reading, what is definitional of the underlier is that it is the subject of a change, whereas the claim that the underlier persists through change is a substantive one based on general considerations about the nature of change. On the second question, in Charles' view, what persists in cases of substantial generation is, simply, the potentiality to become a substance of the relevant kind. As Judson shows, the issues here are partly textual and partly metaphysical: one worry about Charles' view, for instance, is about the direction of fit—whether the sameness of a potentiality is sufficiently robust to explain what is continuous throughout a change if it is not itself grounded in the persistence of some material item.

If both form and matter are metaphysically and explanatorily indispensable in Aristotle's hylomorphism, how are we to understand the priority and posteriority relations between them, and how are we to specify their relations to the compound? Thomas Johansen's 'Matter-Involving Form and Hypothetical Necessity in Aristotle's *De Anima*' takes up these questions as they arise in the context of Aristotle's psychology. For Aristotle, psychological functions, affections, states, and so on are understood analogously to hylomorphic compounds, as consisting of formal and material aspects. For example, anger is a compound of desire for revenge (the formal and teleological aspect) and boiling of the blood and the hot elements around the heart (the material aspect; *De Anima* 1.1, 403a24–b9). In *The Undivided Self: Aristotle on the 'Mind–Body' Problem*, David Charles argues that, in Aristotle's view, a psychological state such as anger is an inextricably psychophysical phenomenon because it has a matter-involving form. Agreeing with this claim, Johansen asks how one should further explicate the involvement of matter. For Charles, the involvement demands an explicit mention of the specific matter of the psychological state in the definition of the form of that state. If so, matter plays a role in defining the form itself, as nose, for example, occurs in the definition of snubness. The alternative Johansen explores is that the specific matter is not present in but follows from the definition of the form. In that case the definition of form, unlike that of snubness, does not explicitly mention matter. Nor, however, is it like the mathematician's account of concavity, which has no implications as to its material realization. Rather, the formal definition of a psychological state may imply a certain material realization by *hypothetical necessity*. Johansen develops this suggestion and considers its strengths against certain objections raised by Charles.

In the example of anger just introduced, we saw that its formal aspect is teleological: anger obtains for the sake of revenge. Aristotle's view more generally is that in the case of artefacts and, more importantly, living beings and their activities, affections, states, etc., a form is (partly) identified with a *telos*. In his 'Life, Agency, and Value' James Lennox discusses David Charles' studies of the relation of goal-oriented beings and processes to normativity in Aristotle and more generally. In particular, Lennox outlines a longstanding disagreement between Charles and Allan Gotthelf over the place of the good in Aristotle's teleology. Lennox compares this debate with recent discussions in the philosophy of biology that seem to suggest that it is necessary to use normative concepts associated with goal-directed agency to characterize properly the activities of living things. As Lennox shows, in light of Charles' and Gotthelf's debate over Aristotle's teleology, these recent discussions have an unmistakable flavour of déjà vu.

Part IV: Modality, Change, and Space

In his hylomorphic theory, Aristotle aligns matter with potentiality (*dunamis*) and form with actuality (*energeia*). In the case of artefacts and living beings, the form or actuality is (partly) identifiable with a *telos*. Moreover, in several places Aristotle suggests that the nature, form, or actuality of living beings is a state of completeness (*entelecheia*), one in which a living being realizes its *telos* (see, e.g., *Metaphysics* Z.17, 1041b28–30; H.3, 1044a6–9; Θ.8, 1050a21–3, b2–3). In 'Reflections on Aristotle's Modal Ontology', Kei Chiba examines the roles of Aristotle's two newly coined technical ontological terms, *entelecheia* and *energeia* (the latter of which Chiba renders 'at-workness'). Chiba examines these terms in connection with three traditional terms that Aristotle inherited from earlier thinkers: *dunamis* ('potentiality'), *ergon* ('work'), and *logos* ('account'). The guiding thought throughout Chiba's discussion is that *entelecheia* is the link between *logos* and *ergon*. In particular, Aristotle uses the term 'completeness' (*entelecheia*) to establish the fundamental connection between a thing's form or substance as what is defined (*logos*) and as what is at work (*ergon*). Moreover, Chiba argues against interpretations that conflate *energeia* with *entelecheia* and that understand Aristotle's modal ontology solely in terms of capacities and their realizations, actualizations, or activities. On Chiba's reading, Aristotle uses the concepts signified by his two new terms, *entelecheia* and *energeia*, to make his ontology subtler and more comprehensive than his predecessors' traditional combinations of work (*ergon*) and potentiality (*dunamis*). Chiba labels Aristotle's investigation conducted in terms of *entelecheia*, *energeia*, and *dunamis* his 'modal ontology'.

A crucial context in which Aristotle deploys his modal ontology is his analysis of change (*kinēsis*) in the *Physics*. This is the focus of Frank Lewis' 'How Aristotle Understands Change: A Reading of *Physics* 3.1–3'. Lewis focuses on an analogy that Aristotle introduces to explain the nature of change. The two sides of the analogy are as follows:

(a) The road up and the road down, together with the road between the two destinations.

(b) The activity of the teacher and the activity of the learner, together with the change that is the student's coming to know that *P*.

The first step in the analogy is to think that just as in (a) the road up is paired with the road down, so in (b) a given episode of the teacher's teaching the learner that *P* is paired with the learner's learning from the teacher that *P*. These pairings are bolstered by the claim that both 'heading up' and 'heading down' on the one hand and the activities of teaching and learning on the other are 'relatives that reciprocate'. From this it follows that there is an intimate metaphysical interdependence between the road up and the corresponding road down, as well as between teaching and learning. Contrary to many alternative readings, Lewis insists that Aristotle does not take a 'projectivist' view of the road up and the road down, in which the distinction between them (as also between teaching and learning) is merely intensional, reflecting different ways of describing or thinking about one and the same thing, without there being any real-world difference between individuals. Contrary to projectivist accounts, Lewis argues that the roads analogy involves relations of sameness—strict sameness in some cases, less-than-strict sameness in others—among real entities, with accidental sameness playing an especially important role in Aristotle's account. Lewis concludes that Aristotle offers a 'two-constituent' analysis of change, in which the activities of teaching and learning combine in the change that is the learner's coming to know that *P*.

Aristotle's account of change is also the topic of Ursula Coope's 'Aristotle: Processes and Continuants'. She discusses David Charles' view that a *kinēsis* corresponds more closely to what we in contemporary philosophy would call a 'process' than to what we would call an 'event'. Charles argues that like a process, but unlike an event, a *kinēsis* (1) has 'modal depth' (meaning that it could have developed differently from the way it in fact did develop) and (2) can take on contrary properties at different times. Coope points out that both of these claims imply that a *kinēsis* is in important respects like an enduring substance or continuant, an implication she closely scrutinizes. She argues that Aristotle's works suggest two different views on the ontological status of *kinēsis*. The *Categories* and *Physics* 5–6 present a view on which, contra Charles, a *kinēsis* is not like an enduring substance or continuant: it is not the kind of thing that can have different properties at different times, nor is it the kind of thing that could have modal depth. However, elsewhere in the *Physics*, Aristotle suggests a different view of *kinēsis*, a view that is compatible with Charles' account. On this second view, Coope argues, a *kinēsis* is still importantly different from an enduring substance or continuant. For unlike a substance, but like an event, a *kinēsis* has temporal parts. Coope concludes that Aristotle's second account of *kinēsis* allows for a category of entity that is neither quite like an enduring substance or continuant nor quite like an event. Such an entity is not, like a substance, present as a whole at each moment at which it exists, but nor is it related to its temporal parts in the way an event is usually taken to be related to its temporal parts.

For Aristotle, natural science studies objects that are metaphysically dependent on matter and change and studies them as such, whereas mathematics studies objects that are metaphysically dependent on matter and change but studies them in abstraction (*Physics* 2.2, 193b33–4). In his 'Why Is Space Discontinuous? *De Lineis Insecabilibus* 968b5–22', Vassilis Karasmanis discusses a question that arises at the intersection of Aristotelian natural science and mathematics: the continuity of magnitude. Karasmanis deals with this question by focusing on a difficult passage from *De Lineis Insecabilibus*. This short pseudo-Aristotelian treatise was written to refute the theory of 'indivisible lines', according to which lines (and therefore magnitudes) are not continuous but are constituted by small, discrete line-atoms. In the *Physics* (206a17) Aristotle mentions this theory *en passant*, saying that 'it is not difficult to refute' it. *De Lineis Insecabilibus* opens with five arguments advanced by the supporters of indivisible lines and then seeks to refute them. Karasmanis focuses on the fifth argument. If correct, this argument would undermine the whole science of geometry. In Karasmanis' view, this argument has been misunderstood not only by the Aristotelian author but also by modern scholars. Karasmanis' first task is to establish which text is to be preferred and how it should be translated. Second, he examines the logical formulation of the argument. Finally, he seeks to show the importance of the argument, and considers plausible ways to escape the difficulties it raises using the Aristotelian theory of the infinite and the continuous.[4]

Works Cited

Charles, David. 1984. *Aristotle's Philosophy of Action*. Duckworth.

Charles, David. 2000. *Aristotle on Meaning and Essence*. Clarendon Press.

Charles, David. 2021. *The Undivided Self: Aristotle and the 'Mind–Body' Problem*. Oxford University Press.

Feser, Edward (ed.). 2013. *Aristotle on Method and Metaphysics*. Palgrave Macmillan.

Groff, Ruth and John Greco (ed.). 2013. *Powers and Capacities in Philosophy: The New Aristotelianism*. Routledge.

Novotný, Daniel D. and Lukáš Novák (eds.). 2014. *Neo-Aristotelian Perspectives in Metaphysics*. Routledge.

Reece, Bryan C. 2022. Review of *The Undivided Self: Aristotle on the 'Mind–Body' Problem* by David Charles. *Notre Dame Philosophical Reviews*.

Tahko, Tuomas E. (ed.). 2012. *Contemporary Aristotelian Metaphysics*. Cambridge University Press.

---

[4] The editors thank Peter Momtchiloff for his help and support in bringing this volume to publication and Demosthenes Patramanis for assistance in preparing the Index Locorum. David Bronstein gratefully acknowledges financial support provided by the Australian Research Council (FT220100615).

List of David Charles' Publications

Monographs

1984. *Aristotle's Philosophy of Action*. Duckworth.
2000. *Aristotle on Meaning and Essence*. Clarendon Press.
2021. *The Undivided Self: Aristotle and the 'Mind–Body Problem'*. Oxford University Press.
In progress. *Aristotle's* Metaphysics: *The Philosophical Project of the Central Books* (with M. Peramatzis).

Edited Volumes

1992. *Reduction, Explanation, and Realism* (with K. Lennon). Clarendon Press.
1994. *Unity, Identity, and Explanation in Aristotle's* Metaphysics (with T. Scaltsas and M. L. Gill). Clarendon Press.
2000. *Aristotle's* Metaphysics Lambda: *Symposium Aristotelicum* (with M. Frede). Clarendon Press.
2001. *Wittgensteinian Themes: Essays in Honour of David Pears* (with W. Child). Clarendon Press.
2010. *Definition in Greek Philosophy*. Oxford University Press.
2023. *The History of Hylomorphism: From Aristotle to Descartes*. Oxford University Press.

Journal Articles and Book Chapters

1983. 'Rationality and Irrationality', *Proceedings of the Aristotelian Society* 83, 191–212.
1986. 'Aristotle: Ontology and Moral Reasoning', *Oxford Studies in Ancient Philosophy* 4, 119–44.
1988a. 'Hypothetical Necessity and Irreducibility', *Pacific Philosophical Quarterly* 69, 1–53.
1988b. 'Perfectionism in Aristotle's Political Theory: Reply to Martha Nussbaum', *Oxford Studies in Ancient Philosophy* (supplementary volume), 185–206. (Reprinted in *Aristoteles' 'Politik': Akten des Xi. Symposium Aristotelicum, Friedrichshafen/Bodensee 25.8–3.9. 1987* (ed. G. Patzig). Vandenhoeck and Ruprecht, 1990.)
1989. 'Intention', in *Cause, Mind, and Reality: Essays Honoring C.B. Martin* (ed. J. Heil). Kluwer, 33–52.
1990. 'Natural Kinds and Natural History', in *Biologie, logique et métaphysique chez Aristote* (ed. D. Devereux and P. Pellegrin). Editions du centre national de la recherche scientifique, 145–67.
1991. 'Aristotle on Substance, Essence and Biological Kinds', *Proceedings of the Boston Colloquium in Ancient Philosophy* 7, 227–62. (Reprinted in *Aristotle: Critical Assessments*, Volume 2 (ed. L. P. Gerson). Routledge 1999, 227–55.)
1992. 'Supervenience, Composition, and Physicalism', in Charles and Lennon (eds.) 1992, 265–96.

XXX   LIST OF DAVID CHARLES' PUBLICATIONS

1994a. 'Aristotle on Names and their Signification', in *Language: Companions to Ancient Thought 3* (ed. S. Everson). Cambridge University Press, 37–74.

1994b. 'Matter and Form: Unity, Persistence, and Identity', in Scaltsas, Charles, and Gill (eds.) 1994, 75–106.

1996. 'Aristotle and Modern Moral Realism', in *Aristotle and Moral Realism* (ed. R. Heinaman). Routledge, 135–72.

1997a. 'Aristotle and the Unity and Essence of Biological Kinds', in *Aristotelische Biologie: Intentionen, Methoden, Ergebnisse* (ed. W. Kullman and S. Follinger). Franz Steiner Verlag, 27–42.

1997b. 'Method and Argument in the Study of Aristotle: A Critical Notice of *The Cambridge Companion to Aristotle*', *Oxford Studies in Ancient Philosophy* 15, 231–57.

1999. 'Aristotle on Well-Being and Intellectual Contemplation', *Proceedings of the Aristotelian Society* 73, 205–23.

2000. '*Metaphysics* Λ 2: Matter and Change', in Frede and Charles (eds.) 2000, 80–110.

2001. 'Wittgenstein's Builders and Aristotle's Craftsmen', in Charles and Child (eds.) 2001, 49–80.

2002. 'Some Comments on Prof. Enrico Berti's "Being and Essence in Contemporary Interpretations of Aristotle"', in *Individuals, Essence and Identity* (ed. A. Bottani, M. Carrara, and P. Giaretta). Kluwer, 109–26.

2004a. 'Simple Genesis and Prime Matter', in *Aristotle's* On Generation and Corruption, *Book I: Symposium Aristotelicum* (ed. F. de Haas and J. Mansfeld). Clarendon Press, 151–69.

2004b. 'Emotion, Cognition and Action', in *Agency and Action* (ed. J. Hyman and H. Steward). Cambridge University Press, 105–36.

2006a. 'Types of Definition in the *Meno*', in *Remembering Socrates: Philosophical Essays* (ed. L. Judson and V. Karasmanis). Clarendon Press, 110–28.

2006b. 'Aristotle's Desire', in *Mind and Modality: Studies in the History of Philosophy in Honour of Simo Knuuttila* (ed. V. Hirvonen, T. Holopainen, and M. Tuominen). Brill, 19–40.

2007. 'Aristotle's Weak *Akrates*: What Does Her Ignorance Consist In?', in Akrasia *in Greek Philosophy* (ed. C. Bobonich and P. Destrée). Brill, 193–214.

2008. 'Aristotle's Psychological Theory', *Proceedings of the Boston Area Colloquium in Ancient Philosophy* 24, 1–29.

2009a. 'Aristotle on Desire and Action', in *Body and Soul in Ancient Philosophy* (ed. D. Frede and B. Reis). De Gruyter, 291–308.

2009b. '*Nicomachean Ethics* VII.3: Varieties of Akrasia', in *Aristotle's* Nicomachean Ethics, *Book VII: Symposium Aristotelicum* (ed. C. Natali). Oxford University Press, 41–71.

2010a. 'The Paradox in the *Meno* and Aristotle's Attempts to Resolve it', in Charles (ed.) 2010, 115–50.

2010b. 'Definition and Explanation in the *Posterior Analytics* and *Metaphysics*', in Charles (ed.) 2010, 286–328.

2010c. '*Metaphysics* Θ.7 and 8: Some Issues Concerning Actuality and Potentiality', in *Being, Nature, and Life in Aristotle: Essays in Honour of Allan Gotthelf* (ed. J. G. Lennox and R. Bolton). Cambridge University Press, 168–97.

2010d. 'Weakness and Impetuosity', in *Mind, Method, and Morality: Essays in Honour of Anthony Kenny* (ed. J. Cottingham and P. Hacker). Oxford University Press, 46–67.

2011a. 'Desire in Action: Aristotle's Move', in *Moral Psychology and Human Action in Aristotle* (ed. M. Pakaluk and G. Pearson). Oxford University Press, 75–93.

2011b. 'Akrasia: The Rest of the Story?', in *Moral Psychology and Human Action in Aristotle* (ed. M. Pakaluk and G. Pearson). Oxford University Press, 187–209.

2011c. '"ΠΡΟΤΑΣΙΣ" in Aristotle's *Prior Analytics*' (with P. Crivelli). *Phronesis* 56, 193–203.

2012a. 'Some Remarks on Substance and Essence in Aristotle's *Metaphysics Z.6*', in *Episteme, etc. Essays in Honour of Jonathan Barnes* (ed. B. Morison and K. Ierodiakonou). Oxford University Press, 151–71.

2012b. 'Teleological Causation', in *The Oxford Handbook of Aristotle* (ed. C. Shields). Oxford University Press, 227–66.

2012c. 'The *Eudemian Ethics* on "the Voluntary"', in *The* Eudemian Ethics *on the Voluntary, Friendship, and Luck* (ed. F. Leigh). Brill, 1–27.

2013. 'Essence, Modality and the Master Craftsman' (with S. Williams), in *Aristotle on Method and Metaphysics* (ed. E. Feser). Palgrave Macmillan, 121–45.

2014. '*Eudaimonia, Theōria*, and the Choiceworthiness of Practical Wisdom', in *Theoria: Studies on the Status and Meaning of Contemplation in Aristotle's Ethics* (ed. P. Destrée and M. Zingano). Peeters, 89–110.

2015a. 'Aristotle on Practical and Theoretical Knowledge', in *Bridging the Gap between Aristotle's Science and Ethics* (ed. D. Henry and K. M. Nielsen). Cambridge University Press, 71–93.

2015b. 'Aristotle on the Highest Good: A New Approach', in *The Highest Good in Aristotle and Kant* (ed. J. Aufderheide and R. M. Bader). Oxford University Press, 60–82.

2015c. 'Aristotle's Processes', in *Aristotle's* Physics: *A Critical Guide* (ed. M. Leunissen). Cambridge University Press, 186–205.

2016. 'Aristotle on Truth-Bearers' (with M. Peramatzis), *Oxford Studies in Ancient Philosophy* 50, 101–41.

2017a. 'Aristotle on Agency', in *The Oxford Handbook of Topics in Philosophy*. Online edition, Oxford Academic. https://doi.org/10.1093/oxfordhb/9780199935314.013.6

2017b. 'Aristotle on Virtue and Happiness', in *The Cambridge Companion to Ancient Ethics* (ed. C. Bobonich). Cambridge University Press, 105–23.

2017c. 'Aristotle's Nicomachean Function Argument: Some Issues', *Philosophical Inquiry* 41, 95–104.

2018a. 'Practical Truth: An Interpretation of Parts of *NE VI*', in *Virtue, Happiness, Knowledge: Themes from the Work of Gail Fine and Terence Irwin* (ed. D. O. Brink, S. S. Meyer, and C. Shields). Oxford University Press, 149–68.

2018b. '*Physics I.7*', in *Aristotle's* Physics I: *A Systematic Exploration* (ed. D. Quarantotto). Cambridge University Press, 178–205.

2018c. 'Processes, Activities, and Actions', in *Process, Action, and Experience* (ed. R. Stout). Oxford University Press, 20–40.

2018d. 'Comments on Aryeh Kosman's *The Activity of Being: An Essay on Aristotle's Ontology*', *European Journal of Philosophy* 26, 860–71.

2019. 'The Fine Shines Through: EN I 8–11', in *Êthikê theôria: studi sull'*Etica nicomachea *in onore di Carlo Natali* (ed. F. Masi, S. Maso, and C. Viano). Edizioni di storia e letteratura, 27–42.

2020. 'Aristotle on the Perception of Objects', in *Aristote et L'âme Humaine: Lectures de* De Anima *III Offertes à Michel Crubellier* (ed. G. Guyomarc'h, C. Louguet, and C. Murgier). Peeters, 19–38.

2023. 'Introduction: The History of Hylomorphism: From Aristotle to Descartes', in Charles (ed.) 2023.

PART I
DEFINITION, MEANING, AND LANGUAGE

1

A Puzzle in Aristotle's Theory of Definition

David Bronstein

Plato had defined human as an animal, biped, and featherless, and was applauded. Diogenes plucked a fowl and brought it into the lecture-room with the words, 'Here is Plato's human'. In consequence of which there was added to the definition, 'having broad nails'. (Diogenes Laertius 6.40, 5–9; Hicks' translation, altered slightly)

Introduction

One of David Charles' most significant contributions to the study of ancient philosophy is his discussion in *Aristotle on Meaning and Essence* of Aristotle's theory of definition and essence.[1] I want to pick up one idea from Charles' deep and sophisticated account and apply it to an important but relatively neglected Aristotelian text. The idea I take from Charles is that the essence of an object must be both (1) a unity and (2) the cause of other necessary features of that object. The text is *Posterior Analytics* 2.13, which contains arguably Aristotle's most important discussion of the method of defining by division. My principal claims are that in *APo.* 2.13 Aristotle is pulled in opposite directions by the two requirements on essence and that, as a result, his account involves a puzzle of significant philosophical interest.

The puzzle is this. Aristotle presents two different and incompatible conceptions of what an essence is and two different conceptions of the method of division corresponding to them. The first conception of essence requires that the items in an essence be of a specific sort. The second requires that the items in an essence stand to each other in a relation of a specific sort. However, the items required by the first conception cannot all stand to each other in the relation required by the second. I hope to show that this puzzle is connected to a difficulty that Aristotle faces in reconciling the two requirements on essence—unity and causality—to which Charles has drawn attention.

I begin with a scholarly dispute about the subject-matter of *APo.* 2.13. I then discuss the two requirements on essence (section 2) and two approaches to

---

[1] See also Charles 2010.

David Bronstein, *A Puzzle in Aristotle's Theory of Definition* In: *Aristotelian Metaphysics: Essays in Honour of David Charles.*
Edited by: David Bronstein, Thomas Kjeller Johansen, and Michail Peramatzis, Oxford University Press.
© Oxford University Press 2024. DOI: 10.1093/oso/9780198908678.003.0001

4   DAVID BRONSTEIN

definition they suggest (section 3). In sections 4–6 I discuss the first conception of essence in *APo.* 2.13 and in sections 7–10 I discuss the second. I conclude in section 11 with the puzzle that results.

1. The Subject-Matter of *APo.* 2.13

APo. 2.13 begins as follows:

[T1]   We stated earlier how the what it is (*to ti estin*) is set out into definitions (*tous horous*)[2] and in what way there is and is not demonstration or definition of it. But let's now discuss how we should hunt out (*thēreuein*) the things predicated in the what it is (*ta en tō(i) ti esti katēgoroumena*).[3,4] (96a20–3)

The first sentence refers back to the catalogue of the types of definition in *APo.* 2.10 and to the method of discovering definitions by demonstration in *APo.* 2.8. The second sentence announces that the present chapter will discuss the method(s) by which we seek ('hunt out') the essence of a thing.[5] It soon becomes clear that the main method on which the chapter focuses is division.[6]

Commentators disagree over two questions about the role of division in 2.13.[7] First, does Aristotle present it as a method for seeking and discovering essences and definitions or merely for displaying essences and definitions sought and discovered by other means?[8] Second, does division (whatever its aim) apply to the

---

[2] Charles (2000, 222) argues persuasively that *horous* in [T1] means 'definitions' not 'terms', which is how some scholars interpret it (see the translations in Barnes 1993, Detel 1993, and Pellegrin 2005; see also Bolton 1993, 208 and Ross 1949, 653).

[3] By 'the things predicated in the what it is' of an object, I take it Aristotle means the essential attributes of that object. In the context of *APo.* 2.13, these are the genus and differentia(e) of that object. By 'the what it is' (*to ti esti*), Aristotle means the essence, which in *APo.* 2.13 he also calls '*ousia*' (see, e.g., 96a34, b6). Throughout 2.13, the expressions '*ti esti*' and '*ousia*' are synonymous and mean 'essence'.

[4] Translations are my own, unless noted otherwise.

[5] Aristotle can move easily between talk of definition and talk of essence because he thinks that to define an object is to answer the 'what is it?' question and that to answer the 'what is it?' question is to formulate the object's real essence. A definition, therefore, is a formula of the real essence of an object: 'A definition is said to be a formula (*logos*) of the what it is (*tou ti esti*)' (*APo.* 2.10, 93a29).

[6] Aristotle also discusses division in *APr.* 1.31 and *APo.* 2.5–6 (where he raises several puzzles, which he then solves in 2.13), in *Met.* Z.12, and in *PA* 1.2–3 (where he is critical of the method of dichotomous division he presents in the *Analytics* and *Metaphysics*; see n. 24 below). I discuss some of the similarities between Aristotle's accounts in *APo.* 2.13 and *Met.* Z.12 below.

[7] On *APo.* 2.13 in general see Bolton 1993, Bronstein 2016, 189–222, Charles 2000, 221–39, Falcon 1997, Ferejohn 1991, 15–32, Goldin 2004, McKirahan 1992, 111–15, and Vlasits 2017, 56–98. For an account of division focusing mainly on the *Metaphysics* and *Parts of Animals*, see Balme 1987. For an earlier discussion, see Lloyd 1961. For an overview of division in Plato and Aristotle, see Deslauriers 2007, 11–42.

[8] Discovery: see, e.g., Barnes 1993, 240, 244, Bronstein 2016, 196–7, Charles 2000, 221–9, and Vlasits 2017, 56, 94–8. Display: see, e.g., Ferejohn 1991, 23–4, Goldin 1996, 88, and Modrak 2001, 93–4.

same definitions Aristotle discusses in *APo.* 2.8—namely, those that have a complex causal structure and are discovered by, and can be represented in, a demonstration, such as the definition of eclipse: 'loss of light from the moon because of the screening of the sun by the earth'—or to different definitions?[9]

Charles has argued powerfully that Aristotle presents division in *APo.* 2.13 as part of the method for discovering definitions by demonstration Aristotle introduces in *APo.* 2.8–10 and, according to Charles, develops in 2.13–18.[10] So Charles sees a role for division in discovering the same definitions discussed in the earlier chapters: namely, definitions that have a complex causal structure and that can be represented in a demonstration, such as the definition of eclipse stated above. I have argued by contrast that in 2.13 Aristotle presents division as a method for discovering a different type of definition—definition by genus and differentia— which applies to a different type of item than the type of item to which the definitions discussed in 2.8–10 apply: not demonstrable attributes but species such as human and horse.[11] These definitions lack a complex causal structure and cannot be represented in a demonstration. The definition of human in *APo.* 2.13 (96b31–5) is an example: 'two-footed tame animal'. So while I agree with Charles that division plays a role in discovery, I disagree about the definitions and essences discovered thereby.

Be that as it may, my aim is not to replay this dispute but to ask the following question. Let's assume for the sake of argument that I am right that the definitions by division Aristotle discusses in *APo.* 2.13 are definitions by genus and differentia, that these definitions apply to species such as human and horse, and that they differ from the demonstrative definitions discussed in *APo.* 2.8–10. Let's also assume that Charles is right that for any definition, the essence formulated therein must be (a) a unity and (b) the cause of other necessary features of the object whose essence it is. The question is, do the essences composed of genus and differentia(e) discussed in 2.13 meet these two conditions?

2. Unity and Causality

Let me first consider the two conditions in more detail, drawing further from Charles' work.[12] For Aristotle, the primary essence-bearers are natural kinds such as human and horse. Take a kind K and its essence E:

---

[9] The same definitions: see, e.g., Charles 2000, 221–9 and Barnes 1993, 240. Different definitions: see, e.g., Bolton 1993, Bronstein 2016, 196–7, and Ross 1949, 633, 656.

[10] Charles 2000, 179–244.

[11] Bronstein 2016, 189–222. See also Ross 1949, 78, 633 and Goldin 1996, 12, 126–41. A similar view is suggested (but not as far as I can tell endorsed) by Gotthelf 2012, 197.

[12] Especially Charles 2000, 179–220.

6 DAVID BRONSTEIN

Unity Condition: E must be a single feature of K or a unified group of features, and not merely an agglomeration of features.

Causality Condition: E must be causally prior to K's other necessary features in that it explains why they belong to K and none of them explains why E belongs to K.

According to Charles, Aristotle lays down the Unity Condition in his discussion, prior to *APo.* 2.13, of certain problems with the method of division.[13] In *APo.* 2.6, Aristotle establishes that, in Charles' words, 'The appropriate method for arriving at definitions should legitimize the claim that the *definiens* is a unity'.[14] In that chapter Aristotle worries that a definition by division such as 'human being is a two-footed terrestrial animal' is not a genuine unity (92a27–33). First, the definition mentions not just one single feature but several different ones. Second, these several features seem like a mere agglomeration—they seem not to constitute any sort of unity. Since Aristotle worries that definitions by division may not be unities, we can see that he is committed to the Unity Condition.[15]

Why is it important, for Aristotle, that the *definiens* (and the essence stated therein) be a unity? The reason has to do with the nature of the objects that are defined and the relationship between an object and its essence. For Aristotle, if a natural kind K is to be defined, then K must be a unity. We can see this in his discussion of the definition of magnanimity in *APo.* 2.13 (97b15–25). Suppose we find that some magnanimous people are characteristically intolerant of insult and others are characteristically indifferent to good and bad fortune. Aristotle states that if these two features do not share some more general feature in common, then we must conclude that magnanimity is not one thing but two and that it therefore requires two separate definitions. So, if a natural kind is to admit of a single definition, then it must be a unity. Furthermore, Aristotle thinks that when we do have a *definiendum* that is a genuine unity, such as the human species, the *definiendum* is unified because its essence is. As Richard Sorabji has put it, an essence does not merely possess unity, it confers unity on the object whose essence it is.[16] Or as Charles puts it, the essence of an object 'underwrites' its unity.[17] Since each object that has an essence is a unity, and is so because of its essence, Aristotle concludes that each essence is a unity.

Let's now consider the Causality Condition. It is of a piece with Aristotle's distinctive form of essentialism. Aristotle famously holds that while all essential attributes of a natural kind K are necessary attributes of K, not all necessary attributes of K are essential attributes of K. If A is a necessary, non-essential attribute of K, then either there is an explanation of why A belongs to K or there is not. If there is

---

[13] See Charles 2000, 191–6 on *APr.* 1.31 and *APo.* 2.5–6.   [14] 2000, 192.
[15] See also *Met.* Z.12 and H.6. For two discussions of these texts, see Code 2010 and Gill 2010.
[16] Sorabji 1980, 194.   [17] Charles 2000, 203.

not, then A belongs to K indemonstrably.[18] If there is, then A belongs to K because of the essence of K. That is, all of the demonstrable necessary, non-essential attributes of K are explained by the essential attributes of K. By contrast, the essential attributes stated in the definition of K are not explained by anything—they belong to K immediately and indemonstrably. Demonstration is the mechanism for displaying the explanations of K's demonstrable necessary, non-essential attributes. A science is partly made up of demonstrations showing that and why certain objects have the demonstrable necessary, non-essential attributes that they have. Definitions are among the first, indemonstrable principles of these demonstrations.

The result of combining the Unity and Causality Conditions is that the essence E of a natural kind K must be unified and explanatorily basic. E must be unified because it must account for K's unity. E must be explanatorily basic because it must be the cause of all of K's demonstrable necessary, non-essential attributes and not caused by any of them (or by anything else). The question I explore in the rest of this chapter is whether definitions by genus and differentia discovered by the method of division can meet these requirements.

3. Defining by Division: Two Approaches

Let's now turn to the sort of definition discussed in *APo.* 2.13: definition by genus and differentia. My aim in this section is to argue that the Unity and Causality Conditions each suggest a different approach to such definitions.

The objects of definitions by genus and differentia are species (e.g., the number three, human). A genus (e.g., animal) is a natural kind that encompasses several species and provides the subject-matter for a distinct science (e.g., biology). A differentia is a feature that qualifies a genus, belongs to one or more species within it, and distinguishes them from one another.[19] It does so by specifying a determinate way of being the genus, a way of being exhibited by all and only those species to which it belongs. For example, *winged* is a differentia of the genus *animal*. As such, being winged is a determinate way of being an animal, a way of being exhibited by all and only those species of animal to which the attribute of being winged belongs. Aristotle holds that each differentia is a differentia of only one genus, which it entails in the following sense: if D is a differentia of the genus

---

[18] For the view that some necessary, non-essential attributes of K belong to K indemonstrably, see Malink 2022, 169 with n. 26. The indemonstrable necessary, non-essential attributes of K cannot be explained to belong to K from K's essence (or otherwise). Hence in the main text I attribute to Aristotle the weaker claim that all demonstrable necessary, non-essential attributes of K belong to K because of K's essence, not the stronger claim, which is sometimes attributed to him (see, e.g., Charles 2000, 203), that all necessary, non-essential attributes of K belong to K because of K's essence.

[19] *Top.* 4.6, 128a20–9.

8 DAVID BRONSTEIN

G, then G belongs to everything to which D belongs (but not vice versa).[20] (That is, for any x, if x is D, then x is G.) Definitions by genus and differentia include some of the most familiar examples of Aristotelian definitions: for example, human being is a rational animal.

We establish definitions by genus and differentia by the method division, which works in two steps. First we distinguish the species from other things in general by selecting its genus. Then we distinguish it from other species in the same genus by selecting differentiae.[21] The goal of defining by division is to mark off the species from all other things by carving out its distinctive niche within the broader kind to which it belongs. There is a question, however, about how Aristotle thinks the definer should accomplish this goal. The question concerns the nature of the differentiae she should seek.

Take the above example: human being is a rational animal. If this is a definition, then all and only humans are rational. In that case, it seems that our aim in defining the human species is to find a differentia that belongs uniquely to the species and thereby defines it: for example, rational. However, not any unique feature will do. Rather, as Aristotle says in the *Metaphysics*, the essence of an object is its form, and a form is that unique feature of an object that provides the fundamental metaphysical ground of its existence: for example, in the case of humans, being rational (or having a rational soul).[22] The conclusion we might draw for Aristotle's theory of definition is that in defining a species the goal is to find *a single unique differentia*, which identifies the species' form and essence and thereby succeeds in defining it.[23] Call this *the single differentia approach* to definition.

Finding a single unique differentia is not the only way of defining by genus and differentia, however. The definer might instead seek several differentiae, which collectively, together with the genus, belong uniquely to the species, but where no single differentia belongs uniquely to it. For example, Plato's definition of human (*Statesman* 266e4–7), mocked by Diogenes of Sinope, as a featherless two-footed animal seems to be a definition of this sort. Humans are not the only featherless animals nor are they the only two-footed ones. They are, however, the only animals that possess both features. And if they are not, as Diogenes' plucked chicken

---

[20] See *Top.* 6.6, 144b12–30 and *APo.* 2.13, 96a24–32 (quoted and discussed below). See also Ackrill 1963, 77, Falcon 1996, and Granger 1981.

[21] *Top.* 6.3, 140a27–8.

[22] See *Met.* Z.7, 1032b1–2, Z.17, 1041b7–9. Aristotle's function argument in *Nicomachean Ethics* 1.7 relies on a similar line of thought. In order to determine what the highest human good is we must determine what the human function is. The human function must be unique to humans, which is why nutrition (shared with plants and non-human animals) and perception (shared with non-human animals) are excluded. But the human function must also be central to what it is to be human—it must be the human form. This leaves rationality as the only candidate. Since the function of a thing is its form and the form is the essence, which is what gets expressed in the definition, rationality is (or is part of) the human essence.

[23] This seems to be Aristotle's recommendation in *Met.* Z.12, which I discuss below.

A PUZZLE IN ARISTOTLE'S THEORY OF DEFINITION   9

perhaps demonstrates, then the attribute Plato allegedly added to the definition, having broad nails, succeeds in repairing it not because humans are the only broad-nailed animals but because we are the only broad-nailed featherless two-footed ones. Understood in this way, the essence of a species does not contain a single unique feature (along with the relevant genus) but rather a unique combination of shared features. Call this *the multiple differentiae approach* to definition. Although perhaps less familiar than the single differentia approach, there is strong evidence for it in our text, *APo.* 2.13, as we shall see.[24]

The single differentia approach is well suited to meeting the Unity Condition on essences. If an essence E is made up of just two items, the genus and a single differentia, then, assuming the differentia is a genuine and determinate way of being the genus (as explained above), we can see how E is a unity. As Aristotle seems to indicate in *Metaphysics* Z.12 (1038a18–26), in a definition of this sort, stating the genus is superfluous, since it is already contained in the differentia. It is not so clear, however, that this approach is well suited to meeting the Causality Condition. For the Causality Condition stipulates that the essence must explain a broad range of the object's features: all of its demonstrable necessary, non-essential attributes. It is difficult to see how a single differentia, combined with the relevant genus, could do this. What is the one, unique differentia of horse that explains all of that species' demonstrable necessary, non-essential attributes? It seems doubtful that any single differentia could fill in the ellipsis in the expression 'a horse is a…animal' in such a way as to meet the Causality Condition. Or consider the above example: 'rational animal' as the definition of human. It seems doubtful that being a rational animal could be the cause of all of the human species' demonstrable necessary, non-essential attributes, such as having two legs, being social, etc. The multiple differentiae approach seems much better suited to meeting the Causality Condition. For the more attributes of a species that the essence needs to explain, the more items we will want the essence to contain so

---

[24] What I am calling the multiple differentiae approach to definition should not be confused with Aristotle's recommendation to divide a genus by multiple differentiae in *PA* 1.3, 643b9–16. (Thanks to Thomas Johansen for raising this issue.) In *PA* 1.3, Aristotle criticizes what he calls 'dichotomous' division, where we attempt to define an indivisible species by applying dichotomous divisions one at a time within a single line of division: for example, in defining human, we divide animal into tame and wild, tame into footed and non-footed, etc. As we shall see below, this is the method Aristotle recommends in *APo.* 2.13. Evidently by the time he writes *PA* 1.3, he has changed his mind. For he now argues that, as David Balme puts it, '[division] must be conducted by a plurality of differentiae applied simultaneously. The genus—e.g. animal—must be differentiated straightaway by all the differentiae that are exhibited by the definiendum. If it is a species of bird, then it is biped, winged, has beak, neck, tail, etc; these are its generic differentiae. Having stated all of these, we must then further differentiate each—the legs are long/short, the wings are broad/narrow and long/short, etc.—until the species is uniquely characterized' (Balme 1987, 73). Thus the claim in *PA* 1.3, 643b9–16 is that each indivisible species is to be defined by multiple differentiae appearing in multiple lines of division, whereas the claim I will attribute to at least part of *APo.* 2.13 is that each indivisible species is to be defined by multiple differentiae appearing in a single line of division. It is the latter that I am calling the multiple differentiae approach to definition.

10   DAVID BRONSTEIN

as to ensure that it achieves the required explanatory coverage. If a horse is essentially an A, B, C, D, E, F animal, then each of these seven (counting animal) features can in principle do some explanatory work and make a contribution to the essence's overall explanatory power.[25] Similarly if a human is essentially a two-footed wingless mortal animal. The problem with the multiple differentiae approach, however, is that it is difficult to see how the proposed essences meet the Unity Condition. For what is it that makes two-footed, wingless, mortal, and animal one?

In this section I have argued that the Unity and Causality Conditions each seem suited to a different approach to defining by division. The Causality Condition speaks in favour of the multiple differentiae approach, the Unity Condition in favour of the single differentia approach. The single differentia approach yields essences that are unified but do not seem sufficiently explanatorily powerful. The multiple differentiae approach yields essences that may be explanatorily powerful but do not seem sufficiently unified. My claim is not that the two conditions are in principle irreconcilable. My claim is only that there is a *prima facie* tension between the two approaches to definition that the two conditions suggest. And in my view *APo.* 2.13 is profitably read with this tension in mind.

4. The D Attribute Rule

Let's turn now to *APo.* 2.13.[26] Throughout the chapter, Aristotle explains how to seek the essences of species by the method of division. In this section and the following two, I discuss the first conception of essence and division we get in *APo.* 2.13, suggesting that it is aligned with the Causality Condition and the multiple differentiae approach. In section 7, I turn to the second conception of essence and division, arguing that here Aristotle tries but fails to reconcile the two conditions and approaches.

Aristotle's first move is to introduce a type of attribute that will play a crucial role in the first part of his account:

[T2]   Of the things that belong always to each thing, some extend further, but not outside of the genus. By extending further I mean whatever belongs universally to each thing but also to another thing. For example, there is

---

[25] The claim is not that, for any given demonstrable necessary, non-essential attribute P of an indivisible species S, the more essential attributes S possesses, the more essential attributes explain P. The claim is rather that different essential attributes are likely to explain different demonstrable necessary, non-essential attributes—thus the more essential attributes, the more explanatory coverage, at least potentially. I am grateful to Michael Peramatzis for raising this issue.

[26] Sections 4–6 summarize and build on my discussion in Bronstein 2016, 199–210.

something that belongs to every three but also to what is not three: being belongs to three but also to what is not a number, but odd belongs both to every three and extends beyond it, for it also belongs to five. But [odd] does not [extend] outside the genus [of number]. For five is a number, and nothing outside of number is odd. (96a24–32)

The type of attribute that belongs universally to one thing and extends beyond it but not outside the genus I will call a D attribute:

D attribute: D_x is a D attribute within a genus G if and only if D_x belongs universally to at least two indivisible species of G and to nothing outside of G.[27]

For example, odd belongs universally to three, and to other numbers (five, seven, etc.), but it does not belong to anything that is not a number. So odd is a D attribute within the genus number. D attributes include differentiae, such as odd. But they also include genera: since number belongs universally to three and to other numbers but not to anything that is not a number, number is a D attribute within the genus number.[28]

Aristotle's next move is to introduce a rule for discovering the essences and definitions of indivisible species:

[T3]   We should take things of this sort [namely, D attributes] up to the point at which we have first taken just so many that, while each extends further [than the object], all [of them together] do not extend further; for this must be the essence (*ousian*) of the object. For example, number belongs to all threes, and so do odd and prime (in both senses—both as not being measured by number [= $prime_1$] and as not being compounded from numbers [= $prime_2$][29]). This, then, is exactly what three is: a number that is odd, prime [= $prime_1$], and prime in this sense [= $prime_2$]. [Taking] each of these [severally], some also belong to all odds, and the last [two] belong to two, but all belong to nothing [other than three]. (96a32–b1)

The rule is that in seeking the essence of an indivisible species S we should select D attributes until the first point at which the conjunction of the D attributes we have selected belongs universally only to S. Since each D attribute must extend

---

[27] At *Top.* 6.3, 140a27–32 Aristotle states that a definition should not contain any items (apart from the genus) that apply to all things in the same genus. Below I note that both genera and differentiae are D attributes. If a D attribute D_x is a differentia of a genus G, we should add that D_x does not belong to every indivisible species of G.

[28] At *Top.* 1.8, 103b12–16, Aristotle says that the genus and the differentia each extend beyond the species to be defined. Thus according to *Top.* 1.8, genera and differentiae are D attributes.

[29] A number is $prime_1$ iff it is not the product of two whole numbers. A number is $prime_2$ iff it is not the sum of two whole numbers. (For Aristotle, one is not a number.)

12 DAVID BRONSTEIN

beyond S (i.e., belong universally to at least one other indivisible species within the same genus as S), we are looking for the first set of D attributes that conjunctively belong universally only to S but severally extend beyond it. For example, applying the rule yields the following as the essence of three: prime$_2$ prime$_1$ odd number. Stated more precisely, the rule is as follows:

D Attribute Rule: In defining an indivisible species S by the conjunction of the members of set E {D$_1$,..., D$_n$}, ensure that (a) each member of E is a D attribute within the genus that encompasses S, (b) the conjunction of the members of E belongs universally only to S, and (c) E is the first set of D attributes, the conjunction of which belongs universally only to S, that you obtain.

Aristotle clearly thinks that correctly applying the D Attribute Rule is sufficient for obtaining the essence. In [T3], he says that 'this must be the essence (*ousian*) of the object' (96a34–5) and 'this is exactly what three is' (96a37–8). A few lines below he offers an argument that begins 'that it is the essence (*ousia*) [of three] is clear from the following' (96b6).[30] He also thinks that correctly applying the D Attribute Rule is necessary for obtaining the essence. At the start of [T3], he says: 'We should take things of this sort [namely, D attributes] (*ta...toiauta lēpteon*)'. The impersonal construction with the verbal adjective *-teon* is equivalent to *dei*, 'it is necessary'.[31] Thus the opening sentence of [T3] has strong modal force: it is necessary to take only D attributes until the first point at which their conjunction belongs universally only to the indivisible species to be defined. Aristotle's claim is not that if we are attempting to obtain the essence and we are limiting ourselves to D attributes, then we must select them until we reach the point mentioned. His claim is that if we are attempting to obtain the essence, then we must limit ourselves to D attributes and select them until we reach the point mentioned. Correctly applying the D Attribute Rule is not only sufficient but also necessary for obtaining the essence. Whether this claim is philosophically plausible, and whether it is consistent with Aristotle's other commitments, are two of the main questions I raise in this chapter.

The D Attribute Rule stipulates that we define using only shared features. This tells us something important about how Aristotle (here) sees the task of defining: he is committed to the multiple differentiae approach. In every essence that conforms to the rule, the differentiae and the genus are D attributes. Therefore, every combination of a genus and a single differentia belongs to at least two indivisible species. For every differentia, in virtue of being a D attribute, belongs to at least two indivisible species. Therefore, no combination of a genus and a single differentia is the essence of any indivisible species. Rather, the

---

[30] See also 97a19: 'one will have the account of the essence (*ousia*)'.   [31] Smyth 1956, 933b.

essence of every indivisible species is made up of at least three attributes: the genus and at least two differentiae. The single differentia approach to definition is ruled out.

This has some significant consequences. Notably, rational animal cannot be the essence of human. If humans are the only rational animals, then rational is not a D attribute and so it cannot be part of the essence. And if humans are not the only rational animals, then this does not uniquely define the species.[32] So [T2–3] rule out one of the most familiar Aristotelian definitions. Indeed, they rule out a whole familiar approach to definition. For according to the D Attribute Rule *no* attribute of an indivisible species unique to it can be part of its essence. To define human (or any other indivisible species) is not to find the one feature that makes humans different from all other animals. It is rather to find the one set of features each of which makes humans the same as other animals but collectively make them different. So Aristotle, in [T2–3], favours the multiple differentiae approach to definition: the definer aims not at a unique feature but at a unique combination of shared features.

What might have motivated Aristotle to introduce the D Attribute Rule? I suggest that one factor might have been the Causality Condition. For the D Attribute Rule guarantees that the essence of an indivisible species will contain at least two differentiae, in addition to the genus, and, as I suggested above, essences with more than one differentia are more likely to meet the Causality Condition than are essences with only one differentia. My claim is not that there is a direct line from the Causality Condition to the D Attribute Rule. My claim is rather that these two aspects of Aristotle's theory share this in common: they both point in the direction of the multiple differentiae approach to definition, as opposed to the single differentia approach.

The D Attribute Rule seems to fit well with the Causality Condition. It does not, however, seem to fit well with the Unity Condition. For it is not clear that an essence composed of a genus and multiple differentiae possesses the requisite unity. If, for example, the essence of three is prime$_2$ prime$_1$ odd number, why think that being three is just one thing and not many—being a prime$_2$ number, being a prime$_1$ number, and being an odd number? I will return to this worry in section 6, but I first want to say more about the method of division.

---

[32] It will not help to suppose that humans are the only rational *animals* and that some non-animals are rational. For then rational will not be a D attribute, given that each D attribute, if it is a differentia, belongs to only one genus. Now rational mortal animal may conform to the D Attribute Rule and succeed as a definition of human being, provided there are rational immortal animals (i.e., the gods). However, this definition departs from the single differentia approach: we are no longer defining the human species by a single attribute (in addition to the genus) that belongs uniquely to us. Therefore, the worry about unity, raised above, reappears: it seems that to be human is to be two different things, a rational animal and a mortal one.

14 DAVID BRONSTEIN

5. Exhaustive Division

In [T2–3] Aristotle says what an essence is. Later in *APo.* 2.13 he argues that division ensures that no essential attributes are omitted from the essence:

[T4]   Next, only in this way [namely, by making divisions] is it possible to omit nothing from the what it is (*tō(i) ti estin*). For whenever the first kind has been taken, if one then takes one of the lower divisions, not everything will fall into it. For example, not every animal is either whole-winged or split-winged; rather, every winged animal is (for it is this of which this is a difference). A first difference of animal is that into which every animal falls. And similarly for everything else, both the kinds outside it and the [kinds] under it. For example, [the first difference] of bird is that into which every bird [falls], and [the first difference] of fish is that into which every fish [falls]. If one proceeds in this way one can know that nothing has been omitted: otherwise it is inevitable that one will omit something without knowing it. (96b35–97a6; Barnes' translation, altered slightly)

Division ensures that no essential attributes are omitted from the essence, if the divisions are exhaustive—that is, if everything in the kind that is divided falls into the sub-kinds marked out by the differentiae that divide it. Let 'G' stand for any kind that admits of division, whether it is the highest relevant genus or a sub-kind of that genus:

Exhaustive Division: D_1/D_2 is an exhaustive division of G if and only if all Gs are either D_1 or D_2 (and some Gs are D_1 and some are D_2 and none are both).[33]

To illustrate exhaustive division, let's take the essence of human that Aristotle presents just before [T4], at 96b31–5: two-footed tame animal. It is derived from the set of divisions shown in Figure 1.1.[34]

There are several things to notice here. First, we are to assume that each division is exhaustive: all animals are tame or wild; all tame animals are footed or non-footed, and so on. Second, the method of exhaustive division permits us to employ the same pair of differentiae in more than one part of the tree. For example, we can use footed/non-footed as an exhaustive division of both tame animal and wild animal; we can similarly use two-/four-footed (Figure 1.2).

---

[33] In *APo.* 2.13, Aristotle also discusses exhaustive division at 97a14–22 and 35–7.
[34] Non-footed and other privative differentiae might seem not to entail their respective genera. (It might seem that some non-footed things are not animals.) However, Aristotle could stipulate that the only species capable of being non-footed are members of a genus some of whose members are footed. In general, if non-D is a differentia of a genus G, then D is a differentia of G.

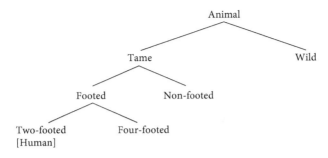

Figure 1.1 First division tree

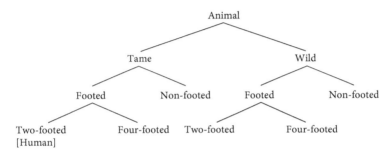

Figure 1.2 Second division tree

This is just what we would want, if our divisions are to carve up the genus accurately and reveal the natural kinds it contains. For all tame animals *and* all wild animals are footed or non-footed, and all footed tame animals *and* all footed wild animals are two-footed or four-footed (let's suppose). In addition, adding the same divisions to wild animal allows us to see that the final differentia in the human essence (two-footed) is a D attribute. For there are other indivisible species to which it belongs: whichever fall under two-footed footed wild animal. Indeed, the method of exhaustive division permits every final differentia in a given line of division to be a D attribute. For the method permits any differentia-pair that appears in one line of division to appear in a different line of division within the same genus.

6. Worries about Exhaustive Division

There is a problem with our division tree, however. Although each division is exhaustive, it is not obvious that this tree represents the only order in which we might apply the same set of divisions and reach the essence of human. Consider an alternative tree, shown in Figure 1.3.

16 DAVID BRONSTEIN

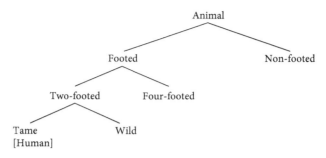

Figure 1.3 Third division tree

Just as with the previous tree, each division is exhaustive. In addition, this version of the human essence contains the same D attributes, although they are arranged differently: human being is a tame two-footed animal. For Aristotle, the order of the attributes in an essence matters: the same attributes placed in two different orders yield two different essences.[35] He thinks that each species has only one correctly ordered essence, which we obtain via the method of exhaustive division. Therefore, there must be a problem with the second division tree and the differently ordered essence it yields. But what is the problem? What reason do we have to prefer the first? We might think the answer lies in Aristotle's account of a differentia as a determinate way of being that which it helps divide. As he says in *Metaphysics* Z.12 (1038a9–10), the differentia must be a differentia of the differentia (or of the genus). But this only introduces the problem anew: what grounds does Aristotle have for saying, for example, that being footed is a determinate way of being tame and not-vice versa? What secures the asymmetry? Since each of the two differentiae, when paired with its contrary, exhaustively divides the kind marked off by the other differentia, Aristotle's method of exhaustive division alone cannot help us determine which of the two essences is the correct one or why. But there can be only one correct essence, so Aristotle needs to supplement exhaustive division with some other principle. What is it?

There is another problem: our candidate for the human essence, two-footed tame animal, is not sufficiently unified. Each of the two differentiae is a determinate way of being the genus, animal, and, it is plausible to assume, entails it. So two-footed-animal and tame-animal each seems to be a unity. In addition, since the essence contains two differentiae, the essence is more likely to be able to meet the explanatory burden placed on it by the Causality Condition than it would be if it contained just one differentia. The problem is that it is not clear how two-footed and tame form a unity. Being human seems to be two things, not one.

---

[35] See 96b25–35. See also *Met.* Z.12, 1038a30–5.

These worries indicate what we should look for in the rest of *APo.* 2.13. To meet the Unity and Causality Conditions, a given essence must be both unified and explanatorily powerful. To be unified, it must be one. To be explanatorily powerful, it must be many. Aristotle needs to show how it can be both. The two conditions could both be met and made consistent with the D Attribute Rule, if Aristotle could show how an essence is a complex unity composed of a genus and multiple differentiae all of which are D attributes related in such a way as to form a unity. Since such essences would contain only D attributes, they would conform to the D Attribute Rule (provided the other conditions are met), thus guaranteeing multiple differentiae. Since they would contain multiple differentiae, they would have a good chance of meeting the Causality Condition. And since they would be unified, they would meet the Unity Condition. In the remaining sections I shall argue that Aristotle attempts to present a conception of essence with just these features, but that he fails in one crucial respect.

7. The Entailment Requirement

In the second half of *APo.* 2.13, Aristotle returns to the question of the structure and arrangement of the essence. His account begins:

[T5]   In constructing a definition through divisions it is necessary to aim at three things: to grasp the things predicated in the what it is (*en tō(i) ti esti*), to order these, which is first and second, and to grasp that these are all [the things predicated in the what it is]. (97a23–6)

The definer's aim is to discover the essence. Her search is successful only if she finds all of the attributes in the essence *and* grasps their correct order. As Aristotle immediately goes on to say (97a26–8), discovering the essence of a species requires in the first place correctly identifying its genus and dividing it correctly.[36] So far his account is consistent with his previous discussion. However, his discussion of the second task (correctly ordering the attributes) is not, as I will eventually try to show.

About the second task Aristotle says this:

[T6]   You will order [the things predicated in the what it is] as you should if you take the first one; and you will do this if you take the one that follows all the others but is not followed by them all (there must be some such thing). Once this is taken, the same now goes for the lower ones: the second will be the one that is first of the others, and the third the one that is first of the next group

---

[36] See Ross 1949, 660.

18   DAVID BRONSTEIN

> (if the topmost one is removed, the next will be first of the others). Similarly
> in the remaining cases. (97a28–34; Barnes' translation, altered slightly)

In the scenario Aristotle has in mind, a definer has before her all of the attributes in the essence. The question is, how can she know whether she has ordered them correctly? Or again, if she has selected the attributes by means of division, how can she know whether she has divided and selected correctly? Aristotle's recommendation is this. Suppose the species defined is human and the attributes in the essence are animal, two-footed, tame, and footed. Start with the first attribute, the genus. To know which one this is, find the attribute that is such that it belongs universally to all of the other attributes but none of the others belongs universally to it (i.e., find the one that 'follows all the others but is not followed by them').[37] Only animal passes both parts of the test:

All two-footed things, all footed things, and all tame things are animals.

But:

Not all animals are two-footed, not all animals are footed, and not all animals are tame.

Now apply the same test in order to determine which is the second attribute. That is, find the attribute that is such that it belongs universally to any remaining attributes but they do not belong universally to it. It is tame:

All two-footed things and all footed things are tame (let's suppose).[38]

But:

Not all tame things are two-footed and not all tame things are footed.

Continue with the third attribute, footed:

All two-footed things are footed.

But:

Not all footed things are two-footed.

This leaves two-footed as the final attribute in the essence, the final differentia. Each of the other three attributes belongs universally to it, but it does not belong

---

[37] 'Follows' (akolouthei) is a standard term in Aristotle's logic synonymous with 'belongs to' (huparchei). (See, e.g., APr. 1.4, 26a2.)

[38] This is clearly false: some two-footed things are wild. As we shall see, there are a number of other false claims generated by the proposed essence. So there is clearly a problem with fitting two-footed (footed) tame animal—Aristotle's own example of an essence—into his discussion in this part of 2.13, although this essence does fit well with his previous account in [T2–4]. This illustrates the point I eventually want to make: the proposed essence fits with one part of the text but not the other because the two texts contain different and incompatible conceptions of what an essence is. The same is true of the essence of three Aristotle proposes in [T3].

universally to any of them. We now know the attributes' proper order and so we know the human essence: two-footed footed tame animal.

One feature of this essence to notice is that, reading left to right (or, looking at the relevant division tree, bottom to top), each attribute entails the one next to (or above) it, if there is one, so that the left-most (or bottom-most) one, two-footed, entails all the rest. (I take it that one attribute B entails another A iff A belongs to everything to which B belongs.) Two-footed entails footed, which entails tame, which entails animal. Hence two-footed, the final differentia, entails footed, tame, and animal. I will call this 'the Entailment Requirement':

Entailment Requirement: The attributes in the essence of a species must form an ordered series in which the prior attribute entails the posterior attribute, if there is one, and not vice versa.

This is a strong requirement. It holds that in any essence of a species S of the form $D_3 D_2 D_1 G$, where G is S's genus and D_1 etc. are its differentiae, everything D_3 is D_2 and not vice versa, everything D_2 is D_1 and not vice versa, and everything D_1 is G and not vice versa. These asymmetric relations of entailment determine the proper order of the items in the essence.

On a different reading of [T6], Aristotle presents a considerably weaker requirement.[39] Start with the fact that in the method of division we divide a genus not into differentiae but into species by means of differentiae.

For example, in Figure 1.4 we divide the genus animal into two species by means of the differentia-pair tame/wild: the species tame animal and the species wild animal. Each of these species is constituted by the conjunction of the genus animal and the relevant differentia (tame or wild). We then divide the species tame animal into two species by means of the differentia-pair footed/non-footed: the species footed tame animal and the species non-footed tame animal. Each of these species is constituted by the conjunction of the species tame animal and the relevant differentia (footed or non-footed). We can represent this as shown in Figure 1.5.

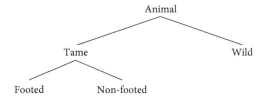

Figure 1.4 Fourth division tree

---

[39] See Vlasits (2017, 89–93) for an interpretation along these lines. Vlasits uses this interpretation as the basis for a solution to the problem I raise below. However, since, as I argue in the main text, this interpretation of [T6] should not be accepted, the solution will not work.

20 DAVID BRONSTEIN

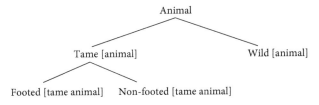

Figure 1.5 Fifth division tree

Now suppose that the items that are to be ordered according to the procedure Aristotle recommends in [T6] are such species (in addition to the genus). In that case, the Entailment Requirement is trivially satisfied. For example, footed entails tame because footed is a species constituted by the conjunction of (i) footed and (ii) the species constituted by the conjunction of tame and animal, and this conjunction entails the species constituted by the conjunction of tame and animal, and hence it entails tame. Put more simply, footed entails tame because footed is the conjunction of footed, tame, and animal, and this conjunction entails tame. Notice that it does not follow from this that footed entails tame in the stronger way I presented above: that is, it does not follow (although neither is it ruled out) that all footed things are tame things. On this reading, then, the Entailment Requirement is significantly weakened: it is possible both for footed to entail tame in the way just described and for some footed things not to be tame things. In this way, the requirement, so interpreted, is consistent with exhaustive division.[40]

There are two reasons why the Entailment Requirement should not be interpreted in this weaker way.

First, if we take [T5] and [T6] together, it is clear that the items that are to be ordered according to the procedure Aristotle recommends in [T6] are 'the things predicated in the what it is'. However, it is clear from the *Topics* that these are the genera and differentiae of species, not species themselves. This indicates that we should interpret, for example, footed not as the conjunction of footed, tame, and animal but as the attribute of being footed, which may or may not be conjoined with tame and animal.

Second, the proposed interpretation renders the Entailment Requirement otiose. To see this, imagine we are presented with three items—A, B, and C—that are predicated in the essence of a species, and we are asked to determine their order by using the procedure recommended in [T6] as understood on the weaker reading. To do so would consist in determining which of these items is the genus and which are species constituted by the conjunction of the genus and one or more differentiae. However, the Entailment Requirement, so understood, gives no

---

[40] This is significant for reasons that will be soon be apparent: the stronger interpretation of the requirement I have proposed is not consistent with exhaustive division. But, as I now argue in the main text, other considerations rule out the weaker interpretation.

guidance as to how to accomplish this over and above the recommendations that Aristotle states elsewhere in the text and that I have set out above. [T6], so understood, amounts to saying that to determine the proper order of the items in an essence, figure out what is a species of what by figuring out what is a differentia of what. But how to do this, [T6] does not say. If this is right, then [T6] disappoints. For it has the appearance of saying something new and significant, but this is cancelled out on the weaker reading.

For these reasons, we should interpret the procedure recommended in [T6] as involving the strong entailment requirement that I have presented. As we shall see, however, its strength causes difficulties for the overall coherence of Aristotle's account.

8. Answering the Worries

The Entailment Requirement seems to be the principle missing from Aristotle's account of exhaustive division. The worry was that exhaustive division alone is insufficient to secure the required asymmetries among the attributes in an essence and ground the claim that, for example, footed is a differentia of tame and not vice versa. The Entailment Requirement secures the asymmetries: footed is a differentia of tame and not vice versa because, in addition to the fact that footed is part of an exhaustive division of tame, it is also the case (let's suppose) that being footed entails being tame and not vice versa. As such, being footed serves as a determinate way of being tame (and not vice versa). So Aristotle has principled grounds for preferring one candidate for the human essence over the other: two-footed (footed) tame animal is right and tame two-footed (footed) animal is wrong because in the first but not the second each posterior attribute entails each prior attribute (if there is one) and not vice versa.

In addition, the Entailment Requirement addresses the problem of the unity of the essence. It is not the case that the human essence is several things, being two-footed, being footed, being tame, and being an animal. For being two-footed entails being footed, being tame, and being an animal. The parts of the human essence form a unity because the final differentia entails the other essential attributes. In this way the human essence is one thing—two-footed—but also many, since being two-footed entails the other essential attributes. These other attributes are not other candidates for the human essence; rather, they are of a piece with the determinate way of being that is being two-footed. And since being two-footed is a single thing, the essence possesses the unity required to account for the unity of the species. So we can see how essences that conform to the Entailment Requirement will meet the Unity Condition.

The Entailment Requirement also seems to show how the essence can meet the Causality Condition. The explanatory burden is distributed among all of the species' essential attributes. Some of the human species' demonstrable necessary,

22 DAVID BRONSTEIN

non-essential attributes are explained by two-footed; some by footed; some by tame; some by animal. But since three of these attributes converge on, and are entailed by, a single attribute, two-footed, the essence achieves explanatory coverage without sacrificing unity.

In sum, if we can combine the Entailment Requirement with the D Attribute Rule, we can unite the two approaches to definition we had previously found to be in tension. In one way, Aristotle favours the multiple differentiae approach: the final differentia defines the species only in conjunction with the other attributes in the essence. In another way, he favours the single differentia approach: the other attributes converge on, and are entailed by, the crucial final differentia. Thus Aristotelian essences can be both unified and explanatorily powerful. They are explanatorily powerful because they are guaranteed by the D Attribute Rule to contain several differentiae, each of which carries some of the explanatory burden. But they are also unified because the Entailment Requirement ensures that the final differentia is a single feature that entails the rest.

It is worth noting that Aristotle's account in [T5-6] is similar to *Metaphysics* Z.12, a chapter that explicitly mentions the account of division in the *Analytics* (1037b8-9, 27-9). In Z.12 Aristotle states that the entailment requirement is a feature of essences obtained by division and that it ensures the unity of the essence (1038a9-34). He calls the final differentia the essence (*ousia*), the definition (*horismos*), and the form (*eidos*) of the species (1038a19-20, 25).

I have argued that if we can combine the Entailment Requirement with the D Attribute Rule, then Aristotle's two approaches to definition—single differentia vs. multiple differentiae—can be united and his two conditions on essences—unity and causality—can be met. But can we combine them? In particular, are all of the attributes in an essence that meets the Entailment Requirement D attributes? I am now going to argue that the final attribute cannot be a D attribute, if the thing defined is an indivisible species.

9. Subsumptive Division

First, it is important to see that the Entailment Requirement presupposes a more robust conception of division than the method of exhaustive division. Exhaustive division is not sufficient for securing the required entailment relations among the attributes in an essence. For it requires only that each division captures all of the kind it divides without further requiring that the kind each division divides captures all of it. This second requirement is a feature of what I will call 'subsumptive division'. As above, let 'G' stand for any kind or sub-kind that admits of division:

Subsumptive Division: D_1/D_2 is a subsumptive division of G if and only if (a) D_1/D_2 is an exhaustive division of G and (b) all D_1s are G and all D_2s are G (i.e., D_1 and D_2 each entail G).

A PUZZLE IN ARISTOTLE'S THEORY OF DEFINITION   23

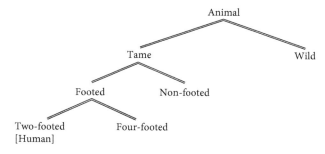

Figure 1.6 Sixth division tree

(In subsequent division trees I will continue to use single lines '/' and '\' to indicate exhaustive division, but I will now use double lines '⫽' and '⫼' to indicate subsumptive division.)

Figure 1.6 shows the division tree for the essence of human we examined just above, with the divisions set out subsumptively. From this tree we can read off the essence of human: two-footed (footed) tame animal. The double lines indicate that the attributes stand to each other in the required entailment relations: all two-footed things are footed (and not vice versa), all footed things are tame (and not vice versa), and all tame things are animals (and not vice versa).

The problem is that at least one of these claims is clearly false. It is not true that all footed things are tame. Rather, even granting that all footed things are animals, it is clear that some footed animals are tame and others are wild. Indeed, this is just what the division tree represented in Figure 1.2 tells us.

The method of exhaustive division permits us to use footed/non-footed as a division of both tame animal and wild animal. However, the method of subsumptive division does not. For if all footed animals are tame (if footed entails tame), given that tame and wild are contraries, no footed animals are wild. Therefore, footed is not a differentia of wild animal. The problem is that footed is a differentia of wild animal (and of tame animal): some wild animals are footed. So Aristotle's main example of an essence in *APo.* 2.13 does not fit with the second part of his account of essence and division [T5–6].[41]

10. The Final Differentia

But the problem is more serious than this. For suppose that two-footed (footed) tame animal did meet the Entailment Requirement. The difficulty is that there is a strong case to be made that in any essence of this sort the final differentia does not extend beyond the indivisible species defined and thus is not a D attribute,

---

[41] The essence of three in [T3] does not fit either. 'Prime$_2$' entails 'prime$_1$', but neither 'prime$_2$' nor 'prime$_1$' entails 'odd'. For two is prime$_2$ and prime$_1$ and even. See Granger 1980, 43–4.

24 DAVID BRONSTEIN

which violates the D Attribute Rule. (Recall that the rule stipulates that each differentia in an essence must extend beyond the indivisible species defined.)

There are two steps to the claim that the final differentia (e.g., two-footed) in an essence obtained by subsumptive division (and thus meeting the Entailment Requirement) is not a D attribute. The first step is that the sub-kind two-footed-footed-tame-animal admits of no further division into sub-kinds encompassing distinct species. Suppose it did divide, say, into feathered and featherless (Figure 1.7).

If this were a correct division of two-footed, then our initial essence of human—two-footed (footed) tame animal—would not belong uniquely to that species, for it would belong to (an)other species (whichever is (are) encompassed by the sub-kind feathered-two-footed-footed-tame-animal). Therefore, if it were possible to divide two-footed into feathered and featherless, then featherless would have to be the final differentia in the human essence. And in that case we would say about featherless what we said about two-footed, that it cannot be divided into sub-kinds encompassing distinct species. The point is simply that the final attribute in any indivisible species' essence obtained by division does not divide into sub-kinds encompassing distinct species. This is part of what it is for it to be *final*—beyond it there is no dividing.[42]

The second step to the conclusion that two-footed is not a D attribute is this. Since (*ex hypothesi*) two-footed entails footed and then tame and then animal, it cannot appear in any other line of division in the same tree. For example, it cannot appear as a differentia of wild animal, for then it would not entail tame. This is a feature of every subsumptive division tree composed entirely of pairs of contrary differentiae.[43] Since each differentia entails the one immediately above it, right up to the genus, each differentia can occupy only *one* position in the tree.

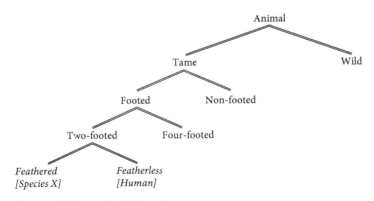

Figure 1.7 Seventh division tree

---

[42] For an argument along these lines, see *APo.* 2.13, 97a35–b6.
[43] For the assumption that all divisions employ contrary differentiae, see *APo.* 2.13, 97a14–22.

A PUZZLE IN ARISTOTLE'S THEORY OF DEFINITION 25

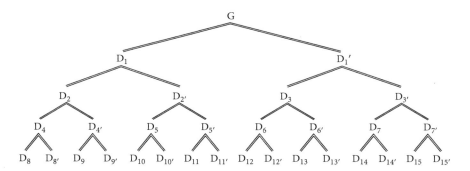

Figure 1.8 Eighth division tree

Consider the division tree shown in Figure 1.8. We can pick any differentia we like and we will find that the position it occupies in the tree is the only one it can occupy. Take D_{10}. Since all D_{10}s are D_5s, D_{10} cannot also be a differentia of $D_{5'}$. For if it were, then it would entail D_5 and $D_{5'}$, which are contraries. Next, since all D_{10}s are D_5s and all D_5s are D_2s, all D_{10}s are D_2s. Therefore, D_{10} cannot also be a differentia of D_4 or $D_{4'}$. For each of these entails D_2, so if D_{10} were also a differentia of either one, it would entail D_2 and $D_{2'}$, which are contraries. Finally, since all D_{10}s are D_5s and all D_5s are D_2s and all D_2s are D_1s, all D_{10}s are D_1s. Therefore, D_{10} cannot also be a differentia of D_6, $D_{6'}$, D_7, $D_{7'}$, D_3, or $D_{3'}$. For each of these entails $D_{1'}$, so if D_{10} were also a differentia of any one of these, it would entail D_1 and $D_{1'}$, which are contraries.[44]

In sum, in every subsumptive division tree composed entirely of pairs of contrary differentiae, each differentia occupies exactly one position in the tree. This makes subsumptive division trees significantly different from exhaustive division trees, which, as we saw above, permit us to use the same differentia-pair in more than one position.

We can now conclude that two-footed is not a D attribute in the genus animal, if it is the final attribute in an essence that meets the Entailment Requirement. It follows from what I have argued that every final differentia in a subsumptive division tree belongs uniquely to the one indivisible species that falls under it. There are no other species below the final differentia to which it can belong, given that it is final. And there are no species marked off by differentiae elsewhere in the division tree to which the final differentia can belong, since, as I have just argued, it cannot appear anywhere else in the tree. Since (*ex hypothesi*) two-footed is a final differentia in a subsumptive division tree, it belongs to only one indivisible

---

[44] The same reasoning shows that D_{10} cannot also be a differentia of any differentiae at its level: if it were, it would entail contraries. For example, D_{10} cannot also be a differentia of $D_{15'}$, for then it would entail D_1 and $D_{1'}$.

26 DAVID BRONSTEIN

species: human. But no D attribute belongs to only one indivisible species. Therefore, two-footed is not a D attribute. In general, no final differentia in a subsumptive division tree is a D attribute.

11. The Puzzle

I have argued that in the second part of *APo.* 2.13 [T5–6], Aristotle introduces a conception of essence according to which the final differentia entails all of the remaining differentiae and the genus and as such belongs uniquely to the indivisible species defined. He discusses the same conception of essence in *Metaphysics* Z.12, where, as I mentioned above, he calls the final differentia the essence (*ousia*), the definition (*horismos*), and the form (*eidos*) of the species defined (1038a19–20, 25), which strongly suggests that it belongs uniquely to it, as I have argued it must on the second *APo.* 2.13 account. Since an attribute that belongs uniquely to an indivisible species cannot be a D attribute, *Metaphysics* Z.12 and *APo.* 2.13 [T5–6] articulate a conception of essence at odds with Aristotle's initial account in 2.13 [T2–4].[45]

We have now come to the main difficulty in *APo.* 2.13. Aristotle presents two different and incompatible conceptions of essence. According to the first, each attribute in the essence of an indivisible species must be a D attribute. According to the second, each attribute in an essence must entail the previous one, which means that the last cannot be a D attribute. No essence can meet the Entailment Requirement and conform to the D Attribute Rule.[46]

I suggested earlier that we can see a connection between the Causality Condition and the D Attribute Rule and a connection between the Unity Condition and the Entailment Requirement. It would be too hasty to conclude that since the D Attribute Rule and the Entailment Requirement are inconsistent with each other, so too are the Causality and Unity Conditions. Aristotle may still have the resources for a theory of essence that makes room for both conditions. Indeed, an obvious solution to the difficulty in *APo.* 2.13—obvious because it is the solution he evidently opts for in *Metaphysics* Z.12—is to give up the D Attribute Rule and embrace the Entailment Requirement. Although, as I have suggested, there is a natural affinity between the Causality Condition and the D Attribute Rule, it may very well be that essences that meet the Entailment

---

[45] Falcon (1997, 140) argues that the *Analytics* and *Met.* Z.12 present inconsistent models of division because on the Z.12 model the final differentia entails all of the preceding ones and the genus whereas on the *Analytics* model it does not. However, Falcon overlooks the fact that this same inconsistency is present within *APo.* 2.13 itself, and that the second model of division in 2.13 is the same as that in *Met.* Z.12.

[46] McKirahan (1992, 114–15) briefly mentions this difficulty.

Requirement can also meet the Causality Condition. We should note, however, that this solution comes at a cost.

First, recall my suggestion that part of what motivates the D Attribute Rule is Aristotle's desire to build into his definitional method a guarantee that each essence will contain more than one differentia in order to increase the chances that the method will yield essences that meet the Causality Condition. The idea, in other words, is to ensure that the single differentia approach to definition is excluded from his method. However, the single differentia approach is consistent with the Entailment Requirement. For if an essence contains a genus and a single differentia, then, so long as the differentia entails the genus, the Entailment Requirement is met. Therefore, the correct approach to definition—the multiple differentiae approach—is not guaranteed by Aristotle's preferred method (although it should be said that neither is it excluded).

Second, the method of Subsumptive Division imposes severer constraints on our practice of division than the method of Exhaustive Division does. For in Subsumptive Division, each differentia-pair can be used only once in a division tree, whereas in Exhaustive Division, some differentia-pairs can appear in multiple places. This suggests that Exhaustive Division is more likely to succeed in carving nature at its joints. For, as we saw above, we want to be able to use the footed/non-footed division in more than one place in the division tree because both all tame animals and all wild animals are footed or non-footed. However, Subsumptive Division does not permit us this flexibility. In addition, for a genus as complex and varied as animal, it seems highly unlikely, perhaps impossible, to come up with a single set of subsumptive divisions encompassing all relevant indivisible species, but this is just what would be required if Aristotle is committed to the Entailment Requirement.

Conclusion

We should not conclude from my discussion that Aristotle fails to come up with a coherent theory of essence in the *Posterior Analytics*. We should rather conclude that the task he sets for himself faces significant philosophical challenges, not the least of which is the challenge of combining the two conditions on essence—unity and causality—on which David Charles has rightly focused our attention.[47]

---

[47] It is a great pleasure and honour to dedicate this paper to David Charles. David generously served as my postdoctoral supervisor at Oxford. His mentorship then and since—equal parts wisdom, kindness, and humility—has been one of the great blessings of my career. For their helpful questions and comments on previous drafts of this chapter, I thank audiences at the University of Campinas, Georgetown University, Indiana University, the University of Chicago, and a meeting of the Pacific APA in San Diego. For particularly helpful discussion and comments, I also thank David Ebrey, Thomas Johansen, Ben Morison, Michael Peramatzis, and Justin Vlasits.

Works Cited

Ackrill, J. L. 1963. *Aristotle* Categories *and* De Interpretatione. *Translated with Notes and Glossary.* Clarendon Aristotle Series. Clarendon Press.

Balme, D. M. 1987. 'Aristotle's Use of Division and Differentiae', in *Philosophical Issues in Aristotle's Biology* (ed. A. Gotthelf and J. Lennox). Cambridge University Press, 69–89.

Barnes, Jonathan. 1993. *Aristotle* Posterior Analytics. *Translated with a Commentary.* 2nd edition. Clarendon Aristotle Series. Clarendon Press.

Bolton, Robert. 1993. 'Division, Définition et Essence dans la Science Aristotélicienne', *Revue Philosophique* 2, 197–222.

Bronstein, David. 2016. *Aristotle on Knowledge and Learning: The* Posterior Analytics. Oxford University Press.

Charles, David. 2000. *Aristotle on Meaning and Essence.* Clarendon Press.

Charles, David. 2010. 'Definition and Explanation in the *Posterior Analytics* and *Metaphysics*', in *Definition in Greek Philosophy* (ed. D. Charles). Oxford University Press, 286–328.

Code, Alan. 2010. 'An Aristotelian Puzzle about Definition: *Metaphysics* Z.12', in *Being, Nature, and Life in Aristotle* (ed. J. G. Lennox and R. Bolton). Cambridge University Press, 78–96.

Deslauriers, Marguerite. 2007. *Aristotle on Definition.* Brill.

Detel, Wolfgang. 1993. *Aristoteles, Analytica Posteriora: Übersetzung und Erläuterung.* 2 vols. Akademie Verlag.

Falcon, Andrea. 1996. 'Aristotle's Rules of Division in the *Topics*: The Relationship between Genus and Differentia in a Division', *Ancient Philosophy* 16, 377–87.

Falcon, Andrea. 1997. 'Aristotle's Theory of Division', in *Aristotle and After* (ed. R. Sorabji). Bulletin of the Institute of Classical Studies, Supplementary Volume 68, 127–46.

Ferejohn, Michael. 1991. *The Origins of Aristotelian Science.* Yale University Press.

Gill, Mary Louise. 2010. 'Unity of Definition in *Metaphysics* H.6 and Z.12', in *Being, Nature, and Life in Aristotle* (ed. J. Lennox and R. Bolton). Cambridge University Press, 97–121.

Goldin, Owen. 1996. *Explaining an Eclipse: Aristotle's Posterior Analytics 2.1–10.* University of Michigan Press.

Goldin, Owen. 2004. 'Atoms, Complexes, and Demonstration: *Posterior Analytics* 96b15–25', *Studies in History and Philosophy of Science* 35, 707–27.

Gotthelf, Allan. 2012. *Teleology, First Principles, and Scientific Method in Aristotle's Biology.* Oxford University Press.

Granger, Herbert. 1980. 'Aristotle and the Genus-Species Relation', *Southern Journal of Philosophy* 18, 37–50.

Granger, Herbert. 1981. 'The Differentia and the Per Se Accident in Aristotle', *Archiv für Geschichte der Philosophie* 63, 118–29.

Hicks, R. D. 1925. *Diogenes Laertius, Lives of Eminent Philosophers*. Two volumes. Loeb Classical Library. Harvard University Press.

Lloyd, G. E. R. 1961. 'The Development of Aristotle's Theory of Classification of Animals', *Phronesis* 6, 59–81.

McKirahan, Richard. 1992. *Principles and Proofs: Aristotle's Theory of Demonstrative Science*. Princeton University Press.

Malink, Marko. 2022. 'The Discovery of Principles in *Prior Analytics* 1.30', *Phronesis* 67, 161–215.

Modrak, Deborah K. W. 2001. *Aristotle's Theory of Language and Meaning*. Cambridge University Press.

Pellegrin, Pierre. 2005. *Aristote: Seconds Analytiques*. Flammarion.

Ross, W. D. 1949. *Aristotle's* Prior and Posterior Analytics. *A Revised Text with Introduction and Commentary*. Clarendon Press.

Smyth, Hebert Weir. 1956. *Greek Grammar*. Revised by Gordon M. Messing. Harvard University Press.

Sorabji, Richard. 1980. *Necessity, Cause and Blame: Perspectives on Aristotle's Theory*. Cornell University Press.

Vlasits, Justin. 2017. 'Platonic Division and the Origins of Aristotelian Logic'. Ph.D. dissertation, University of California, Berkeley.

2

Antisthenes on Definition

Metaphysics H.3

Marko Malink

Introduction

In *Metaphysics* H.3, Aristotle discusses a difficulty raised by Antisthenes and his followers concerning the possibility of definition. The difficulty led the Antistheneans to conclude that it is impossible to define what a thing is (1043b23–32). While this passage is one of the major sources on the thought of Antisthenes, it poses a number of interpretive problems. It is, as Myles Burnyeat puts it, an 'obscure passage... which lacks an agreed interpretation'.[1] In particular, it is not clear what the difficulty raised by the Antistheneans was, and why Aristotle chooses to address it in his discussion of hylomorphism in *Metaphysics* H.3. The aim of this chapter is to contribute to a better understanding of the Antisthenean difficulty by providing fresh answers to these questions.

I begin by considering the context of Aristotle's discussion of the Antisthenean difficulty in *Metaphysics* H.3 (section 1). I then turn to his discussion of the difficulty itself (section 2). I argue that, contrary to what is often thought, the difficulty derives from an argument to the effect that any attempt at defining what a thing is leads to an infinite regress of definitions (section 3). More specifically, the Antisthenean argument is based on a compositional conception of definition, according to which the definition of a thing must mention the constituents of which the thing is composed (section 4).

1. Genus and Differentia as Material Constituents of the Species

Antisthenes, a pupil of Socrates and opponent of Plato, examined the nature of definitions. According to Diogenes Laertius, Antisthenes required that the definition of a thing specify what the thing is or what it was:

---

[1] Burnyeat 1970, 111; similarly, 1990, 171 n. 54.

Marko Malink, *Antisthenes on Definition:* Metaphysics *H.3* In: *Aristotelian Metaphysics: Essays in Honour of David Charles.*
Edited by: David Bronstein, Thomas Kjeller Johansen, and Michail Peramatzis, Oxford University Press.
© Oxford University Press 2024. DOI: 10.1093/oso/9780198908678.003.0002

ANTISTHENES ON DEFINITION   31

Antisthenes was the first to define 'definition', saying: 'A definition is an account revealing what a thing was or is.'[2]

πρῶτός τε ὡρίσατο λόγον εἰπών, 'λόγος ἐστὶν ὁ τὸ τί ἦν ἢ ἔστι δηλῶν.' (Diogenes Laertius 6.3, 1–2)

This corresponds to Aristotle's view, stated in *Metaphysics* H.1 and elsewhere, that a definition (*horismos*) of a thing is an account (*logos*) specifying its essence or what it was for the thing to be (*to ti ēn einai*).[3] Unlike Aristotle, however, Antisthenes was led to adopt a sceptical attitude to definitions. As Aristotle reports in H.3, Antisthenes and his followers maintained that 'it is not possible to define what a thing is' (*ouk esti to ti estin horisasthai*, 1043b25).

Aristotle's discussion of Antisthenean scepticism in H.3 is preceded by a series of considerations on the nature of composites (*suntheta*). Aristotle emphasizes that the mode of composition by which a composite is formed from its constituents is not itself a constituent of the composite. For example, the mode of composition by which a syllable is formed from its constituent letters is not itself a constituent of the syllable:

On investigation it is evident that a syllable is not constituted by the letters and their composition, and a house is not bricks and composition. And this is correct, for the composition and the mixture are not themselves constituted by the things that are mixed or composed, and the same holds of all other cases.

οὐ φαίνεται δὴ ζητοῦσιν ἡ συλλαβὴ ἐκ τῶν στοιχείων οὖσα καὶ συνθέσεως, οὐδ᾽ ἡ οἰκία πλίνθοι τε καὶ σύνθεσις. καὶ τοῦτο ὀρθῶς· οὐ γάρ ἐστιν ἡ σύνθεσις οὐδ᾽ ἡ μῖξις ἐκ τούτων ὧν ἐστὶ σύνθεσις ἢ μῖξις. ὁμοίως δὲ οὐδὲ τῶν ἄλλων οὐθέν. (*Met.* H.3, 1043b4–8)

In this passage, Aristotle recalls some results established in *Metaphysics* Z.17 concerning composites that are unified not like a heap but like a syllable or like homoeomerous bodies such as flesh (1041b11–16). In Z.17, he argued that any such composite is something over and above the elements of which it is composed, something that is not itself an element (1041b16–33). He characterizes this entity as the substance of the composite and the first cause of its being (1041b27–8). Although Aristotle does not explicitly say so, it seems clear that the entity in question is the form (*eidos*) of the composite.[4] In the present passage from H.3, Aristotle identifies this form with a mode of composition (*sunthesis*) in the case of syllables, and with a mode of mixture (*mixis*) in the case of flesh.[5] Just

---

[2] All translations are my own.
[3] *Met.* H.1, 1042a17–21. See also *Met.* Z.4, 1030a6–7, 1030b5–7, Z.5 1031a11–12, *Top.* 7.5, 154a31–2.
[4] Ps.-Alex. Aphr. *In Metaph.* 542.12–543.26, Bonitz 1849, 360, Witt 1989, 116–17, Harte 2002, 133.
[5] See Bostock 1994, 262.

32 MARKO MALINK

like in Z.17 (1041b19–25), he states that this mode of composition or mixture is not itself constituted by elements.

Aristotle proceeds, in H.3, to apply this account of composites to a case he did not consider in Z.17: the case of definition by genus and differentia.[6] Using the example of the species *human* defined by means of the genus *animal* and the differentia *biped*, he writes:

> Nor, then, is man animal and biped. But if these are matter, there must also be something over and above them, something which is not an element and not constituted by an element but is the substance; and this they eliminate when they state only the matter. So, if this is the cause of the thing's being, and this is the substance, they will not be stating the substance itself.
>
> οὐδὲ δὴ ὁ ἄνθρωπός ἐστι τὸ ζῷον καὶ δίπουν, ἀλλά τι δεῖ εἶναι ὃ παρὰ ταῦτά ἐστιν, εἰ ταῦθ' ὕλη, οὔτε δὲ στοιχεῖον οὔτ' ἐκ στοιχείου, ἀλλ' ἡ οὐσία· ὃ ἐξαιροῦντες τὴν ὕλην λέγουσιν. εἰ οὖν τοῦτ' αἴτιον τοῦ εἶναι, καὶ οὐσία τοῦτο, αὐτὴν ἂν τὴν οὐσίαν οὐ λέγοιεν. (*Met.* H.3, 1043b10–14)

Aristotle here describes the species as a composite composed of the genus and the differentia. Just as the letters 'B' and 'A' are constituents of the syllable 'BA', and the elements fire and earth are constituents of the composite body flesh, the genus *animal* and the differentia *biped* are regarded as constituents of the species *human*. In Z.17, the letters are taken to be the matter (*hulē*) of the syllable (1041b32). Similarly, in the present passage, both the genus and the differentia are viewed as matter (*hulē*) of the species (1043b11).[7] Thus, both *animal* and *biped* are material constituents of the species *human*. Aristotle emphasizes that, on this account, the species is something over and above the genus and the differentia, something which is not itself an element or a material constituent of the species. The item in question is the cause of being and the substance of the species. Consequently, if *human* is defined simply as *biped animal*, this definition 'states only the matter', but fails to specify the cause of being and the substance of the thing defined.

In the passage just quoted, both the genus and the differentia are regarded as 'matter' of the species. By contrast, in *Metaphysics* Z.12 Aristotle states that, in a definition by genus and differentia, only the genus but not the differentia plays the role of matter (1038a5–9).[8] This is in line with his statement in Δ.28 that 'that of which the differentia or quality is a differentia or quality is the underlying subject, which we call matter' (1024b8–9). Similarly, Aristotle states in *Metaphysics* I.8 that 'the genus is the matter of that of which it is called the genus' (1058a23–4).[9] In these passages, Aristotle implies that the differentia should not be regarded as

---

[6] Bostock 1994, 263.   [7] Ross 1924, vol. ii 231–2, Prince 2015, 453–4.
[8] See Gill 2010, 104–9.   [9] Similarly, 1057b37–1058a2. See Castelli 2018, 216–17.

matter.[10] This is in tension with the account presented in H.3, on which genus and differentia alike count as matter of the species. In light of this, Dittenberger concludes that the passage from H.3 should be regarded as an interpolation since it conflicts with Aristotle's considered view.[11] Against this, Menn and others argue that this passage is not meant to describe Aristotle's own position, but an account of definition by genus and differentia which was maintained by some Platonists.[12] This is supported by the fact that, in Z.14–15, Aristotle attributes to some Platonists the view that the species contains both the genus and the differentia as constituents.[13] These Platonists maintain that the species is constituted by the genus and the differentiae (*to eidos ek tou genous poiousi kai tōn diaphorōn*, 1039a26). Accordingly, they hold that both the genus and the differentiae are parts of and prior to the species (*protera g' onta kai merē tou sunthetou*, 1040a18).[14] This fits with the account of definition by genus and differentia described by Aristotle in H.3. Thus, when Aristotle contends in H.3 that those who define *human* as *biped animal* state only the matter but ignore the cause of being of the thing defined, this is not a criticism of the method of definition by genus and differentia as such. Instead, it is a criticism of a Platonist account of this type of definition, an account on which both the genus and the differentia are viewed as material constituents of the species.

2. The Antisthenean Difficulty

Aristotle continues his discussion in H.3 by elaborating on the form of composites, their mode of composition or mixture (1043b14–23). He states that the form neither comes into being nor perishes, referring to his earlier argument for this claim in Z.8 (1033a24–b19). With this background in place, Aristotle turns to the Antisthenean difficulty concerning the possibility of definition:

> [i] Therefore the difficulty which was raised by the Antistheneans and other such uneducated people has some appropriateness here. [ii] They stated that it is not possible to define what a thing is, since the definition would be a long account; [iii] but one can specify and teach[15] of what sort a thing is. For example, one cannot define what silver is, but one can specify that it is like tin. [iv] Therefore

---

[10] Moreover, Aristotle is often taken to assert at H.6, 1045a23–5 that the genus is the matter and the differentia the form of the species; Ps.-Alex. Aphr. *In Metaph.* 561.33, Schwegler 1848, 151–2, Bonitz 1849, 375–6, Ross 1924, vol. ii 238, Charles 1994, 87, Gill 2010, 98 and 109. However, Bostock (1994, 280–3) and Harte (1996, 283–94) argue against this reading of 1045a23–5.

[11] Dittenberger 1869, 18.

[12] Menn 2001, 104, 123, 127–8, 2011, 186, Galluzzo 2018, 312–15.

[13] Z.14, 1039a24–6 and 1039a30–2; see Lewis 2013, 241–2.   [14] Ross 1924, vol. ii 216.

[15] For this translation of *endechetai kai didaxai*, see Bonitz 1890, 170, Prince 2015, 447 and 460–1.

34 MARKO MALINK

there can be a definition and an account of one kind of substance, namely of composite substance, whether it be the object of sense or of reason; [v] but the primary constituents of which this is composed cannot have a definition, [vi] since a defining account signifies something of something, and the one item must be like matter and the other like form.

[i] ὥστε ἡ ἀπορία ἦν οἱ 'Αντισθένειοι καὶ οἱ οὕτως ἀπαίδευτοι ἠπόρουν ἔχει τινὰ καιρόν, [ii] ὅτι οὐκ ἔστι τὸ τί ἔστιν ὁρίσασθαι (τὸν γὰρ ὅρον λόγον εἶναι μακρόν), [iii] ἀλλὰ ποῖον μέν τί ἐστιν ἐνδέχεται καὶ διδάξαι, ὥσπερ ἄργυρον, τί μέν ἐστιν οὔ, ὅτι δ' οἷον καττίτερος· [iv] ὥστ' οὐσίας ἔστι μὲν ἧς ἐνδέχεται εἶναι ὅρον καὶ λόγον, οἷον τῆς συνθέτου, ἐάν τε αἰσθητὴ ἐάν τε νοητὴ ᾖ· [v] ἐξ ὧν δ' αὕτη πρώτων, οὐκ ἔστι,[16] [vi] εἴπερ τὶ κατὰ τινὸς σημαίνει ὁ λόγος ὁ ὁριστικὸς καὶ δεῖ τὸ μὲν ὥσπερ ὕλην εἶναι τὸ δὲ ὡς μορφήν. (Met. H.3, 1043b23–32)

In points [i]–[iii] of this passage, Aristotle describes the difficulty raised by the Antistheneans and 'other such uneducated people'. The use of *hōste* in point [i] indicates that the difficulty is related to Aristotle's earlier discussion in H.3. In particular, it appears to be related to the discussion of composites at 1043b4–10 and the account of definition by genus and differentia given at 1043b10–14.[17]

It is debated whether points [iv]–[vi] continue the description of the Antisthenean difficulty or whether they contain Aristotle's own conclusions.[18] The terminology in this part of the passage, especially the reference to matter and form in [vi], is more Aristotelian than in the preceding part. Moreover, Aristotle's statement in [iv] that there is a definition of composite substances seems to contradict the sceptical position attributed to Antisthenes in [ii] that 'it is not possible to define what a thing is'.[19] In view of this, it seems unlikely that points [iv]–[vi] constitute a direct report of Antisthenes' position. Nevertheless, the presence of *hōst'* in point [iv] makes it clear that the discussion in [iv]–[vi] is closely related to the Antisthenean difficulty. Thus, even if this discussion does not fully match Antisthenes' position, it bears on the Antisthenean difficulty and can help to shed light on it.[20]

In point [vi], Aristotle states that a definition signifies 'something of something' (*ti kata tinos*), the first item playing the role of form and the latter that of matter. With respect to definitions by genus and differentia, this remark is sometimes taken to mean that the differentia plays the role of form and the genus that

---

[16] Reading οὐκ ἔστι with E and J (Bekker, Bonitz, Schwegler) instead of οὐκέτι (Ross, Jaeger).

[17] Ross 1924, vol. ii 232, Caizzi 1964, 51.

[18] Points [iv]–[vi] are taken to be part of Aristotle's description of the Antisthenean difficulty, e.g., by Ps.-Alex. Aphr. In Metaph. 554.22–33, Bonitz 1849, 369, Zeller 1875, 253 n. 1, Dümmler 1901, 1–2 and 309, and von Fritz 1927, 463–4. Against this, others have denied that [iv]–[vi] constitute a report of the Antisthenean difficulty; e.g., Barlen 1881, 4–5, Grube 1950, 21–3, Hicken 1958, 138, Burnyeat 1970, 114, Rankin 1970, 525–6, Burnyeat et al 1984, 18, Kalouche 1999, 21 n. 29.

[19] Grube 1950, 23, Hicken 1958, 134.   [20] Prince 2015, 461–2, Caizzi 1964, 51.

of matter.[21] However, this is not in accordance with the account of definition by genus and differentia given earlier in H.3, on which both genus and differentia are regarded as matter. Aristotle gives no indication in H.3 of a transition from this Platonist account to the one presented in Z.12, on which only the genus but not the differentia is regarded as matter. Thus, insofar as his remark in point [vi] applies to definitions by genus and differentia, it should be taken to rely on the Platonist account of these definitions described at the beginning of H.3.[22] On this account, both genus and differentia are material constituents of the species, thus giving rise to Aristotle's criticism that a proper definition of the species must mention not only the material constituents but also the form (1043b10–14). According to point [vi], the form is in some way predicated of the material constituents. As Aristotle puts it in H.2, in any definition, 'the actuality itself [i.e., the form] is predicated of the matter' (1043a5–7).[23] This is the case for the definitions of, for instance, a threshold, a house, ice, and harmony (1043a7–12). It is also the case for definitions by genus and differentia as understood by the Platonist account, on which a species is a composite (*suntheton*) composed of genus and differentia.

In points [iv] and [v], Aristotle states that composite substances have a definition while their primary constituents, being themselves incomposite, lack a definition. He seems to assume that a definition of a thing is an account mentioning the constituents of which the thing is composed, and that incomposites, since they do not have any constituents, lack a definition. Aristotle appeals to this view in his argument against Platonic universal substances in Z.13, when he implies that no incomposite substance has a definition (1039a17–19). The view has a notable precedent in the dream theory presented by Socrates in the final part of the *Theaetetus* (201e1–202b5). In point [iv], Aristotle states that this view applies to both perceptible and intelligible substances. He does not explain what kind of intelligible substance he has in mind, but when he distinguishes between perceptible and non-perceptible substances in H.1, he lists Platonic ideas and mathematical objects as examples of non-perceptible substances (1042a22–4). Accordingly, the discussion of the Antisthenean difficulty in H.3 appears to be concerned with Platonist conceptions of universals, whereas the remainder of the chapter deals with Platonist conceptions of number (1043b32–1044a11). When Aristotle refers to intelligible composites and their elements in *Metaphysics* Λ.4, the composites are Platonic ideas and their elements are the highest genera by means of which they are defined (1070b7–8).[24] An element, for Aristotle, is a primary material constituent that is indivisible in the sense that it has no further

---

[21] Ross 1924, vol. ii 233, von Fritz 1927, 463 n. 1, Burnyeat 1970, 114, Galluzzo 2018, 312 n. 36.

[22] See Prince 2015, 453–4 and 465.

[23] Kung 1978, 155. See also the related use of the phrases *ti kata tinos* and *allo kat' allou* at *Met.* Z.17, 1041a23–6.

[24] See Crubellier 2000, 146–8.

36   MARKO MALINK

material constituents (Δ.3, 1014a26–30). Thus, when in point [v] Aristotle refers to the primary constituents of a species, these are the highest genera and differentiae by means of which the species is defined but which do not themselves have a definition by genus and differentia.[25] In this way, the account of definition described by Aristotle in points [iv]–[v] is applicable not only to composite perceptible substances such as syllables and houses but also to intelligible composite substances such as Platonic universals and numbers.

According to point [ii], the difficulty raised by the Antistheneans led them to claim that it is impossible to define anything. On what grounds did the Antistheneans reach this sceptical conclusion? Pseudo-Alexander and Bonitz, among others, take the difficulty in question to turn on the fact that the definiens of a definition is a complex expression consisting of two or more syntactic constituents.[26] In support of this interpretation, Bonitz cites a passage from *Metaphysics* Δ.29 in which Antisthenes is credited with the view that nothing can be said of a thing except its peculiar formula (*oikeios logos*):

> Antisthenes was thinking foolishly when he maintained that nothing can be spoken of except by its peculiar formula, one formula for one thing, from which it followed that contradicting is impossible and speaking falsely virtually impossible too.
>
> Ἀντισθένης ᾤετο εὐήθως μηθὲν ἀξιῶν λέγεσθαι πλὴν τῷ οἰκείῳ λόγῳ, ἓν ἐφ' ἑνός· ἐξ ὧν συνέβαινε μὴ εἶναι ἀντιλέγειν, σχεδὸν δὲ μηδὲ ψεύδεσθαι. (*Met.* Δ.29, 1024b32–4)

Antisthenes maintained that, for any given thing, there is exactly one 'peculiar formula', and that this formula is the only predicate that can be said of the thing. This implies that it is impossible to make any statements, true or false, which attribute to a thing anything else than its peculiar formula (1024b34–1025a1). Antisthenes inferred from this that it is impossible for speakers to contradict one another.[27] If I say that Theaetetus is sitting, you cannot contradict me by saying that Theaetetus is not sitting. For if you contradict me, then you and I ascribe two distinct predicates—sitting and not sitting—to the same thing, which is impossible given that no more than one predicate, the peculiar formula, can be said of a thing.[28] Moreover, provided that a thing's peculiar formula is true of the thing, Antisthenes' view implies that it is impossible to speak falsely; for any false statement would attribute to the thing something else than its peculiar formula.

---

[25] See Menn 2001, 117 and 121.

[26] Ps.-Alex. Aphr. *In Metaph.* 554.2–5, Bonitz 1849, 369, von Fritz 1927, 463, Brancacci 1990, 234, 1999, 385, Denyer 1991, 31–2, Bostock 1994, 266.

[27] This is confirmed by Aristotle at *Top.* 1.11, 104b20–1.

[28] Alex. Aphr. *In Metaph.* 435.5–14.

ANTISTHENES ON DEFINITION   37

According to Bonitz, this is the view that underlies the Antisthenean difficulty described in H.3. Bonitz argues that, if 'nothing can be designated except by its own concept and this is unique and singular, a definition cannot be complex and contain in itself several marks'.[29] For example, if *human* is defined as *biped animal*, each of the two marks *biped* and *animal* is said of the subject *human*, violating Antisthenes' doctrine that only one thing can be said of any given subject.

Although Bonitz's interpretation can explain how the Antistheneans reached the conclusion that definition by genus and differentia is impossible, it does not fit well with Aristotle's text in H.3. For one thing, the doctrine attributed to Antisthenes in Δ.29 entails the impossibility not only of definition by genus and differentia but of any declarative statement which attributes to the subject anything else than its peculiar formula. The doctrine entails that, for any given subject, there is only one statement that can be made about it. If this statement is true, no false statement can be made about the subject. Thus, the doctrine from Δ.29 has much broader scope and more extreme consequences than the more limited thesis that definition is impossible. The doctrine is, as Burnyeat puts it, 'stronger and stranger than' any argument that merely denies the possibility of definition.[30] The proper place to engage with such a doctrine is in a general discussion of true and false statements. This is what Aristotle does in his treatment of false *logoi* in Δ.29, in which he refutes Antisthenes' doctrine and dismisses it as foolish (*euēthōs*, 1024b29–1025a1). It is not clear why Aristotle should revisit the doctrine in H.3, and why he should do so by limiting himself to the special case of definition without mentioning the more general and egregious consequences of the doctrine. Aristotle introduces the Antisthenean difficulty in point [i] by stating that it has 'some appropriateness' (*tina kairon*). Yet, on Bonitz's interpretation, it is mysterious what appropriateness the difficulty might have at this stage of Aristotle's discussion in *Metaphysics* H.3.

Moreover, Bonitz's interpretation is in tension with the view attributed to Antisthenes in point [iii], that 'one can specify and teach of what sort a thing is'. Antisthenes maintained that, while one cannot define what silver is, one can specify and teach that it is like tin. This will involve the making of a relational statement such as *Silver is like tin*, a statement which presumably does not express the unique 'peculiar formula' of silver.[31] Thus, as Barlen and others have pointed out, the acceptance of such relational statements in point [iii] conflicts with the doctrine of a unique peculiar formula ascribed to Antisthenes in Δ.29.[32] Given that point [iii] is part of Aristotle's report of the Antisthenean argument against

---

[29] Bonitz 1849, 369; similarly, Denyer 1991, 32, Bostock 1994, 266.

[30] Burnyeat 1990, 167; similarly, 1970, 120–1.

[31] In *Metaphysics* Δ.29, Aristotle denies that the statement *Eight is a double* expresses the unique peculiar formula of *eight* since it involves the formula of *two* (1024b34–1025a1). Similarly, *Silver is like tin* will fail to express the peculiar formula of *silver* since it involves the formula of *tin*.

[32] Barlen 1881, 5, Grube 1950, 22–3.

38   MARKO MALINK

definition, it is not plausible to take this argument to be based on the doctrine of
Δ.29. Instead, it is preferable to take the argument to be independent of that doctrine. Thus, relational statements such as *Silver is like tin* are admissible in the
context of the Antisthenean argument against definition presented in H.3, even if
they are ruled out by the more extreme doctrine attributed to Antisthenes in Δ.29.

Finally, Bonitz's interpretation does not sit well with Aristotle's claim in point
[ii] that, for the Antistheneans, any putative definition is a *logos makros* ('long
account'). The interpretation implies that, for example, *biped animal* is a *logos
makros*, given that it is the putative definition of *human*. Accordingly, it is sometimes thought that a *logos makros* here is simply an account which is syntactically
complex. For example, Bostock takes it to be any account which is 'longer than a
single name'.[33] This, however, is not a natural reading of the qualification *makros*.
For this qualification does not indicate mere syntactic complexity, however low it
may be, but rather signifies length of expression. We know that, in his *Ajax*,
Antisthenes uses the phrase *makroi logoi* to refer to long-winded and vain
speeches (Caizzi 14.8, Prince 53.8). Similarly, in *Metaphysics* N.3 (1091a7–8)
Aristotle uses the phrase *makros logos* to describe 'evasive verbiage such as slaves
tell to cover up failure to do the job assigned to them'.[34] When the Eleatic Stranger
invites Theaetetus to consider the statement *Theaetetus is sitting*, asking 'This
logos is not long, is it?' (*mōn mē makros ho logos*), Theaetetus' answer is: 'No, not
long but fitting' (*Ouk, alla metrios*).[35] By the same token, the definition *biped animal*, while syntactically complex, is not a *makros logos*.

Of course, these considerations are not decisive against Bonitz's interpretation.
Nevertheless, taken together they provide good reason for exploring alternative
interpretations. If the extreme *oikeios logos* doctrine discussed in Δ 29 cannot
account for the Antisthenean difficulty in H.3, what else is the rationale underlying this difficulty?

3. Infinite Regress of Definitions

When Aristotle introduces the Antisthenean difficulty in H.3, he refers to
Antisthenes and his followers as 'uneducated' (*apaideutoi*). There are two more
passages in the *Metaphysics*, both of them in book Γ, in which Aristotle mentions
a group of people who are, in his view, uneducated. In the first passage, Aristotle
targets students who attend a lecture on first philosophy without prior education
regarding 'the manner in which truth should be accepted':

---

[33] Bostock 1994, 266. Similarly, Ps.-Alex. Aphr. *In Metaph.* 554.2–5, Gillespie 1913, 482, von Fritz
1927, 463, Kapp 1965, 68 n. 17.
[34] Prince 2015, 460; similarly, Ross 1924, vol. ii 233 and 482–3.   [35] *Sophist* 263a2–3.

ANTISTHENES ON DEFINITION 39

The attempts of some of those who discuss the manner in which truth should be accepted are due to a lack of education in the *Analytics*. For a student ought to come to the lecture already equipped with knowledge of these things, but not seek it while listening.

ὅσα δ' ἐγχειροῦσι τῶν λεγόντων τινὲς περὶ τῆς ἀληθείας ὃν τρόπον δεῖ ἀποδέχεσθαι, δι' ἀπαιδευσίαν τῶν ἀναλυτικῶν τοῦτο δρῶσιν· δεῖ γὰρ περὶ τούτων ἥκειν προεπισταμένους ἀλλὰ μὴ ἀκούοντας ζητεῖν. (*Met.* Γ.3, 1005b2–5)

Aristotle maintains that, when attending a lecture, 'one must already be educated on how to accept each' sort of argument (*dei pepaideusthai pōs hekasta apodekteon*, *Met.* α.3, 995a12–13). In Γ.3, Aristotle is clear that this education is provided, at least in part, by the *Analytics*. The education involves, among other things, a recognition of the fact, emphasized in *Posterior Analytics* 1.3, that there is not a demonstration of every truth but that there are fundamental, indemonstrable truths. Those who fail to recognize this fact and demand a demonstration of fundamental laws such as the principle of non-contradiction lack education:

Some demand that even this [i.e., the principle of non-contradiction] shall be demonstrated, but they do so through lack of education. For it is lack of education not to recognize of which things demonstration ought to be sought, and of which not. For it is impossible that there should be demonstration of absolutely everything, since it would go on to infinity so that even in this way there would be no demonstration.

ἀξιοῦσι δὴ καὶ τοῦτο ἀποδεικνύναι τινὲς δι' ἀπαιδευσίαν· ἔστι γὰρ ἀπαιδευσία τὸ μὴ γιγνώσκειν τίνων δεῖ ζητεῖν ἀπόδειξιν καὶ τίνων οὐ δεῖ· ὅλως μὲν γὰρ ἁπάντων ἀδύνατον ἀπόδειξιν εἶναι· εἰς ἄπειρον γὰρ ἂν βαδίζοι, ὥστε μηδ' οὕτως εἶναι ἀπόδειξιν. (*Met.* Γ.4, 1006a5–9)

The two passages from Γ just quoted and Aristotle's discussion of the Antisthenean difficulty in H.3 contain all references to lack of education (*apaideusia*) in the *Metaphysics*. In view of this, Maier and Ross argue that the uneducated people targeted in the first two passages are the same as those targeted in H.3: namely, Antisthenes and his followers.[36] Whether or not this is correct, it is reasonable to suppose that the lack of education ascribed to the Antistheneans in H.3 is of a similar kind as the one criticized in Γ. In Γ.4, the lack of education manifests itself in the demand to provide a demonstration of fundamental principles which are in fact indemonstrable. In Aristotle's view, this demand leads to an infinite regress of demonstrations, and hence to the annihilation of demonstration and

---

[36] Maier 1900, 11 n. 3 and 15 n. 2, Ross 1949, 514. On the other hand, Barnes (1976, 282 n. 8) casts doubt on Maier's argument.

40 MARKO MALINK

demonstrative knowledge. Aristotle describes this sort of sceptical position in *Posterior Analytics* 1.3 as follows:

> Some maintain that there is no knowledge because this would require knowing the first premises.... They suppose that there is no way of knowing other than by demonstration, and claim that we are led back *ad infinitum*, seeing that we will not know the posteriors on account of the priors if there are no first premises behind the priors. And they argue correctly, for it is impossible to traverse infinitely many things. And if it comes to a stop and there are principles [i.e., first premises], they say that these are unknowable since there is no demonstration of them, which they say is the only way of knowing. But if we cannot know the first premises, neither can what depends on them be known *simpliciter* or properly, but only from a hypothesis, on the supposition that these hold.

> ἐνίοις μὲν οὖν διὰ τὸ δεῖν τὰ πρῶτα ἐπίστασθαι οὐ δοκεῖ ἐπιστήμη εἶναι,...οἱ μὲν γὰρ ὑποθέμενοι μὴ εἶναι ἄλλως ἐπίστασθαι, οὗτοι εἰς ἄπειρον ἀξιοῦσιν ἀνάγεσθαι ὡς οὐκ ἂν ἐπισταμένους τὰ ὕστερα διὰ τὰ πρότερα, ὧν μὴ ἔστι πρῶτα, ὀρθῶς λέγοντες· ἀδύνατον γὰρ τὰ ἄπειρα διελθεῖν.εἴ τε ἵσταται καὶ εἰσὶν ἀρχαί, ταύτας ἀγνώστους εἶναι ἀποδείξεώς γε μὴ οὔσης αὐτῶν, ὅπερ φασὶν εἶναι τὸ ἐπίστασθαι μόνον· εἰ δὲ μὴ ἔστι τὰ πρῶτα εἰδέναι, οὐδὲ τὰ ἐκ τούτων εἶναι ἐπίστασθαι ἁπλῶς οὐδὲ κυρίως, ἀλλ' ἐξ ὑποθέσεως, εἰ ἐκεῖνα ἔστιν. (*APo.* 1.3, 72b5–15)

The sceptics under consideration in this passage assume that the only way of having knowledge of a given proposition is by possessing a demonstration of it. Based on this assumption, they argue that it is impossible to have knowledge of anything. For, to have knowledge of a proposition P, one must demonstrate it from further premises. In order for this demonstration to confer knowledge of P, the demonstrator must know the premises. Hence, the demonstrator must possess demonstrations deriving each of these premises from further premises, and so on. If the regress stops, the chain of demonstrations will not confer proper knowledge of P but only hypothetical knowledge: that is, knowledge on the supposition that the ultimate premises employed in the demonstration hold. If, on the other hand, the chain of demonstrations proceeds to infinity, it fails to confer knowledge of P because 'it is impossible to traverse infinitely many things.'[37]

While sceptical positions of this sort may have been adopted by various thinkers associated with the Academy, Cherniss argues that Aristotle's main target in the passage just quoted is Antisthenes.[38] Cherniss's argument has been widely accepted by scholars.[39] On this reading, Antisthenes denied not only the possibility of definition but also that of demonstrative knowledge. Thus, it stands

---

[37] See Code 2010, 101.   [38] Cherniss 1944, 65.
[39] Ross 1949, 513–14, Tredennick 1960, 36, Mignucci 1975, 44, Dillon 2003, 152, Long 2006, 49 n. 12 and n. 14.

to reason that the difficulty concerning definition raised by Antisthenes and his followers is analogous to the sceptical argument against demonstrative knowledge described by Aristotle in *Posterior Analytics* 1.3. Specifically, the Antistheneans can be taken to hold that, for any universal X, the only way of knowing what X is is through a definition by genus and differentia. For example, to know what *human* is, one must define it by genus and differentia, say, as *biped animal*. In order for this definition to confer knowledge of what *human* is, the definer must know what the universals *animal* and *biped* are. Hence, the definer must provide definitions of the latter universals by means of further genera and differentiae, and so on. If the regress stops, the chain of definitions does not confer knowledge of what *human* is, since the definer does not have the requisite knowledge of the ultimate genera and differentiae employed in these definitions.[40] If, on the other hand, the chain of definitions proceeds to infinity, it fails to confer knowledge because it is impossible to traverse infinitely many things.

Aristotle mentions a group of people who posit such an infinite regress of definitions in *Metaphysics* α.2:

> The essence cannot be referred always to another definition which is expanded in account. For the prior definition is always more of a definition, and not the posterior one; and in a series in which the first thing does not obtain, the next one does not obtain either. Moreover, those who say this destroy knowledge, for it is not possible to know until one comes to what is indivisible. There will also be no cognition, for how can one think things that are infinite in this way?
>
> ἀλλὰ μὴν οὐδὲ τὸ τί ἦν εἶναι ἐνδέχεται ἀνάγεσθαι εἰς ἄλλον ὁρισμὸν πλεονάζοντα τῷ λόγῳ· ἀεί τε γὰρ ἔστιν ὁ ἔμπροσθεν μᾶλλον, ὁ δ' ὕστερος οὐκ ἔστιν, οὗ δὲ τὸ πρῶτον μὴ ἔστιν, οὐδὲ τὸ ἐχόμενον· ἔτι τὸ ἐπίστασθαι ἀναιροῦσιν οἱ οὕτως λέγοντες, οὐ γὰρ οἷόν τε εἰδέναι πρὶν εἰς τὰ ἄτομα ἐλθεῖν· καὶ τὸ γιγνώσκειν οὐκ ἔστιν, τὰ γὰρ οὕτως ἄπειρα πῶς ἐνδέχεται νοεῖν; (*Met.* α.2, 994b16–23)

While this passage raises a number of interpretive questions, it is clear that it deals with a sceptical position according to which any putative definition leads to an infinite regress of definitions. In this regress, the definer is led from one defin-ition to another which is 'expanded in account'. For example, if *human* is defined as *biped animal*, the definiens will be expanded into, say, *biped perceiving body*.[41] The latter definiens will be expanded into yet another more complex account, and so on. At any given stage, the expanded definiens is prior (ἔμπροσθεν) to the less

---

[40] This is in accordance with Gillespie's view that 'Antisthenes held all definition to be incomplete as ultimately employing indefinable terms' (Gillespie 1913, 480 n. 1; similarly, Maier 1900, 13–14, Ross 1924, vol. ii 232–3).

[41] For this kind of expansion of definitions, see *Top.* 2.2, 110a4–9, 6.7, 146a33–5.

42   MARKO MALINK

expanded definiens from which it is obtained.[42] The prior, expanded definiens constitutes more (*mallon*) of a definition than the posterior, less expanded one. According to the sceptical position under consideration, there is no first definiens: that is, a definiens which cannot be further expanded. In Aristotle's view, this means that no posterior definiens constitutes a proper definition, and hence that there is no genuine definition at all.[43] In this way, those who posit an infinite regress of putative definitions do away with the possibility of definition. Consequently, they also do away with knowledge (*epistasthai*).

Aristotle does not further specify the group of people (*hoi houtōs legontes*) who posit this infinite regress of putative definitions. But, if I am correct, his description fits Antisthenes and his followers. For, according to the Antisthenean position under consideration, any putative definition by genus and differentia leads to a regress of definitions, at each stage positing new definitions of the genera and differentiae appearing in the definiens. In this way, any attempt at defining a thing by genus and differentia results in a truly long account, a *makros logos*.

In the passage from *Metaphysics* α.2 just quoted, Aristotle firmly denies, against the Antistheneans, that there is an infinite regress of definitions. He also denies the existence of an infinite regress of definitions in H.3. Shortly after his discussion of the Antisthenean difficulty at 1043b23–32, he asserts that definitions are like numbers in that they are divisible into indivisibles on the grounds that 'the accounts are not infinite':

A definition is a sort of number since it is divisible into indivisibles (for the accounts are not infinite), and number is also of such kind.

ὅ τε γὰρ ὁρισμὸς ἀριθμός τις· διαιρετός τε γὰρ καὶ εἰς ἀδιαίρετα (οὐ γὰρ ἄπειροι οἱ λόγοι), καὶ ὁ ἀριθμὸς δὲ τοιοῦτον. (*Met.* H.3, 1043b34–6)

A definiens such as *biped animal* is divisible into its constituents *biped* and *animal*. Each of these may in turn be divisible into further constituents, and so on. Aristotle insists, however, that this type of regress does not go on to infinity ('the accounts are not infinite'), but comes to a stop at indivisible items that do not have a definition by genus and differentia.[44] In this way, Aristotle indicates how his own position differs from that of the Antistheneans and how it avoids the Antisthenean regress argument against the possibility of definition.

Of course, regress arguments against the possibility of definition and demonstration need not be exclusive to the Antistheneans, but may also have been put forward by other thinkers. As Cherniss notes with respect to Antisthenean regress

---

[42] Alex. Aphr. *In Metaph.* 162.6–10, Crager 2015, 147–8.
[43] Aristotle writes, οὗ δὲ τὸ πρῶτον μὴ ἔστιν, οὐδὲ τὸ ἐχόμενον (994b19–20). This corresponds to his description of the sceptical argument against demonstrative knowledge in *Posterior Analytics* 1.3: ὡς οὐκ ἂν ἐπισταμένους τὰ ὕστερα διὰ τὰ πρότερα, ὧν μὴ ἔστι πρῶτα (72b9–10).
[44] Ps.-Alex. Aphr. *In Metaph.* 555.6–10.

ANTISTHENES ON DEFINITION   43

arguments, 'there is no likelihood that such an attitude was restricted to a single group or school; anyone who was inclined to scepticism would be likely to maintain it as is shown by its reappearance in the work of Sextus'.[45] Sextus gives an argument based on the mode of infinite regress against the possibility of definition (*PH* 2.207). There is thus good reason to think that this type of regress argument was employed by a number of sceptics before Sextus.[46] Crucially, this regress argument does not rely on the *oikeios logos* doctrine attributed to Antisthenes in Δ.29, but on more general and less idiosyncratic assumptions that would likely be shared by a wide variety of sceptic thinkers in the vicinity of Plato's Academy. Accordingly, Aristotle notes that the regress argument against the possibility of definition was given not only by Antisthenes and his followers (*hoi Antistheneioi*) but also by 'other such uneducated people' (*kai hoi houtōs apaideutoi*, 1043b24).

4. Definition and Composition

As we have seen, Aristotle's discussion in H.3 relies on the Platonist assumption that, in a definition by genus and differentia, the species to be defined is a composite containing the genus and the differentia as constituents. Aristotle suggests that the Antisthenean regress argument applies not only to species composed of genus and differentia but more generally to any 'composite substance' (1043b28–9). So understood, the regress argument concerns not only definitions by genus and differentia but any definitions in which a composite is defined by reference to its constituents. The argument assumes that, for any X, the only way of knowing what X is is through a definition that mentions the constituents of X. If X does not have constituents, it is not definable and one cannot know what it is. If, on the other hand, X has constituents, then, in order for a definition to confer knowledge of what X is, the definer must know what each of X's constituents is. Thus, the definer must in turn provide definitions of these constituents in terms of their constituents, and so on. If the regress stops, the series of definitions does not confer knowledge of what X is, since the definer does not have the requisite knowledge of the ultimate constituents. But if the series of definitions proceeds to infinity, it fails to confer knowledge because it is impossible to traverse infinitely many things. Hence, there is no definition conferring knowledge of what X is.

---

[45] Cherniss 1944, 65.

[46] In addition, this sort of regress argument was also given by thinkers after Sextus. For example, Descartes writes in the *Meditationes*: 'So what in fact did I antecedently think I was? A human being, of course. But what is a human being? Shall I say, a rational animal? No, for then I should have to examine what an animal is, and what rational is, and hence, starting with one question, I should stumble into more and more difficult ones. Nor do I now have so much leisure that I can afford to fritter it away on subtleties of this kind' (*Meditationes de prima philosophia*, 2nd Meditation).

44 MARKO MALINK

This regress argument applies whether X is a perceptible substance such as a house or a piece of silver or an intelligible substance such as a Platonic universal or a number. The argument is based on a compositional conception of definition according to which the definition of X must make reference to the constituents of which X is composed. In his discussion of the Antisthenean difficulty, Aristotle expresses this compositional conception of definition in points [iv]–[v] as follows:

> [iv] Therefore there can be a definition and an account of one kind of substance, namely of composite substance, whether it be the object of sense or of reason; [v] but the primary constituents of which this is composed cannot have a definition.
>
> [iv] ὥστ' οὐσίας ἔστι μὲν ἧς ἐνδέχεται εἶναι ὅρον καὶ λόγον, οἷον τῆς συνθέτου, ἐάν τε αἰσθητὴ ἐάν τε νοητὴ ᾖ· [v] ἐξ ὧν δ' αὕτη πρώτων, οὐκ ἔστι. (*Met.* H.3, 1043b28–30)

In point [iv], Aristotle claims that composite substances can have an account and a definition. It is sometimes thought that this claim is not part of Aristotle's report of the Antisthenean argument since it contradicts Antisthenes' contention that it is impossible to define anything.[47] This, however, is not the case. Point [iv] is not intended to attribute to Antisthenes the view that composite substances have genuine definitions producing knowledge of what these substances are. Instead, as Dümmler has pointed out, Aristotle's intention in [iv] and [v] is to state an underlying assumption of the Antisthenean argument: namely, that the only possible way to provide a definition of X is by means of an account making reference to the constituents of which X is composed.[48] Thus, Aristotle indicates that the Antisthenean argument is based on the compositional conception of definition.

The compositional conception of definition was widely known in the Academy from the dream theory presented by Socrates in the *Theaetetus*. In fact, some commentators have taken Aristotle's remarks in points [iv]–[v] to indicate that the dream theory originated with Antisthenes.[49] In a similar vein, Burnyeat maintains that if the dream theory 'does derive—in whole or in part—from an actual historical thinker, the most likely candidate is Antisthenes', although Burnyeat also allows for the possibility that 'Socrates in the *Theaetetus* is not restating Antisthenes but making creative use of some Antisthenean materials'.[50] Whether or not Antisthenes is in fact the originator of the dream theory, though, it seems clear that, like most thinkers associated with the Academy, he was well acquainted with some version of this theory. Thus, Antisthenes may well have employed the dream theory's compositional conception of definition in a sceptical argument against a central tenet of Platonic thought, the possibility of defining what

---

[47] Barlen 1881, 4–5; Grube 1950, 22–3; similarly, Burnyeat et al. 1984, 18.
[48] Dümmler 1901, 309.   [49] Schwegler 1848, 144, Zeller 1875, 253 n. 1.
[50] Burnyeat 1990, 165–6.

something is. This would also help to explain why Aristotle takes the Antisthenean argument to have 'some appropriateness' (*tina kairon*, 1043b25) in his discussion in H.3. For, as we have seen, the first part of H.3 contains a discussion of the nature of composites, including the Platonist view that in a definition by genus and differentia the species is composed of the genus and the differentia (1043b4–14). On this Platonist view, definition by genus and differentia is a special instance of the compositional conception of definition. Thus, given that the Antisthenean argument against definition was based on this compositional conception, it is directly pertinent to Aristotle's discussion in H.3. For the argument poses an important challenge for any Platonist adopting the compositional conception of definition.

In the case of the sceptical regress argument against the possibility of demonstrative knowledge discussed in *Posterior Analytics* 1.3, Aristotle mentions a group of thinkers who rejected the argument by appealing to the possibility of circular demonstration. These thinkers defended the existence of demonstrative knowledge by arguing that 'nothing prevents there being demonstrations of everything; for it is possible for demonstrations to proceed in a circle or reciprocally'.[51] Similarly, one might respond to a regress argument against the possibility of definition by appealing to the possibility of circular definition.[52] This possibility, however, is precluded by the compositional conception of definition, on the grounds that nothing can be a constituent of itself. As Aristotle puts it, 'it is not possible that any of the elements is the same as that which is composed of the elements, for example, that either B or A is the same as BA' (*Metaphysics* Λ.4, 1070b5–6). More generally, he maintains that if X is a constituent of Y, the converse does not hold (Δ.2, 1013b9–11). Thus, given that the relation of being a constituent is transitive, it follows that this relation is acyclic in the sense that there are no $X_1, \ldots, X_n$ such that X_1 is a constituent of X_2, X_2 is a constituent of $X_3, \ldots$, and X_n is a constituent of X_1. Consequently, the compositional conception of definition implies that the Antisthenean regress of definitions is not circular. For, when a definer seeks to obtain knowledge of what X is by decomposing X into its constituents, none of the constituents appearing in the regress of compositional definitions is identical with X. As a result, the Antisthenean regress of compositional definitions is neither finite nor circular but proceeds to infinity, thus giving rise to a *makros logos*.[53]

---

[51] *APo.* 1.3 72b16–18; see also 72b6–7. See Barnes 1976, 279, Code 2010, 101.

[52] Fine (1979, 386–97) argues that Plato adopts this position in the *Theaetetus*, embracing circular definition in response to the problems raised by the dream theory.

[53] This chapter grew out of discussions with David Charles during a series of joint seminars on *Metaphysics* Z and H that we organized in 2016–17 at New York University and Yale University. David provided helpful comments on an earlier draft of this chapter during a workshop on Aristotle's *Metaphysics* at Université Paris1 Panthéon-Sorbonne in 2018. I am very grateful to David for illuminating and inspiring discussions on these and numerous other occasions over the past two decades. In addition, the paper benefited enormously from detailed comments by Gábor Betegh, Michel Crubellier, Roberto Granieri, Anne Siebels Peterson, Christian Pfeiffer, and three anonymous referees. Thanks are also due to audiences at Cambridge University, Renmin University, and the University of Toronto.

46 MARKO MALINK

Works Cited

Barlen, K. 1881. *Antisthenes und Plato*. Strüder.

Barnes, J. 1976. 'Aristotle, Menaechmus, and Circular Proof', *Classical Quarterly* 26, 278–92.

Bonitz, H. 1849. *Aristotelis Metaphysica, pars posterior*. Marcus.

Bonitz, H. 1890. *Aristoteles: Metaphysik*. Reimer.

Bostock, D. 1994. *Aristotle's Metaphysics: Books Z and H*. Clarendon Aristotle Series. Clarendon Press.

Brancacci, A. 1990. *Oikeios Logos: La filosofia del linguaggio di Antistene*. Bibliopolis.

Brancacci, A. 1999. 'Eutidemo e Dionisodoro, gli ΟΨΙΜΑΘΕΙΣ del *Sofista* e un passo dell'*Eutidemo*', *Elenchos* 20, 280–300.

Burnyeat, M. F. 1970. 'The Material and Sources of Plato's Dream', *Phronesis* 15, 101–22.

Burnyeat, M. F., et al. 1984. *Notes on Books Eta and Theta of Aristotle's Metaphysics*. Faculty of Philosophy, University of Oxford.

Burnyeat, M. F. 1990. *The Theaetetus of Plato*. Hackett.

Caizzi, F. 1964. 'Antistene', *Studi Urbinati di storia, filosofia e letteratura* 38, 48–99.

Castelli, L. M. 2018. *Aristotle: Metaphysics Book Iota*. Clarendon Aristotle Series. Clarendon Press.

Charles, D. 1994. 'Matter and Form: Unity, Persistence, and Identity', in *Unity, Identity, and Explanation in Aristotle's Metaphysics* (ed. T. Scaltsas, D. Charles, and M. L. Gill). Clarendon Press, 75–105.

Cherniss, H. F. 1944. *Aristotle's Criticism of Plato and the Academy*. Johns Hopkins Press.

Code, A. 2010. 'Aristotle and the History of Skepticism', in *Ancient Models of Mind: Studies in Human and Divine Rationality* (ed. A. Nightingale and D. Sedley). Cambridge University Press, 97–109.

Crager, A. D. 2015. 'Meta-Logic in Aristotle's Epistemology'. Ph.D. Dissertation, Princeton University.

Crubellier, M. 2000. '*Metaphysics Λ* 4', in *Aristotle's Metaphysics Lambda: Symposium Aristotelicum* (ed. M. Frede and D. Charles). Clarendon Press, 137–60.

Denyer, N. 1991. *Language, Thought and Falsehood in Ancient Greek Philosophy*. Routledge.

Dillon, J. 2003. *The Heirs of Plato: A Study of the Old Academy (347–274 BC)*. Clarendon Press.

Dittenberger, W. 1869. *Exegetische und kritische Bemerkungen zu einigen Stellen des Aristoteles (Metaphysik und de anima)*. Hofbuchdruckerei.

Dümmler, F. 1901. *Kleine Schriften, Erster Band: Zur griechischen Philosophie*. Hirzel.

Fine, G. J. 1979. 'Knowledge and *Logos* in the *Theaetetus*', *Philosophical Review* 88, 366–97.

Galluzzo, G. 2018. 'Substantiae sunt sicut numeri: Aristotle on the Structure of Numbers', in *Revolutions and Continuity in Greek Mathematics* (ed. M. Sialaros). de Gruyter, 295–318.

Gill, M. L. 2010. 'Unity of Definition in *Metaphysics* H.6 and Z.12', in *Being, Nature, and Life in Aristotle: Essays in Honor of Allan Gotthelf* (ed. J. G. Lennox and R. Bolton). Cambridge University Press, 97–121.

Gillespie, C. M. 1913. 'The Logic of Antisthenes', *Archiv für Geschichte der Philosophie* 26, 479–500.

Grube, G. M. A. 1950. 'Antisthenes Was No Logician', *Transactions and Proceedings of the American Philological Association* 81, 16–27.

Harte, V. 1996. 'Aristotle *Metaphysics* H6: A Dialectic with Platonism', *Phronesis* 41, 276–304.

Harte, V. 2002. *Plato on Parts and Wholes: The Metaphysics of Structure.* Oxford University Press.

Hayduck, M. (ed.). 1891. *Alexandri Aphrodisiensis in Aristotelis Metaphysica Commentaria.* Reimer.

Hicken, W. 1958. 'The Character and Provenance of Socrates' 'Dream' in the *Theaetetus*', *Phronesis* 3, 126–45.

Kalouche, F. 1999. 'Antisthenes' Ethics & Theory of Language', *Revue de Philosophie Ancienne* 17, 11–41.

Kapp, E. 1965. *Der Ursprung der Logik bei den Griechen.* Vandenhoeck & Ruprecht.

Kung, J. 1978. 'Can Substance Be Predicated of Matter?', *Archiv für Geschichte der Philosophie* 60, 140–59.

Lewis, F. 2013. *How Aristotle Gets By in Metaphysics Zeta.* Oxford University Press.

Long, A. A. 2006. *From Epicurus to Epictetus: Studies in Hellenistic and Roman Philosophy.* Oxford University Press.

Maier, H. 1900. *Die Syllogistik des Aristoteles, ii/2. Die Entstehung der Aristotelischen Logik.* Laupp.

Menn, S. 2001. '*Metaphysics* Z10–16 and the Argument Structure of *Metaphysics* Z', *Oxford Studies in Ancient Philosophy* 21, 83–134.

Menn, S. 2011. 'On Myles Burnyeat's *Map of Metaphysics Zeta*', *Ancient Philosophy* 31, 161–202.

Mignucci, M. 1975. *L'argomentazione dimostrativa in Aristotele.* Editrice Antenore.

Prince, S. 2015. *Antisthenes of Athens: Texts, Translations, and Commentary.* University of Michigan Press.

Rankin, H. D. 1970. 'Antisthenes a "Near-Logician"?', *L'Antiquité Classique* 39, 522–27.

Ross, W. D. 1924. *Aristotle's* Metaphysics: *A Revised Text with Introduction and Commentary.* 2 vols. Clarendon Press.

Ross, W. D. 1949. *Aristotle's* Prior and Posterior Analytics. *A Revised Text with Introduction and Commentary*. Clarendon Press.

Schwegler, A. 1848. *Die Metaphysik des Aristoteles: Vierter Band, des Commentars zweite Hälfte*. Fues.

Tredennick, H. 1960. *Aristotle: Posterior Analytics*. Loeb Classical Library. Harvard University Press.

Von Fritz, K. 1927. 'Zur Antisthenischen Erkenntnistheorie und Logik', *Hermes* 62, 453–84.

Witt, C. 1989. *Substance and Essence in Aristotle: An Interpretation of Metaphysics VII–IX*. Cornell University Press.

Zeller, E. 1875. *Die Philosophie der Griechen in ihrer geschichtlichen Entwicklung II.1: Sokrates und die Sokratiker, Plato und die alte Akademie*. 3rd edition. Fues.

3

Focality, Analogy, and the Articulation of Concepts

S. G. Williams

1.

The conspicuous failure of the great programmes of analysis of the twentieth century—most notably, the different forms of foundationalist epistemology that use modern logic—alongside the seemingly futile attempts of conceptual analysts to understand important philosophical concepts piecemeal, has contributed (or so it can sometimes seem) to a dispiriting holistic backlash. Serious analysis is forsworn entirely, and all that is properly left to analytical philosophers is the diagnosis of mistakes in past and future attempts at constructive philosophy. In this dismal narrative, nothing remains of the creative impulse to understand the world analytically save this or that Ozymandian wreck. This is not to say that no concept at all is analysable. Indeed, that some are follows from trivial one-line definitions like that of *oculist* as *eye-doctor* or *bachelor* as *unmarried man*. But the banality of such examples contrasts badly with the aims of the great programmes. The question for anyone wishing to resist the dismal narrative is whether any hope remains of something beyond the banal.

One response has been to set aside the strict project of analysing concepts—of understanding them in terms of simpler, more basic ones—in favour of providing what David Wiggins once called *elucidations* of them. Here an elucidation of a concept is something that 'illuminates [it] by employing it in a set of true judgments that involve it revealingly and interestingly with distinct, coeval, collateral concepts'.[1] Some elucidations may even turn out to be circular, if the coeval or collateral concepts are themselves elucidatable in terms of the original—and they may be none the worse for that. Indeed, this allows for the possibility that some failed analyses—not the ones that are vulnerable to counterexamples, but rather those that are rejected because circular—may be perfectly acceptable as elucidations.

Wiggins himself provides a good illustration of the method of elucidation, using the concept of identity.[2] He suggests that although we can illuminate this

---

[1] Wiggins 1998, n. 4. Wiggins takes himself to be echoing Frege and Wittgenstein.
[2] See Wiggins 2001, ch. 1.

S. G. Williams, *Focality, Analogy, and the Articulation of Concepts* In: *Aristotelian Metaphysics: Essays in Honour of David Charles*. Edited by: David Bronstein, Thomas Kjeller Johansen, and Michail Peramatzis, Oxford University Press.
© Oxford University Press 2024. DOI: 10.1093/oso/9780198908678.003.0003

50   S. G. WILLIAMS

concept through the *Law of Identity* (the claim that every object is identical to itself) and *Leibniz's Law* (in one form, the claim that any property of an object is a property of anything identical to that object), these principles are unlikely to constitute an analysis of identity. For such an analysis, we would need conditions that were both necessary and sufficient for identity. And these principles are only indisputably sufficient for identity—in the sense that any relation that correctly replaces identity in them will be equivalent to identity—if the notion of *property* used here is interpreted so widely as to include properties that themselves involve identity.[3] Almost certainly, therefore, the principles do not constitute an analysis of identity—either because the conditions they embody are insufficient, or because they presuppose the very concept they are meant to be an analysis of. Nevertheless, these principles constitute an elucidation of the concept of identity: they are true and illuminating principles governing identity, the second of which (Leibniz's Law) deploys the collateral concept of *property*.

Examples like this suggest that the method of elucidation embodies a powerful analytical tool in philosophy. (Think only of the way in which the Leibnizian component of the elucidation of identity, if used sensitively via its contrapositive, can be used to establish distinctness.) For reasons that will emerge presently, however, I doubt that it will supplant conceptual analysis, strictly understood. In fact, the two methods function as important, complementary tools in the understanding of concepts. But as things stand, given the piecemeal fashion in which each is currently pursued, neither can plausibly lay claim to any kind of systematicity, whether it be in the uncovering of concepts or in their understanding. What I wish to suggest in this chapter is that through resources supplied by Aristotle we can begin to fill this gap: to give system to the uncovering of important concepts and to the kinds of analysis and elucidation they might receive. With his help, we can continue to chart a course between the great programmes of analysis and the holistic backlash.

2.

To understand how to do so, it is important to highlight first a question the answer to which might seem orthogonal to our discussion of analysis and elucidation. This is the question whether individual concepts are unitary or fragmented. (Here I take a unitary concept to be one that is not fragmented, and a fragmented concept to be one that is analysable as a concept that is essentially disjunctive or

---

[3] Although familiar, the proof of this claim bears repetition. Suppose we have another relation R such that for arbitrary a and b (i) Raa, and (ii) if Rab, then every property of a is a property of b. Then Rab is equivalent to a = b. Right to left is trivial from (i) and Leibniz's Law. For left to right, we know by (ii) that every property of a is a property of b. Hence if a has the property that a thing has when a = it, then so will b. But a does have this property, by the Law of Identity. So b does too. Hence a = b.

FOCALITY, ANALOGY, AND THE ARTICULATION OF CONCEPTS 51

essentially a cluster concept.[4]) It is perhaps fair to say that the Platonic philosophical culture in which Aristotle found himself took it for granted that important philosophical concepts were unitary. And to the extent that they are, analysis and elucidation can certainly aid our understanding of their unity—particularly by being sufficiently thorough to ensure that no fragmentation is hidden.[5] The problem, however, is that the investigation of many concepts can reveal them to be seriously fragmented, properly capturable only disjunctively or through cluster concepts. And it was this insight, which we owe in essence to Aristotle, that seriously undermined the Platonic culture. For *pace* Plato, he thought—and often rightly, to my mind— that some of our most important philosophical concepts, concepts like *being*, *goodness*, and *justice*, were non-unitary.

Given their fragmented status as disjunctive or cluster concepts, the question naturally arises how to understand them. Here their analysis or elucidation—or what I shall from now on refer to as their *articulation*—can again play a part. In the first instance, this will consist in using analysis to display them as appropriate disjunctive or cluster concepts, the resulting disjuncts or sub-concepts of which may then be elucidated or analysed further. However, both can play an additional role. For what is important about fragmented concepts is that many of them are not *just* disjunctive or cluster concepts—they are not, for instance, like the concept expressed by Goodman's 'grue' predicate or the many whimsical disjunctive concepts that emerged in its wake. For the disjuncts of such fanciful concepts are typically so constructed that their disjuncts have almost nothing of significance in common. But this is untrue of the concepts that Aristotle had in mind, whose articulations often reveal disjuncts or sub-concepts that are intimately related. In such cases, the methodology of analysis and elucidation can help us not only to understand certain concepts through the articulation of, say, their sub-concepts, but also to reveal connections among those sub-concepts. And, of course, this in turn can contribute towards a wider taxonomy of such connections. It is here, I suggest, that we can follow in Aristotle's footsteps. For despite the subtlety and intricacy of many of the connections, he nevertheless managed to bring some measure of system and order to them—ensuring thereby a corresponding systematicity to the articulations of the fragmented concepts themselves.

The Aristotelian resources I want to deploy, then, in trying to resist the dismal narrative are initially those that can be used systematically to articulate and

---

[4] I take C to be essentially a cluster concept if there is a family, C*, of sub-concepts of C, none of which is redundant, such that it's analytic that x falls under C iff x falls under a member of C*. Similarly, C is an essentially disjunctive concept if it is a disjunctive concept with no redundant disjuncts. Note that for simplicity, I often omit the qualifier 'essentially' in what follows. Although formally equivalent, I have mentioned both disjunctive concepts and cluster concepts here partly to echo the lexicographers' practice of providing both disjunctive entries and separate entries for words.

[5] I take this, in effect, to be Wiggins' view about identity. I shall modify and extend it later; see section 13. Note here that a more nuanced view of unity will emerge later in the chapter; see sections 5 and 13.

52 S. G. WILLIAMS

categorize appropriate non-unitary concepts in the manner just adumbrated. However, a second way of resisting the narrative would be provided by giving system to the very uncovering of the concepts that can be subjected to the methods of articulation. It turns out that the same—or at least some of the same— resources can be deployed in this task too.

3.

What then are these resources? In effect, they are what are supplied by the twin Aristotelian notions of *focality* and *analogy*. It would be too large an enterprise to cover both in detail here, and I shall devote most of my efforts to focality. Nonetheless, it is impossible to avoid the topic of analogy entirely. Not only does analogy provide a nice contrast with focality in the manner in which the two ideas allow us to resist the dismal narrative, it also occurs in a proper understanding of focality. In broaching these topics, it will help if we have a working characterization of both. We begin with analogy.

In the spirit of Aristotle, we distinguish two general types of analogy: *the simple* and *the structural*; and we consider simple analogies first. Calling a relation which holds between two objects and is of the form *x is like y* (or *x resembles y, x is similar to y*, etc.) a 'simple analogical relation', we can discern two sub-types, depending upon whether:

(1) we can learn the feature in virtue of which the likeness holds through the simple analogical relation, but the concept corresponding to this feature can be properly articulated without reference to such likenesses; or

(2) we can learn the feature in virtue of which the likeness holds through the simple analogical relation, but the concept corresponding to this feature cannot be properly articulated without reference to such likenesses.

An example of (1) might arise if we learnt the concept of being spherical by noting, for example, the resemblance between a tennis ball and a marble. In this case the analogy would furnish us with a concept whose articulation does not subsequently require the inclusion of this or any other relevant simple analogical relation. What it is to be spherical can be directly defined geometrically. By contrast, as an example of (2), we might cite a secondary quality like being red. Thus suppose we learn the concept of being red by noting the resemblance between a British pillar box and an old British telephone box. In this case, the analogy furnishes us with a concept whose articulation requires an instance of a simple analogical relation.[6] It needn't be the one just noted; it could be any instance that is

---

[6] I assume here that analytical physicalism about colours is incorrect.

FOCALITY, ANALOGY, AND THE ARTICULATION OF CONCEPTS   53

sufficiently similar. (An imaginative dictionary might refer to paradigms on an accompanying colour chart.) Crucially, then, in the first case, analogy figures only in the uncovering of the concept; in the second, it figures both in its uncovering and in its articulation. Where it figures in its articulation, I shall say that a simple analogical concept is *essentially* analogical. The concept of being red is such a concept.

Similar remarks apply to structural or higher-order analogies—the analogies that we most naturally associate with Aristotle's name. In this case, we say that concepts are *related* by higher-order analogy if they are related in accordance with his famous fourfold schema: *just as A is to B, so C is to D*. Any such schema will hold, if it holds at all, in virtue of a relation between A and B that is common to C and D or resembles one between them. Thus Aristotle tells us that just as feathers are to birds, so scales are to fish, thereby indicating, at least given a sufficiently rich background context, the idea of a natural protective covering.[7] But—and it is here that matters resemble the first type of simple analogy—such instances of the schema are unlikely to be constitutive of our understanding of this idea; they merely provide a partial route to it.

On the other hand, consider the following instance of the schema: just as a ripe strawberry is to the palate, so the voice of a trained child soprano is to the ear.[8] Anyone propounding this instance of the schema might well be trying to get us to latch on to the concept of sweetness. However, any resemblance between ripe strawberries and the voices of trained child singers is not a simple analogical one; rather it holds between the salient relation that the strawberries bear to the palate and the corresponding relation that the voices bear to the ear. It is a higher-order analogical relation between what are, minimally, relations of gratification. But since the similarities between the different modes of gratification for each sense are unlikely to be graspable except through an appreciation of instances like the above, it will be correspondingly unlikely that the concept of being sweet over all senses will receive a characterization independent of the analogical relation.[9] So any proper articulation of the analogy will have to refer to the relation or something similar; and when this is so, I shall speak of a higher-order analogical concept's being *essentially* analogical. Such considerations, then, suggest that simple and structural analogies often act as a catalyst for concept acquisition in that, at least when the analogies are successful, they allow people to be inducted into concepts that they may hitherto have not understood or not understood properly. However, they also indicate that in certain cases the analogies may function as

---

[7] See his *PA* 1.4, 644a14–24.
[8] I here riff on an example of Richard Whately's; see Whately 1870, Bk. III, §10.
[9] I assume here not only that analytical physicalism about each such quality is false, but that any such physicalism won't in any case generalize across different senses.

a component in the articulation of the concepts; these will be the essentially analogical concepts.

Such examples indicate how analogies can play an important role in both the uncovering of concepts, and, in the case of essentially analogical concepts, their articulation. What they gloss over, however, are the factors that determine not just which analogical concept is appropriate, but even whether there is a genuine analogy there at all. Thus, returning to the birds and the fish, we can imagine, first, a situation in which we don't yet know whether fish have features that correspond to feathers in birds. We may have found plausible the conjecture that gills and fins in fish are analogous to nostrils and wings in birds, but we may also have discovered that nothing in fish corresponds to the outer ear of a bird. Are scales and feathers like the pairs in the conjecture, or do feathers in birds, like their outer ears, correspond to nothing in fish?

Suppose, however, that we do find the pairing of feathers and scales plausible. Perhaps this is because of their respective locations on the surface of birds and fish, along with an attractive explanation of why fish have no outer ears—for example, that water in any such ears would otherwise interfere with their ability to hear. There would remain the question which analogical concept best captures the analogy. And this may not be at all obvious. Aristotle wanted the concept in question to be that of a natural protective covering. But just knowing that feathers and scales are analogous would be consistent with their both being crucial to camouflage, say, or to sexual attractiveness, or to easy motion through their respective mediums (namely, air and water), and so on. It follows that any comprehensive treatment of analogy must help us decide not only whether there is an analogy at all, but also between competing interpretations of the analogy.

These considerations suggest in principle a quasi-inferential structure. Sticking to structural analogies, for simplicity, and articulating them in the Aristotelian manner—just as A is to B, so C is to D—we may set it out as follows:

1. We amass evidence about features of B and of D.
2. We conclude, at least provisionally, that to feature A in B, there corresponds C in D.
3. We abstract an analogical concept (that in virtue of which the correspondence holds) through at least a partial articulation of it.
   And finally, where the concept is not essentially analogical,
4. We provide an articulation of the concept independent of the analogy.

This means that if we want to create an alternative to the dismal narrative along the present lines, we must show how basic analogical inferences (stage 1 to 2), along with the subsequent uncovering and articulation of the corresponding concepts (stages 2 to 3 and 3 to 4), can both be set out in a broadly systematic way. The history of the theory of analogy suggests that formal, exceptionless criteria

FOCALITY, ANALOGY, AND THE ARTICULATION OF CONCEPTS   55

will be thin on the ground for either of these projects. Nevertheless, the materials for thinking that we can offer *defeasible*, structured guidelines, both for establishing the existence of analogies and for providing at least partial articulations of the analogical concepts abstracted from the analogies, are already available within much of the same literature.[10]

<h2 style="text-align:center">4.</h2>

As I said earlier, however, the principal tool I wish to use here in resisting the dismal narrative is the notion of *focality*. At its heart is the idea of a *focal concept*, which, roughly speaking, consists of a disjunction or cluster of sub-concepts, in terms of one of which (its *focus*) the others (its *satellites*) can be defined. We will discuss later whether, and if so, how, to finesse this characterization. (Most notably, we need to know how, if at all, it should be supplemented.) But for illustrative purposes now, we note one of Aristotle's favourite examples: namely, the concept of being healthy. This is partly focal, since many of its sub-concepts can be understood in terms of the concept of a healthy body: healthy exercise contributes to a healthy body, a healthy regimen aims at a healthy body, a healthy lung is partly constitutive of a healthy body, and so on.[11] Focality, therefore, contributes to our understanding of such concepts through the static description of the relationships between its focus and its satellites; and crucially these relationships remain part of our understanding of them.

Focality, then, seems to be a much simpler notion than analogy. Most notably, there is nothing that corresponds to the distinction between simple and structural analogies, nor to that between analogical concepts that are essentially analogical and those that are not. For given that the relations between its satellites and its focus remain part of our understanding of a focal concept, every such concept will be essentially focal. It follows that nothing corresponds to stage 4 in the schema above.[12] Indeed, it also highlights an important connection with fragmented concepts. For while focal concepts are invariably fragmented—they're defined as such—only *essentially* analogical concepts have to be. To be sure, it may turn out that analogical concepts that are not essentially analogical are in fact fragmented; but having spun free of the analogy, they could equally well turn out to be strictly unified (understood neither as disjunctive nor as a cluster concept).

---

[10] I take Aristotle himself to be a principal figure in this undertaking; see, e.g., *Top.*, 1.17. And whatever their own take on it might be, other key thinkers in it include Keynes 1921, chs 18–19, Hesse 1966, esp. chs 2–4, and Bartha 2010, esp. chs 1–2, 4.

[11] Aristotle also allows the focus of a focal concept to be the concept expressed by the substantive corresponding to the salient sub-concept—in this case, 'health' (in contrast to the dictionary entry in n. 22 below, which, pleonastically in context, uses 'good health').

[12] This is not to say that there would be no scope for further articulation of the focus.

56 S. G. WILLIAMS

For all I know, the concept of a natural protective covering is just such a concept. Furthermore, on the face of it, there seems to be nothing corresponding to the schema's dynamic phases. For example, there are no focal inferences that match the analogical inferences that take us from stage 1 to stage 2. As we shall see, however, this is not to say that there is no system in the uncovering of focal concepts. Some such system will emerge when we introduce the linguistic side of Aristotle's thinking in section 6, one grounded in meaning. Indeed, in principle, this also provides an additional way of seeing whether this or that concept is analogical.

5.

I submit, then, that exploration of connections forged by focality and analogy enables us to understand important fragmented concepts, and along with analogy's double role in helping to uncover concepts, it thereby allows us to create an alternative to the dismal narrative. But if I am right, it also brings with it a puzzle. For commentators like David Charles are apt to speak of essences, described through individual principles that may exploit focality and analogy, as counting for Aristotle as unitary.[13] But how can this be? Doesn't it undermine the contrast with Plato? Not really. To see this, first note that although focality and analogy can furnish us with fragments of concepts that are linked in quite tenuous ways—we will see examples later—the fragments of some concepts overlap so closely that it is as if the concepts themselves are unitary: they are unitary for most practical or theoretical purposes. Indeed—in the spirit of Hume, Reid, and Chisholm[14]—we might with justification call such concepts 'loosely unitary' or 'loosely unified', reserving the term 'strict unity' for the concepts we referred to earlier as unified. With this in mind, we may then say that from a philosophical perspective in which the only kind of unity that is available to us is strict unity, Plato will be a unitarian regarding the concepts whose articulation he and Aristotle disagree about, and Aristotle not; but from a wider, more liberal perspective, which allows us to embrace both strict and looser conceptions of unity, even Aristotle can count as a unitarian about such concepts. So although Aristotle remains *strictly* at odds with Plato, the fact that he is in some sense a unitarian means that they are much closer than it might seem initially. It follows that Charles can be perfectly correct in describing an essence whose characterization exploits focality and analogy as unitary; it's just that the unity will be loose rather than strict. Admittedly, we still need to be able to characterize strict and loose unity. But if we can avail ourselves of the notion of loose identity—something we discuss in more detail in section 13—we might offer the following gloss. A concept is *strictly unitary* iff it is not a fragmented concept. (This is our earlier definition of unity *simpliciter*.) It is

---

[13] See, e.g., Charles 2015, esp. 72.
[14] See Hume 1978, I, IV, 6, Reid 1969, III, ch. 4, esp. 343–4, and Chisholm 1976, ch. 3, esp. §2.

loosely unitary if (a) it is a cluster concept, and there is a member of the cluster that is *loosely* identical to the others; or (b) it is disjunctive, and one of the disjuncts is *loosely* identical to the others.

6.

In our discussion so far, the notions of focality and analogy have been presented in conceptual rather than linguistic terms. But as I intimated earlier, there is a familiar Aristotelian tradition that uses a more language-oriented approach, one grounded in the notion of homonymy. Is there anything to be said for this more indirect approach? I think there is—but to understand why, it is important to get clear first on the notion of homonymy.[15] The straightforward interpretation of the term 'homonymy' is: *having the same name*, where the name may be common or proper. Thus, I and the founder of Radio Luxembourg are homonyms, according to this interpretation, since we are both called 'Stephen Williams'; and so are the relevant kinds of riverside and financial institution, both being called 'bank'. It is common now, however, to find the term being used as a property of the names rather than of what they name. Theoretical linguists, in particular, are apt to use it as a synonym for 'ambiguity', at least for common and proper names. This would not matter if the uses were equivalent, modulo the change in subject. (Sentences involving one would naturally translate into sentences involving the other.) But they are not, as the existence of coreferential ambiguous names demonstrates.[16]

Following Christopher Shields, however, we can ensure that the uses of the term are indeed appropriately equivalent by defining 'homonymy' in terms of names with the same *signification*, 'signification' being construed as a variant on 'meaning' rather than 'reference'.[17] In particular, provided we take the things that words signify to be concepts, the two uses of homonymy can go hand in hand. Thus we may say that a name is homonymous iff it signifies two or more concepts; but equally, we may say that two or more concepts are homonymous iff they share a name which signifies them. So a name is homonymous (in the first of these senses) iff the concepts it signifies are homonymous (in the second sense) with respect to that name. For present purposes, it will be convenient to use 'homonymy' in both senses here.

---

[15] How to interpret the term 'homonymy' in Aristotle is a longstanding and vexed question among commentators; see, e.g., Irwin 1981, Shields 1999, ch. 4, and Ward, 2008, ch. 2.

[16] Suppose, for example, that the different explorers who by geographical necessity learnt about Frege's fictional mountain, Afla, through its different modes of presentation had, by a staggering coincidence, both called it 'Afla' (rather than 'Afla' and 'Ateb'). 'Afla' would then have been ambiguous even though in its different uses it names the same thing. Of course, in the unlikely event that one of the same-reference-same-sense pictures of reference proves right for proper names, then the equivalence of the two uses of 'homonymy', for proper names at least, would follow trivially. For Frege's example, see Frege 1997.

[17] See Shields 1999, ch. 3.

58   S. G. WILLIAMS

So I return to the question: is there anything to be gained from broaching questions of focality and analogy using the more indirect approach? To see that there is, we need only appeal to a general feature of Aristotle's method of successful scientific enquiry, which, according to David Charles, begins canonically with an exploration of what salient names or name-like expressions signify.[18] This is no more than a recognition of the fact that scientific inquiry does not exist in a hermeneutic vacuum, and most notably of the fact that we already have names for many of the concepts—or close relatives of such concepts—that should properly interest us. So by investigating whether their names are homonyms, we open up the possibility of discovering whether the concepts they signify are indeed focal or analogical. In effect, we can look at their different meanings, and explore how such meanings are related. In some cases, they may be completely unrelated, and the salient ambiguity will therefore be accidental. But most cases of interest to us will involve what we may call 'connected homonymy'. The connections might be distantly figurative or emerge only through etymology; but they could equally well have the hallmarks of focality or analogy, since the concepts that the names signify may be focally or analogically related. (In these circumstances, we may speak of 'focal' or 'analogical' terms—and similarly with their meanings.)

It follows that investigating focality and analogy through homonymy and the meanings of words has the merit of allowing us to build straightforwardly upon the analytical and taxonomic endeavours of our predecessors, however informal such endeavours might have been. It is true that working in this way is vulnerable to the whims of contingency. After all, the names we do have may not signify quite the right concepts, and so an examination of their meanings might set us off on the wrong tack; equally, not every concept has a name, and so we might miss relevant concepts altogether. In themselves, however, these objections should simply encourage us to be vigilant, to be careful and thorough in our investigations. Unless we are lexicographers or literary critics, we must not become distracted by the distantly metaphorical or the merely etymological; and we must always be on the lookout for nameless neighbouring concepts that might be connected to those we are already investigating.

7.

The Aristotelian interrogation of focality and analogy through the linguistic expression of the concepts in question, or their near neighbours, has then

---

[18] According to Charles, this is stage one of three, the other two consisting, first, of establishing that objects or kinds corresponding to the name exist, and secondly, of discovering the essence of the kind. See, e.g., Charles 2015, 72 for a brief rehearsal of the three-stage view; for detailed defence and elaboration, see Charles 2000, esp. ch. 2.

FOCALITY, ANALOGY, AND THE ARTICULATION OF CONCEPTS   59

considerable methodological value. It provides us, in particular, with a way of investigating whether this or that concept is focal or indeed analogical.[19] And in saying this, we are, like Aristotle, taking language to be an *object* of scientific investigation. However, from his broadly scientific perspective, he seems to have thought that *using* strictly homonymous terms that are related through focality and analogy also has merit, provided we have properly articulated the concepts the terms express. In effect, the fragments of some concepts *warrant* having the same name. Such a view, however, has not always found favour. For example, according to Locke, for whom the scientific perspective was paramount, homonymous uses of the same word are in fact abuses of those words, to be avoided in a properly constructed scientific-cum-philosophical language.[20] For him, one of the principal reasons why philosophers and scientists talk across each other is their failure to appreciate when they are speaking ambiguously; and they can avoid such confusion by using terms that are commonly and correctly understood to be unambiguous.

Now Aristotle would doubtless have agreed that univocity is a worthwhile aim in a scientific-cum-philosophical language, but his practice suggests—and rightly—that like all such aims it is unlikely to be indefeasible. Thus, we may sometimes find it *attractive* to use a word homonymously, if only to signify that there are important connections between its different uses.[21] Cautious collaborators will then be able to infer in any given case that they have either synonymous uses of a term, or ones that are so connected. Indeed, transparency about the homonymous uses of terms will enable them to avoid confusion entirely. It follows that it may be quite proper for a word to be homonymous, provided the connections between the concepts that its different uses signify are of the right sort. Notice that should the fragments of a named concept be so closely connected that they form a loose unity—something we have already made provision for—the different meanings of the name may be similarly thought of as also possessing a loose unity.[22] As we might put it, the uses of the name will be loosely synonymous, if strictly homonymous. It follows that Locke and Aristotle are closer

---

[19] This is what I meant earlier (section 6) when I said that both focal and analogical notions might be investigated linguistically, through the meanings of terms.

[20] Locke 1975, Bk. III, ch. X, §§28–9.

[21] For detailed discussion of Aristotle's commitment to the importance of univocity in scientific reasoning, alongside his freewheeling, and arguably essential, use of homonymy in certain kinds of scientific exposition, see Lloyd 1996, esp. ch. 4 on 'concoction' (*pepsis*). Compare also here Beere 2009, 180–1.

[22] And this can be so even if the principal meaning specification of a name is itself essentially disjunctive. For its meanings may also include the specification's disjuncts. Thus, consider the following sub-entry for 'healthy' in the *Concise Oxford English Dictionary*: 'indicating or promoting good health'. Here although the word is treated univocally but with an essentially disjunctive meaning, it can in certain contexts still mean, literally, one or other of the disjuncts. Take 'healthy complexion', for instance, which ordinarily means a complexion that *indicates* good health.

60 S. G. WILLIAMS

than we might initially have thought; and in this regard, Aristotle's relationship to Locke is similar to his relationship to Plato.

8.

Let us try to illustrate some of the ideas developed so far, using the concept of knowledge—in the first instance concentrating on propositional knowledge or *knowing that*. Here we arguably find a strictly unitary concept. For suppose initially that the notion of being a *non-accidental belief* is itself analysable in a way that is neither fragmented nor presupposes, even indirectly, the concept of *knowing that*. Then any analysis of propositional knowledge along the lines of non-accidental *true* belief might provide a deep, strictly unified understanding of what such knowledge consisted in. On the other hand, suppose that the idea that propositional knowledge is non-accidental true belief is true, but only our best *shot* at analysing the concept; and that in fact we cannot understand what it is to be relevantly non-accidental except through concepts coeval or collateral with it. Then the concept would be primitive, and therefore a strictly unitary concept with the biconditional:

(K)   A knows that p iff it's true that p, A believes that p, and it is not accidental that A believes that p

constituting an important elucidation of it. Either way we would find a strictly unitary concept nicely articulated.

All well and good. Here analysis and elucidation are doing the kind of work that a Platonic culture might endorse. But now consider the apparently more generic notion of knowledge that includes not only *knowing that*, but also *knowing how*, *knowing whether*, *knowing why*, *knowing which*, etc. In this case, despairing of a unitary account, we might try analysing the seemingly generic notion as an essentially disjunctive concept or a corresponding cluster concept, each disjunct or member of the cluster representing one of these apparent sub-notions and being analysed or elucidated as appropriate. In line with our previous remarks, such a picture would enable us to appreciate nicely the concept's lack of unity. But then the questions emerge what the disjuncts or members of the cluster have in common, whether these connections warrant the fragments being given the same name, and finally, whether it would be appropriate to think of them as being *loosely* unified.

We begin with the question of what links, directly or indirectly, the disjuncts or the members of the cluster. Here although the notion of focality can play an important role, matters are not at all straightforward. A tempting first thought would be to articulate each disjunct or member of the cluster focally, taking

FOCALITY, ANALOGY, AND THE ARTICULATION OF CONCEPTS   61

knowing that as the focus. Thus, we might articulate *knowing whether* and *knowing how* through the following biconditionals:

(1) A knows whether p iff [A knows that p or A knows that not p]
(2) A knows how to ϕ iff for some w, A knows that w is a way of ϕ-ing[23]

Unfortunately, this cannot explain properly what makes it appropriate to use the term 'know' in both cases, let alone why we might think of them as unified, if indeed they are. It can't *simply* be that *knowing how* can be articulated in terms of *knowing that*. After all, *ignorance whether p* can be defined as *not knowing that p and not knowing that not p*. But this is scarcely a good reason to label ignorance 'knowledge'.

What can we appeal to? For *knowing whether*, little more is needed, I suspect, than the fact that any genuine instance of the concept is actually *constituted* by a specimen of the focus, *knowing that*: when I know whether p, my doing so consists either in my knowing that p or in my knowing that not p, and so one way or the other what makes it true that A knows whether p is an instance of *knowing that*. (Conversely, of course, when I know that p, that fact constitutes my knowing whether p.) These considerations are surely enough for them to be properly called by the same name, and perhaps even for them to constitute a loose unity.[24]

Knowing how, on the other hand, is more complicated. In this case, it is perhaps enough to appeal to the common analytical or elucidatory structures that (2) ensures *knowing how* inherits from *knowing that*. For example, we might think that in knowing how to ϕ, I know by (2) that the relevant w is a way of ϕ-ing, and so, by (K), I non-accidentally believe as much; hence, I have a non-accidental belief as to how to ϕ. Moreover, in so far as I know that w is a way of doing ϕ, w must work; hence if I know how to ϕ, what I believe must work. We therefore have a tripartite analytical or elucidatory structure for *knowing how* that mirrors exactly the corresponding structure for propositional knowledge sketched above.[25] Although not materially identical, they are at the level of proper articulation structurally identical: they are exactly analogous. And as we shall see later (section 11), when these matters are spelt out in more detail, this should be

---

[23] I say *articulate* here with good reason. For although (1) surely counts as an analysis, (2) is meant to echo Stanley and Williamson's much-discussed proposal for analysing *knowing how to φ* in terms of *ways of φ-ing*, a proposal, even if true, that has not commanded universal assent as an analysis of *knowing how*. Not counting as an analysis, however, wouldn't preclude its counting as an *elucidation*. Hence my use of the term 'articulate'. For details of their proposal, see Stanley and Williamson 2001; and for criticism of it as circular, see Wiggins 2012 and Lovibond 2022, ch. 6. The most influential proponent of the irreducibility of *knowing how* to *knowing that* is, of course, Ryle 1949, ch. 2.

[24] Everything here depends upon whether this kind of reciprocal instantiation is enough for loose identity; see section 5. I suspect that it is, but this needs further work.

[25] We might put it like this: A knows how to φ iff A has a belief as to how to φ, A's coming to have this belief is non-accidental, and what A believes works.

62 S. G. WILLIAMS

enough to warrant their both having the same name: for having the same name here points to a substantial commonality of understanding. I remain agnostic, however, whether *knowing that* and *knowing how* constitute a loose unity.

9.

Our initial question was how to avoid making analytical philosophy vulnerable to the dismal narrative. And as a first step, I suggested that we divorce it from its associated foundational programmes and allow it to embrace not merely analysis per se, but also the elucidation of concepts. For in so doing, we would be able to create maps of properly separable but interrelated concepts that guide us through parts of our conceptual scheme and doubtless suggest similarities elsewhere. Such a reply, however, still lacks much by way of system. Only if we can find other, more bounded, ways of introducing system both into the articulation of the concepts and into their discovery can we give significant content to a contrary narrative. As I highlighted in section 4, I think focality provides us with such ways; and in the remaining sections, I want to indicate in some detail why this is so. Because the linguistic and the conceptual perspectives are interchangeable, I shall switch between them broadly without comment.

Post-war thinking about focality received an initial impetus from its deployment by J. L. Austin, Herbert Hart, and G. E. L. Owen.[26] Indeed, it was Owen who first coined the term 'focal' (as a gloss on the Greek term *pros hen*).[27] However, current understanding of the notion has been greatly enhanced by Christopher Shields' uncovering of an elegant idea in the work of the Thomist philosopher, Thomas Cajetan.[28] To see what this idea amounts to, we return to Aristotle's example of 'healthy' (*hugiēs*).[29] In line with what we said earlier (section 4), uses of this word within a certain range are for him articulable in terms of the meaning of a core use of it: namely, that of 'healthy' as it occurs in 'healthy body'.[30] Thus 'healthy' in 'healthy exercise' typically means *productive of a healthy body*; in 'healthy regimen' it means *designed to produce a healthy body*; in 'healthy lungs' it means *partly constitutive of a healthy body*; and so on. (As before, the core use of the term will be its *focus*, the other uses its *satellites*.) To be sure, not every use of 'healthy' fits this focal template. Some uses are clearly metaphorical, as in 'healthy economy' or 'healthy bank balance'; others—like 'healthy appetite' or 'healthy mind'—remain unclear. If it should turn out that a healthy appetite—which is normally taken to indicate a *sizeable* appetite—generates a healthy body, then we

---

[26] See Austin 1962, 64, Hart 1961, ch. 1, §3, and Owen 1986.   [27] Owen 1986, 184.
[28] See Shields 1999, esp. §4.4. Cajetan's proposal may be found in Cajetan 2009, 8–16.
[29] See, e.g., *Metaphysics* Γ.2, 1003a33ff.
[30] Or, echoing what we said earlier, in terms of the corresponding substantive 'health'.

FOCALITY, ANALOGY, AND THE ARTICULATION OF CONCEPTS 63

could imagine it fitting the template; similarly with a healthy mind, if Juvenal is right and healthy minds are grounded in healthy bodies.

Does this example point to anything more general? On the face of it, it does. For not only are the different uses of 'healthy' definable in terms of a healthy body, but each such definition employs one or other of at least three of Aristotle's four causes—material, efficient, final, or formal.[31] Thus, healthy exercise is an efficient cause of a healthy body; a healthy body is a final cause of a healthy regimen, since such a body will be the aim of the regimen; and in partly constituting a healthy body, a healthy lung will be a material cause of a healthy body. And it is here that Shields' appropriation of Cardinal Cajetan kicks in. For according to Cajetan, in cases of genuine focal meaning, the relation between a term's satellite uses and its focus must be drawn from four types of causal relation; and it is natural to construe these four types of cause as tantamount to Aristotle's four causes. In other words, using essentially Shields' gloss, if F is a focal concept, with a being a focal case of being F and b a satellite of being F, then:

(F) b's being F must stand in the relation of one or more of the four Aristotelian causes to a's being F.

Notice that when the focus and one of its satellites stand in a specific relation of causation, the direction of causation might run either way. In the case of 'healthy exercise', which connotes being *productive* of health, the direction is from satellite to focus, while in the case of 'healthy complexion', which connotes being *indicative* of health, it is the other way round. But both are examples of efficient causation. Nevertheless, all the examples require understanding of the focus ('healthy body') to understand the satellites. And in consequence, Shields adds a second condition, which he calls the *priority* condition:

(P) It is impossible to understand what it is for b to be F without understanding what it is for a to be F, though not vice versa.[32]

Elegant though it is, this picture has not gone unquestioned. In particular, there has been interpretational controversy about whether Aristotle, and indeed Cajetan, intended to include formal causes in the definition of focality. According to Shields, convincing examples in Aristotle of the use of formal causes in the characterization of individual focal terms have been hard to come by; and Cajetan appears to replace formal cause with something that he calls an *exemplary cause*:

---

[31] For Aristotle, a *material cause* of something is constitutive of it; a *formal cause* of something is its form, or that which makes it what it is; an *efficient cause* is that which brings about change or rest in it; and a *final cause* of something is that for the sake of which it is produced; see, e.g., *Metaphysics* Δ.2, 1013a24–b2.

[32] For Shields' discussion of this extra condition, see Shields 1999, §4.5.

64 S. G. WILLIAMS

that is, one which, as Julie Ward puts it, is 'related to the thing caused as the model is related to the product made or the thing done'.[33] Moreover, there appears to be a principled reason for excluding formal causes from the definition of focality. Because it seems to be a necessary condition on definitions fully grounded in formal causation that the *very same quality* be preserved from *definiens* to *definiendum*, we will not, in any genuine instance of formal causation, have two things with the same name, but one. We will no longer have an instance of homonymy.[34]

Replying to this is not straightforward. But in the first instance we can at least say that Aristotle himself seems not only to have been aware of the existence of exemplary causes, but also to have recognized them as formal causes.[35] Admittedly, this does not show that he was entitled to recognize them as such,[36] but with the conceptual resources that we are allowing ourselves regarding identity and unity, we can, I think, see that he was. For even if with Ward we insist that the same property should be preserved in focal definitions that use formal causation, there is nothing to stop us, in line with our previous discussion, from allowing property-preservation from *definiens* to *definiendum* in formal causation to be tied to loose identity. That way, in one sense of identity, identical properties can be preserved, while strict homonymy is maintained. Plainly this will accommodate those cases in which (as we might say) a feature of a product created properly in the image of a model or paradigm is only loosely identical to the corresponding feature of the model or paradigm itself. It follows that even with the restriction, we may count exemplary causes as formal causes, provided we permit ourselves a conception of property-preservation that can be tied to loose identity.

For all that the interpretational controversy tells us, the four-causes framework seems to come through unscathed. Nevertheless, I remain uneasy about it as a comprehensive account of focality. For although it may well be able to accommodate the Aristotelian examples we have considered so far, it is not yet clear why it is anything more than a historical curiosity. What we need to understand better is: why introduce focality at all? In light of our preceding discussion, however, it is natural to take it as providing a criterion of when it is appropriate to reserve the same name for certain concepts, and perhaps also of when the concepts are loosely unified, even if they are not strictly so. Hence, to test the framework, we should ask how it stacks up against the purpose of focality so understood. In other words:

---

[33] Ward 2008, 85. [34] See Ward 2008, 81–3.
[35] See, e.g., *Physics* 2.2, 194b26 where paradigms are used as an example of a formal cause. Thanks here to David Charles, who has long understood this feature of Aristotle's thinking; see, e.g., Charles 1999.
[36] Ward evidently thinks that he wasn't.

FOCALITY, ANALOGY, AND THE ARTICULATION OF CONCEPTS   65

(1) Do relations captured in the four-causes account invariably yield disjunctive or cluster concepts that it is proper to think of as warranting the same
name, or even as being loosely unified?

(2) Are there other relations than those in the four causes account that fit the
focus-satellite template, and which yield similar disjunctive or cluster concepts with these same features?

Unfortunately for the framework, however, not only is the answer to (1) 'no', the answer to (2) seems to be 'yes'.

Consider (1). It is not hard to find cluster concepts that fit the four-causes framework but which we would struggle to suppose should have the same name, let alone think of as loosely unitary. The sun plays an important role in the main-tenance of human health, but would it be appropriate to call it 'healthy'? Or think of a lecture on public health. This may promote health and healthy bodies, but again would it be appropriate to call it 'healthy'? I doubt these things. It is true, as Shields points out, that the notion of focality, understood in the broadly causal manner he advocates, is almost certainly open-textured. Thus should we discover that, for example, a healthy appetite really does stand in the relation of efficient cause to healthy bodies, we might properly allow the expression 'healthy appetite' to be in the list of terms focally related to 'healthy body'. But as things stand, it does not seem appropriate to add any of 'healthy appetite', 'healthy sun', and 'healthy lecture' to the list.

Question (2) is less straightforward, but there do seem to be cases that warrant an affirmative answer. For instance, take 'healthy wound'. We can think of this as typically connoting a wound that was once serious but is now sufficiently recovered to be visibly indicative of future healthy tissue, something that in turn is part of a healthy body. But although this certainly fits the template—healthy wounds have got *something* to do with health and healthy bodies—it is not entirely clear how. As a first go, however, we might say that a healthy wound is indicative of something that is an efficient cause of something else—healthy tissue—that is a material cause of a healthy body. From which it follows that the wound is connected to a healthy body at least through a combination of efficient and material causes. But then, although it would fit the template, it won't satisfy (F) as it stands.

Equally, consider Shields' example of vitamins that are called 'healthy' because they *preserve* or *guard health*. They evidently fit the template too, but do they really satisfy (F)? According to Shields, they do since they contribute towards health or a healthy body, thereby exemplifying efficient causation. But I wonder if this is right. Surely, they contribute to a healthy body, by *keeping* it healthy or even by *warding off* ill-health; and it takes quite a bit of shoe-horning to think of this as efficient causation. Merely preserving health is preserving the status quo, not, as our definition of efficient causation (in n. 31) has it, bringing about change or rest. Indeed, something—a healthy balm, say—might succeed in guarding health, possibly in tandem with other factors, without itself inducing any change in the body. (Its role, for instance, might be to fight off harmful invading micro-organisms.) Admittedly, preserving the status quo in this way might well *involve* the bringing about of change or rest in the body, something we could discover by looking deeply enough into the preservation mechanism. But for all 'preservation of the status quo' means, it could happen if absolutely nothing changed. And even if it should turn out that preservation of the status quo necessarily *supervenes* on bodily change, that would not make it an efficient cause in itself.

Faced by these examples, we can, I think, conclude that the answer to (2) is indeed 'yes'. It is true that we might try to retain the spirit of the proposal by first adjusting (F) so that it includes combinations of the causal relations we have deployed so far. (This would accommodate healthy wounds.) Indeed, if combinations of such relations are subsumable under the general banner of supervenience upon the four causes, we might even be able to accommodate both healthy wounds and healthy vitamins, via the following:

(F*)   *b*'s being F must stand in the relation of one or more of the four Aristotelian causes to *a*'s being F—or in a relation to *a*'s being F that *supervenes upon* such relations.

The trouble with the first adjustment is that we don't know how causes may be legitimately combined to ensure focality; and the introduction of the catch-all term 'supervenience' in (F*) merely masks this fact.[37]

10.

Although the four-causes model of focality as conceived by either Cajetan or Shields must be deemed incorrect, it would be wrong to dismiss it out of hand. The mistake, I suspect, lies in thinking that the model should match exactly the cases we like—the cases in which the satellites are so intimately related to the focus that they at least warrant the same name, and perhaps even count as loosely identical. I suggest instead that we treat the four-causes model as providing non-exhaustive, defeasible guidelines to the same end—and that exposing a concept as focal is just the first step.

---

[37] An important, related question that the above considerations throw up is whether they provide grounds for extending the list of types of cause. Maybe combinations of causes can generate further types of cause, maybe things that *preserve* a state of affairs can count as special *preservative* causes, and so on. Notice that there need be nothing anti-Aristotelian about this: for some observations relating to the provisional nature of Aristotle's deliberations about causality, see Williams and Charles 2013, §2.

FOCALITY, ANALOGY, AND THE ARTICULATION OF CONCEPTS   67

However, this means we need a different way of thinking about focality; and for this I propose that we return to the rough characterization in section 4. According to that suggestion, a focal concept is a disjunction or cluster of sub-concepts, in terms of one of which (its *focus*) the others (its *satellites*) can be understood. But we left it open whether it should be refined in any way. What I suggest now is that we keep any refinements to a minimum, and that we simply use the literal meaning of the original Aristotelian term *pros hen* (i.e., *pertaining to one thing*), along with the notions of analysis and articulation, to make the connection between the satellites and the focus. More precisely, we define a focal concept as one that can be analysed as a disjunction or cluster of sub-concepts to one of which (the focus) the others may be articulated as pertaining; a focal term will then be a term that expresses a focal concept, and each disjunct of its disjunctive meaning or each member of its cluster of meanings will be articulated as pertaining to the focus.[38] Notice that such a definition does not include anything corresponding to Shields' priority condition (section 9); but while it *may* be appropriate to add such a condition explicitly, I am inclined to resist doing so. Underpinning it, I suspect, is the idea that the satellites must be *analysed* in terms of the focus, but if the notion of articulable pertinence is not restricted to analysis, and can involve elucidation, then there may well be cases in which priority fails. (The proposed articulation of *knowing how* in terms of *knowing that* in section 8 would be an illustration, if biconditional (2) there amounts only to an elucidation, not to an analysis.) In fact, some cases might even involve *reciprocal* pertinence.

Given that this proposed definition is just a modest precisification of our rough characterization of focality, our initial examples involving 'healthy' will be accommodated as before. (Healthy exercise, healthy regimens, healthy lungs, and even healthy complexions, healthy wounds, and healthy vitamins are all in their different ways articulable as pertaining to health or to a healthy body.) And that is all to the good. On the other hand, it must be conceded that the proposal is much more permissive than the four-causes model. Not only will it allow in oddities like 'healthy hospital' (designed to promote health), 'healthy lecture', and 'healthy textbook' (if both are about health), it will even let in, for example, 'healthy pen' (for any pen that has the logo of a well-disinfected hospital on it); and so on. But with such examples satisfying it, surely the proposal is useless.[39]

I doubt that the notion of pertinence here is quite that feeble, but in any case, from our new perspective, where we are released from the task of trying to define focality so that it matches exactly the cases we like, there is nothing to prevent us from adopting the more permissive definition as a first step and then, via what I shall refer to as *rich* or *wide-ranging* pertinence, distinguishing good illustrations of focality from bad ones. Here the idea is that in the absence of countervailing

---

[38] Wiggins proposes and then rejects what is in effect this suggestion in Wiggins 1971, 32 n. *b*.
[39] The permissiveness of the account was essentially Wiggins' reason for rejecting it; see Wiggins 1971, 32 n. *b*, again.

68   S. G. WILLIAMS

considerations, richly pertinent cases will meet the designated purpose of focal terms: that is, they will warrant the use of the same name, and sometimes make it appropriate to think of the relevant disjunctive or cluster concept as unitary. As we shall see, our original examples, those involving healthy exercise, regimens, and lungs, will emerge as good illustrations of focality, since each is richly pertinent to a healthy body; and even some of the oddball cases like 'healthy hospital' may be too. But others will definitely not be. Thus (filling out the example of the healthy pen) we could define a healthy pen as one which has on it the logo of a hospital that promotes health or regularly turns out healthy patients. Although it would certainly pertain to healthy bodies, its pertinence is seriously limited. The fact that a hospital has such a logo does not mean that it really does promote health or turn out healthy patients: the connection between a healthy pen (so defined) and healthy patients is too flimsy.

11.

Such a picture evidently calls for an explanation of what rich or wide-ranging pertinence amounts to. I propose the following. Suppose that F is a focal concept whose focus is F_1 and one of whose satellites is F_2. Then F_2 is *richly pertinent* to F_1 if there is a substantial, non-accidental correspondence between features that F_1 and F_2 have, or between features that things have by virtue of satisfying F_2 and features that things have by virtue of satisfying F_1. For any given case, whether there is such a correspondence will emerge through the details of the articulated pertinence relation in question. More specifically, we can expect the correspondence to be substantial, and the pertinence to be rich or wide ranging, when this relation in context manifests any of:

 (a) a close approximation to identity (exemplary causes);
 (b) a highly integrated form of the part-whole relation (material causes);
 (c) extensive explanation (efficient and final causes);
 (d) rich structural analogy (*knowing how* and *knowing that*).

Let us look briefly at how these thoughts play out in practice, beginning with exemplary causes. By way of illustration, we return to the crusty debate between Susan Stebbing and Arthur Eddington about whether tables are solid, with Eddington insisting that they aren't, on the grounds that there is a great deal of space between the atoms that individually make up the tables, and Stebbing arguing that they are, on the grounds that part of what we mean by 'solid' is that tables are solid.[40] By using the notion of an exemplary cause, we can see that in a way

---

[40] For details, see Eddington 1928, introduction, and Stebbing 1944, ch. 3.

FOCALITY, ANALOGY, AND THE ARTICULATION OF CONCEPTS   69

both were right; they were just using the terms slightly differently, with Eddington's use being a kind of ideal use, and Stebbing's being definable as an approximation to the ideal. Here we have an example of the meaning of a focal term being grounded in an exemplary cause, the focus being an ideal use of 'solid', and the approximations being the satellites.

Calling the two conceptions of solidity *Eddington-solidity* and *Stebbing-solidity*, (or *E-solidity* and *S-solidity*, for short), we now ask whether there is a substantial non-accidental correspondence in features that things have in virtue being E-solid and features that things have in virtue of being S-solid. And plainly there is. E-solids will be impenetrable and possess rigidly positioned parts between which there will be no gaps; and quite generally they will possess none of the properties that mark out liquids or gases. But given that S-solidity is defined as a close approximation to E-solidity, if F is a feature of an E-solid (*qua* solid), then the fact that the E-solid is F will constitute strong grounds for supposing that S-solids also have it, or at least an approximation to it. For example, it is a feature of an E-solid that it won't in any circumstances drip. But this provides strong grounds for thinking that at any given moment an S-solid like a metal trunk, or a pebble on a beach, or a piece of properly preserved mahogany won't drip either. Equally, just as E-solids are rigid, impenetrable, and lack gaps between their parts, etc., so S-solids will be all but rigid, impenetrable for all everyday purposes, and lack macroscopic gaps between their parts, etc. Thus, it is safe to say that the non-accidental correspondence between the features of the two kinds of solidity (*qua* solidity) is sufficiently widespread to allow us to take S-solidity to be richly pertinent to E-solidity. At the very least, therefore, it is quite proper to allow S-solids and E-solids to be homonymous: having the same name in context highlights the large non-accidental correspondence of features.

Consider now (b), material causation, as exemplified by the relation between healthy lungs and healthy bodies. In being a material cause of a healthy body, healthy lungs are partly constitutive of the healthy body, but not—or not merely—in the sense of abstract mereology. They are constitutive of it insofar as they are part of a network of *organs* that constitute the healthy body. What we need to know is whether there is a substantial correspondence of features that healthy lungs and a healthy body have by virtue of their each being healthy. And the answer is surely yes. On the one hand, healthy bodies share with healthy lungs any property that an organ has just by virtue of its being healthy. Thus just as a healthy body must be disease-free, uninjured, and functioning properly, so the corresponding lungs must be too. On the other hand, even though a healthy lung won't have all the health-related properties of a healthy body—healthy bodies have a healthy heart, but healthy lungs don't—the fact that it is an organ partly constitutive of a healthy body means that it can at least be a *sign* of a healthy body, and hence of the features that a healthy body possesses, given the interrelatedness of a body's organs. So there is a substantial non-accidental *correspondence* of related properties, some of which are shared properties and some not. It follows that the pertinence relation between a healthy lung and a healthy body is rich, and therefore to allow them to be homonymous is warranted.

For efficient causes like healthy exercise, there will be almost no sharing of relevant features between them and healthy bodies. (Thus, the fact that a healthy body has some feature—a healthy heart, say—by virtue of its being healthy provides no grounds for thinking that healthy exercise will have the feature or something similar.) Nevertheless, there is a substantial non-accidental correspondence between features that healthy exercise possesses by virtue of its being healthy and features that healthy bodies possess by virtue of their being healthy. For comprehensive healthy exercise will result, through its different facets, in the health of a healthy body's material causes—a healthy heart, lungs, muscles, bones, and so on—and hence in the features that these organs have by virtue of their being healthy. Thus through a constellation of salient facts that surround healthy exercise, we can see how it can explain a wide range of features of healthy bodies. Similar remarks apply to healthy regimens, which healthy bodies are final causes of. For the different facets of a good regimen—including healthy exercise—will also take in features of the organs that are the material causes of healthy bodies. So again there will be a substantial non-accidental correspondence. And when the regimen is successful, its different aspects will explain these features. Homonymy in both cases will be warranted. Notice that such considerations are in contrast to a healthy appetite or our so-called healthy pen. A healthy appetite or a healthy pen can explain very little about the health-related features of their foci, and similarly, vice versa. In their case, homonymy is certainly not warranted.

Finally, we have the case of structural analogy, (d). Given the fourfold schema, any Aristotelian account of structural analogy will always involve some correspondence of features; but a good structural analogy will at least presuppose a substantial non-accidental correspondence of such features. Let us return to our example earlier (section 8) of *knowing how* and *knowing that*. I suggested that these concepts should be articulated together through the focal equivalence:

(2)   A knows how to ϕ iff for some w, A knows that w is a way of ϕ-ing,

and individually through their matching tripartite clauses. But I also suggested these articulations instantiate a structural analogy between the two concepts. How rich is this analogy? In fact, (2) along with the matching individual articulations ensures a wealth of matching inferential features. Letting 'AKp' mean A knows that p, and 'AK how to ϕ' mean A knows how to ϕ, we can discover that

   (i) Just as 'AK[p and q]' entails '[AKp and AKq]', so 'AK how to [ϕ and ψ]' entails '[AK how to ϕ and AK how to ψ]';

FOCALITY, ANALOGY, AND THE ARTICULATION OF CONCEPTS 71

(ii) Just as '[AKp or AKq]' entails 'AK[p or q]', so '[AK how to ϕ or AK how to ψ]' entails 'AK how to [ϕ or ψ]'; and

(iii) Just as 'AKp' and 'AK[p → q]' entails 'AKq', so '[AK how to ϕ and AK[A ϕs → A ψs]]' entails 'AK how to ψ'.[41]

And so on. All are deducible through (2), and accordingly, we surely have good reason to conclude that *knowing that* and *knowing how* are warranted homonyms.[42]

I submit that all four examples yield warranted homonyms, and none involves an abuse of terms from a properly nuanced Lockean perspective. Of course, this still leaves the question whether it is appropriate to think of these homonyms as constituting a loose unity. As I shall argue in section 13, given that the salient articulated pertinence relation between E-solidity and S-solidity manifests a close approximation to identity, the two conceptions of solidity do indeed form a loose unity. But I remain agnostic about the other cases.

12.

As advertised in section 10, considerations like the above that favour warranted homonymy are defeasible. If, for example, it should turn out that a particular kind of physical exercise had all along been utterly deadly, then no matter how rich the pertinence, no matter how extensive the correspondence in features, it would not warrant the label 'healthy'. And it might seem in consequence that we are edging our way back to the dismal narrative—or at least back to the merely haphazard exploration of concepts and their articulations. But this would not be right. What our discussion of focality shows is something like the following investigative strategy—a strategy I take to be of a piece with Charles's understanding of Aristotle's general scientific methodology (section 6), along with the quasi-inferential structure we associated with the uncovering of analogical concepts (section 3):

1. We investigate individual words to see whether they are used homonymously.
2. We uncover (minimally) focal uses.
3. We deploy causal-cum-analogical guidelines of the sort exploited in our discussion of examples (a)–(d) of section 11 to see whether the pertinence is rich.

---

[41] On both sides of the schema in (iii), we might add, 'provided A puts the premises together'.

[42] Of course, not *all* such inferential features match. For example, although 'AK not p' entails 'not AKp', 'AK how not to φ' does not entail 'not AK how to φ'. (I know how not to speak, but I also know how to speak.) However, this does not mean that the homonymy through analogy is no longer warranted. For there is still a substantial overlap of such inferential features. At any rate, given equivalence (1) and the matching tripartite articulations of *knowing how* and *knowing that*, alongside such features, the onus is surely on those who think the homonymy is not warranted to explain why not.

72 S. G. WILLIAMS

4. On the assumption that no defeating considerations obtain, we conclude that they warrant being homonyms even from our nuanced Lockean perspective.
5. We find the connections appropriate for a determination of loose unity.

In pursuing matters in this way, not only are we able to investigate a range of concepts in a broadly systematic way, but also we are able to uncover a multitude of causal and a priori connections, some of which may yield a deep articulation of the concepts in question. Through the defeasible heuristic devices provided by the guidelines, we are already a far cry from the haphazard activity of conducting analysis and elucidation piecemeal—and certainly from the dismal narrative.

13.

Aristotle thought his focal-cum-analogical picture would help us to understand a variety of important but strictly fragmented philosophical concepts. And in this I think he is right. I wish to conclude the chapter by discussing briefly one such concept—*identity*.[43] In section 1, we used this concept to illustrate the distinction between elucidation and analysis, employing Wiggins' idea that it could be elucidated, though not analysed, through what seem to be the fundamental logical principles that govern it: namely, the Law of Identity and Leibniz's Law. There was nothing in this elucidation, however, to suggest that it was a fragmented concept. (Wiggins evidently thinks it isn't.) I want now to indicate how we might revise this elucidation so that it allows us sometimes to think of identity quite properly as both a fragmented and a unitary concept: it is strictly fragmented, but loosely unitary. Of course, the idea that identity might be loosely unitary itself presupposes the notion of loose identity: concepts C_1 and C_2 are loosely unified if C_1 is loosely identical to C_2. But to the extent that there is a circularity here, it is not vicious. It simply shows that if we can make sense of loose identity independently of loose unity—and what follows indicates that we can—the concept of loose unity makes sense too, and loose identity falls under it.

I shall take at least a modified version of Wiggins' suggestion to be an elucidation of *strict* identity, and then indicate how this elucidation might be modified further to accommodate looser forms of identity. In effect, the modifications will reflect the idea that identity is a focal concept with strict identity as its focus and looser conceptions as its satellites. The relation of articulated pertinence will in any given case amount to a close approximation to strict identity. It will therefore be exemplary causes here that are acting as our methodological guide. It should

---

[43] Other concepts, I think, that are articulable in a focal/analogical way include existence and truth. For a non-Aristotelian analogical account of existence, see Williams 1996/2000, §3, §16; and for the beginnings of a focal treatment of truth, see Williams 2004, §6.

FOCALITY, ANALOGY, AND THE ARTICULATION OF CONCEPTS   73

be borne in mind that what counts as a close approximation will change as the examples vary. Artefacts will typically depend on some combination of purpose and constitution, universals on their articulated natures, and so on.

How then should we elucidate loose identity? Since, as far as I can see, there are no possible circumstances in which something could in any sense be distinct from *itself*, the corresponding Law of Identity seems difficult rationally to deny. Accordingly, I shall take loose forms of identity, henceforth represented by the symbol '≈', to be such that for all x, x ≈ x. This means that any modification of the elucidation of strict identity that will accommodate loose forms has to concern Leibniz's Law. To see how, three points need highlighting.

The first is that the form in which Leibniz's Law is presented in elementary logic textbooks is typically already an ideological abstraction. In order to accommodate change in objects, which seems to conflict with the law, its advocates are apt to follow Frege and introduce the notion of temporal relativity. They say that although a bicycle tyre might be both flat and hard, this does not conflict with their form of Leibniz's Law, since *being flat* and *being hard* are time-relative properties: the tyre will be flat at t and hard at t′. But as David Lewis has pointed out, this contradicts the fact that such properties as *being flat* and *being hard* are not relations to times at all: *being flat at t* and *being hard at t′* are abstractions from these properties.[44] On the assumption that Leibniz's Law preserves properties across identities, this seems to leave us with no explanation of how our tyre can persist through the change from flat to hard. Being wedded to a similarly broad conception of Leibniz's Law, Lewis himself responds to the conundrum by claiming that we have different *objects* at times t and t′: the tyre-at-t and the tyre-at-t′. But this seems even more implausible than the claim that *being hard* and *being flat* are temporal relations. Although I would not deny that there are such things as the tyre-at-t and the tyre-at-t′, again they are surely abstractions from the continuant that is the tyre.

I conclude from this that we need an alternative way of thinking about Leibniz's Law, one that allows for the existence of ordinary properties and objects and doesn't require time-relative abstractions to maintain the law's truth. I suggest that for strict identity between any objects of any kind, we confine ourselves to *essential* properties, properties that objects have by virtue of their being those objects.[45] Thus, if our property is *being made of rubber* then if tyre b has it and b is identical to c, then c has it too, for being made of rubber is an essential property of any tyre that has it: it is a property such that if a tyre has it then it has it by virtue of

---

[44] See Lewis 1986, 203–4. Lewis calls such properties 'intrinsic'. I steer clear of the term here to avoid being caught up in the web of alternative characterizations; see next footnote.

[45] This is one of Lewis's ways of characterizing *intrinsic* properties. But given the number of non-equivalent ways of doing so, I stick with the term 'essential' and this reasonably uncontroversial way of understanding it. Note that Aristotle seems to foreshadow the restriction to essential properties in *Sophistical Refutations* 24, 179a35–8. For development of this thought, see Charles 2000, 95ff.

74   S. G. WILLIAMS

being a tyre. Let us call this the *core form* of Leibniz's Law. We might express it as follows:

(LL$_1$)   Given b = c and Pb, it follows that Pc, provided that P is essential to b.[46]

It should be noted that the properties in question can themselves involve relations. For example, if b is identical to c, then being identical to c is essential to b.[47]

The second point that needs highlighting is that much talk of loose forms of identity emerges from the consideration of vagueness—and especially sorites puzzles about identity.[48] And it is these that bear directly on Leibniz's Law. For all such puzzles involve a sequence of apparent identities between things that are close in nature, even though the first and last are far enough apart to be distinct. The problem is that if the identities are strict, then the transitivity of strict identity will ensure that the first and the last of the objects are identical, which is a contradiction. Evidently, we can avoid this contradiction if we introduce a form of identity that is not transitive. And loose identity seems to fit the bill. But our problem is that Leibniz's Law ordinarily entails transitivity. It follows that we must restrict the law further to block the deduction.[49] How so?

Since sorites problems about identity tend to involve diachronic identity—think of Theseus's Ship—it is tempting to think that any (further) restrictions should apply to loose identity over time. However, I doubt this can be the heart of the matter. And this brings me to my third point. Since one of our principal concerns in this chapter lies with the loose unity of cluster concepts, and with loose identity between some of its sub-concepts, we need to apply any restriction of Leibniz's Law to universals as well. But given that universals are by nature atemporal, any adjustment to LL$_1$ that applies merely to diachronic identities will be of no use in accommodating sorites series that involve loose identities between (say) strictly distinct but neighbouring universals. So how might we do so? To conclude the chapter, I offer the following rough-and-ready sketch.

---

[46] I noted in section 1 that care is always needed when trying to establish distinctness through the contrapositive. We can now see why. In order to establish that tyres a and b are distinct, it's not enough that a should be flat and b hard. We need to know further that being flat or being hard is a property that the objects have by virtue of being the objects they are. But they are plainly not: after all, b's hardness may simply be the result of my pumping up a. Notice that the core form does not entail that the *only* properties that are preserved are the essential ones. For instance, if a is flat and remains unchanged throughout its life, then if a is identical to b, then b is flat too. And, of course, the abstracted property of being flat at t will also be preserved.

[47] This means that in conjunction with the Law of Identity even LL$_1$ is sufficient for identity, in the sense of n. 3.

[48] See again Chisholm 1976, ch. 3.

[49] As a rule of inference, transitivity follows immediately from LL$_1$. For replacing the variable P in LL$_1$ by the open sentence 'a = ξ' that in effect designates the essential property of being identical to a, we obtain as premises: b = c, a = b. So by LL$_1$, we can infer a = c. I should emphasize that the failure of transitivity is not the only vagueness-related problem that affects the present discussion. See Williams 2004, esp. §6, for a picture that uses some of the present considerations to ameliorate such difficulties.

FOCALITY, ANALOGY, AND THE ARTICULATION OF CONCEPTS   75

Given that we are taking loose identity to be an approximation to strict identity, no version of Leibniz's Law can allow loose identities to preserve strict properties that are essential to non-vague objects. For example, associated with E-solidity will be the property of *being gapless internally*. But if we allow this property to be preserved across loose identity, then we will reach the false conclusion that S-solidity will be associated with it too. On the other hand, properties like *being nearly gapless internally* will apply to both.[50] And I suggest we use this as a model. Call a property 'potentially soritical' (PS) if things can have it more or less, or to a greater or lesser degree. Many such properties will be expressible using gradable adjectival phrases: that is, adjectival phrases that, typically, can properly be prefixed by intensifiers like 'very', 'highly', or 'extremely'. Examples include the properties of being bright, tall, tubby, and even being rigid or solid. And, as the example of *being internally gapless* illustrates, we can often turn properties that are not PS into ones that are by prefixing adverbs like 'nearly', 'almost', or 'close to' to adjectival phrases that express them. Then we might try the following version of Leibniz's Law, which would apply to all loose identities, diachronic or otherwise:

Given $b \approx c$ and Pb, it follows that Pc, provided P is a PS-property that is essential to b.

Unfortunately, this will not prevent paradox from ensuing. On the assumption that being loosely identical to c is essential to b, if it holds of it at all, we can generate a straightforward sorites series: apply the property represented by '$a_1 \approx \xi$' to the sequence $a_1 \approx a_2, \ldots, a_{n-1} \approx a_n$. However, we can remove this consequence if instead of thinking of Leibniz's Law as *conclusive*, we view it as *presumptive*: we take the premises as providing a presumption in favour of its conclusion.[51] This results in the following version of the law:

(LL$_2$)   Given $b \approx c$ and Pb, there is a presumption in favour of Pc, provided P is a PS- property that is essential to b.

Evidently this can apply to ordinary PS-properties. Thus suppose that (i) $a \approx b$, (ii) being close to consisting entirely of wood is essential to a boat, if it has that property at all, and (iii) a is a boat with that property. Then there will be a presumption in favour of b's having it too. But since a presumption in favour is not an inevitability, it won't apply right across a sorites spectrum. Eventually the

---

[50]   I here take the connection between 'nearly F', 'close to being F', 'almost F', etc., and 'being not F' to be an implicature not an entailment. For helpful discussion of these issues, see Atlas 2005, ch. 5.

[51]   We may gloss presumption as follows: there is a presumption in favour of q (given p) iff one may properly take it that q is the case (given p) unless or until one has (sufficient) reasons to believe that q is not the case. This is a variant on a rule of presumption developed by Edna Ullman-Margalit in connection with practical deliberation. (See Ullman-Margalit 1983, esp. 147.)

76   S. G. WILLIAMS

presumption will be trumped by other considerations—most notably by the fact that it will yield a contradiction otherwise. Admittedly, where exactly this is will remain blurred; but that's how it is with vagueness. And the same applies to loose identity itself, whether the identities are diachronic, synchronic, or atemporal. Consider the PS-property essential to a that is represented by 'a $\approx \xi$'. Given that b $\approx$ c and that a $\approx$ b, there is undoubtedly a presumption in favour of a $\approx$ c. So transitivity is presumptively valid.[52] But because it would otherwise lead to paradox when applied in sequence to (say) $a_1 \approx a_2, \ldots, a_{n-1} \approx a_n$, the presumption can be trumped or overridden by other considerations. To be sure, it will be confirmed for initial members of the series: $a_1 \approx a_2$ and $a_1 \approx a_3$, say; but to avoid contradiction, the presumption will eventually have to be trumped. As before, it will be blurred when exactly this is so—but again that's how it is with vagueness.

I propose LL_2, along with the Law of Identity, as an elucidation of loose identity. It is an approximation to strict identity, and it can apply without paradox to universals like E- and S-solidity just as much as to vague spatiotemporal objects. Indeed, we can even argue by analogy with examples like E- and S-solidity that strict and loose identity are themselves loosely identical. The disjunctive concept of identity will therefore count as a loosely unified concept.[53]

Works Cited

Atlas, Jay David. 2005. *Logic, Meaning, and Conversation: Semantical Underdeterminacy, Implicature, and Their Interface*. Oxford University Press.

Austin, J. L. 1962. *Sense and Sensibilia* (ed. G. Warnock). Oxford University Press.

Bartha, Paul. 2010. *By Parallel Reasoning*. Oxford University Press.

Beere, Jonathan. 2009. *Doing and Being: An Interpretation of Aristotle's* Metaphysics Theta. Oxford University Press.

Cajetan, Tommaso de Vio. 2009. *The Analogy of Names, and the Concept of Being* (trans. E. A. Bushinski and H. J. Koren). Wipf and Stock.

---

[52] Notice that it is the fact that loose identity is presumptively transitive that distinguishes it from similarity.

[53] For suggestions and comments on matters both ancient and modern, I would like to thank the editors and two anonymous readers for OUP, alongside Gary Jenkins, Sabina Lovibond, Martin Pickup, and especially David Charles. During the summer of 1986, David and I drove across the United States from Washington DC to San Francisco. On this trip, not only did I learn how to drive properly, but I also first stumbled upon the claim that identity was a focal concept. Not that I had much idea what a focal concept was then, it just sounded right. But through what seems in retrospect to be a single, albeit fragmented, conversation with him, one that started (I like to think) in the wilds of North Dakota and has continued ever since, I have slowly and tortuously tried to develop a framework in which the claim might make sense, and even assume a degree of plausibility. This chapter is my latest effort, and it is a privilege to be asked to present it as part of this celebration of David's work in philosophy.

FOCALITY, ANALOGY, AND THE ARTICULATION OF CONCEPTS 77

Charles, David. 1999. 'Aristotle on Well-Being and Intellectual Contemplation', *Proceedings of the Aristotelian Society Supplementary Volume* 73, 205–23.

Charles, David. 2000. *Aristotle on Meaning and Essence*. Clarendon Press.

Charles, David. 2015. 'Aristotle on the Highest Good', in *The Highest Good in Aristotle and Kant* (ed. J. Aufderheide and R. M. Bader). Oxford University Press, 60–82.

Chisholm, Roderick. 1976. *Person and Object*. George Allen & Unwin.

The Concise Oxford English Dictionary. 2011. 12th edition. Oxford University Press.

Eddington, Arthur. 1928. *The Nature of the Physical World*. Dent.

Frege, Gottlob. 1997. 'Letter to Jourdain, Jan. 1914', in *The Frege Reader* (ed. M. Beaney). Blackwell, 319–21.

Hart, H. L. A. 1961. *The Concept of Law*. Oxford University Press.

Hesse, Mary. 1966. *Models and Analogies in Science*. University of Notre Dame Press.

Hume, David. 1978. *A Treatise of Human Nature* (ed. L. S. Selby-Bigge). Oxford University Press.

Irwin, Terence. 1981. 'Homonymy in Aristotle', *Review of Metaphysics* 34, 523–44.

Keynes, J. M. 1921. *A Treatise on Probability*. Macmillan.

Lewis, David. 1986. *On the Plurality of Worlds*. Blackwell.

Lloyd, G. E. R. 1996. *Aristotelian Explorations*. Cambridge University Press.

Locke, John. 1975. *An Essay Concerning Human Understanding* (ed. P. H. Nidditch). Oxford University Press.

Lovibond, Sabina. 2022. *Essays on Ethics and Culture*. Oxford University Press.

Owen, G. E. L. 1986. 'Logic and Metaphysics in Some Earlier Works of Aristotle', in G. E. L. Owen, *Logic, Science, and Dialectic: Collected Papers in Greek Philosophy* (ed. Martha Nussbaum). Duckworth, 180–99.

Reid, Thomas. 1969. *An Essay on the Intellectual Powers of Man*. MIT Press.

Ryle, Gilbert. 1949. *The Concept of Mind*. Hutchinson.

Shields, Christopher. 1999. *Order in Multiplicity: Homonymy in the Philosophy of Aristotle*. Oxford University Press.

Stanley, Jason and Timothy Williamson. 2001. 'Knowing How', *Journal of Philosophy* 98, 411–44.

Stebbing, L. S. 1944. *Philosophy and the Physicists*. Penguin.

Ullman-Margalit, Edna. 1983. 'On Presumption', *Journal of Philosophy* 80, 143–63.

Ward, Julie K. 2008. *Aristotle on Homonymy*. Cambridge University Press.

Whately, Richard. 1870. *Elements of Logic*. 9th edition. Longmans, Green, Reader and Dyer.

Wiggins, David. 1971. 'Sentence Sense, Word Sense, and Difference of Word Sense: Towards a Philosophical Theory of Dictionaries', in *Semantics: An Interdisciplinary Reader* (ed. D. Steinberg and L. Jakobovits). Cambridge University Press, 14–34.

Wiggins, David. 1998. 'Truth, and Truth as Predicated of Moral Judgments', in David Wiggins, *Needs, Values, Truth*. 3rd edition. Oxford University Press, 139–84.

Wiggins, David. 2001. *Sameness and Substance Renewed*. Cambridge University Press.

Wiggins, David. 2012. 'Practical Knowledge: Knowing How To and Knowing That', *Mind* 121, 97–130.

Williams, S. G. 1996/2000. 'Ambiguity and Semantic Theory', in *Identity, Truth and Value: Essays for David Wiggins* (ed. S. Lovibond and S. G. Williams). Blackwell, 49–72.

Williams, S. G. 2004. 'Indeterminacy and the Rule of Law', *Oxford Journal of Legal Studies* 24, 539–62.

Williams, S. G. and David Charles. 2013. 'Essence, Modality and the Master Craftsman', in *Aristotle on Method and Metaphysics* (ed. E. Feser). Palgrave Macmillan, 121–45.

4

David Charles on Wittgenstein, Aristotle, and Artisans

Paul Snowdon

Introduction

In this chapter I wish to reflect on some ideas that David Charles has expressed in a comparison between some of the things that Wittgenstein and Aristotle say about the unlikely trio of concepts, understanding, and manual workers. I shall express some gentle reservations about what Professor Charles says, but also about what Wittgenstein says too. However, before doing so I want to say a few words about David's role in my own philosophical life in Oxford, both by way of describing that role and also to express my immense gratitude to him for it.

1. David's Group

I was enormously lucky in the philosophical education that I received as a student in Oxford, about which I have written elsewhere.[1] But I was also very fortunate in the colleagues I had in Oxford once I started working there as a tutor, and the most significant one was David Charles.

His major contribution to my life in Oxford was the philosophical discussion group that he ran for more or less the whole time I was there. I am not aiming to write the history of what was called 'David's group'. Rather, I want to say how absolutely central it was to my philosophical life and development and to thank David for his colossal efforts in running it.

The group met once a week during term time, early on in different places but for most of the time in his light and airy rooms on the main quad in Oriel College. Sometimes we had to wait on the stairs leading to his rooms for a tutorial to finish, but once inside we could sit on comfortable chairs, or sofas, or perch on ledges beneath windows. The speaker sat at the front next to a table and a white board, which was often scribbled on. David's easy chair was to the speaker's left.

---

[1] See Snowdon 1998, 293–4.

Paul Snowdon, *David Charles on Wittgenstein, Aristotle, and Artisans* In: *Aristotelian Metaphysics: Essays in Honour of David Charles.* Edited by: David Bronstein, Thomas Kjeller Johansen, and Michail Peramatzis, Oxford University Press.
© Oxford University Press 2024. DOI: 10.1093/oso/9780198908678.003.0004

80 PAUL SNOWDON

Meetings lasted two hours with an initial presentation, usually interrupted, taking about an hour, followed by discussion. Discussion, though, might well continue longer, or carry on over lunch.

The group's history can be divided roughly into two stages. Initially it was mainly devoted to reading and discussing philosophical literature, to a large extent works coming from the States, though we also, and this was important, read our own papers. As I remember, we read works by Dennett, Stitch, Fodor, the literature by and on Quine, and Davidson, and Putnam, and of course many others, but also work related to philosophy, such as Marr's work on perception and computing. In the second phase we read and discussed more of our own papers, but we would return to close reading of texts when what we thought of as really significant books came out, such as works by Evans and Dummett. The participants were mainly the younger philosophers given permanent appointments in Oxford from the early 1970s onwards, although the membership was to some extent fluid with some people attending for a time and then dropping out. It included Bill Brewer, John Campbell, Quassim Cassam, Bill Child, Adrian Cussins, Imogen Dickie, Dorothy Edgington, Elizabeth Fricker, Jennifer Hornsby, Oliver Pooley, Ian Rumfitt, Helen Steward, Stephen Williams, and Timothy Williamson (plus others), but also a series of members on non-permanent appointments there or from other universities, including Justin Broackes, David Mackie, Michael Martin, Michael Morris, Ralph Wedgwood, and Rowland Stout, to name but a few.[2] Visitors to Oxford would also attend, including as I remember Tyler Burge, Donald Davidson, Charlie Martin, John McDowell, Richard Rorty, Nathan Salmon, and Sydney Shoemaker.[3]

From it I acquired what I am tempted to call a philosophical education while already a philosopher. I learnt about developments in philosophy, and I learnt a plethora of ways to think about them. I learnt, too, about the topics and ideas that my colleagues were exploring. I also received critical feedback on my own ideas, which were often given their earliest presentations to David's group. This feedback could be brutal, but David's chairing of the meetings ensured they were courteous, friendly, and constructive. It can be said that he conferred upon the meetings the virtues he himself possesses. David's primary goal when discussing things was

---

[2] Of course, in a philosophical centre like Oxford, there were many discussion groups, but there were at least what I think of as three leading groups in Oxford which were not single-topic focused, at the time that I am describing. One was David's, a second was run by Ralph Walker, and contained philosophers of what might be called the then middle generation in Oxford, including, I think, Lesley Brown, David Bostock, Bill Newton-Smith, and John Kenyon, and the third one was called the Ayer group, having been set up by Ayer when he arrived in Oxford as a professor, containing the more longstanding senior Oxford philosophers, such as Michael Dummett, P. F. Strawson, Philippa Foot, David Pears, Brian McGuinness, Jonathan Cohen, Michael Woods, David Wiggins, Dan Isaacson, Chris Peacocke, and Colin McGinn. Some belonged to more than one group, and some famous philosophers, the mavericks and the loners, belonged to none.

[3] I am sure my list is incomplete, and I wish to apologize to anyone overlooked. I am grateful to David Charles for jogging my memory.

not to tell you why it is wrong, and what the right way is to think about the matter (the standard reaction of philosophers on hearing anything), although he was as adept at doing so as anyone else, but, rather, to ensure the ideas were fully formulated, and to explore the proposal's resources. For someone trying to develop their thinking, his was the ideal response. I have highlighted David's chairmanship, but of considerable significance also was the outstanding quality, both critical and constructive, of the members he assembled in his group—a true galaxy of philosophical talent. I should add that we were not like the Vienna Circle, in more ways than one, no doubt, but principally in that there was no basic philosophical idea we were, as a group, committed to.

I want to stress that the running of the group was extremely onerous. Persuading people to deliver papers, and to attend, and chairing the meetings took masses of time and energy, sustained by David's conviction, which was clearly true, that the continuation of the group was something of incredible value. When I left Oxford, the greatest downside was that I was no longer able to participate in the group in the way I had done. In consequence, I think, my philosophical horizons narrowed.

As a postscript it can be said that David's group ceased well before David himself left Oxford. It was the victim of the emergence of a feeling, not on David's part but that of his then colleagues, that the pressures of academic life in Oxford meant it was more or less impossible to spare the time needed to keep such a group alive. This was, surely, a very sad development, and it leads me to say that in some respects the period in Oxford during which it ran was a golden age to be a philosopher of my generation there. Speaking personally, it is thanks to David that I can say that.

2. David Charles on Wittgenstein, Builders, and Craftsmen

I want to offer some reflections on David Charles' paper 'Wittgenstein's Builders and Aristotle's Craftsmen', which is his contribution to a collection of essays in honour of David Pears that he edited along with Bill Child.[4] Charles' contribution is typically ingenious and imaginative. He takes some central ideas, as he sees them, of Wittgenstein, and which he reads Wittgenstein as supporting by reflection, among other things, on the little language games described at the beginning of the *Investigations*. Now, in the discussion of these language games, Wittgenstein often brings in people engaged in construction, workers and builders, and so Charles relates these examples and Wittgenstein's treatment of them to Aristotle's reflections on craftsmen, thereby linking the philosopher on whom Pears worked most with the philosopher Charles himself has written about most. In Charles' view, Aristotle's reflections on craftsmen are superior to those of Wittgenstein on

---

[4] Charles 2001, 49–79.

82   PAUL SNOWDON

builders, and provide us with a way (or part of a way) to avoid the conclusions that Wittgenstein draws. That is the upshot of his comparison of Aristotle and Wittgenstein. As a compliment to a Wittgenstein specialist from an Aristotelian specialist, this is highly ingenious.

In my discussion of Charles' approach, I do not intend to criticize his exposition of Aristotle's account and distinctions. I have too little knowledge of Aristotle to do that. I want, rather, to try to work out whether Charles is right to bring the Aristotelian account in as a potential answer to what Wittgenstein thinks.

I want to focus on two aspects of the discussion. The first is his exposition of the issues that Wittgenstein is raising about the basis of meaning and understanding, which, to some extent, I want to query. The second is his invocation of the Aristotelian craftsman as an antidote to Wittgenstein. I want to consider these elements because they are of real interest, but also because there are things I wish to propose myself about the Wittgenstein passages, and I can do that while looking at Charles' ideas.

Charles' understanding of the debate initiated by Wittgenstein is complex. He starts his discussion with Wittgenstein's reaction at the beginning of the *Investigations* to Augustine's description of how he learnt language. How should we understand that engagement? Wittgenstein, as everyone knows, quotes a passage from Augustine about how he learnt language. It is clear that Wittgenstein is unhappy about the view of language that the passage incorporates. But it is not child's play to say precisely what, according to Wittgenstein, is wrong with the so-called Augustinian picture. Nor is it child's play to say what Wittgenstein is up to in his engagement with language in these first few sections of his book.

Obviously, one of his goals in these early sections of his book is to introduce in the *Investigations* his notion of a language game. Thus, in section 7 Wittgenstein tries to produce a satisfactory elucidation of what counts as a language game, a notion that figures prominently in his arguments. It is clear that for this task Wittgenstein does not need to criticize Augustine. In that section he is merely introducing a technical term of his own by citing examples. Of course, it is while performing this task that Wittgenstein brings forward examples of artisans or workers reacting to bits of language.

A second theme in the passage is what we might call Wittgenstein's *anti-generalism*. He is trying to convince us that the elements in our sorts of very complex languages are various and radically different, and that it is unhelpful to try to offer a unified account of the role of all expressions. One way to put Wittgenstein's point is as the claim that there is no universal essence shared by all parts of language. Now, Wittgenstein links the idea he is opposed to with what Augustine says. Thus, Wittgenstein says: 'These words [he means Augustine's], it seems to me, give us a particular picture of the essence of human language.'[5] Whether Wittgenstein is

---

[5] Wittgenstein 2001, §1.

DAVID CHARLES ON WITTGENSTEIN, ARISTOTLE, AND ARTISANS   83

right or wrong about the claim that there is no such essence, it does not look as if what Augustine says in any way carries the implication that there is such an essence. Augustine could perfectly well accept that his description of language learning is restricted to one central group of terms and concede that there are other elements that his little account misses out. Augustine does not really commit himself to any view about the 'essence of language'. These two purposes, then, seem to have nothing to do with what Augustine says.

Another observation about Wittgenstein's approach to Augustine is that, in so far as Wittgenstein wants to extract from the passage something approaching a conception of the essence of language, it must relate to the type of semantic description that Augustine employs: namely, that words name objects. This, indeed, is what Wittgenstein says. Now, if that is the significance of the passage, it becomes quite incidental how Augustine describes *language learning*, or whatever problems there are with that. However, leaving that aside, as Charles points out, Wittgenstein alleges, and as I read him Charles himself agrees with this criticism, that Augustine's description credits the young Augustine with possession of a language prior to learning his first language. Wittgenstein says: 'And now I think we can say: Augustine describes the learning of human language as if the child came into a strange country and did not understand the language of the country; that is, as if it already had a language, only not this one.'[6] Now, if this allegation were true, it would of course refute Augustine's account, on any normal understanding of language learning, which does not posit something like an innate and not learned language for the child to employ, since he is meant to be describing the learning of a *first* language, not a second one. However, it is not at all clear that Wittgenstein's criticism is sound. Wittgenstein's criticism depends on two assumptions. The first is that Augustine's account rests on the idea that the learner is thinking about what words stand for, asking themselves what thing or things a term picks out. The second is that such thinking requires the possession of language in which it needs to be formulated. In fact, neither assumption need be granted. It seems clear that we, ordinary human beings, do employ, in some sense, language when we occurrently think, but that hardly shows that thinking in general or universally requires language. It is also not obvious that Augustine's account involves taking the learner to be thinking in terms of what objects are called what, as he or she goes through the process described by Augustine. He certainly captures what is learnt, which is to say he characterizes the cognitive *upshot* in such terms, but that does not mean that those notions are being read back into the reflective process of the learner; further, as a description of what is

---

[6] Wittgenstein 2001, §32. It can be pointed out that the notion of coming into a new linguistic community or society that Wittgenstein alludes to here is one that he cites on different occasions, and which seems to have been of some significance for him. We can conjecture that part of its meaning for him is that he made such a transition in his own life, the new society being for him that very unusual society known as Cambridge University.

84 PAUL SNOWDON

learnt eventually by the learner, it is surely totally natural and really (dare one say?) undeniable. Augustine is also surely right in singling out aspects of the behaviour of the teachers as what enables the learner to pick up what he or she eventually learns.

I have just queried the legitimacy of one of Wittgenstein's criticisms of Augustine, which I suspect Charles thinks is sound, but Charles, in his discussion, also presents the same criticism to the employment of the notion of the *radical interpreter* by theorists of meaning. He says:

> Consider the radical interpreter. She comes to meet her native, already equipped with her own linguistic notions. Her task is to map the native's language on to one which she already understands. In doing so, she aims to maximize agreement, to make the native come out speaking the truth by her lights. But, one can ask, how did she come to possess the notions she employs as the basis of her translation? How did she acquire the grasp of the meanings of her own expressions?[7]

He calls this an 'uncanny resemblance' to Augustine's child.

A reply to this that deserves consideration is to say that introducing the radical interpreter into the theory of meaning, which Quine did, is to introduce a device that is meant to shed light on what meaning is, what it consists in. The device is supposed to help by making us focus on what the translator looks at when determining that an expression in her language means the same as an expression in the foreign language. It is natural to assume that if we can work that out then the constituents of meaning will be visible. Quine's view, if asked how the translator originally learnt her own language, would be to say that, as revealed by studying the translator, her mastery of meaning consists in L (whatever that is), and her learning consisted in her undergoing a natural process that instilled L into her. As a device aiding philosophical investigation, this seems to me beyond criticism. As Davidson pointed out, though, Quine did misemploy his own device, in concluding that what needs looking at is stimulus meaning, thereby excluding the more distal surrounding and impacting world, which is clearly a component in determining meaning. However, as a potential *device* for exploring the nature of meaning, it seems not to be objectionable.

3. Charles' Reading of the Debate

I have so far queried two thoughts that Wittgenstein proposes about the Augustinian picture, and also queried something that Charles says about the idea of the radical interpreter. But I want, next, to engage with the core proposals that

---

[7] Charles 2001, 51.

DAVID CHARLES ON WITTGENSTEIN, ARISTOTLE, AND ARTISANS   85

Charles makes about how to understand that debate about language and understanding that Wittgenstein generates. In section 2 of his paper, Charles summarizes his reading of Wittgenstein's approach, at the end of which we are supposed to have reached an understanding of it which should make an invitation to unearth ways to oppose it attractive. What is that understanding? And what understanding of the support for it that Wittgenstein gives does Charles offer?

The central and objectionable consequence of Wittgenstein's views, on Charles' reading, is that Wittgenstein challenges a 'realist' conception of thought and language. Charles' view, which is completely natural, is that we achieve a grasp of what he calls 'ratification independent truth conditions', and so Wittgenstein must have gone wrong in recommending a view of thought and language that rejects that possibility. This seems to be treating Wittgenstein as an 'anti-realist' in the terminology deriving from Dummett. At this point two very large questions arise. First, was Wittgenstein an anti-realist? Second, is anti-realism unacceptable? Although these are large questions, here is not the place to attempt to answer them. I am myself perfectly happy to go along with Charles' assumption that anti-realism is objectionable. About the first question I feel that it remains unclear what Wittgenstein's account of understanding is. The so-called rule-following sections in the *Investigations*, which have been so analysed, are very hard to interpret. These remarks may seem like two pieces of intellectual cowardice, but my purpose here is, primarily, to try to draw guidance from Charles' approach, so I shall concentrate on that.[8]

It is in section 2 of his paper that Charles expands his account of what Wittgenstein is himself doing. According to Charles, Wittgenstein's opponent and so his target, labelled a 'Platonist' by Charles, accepts two things. As he puts it: 'First, we grasp terms for objects and properties when they impact on us. Thus the meaning of these terms is fixed, when all goes well, by objects and properties in the world. We are justified in having such terms because they represent the world's objects and properties.' To which he adds that the Platonist also says: 'Second, our sentences are true (or false) when the world contains (or fails to contain) objects related as we say they are related.'[9]

Now, one remark, which may well be of no importance, is that in the passage from Augustine nothing like these claims seems to be made. In relation to the second element, Augustine does not talk *about truth* at all. Rather the upshot of language mastery that he mentions is expression of desire. Augustine is, surely, right to mention this; children do use their acquired terms to signal desire or, more crudely, to get things. Surprisingly, in citing this, Augustine stresses something that is present in Wittgenstein's language games, where a character often

[8] I have tried to say something about the interpretation (and assessment) of Wittgenstein on rule-following in Snowdon 2018a and Snowdon 2018b.
[9] Both sentences are from Charles 2001, 52.

86   PAUL SNOWDON

uses language to get bricks or apples. In relation to the first claim, things are more complicated. The difficulty in reading Augustine as committed to this is that he really says nothing about what 'grasping a term for an object' consists in. He, Augustine, thinks that the learner in normal cases learns that a certain term names an object or type of object, but he gives us no indication as to what he thinks such learning consists in. It is surely obvious that a child experiencing feature F, say the colour red, and having names for the colour used at the same time, does not automatically learn the significance of the terms. Something or other has to develop in the child for that learning to occur, and Augustine does not advance any view as to what that is. So, Augustine seems not to be a representative of Platonism. And one thing this means is that Charles' reading of Wittgenstein cannot be supported by Wittgenstein's opposition to Augustine.

I wish now to leave aside the question whether Augustine's passage expresses Platonism as defined here, but I want to add that the distinction brought out in the previous paragraph between saying that the understander knows what things in the environment words stand for (or refer to, or designate), and saying in some more analytical way what this knowledge consists in or amounts to, is a distinction that is fundamental to this whole debate. It is the distinction between characterizing understanding in terms of what we might call the understander's knowledge specified in semantic terms, and providing an account of what possession of that knowledge *consists in*, in some informative and illuminating way.

It is a distinction that Wittgenstein himself seems to accept. Thus, somewhat surprisingly, in section 2, Wittgenstein says; 'Let us imagine a language for which the description given by Augustine is right.' Now, when describing Augustine's passage Wittgenstein characterizes it this way: 'the individual words in the language name objects'. This is a semantic characterization which Wittgenstein is not objecting to in the case of the second language game he specifies, the one involving builders and bricks. But it is clear that Wittgenstein regards the *use* of the words between people as *grounding* this semantic description. Indeed, the basic conception of meaning that Wittgenstein favours is captured in his famous slogan: 'For a large class of cases—though not for all—in which we employ the word "meaning" it can be defined thus; the meaning of a word is its use in the language.'[10] It is also surely very tempting to read these early sections of the *Investigations* as, in part, an effort to bring out the significance of use as the basis of meaning. Viewing his overall argument in a general way, we can say that he is proposing what (in the main) constitutes *meaning*, and that is *use*, but later, when he is discussing rule-following (or understanding), what he is doing is trying to determine the nature of *understanding*, the nature of that which is possessed by people who understand the language. And this problem is *generated*, at least in part, by

---

[10] Wittgenstein 2001, §43.

the very fact that meaning, which is what an understander grasps, is *constituted by use*. Thus he poses an introductory question in the rule-following section in these words: 'when someone says the word "cube" to me, for example, I know what it means. But can the use of the word come before my mind, when I understand it in this way?'[11] Wittgenstein's problem about understanding seems to be generated by the idea of meaning as use. Now, saying this is to advance a highly general reading of Wittgenstein, though without any account, so far, of where he gets to in his discussion of what understanding is. I hope, though, that it might help us in considering Charles' reading of the debate.

As we have seen, Charles thinks of Wittgenstein's target as the two-sided Platonism that he defines. Should we view the debate this way? My worry is two-fold. The first thesis of Platonism is simply that as a result of our interaction with our environment we acquire terms which refer to or pick out things and features in that environment. Now, it seems to me that Wittgenstein would be prepared to say that. He seems happy to talk of words standing for objects, and he need not think that language learning has to be difficult. So I am unsure that he is an opponent of the first clause in Platonism. We can agree that he would be opposed to it as a complete account of what language learners learn, but not that he would oppose it as a partial account. The problem with the second thesis, which thus becomes his principal target on Charles' reading, is that it is unclear that he opposes it: that is, that he is an anti-realist.

Charles builds up his account by saying that Wittgenstein's proposal is that 'we should think of concept mastery in terms of mastering techniques which allow us to determine whether something is yellow, or gold, or elm-wood'.[12] Now, it is not entirely clear what this proposal amounts to. The crucial question, given the centrality of anti-realism in Charles' account of the debate, is whether we conceive of this technique in the judgement case as requiring that it gives a verdict in all cases, or whether it requires giving a verdict only in some. If Wittgenstein favours the second option, then he is not an anti-realist. Now, according to Charles himself the analogous cases of acquiring a technique are, for example, learning to cook or learning to build.[13] But when he characterizes these techniques himself he says that 'in learning to cook we do not at some point...grasp the answer to all questions that could be asked about cooking'.[14] But in that case, treating concept mastery in a parallel fashion, which, according to Charles is what Wittgenstein is requesting us to do, we should see it as, maybe, involving the capacity to determine the truth in some cases, but not in all.

Charles also indicates how the types of argument in the rule-following sections are meant to support this view. He says: 'he argues that we could not grasp a concept simply by being given a definition of the relevant form. For what makes the

---

[11] Wittgenstein 2001, §139.   [12] Charles 2001, 52.   [13] Charles 2001, 52.
[14] Charles 2001, 52–3.

88   PAUL SNOWDON

definition itself determinate or unambiguous?'[15] This is Charles' highly con-
densed exposition of Wittgenstein's famous claim that lies behind his remark that
'no course of action can be determined by a rule, because any course of action can
be made out to accord with the rule'.[16] At this point Wittgenstein brings in the
term 'interpretation', by which he understands 'the substitution of one expression
of the rule for another'. So offering a definition involves an interpretation, and his
conclusion is that 'there is a way of grasping a rule that is not an interpretation'.

Now, care surely needs to be exercised here. Wittgenstein cannot really mean
that the significance of a term cannot be conveyed in a definition, presented, as it
were, on a single occasion, since that is clearly one way we do convey meanings
(or, perhaps, create meanings). What Wittgenstein means is that *solely* having one
expression linked to another is not what understanding is. Put that way, the conclusion seems fairly undeniable, but it turns out not to be a remark which says
anything about how meanings are *actually* explained. It fails to say anything about
how meanings are actually conveyed by offering definitions (or what Wittgenstein
calls 'interpretations'), since that process actually works because the expression
offered is not in fact a free-standing uninterpreted sequence of expressions. More
important, though, the conclusion that Wittgenstein himself draws is this: 'What
this shows is that there is a way of grasping a rule which is not an interpretation,
but which is exhibited in what we call "obeying the rule" and "going against it" in
actual cases.'[17] This is taken to be, and is clearly intended to be, an important
conclusion. But Wittgenstein's response should elicit the following query: what
exactly does the remark mean, and why is it the only alternative to the myth that
understanding can consist simply in pairing a term with another expression?

One way of interpreting Wittgenstein's proposal is that the conditions we are
picking out when we say someone grasps a rule are that they have done something which amounts to obeying the rule. So, to take a silly case, my grasping the
rule 'Always say "thank you" when given a gift' comes down to having, on receiving a gift, said 'thank you'. It is not easy to read the final part of the sentence
along these lines but let us ignore that. There are two obvious problems with
Wittgenstein's remark. The first is that having responded with 'thank you' after
receiving a gift does not in fact mean that I am following the rule, nor that I have
understood the rule. Who knows why I said 'thank you' or what understanding
I have? The second problem is that I can, surely, grasp the rule and accept it, without having had occasion actually to act in accordance with it. Thus, I can be given
a rule which I understand and accept to cover circumstances which have not yet
arisen for me. So, on the present reading, Wittgenstein's approach to what grasping a rule consists in looks rather mysterious. This should add to our sense that
interpreting him is very tricky.

---

[15]   Charles 2001, 53.   [16]   Wittgenstein 2001, §201.   [17]   Wittgenstein 2001, §201.

This seems to be a criticism that Charles is unsympathetic to. Thus, he says: 'Looking at one case cannot by itself make us masters of the relevant technique. For getting it right in a variety of cases is (partially) constitutive of what it is to master a technique.'[18] Now it might be correct as a remark about the English language expression 'has mastered the technique of' that it can only apply to someone who has exhibited his mastery of the technique. That would make the expression like the phrase 'is good at learning languages', which can only apply to someone who has actually learnt languages. It is not a pure dispositional expression. But if so, since the real topic of the rule-following section is understanding and grasping rules, given the point made above, this amounts to showing that 'mastery of a technique' is not the right thing to compare understanding with.

I want finally to look at Charles' general characterization of Wittgenstein's approach. Charles represents Wittgenstein's position as having two basic elements and an important consequence. The two basic features are:

(A) In acquiring a concept (such as that of yellow) the learner acquires a technique for discriminating yellow objects. Mastery of such techniques is partially constitutive of what it is to master the concept. (*Centrality of technique*).

(B) We cannot say what the relevant techniques are without reference to the objects on which we practise our techniques. We cannot say what it is to discriminate yellow objects without reference to the yellow objects thus discriminated. (*Externalism*).[19]

Now, ignoring for a moment the supposed implication from these, it is hard not to feel some sympathy for both claims. Since Charles uses 'yellow' as his example of a term, we can ask: how do we tell that a child has acquired an understanding of the term 'yellow'? The obvious answer is that we check to see whether she agrees that 'yellow' applies to perceptually presented yellow objects and agrees that 'yellow' does not apply to perceptually presented non-yellow things. That is the central requirement for terms like 'yellow'.

Three things need adding, though. It seems obvious that we cannot say the same about all terms. Suppose we are teaching someone the word 'spinster'. We would not present them with spinsters and test whether they recognized them as such. Nor would we expect them to recognize perceptually presented non-spinsters as non-spinsters. What is plausible to say is that we would look for evidence that the child has appreciated the condition for counting as falling under the term 'spinster'. This is just another sort of case, and it is not being claimed that it is the only other case to be contrasted with the 'yellow' case. Second, what is

---

[18] Charles 2001, 53. I may be misunderstanding Charles' claim here. Perhaps it is simply a report of what Wittgenstein himself would claim.
[19] Charles 2001, 54.

90   PAUL SNOWDON

special about terms like 'yellow' is that they are attached to conditions that we, as normal humans, can, in normal conditions, simply tell or observe are present: that is to say, conditions given to us by the perceptual/cognitive mechanisms that come with our nature. Given those, we can test for understanding by seeing what the child is prepared to say about perceptually presented examples. Most conditions or features do not relate in that way to our perceptual/cognitive nature. Third, we should not exaggerate our recognitional capacity vis-à-vis yellow things. Or at least we should notice there are complexities. Where we would test understanding of 'yellow' is with cases that the presented object is plainly yellow. If the object is plainly yellow and the child is unsure whether it is yellow, then we would think she had not understood the term. This does not mean that there might not be cases where even someone with the technique for recognizing yellow things might be unsure or wrong about whether a presented item is yellow. It is not hard to imagine such cases. This means that in developing implications from (A) care needs to be taken.

Claim (B) does seem obvious. Indeed, it would seem to be part of the basic logic of dispositional ascriptions that what the disposition is a disposition for requires specification of the external feature to which it relates. Thus, a disposition that salt possesses is being water-soluble because it dissolves in water, that surrounding stuff. So if we acquire a technique for discriminating yellow things, then that is what the technique is a technique for. Further, what Wittgenstein surely accepts is that our language is without doubt a language about external things—such as tables and bricks and colours. He is, that is, an 'it goes without saying' externalist. He sees no need to argue, along lines presented by Putnam or Burge, that language has external significance. He takes that for granted from the very beginning of his discussion of language. Indeed, the very idea of internalism, as it is known, would have struck him as a typical philosophical distortion or illusion, as it, surely, is.

Now, according to Charles, Wittgenstein arrives at his objectionable view by regarding it as an implication of (A) together with (B). One way he states the consequence is that 'we can make no sense of what is really yellow beyond that which our skilled judges...discriminate as yellow'.[20] This is meant to be Wittgenstein's anti-realism. Now, Charles' reading might be right as an interpretation, but it is hard to see that such an inference, given that the premises are formulated in a reasonable and qualified way, can imply any such thing. One oddity in the conclusion is the reference to skilled masters of the technique. Since anyone who understands the term 'yellow' must have mastered the technique, on this account of language learning there are no skilled masters to be contrasted with non-skilled masters. Further, let us suppose we take the concept of 'yellow', and

---

[20] Charles 2001, 54.

terms like it, since other terms are not even *prima facie* tied to observer authority, but we treat the required recognitional ability as restricted to plain cases. There seems to be no implication that people understanding the term cannot go wrong in some cases, or fail to recognize things in other cases.

4. Charles' Response

The most original part of Charles' discussion of Wittgenstein is the response that he develops. His idea is, as he says, 'to show that there is more involved in our grasp of objects than Wittgenstein allows'.[21] This requires 'us to show realist truth conditions can emerge, by comprehensible steps, out of the primitive situation so far described'. The implementation of this strategy begins with Charles remarking that 'Wittgenstein's characterization of life on the building site does not seem fully to capture the range of skills and know-how employed in the building trade'.[22] To bring this out Charles presents the threefold distinction that Aristotle draws between low-level artisans, the empirical doctor, and the master craftsman. I can only sketch these categories here. The low-level artisan has been trained to carry out a few techniques, which he does not understand, and if not employed doing them then says he has no idea what to do. The empirical doctor follows evidence of effectiveness but does not understand why the treatment is effective. The master craftsman, by contrast, 'can explain why we act one way, rather than another'.[23] He has 'a grasp on a variety of types of wood; what each is good for, what can be done with one and not another'. He can devise new methods and criticize existing methods. What is particularly important is that he has 'a grasp on the nature of the wood, in terms independent of what he can do with it, which explains why he should act in one way and not another. It is this which appears to give him the ability to underwrite our discriminatory practices in a recognizably realist way'.[24]

Charles seems to identify two aspects of the craftsman practices that he regards as especially significant. The first is that he is not tied to the initial practices that he was taught, unlike the labourers, but can criticize them, and introduce new, more intelligent, practices. The second is that his use of kind terms can be defended by him on the basis of his knowledge of the character of the substances around him.

I hope that I have picked out the two basic elements that Charles regards as significant. Further, I do think that we can say that both points are correct. In these respects, the master craftsman transcends the practices of the labourer, and in between them comes the empirical doctor.

[21] Charles 2001, 58. [22] Charles 2001, 59. [23] Charles 2001, 61.
[24] Charles 2001, 63–4.

92 PAUL SNOWDON

Now, with a doctrine such as anti-realism which Charles regards as the bad place that Wittgenstein reaches, there are two ways to criticize it. The first is to present evidence that our thought does not conform to the anti-realist account. Thus, we might locate plainly intelligible thoughts which have recognition-transcendent truth-conditions. The second way is to provide what look like refutations of the considerations provided by anti-realists in favour of their approach. With this distinction in mind, the question I want to raise is: which of the two roles is the example of the master craftsman supposed to play? Is he meant to provide an example of bona fide realist thinking or is he meant to make us realize where the fault lies in pro-anti-realist arguments?

It is reasonable, I want to suggest, to be sceptical about the idea that the master craftsman is an undeniable example of realist thinking. It surely cannot be that the anti-realist approach to thought and truth rules out a craftsman devising new and better techniques for manipulating wood. If we should think of concept mastery—that is, understanding—as internalizing a technique for judgement, which seems to be Charles' reading of Wittgenstein's anti-realism, then since that technique is definitive of the presence of the concept in question, it cannot, presumably, be improved or corrected. But techniques for manipulating wood, or responding to illness, are not techniques definitive of concepts, and so can, of course, be corrected or improved as knowledge increases. Equally, it is hard to think that the anti-realist account of understanding is inconsistent with a growth in someone's knowledge of the kinds of thing around them. If the crucial anti-realist claim is that there are no recognition-transcendent truths, this would not seem to rule out someone detecting new truths about a kind which people already had a way of thinking about. Thus, the low-level artisan could have a term for the kind of wood he is dealing with, a term shared with the master craftsman, but the master craftsman knows about it far more than the artisan. I think, therefore, that there is nothing, or at least nothing obvious, about the master craftsman's understanding that makes him a clear example of a realist.

Now, in the light of the distinction sketched above between two ways an example such as the master craftsman might figure in the debate about anti-realism, this means that as an example he must undermine somehow a consideration offered in favour of anti-realism. But, again, I think one might wonder how that could be. For it to be so, it must be that Wittgenstein's grounds for his anti-realism (which is not to say everyone's grounds for anti-realism) rest on assuming that human cognizers are somehow restricted in their intellectual engagement with language to the levels of the labourers and shopkeepers whom Wittgenstein describes in his examples at the beginning of the *Investigations*. The argument, however it went, could be stopped in its tracks by using the master craftsman to show such a restrictive conception was illegitimate. But the doubt about regarding the case as relevant in that way is that it is quite unclear that the labourers and shopkeepers imagined by Wittgenstein are meant to define the cognitive resources involved in language learning. Thus, when Charles says that Wittgenstein's characterization of life on the building site does not seem fully to capture the range of skills and know-how employed in the building trade, he says something that is undoubtedly true, but why suppose that that truth undermines Wittgenstein's grounds for his anti-realism? It may be that Wittgenstein's purpose in giving his supposed examples of language games in the early sections of the *Investigations* is to persuade us that the kinds of interaction in them between the agents and the expressions amount to enough to count as the expression having meaning, but he would not seem to be committed to the claim that among the grounds or uses that constitute meaning there are not any which involve cognitively more advanced 'uses'. Since I cannot see that Wittgenstein is committed to this restriction, I am doubtful that Aristotle's master craftsman, cognitively admirable creature that he is, can block Wittgenstein's reflections on the nature of understanding.

There is, though, something remarkably odd, I want to suggest somewhat in the spirit of Charles' approach, about the examples that Wittgenstein presents in the early stages of the *Investigations*. In the very first section he presents his example of someone being sent shopping with a slip on which are written the words 'five red apples'. The shopkeeper to whom the slip is given then hands over five red apples. However, he selects the apples by taking objects out of a drawer marked 'apples', and he selects the red ones on the basis of checking their colour against a colour chart, and to determine the number he picks out one for each numeral he recites up to 'five'. Wittgenstein seems to think that we can call this a use of language, and it can reveal that what we tend to think of as necessary for meaning need not be present for there to be such a use. Ultimately, he proposes that use is the core ground of meaning, as it were, properly conceived. But the real oddity about such an example is that the shopkeeper plainly does not understand the language, although he can respond to uses of the terms. He does not know what 'red' means, since he has to look up the colour on a chart, and he does not know what 'apple' means, since he would hand over whatever was in the drawer. Nor does he understand 'five' as a term for counting. It is quite fair to ask, given this, and in the spirit of Charles' reservations about Wittgenstein's approach, whether such examples of use can shed much light on the nature of real language as it is shared by groups of humans. We confront here a problem that Wittgenstein's writings always generate—what exactly are we supposed to learn from these examples?

Conclusion

Given the obscurities of Wittgenstein's writings, it is hard to attribute conclusions to him, and hard to discern his grounds for thinking things, but I have expressed some reservations about some of the readings that David Charles seems to incline to, and also about some of his arguments. Mixed in with this, I have also expressed some reservations of my own about Wittgenstein's arguments. However, the spirit in which I have written here is as if I were encountering David's paper as presented to his group, responding to it, sympathetically and questioningly, but also expecting to receive further illumination from his responses.

Works Cited

Charles, David. 2001. 'Wittgenstein's Builders and Aristotle's Craftsmen', in *Wittgensteinian Themes: Essays in Honour of David Pears* (ed. D. Charles and W. Child). Clarendon Press, 49–80.

Snowdon, P. F. 1998. 'Strawson on the Concept of Perception', in *The Philosophy of P. F. Strawson* (ed. L. E. Hahn). Open Court, 293–310.

Snowdon, P. F. 2018a. 'Wittgenstein on Rule Following: Some Themes and Some Reactions', in *Mind, Language and Morality* (ed. G. Ortiz-Millan and J. A. C. Parcero). Routledge, 97–114.

Snowdon, P. F. 2018b. 'Wittgenstein and Naturalism', in *Wittgenstein and Naturalism* (ed. K. M. Cahill and T. Raleigh). Routledge, 15–32.

Wittgenstein, Ludwig. 2001. *Philosophical Investigations*. Blackwell.

PART II
CATEGORIES, SUBSTANCE, AND ESSENCE

5

Plato's Butcher

Realism and Platonic Classification

Verity Harte

Introduction

My title evokes a phrase, based on a famous image in Plato's *Phaedrus*, but with a
life of its own in present-day philosophical discussion: 'carving nature [or sometimes: "reality"] at its joints'.

One recent invocation is in Ted Sider's *Writing the Book of the World*, where
he writes:

> Metaphysics, at bottom, is about the fundamental structure of reality....
> Discerning 'structure' means discerning patterns. It means figuring out the right
> categories for describing the world. It means 'carving reality at its joints', to
> paraphrase Plato. It means inquiring into how the world fundamentally is, as
> opposed to how we ordinarily speak or think of it. (Sider 2011, 1)

Distinctive as Sider's position is on what to *include* among the joints of reality, his
framing of the position in terms of what he calls 'knee-jerk realism' captures the
general spirit of invocations of Plato's image. Here is how he frames such realism:

> The point of human inquiry—or a very large chunk of it anyway, the chunk
> that includes physics—is to *conform* itself to the world, rather than to *make* the
> world. The world is 'out there', and our job is to wrap our minds around it. (Sider
> 2011, 18)

This is the kind of realism I am interested in here: the view that there is, at least
fundamentally, some unique and global, mind- or language-independent structure of reality that it is the business of philosophy or science to know.[1] It is the
'externalist perspective' of Putnam's 'Two Philosophical Perspectives' (Putnam
1981, 49–74); the contrast to Goodman's 'worldmaking' (Goodman 1978). If

---

[1] The focus on fundamentality goes with Sider's cautious restriction and focus on physics. I shall
come back to this feature of modern invocations of Plato's image.

Verity Harte, *Plato's Butcher: Realism and Platonic Classification* In: *Aristotelian Metaphysics: Essays in Honour of David Charles.*
Edited by: David Bronstein, Thomas Kjeller Johansen, and Michail Peramatzis, Oxford University Press.
© Oxford University Press 2024. DOI: 10.1093/oso/9780198908678.003.0005

98   VERITY HARTE

Plato seems to you a 'poster child' for robust realism of this sort, that is all well and good.

My chapter starts from a historian's curiosity about some key differences between modern invocations and Plato's original image. I build out from this to put some philosophical pressure on Plato's own credentials as a knee-jerk realist. My project is *not* to offer an anti-realist Plato. Instead, by considering the character and contours of Plato's realism and by identifying the moves that keep him in the realist fold, I want to open the way for broader questions both about the metaphysics of Platonic classification and about the potentially recombinable elements of his classificatory realism.[2] One way to put my central thought is: given Plato's conception of 'the real', there is room for manoeuvre or slippage between the reality to which classification gives us access and the everyday 'reality' from which we begin, and not, or not just, in how we think about the latter.

1. *Phaedrus* 265c8–266c1

I begin with the ur-text in its immediate context as translated by Nehamas and Woodruff in Cooper 1997:

> SOC: Well, everything else in it really does appear to me to have been spoken in play. But part of it was given with Fortune's guidance, and there were in it two kinds of things the nature of which it would be quite wonderful to grasp by means of a systematic art.
>
> PH: Which things?
>
> SOC: <u>The first consists in seeing together things that are scattered about everywhere and collecting them into one kind, so that by defining each thing we can make clear the subject of any instruction we wish to give.</u> Just so with our discussion of love: Whether its definition was or was not correct, at least it allowed the speech to proceed clearly and consistently with itself.
>
> PH: And what is the other thing you are talking about Socrates?

---

[2] Charles 2001 carefully articulates a moderate form of realism for Aristotle, in contrast to Wittgenstein's Augustinian Platonist. Charles's focal points are distinct from mine: realist forms of truth conditions for thought and language and the relation between concept-acquisition and skill, and the 'Platonist' is here presented as both Wittgenstein's and Aristotle's hyper-realist foil. These differences notwithstanding, I think of my reflections on Plato here, at least indirectly, as in conversation with this insightful paper. It is a great pleasure to offer them in a volume in his honour, in thanks both for his contributions to the field and for collegial friendship, beginning long ago when I was a new Junior Research Fellow in Oxford and continuing more recently when, to my delight, he became my colleague at Yale.

SOC: <u>This, in turn, is to be able to cut up each kind according to its species along its natural joints, and to try not to splinter any part, as a bad butcher might do.</u> In just this way our two speeches placed all mental derangements into one common kind. Then, just as each single body has parts that naturally come in pairs of the same name (one of them being called the right-hand and the other the left-hand one), so the speeches, having considered unsoundness of mind to be by nature one single kind within us, proceeded to cut it up—the first speech cut its left-hand part, and continued to cut until it discovered among these parts a sort of love that can be called 'left-handed', which it correctly denounced; the second speech, in turn, led us to the right-hand part of madness; discovered a love that shares its name with the other but is actually divine; set it out before us, and praised it as the cause of our greatest goods.

PH: Yes, you are absolutely right.

SOC: <u>Well, Phaedrus, I am myself a lover of these divisions and collections, so that I may be able to think and to speak;</u> and if I believe someone else capable of looking to a one and at a natural many, I follow 'straight behind, in his tracks, as if he were a god'. God knows whether this is the right name for those who can do this correctly or not, but so far I have always called them 'dialecticians'. (Plato *Phaedrus* 265c8–266c1)[3]

This is a well-known passage. In context, Socrates is drawing attention to two important and admirable features of philosophical method that he suggests were illustrated in two preceding speeches he gave, one speech criticizing love as a form of madness, the other speech praising love as a form of madness. I will not comment on this broader context, except to say that one might think an investigation into love or madness somewhat far removed from modern focus on an inquiry into nature or the fundamental structure of reality.

The first feature Socrates draws attention to is described in the first underlined passage (but I will not focus on this); the second feature is in the second underlined passage—this is the ur-text; and the third underlined passage refers to one or both in having Socrates characterize himself as a lover of 'these divisions and collections', which he associates with dialectic. The passage is one of several passages in Plato which either describe (as here) or implement a method generally known, based on this passage, as 'the method of collection and division'. Implementations include the seemingly laborious 'divisions' of the *Sophist* and *Statesman* working towards an identification of sophistry and statesmanship. Based on various points of contrast (some of which I mention below), it is best to think of the various

---

[3] At 266b6 I follow Burnet et al. in reading 'πεφυκόθ' and have lightly adapted the translation accordingly.

100   VERITY HARTE

descriptions and implementations as constituting a *family* of methods and to understand talk of '*the* method of collection and division' accordingly.[4]

I want to make three points about the second underlined passage, the ur-text. First, a small point: 'nature' is not—as the modern descendant often has it—the *domain*, but a constraint on the carving, which must be *natural*.[5] Second, a glance at the diversity that exists in translations of the passage—exemplified in the following selections—suggests uncertainty in scholarship as to what has 'the nature' (the *phusis*) that grounds this claim to naturalness in carving, where options include: the *item carved*; the *points at which it is carved* (the joints); the *carving itself.*

> Hackforth 1952 seemingly opts for the carved: 'The reverse of the other, whereby we are enabled to divide into forms, following the objective articulation; we are not to attempt to hack off parts like a clumsy butcher'.
>
> Rowe 1988 opts either for the carved or for the points at which it is carved, the joints: 'Being able to cut it [viz. the single kind/form mentioned earlier?] up again, form by form, according to its natural joints, and not try to break any part into pieces, like an inexpert butcher' (my supplement).
>
> Yunis 2011, 198 opts for the carving itself: 'that one is able in the opposite direction [i.e., opposite to collecting] to cut up [the general form] into its sub-classes at joints where it is natural [to cut it up]' (his supplements).

The Greek reads:

> Τὸ πάλιν κατ᾽ εἴδη δύνασθαι διατέμνειν κατ᾽ ἄρθρα ᾗ πέφυκεν, καὶ μὴ ἐπιχειρεῖν καταγνύναι μέρος μηδέν, κακοῦ μαγείρου τρόπῳ χρώμενον·

For my own part, I think the most plausible construals are to take the talk of naturalness either (A) with the *joints*—'to cleave through according to the joints in the way in which [*they, the joints*] are of a nature to occur'—or (B) with the

---

[4] Hayase 2016 arrives at a complementary thought by different means, distinguishing the '*distinctively characteristic operations*' (2016: 120–1, his emphasis) of collection and of division from applications of one or both. I appreciate, but do not here engage with his nicely context-sensitive reading of the entire quoted passage.

[5] Contra Henry 2011: 252. Henry's discussion shows that the modern use reflects a (quite possibly, common) reading of the *Phaedrus* image within Platonic scholarship also. Henry 2011: 234–6 has the advantage of clearly articulating the kind of reading of the *Phaedrus* passage I dispute in this chapter, proposing that the passage does indeed articulate a method aimed at identification of natural kinds, so understood. Henry cites *Phaedrus* 266a3 '*pephukos eidos*' understood as 'natural kind' in support of this reading. But the suggested translation of this phrase when taken in context is misleading. In context, the point of the adjective '*pephukos*' or 'natural' is to convey the way in which, in the speeches that have been given, unreasoning love was treated, either as naturally single (with Rowe 1988, 103) or as naturally existing in us (with Yunis 2011, 198). The point of the adjective is not to characterize the status of the form or kind as such.

PLATO'S BUTCHER 101

cutting—'to cleave through according to the joints in the way in which [*it, the cleaving through*] is of a nature of occur'. For evidence that actions in general (*praxeis*) and more specifically the action of cutting (*temnein*, the stem of our *Phaedrus* verb) can have a nature or *phusis*, we may compare the following passage from the *Cratylus*.

> SOC: So an action's performance accords with the action's own nature, and not with what we believe. Suppose, for example, that we undertake to cut something. If we make the cut in whatever way *we* choose and with whatever tool *we* choose, we will not succeed in cutting. But if in each case we choose to cut in accord with the nature of cutting and being cut and with the natural tool for cutting, we'll succeed and cut correctly. If we try to cut contrary to nature, however, we'll be in error and accomplish nothing. (Plato, *Cratylus* 387a1–9; Reeve's translation in Cooper 1997)

Whatever may be the answer to the question as to the location of the relevant nature, my third point about the ur-text is that, directly or indirectly, the naturalness is tied to the carving. This is partly a function of the talk in the ur-text of 'joints', to which the carving must conform. A 'joint'—in Greek, an '*arthron*', a general term for a bodily joint, often used of the ankle, sometimes more specifically referring to the ball or socket—while it is a real feature of the animal, comes into focus in the context of carving because of the ease or appropriateness of carving at joints.

The butcher image confirms that we should be thinking of the activity of a *mageiros* (mentioned at 265e3), a skilled professional combining the roles of slaughterman, butcher, and cook, carving up an animal's body, typically for the dual purpose of providing sacrificial offerings and food.[6] Absent this context, it is far from obvious that a natural division of the animal in question would focus on its joints (as opposed to its limbs or its organs). Joints, though they exist independently, are tied up with carving insofar as they are the points at which carving is most readily *possible*, given the character and aim of carving.

This close tie to carving is only underlined if both Hackforth and Yunis are right, in their translations above, to talk not of dividing 'according to forms', as if forms *orient* the division, but of dividing '*into* forms', a reading recently defended by Lesley Brown.[7] Understood thus, forms emerge in the context of a division undertaken with a given purpose, though this is not to suggest they exist only because of the division. To say that forms emerge in the context of a division is

---

[6] Berthiaume 1982 remains the authoritative study of the *mageiros*. §III is focused specifically on the aspect of this professional's role involving butchery.

[7] Brown 2010. (Yunis speaks of dividing 'into subclasses' rather than forms, but I like this terminology less.) Scepticism about the construal is expressed by Muniz and Rudebusch 2018, n. 15. The adoption of Brown's reading is not essential to my point.

102   VERITY HARTE

not to say that forms are miraculously brought into being *by* the division. But it is to tie the forms divided and made salient to the context—and *project*—of the division. In turn, this complicates the relation between these forms and the 'world' articulated by the division.

Again, reflection on carving helps. The *Cratylus* underscores that we cannot carve however we like, nor with whatever tool we may choose. However, as the *Phaedrus* image also reminds us, such object-responsive carving is undertaken by the *mageiros* as part of a specific (ritual) practice and with project-determined aims. These too partly determine the carving, in its selection of joints. In its most canonical occurrence at a public sacrifice (*thysia*), the *mageiros* first carves specific choice parts of the animal (including certain 'joints' in the culinary sense) for the priest or priestess and for other civic functionaries; then the *mageiros* carves the remaining edible portions for distribution to the remaining participants in the festival according to the principle that each person receives a share of equal weight (if not, of necessity, of equal *quality*).[8] Thus, while carving no more conjures into being the results of carving than it does the joints in accordance with which it carves, *which* joints carving accords with and *in what manner* are a function not solely of what is carved, but also of the project of the carving. In consequence, the articulation of the animal that is revealed by any given carving is specific and limited in perspective.

The points I have made regarding the ur-text put no pressure on modern use of the butcher image, which has taken on an independent life of its own. Nevertheless, I want to build on these observations to put some pressure on *Plato's* credentials to knee-jerk realism, at least to complicate the picture somewhat, with potentially broader implications for what the butcher image contributes to realism. If I am correct, this image is not what does the heavy lifting in Plato's realism.

The key lever I will use is the point that the naturalness at issue for Plato seems tied to the project of the carving. In principle, this opens the way to different, equally natural ways of dividing into forms according to different projects.[9] I shall now point to evidence from Plato's *Philebus* that the method does indeed allow for such variance.

2. *Philebus* 16c5–17a5: Socrates' Promethean Method

In *Philebus* 16c5–17a5 Socrates describes a method associated in context with dialectic and of which he calls himself a 'lover', just as in the *Phaedrus* he described

---

[8] See, for example, Berthiaume 1982, 50–1 and Ekroth 2014 for evidence of this pattern and norm. My description here is limited to the butchery proper, setting aside prior phases of the sacrificial event, other elements of which include the killing, exsanguination, and evisceration of the animal; and the preparing and burning of 'portions' for the gods.

[9] Contrast here Gill 2012, 183, who thinks such permissiveness *is* in evidence in the divisions of the *Sophist* and *Statesman* but goes against the model of the *Phaedrus* with its butcher image.

himself as a 'lover of these divisions and collections'.[10] I take this intertextuality to be good evidence that Plato regarded these two methodological passages as importantly connected. The *Philebus* passage raises many difficult exegetical questions that have been much worked over. I will tread lightly here, which means I will in places be somewhat dogmatic.

> It's a gift of the gods to men, as it seems to me at least, cast down from the region of the gods by some Prometheus along with shining fire. And the ancients, superior to us and living closer to gods, handed down this saying [1] that whatever are said to be are made up of one and many, but have limit (*peras*) and lack of limit (*apeiria*) fused together within them.
>
> [2] Given that these things [whatever are said to be] are organized in this way [according to [1]] <they said that> we must investigate by [2a] on each occasion positing one form in connection with everything, since we will find it if/because it is present; if we got hold of it, [2b] after one we must examine two, if there are so many, but, if not, three or some other number, and [2c] <we must> in turn <examine> each of these ones likewise until [2d] one should see with respect to the one at the start [the single form identified at [2a]] not only that it is one and many and lacking limit (*apeira*) but also how many <it is>; [2e] that <we should> not apply the form of what lacks limit (*to apeiron*) to the plurality until one should discern the entire number of it [the plurality] between both what lacks limit (*to apeiron*) and the one, at that point leaving be each one of them all, having released them into what lacks limit (*to apeiron*).
>
> [3] The gods, then, as I said, handed down to us to investigate in this fashion and to learn and to teach one another. But the wise amongst mankind nowadays make a one at random and a many more quickly and more slowly than they ought; after the one, they skip straight to what lacks limit, but the intermediates escape them, the things by means of which a dialectical or eristical manner of producing arguments for one another are to be separated from each other. (Plato, *Philebus* 16c5–17a5; my translation and enumeration for ease of reference)[11]

In this passage, the section marked [2] contains Socrates' description of a method, described in [3] as a divinely ordained method for investigating and for teaching

---

[10] While I will talk in terms of this being a 'method', I do not mean this label in and of itself to settle the question of whether performing (all and only) the tasks described in this passage is intended to help a practitioner *acquire* expertise, as opposed, for example, to *present* the results of expertise otherwise acquired. To this question, see the judicious reflections of Fossheim 2012.

[11] '[…]' marks exegetical supplements I have added; '<…>' marks textual/grammatical supplements. I have used 'lack of limit' and related expressions to capture the alpha-privative in '*apeiria*', '*apeiron*' and so on. I mark the difference between the noun '*apeiria*' ('lack of limit') and the adjectival noun phrase '*to apeiron*' ('what lacks limit'), but the latter may refer to the feature in virtue of which something lacks limit (lack of limit) rather than to something that lacks limit.

and learning, and as one whose correct implementation is said to be key to a dialectical manner of proceeding in argument. The method, as described in [2], is explicitly said to rely on a—notably obscure—view about the structure of reality reported in [1]. I call this method Socrates' 'Promethean Method' because of his explicit allusion to the Prometheus myth. This Promethean Method belongs to the *family* of scholarship's 'method of collection and division'. The broader context of the *Philebus* suggests the Promethean Method in its turn comprises different possible implementations, not all of which mirror Socrates' tidy description here.[12]

The Promethean Method as characterized in [2] is clearly a method of classification, the stages of which are itemized in [2a] through [2c]: a series of forms are posited by the method's user; forms in the series are related in such a way that the two, three or *n* forms posited at step 2, in [2b], are forms of—somehow within or under—the one form initially posited at step 1, in [2a], and so on.[13] *Classification*, of course, might be undertaken in different ways and for different reasons. Faced, for example, with the three shapes, A, B and C in Figure 5.1, one might embark on a classification of *shape* or of *polygon* or of *triangle*. In so doing, one might be focused on using the classification to come up with a definition of 'shape' or of 'polygon' or of 'triangle', or with a view to mapping out the entire geometrical space of options to understand the domain.

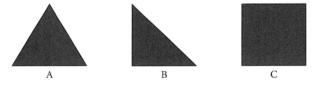

Figure 5.1 Three shapes

In the *Philebus*, the latter project—mapping the entire space—is closest to the character of the description of the Promethean Method and to the project of the dialogue to which it is relevant. In this respect, Promethean division has a different structure than the definition-oriented divisions produced in the *Sophist* or *Statesman*.[14] Consider, by way of illustrating this contrast, the exemplary account of angling offered in the *Sophist* by the Eleatic Stranger (ES).

> ES: Concerning angling, you and I have now not only agreed the name, but we have also sufficiently grasped the account concerning the work itself. For of skill

---

[12] 'Method' should be understood in a manner closer to its use in a phrase such as 'the scientific method' than to some specific *technique*.

[13] I speak of 'classification' as the term is used informally, rather than its technical biological usage. For discussion and a defence of the distinction between classifying and characterizing, see Lambert and Simons 1994.

[14] Gill 2012, 214–15 rightly emphasizes this difference.

as a whole, one half part was acquisitive, and of the acquisitive part one half part was taking by force, and of taking by force one half part was hunting, half of hunting was animal hunting, half of animal hunting was aquatic hunting, the whole lower portion of aquatic hunting was fishing, and of fishing doing so by blows, and of doing so by blows hooking. Of this, the part that involves a blow drawing a thing up from below, the name being likened to the action itself has come to be by designation 'angling', the thing being sought. (*Sophist* 221a7–c3; my translation)

In dividing the single form or kind, labelled 'skill as a whole' (*sumpasa technē*), in pursuit of an account of the skill that is angling, ES divides skill into two, takes up one of the resulting parts and divides it into two and repeats the process until concluding.[15] In the *Philebus*, by contrast, Socrates' Promethean method requires a complete enumeration of sub-forms of whatever number at every level.

Socrates' Promethean Method is clearly presented as being answerable to reality, and this in a couple of different ways. First and as already noted, the method is *premised* on a description of reality; I shall return to this aspect. Second, Socrates writes a connection to reality into the method's description. In [2a], the Greek is ambiguous between the claim that one will discover the first form posited *if* or *because* it is present, but either version holds the posit accountable to reality. The conditional reading may be especially suited to this being the *first* step of the method.[16] This would underscore that, in positing one form 'in connection with everything', there is no commitment to there being a single form for everything just as we like. Context suggests that there will be a single form in every complex domain of inquiry determining a skill (*technē*).[17] Presumably, failure properly to identify a salient, single form does not mean one should give up and go home, but that one should revisit one's initial posit. But a failure at this first step takes one back to the drawing board entirely, which in turn supports particular emphasis on the provisional character of this first move. Here—and throughout—nothing is said to indicate how one might *detect* this or any comparable methodological error.

Being answerable to reality in positing the series of forms helps to explain how the Promethean Method could have the natural and determinate stopping point that Socrates' description implies and describes in [2d] and [2e], especially given the following fact that the description itself emphasizes: that each form

---

[15] In line with Vlasits 2017, 23–5 (who also helpfully refers to a broad range of scholarship on this question), I do not take *dichotomous* division to be mandated by the method applied in the *Sophist* and *Statesman*, though it is frequently exemplified.

[16] Thanks to Gail Fine (pers. comm.) for this suggestion.

[17] For the connection with *technē*, see, for example, 16c2, and further discussion in section 3. In the context of the *Philebus*, the term has broad scope, seemingly coextensive with branches of knowledge (*epistēmai*) or the 'disciplines' (*ta mathēmata*).

posited seems at least in principle open to the same investigative treatment. As indicated in [2d] an application of the method can and should cease at the point where the plurality of forms existing for discovery from steps 2 through n has been fully enumerated, when one knows 'how many' the original one is. The procedure for counting here is striking: the plurality enumerated does not include the original one—hence its number is said in [2e] to be '*between*' what lacks limit and 'the *one*'. Nor do we keep a tally of forms per layer: at step 2, step 3, and so on. Thus, the count arrived at neither includes all forms identified nor discriminates between forms of different layers. I take the focus on knowing this count to arise less from concern for enumeration as such (still less from some Platonic fetish for numbers) and more to reflect a concern for completion, ensuring *every* sub-form of the original form is accounted for.[18] Again, there is no indication how an investigator might determine that this point has been reached. In general, the method is silent about this aspect of its epistemology.

In [2d] and [2e] Socrates focuses on the point of completion of some instance of the method, emphasizing that this point is reached only when its practitioner knows *how many*, the *entire number* of the plurality of sub-forms of the original single form. He also insists that 'the form of what lacks limit' should not be ascribed to this plurality until this point is reached. Note that this shows that 'the form of what lacks limit'—whatever that may be—*does apply* to the plurality, alongside possession of some determinate number.[19] Note, further, that it seems to apply to it *all along*. Socrates' point is methodological—the method's user should not *ascribe* it until in possession of that plurality's determinate number: that is, as I understand it, until the plurality has indeed been completely identified.

What feature of the plurality grounds the ascription of the form of what lacks limit? It is natural to connect this to the mention of 'lack of limit' in the description of reality in [1] on which the method is based. However, though there no doubt is some connection of this kind, it does not much help us here, since the mention in [1] is just that, a *mention*, nothing more. One way to understand the relevant feature—a way I reject—is to regard it as pointing to the fact that each sub-form is instantiated in an indefinite number of particulars. A second way—a way I accept—is to understand the plurality's possession of lack of limit as pointing to the fact that, no matter where the enumeration of existing sub-forms of the original form runs out, the plurality has features that remain open to further—if *ex hypothesi* inapt—points of division.

To illustrate: suppose one were embarked on an exhaustive investigation of *shape* with the object of identifying and classifying all existing varieties of shape, a non-trivial geometrical research project. Shape includes polygons of various kinds, including those in Figure 5.1. Polygons A and B exemplify two

---

[18] Compare Frede 1997, 155–7.
[19] Does it apply to the plurality collectively, individually, both? I am tempted to answer 'both'.

representative varieties of three-sided polygon or triangle: equilateral and isosceles. Triangle B is a triangle and, more specifically, an isosceles right-angled triangle. Both features, let us assume, are sub-forms of shape that it displays. It is also an isosceles right-angled triangle with side of some specific length, printed in Figure 5.1. *These* features of it, however, let us also assume, are not sub-forms of shape and may be rightly ignored in an exhaustive classification of shape. Nor is the possibility of inapt division a feature of the plurality only at the bottom layer. Suppose a correct first move in classifying shape would be to distinguish curvilinear and rectilinear shape; nevertheless, one could erroneously make an initial threefold division into curvilinear shape, rectilinear polygon of fewer than ten sides and rectilinear polygon of ten or greater sides. In general, on the interpretation I accept, the plurality's lack of limit consists in the apparent availability of these inapt divisions.

Arguably, this way of interpreting what it is for the plurality to lack limit does a better job of explaining Socrates' methodological caution. On this way of understanding the feature, if one *were* to ascribe the form of what lacks limit to the plurality before having completely enumerated it, one would wrongly ascribe it, having failed to identify all and only the genuine sub-forms of the original form.[20] Further, this interpretation can help to explain why it sometimes seems as if Socrates' talk of 'what lacks limit' refers, at least extensionally, to the indefinite number of particular instances of some form (giving support to the alternative reading). This is because, as with the triangles in Figure 5.1, routes to other, apparent, but unreal divisions of salient formal characters are made visible by and in such particulars.

Let me pause to take stock. Thus far, my interpretation of Socrates' Promethean Method is conducive to the conventional understanding of the *Phaedrus* butchery image, and the method is certainly realist in tenor. But I want also to point to the way in which the ascription to the plurality of the form of what lacks limit makes room for a kind of 'gap', as it were, between, on the one hand, the reality in which the classification is made and to which it applies and, on the other, the classificatory entities posited: the initial single form and its determinate plurality of sub-forms. This gap indicates some domain of resistance to or lack of salience for any individual application of the Promethean Method. I want next to suggest that this gap is supported both by the description of reality on which the method is founded, in [1], and by the broader context of the passage, and that it invites further reflection on the character and robustness of the method's realism.

---

[20] Of course, one could know *generally* that the domain allows for inapt divisions of indefinite number, prior to successfully completing the correct division, but one would not then know which potential divisions would be inapt, especially allowing that it remains possible that one may need to correct one's initial starting-point.

108   VERITY HARTE

Start with [1]: Socrates reports 'the ancients' as handing down the saying that 'whatever are said to be are made up of one and many but have limit and lack of limit fused together within them'. The phrase I translate 'whatever are said to be' is sometimes translated—less naturally, I think—as 'things said always to be', restricting the title to permanent beings. Gisela Striker (Striker 1970, 17–23) is the principal defender of this latter view, on the grounds that it would be false to suggest that perishable particulars are unlimited: that is, that some particular *itself* lacks limit in some way, as opposed to there being an unlimited number *of such particulars* under any given form.[21]

The objection ignores the way in which the ancients' saying is focused on *ascriptions* of being, on things *said to be*. This focus develops out of the preceding context. Earlier, Socrates had mentioned certain puzzles arising if one identifies something as both one and many. Such puzzles were said to arise both in connection with perishable particulars and in connection with imperishable forms, though the latter is the context that Socrates said gave rise to specific concern. Within this broader context, the ancients' focus on *ascriptions* of being picks up a point Socrates more recently made, in language echoed in the ancients' saying, that one–many identifications arise in the context of language, 'statements', and are an inevitable feature of language.[22]

> SOC: We say, I suppose, that the same thing, becoming one and many as a result of statements (*logoi*), runs round everywhere according to each of the things said on every occasion, both long ago and now. (*Philebus* 15d4–6; my translation)

Socrates' point about language—I would argue—reflects the truism that statements ascribing features to things or articulating the constituents of things are a staple of informative speech. When, then, the ancients speak of things that are 'said to be' in [1], we should think of statements of the form 'X is Y', where Y is some feature or constituent of X. Statements of this form may be made *about* perishables or imperishables, which is why the talk of 'whatever are said to be' may be given its natural reading. But the ancients' saying focuses our attention on ascriptions of being (sayings *to be*...). That does not mean we are to attend to what is accorded the title 'being'. Rather, it directs attention to the beings ascribed—the characteristics and constituents picked out by the '... is Y' element in statements of the relevant form.[23]

---

[21] Striker is followed in this, more recently, by Crivelli 2019, 44 with n. 35.

[22] Gosling 1975, 83–4 notes the connection. Delcomminette 2006, 96–101 develops it in ways most similar to my proposal, save that his reading is linguistically oriented, taking the focus to be the sense of certain general expressions.

[23] As often in Plato (and in Attic Greek), the verb 'to be' is best understood here as syntactically incomplete (admitting completion).

It is the *beings ascribed* that are identified and articulated in an application of the subsequent method: as the one form and the determinate plurality of sub-forms identified. Given their designation as forms, it is reasonable to suppose that these are, for Plato, imperishable. (Socrates does not *say so*, but the broader context supports the decision nonetheless.) These, when properly identified and articulated, are what I mean by talk of 'the classificatory entities posited'. It is unsurprising to find Plato associating dialectical method with a method whose application deals only in (putatively imperishable) forms.[24] But the 'gap' that I posited between these classificatory entities and the reality in which the classification is made and to which it applies gets some additional support from the thought that the subject of the relevant ascriptions (the X that is Y) may be perishable or imperishable. Indeed, I take the best understanding of the *extension* of the ascriptions of being (as opposed to the *beings* ascribed) to be just 'reality', loosely speaking.

I shall return to this gap, which is crucial to the possibility of different, legitimate classifications of the same broad domain, a possibility Socrates' examples of the Promethean Method illustrate.

3. The Broader Context: Realism and Skill (*Technē*) in Socrates' Promethean Method

Socrates' examples pick up the broader context of his Promethean Method. When Socrates introduced the method, he credited to it every discovery in the domain of craft-expertise or skill (*technē*).

> SOC:...There is not, nor could there be a finer path than that of which I am ever a lover, but which, oftentimes, having escaped me has left me desolate and at a loss.
>
> PRO: What is it? Just say.
>
> SOC: One that is not very difficult to describe, but very difficult to use. Everything that has been discovered in the domain of craft-expertise/skill (*technē*) has come to light through this....(*Philebus* 16b5–c3; my translation)

Socrates' description of the method has not yet filled out this connection to skill. But both this introductory remark and the attribution of the discovery of the method to 'some Prometheus' underline its centrality: Prometheus—in many Greek accounts of the legend, including Plato's own in the *Protagoras*—is given

---

[24] I do not mean to suggest the forms articulated do not have *application* to perishables.

credit for giving humanity, not just fire, but also the *technai*—the productive and practical skills necessary for successful human living, whatever one might take that to involve.

The connection to skill is filled out by three examples Socrates offers to illuminate his terse description of the method. Arguably, the central object of these examples is to tie a grasp of the complex structures elaborated in a successful application of the method to the conditions for wisdom (*sophia*) as these are exemplified by two presumptively familiar forms of expertise (*technai*): *grammatikē*, the body of phonetic knowledge associated with the ability to read and write, and *mousikē*, the body of acoustic knowledge associated with musical composition and/or performance. I will call these forms of expertise 'literacy' and 'musical expertise', respectively, though neither term in English is an ideal match. Regarding literacy, note that the relevant body of phonetic knowledge is bound up with the distinction of those phonemes that, through association with written symbols, make up the alphabet; despite its verbal resemblance '*grammatikē*' is nothing like '*grammar*', as we understand it.[25]

Here are all or part of each of the three illustrations offered.

[ILLUSTRATION 1]

SOC: Voice (*phonē*) issuing through our mouth, for each and all of us, is one, presumably, but in turn lacking limit as to plurality.

PRO: Indeed.

SOC: But we are not yet at all wise in virtue of either of these, neither that we know the lack of limit of it, nor that we know the one. Rather, <knowing> both how many <are the forms of voice> and of what sort, this is what makes each of us literate.

PRO: Absolutely true.

[ILLUSTRATION 2, first part]

SOC: Further, this same thing is what makes one musically expert.

PRO: How so?

SOC: Voice (*phonē*) corresponding to that craft-expertise/skill (*technē*) is presumably one in it.[26]

PRO: Of course.

SOC: But we posit two, low and high, and a third, even-pitch. Isn't that so?

PRO: It is.

---

[25] For a helpful discussion of the term and its meaning, see Graham and Barney 2014.

[26] T (followed by Burnet) reads που καὶ τὸ κατ'; B (followed by Diès and translated here) reads που κατ'.

SOC: But you would not yet be wise with respect to music knowing just these, though without knowing them, you would be practically worthless regarding these matters. (*Philebus* 17b3–c9; my translation)

[ILLUSTRATION 3]

SOC: When some god or even a divine human discerned voice (*phonē*) lacking limit—as the story goes in Egypt, this was a certain Theuth, who first discerned the vowels in what lacks limit, being not one but a greater number, and in turn respecting others, having a share not of voice, but of a type of sound, that there is a certain number of these too, and he distinguished as a third form of letters what we today call 'unvoiced'. Next, he divided the ones lacking voice and sound as far as each one and the vowels and the intermediates in the same fashion until grasping their number he gave the name 'phonetic element' (*stoicheion*) both to each individually and to them all together. Seeing distinctly that no one among us would learn/understand even one in isolation without them all, and, in turn, reckoning this bond as being one and making all these one in a way, he designated a single expertise (*technē*) set over them, giving it the name 'literacy' (*grammatikē*). (*Philebus* 18b6–d2; my translation)[27]

A lot could be said about these illustrations, but I will focus on three main points, two tied to the way in which they are connected to each other. Socrates offers *three* illustrations, but the first and third concern the same form of expertise, literacy. What distinguishes the two illustrative discussions of literacy, and, more generally, distinguishes the first two illustrations from the third, is perspective. One perspective is pedagogical: in the first appeal to literacy, what one must know respecting (spoken) voice to count as *literate* (in possession of *grammatikē*), where the answer is that one must know both how many are the relevant forms of voice and what they are like (17b8).[28] The second discussion of literacy—in the passage's third illustration—adopts the perspective of discovery, telling the story of how the Egyptian god, Theuth, discovered and mapped out the various phonemes making up the alphabet, and gave the name of 'literacy' to their systematic understanding.[29]

---

[27] This passage is tricky to parse. At 18b6, I use 'discerned voice lacking limit' to preserve an ambiguity as to whether lacking limit is *the fact discerned* about voice or (as I prefer) a feature of voice with the discernment being specified in what follows ('discerned the vowels'). At 18c8–d1, Theuth's twin reckonings—'reckoning this bond as being one *and* making all these one in a way'—should, I think, be taken closely together, though I do not go so far as to suggest the 'and' is epexegetical. I discuss this final part of the passage further below.

[28] The appeal to musical expertise in the second illustration adopts a similarly pedagogical perspective.

[29] The story of Theuth's discovery of the alphabet is also told in the *Phaedrus* 274c5–275c4 in explaining the origins of writing with a view to assessing the merits and demerits of writing. There too the *grammata*—the phonetic elements and their written symbols—are framed as a *discovery*, on Theuth's part, not an *invention*. See especially '*heurein*' at 274c8.

My first main point is that the illustrations' different perspectives indicate that implementations of the Promethean Method in teaching and learning and in discovery—contexts of use to which Socrates referred in his general comment on the method ([3])—should be kept distinct. This in turn helps to make clear that the tidy description of the method that Socrates has given can be tidy in part because—in the manner of a pedagogical implementation of his method—his description is parasitic on the successful completion of the rather messier business of its implementation in a discovery context of the sort Theuth illustrates.

Because Theuth is said to start not with the one form (as in Socrates' description) but with what lacks limit, Theuth's procedure might be thought simply to reverse Socrates' originally described manner of proceeding. But that would be an oversimplification of what Theuth is represented as doing.[30] Without getting into the details of the phonetic system underlying what Theuth is described as doing, the way he is said to proceed is instructive.

Theuth begins—Socrates suggests he is compelled to begin—with what lacks limit, which I understand to mean he begins with voice as it presents itself in the form of actual speech. Compared to Socrates' sequence of phases in [2] Theuth begins his classification in the middle. He does not begin with the single overarching form that will be identified for this domain: 'phonetic element' (*stoicheion*).[31] Nor, having begun, does he move straight on to this single form. Confronted with voice as presented by actual speech, Theuth first identifies certain phonetic types, beginning with the vowel. These initially identified types are located in the middle of the completed classificatory system Theuth is in the course of discovering. Having begun there, he next goes on to divide each of those intermediate types into its various constituent sub-types before identifying and classifying all the types and sub-types as forms of 'phonetic element'.[32]

Theuth operates in this way in part because, prior to him, no one had established that there *was* a complex single form to be identified as a legitimate object of study and expertise. My second main point is that Socrates' description of Theuth's activity suggests that the existence of a systematic body of understanding in the domain not only licenses the identification of a unitary expertise—literacy—that pertains to the domain but bears on the standards for success of Theuth's classificatory activity.

To explain: the talk of Theuth 'discerning' various phonetic forms supports a realist understanding of his manner of proceeding. The phonetic elements that he

---

[30] On this point and, in general, for a careful discussion of the illustration involving Theuth with which I am very sympathetic, see Menn 1998.

[31] 'Stoicheion' can also be translated 'letter', picking up the alphabetical character of these phonetic elements and their association with a written symbol.

[32] As Menn 1998 argues, this careful stepwise procedure is crucial to the difficult (and, in the passage, still seriously oversimplified) process in fact necessary to generate a phonetic alphabet for a language for the first time.

identifies and classifies are correctly identified only if and because they are there for discovery. However, the passage also suggests that the apportionment of voice as presented to us in actual human speech into a unitary domain with the relevant structure is constrained by the structure of human understanding reflected in the newly baptized *technē*, literacy. I have in mind here the claim at the very end of the passage:

> Seeing distinctly that no one among us would learn/understand even one in isolation without them all, and, in turn, reckoning this bond as being one and making all these one in a way, he designated a single expertise (*technē*) set over them, giving it the name 'literacy' (*grammatikē*). (*Philebus* 18c7–d2; my translation)

The Greek is this:

> καθορῶν δὲ ὡς οὐδεὶς ἡμῶν οὐδ᾽ ἂν ἓν αὐτὸ καθ᾽ αὑτὸ ἄνευ πάντων αὐτῶν μάθοι, τοῦτον τὸν δεσμὸν αὖ λογισάμενος ὡς ὄντα ἕνα καὶ πάντα ταῦτα ἕν πως ποιοῦντα μίαν ἐπ᾽ αὐτοῖς ὡς οὖσαν γραμματικὴν τέχνην ἐπεφθέγξατο προσειπών.[33]

At minimum, it seems here that *alongside* the way in which the notion of letter or phonetic element (*stoicheion*) captures and unites all the entities in the domain, *in turn* the status of these entities with respect to human understanding—the fact that their understanding is and must be in some way systematic in character—is a crucial step in Theuth's conclusion that his work is done; a complex, but unitary domain has been correctly marked off and suitably classified.

Theuth's baptism of literacy is traced to two key insights. The first ('Seeing distinctly...in isolation without them all') might seem to suggest that no person can have knowledge of one phonetic element without knowing them all. This reading, however, conflicts with Socrates' earlier explicit acknowledgement that a person could know the three musical pitches (high, low, even-pitch) without yet knowing all the forms required for expertise in music.[34] I take Theuth's first insight instead to be, not that knowing any one phonetic element depends on knowing them all, but rather that each phonetic element's availability as an object of knowledge depends on its being part of this system of phonetic elements. No element is isolated as an object of knowledge; each is a part of a system, more specifically an alphabet. This is true even if a child may learn the elements of the alphabet piecemeal. Still, she learns them *as* elements of an alphabet, as constitutive parts of her progress towards literacy.

This understanding of Theuth's first insight helps interpret his second ('reckoning this bond...in a way'). It is rather odd to speak of reckoning 'this bond'

---

[33] The translation of the passage varies quite significantly across different translations and commentaries. For details of my construal, see n. 27 above.

[34] 17c4–9, quoted above [ILLUSTRATION 2, first part].

114   VERITY HARTE

(singular) as 'being one', as if there might be doubt about this. I suggest that we take the twin aspects of Theuth's reckoning to be closely connected. The phonetic elements that Theuth enumerates and distinguishes make possible human learning by collectively constituting an interconnected system for learning and knowledge. This is Theuth's first insight. The grounds of this epistemic feature of the elements in the elements' mutual dependence on each other as parts of an alphabetical system constitutes the bond Theuth reckons in his second insight. In recognizing the *system* the elements comprise ('reckoning the bond as being one'), Theuth recognizes what makes all these (and only these) elements into a domain that can be treated as one ('and as making all these one in a way'). These elements form a unitary domain from the perspective of enabling the *technē* he baptizes 'literacy'. This *technē* sets standards of success for the adequacy of any given system of forms identified for it, given its project: a phonetically sensitive alphabetized writing system.

Theuth's discovered single, complex form is *stoicheion*, which captures the idea of a phonetic *element*, something both foundational and generative or combinable. Theuth's discovery of this single form comes as a package with his articulation of it. Both are answerable not only to the ways in which actual human speech is differentiable into distinguishable component phonetic elements but also to the way in which the phonetic elements so distinguished may act in concert with each other to make up larger units of speech, the syllables and words that are to be represented as made out of them in an alphabetized system of writing, expertise in which will constitute the skill of literacy.

This two-way responsiveness leads on to my third main point, which again picks up a connection between Socrates' three illustrations. While Socrates' first and third illustrations each focus on literacy, his second is focused on musical expertise. However, although literacy and music are distinct varieties of expertise, they each concern what, from the perspective of our sensory experience, is a single phenomenon: namely, *voice* (*phonē*).[35] Literacy is an expertise in (spoken) voice, including its representation in alphabetized writing and in the reading of such written representations aloud.[36] Ancient Greek music too is focused on voice, primarily the human voice in song, though accompanying instruments could, by extension, be ascribed voice.[37]

The passage seems, if anything, to emphasize this connection between the domains of the different forms of expertise appealed to in the illustrations. Each illustration starts with a focus on voice (*phōnē*). In the first illustration, this is voice characterized as 'issuing through the mouth' (17b3–4) and regarded as a

---

[35]   On the translation of '*phonē*', see Striker 1970, 24–30 and Menn 1998, 293–5, each of whom treats the term as more narrowly linguistic than I do. I do, however, agree with them that Theuth is confronted by voice in the form of *speech* rather than *sound*.

[36]   Reading aloud, not silently, was the default for ancient Greek readers.

[37]   See, for authoritative discussion, West 1992, 39–47.

complex unity. As the third illustration makes clear, to recognize voice as it issues through the mouths of humans in speech as a complex unity is made possible by the foundational work of Theuth, who in turn is described as beginning with voice (*phōnē*, 18b6) not yet discriminated in the relevant way. In the second illustration, Socrates' discussion kicks off with the contention that 'voice corresponding to that *technē*' is to be presumed one 'in it' (17c1): that is, in the context of the skill. Thus, there is, it emerges, not one, but (at least) two distinct, but appropriate ways of dividing voice, considered as such, ways corresponding to the two skills appealed to. Literacy and musical expertise are each responsive to real features of voice, but the features to which they are responsive are skill specific. The character and project of these forms of expertise are integral to the classificatory schemata in ways surprising both from the perspective of a traditional picture of Plato's realism and against the backdrop of later use of his butchery image.

4. Implications

In closing, I will set up some broader questions about realism to which these reflections point. As far as Plato goes, I have argued that, alongside the realism we might expect of him, a commitment to any classification being responsive to reality, there is evidence of a complementary skill-responsiveness too. Of course, human skills and the projects they serve are parts of reality too. But they are also methodologically integral to Platonic classification.

This goes back to a feature of the ur-text and its context: Plato's classificatory method does not focus on the *natural* or *fundamental* as the domain of the activity of classification. To the contrary, his focus is domains of human expertise. This point might be misunderstood. I do not mean that Plato's classificatory method focuses on domains of human expertise *in contrast* to the natural or fundamental. Given Plato's understanding of the natural world as the product of divine demiurgy, he does not in the same way draw an (Aristotelian) contrast between the artificial and the natural.[38] Instead, I mean to draw attention to the ways in which Plato's classificatory method applies to domains of experience whose systematic understanding constitutes varieties of human expertise or organized bodies of knowledge without privileging one over others as more fundamental. At least, none are privileged as fundamental in the way I take this to be meant in, for example, Sider's talk of 'the fundamental structure of reality' (2011, 1, quoted at start), which implies levels within the reality classified.[39]

---

[38] For discussion, see Lennox 1985.

[39] Dialectic, which seems to be counted as a *technē*, is accorded priority ahead of other *technai* or branches of knowledge (*epistēmai*) in the *Philebus* (57e6–59d6) and is distinctive in the character of its objects, but its priority is to do with its epistemic character (its truth, stability, and purity) rather than its concern with some putative, fundamental structure of reality.

116   VERITY HARTE

Perhaps, however, Plato does not so much *lack* interest in what is fundamental as have a very broad notion of what counts as such. For all I have shown, one might argue, we have here nothing more than robust realism, combined with a high degree of confidence in how well the structure of various forms of human expertise in fact responds to (some, nevertheless unique and fundamental) portion of reality.[40] In the case of voice, for example, the situation might be one in which the impression that we are dealing here with a *single* phenomenon, organized in different ways in response to literacy and by musical expertise, turns out to be mistaken.[41] Instead, *phonetic voice* and *musical voice* turn out to be two distinct portions of reality, properly classified by two distinct forms of expertise.

There may be *a* sense in which this is right at least for voice, literacy, and musical expertise. Even here, however, I would suggest that the Platonic basis for saying so at the very least points to a rather different source of support for his realism. One key complication is that there are for Plato two very distinct routes by which we may access reality: our sensory experience, uninformed by reasoning in terms of intelligible forms, and our reasoning so informed.[42] The only sense in which there are two distinct, real domains of voice for classification is the one in which we are concerned with reality already intelligibly informed. But these are competing equally legitimate formations of a single phenomenon from the point of view of sensory experience.

Put this another, more general way: just as, I observed, Plato's butcher carves an animal at its joints because joints are *suited to carving*, so Platonic classification carves at intelligible joints, which joints are *suited to intelligizing*. Literacy and musical expertise are both examples of such intelligizing and, I take it, a figure for intelligizing the world generally (with the project, *to do so*).

Certainly, Plato writes in the language of discovery and does not think that intellectual carvings are at the whim of human invention; nor does he think that any arbitrary carving we might come up with might do. But the basis for this in his thought seems to me tied up with other positions he has: that what are being discovered, identified, and enumerated in the method are forms; that, through such forms, the world is structured so as to be intelligible; and, at least in the *Philebus* and *Timaeus*, that such structuring of the world as we encounter in

---

[40] I am grateful to Ursula Coope (pers. comm.) for pressing this question.

[41] Another option would be to treat voice (*phonē*) in the passage as a unitary form of which phonetic and musical voice are each (complex) sub-forms. But there is no indication of such a relation in the passage itself and it would, I think, put unreasonable pressure on the individuation of literacy and musical expertise to adopt this view.

[42] I do not here assume—and indeed would reject—the view that *what* portion of reality is accessed in these ways differs, so that forms are exclusively objects of reason and cannot inform our sensory judgements, whereas the objects of our sensory judgements are exclusively the objects of unreasoning sensory experience. Compare Harte 2017.

classifying is in turn the product of divine, intelligent intervention. Thus, if there is a sense in which it is true that these 'joints' exist in reality independently of the operation of human thought and action, that is because they are secured by the reality of forms that are precisely objects for human intelligence.

In *Ways of Worldmaking*, strikingly, Goodman at one point aligns his own view with the Platonist over the physicalist, suggesting his principal disagreement with Platonism is his nominalism (Goodman 1978, 94–5). There seems to me something importantly right about this, with implications both for how robust Plato's realist credentials are; and for how legible they become once transposed to the (presumably, very different) intellectual landscape of modern discussion.

Let me close by gesturing at a tentative, very general claim about what I take voice, in the illustrations of the *Philebus*, to be a figure for: reality as a whole independently of any specific classification or division into forms, from which different structures emerge as salient to different varieties of expertise. This goes back to the 'gap' I suggested there is between the classificatory entities identified and articulated through an application of the method and the independently perceptually accessible reality in which any given application of the method takes place.

I have argued that, for any given classification, the way in which the classification responds to reality, though respond to reality it does, is bound up with the character and objects of some domain of expertise to which that classification contributes. I have also suggested that, for any given such classification, there will be aspects of reality that resist or fall outside the relevant classification. Pitch and rhythm, for example, are features of voice in speech and in song. However, while central to the classificatory articulation of voice that constitutes the domain for musical expertise, they are legitimately neglected by Theuth in his articulation of voice as the domain for literacy.[43]

If there is no single, privileged, overarching classification of reality, then, once transposed to the whole of reality, the presence of such a gap suggests that there is some aspect of the classification-independent reality in which human classificatory activity takes place that resists classification.[44]

---

[43] In the fuller version of Socrates' second illustration of the conditions on wisdom in respect of music, pitches are the focus of 17c4–d3, rhythms the focus of 17d3–6. Pitch would be pertinent to the written representation of any *tonal* language, but nothing hangs on the specifics of my examples.

[44] Earlier versions of this chapter were given at Oxford, Pittsburgh, Berkeley, the University of Connecticut, and the University of Chicago. In addition to my audiences on all five occasions, I am grateful for additional conversation, discussion, and comments to David Charles, Tim Clarke, Ursula Coope, Gail Fine, Hannah Ginsborg, Harvey Lederman, Jim Lennox, MM McCabe, Vasilis Politis, Evan Rodriguez, Pauline Sabrier, Lea Schröder, Lorenzo Simpson, Amia Srinivasan, Justin Vlasits, and Jennifer Whiting, as well as to the volume's editors and to two anonymous readers for the Press.

118 VERITY HARTE

Works Cited

Berthiaume, Guy. 1982. *Les Rôles du Mágeiros: Étude sur la boucherie, la cuisine et le sacrifice dans la Grèce ancienne.* Brill and Les Presses de l'Université de Montréal.

Brown, Lesley. 2010. 'Definition and Division in Plato's *Sophist*', in *Definition in Greek Philosophy* (ed. D. Charles). Oxford University Press, 151–71.

Charles, David. 2001. 'Wittgenstein's Builders and Aristotle's Craftsmen', in *Wittgensteinian Themes: Essays in Honour of David Pears* (ed. D. Charles and W. Child). Clarendon Press, 49–80.

Cooper, John M. (ed.). 1997. *Plato Complete Works*. Hackett.

Crivelli, Paolo. 2019. 'Division and Classification: *Philebus* 14c–20a', in *Plato's Philebus: A Philosophical Discussion* (ed. P. Dimas, R. E. Jones, and G. R. Lear). Oxford University Press, 34–54.

Delcomminette, Sylvain. 2006. *Le Philèbe de Platon*. Brill.

Ekroth, Gunnel. 2014. 'Animal Sacrifice in Antiquity', in *The Oxford Handbook of Animals in Classical Thought and Life* (ed. G. L. Campbell). Oxford University Press, 324–54.

Fossheim, Hallvard. 2012. 'Division as a Method in Plato', in *The Development of Dialectic from Plato to Aristotle* (ed. J. L. Fink). Cambridge University Press, 91–112.

Frede, Dorothea. 1997. *Platon Philebos*. Vandenhoeck & Ruprecht.

Gill, Mary Louise. 2012. *Philosophos: Plato's Missing Dialogue*. Oxford University Press.

Goodman, Nelson. 1978. *Ways of Worldmaking*. Hackett.

Gosling, J. C. B. 1975. *Plato Philebus*. Oxford University Press.

Graham, Daniel W. and Justin Barney. 2014. '*Γραμματική* in Plato and Aristotle', *Apeiron* 47, 513–25.

Hackforth, R. 1952. *Plato's Phaedrus*. Cambridge University Press.

Harte, Verity. 2017. 'Knowing and Believing in *Republic 5*', in *Rereading Ancient Philosophy: Old Chestnuts and Sacred Cows* (ed. V. Harte and R. Woolf). Cambridge University Press, 141–62.

Hayase, Atsushi. 2016. 'Dialectic in the *Phaedrus*', *Phronesis* 61, 111–41.

Henry, Devin. 2011. 'A Sharp Eye for Kinds: Plato on Collection and Division', *Oxford Studies in Ancient Philosophy* 41, 229–56.

Lambert, Karel and Simons, Peter. 1994. 'Characterizing and Classifying: Explicating a Biological Distinction', *The Monist* 77, 315–28.

Lennox, James G. 1985. 'Plato's Unnatural Teleology', in *Platonic Investigations* (ed. D. J. O'Meara). The Catholic University of America Press, 195–218.

Menn, Stephen. 1998. 'Collecting the Letters', *Phronesis* 43, 291–305.

Muniz, Fernando and Rudebusch, George. 2018. 'Dividing Plato's Kinds', *Phronesis* 63, 392–407.

Putnam, Hilary. 1981. *Reason, Truth and History*. Cambridge University Press.

Rowe, C. J. 1988. *Plato Phaedrus*. Aris and Phillips.

Sider, Theodore. 2011. *Writing the Book of the World*. Oxford University Press.

Striker, Gisela. 1970. *Peras und Apeiron: Das Problem der Formen in Platons Philebos*. Vandenhoeck & Ruprecht.

Vlasits, Justin Joseph. 2017. 'Platonic Division and the Origins of Aristotelian Logic'. Ph.D. dissertation, University of California, Berkeley.

West, M. L. 1992. *Ancient Greek Music*. Clarendon Press.

Yunis, Harvey. 2011. *Plato Phaedrus*. Cambridge University Press.

6

Non-substance Individuals
in Aristotle's *Categories*

Jennifer Whiting

Introduction

I first encountered David Charles in his Oxford seminar on Donald Davidson's theory of action. So it seems apt to begin with Isaiah Berlin's account of the best class he ever took, Oxford's first (as far as he knew) on the work of a contemporary philosopher: J. L. Austin teaching C. I. Lewis.

> 'If there are three vermilion patches on this piece of paper, how many vermilions are there?' 'One,' said I. 'I say there are three,' said Austin, and we spent the rest of the term on the issue. (Berlin 1973, 8)

Oxford Aristotelians are no less capable of spending entire terms debating where Aristotle stood, at least when he wrote his *Categories*, on more or less the same question: whether the 'individual white' (*to ti leukon*) that Aristotle says is 'in' a particular body is peculiar to that particular body and incapable of existing apart from it; or whether the 'individual white' that is 'in' a particular body is rather something sharable and capable of 'inhering' in other, numerically distinct bodies. Ditto for 'the individual knowledge of grammar' (*hē tis grammatikē*, with *epistēmē* understood from 1b1): is it peculiar to the individual soul to which it belongs or is it a sharable item capable of 'inhering' in the soul of any (and every) one who has learnt the relevant form of grammar?[1]

Please note that I refer to the items in question as 'non-substance *individuals*', *not* (as some commentators do) 'non-substance *particulars*'. I take the relevant conception of an individual to be captured by Aristotle's use of 'one in number' (*hen arithmō(i)*) as a one-place predicate, as in 3b10–13 (in [B] below). The primary substances of Aristotle's *Categories* are individuals in this sense. They are individual men and horses, each *itself* one in number while being one *in species* with other men or horses and one *in genus* with other animals. But the species and genera to

---

[1] I follow Owen 1965 in using 'inherence' and its cognates to refer to what the *Categories* calls 'being in a subject'. Translations, except where noted, are from Ackrill 1963.

Jennifer Whiting, *Non-substance Individuals in Aristotle's* Categories In: *Aristotelian Metaphysics: Essays in Honour of David Charles.* Edited by: David Bronstein, Thomas Kjeller Johansen, and Michail Peramatzis, Oxford University Press.
© Oxford University Press 2024. DOI: 10.1093/oso/9780198908678.003.0006

which they belong are *not* one *in number*: each is by nature such as to be predicated of many 'particulars' (*kath' hekasta*), and so what *De Interpretatione* 7 (quoted in [C] below) calls a 'universal' (*katholou*). I suspend judgement for now on whether Aristotle took the non-substance individuals of his *Categories* to be particulars in the way in which Callicles is a particular, which involves having a determinate spatiotemporal location or continuous series of such locations. For the *Categories* never refers to these items as *kath' hekasta*. I return to this question in section 4.

J. L. Ackrill (1963) took the non-substance individuals of Aristotle's *Categories* to be particulars. His paradigms are numerically distinct tokens of a determinate shade of white, one for each page of the book you hold in your hands; and numerically distinct tokens of the relevant knowledge of grammar, one (let us suppose) for each competent reader of this paragraph. Heinaman (1981) and Irwin (1989) followed suit. Heinaman calls this the 'traditional' reading (henceforth 'TR').

G. E. L. Owen (1965) challenged this reading, calling it a 'fashionable dogma'. He and Michael Frede (1987) have made strong cases for an alternative reading according to which non-substance individuals are fully determinate properties, each capable of being in a plurality of numerically distinct subjects (henceforth 'AR'). Consider, for example, knowledge of how to conjugate some irregular verb in Greek. According to Owen and Frede, this very knowledge may inhere in a plurality of numerically distinct souls. It might seem to follow that this knowledge is what *De Interpretatione* 7 calls a universal. But there are ways, discussed below, to avoid this conclusion.

Irwin rejects AR by appeal to an argument (italicized here) and a few examples from the *Categories*.

> *Since individual non-substances are particulars, they must be numerically one, and therefore cannot inhere in more than one particular substance.* Particular relatives included particular slaves and particular fathers, each of whom inheres in only one particular substance, *Catg.* 6b28–30, and when Aristotle refers to particular relatives 8b13–15, these particulars limited to one particular substance seem to be intended. Similarly, when he says that the same numerically one action cannot be both good and bad, he ought to be referring to an action-token; the point would not be correct for an action-type, 4a15–16. (Irwin 1989, 502)

I have already noted that the *Categories* does not refer to non-substance individuals as *kath' hekasta*. But the premise that non-substance individuals are particulars is idle if Irwin's argument turns on the claim that what is numerically one *cannot* be in a plurality of numerically distinct subjects. And that is my question: does Aristotle recognize the existence of anything 'numerically one' that *can* be in a plurality of numerically distinct subjects?

Citing examples of the sort of individuals that *cannot* be in a plurality of numerically distinct subjects does not settle the issue if there are individuals of

122   JENNIFER WHITING

other sorts that *can* be. The example of the slave is not probative.[2] Much hangs then, for proponents of TR, on their 'star example', the action-token.

Readers familiar with David Charles' first book, which is focused on the individuation of action-tokens and stems from a dissertation supervised by Ackrill, might expect Charles to side with Ackrill and Irwin.[3] But action-tokens aside, Charles has been remarkably silent for an Oxford Aristotelian on the *Categories'* conception of non-substance individuals. So I want to take this opportunity to honour one of Oriel's, and hence Oxford's, pre-eminent Aristotelians by recommending to him a reading that can accommodate TR's star example without having to adopt TR hook, line, and sinker.

The reading I recommend is closest to that of Frede but ultimately a kind of hybrid. I read the *Categories* as allowing—perhaps even demanding—different kinds of account in different categories. Acknowledging such differences may even be part of Aristotle's point in introducing a theory of categories in the first place. So even if individuals in the category of *poiein* are action-tokens, we cannot simply generalize and conclude that *every* non-substance individual in *every* non-substance category must be a token of some fully determinate type, a token that is spatiotemporally unified in the way an action-token is. It may even be problematic to generalize within a single category from one sort of predicate to others. For different sorts of predicates obey different logics. Consider, for example, the differences between count and mass nouns (on which more in section 5).

Proponents of TR tend to acknowledge that the *Categories* itself provides little direct support for it. Heinaman defends TR by arguing that Aristotle's *later* works assume the traditional conception. But Ackrill rests his case on *Categories* 1a24–5, to which I now turn. For despite all the ink spilt over these lines, there is in the surrounding context a detail whose significance has not yet been registered, one that counts strongly against any generalized version of TR.

1. The *Exegetical* Dispute

The lines appear in *Categories* 2, where Aristotle presents a fourfold classification of 'the things that *are*' (*ta onta*), as distinct from 'the things that *are said*' (*ta*

---

[2] 6b28–30 is about 'the slave' (*ho doulos*, a generic) and not about 'a particular slave' (for which Aristotle would have used something like '*ho tis doulos*'). And even if 8b13–15 is about some particular, his point is epistemological, not ontological. Aristotle is contrasting (a) the conditions for knowing determinately of 'some this' *that to which* it is relative (e.g., knowing of some slave *whose* slave it is) with (b) the conditions for knowing indeterminately of 'some this' that it stands in the relevant relation to some relatum or other of the relevant kind (in this case, to some master or other). And it is compatible with this that Aristotle should conceive of the relations in which particular relatives stand to one another to obtain among multiple pairs (and triples etc.) of particulars.

[3] Charles 1984.

NON-SUBSTANCE INDIVIDUALS IN ARISTOTLE'S *CATEGORIES*   123

legomena). The classification turns on a distinction between two forms of predication, each of which is primarily *ontological* but associated with various linguistic phenomena. Aristotle signals each form by turning an ordinary language expression into a technical term (indicated henceforth with small caps): some of the things predicated are SAID OF their subjects, others are IN their respective subjects. The subjects are routinely designated, following Aristotle's general practice, with a substantive formed from the neuter participle '*hupokeimenon*'. But stay tuned: *Categories* 2 harbours a pair of significant exceptions.

SAID-OF predication is commonly viewed as a form of essential predication.[4] The thing predicated *classifies* its subject by answering the *ti esti* (or 'what is it?') question about that subject. This explains Aristotle's claim that whenever the thing predicated, P, is SAID OF some subject, S, not only the name 'P' but also the definition of P is predicated of S (2a19ff.).[5] Human is SAID OF Socrates and Plato because each is (essentially) human, so the definition of Human tells us *what* each of them *is*. Animal is SAID OF Human, Horse, and Dog because each of these *is* (essentially) a certain kind of Animal, so Animal is part of the definition of each. Similarly, Colour is SAID OF Black and Blue because each is (essentially) a colour, so Colour is part of the definition of each; and Virtue is SAID OF Courage and Justice because each is (essentially) a kind of virtue, so Virtue is part of the definition of each. But neither Colour nor any determinate shade of Colour is SAID OF a human, a horse, or any other substance. For even if there are some cases in which the *name* of a determinate colour appears to be predicated of a substance—as, for example, when 'tan' is predicated of Socrates or his skin—the *definition* of that colour is *never* predicated of any substance: neither Socrates nor his skin *is* a form of Colour.[6]

I have introduced the examples of Colour and Virtue to indicate that SAID-OF predication occurs in *all* categories and not just the category of substance, which seems in the *Categories* to be restricted to individual organisms and the species and genera to which they belong.[7] Though SAID-OF predication can occur in any category, it is itself (at least on the common account) *intra-categorial*. IN predication, by contrast, is *cross-categorial* and the things predicated are coincidents of the subjects in which they 'inhere'. Among such coincidents are the subjects' quantities (e.g., 6-foot, 180 pounds), qualities (white, wisdom), locations (in-Oxford, at-Yale), and actions (teaching, writing).

---

[4] I accept the common account. For an alternative, see Crivelli 2017. For a critique of Crivelli and defence of the common account, see Rapp in Chapter 7 of this volume.

[5] The definition here is of *P itself* and not simply its name.

[6] I say 'appears' because the predicate (which is an adjective) is a homonym, or disguised paronym, of the name (which is a common noun).

[7] I oversimplify a bit, since the *Categories* sometimes speaks of Soul and Body as if they were substances (as Aristotle later takes them to be).

124   JENNIFER WHITING

The distinction between beings that are IN subjects and beings that are not IN subjects is generally one between *non-substance* items and the *substances* of which they are predicated: between (on the one hand) the colours, sizes, and actions of animals, and (on the other hand) the individual animals of which these things are predicated and the species and genera to which these individual animals belong. For when *white*, *6-foot*, and *teaching* are predicated of an individual human, they are also predicated of the *species* Human as well as the *genus* Animal.[8]

The distinction between beings that are SAID-OF subjects and beings that are not SAID-OF subjects is between *universals* and what I call *individuals*. So the classification yields (a) *substance universals* ('SAID OF some subject but *not* IN any subject'); (b) *non-substance individuals* ('IN a subject but *not* SAID OF any subject'); (c) *non-substance universals* ('both SAID OF a subject and IN a subject'); and (d) *substance individuals* ('neither SAID OF any subject nor IN any subject').

Our concern is with the items in (b). Let us turn, then, to Aristotle's attempt to explain the technical use of 'in' employed in this classification. Ackrill puts the disputed lines in parentheses and translates as follows:

(By 'in a subject' I mean what is in something (*ho en tini*), not as a part, and cannot exist separately from what it is in (*tou en tō(i) estin*).) (1a24–5)

Aristotle continues with the examples mentioned above.

For example, the individual knowledge-of-grammar (*hē tis grammatikē*), is in a subject, the soul, but is not said of any subject; and the individual white (*to ti leukon*) is in a subject, the body (for all colour is in body), but is not said of any subject. (1a25–9)

Ackrill (1963, 74) reads the disputed lines as defining the *relation* being-IN-subject. He interprets them as follows.

[ACK]   for any being x and any being y, x is IN y as its subject *if and only if*
    (i)   x is (colloquially speaking) 'in' y,
    (ii) x is not a part of y, and
    (iii) x cannot exist separately from y.

It follows from this that *if* y is an individual substance and x is IN y, then x cannot exist apart from the *individual* substance, y, in which it inheres. This leads Ackrill

---

[8]   I say 'generally' so as to acknowledge the problematic status of differentiae, which are (according to 3a12ff.) neither in a substance nor themselves substances. I bracket the problems but am inclined to agree with Frede (1987, 61–2) that Aristotle says 'not as a part' to indicate that he is not talking about differentiae or any other 'conceptual' parts (e.g., species and genera).

NON-SUBSTANCE INDIVIDUALS IN ARISTOTLE'S *CATEGORIES*   125

to say that non-substance universals are not strictly speaking IN individual substances: they are instead SAID OF non-substance individuals, which are (according to this definition) the *only* items that can strictly speaking be IN individual substances. On this account, Aristotle's characterization of non-substance universals in (c) is misleading: these items are IN individual substances only insofar as they are SAID OF individual tokens that are themselves IN individual substances.

Ackrill is not sufficiently troubled by this: he discounts the formulation of Aristotle's claims about non-substance universals as 'compressed and careless' (1963, 83). I think he is willing to countenance this because he reads the *Categories*' account of non-substance universals as presenting a nominalist alternative to Plato's manifestly realist theory of Forms, an alternative according to which the only qualities, quantities, positions, etc., there are, are the fully determinate qualities, quantities, positions, etc. of whatever individual substances happen to exist.[9] For on Ackrill's account, the species and genera of these qualities, quantities, positions, etc. are assimilated to sets and identified with their (contingent) extensions.

> The inseparability requirement has *the consequence* that only individuals in non-substance categories can be 'in' individual substances. Aristotle could not say that generosity is in Callias as subject, since there could be generosity without any Callias. Only this individual generosity—Callias' generosity—is in Callias.... For a property to be in a kind of substance it is not enough that some or every substance of that kind should have the property, nor necessary that every substance of that kind should have it; what is required is that every *instance* of that property should belong to some individual substance of that kind. *Thus, the inherence of a property in a kind of substance is to be analysed in terms of the inherence of individual instances of the property in individual instances of that kind.* (Ackrill 1963, 74–5; my italics)

But there is a plausible and recognizably Aristotelian alternative to "extensional" (and implicitly nominalist) readings of this sort.

Even if Aristotle takes every instance of Colour to be the colour of some individual body, this need not be what explains his claim that Colour is IN body in the technical sense at issue. His point may instead be that Colour is *by definition* the sort of entity that cannot exist apart from a *specific kind* of subject: namely, Body. To understand *what* Colour *is*, you have to understand the *kind of subject* to which it, insofar as it is *the kind of thing it is*, belongs.

To see the plausibility of ascribing some such view to Aristotle around the time he wrote the *Categories*, compare the sense in which the *Categories* treats Colour as IN Body with the sense in which *Posterior Analytics* 1.4 treats Odd and Even as

---

[9] I take Ackrill to combine this with a realist account of *substance* universals, which (as *Apo.* 1.11, 77a5–7 makes clear) need not presuppose the existence of Platonic Forms.

126   JENNIFER WHITING

belonging *kath' hauto* (or 'in itself') to number. Odd and Even are *by definition* predicates (in the ontological sense) of Number: one cannot understand *what it is to be* Odd or Even without understanding the sort of subject to which it, insofar as it is *what it is*, belongs: namely, a Number. A similar point applies to Male and Female, which are *by definition* predicates of animals. One cannot understand what it is to be Male or Female without understanding the sort of subject to which it, insofar as it is *what it is*, belongs: namely, a living being belonging to a species whose mode of reproduction is sexual.

Frede interprets 1a24–5 in this way: namely, as defining the *sort of entities* that are IN a subject by saying of them that they are entities such that there is, for each of them, some *definite kind of subject* apart from which it cannot exist.

> If we assume...that, for every property there is a species or genus outside of which the property cannot occur *because of how its range of possible objects has been defined*, we shall be able to specify *some universal* without which the property cannot occur. Only living things are healthy or ill, only certain kinds of living things are male or female, only human beings are foolish. (Frede 1987, 61; my italics)

Frede then adds:

> It is important to note that 1a24–25 does not say that if something is in something else as its subject, it *cannot exist* independently of [that].[10] While it is natural and presumably also correct to assume that *tou en hō(i) estin* in 1a25 refers back to *to en tini* in 1a24, the reference of *en tini* is not fixed by the preceding words.[11] As we have seen, everything that occurs in a subject must already have a plurality of subjects, at least some individual object and its species and genera. What is being claimed in 1a24–25 is *not* that for *each* of these subjects the property could not exist without *it*. What is being claimed is, rather, that if something is the kind of thing that occurs in a subject, then there is something, *at least one subject*, without which it cannot exist. (Frede 1987, 61; my italics)

For any given colour, at whatever level of determination, Frede takes the subject in question to be the genus (or universal) Body. Similarly for any given form of knowledge, at whatever level of determination, the subject in question will be the

---

[10] I have altered Mann's translation, replacing 'it' with 'that' to make Frede's point clear.

[11] This is the point missed by Ackrill's reading of 'the inseparability requirement'. Consider, as uttered before same-sex marriage, 'x is a wife if and only if she is married to *some* man'. Elizabeth Taylor was, intermittently, a wife in virtue of being married to Richard Burton; but she was sometimes a wife in virtue of being married to some *other* man. And in a society that tolerated polyandry, she could have been a wife in virtue of being married, simultaneously, to multiple men.

NON-SUBSTANCE INDIVIDUALS IN ARISTOTLE'S *CATEGORIES*   127

genus (or universal) Soul. Frede is thus committed to an "intensional" (and implicitly realist) account of these non-substance universals.

Frede's reading is manifestly superior to Ackrill's, which conflicts with what Aristotle says in the main argument of *Categories* 5. That argument runs (in Ackrill's translation, with my numbers) as follows:

[A]   [1] All the other things are either *said of* the primary substances as subjects or *in* them as subjects (*ē en hupokeimenais autais*).

[2] This is clear from an examination of cases. For example, [A]nimal is predicated of [H]uman (*kata tou anthrōpou katēgoreitai*) and therefore also of the individual human (*kata tou tinos anthrōpou*); for were it predicated of none of the individual humans (*ei gar kata mēdenos tōn tinōn*) it would not be predicated of [H]uman at all.

[3] Again, color is in body (*en sōmati*) and therefore also in an individual body (*en tini sōmati*); for were it not in some individual body (*ei gar mē en tini tōn kath' hekasta*), it would not be in body at all.[12]

[4] Thus all the other things are either said of the primary substances as subjects or in them as subjects (*ē en hupokeimenais autais*). So if the primary substances did not exist it would be impossible for the other things to exist. (*Cat.*, 2a34–b6)

Please note that the bold-face phrase in [1] and [4] is feminine plural and agrees with 'the primary substances' (*hai prōtai ousiai*).

The main problem for TR lies in [3], which seems to say that Colour is in an *individual* body. For Colour can, of course, exist apart from any given individual body provided it is in *some* individual body *or other*. Ackrill seeks to deal with the problem as follows.

As for colour, Aristotle *could have argued* to his final conclusion (sc., [4]) simply by using the definition of 'in' together with the fact, just established, that the existence of secondary substances presupposes the existence of primary substances: if colour is in body it cannot exist if body does not, and body cannot exist if no individual bodies exist. What *is* Aristotle's own argument? It was suggested earlier that to say that colour is in body is to say that every instance of colour is in an individual body. *If so*, Aristotle's present formulation is *compressed and careless*. For he does not mention individual instances

---

[12] I would prefer 'if it were not in one of the particular <bodies>, it would not be in body at all'. This is one of the only places in the *Categories* where Aristotle uses '*kath' hekasta*' (as distinct from '*atoma*') to refer to what Ackrill and I call 'individuals'. But he refers to bodies and not to the items that are IN these bodies. I take this to be significant. These bodies are, of course, particulars with determinate locations and spatiotemporally unified careers. But it does not follow that *non-substance* individuals are particulars in the same way.

of colour; he speaks as if, because colour is in body, colour is in an individual body. Strictly, however, it is not colour, but this individual instance of colour, that is in an individual body; for colour could exist apart from this body (though this individual instance of colour could not). (Ackrill 1963, 83; my italics)

But whether Aristotle *could have argued* to his conclusion in the way Ackrill suggests depends in part on whether Aristotle actually accepted the definition of being-IN-a-subject that Ackrill ascribes to him. So the fact that Aristotle *did not* argue in the way afforded by the alleged definition should have given Ackrill pause.

Consider what Aristotle should have said if Ackrill's reading of the inseparability requirement were correct. On that reading, 'only *individuals* in non-substance categories can be INindividual substances'. So 'all the other things' mentioned in [A][1] and [4] should include not only (as [1] and [4] say) things that are 'SAID OF primary substances as subjects' and things that are 'IN primary substances as subjects', but also (as [1] and [4] do *not* say) 'things that are SAID OF things that are IN primary substances as subjects'. For (on Ackrill's view) a fully determinate shade of white *cannot* be IN an individual substance; it can only be SAID OF some individual instance that is IN an individual substance. The same goes for any other fully determinate species of non-substance being.

Compressed indeed: we are asked to suppose that, in an argument for the *Categories'* fundamental ontological claim, Aristotle omits, from what purports to be an exhaustive list of the kinds of being there are, *all non-substance universals*. I see two more charitable hypotheses. *Either* Aristotle was a nominalist about *non-substance* universals but not about the species and genera to which individual substances belong, in which case there is no careless omission because Aristotle did not think that non-substance universals were genuine beings. *Or* Aristotle did not intend the inseparability requirement the way Ackrill reads it and really did think that non-substance universals are strictly speaking *in* individual substances, which is what [A][3] at least appears to say. Given that Aristotle chose to include non-substance universals in his fourfold classification *of beings*, as distinct from *things said*, charity strongly favours the latter hypothesis.

Let me turn now to the textual detail mentioned above and signalled by bold face in [A][1] and [4]. Aristotle's standard way of referring to subjects as such—the subjects of change as well as ontological predication—is to form a substantive by adding a definite article to the neuter participle '*hupokeimenon*'. He does sometimes use the feminine as an attributive adjective—as in '*hē hupokeimenē hulē*', sometimes just '*hē hupokeimenē*' for short. But his use of the attributive adjective in [1] and [4] (with '*ousiais*' understood) is anomalous, especially given the neuter in his general account of 'being IN a subject'. It is as if he is going out of

NON-SUBSTANCE INDIVIDUALS IN ARISTOTLE'S *CATEGORIES* 129

his way to indicate that non-substance universals are IN the *primary substances themselves*, and not simply SAID OF beings (neuter) that are IN the primary substances (feminine). The relevant bits of [1] and [4] are in fact best translated this way, taking '*autais*' as intensive and understanding '*ousiais*' with '*hupokeimenais*'. In other words, it is as if Aristotle were going out of his way to warn *against* Ackrill's reading.

So why—especially given the availability of an alternative that does not require us to read the argument as 'compressed and careless'—is TR so 'fashionable'?

2. The Philosophical 'Sensibility' behind TR

The answer, I suspect, lies partly in the commentators' own philosophical sensibilities, what they themselves find intuitively plausible and so tend, in acts of Davidsonian charity, to ascribe to Aristotle.[13] I suspect in fact that TR owes much of its popularity to the intuitive plausibility of the following ideas, especially when conjoined.

(I) The distinction between *non-substance* individuals and the species and genera to which they belong is parallel to the distinction between *substance* individuals and the species and genera to which they belong, so Aristotle must construe individuality in non-substance categories *in the same way* that he construes it in the category of substance.

(II) The relevant conception of individuality requires an individual substance to have a determinate spatiotemporal location, the sort of location that allows it to be ostended or picked out by means of a demonstrative such as '*tode*'.

There are two passages in *Categories* 5 that might be read as supporting (II). One is 4a10–22 and invokes TR's star example. I return to it in section 5.

The other is 3b10–18, which distinguishes primary substances, 'such as an individual human or an individual horse' (*hoion ho tis anthrōpos ē ho tis hippos*, 1b4–5), from secondary substances such as Human and Horse (*ho anthrōpos, ho hippos*).

[B]   Every substance seems to signify a certain 'this' (*tode ti*). As regards the primary substances, it is indisputably true that each of them signifies a certain

---

[13] For discussion of a similar case where Oxford-educated commentators with different philosophical intuitions end up with very different readings of Aristotle, see Whiting 2002. I find such comparisons methodologically instructive.

130   JENNIFER WHITING

'this'; for the thing revealed is **indivisible** and numerically one (*atomon gar kai hen arithmō(i)*).[14] But as regards the secondary substances, though it appears from the form of the name—when one speaks of [H]uman or [A]nimal—that a secondary substance likewise signifies a certain 'this', this is not really true; rather it signifies a certain qualification (*poion ti*), for the subject is not, as the primary substance is, one, but [H]uman and [A]nimal are said of many things (*kata pollōn legetai*). (3b10–18)

The point is that Human and Animal are not one in the way that primary substances are: they are not one *in number* and so lack the sort of determinate spatiotemporal location characteristic of particulars. Since they are predicated of numerically distinct individuals that exist at different times and places, they are what *De Interpretatione* 7 calls 'universals':

[C]   I call 'universal' (*katholou*) that which is by its nature such as to be predicated of many things (*ho epi pleionōn pephuke katēgoreisthai*), and 'particular' (*kath' hekaston*) that which is not; [H]uman, for instance, is a universal, Callias a particular. (17a39–b1)

Callias is an example of what the *Categories* calls '*tode ti*' and takes to be '*atomon kai hen arithmō(i)*'. So we might easily take '*atomon kai hen arithmō(i)*' in [B] as an alternative way to express what [C] seeks to express in using '*kath' hekaston*'.[15] And we might infer from the fact that particulars like Callias have determinate locations and unified spatiotemporal careers in a way in which universals do not that *anything* that is *atomon kai hen arithmō(i)* has the sort of determinate location and unified spatiotemporal careers characteristic of particulars like Callias.

I question this inference in section 4. Let us continue here with apparent evidence for (II). Consider *Posterior Analytics* 1.31.

[D]   Nor is it possible to know (*epistasthai*) through perception. For even if there is perception of what is such and not some this (*tou toioude kai mē toude tinos*), it is nevertheless necessary to perceive some this (*tode ti*) at a place and at a time. For it is impossible to perceive what is universal and holds of every case (*to katholou kai epi pasōn*). For that is neither a this nor at a time—<if it were> it would not be universal. (87b28–32; my translation)[16]

---

[14] I have altered Ackrill's translation here, substituting 'indivisible' for 'individual' in rendering '*atomon kai hen arithmō(i)*'. Aristotle is, of course, talking about individuals and does sometimes use '*atoma*' to refer to individuals as such. But Ackrill's rendering of '*atomon*' obscures the way in which Plato's method of division frames the *Categories* argument. Aristotle is better read as speaking of indivisibility and using '*hen arithmō(i)*' to indicate the kind of indivisibility he has in mind here: namely, indivisibility *in number* as distinct from indivisibility *in genus or species*.

[15] [C] uses '*kath' hekaston*' in a special sense explained in section 4 below.

[16] I use angular brackets to indicate material I take to be implied by the text.

NON-SUBSTANCE INDIVIDUALS IN ARISTOTLE'S *CATEGORIES*   131

Though Aristotle means here to allow that we can in some sense perceive a universal *in* perceiving some instance of it, the point is that we perceive universals only insofar as we perceive instances of them *in particular places at particular times*: we can perceive Human or Horse only by perceiving some individual human or some individual horse. And as Aristotle says in *Metaphysics* M.10, 1087a19–21, 'sight sees the universal colour coincidentally (*kata sumbebēkos*) because this colour which it sees is a colour' (my translation). So we might easily extend the point to *non-substance* beings, taking 'the individual white' to be located wherever the individual body in which it 'inheres' is located and 'the individual knowledge of grammar' to be located (so to speak) wherever one finds the individual body to whose soul it belongs.

This fits the sort of extensional (and implicitly nominalist) reading of non-substance universals described above.[17] Those who read the *Categories* in this way sometimes appeal to *Categories* 11, where Aristotle says, 'if everyone were well, health would exist but not sickness, and if everything were white, white would exist but not blackness' (14a7–9). But these lines do not by themselves license a straightforwardly nominalist reading. Aristotle could simply be saying that non-substance species do not exist when they do not have members, without treating the existence of any such species as simply reducible to the existence of its individual members: the existence of a non-substance species may, like the existence of a substance species, require the applicability to its members of a real (as distinct from merely nominal) definition.[18]

So let us leave *Categories* 11 aside. The popularity of TR is surely due more to the idea, resulting from the combination of (I) and (II), that *non-substance* individuals resemble *substance* individuals in having their own spatiotemporal locations and careers, each distinct from the spatiotemporal locations and careers of other such individuals. Here, however, it is important to note that however intuitive this picture may be—especially to philosophers who pride themselves on their 'common sense' and view Aristotle as a kindred spirit—Aristotle may have been working with an alternative conception of individuality, one more closely tied to the method of division employed in Plato's academy. That is the conception with which Frede works, one according to which an individual is, fundamentally, what is *not* SAID OF any subject.[19] The genus Animal, which is a universal, is SAID OF Human and Dog. And the species Human and Dog, which are also universals, are SAID OF their respective members: Human is SAID OF Socrates,

---

[17] Such readings leave room for a realist conception of *substance* universals of the sort explained in n. 3 of Frede 1987: Human is a *res* that exists in its individual parts, as they come and go, in something like the way in which *the Forest* or *the Police* is a *res* that exists in the individual trees or individual officers as they come and go. As Frede says, 'the parts can and do change without the identity of the forest or police changing' (1987, 367).

[18] For a state-of-the-art treatment of Aristotle's views on definition and essence, see Charles 2000.

[19] It seems also to be the conception with which the *Categories* itself works.

132   JENNIFER WHITING

Callias, and Plato, and Dog is SAID OF Bebop, Swizzle, and Jekyll. But these humans and dogs are (on Frede's account) *individuals*: there are *no further subjects OF* which *they* are *SAID*.

It is, of course, true that each has determinate and unified spatiotemporal location and occupies in the end a continuous series of such locations. So each is (on my account) a particular. But this is not, on Frede's view, what *makes* them individuals. So even if spatiotemporal unity is characteristic of individuals in the category of *substance*, it need not be characteristic of *non-substance* individuals: we can retain (I) while rejecting (II). In other words, we can construe the individuality of non-substances in the *same* way we construe the individuality of substances while rejecting the idea that determinate spatiotemporal location and the sort of spatiotemporal unity that tends to go with that is what *constitutes* individuality in the category of substance. We can instead take *not being SAID OF any subject* as the criterion for being *atomon kai hen arithmō(i)*, not only in the category of substance but also in non-substance categories. And this opens the door to the possibility that a non-substance individual can be IN a plurality of numerically distinct individual substances (or particulars), each with its own numerically distinct spatiotemporal location.[20] But why think Aristotle embraced this possibility?

3. The Philosophical 'Sensibility' behind AR

The conception of individuality with which AR works is grounded in Plato's 'method of division'. Aristotle takes division, properly conducted, to play an important (albeit non-apodeictic) role in scientific investigation.[21] But this requires him to revise Plato's conception of that method in two ways.

First, Aristotle rejects 'dichotomous' division, where a genus is exhaustively divided according to a single 'difference'. For this tends to produce divisions in which one 'part' of a genus is simply the 'privation' of the other (e.g., *winged* and

---

[20] Proponents of TR are likely to object that anything predicated of a plurality of numerically distinct subjects is, according to [C], a universal. But if we can read [C] as using '*katēgoreisthai epi*' with the genitive to refer to SAID-OF predication, the objection begs the question against a view according to which Aristotle is working with a conception of universal that is tied to his method of division in ways such that a universal is *by definition* something that is divisible into *subjective* parts (i.e., parts of which not only the name but also the definition of the relevant universal can be predicated). And I think we can legitimately read [C] in this way. For Aristotle clearly uses '*katēgoreisthai kata*' with the genitive in the *Categories* itself to refer to SAID-OF predication: see 2b15–17, where *panta ta kata toutōn katēgoreisthai ē en tautais* seems equivalent to *ta d' alla panta ētoi kath' hupokeimenōn legetai tōn prōtōn ousiōn ē en hupokeimenon* in 2a34–5 (repeated with minor variation at 2b6). Irwin's appeal to the difference between '*kata*' and '*epi*' is weak, especially insofar as the motivation for it is largely to preserve the reading of [A] to which serious objections were raised in section 1 and for which a plausible alternative is presented in section 3. See also *APr.* 1.22 on *katēgoreisthai*.

[21] See Bronstein 2016, especially ch. 12.

NON-SUBSTANCE INDIVIDUALS IN ARISTOTLE'S *CATEGORIES*   133

wingless), with the result that creatures significantly different in kind from one another are grouped together in the privative complement (e.g., wingless mammals, fish, and reptiles). Proper division is 'polythetic': it proceeds along various lines of difference, not only among the parts of animals but also among modes of subsistence, actions, and ways of life.[22]

Second, and more important here, it is crucial that the genera under investigation not be divided along coincidental lines: one must start with proper differentiae (i.e., those that belong to the essence of the relevant kind) and one must divide at each stage by proper differentiae of the differentiae that governed division at the previous stage. In the case of natural kinds, what counts as a proper differentia is determined largely by teleological considerations to do with the role played by the feature in the survival and well-being of individuals belonging to the relevant kind.

Consider an example from *Metaphysics* I.9. If one is dividing Animal according to parts that are present for the sake of locomotion, and one has just taken Footed and Winged as proper differentiae, the next differentiae must be differentiae of *Footed* and *Winged*. They must be *ways of being Footed* and *ways of being Winged*, or *forms of Footedness* and *forms of Wingedness*. The differentiae of *Footed* might be the teleologically significant, such as *Web-footed* and *Cloven-footed*, but not (usually) *White-footed* and *Black-footed*. For though colours can sometimes play the relevant sort of teleological role—as when they serve to attract mates or provide camouflage—differences in colour tend to be coincidental. As Aristotle says in *Metaphysics* I.9, neither *whiteness* nor *blackness* in a human being makes for a difference in species, not even if a single name is applied to each purported kind. These differences, being due to matter rather than form, are merely coincidental.

I.9's parallel treatment of the teleologically significant difference between *male* and *female* is more controversial, but Aristotle supports it by claiming that male and female alike come from the same seed. His idea seems to be that the movements imparted by the seed, which are by nature such as to impose the relevant form on suitable matter, are affected by that matter in ways such that the offspring might prove to be *either* male *or* female. So, although *male* and *female* are affections proper to animals as such, this too is a matter of coincidental difference.

Aristotle must, of course, justify the distinctions he draws between the proper differentiae of any object of division and mere coincidents of it: he must justify his account of where, so to speak, form ends and matter begins. And there will be controversy about where exactly to draw the line, as he himself would be the first to admit.[23] Let me pause then to illustrate the plausibility of his general view by appeal to a somewhat artificial example, one offered in the spirit in which I think

---

[22] See *PA* 1.2–3, usefully discussed in of Lennox 2001, chs. 4 and 7.
[23] See *Met.* Z.10, where Aristotle explicitly says that it is difficult to know where exactly to draw the line. See also *Meteor.* 4.12, 390a14–24.

134   JENNIFER WHITING

he himself presents features of artefacts as analogues (rather than proper exemplars) of features of natural substances.

Suppose that Aristotle regarded Polygon as a genus instead of an ordered series. This will help us to see (a) why he thinks it plausible that dividing a genus according to proper differentiae will lead in the end to kinds that are no longer divisible into further kinds but only (if at all) into numerically distinct individuals; and (b) what is relevant to determining where such division ends. It will also provide a model with reference to which we can seek to determine whether such kinds can also be reached in dividing non-substance genera, and if so, what are to count as the individual units OF which *they* are SAID.

In considering the hypothetical genus Polygon, we start with something *indeterminate* in the sense that there cannot be a polygon that is not a polygon of some particular form or other. Any given polygon must have a determinate number of sides and angles: it must be a triangle or a quadrilateral or pentagon, and so on ad infinitum. Part of the work of the differentiae is to *determine* the indeterminate genus in the ways in which it, *qua* Polygon, can be determined. Successive differentiae will distinguish increasingly determinate polygons. So, for example, the differentia *three-sided* will distinguish the Triangle from all other polygons, while the differentia *having-two-equal-sides* will differentiate the Isosceles Triangle from other forms of Triangle (namely, the Equilateral and the Scalene).[24]

Here, however, you might wonder whether these three forms of Triangle aren't themselves indeterminate in the sense that you cannot have an isosceles triangle the length of whose sides and degrees of whose angles are not determinate in quantity. Treating determinate quantities as differentia and continuing on to congruence classes would yield an infinite number of so-called forms of isosceles triangle, each of which might still be multiply instantiated. But Aristotle should and surely would treat such differences as belonging to matter and so as coincidental. In this case, the ultimate forms appear at the level of Equilateral, Isosceles, and Scalene, rather than similarity or congruence classes.

It does not matter for present purposes where exactly Aristotle would draw the line. The point is simply that *given the distinction between proper differentiae and mere coincidents*, it is intuitively plausible to suppose that there *is* a line to be drawn *somewhere* and that dividing correctly will *eventually* yield indivisible forms or species. But the forms or species thus reached are not absolutely indivisible. At least in the case of substance species, these forms are divisible *in number* in the sense that there are numerically distinct individuals OF which they are SAID: Human is SAID OF Socrates and Plato; Dog is SAID OF Bebop and Swizzle.

---

[24] I assume that Aristotle, unlike modern geometers, would have treated the Isosceles/Equilateral distinction as exclusive. See Euclid Definition 20: the isosceles has *only* two equal sides.

But what about a *non-substance* form like a fully determinate shade of colour? Let's call it 'vanilla white'. Is *vanilla white* divisible in number? Are there individual instances OF which it is SAID?

Proponents of TR are committed to the existence of the individual 'instances' OF which *vanilla white* is SAID. They seem in fact to think it *obvious* that there are such things, perhaps because they assume that non-substance individuals must resemble substance individuals in having determinate spatiotemporal locations. But the existence of such instances is controversial. To see why, we need only take a *vanilla white* piece of paper and tear it, as I tear paper when teaching the *Categories*, into successively smaller pieces. This reveals how arbitrary the identity of any alleged 'instance' of a fully determinate shade is: the identity of the instance is parasitic on the identity of the subject to which it belongs, however arbitrary the boundaries of *that* subject may be. Dividing a fully determinate shade of *vanilla white* (or any other colour) is in this respect *unlike* dividing an Animal species: the subjects OF which Human is SAID are 'self-subsistent' units in a way in which the putative instances OF which the name of some determinate shade of white is supposed to be SAID are *not*.[25]

More importantly, even where the *name* of the relevant shade (or some homonymous paronym of it) can be predicated of the putative instance, the *definition* of that shade cannot. What I am holding in my hand when I tear the paper are bits of paper that *happen to be* vanilla white, not bits of vanilla white itself. For 'vanilla white' tells us only what the things I am holding *are like* (i.e., *poion ti*), not what they *are* (i.e., *ti esti*).

In other words, at least with Colour and the determinate shades of it, there is intuitive plausibility to AR. Once we reach the fully determinate shade, there are no further subjects OF which *it* can be SAID. There may be numerically distinct subjects of which its *name* or some homonymous paronym of that can be predicated, but the predicate indicates what these subjects are *like*, not what they *are*: what each of them is, is always (according to the argument of *Categories* 5) some primary substance, a bird, for example, or a dog.[26] That is why Aristotle says that White and Colour are IN these things, not SAID OF them. It may also be why [A] uses the feminine plural to refer to the underlying subjects of which non-substance beings are predicated—to make it clear that these things are predicated directly of *the primary substances* (*ousiai*, feminine plural) themselves.

Frede invokes the scholastic distinction between 'subjective' and 'integral' parts to elucidate the relevant conception of individual, which he sees both in non-substance categories and in the category of substance. Infimae species and the genera to which they belong are divisible *in the same way* insofar as each is a

---

[25] By 'self-subsistent', I mean not just that they cannot be arbitrarily divided but also that their boundaries are determined by the kinds of thing they are.

[26] Or perhaps some artefact.

136 JENNIFER WHITING

whole that has what the Scholastics called 'subjective' parts. The genus Animal can be divided into various species, each of which is a subjective part of the genus in the sense that each is itself a *subject* to which the name of the whole can be truly applied: Human and Dog are both *Animals*. The species too can be divided into their members, which are subjective parts of them: Socrates is a human and Bebop is a dog. But there are no further subjects into which Socrates or Bebop can in turn be divided: any parts they have are 'integral' parts, such as bodily limbs and organs. Such parts comprise a whole, but in a different way from that in which species comprise a genus; in their case, neither the name nor the definition of the whole can be predicated of the parts.

Frede, relying on the scholastic distinction, formulates what he calls the *Categories* 'definition' as follows:

[FR] x is an individual if (i) it is a subjective part of something and (ii) it itself has no subjective parts. (Frede 1987, 54)

But to call this a 'definition' is misleading. What Frede formulates is a sufficient condition for being an individual, one that leaves open the possibility of other sorts of individuals. Some, like Socrates and Bebop, are subjective parts of wholes but do not themselves have any subjective parts. But insofar as [FR] provides only a sufficient condition for being an individual, it leaves room for the possibility of an individual that is not itself a subjective part of any whole. And this may be significant. For there is evidence that Aristotle recognized the existence of at least one entity that is *atomon kai hen arithmō(i)* ('one in number') but is not itself a subjective part of anything else: namely, the 'first mover' of *Metaphysics* Λ.9.

Aristotle speaks here of cases where one and the same *logos* applies to a plurality of numerically distinct entities, and he says that all such things have matter (1074a31–5). He then says that the 'first essence (*to ti ēn einai to prōton*) does not have matter, for it is *entelecheia*' (1074a35–6): he concludes that that 'the first mover, being without movement (*akinēton*), is one both in *logos* and in number' (1074a36–7). One might take *hen arithmō(i)* ('one in number') to be used here to indicate that the first mover is *unique*, that there is *only one* such thing. But that seems unlikely given the way Aristotle chooses to express his point about the uniqueness in *De Caelo* 1.10, which also associates enmattered form with the possibility, at least in principle, of multiple instantiation. Aristotle treats the heavens, taken as a whole, as a special case: though enmattered forms are in principle multiply instantiable, the heaven (*ho ouranos*) is composed of all the matter there is, so it is in fact one alone or unique (*heis kai monos*, 279a6–11). So I take the point in *Metaphysics* Λ.8 to be that the first mover is one not only in account but also in number: it is what I call an 'individual'.

NON-SUBSTANCE INDIVIDUALS IN ARISTOTLE'S *CATEGORIES*   137

This is relevant insofar as the first mover is supposed to lack *any* spatiotemporal location. It raises the possibility that Aristotle is working in his *Categories* with a conception of individuality according to which having a determinate location or spatiotemporally unified career is not a necessary condition for being an individual. According to this conception, something that is IN but not SAID OF a plurality of numerically distinct subjects can be an individual, however spatiotemporally scattered it may be.

4. The 'Individual' and the 'Particular'

We are now in a position to appreciate the distinction between what is *atomon kai hen arithmō(i)* and what is *kath' hekaston* in the special sense in which I take [C] to speak of Callias as *kath' hekaston*. Let me begin by explaining this special sense.

It is highly probable that Aristotle coined the term '*katholou*' following Plato's use of the propositional phrase '*kath' holou*', which means 'according to <some> whole'.[27] Aristotle often uses '*katholou*' adverbially and he contrasts investigating a genus *katholou* both with investigating a genus *kata meros* and with investigating a genus *kath' hekaston*.

[E]   It is plain that speaking according to <each> part (*kata meros*), we will say the same things many times about many <animals>, for each of the things mentioned belongs to horses and to dogs and to humans, so that if someone states the coincidents (*ta sumbebēkota*) according to each (*kath' hekaston*) <part>, he will have to speak about the same things many times, whatever <coincidents> being the same belong to animals differing in species (*eidei*) but do not themselves contain any difference. (*PA* 1.1, 639a23–30; my translation)

If we examine the genus Animal *katholou*, we examine it with reference to features that belong to each and every 'part', from the higher taxa down to its proper species. If we examine the genus Animal *kata meros*, we examine each 'part' separately, for features that distinguish its members from the members of the other coordinate 'parts'. The parts in question include infimae species, so talk of examining the genus *kath' hekaston* can be understood as referring to the examination of a genus species by species, paying attention to those features that distinguish the members of one infima species from the members of others in the same genus.

It is here that the special sense in which [C] uses '*kath' hekaston*' kicks in. It seems from *Metaphysics* I.9's talk of things that come 'from the same seed' that

---

[27]   von Fritz 1938.

138   JENNIFER WHITING

Aristotle takes something like reproductive isolation to play a fundamental role in the individuation of species. He denies that infimae species are divisible into sub-kinds in the way their higher taxa are: there are no proper sub-kinds, such as Greek and Barbarian, or Beagle and Poodle, into which Human and Dog can be divided. He recognizes, no doubt, that we have labels for different kinds of human being: for example, racialized labels. But he seems to deny that such labels designate real (as distinct from nominal) kinds: the infimae species are in this sense indivisible (*atomon*). But Aristotle allows another sense in which these species are divisible: namely, 'in number' (*arithmō(i)*). So there *is* a sense in which we can examine an infima species *kath' hekaston*: we can examine each of its individual members, one at a time. In that case, we would be examining *ta kath' hekasta* in the special sense in which Aristotle uses that term to refer to particular beings, each with its own determinate spatiotemporal location or unified series of such locations.

It should now be clear how Aristotle's use of the substantives '*to katholou*' and '*to kath' hekaston*' might have evolved, via the addition of neuter articles, from the adverbial uses employed above. And it should be clear from the connection between '*kata meros*' and '*kath' hekaston*' why 'particular' (derived from the Latin *particula*) is so apt for capturing the special sense in which *kath' hekaston* is used in [C]: *ta kath' hekasta* are the smallest 'parts' into which a genus can be divided. But the difference between these parts and those above them is a *difference in ontological kind*. The others are all by nature such as to be predicated of *many* things: the others all have 'subjective' parts of which they, together with their names *and definitions*, are predicated. Human, Horse, and Dog are subjective parts of the genus Animal, for each is (insofar as it is the kind of thing it is) something to which the definition of Animal applies. And Socrates, Callias, and David are subjective parts of the species Human, for each is (insofar as it is the kind of thing it is) something to which the definition of Human applies. But these human beings, unlike the 'universals' above them, are not such as to be predicated of many subjects: each is, as [C] explains, a *particular* in this special sense.

Each is also an *individual* in the sense that it is *atomon kai hen arithmō(i)*. But what it is to be an individual in this sense is distinct from what it is to be a particular; for what it is to be a particular in the sense employed in [C] is to be a subjective part of some indivisible species. But the 'first mover', which is *hen arithmō(i)*, is not a subjective part of any such kind. For though Aristotle acknowledges the existence of a plurality of unmoved movers, at least one for each of the heavenly bodies whose movements need to be accounted for, he does not treat these unmoved movers as belonging to a single kind: these movers belong to what he calls an 'ordered series'.[28]

---

[28] Lloyd 1962.

NON-SUBSTANCE INDIVIDUALS IN ARISTOTLE'S *CATEGORIES*   139

In sum, Aristotle's use of '*kath' hekaston*' is tied, conceptually, to his use of '*katholou*' in a way his use of '*hen arithmō(i)*' is not.[29] And the special sense in which he uses '*kath' hekaston*' in [C] seems to be tied to having a determinate spatiotemporal location.[30] This opens the door to the possibility of an *individual* that is IN a plurality of numerically distinct, spatially as well as temporally discontinuous, subjects.

It is worth noting that there is independent reason to read Aristotle as embracing this distinction between *individuals* and *particulars* insofar as doing so allows us to reconcile his claim that the objects of knowledge are universal with his treatment of the 'first mover' as a paradigmatic object of knowledge. If the primary contrast is between universals and particulars, then we can read him as ruling out knowledge of particulars while remaining silent on the question whether any individual can be known. This is especially plausible if his claims about the objects of knowledge being universal are made in places where his universe of discourse is restricted to the sublunary world, where the presence of coincidents due to matter makes it difficult to determine, by examining many particulars of the same kind, what features of them belong to or follow from their knowable essence, and what features are simply coincidents and so (according to *Metaphysics E*) not proper objects of knowledge. For if the knowable essence of each kind is not only devoid of coincidents but also proper (in the sense of being unique) to the kind, then the knowable essence of each kind resembles the 'first mover' and any other unmoved movers there are. This makes it easier to see how Aristotle might view an unmoved mover as an individual object of knowledge, at least to itself.[31]

My point in introducing unmoved movers is to call attention to the risks involved in generalizing from one sort of case to another. From the fact that individuals such as Socrates and Callias have determinate locations and unified spatiotemporal careers, it does not follow that Aristotle takes anything and everything that is *atomon kai hen arithmō(i)* to have a determinate location and a unified spatiotemporal career. So Aristotle may recognize at least some non-substance individuals of the sort countenanced by Owen and Frede. This would help to explain the *Categories*' failure to speak of such individuals as themselves *kath' hekasta*. Aristotle may refrain from calling them particulars because he does not view them as having the sort of determinate locations and unified spatiotemporal careers that particulars like Socrates and Bebop do.

---

[29] If this is right, then what [FR] provides is a sufficient condition for being a *particular*, not an *individual*. For an *individual* (unlike a *particular*) need not be a subjective part of some whole. But recognizing this leaves intact the main point of AR: namely, that an individual can be IN (though not SAID OF) a plurality of numerically distinct subjects.

[30] I base this on *Met.* N.5, 1092a19–20, where (in arguing against taking numbers as first principles of being) Aristotle says that place (*topos*) is proper (*idion*) to *kath' hekasta*.

[31] I bracket questions about whether, and if so how, the first mover can be an object of human knowledge.

140   JENNIFER WHITING

Though I take this failure to strengthen my case against a generalized version of TR, I do not place significant weight on this. My argument rests primarily on the way in which Aristotle's anomalous use of the feminine plurals in [A][1] and [4] supports taking the argument of [A] not as 'compressed and careless' but as exceptionally careful: the point seems to be that *all* non-substance beings are IN the *primary substances themselves*, and not simply SAID OF beings (neuter) that are IN the primary substances (feminine).

5. The Token-Action Objection and the Possibility of a Hybrid Reading

Here, however, proponents of TR are sure to appeal to the second point mentioned as evidence that Aristotle associates having a determinate spatiotemporal location with being *atomon kai hen arithmō(i)*.

> [F]   It seems most distinctive of substance that what is numerically one and the same (*to tauton kai hen arithmō(i)*) is able to receive contraries. In no other case could one bring forward anything, numerically one, that is able to receive contraries. For example, a colour which is numerically one and the same will not be black and white, *nor will numerically one and the same action be bad and good*. And similarly with everything else that is not substance. A substance, however, numerically one and the same, is able to receive contraries. For example, an individual human (*ho tis anthrōpos*), being one and the same, becomes pale at one time and dark at another, and hot and cold, and bad and good. Nothing like this is seen in any other case. (*Cat.* 5, 4a10–22)

Irwin, in the passage quoted at the outset, follows Heinaman in taking [F] to support TR. Here is Heinaman's argument:

> Numerically one and the same action cannot be both bad and good. On the new [viz., alternative] interpretation an action which is one in number is a specific type of action, and, as any reader of Plato's early dialogues would know, a specific type of action can be both bad and good. So the action which is one in number here is not a type of action but an historical event. *The analogue in the case of 'a color which is numerically one' is not an indivisible shade but an individual instance.* (Heinaman 1981, 300; my italics)

But Heinaman's analogy may fail. Even if Aristotle counts token-actions as non-substance individuals in the category of *poiein* (or Acting), it does not follow that he treats all non-substance individuals as having the sort of determinate and unified spatiotemporal careers that token-actions do. For he clearly thinks that different kinds of being are unified, and thus individuated, in different ways. The unity of an individual colour, such as Vanilla White, is not like the unity of an individual action, such as building or selling a house. And most importantly for present purposes, Aristotle seems reluctant in *Topics* 1.7 to speak of the spatiotemporally unified portion of water in one well, even if it stays put, as constituting an 'individual' that is numerically distinct from other such portions of water: he seems to think that when we reach Water, we have reached an infima species that is not divisible in number in the way that species like Human and Dog are (103a19–23).

We might put the point by noting that 'human' and 'horse', like their Greek counterparts, are *count* nouns, whereas the names of the four elements and of compounds formed from them are (in Greek as in English) *mass* nouns, and then proposing to speak by analogy of 'count forms' and 'mass forms'. We can then say that the forms of Animal (though not perhaps of Plant) are 'count forms' whereas the forms or kinds of Matter are 'mass forms'. And we can say that the forms of Colour resemble the forms of Matter in being 'mass forms', whereas at least some of the forms of Acting are 'count forms'. Consider 'marrying': we can ask a preacher how many marriages she has performed, and we can ask an individual how many times he or she has married. But even if some forms of Acting are clearly count forms, it does not follow that all of the forms of Acting are count forms: for we might take Aristotle's distinction between *kinēseis* (of the sort so astutely discussed in *Aristotle's Philosophy of Action*) and *energeiai* (in the sense in which Aristotle says that seeing and hearing are *energeiai*) to be a distinction between count forms of *poiein* and mass forms of *poiein*. So even within a single category, it may be illegitimate to generalize in the way I've been arguing we should not generalize across categories.

I conclude, then, that the burden of proof is on those who want to generalize and take the appearance of an action-token in [F] as reason for taking the *Categories*' references to 'the individual white' and 'the individual knowledge of grammar' as references to particulars with determinate locations and unified spatiotemporal careers such as those enjoyed by a primary substance. 1a24–5 do not support TR and the star example is of little use to TR once we see the plausibility of reading these lines as allowing for the possibility of a non-substance individual that is IN (but not SAID OF) a plurality of numerically distinct particulars and moreover take Aristotle to view this possibility as actualized in the case of mass forms like 'water' and 'vanilla white'. But proponents of AR should not generalize from these examples with a view to dismissing the idea that Aristotle, when writing the *Categories*, allowed *some* non-substance individuals to be particulars in the sense in which Callias is a particular and so to have determinate locations and spatiotemporally unified careers. For we cannot simply dismiss [F]'s appeal to what is surely a token-action. Fortunately, we can read Aristotle as adopting a

142   JENNIFER WHITING

hybrid view of the sort defended here, with mass forms and count forms demanding different sorts of treatment. So I offer the hybrid reading to David as a token of my appreciation for all that I have learned from him.[32]

Works Cited

Ackrill, J. L. 1963. *Aristotle* Categories *and* De Interpretatione. *Translated with Notes and Glossary.* Clarendon Aristotle Series. Clarendon Press.

Berlin, Isaiah. 1973. 'Austin and the Early Beginnings of Oxford Philosophy', in *Essays on J. L. Austin* (ed. I. Berlin). Clarendon Press, 1–16. (Reprinted in *Personal Impressions.* The Viking Press, 1981.)

Bronstein, David. 2016. *Aristotle on Knowledge and Learning: The* Posterior Analytics. Oxford University Press.

Charles, David. 1984. *Aristotle's Philosophy of Action.* Duckworth.

Charles, David. 2000. *Aristotle on Meaning and Essence.* Oxford University Press.

Crivelli, Paolo. 2017. 'Being-Said-Of in Aristotle's *Categories*', *Rivista di Filosofia Neo-Scolastica* 3, 531–56.

Frede, Michael. 1987. 'Individuals in Aristotle', in Michael Frede, *Essays in Ancient Philosophy.* University of Minnesota Press, 40–71. (English translation by Wolfgang Mann.) (Originally published as 'Individuen bei Aristoteles', *Antike und Abendland* 24 (1978), 16–39.)

Heinaman, Robert. 1981. 'Non-substantial Individuals in the *Categories*', *Phronesis* 26, 295–307.

Irwin, T. H. 1989. *Aristotle's First Principles.* Clarendon Press.

Lennox, James G. 2001. *Aristotle's Philosophy of Biology: Studies in the Origins of Life Science.* Cambridge University Press.

Lloyd, A. C. 1962. 'Genus, Species, and Ordered Series in Aristotle', *Phronesis* 7, 67–90.

Owen, G. E. L. 1965. 'Inherence', *Phronesis* 10: 97–105. (Reprinted in G. E. L. Owen, *Logic, Science, and Dialectic: Collected Papers in Greek Philosophy* (ed. M. Nussbaum). Cornell University Press (1986), 252–8.)

von Fritz, Kurt. 1938. *Philosophie und Sprachlicher Ausdruck bei Demokrit, Plato und Aristoteles.* G. E. Stechert.

Whiting, Jennifer. 2002. 'Strong Dialectic, Neurathian Reflection, and the Ascent of Desire: Irwin and McDowell on Aristotle's Methods of Ethics', *Proceedings of the Boston Area Colloquium of Ancient Philosophy* 17, 61–122.

---

[32] I would like to thank Marko Malink for his comments on an early draft and David Bronstein for comments and editorial assistance above and beyond the call of duty. He is a first-rate midwife.

7

Essential Predication
in Aristotle's *Categories*

A Defence

Christof Rapp

Introduction

Aristotle's *Categories* is a treatise that is mostly concerned with classifications. Many ancient commentators saw the *Categories* as closely connected with the *Topics* and some of the earliest mentions of this treatise in antiquity even used the title *Before the Topics* instead of *Categories*, indicating that it was seen as a sort of propaedeutic to the *Topics*,[1] and thus as closely related to Aristotle's method of dialectic.[2] Still, the *Categories* offers a series of claims, most notably claims associated with the concept of substance (*ousia*), that we would rate as straightforwardly 'metaphysical' ones. This is the reason why the *Categories*' claims about substance are regularly and inevitably compared to the presumably most authoritative treatise on all questions concerning Aristotelian metaphysics—namely, Aristotle's *Metaphysics*—even though this latter treatise is dedicated to an entirely different project. Far from the *Categories*' mostly classificatory interest (and far from, perhaps, merely contributing to the art of dialectic), the *Metaphysics* is meant to unfold Aristotle's most ambitious project of first philosophy, aiming at the identification of the first principles and causes of everything. Because of this unequivocal difference in the status of the two treatises and their respective projects, it is a legitimate question whether the *Categories* is the kind of treatise that can be expected to defend a genuinely metaphysical stance in the first place (especially if one wants to reserve the attribute 'metaphysical' for the kind of project that we see in Aristotle's *Metaphysics*). This is the background against which authors have come to doubt whether one should associate a small, mostly classificatory, dialectically oriented project like the *Categories* with the burden of 'heavy metaphysical

---

[1] See Bodéüs 2002, xxiv–xli.
[2] Which is not to say, to be sure, that it is a 'merely dialectical' project; rather one could infer, as Menn 1995, 315 puts it, 'that the *Categories teaches* the art of dialectic by giving principles for constructing dialectical arguments, no[t] that it *uses* the art of dialectic for anything else'.

Christof Rapp, *Essential Predication in Aristotle's* Categories: *A Defence* In: *Aristotelian Metaphysics: Essays in Honour of David Charles.* Edited by: David Bronstein, Thomas Kjeller Johansen, and Michail Peramatzis, Oxford University Press.
© Oxford University Press 2024. DOI: 10.1093/oso/9780198908678.003.0007

144 CHRISTOF RAPP

baggage'[3] or the 'ontologically loaded'[4] notion of essential predication. In this chapter I will argue that the *Categories*, its peculiar status and its kinship to the *Topics* notwithstanding, demarcates a kind of predication that is meant to be an essential one—even though the essentialism we find in the *Categories* is (still) a far cry from the metaphysical theory of the *Metaphysics*, according to which forms as constituents of hylomorphic compounds are the essences and causes of the being of sensible things.

1. Setting the Stage

The core of the *Categories*, as it has come down to us, is mostly concerned with a tenfold classification of being or beings: every being that is said in isolation (i.e., taken as such and not as part of an assertion) signifies either substance (*ousia*) or quantity or qualification or a relative or where or when or being-in-a-position or having or doing or being-affected (*Cat.* 4, 1b25–7). Traditionally, these ten classes have been dubbed 'categories' (*katēgoriai*) and this is also where the traditional title of the treatise has been taken from. The Greek word *katēgoria* derives from *katēgoreisthai*, which originally means 'accusing someone of something'; in Aristotle, though, it is quite consistently used for 'predicating something of something': that is, some predicate of a subject or of a non-linguistic thing in the world. The use of the word *katēgoria* raises the expectation that the ten categories as enumerated in the *Categories* are meant to be classes of predication or predicates; this, however, is not exactly what Aristotle says in the *Categories*, for this classification of things said without combination (*aneu sumplokē*) in *Categories* 4 seems to refer back to *Categories* 2, where Aristotle clearly intends to classify beings (*onta*), not predicates strictly speaking (1a20). Within the *Categories* he mostly avoids calling the ten items on this list 'categories' (with presumably two exceptions in *Cat.* 8, 10b19 and 21). Furthermore, the focus on items that are 'said without combination' makes it clear that this classification is at least not about actually predicated predicates: that is, items actually stated as building blocks of a predicative combination (although this formulation leaves open the possibility that the classification still concerns predicable, just not actually predicated predicates). Moreover, the list of so-called categories includes one item that is not predicable of anything else (the primary substance), so we should be cautious about subsuming the *Categories*' categories under the generic terms of predication, predicates, predicables, or the like. These concerns notwithstanding, predication is an important issue both for the treatise as a whole and for the list of categories. As for the list of categories, it might well be that, even though the

---

[3] Menn 2018, 21.   [4] Crivelli 2017, 549.

ESSENTIAL PREDICATION IN ARISTOTLE'S *CATEGORIES*   145

Categories does not introduce this list as a classification of predicates, but rather as a classification of beings, the list of ten items originally derives from a list of possible predications, for in *Topics* 1.9 more or less the same list is explicitly introduced as a list of predicates or predications. Moreover, there are passages arguing that the tenfold list pertains to the different meanings of being, just because it captures the different figures of predication.[5]

In *Categories* 2 Aristotle famously distinguishes two ways in which beings (*onta*) can be related to each other (see section 2 below). One of these two relations within the *Categories* is the relation of being SAID OF,[6] which comes to the fore when we ask *what something is*. When X is SAID OF Y, X gives an answer to the question of what Y is or at least provides a part of this answer. It thus indicates either that an individual Y is a member of the universal class of X or that a class Y is included in a more general class X. Most famously, Aristotle points out that what he calls 'secondary substances'—that is, universal species or genera, like the species man or the genus animal—are SAID OF individual 'primary substances', like a particular man, telling us *what* the particular substance *is*, and that the more general genus animal is SAID OF the less general species, telling us *what* the species or all members of the species *are*. 'Human' is SAID OF particular humans, indicating that they are members of the species human, and 'animal' is SAID OF human, indicating that the species human is included in the class of animals. If X is SAID OF Y and Y is SAID OF Z, then X is also SAID OF Z (transitivity principle). If X is a genus, say animal, and Z an individual, say a particular human, one might wonder whether X gives the full and satisfactory answer to the question of *what Z is*, even though the answer is true, for X gives a true, though incomplete, answer to the question of *what Z is*. Perhaps one might say that X only provides a part of the answer to the question of *what Z is*; nevertheless, it is SAID OF Z.

Within the framework of the *Categories*, the relation of being SAID OF and everything that is connected with the answer to the question of what something is then seems to be a natural place to look for essences, even though a particular term for what we call 'essence' is absent from the *Categories* (with the possible exception of *Categories* 1, where Aristotle speaks of *logos tēs ousias*, the implications of which, however, are fairly controversial). The relation of being SAID OF seems to be a particularly promising path to essences, because Aristotle connects this notion with the test that whenever X is SAID OF Y, both the name and the

---

[5] See *Met.* Δ.7, 1017b25–30, where the idea seems to be that being has as many meanings as there are figures of predication, *just because* each and every predication using a verbal predicate (e.g., Socrates suffers) can be turned into a predication using the copula *is* (e.g., Socrates is suffering) and thus implies a specific meaning of *being*.

[6] By capitalizing SAID OF and IN I want to indicate a terminological use; the assumption that there is such a terminological use and that this terminology is important for the overall interpretation of the *Categories* will be justified below in sections 4–6.

146 CHRISTOF RAPP

definition of X must hold of Y (the so-called 'name-and-definition-test'). Although these notions and requirements are most extensively studied in connection with the first category, the category of substance, and as part of the attempt to highlight the distinctiveness of substance compared to all other categories, it is important to note that the relation of being SAID OF can also hold between items of the non-substantial categories. When someone asks, for example, of a particular property or attribute, say white, *what* it *is*, the appropriate answer, say 'colour', will be SAID OF the particular white, and hence will have to pass the name-and-definition-test: that is, the test of whether both the name and the definition of colour would hold of the particular white. If we are willing to accept the application of the SAID OF relation together with the name-and-definition-test as a general hint about essences in the case of substances, we are committed to the view that non-substances have essences no less than substances have them (a view that will be doubted or qualified in *Metaphysics* Z.4–6).

2. Being SAID OF and Being IN Distinguished in the *Categories*

Whenever X is SAID OF Y, both its name and its definition can also be predicated of Y (*Cat.* 5, 2a19–27)—this is what we called the 'name-and-definition-test', for one can use this requirement to test whether some term is really SAID OF a subject in the required sense or whether it is IN it.[7] Now the *Categories* not only introduces the relation of being SAID OF but contrasts this with the relation of being IN a substrate. The contradistinction of these two relations in the *Categories* is often invoked as the ancestor of all distinctions between essential and accidental predications. In chapter 2 of the *Categories*, where these two relations are introduced and preliminarily contrasted, they are used to delineate the famous fourfold ontology of the *Categories*, distinguishing (1) beings (*onta*) that are SAID OF a substrate, but not IN a substrate (namely, species, genera: the secondary substances of the *Categories*), (2) beings that are IN a substrate, but not SAID OF any substrate (i.e., non-substantial particulars), (3) beings that are IN a substrate, but also SAID OF a substrate (i.e., non-substantial universals), and finally (4) beings that are neither IN a substrate nor SAID OF a substrate (i.e., the substantial particulars: the primary substances of the *Categories*). Whereas the relation of being SAID OF is introduced without further comments in this chapter, the relation of being IN a substrate is introduced by a brief account: 'by "in a substrate" I mean what is in something, not as a part, and cannot exist separately from what it is in' (*Cat.* 2, 1a24–5). The first part of this description is meant to forestall a mereological

---

[7] This kind of test is first presented in *Cat.* 5, 2a19–34 (see texts [T2] and [T1], in this order). In *Cat.* 5, 3a17–21 the test is carried out in order to prove that no substance is in anything else as its substrate.

understanding of this relation, for the preposition 'in' could naturally be taken to indicate parts of a whole; according to the first part of this description, we are supposed not to take the 'in' in a mereological sense. This much is clear; it is less clear what the positive implication of the 'in' is. The second part of the description seems to include a modal account of ontological, probably existential, dependence: for an entity that is IN a substrate, it is impossible (*adunaton*) to be in separation from the substrate it is IN (implying that, conversely, it is possible for the substrate to be or to exist in separation from the particular beings that are IN it).[8]

A preliminary worry concerns the status of these two relations: are they meant to be linguistic predications? Or what else are they? In particular, one could be worried about the impression that the first relation, the relation of being SAID OF, seems to appeal to something genuinely linguistic—for, after all, 'being SAID OF' (*legesthai kata*) taken literally refers to things we say—while the other relation, the one of being IN a subject, does not. In addition, this might be confusing because, as we already said (see section 1 above), the *Categories* does regularly appeal to predications, some of which are undoubtedly meant in a linguistic sense.[9] Now, since chapter 2 of the *Categories* uses these two relations to classify beings (*onta*), there is a widespread consensus among scholars that these two relations are meant to hold between things that are and not primarily between linguistic entities.[10] For this reason, some call them 'metaphysical predications'. Still, even if we call them 'metaphysical', it is clear that they are closely connected with and indicated by ordinary linguistic predications. If, for example, human is SAID OF Socrates, this grounds the truth of the ordinary predicative statement 'Socrates is a human' (and according to the name-and-definition-test likewise the truth of the statement 'Socrates is a biped animal'), and if, for example, white or whiteness is IN a particular human being or, as scholars say, 'inheres' in a particular human being (e.g., Socrates), this grounds the truth of the ordinary predicative statement 'Socrates is white'. Considering the striking syntactic similarity of these two statements ('Socrates is a human' and 'Socrates is white'), one might speculate whether the distinction between being SAID OF and being IN originally derives from the attempt to disambiguate predicative statements with the copula 'is' into two genuinely distinct relations.[11] Indeed, the *Categories* uses a third notion for the

---

[8] In the light of recent metaphysical and scholarly research, there would be a lot to say about the interpretation of the peculiar dependence involved here; for the present purpose, I take the formulation at face value, and taken at face value it is a modal account.

[9] For examples, see section 3 below.

[10] See, e.g., Mann 2000, 51: 'a relation between things, not linguistic items', together with the important qualification on p. 53 that 'while things (ὄντα) are being talked about and classified, they are classified on the basis of the expressions (λεγόμενα) used to refer to them or to introduce them into discourse'.

[11] At Aristotle's time, people may have wondered whether the use of 'is' is always meant to indicate what a thing is and whether in this sense anything can be more than one thing (see Plato's *Sophist* 251a). Aristotle imposes a terminology that disambiguates the copula into what something *really* is and into what something *has* as its characteristics (species membership vs. property possession, as one might say). This is the difference that matters above all.

148   CHRISTOF RAPP

metaphysically neutral linguistic relation of being predicated of, which can be contrasted to both 'metaphysical' relations, so to speak; the Greek word that is mostly used for this latter purpose is *katēgoreisthai* with genitive or with the preposition *kata*. In virtually all other contexts, this word could be used interchangeably with *legesthai*, but in this particular context, it seems to be primarily used for the ordinary, linguistic predication that can correspond to either of the two metaphysical relations (unfortunately, things are a bit more complicated, since the *Categories*' shifts from *legesthai* to *katēgoreisthai* are an endless source of confusion—we will get back to this in section 3 below).

As examples for beings that are IN a substrate, Aristotle mentions that (a) 'the individual knowledge-of-grammar is in a substrate, the soul', although it is, of course, not SAID OF any substrate (*Cat.* 2, 1a26–7), that (b) 'the individual white is in a substrate, the body', without being, of course, SAID OF any substrate (*Cat.* 2, 1a27–9), and that (c) knowledge, conceived as a non-substantial universal, is both IN a substrate, namely the soul, and SAID OF a substrate, namely of the knowledge-of-grammar (*Cat.* 2, 1b1–3). The inhering beings are referred to by abstract nouns (i.e., nouns designating properties): namely, particular properties in cases (a) and (b) and universal properties in case (c). We could extend this list by referring to later passages from the *Categories*, where we are told that health and sickness are in an animal's body, whiteness and blackness in a body simply, and justice and injustice in a soul (*Cat.* 11, 14a16–19). Here the author seems not particularly keen to stress that these non-substantial properties must be anchored in a particular substance,[12] emphasizing rather that they require a substance of a certain sort (e.g., souls, bodies in general, and bodies of living beings). Aristotle adds a brief explanation to example (b), consisting in the remark that each colour is 'in body'. Colours are by their nature such that they occur on or in bodies (strictly speaking, on their surfaces), knowledge is by its nature such that it occurs in souls, and health and sickness are by their nature such that they occur in bodies of living beings.

Aristotle substantiates the distinction between being SAID OF and being IN by bringing in the name-and-definition-test.[13] If X is SAID OF Y, both its name and its definition must be predicable of Y; if X is IN Y, this is not the case. So if the

---

[12]   In chapter 5 of *Categories*, the chapter on substance, by contrast, this will be an important point.

[13]   This test is introduced in *Cat.* 5, 2a19–34. Within this particular chapter the test seems to be part of the discussion of substance. However, substance does not play an explicit role in this particular passage (later in the chapter, though, in 3a17–21, the test will be explicitly applied to substances); in a way, the passage 2a19–34 even interrupts the discussion of substance. For this reason, I am in principle sympathetic to Mann's suggestion that this passage and the name-and-definition-test should be taken as a continuation of chapter 2, which introduces the difference between being SAID OF and being IN (possibly together with the first lines—1b10–15—of chapter 3): see Mann 2000, appendix I; it is a different question, though, whether this passage should be actually transposed to this place in the treatise.

ESSENTIAL PREDICATION IN ARISTOTLE'S *CATEGORIES*   149

species human being is SAID OF a particular human, both the name of this species, say 'human', and its definition, say 'biped animal', must be predicable of the
particular human. Given that Socrates is (a) human and that 'biped animal' is the
definition of human, it is true to say that Socrates is a biped animal. In *Topics* 6.1,
139a26–7, Aristotle stresses in a similar vein that the definition of human ought
to be true of each and every human. However, if we try to apply the same test to
beings that are IN a substrate, we'll get the following result:

[T1]   But as for things which are in a substrate, in most cases neither the name nor
the definition is predicated of the substrate. In some cases there is nothing
to prevent the name from being predicated of the substrate, but it is
impossible for the definition to be predicated. For example, white, which is
in a substrate (the body), is predicated of the substrate; for a body is called
white. But the definition of white will never be predicated of the body.[14]

From this passage we are supposed to learn three things: (i) of things being IN a
subject or substrate the definition can never be predicated of this substrate;
(ii) nor for the most part can the name be predicated; (iii) however, there are a
few exceptions to result (ii).

Result (i) seems to be Aristotle's main point, for it marks the crucial difference
with being SAID OF. Let the definition of white be 'bright colour'; a white thing,
be it a body, a wall, or a sheet of paper, cannot be said to be '(a) bright colour' for
the things mentioned are no colours at all. Accordingly, things that are IN a substrate do not tell us *what* the substrate *is*. Even if in some cases the name of the
corresponding property is linguistically predicated of this substrate, the name-
and-definition-test reveals that this predicated name does not tell us anything
about *what* the substrate *is*, even though the linguistic form of this predication,
using the copula *is*, could give us this impression.

Result (ii) can be illustrated by referring to the above-mentioned stock examples:
Knowledge is in the soul, but its name, say 'knowledge', cannot be predicated of
the soul; the assertion 'The soul is knowledge' does not make any sense, nor does
the assertion 'The body is sickness', if sickness happens to inhere in a body. In
cases like these, we do not even need to refer to the definition of the inhering
property in order to see that the predicates '(a) knowledge' or '(a) sickness' do not
tell us *what* their substrates *are*, because not even the name can be predicated of
its substrate.

---

[14] *Cat.* 5, 2a27–34; Ackrill's translation, slightly altered. Greek text by Minio-Paluello: τῶν δ' ἐν
ὑποκειμένῳ ὄντων ἐπὶ μὲν τῶν πλείστων οὔτε τοὔνομα οὔτε ὁ λόγος κατηγορεῖται τοῦ ὑποκειμένου· ἐπ'
ἐνίων δὲ τοὔνομα μὲν οὐδὲν κωλύει κατηγορεῖσθαι τοῦ ὑποκειμένου, τὸν δὲ λόγον ἀδύνατον· οἷον τὸ
λευκὸν ἐν ὑποκειμένῳ ὂν τῷ σώματι κατηγορεῖται τοῦ ὑποκειμένου, – λευκὸν γὰρ σῶμα λέγεται, – ὁ δὲ
λόγος τοῦ λευκοῦ οὐδέποτε κατὰ τοῦ σώματος κατηγορηθήσεται.

150   CHRISTOF RAPP

Result (ii) raises the notorious question of how to express the fact that, for example, knowledge of grammar inheres in the soul within an ordinary predication; for usually, we do not say that wisdom inheres in Socrates, but rather that Socrates is wise. Aristotle does not explain his suggestion in so many words. However, already in chapter 1 of the *Categories* he has equipped his readers with the useful tool of paronymous names: the grammarian (*ho gramatikos*, i.e., the person who is knowledgeable in grammar), he says, gets his name or description (*prosēgoria*) paronymously from *hē grammatikē*, from grammatical knowledge, and the brave one (*ho andreios*) gets his name or description from bravery (*hē andreia*). This inspires the interpretation that in the standard cases mentioned in result (ii), in which not even the name of the inhering property can be predicated, a paronymous form deriving from the name of the inhering property (e.g., a concrete adjective such as 'knowledgeable-in-grammar', 'brave', 'healthy', or 'just') can be predicated given that the corresponding property inheres in the substrate. If this is so, the fact that bravery inheres in a soul would ground the truth of the statement 'This soul is brave.' This interpretation is confirmed by a passage in *Categories* 8 (10a27–b11), where Aristotle points out that for qualities (though not for accidents of all categories) things are called paronymously in accordance with their qualities: for example, the white one (*ho leukos*) from whiteness, the one-who-is-knowledgeable-in-grammar (*ho grammatikos*) from the art of grammar, and the just one (*ho dikaios*) from justice. This, he says, happens 'in most and actually in almost all cases', so it seems to be a standard procedure—at least in the case of qualities.

It might be worth exploring some features of this paronymy-based account. First of all, it matches the expectation that the inherence of knowledge-of-grammar in some substrate should correspond to an ordinary predicative statement of the form 'X is knowledgeable-in-grammar' (or, conversely, the expectation that a predicative statement of the form 'X is knowledgeable-in-grammar' is adequately analysed by saying that knowledge-of-grammar inheres in X). Second, the paronymy-based account promises to supply predicable paronymous nouns in many cases; the procedure of deriving such predicable nouns by way of paronymy is limited only by the factual availability of names and paronyms in a given language (i.e., by the contingent facts that in a certain language, say Greek, there might be either no name for the inhering property or no predicable adjective that could be derived from it); Aristotle dwells on the discussion of this phenomenon (*Cat.* 8, 10a3ff.) and quibbles with the problem that in Greek people are called 'decent' or 'virtuous' (*spoudaios*) according to their virtue, but that the word *spoudaios* is no paronym deriving from *aretē*, the standard word for virtue. Third, the paronym is only a linguistic variation of the name for the property. In speaking of paronyms, commentators usually do not feel inclined to proclaim an additional entity over and above the inhering property and the involved substrate; the paronymous term comes as an 'ontological free lunch', as it were (i.e., it does not require any additional entity). What is predicated when we say that Achilles is courageous is not a different entity but a linguistic name paronymously derived from the name for the property (courage) that inheres in Achilles: *one* inhering entity (courage) with *one* definition, *one* name, and (at least) *one* paronymous name attached to it. Fourth, and this is connected with the previous point, when Aristotle speaks of paronymy in the *Categories*, he never considers the problem that the parony-mously related names, such as 'courage' and 'courageous', could have different definitions in the way homonymous terms do—even though it is obvious that 'courage' and 'courageous' are applied to different things, one to the inhering property and one to the substrate that has the property of courage. Why is this so? Let us speculate! Whereas in the case of homonymy (as defined in *Categories* 1) one word means altogether different things, the paronymous terms 'courage' and 'courageous' do not refer to altogether different things, but rather share a com-mon understanding of what courage consists in. When the one thing (the cour-ageous person) is *named after the other* (the property of courage), this reveals a difference between 'being courage' and 'having or displaying courage', but involves no difference concerning the core meaning of 'courage'.[15] And this again might be connected with our previous point: since it is one and the same entity (revealed by one and the same definition) that the one thing is and the other thing displays, the introduction of the paronymous term is only a linguistic convention and as such ontologically neutral; it does not provide a new item that has to be accom-modated in the fourfold ontology.

So far, we have suggested a solution for the standard case corresponding to result (ii): namely, that for the most part not even the name of the inhering property can be predicated of its substrate. What about the less frequent cases correspond-ing to result (iii): namely, the cases in which the name, though not the definition, can indeed be predicated of the substrate? In our current passage, Aristotle says that these are 'some cases', which are contrasted with 'most cases' in which the predication of the name is not possible; later (*Cat.* 5, 3a16) Aristotle just says that it is 'sometimes' possible to predicate the name. In any case, the example by which he illustrates result (iii) is the following: if white is IN a body, the name 'white' can be predicated of the substrate, for 'a body is called white'. Apparently, this is pos-sible only if we use 'white' (*leukon/to leukon*) in two different ways: on the one hand, as an abstract noun for designating whiteness or the property of being white and, on the other hand, as the concrete neuter adjective 'white' that can be predicated without modifications of a neuter substrate, such as body (*sōma*). Maybe this is one of the reasons why this case is supposed to be relatively rare,

---

[15] This is why scholars have associated *paronymy* in the *Categories* with the famous *pros hen* rela-tion as we know it from the *Metaphysics* and the *Eudemian Ethics*; however, the notion of *pros hen* does not occur in the *Categories* and seems to be restricted to a narrower class of cases; on the two relations, see Tolkiehn 2020, 159–63.

152   CHRISTOF RAPP

since owing to the grammatical requirement of gender agreement a masculine substrate, such as man (*anthrōpos*), would require *leukos* instead of *leukon*, and a feminine substrate, such as surface (*epiphaneia*), would require *leukē*. In *Metaphysics* Z.6, 1031b23–5, Aristotle actually acknowledges that *to leukon* can be used in two ways: for the accidental property and for the substrate that has it. In the passage from *Categories* 8 that we discussed above, Aristotle used the adjective *leukos* together with the abstract noun *leukotēs* (whiteness), thus also acknowledging (though indirectly) the distinctness of the two uses. In this latter passage, *leukos* is clearly a paronymous name, but in our present passage, when the adjective *leukon* corresponds to the abstract noun *to leukon*, it cannot be a case of paronymy, for paronymy would require different endings.

Taken at face value, the *leukon* example seems simpler and more straightforward than the paronymy account in that it does not predicate a merely paronymous name, but the very same name, the abstract noun (i.e., the name for the inhering property), which is strictly speaking *to leukon* (*the white*) and not *leukon*, the latter of which is predicable, while the former is not (Aristotle might have been confused about the use of the neuter article, which in this context can be used either for forming the abstract term *the white* or for indicating—just like a modern quotation mark—that *leukon* is mentioned or quoted). Yet here Aristotle does not show any awareness in this context of the double use of *leukon* or *to leukon*; on the contrary, there is only one syntactical subject, *to leukon*, which is said to be IN the substrate and at the same time predicated of it. One might defend this move by declaring the phonetic aspect—that is, the sequence of sounds, regardless of what it stands for—to be the sole identity criterion of names. Still, the fact that the use of *leukon* is multivocal might cause some trouble.

Several authors have suggested that this is a case of homonymy,[16] since after all the word *leukon* that can be predicated of a substrate does not mean the same as *to leukon*, which refers to the inhering property; and homonymy is given, in a nutshell, when one name corresponds to two different definitions. Similarly, one of Aristotle's stock examples for paronymy is that *hē grammatikē* means knowledge-of-grammar, while the paronymous term *ho grammatikos* (masculine, applying to a masculine subject) refers to someone who is knowledgeable-in-grammar. If we think, however, of a feminine subject, like Aspasia, whom we also want to call 'knowledgeable-in-grammar', the predicative noun must take on the feminine ending *-ē*, so that we get *grammatikē*;[17] and *grammatikē* (as opposed to

---

[16] See Menn 1995, 322, Crivelli 2017, 552, Menn 2018, 17. Ackrill 1963, 72 is a bit more cautious: 'homonymy or something like it'. Mann (2000, 192) defends a somewhat more differentiated view: he says of the homonymy that derives from one thing being called after the other (i.e., of a special case of homonymy in which the definitions do overlap; see n. 21 below) that homonymy is assimilated to paronymy or that it is a 'degenerate case of paronymy', which comes close to the solution suggested below.

[17] I owe this example to Stephen Menn; it is construed by analogy with Simplicius' example (*In Cat.* 37.18–21 (Kalbfleisch)) of a woman who is musical (*mousikē*); the same example is used by Porphyry (*In Cat.* 113.24 (Busse)).

ESSENTIAL PREDICATION IN ARISTOTLE'S *CATEGORIES*   153

the masculine *grammatikos*) is no longer a paronym from *hē grammatikē*, but is fully equivalent to the *leukon* example. Ancient commentators such as Porphyry and Simplicius also accept this feminine example as a case of homonymy. The homonymy account, however, faces some difficulties. Obviously, Aristotle himself refrains from explicitly calling this a homonymous case and he does not refer to different definitions. If a second definition introduces an additional entity apart from whiteness or knowledge-of-grammar, how could this new additional entity be accommodated in the fourfold ontology? It would not be IN a substrate (for it is only the property corresponding to the abstract noun, such as whiteness, that is IN the substrate), nor is it SAID OF a substrate (it is only predicated of it),[18] but still it is no primary substance. At any rate, the ontological free-lunch solution that we suggested for the paronymy account would not be available for fully fledged homonymy. Moreover, it would be surprising if Aristotle construes the standard case (in which the name itself cannot be predicated) in accordance with the paronymy solution, while construing the non-standard case (in which the name can be predicated) as a case of homonymy—especially if, as we argued, the difference between the paronymy and the homonymy account would be ontologically significant, while we would not like to accept ontologically significant differences between the masculine case *grammatikos* and the feminine case *grammatikē*. Finally, if we want to keep the differences between the standard case and the non-standard case manageable, we should acknowledge that, just as the paronymy case presupposes a common understanding of what courage, whiteness, or knowledge-of-grammar consists in (as we argued above), the allegedly homonymous case of *leukon* (or of the feminine predicative noun *grammatikē*) cannot involve different meanings of whiteness (or of knowledge-of-grammar), captured by different definitions. If there are different definitions, they would only capture the difference between 'being whiteness' and 'having whiteness' (analogous to the paronymy case, as analysed above).

This leads us, finally, to the contested question of what exactly Aristotelian homonymy consists in, whether all cases of something being said in many ways (multivocity) are cases of homonymy, and whether homonymy requires that the definitions be completely different or whether it is sufficient for homonymy that the definitions are not exactly the same.[19] On a more liberal understanding of homonymy (the definitions are not exactly the same, but may overlap), the *leukon* example seems to be a clear case of homonymy, even though Aristotle does not say this, while on a narrow understanding (the definitions are strictly distinct), this would not be a case of homonymy. And one might wonder whether the

---

[18] Unless one accepts one of the 'apostate' readings discussed in section 3 below.

[19] This latter difference corresponds to Shields' distinction (in Shields 1999) between discrete and comprehensive homonymy. Tolkiehn 2020 makes a case for a narrow concept of homonymy, which excludes overlapping definitions and therefore the *pros hen* relation.

154 CHRISTOF RAPP

Categories' full definition of homonymy aims at a narrow understanding when it introduces the qualification that the account of being (*logos tēs ousias*) is different *kata tounoma* (i.e., with respect to the name),[20] which could be taken to mean that what it means to be an *F* (if *F* stands for the involved name) must be different. At any rate and irrespective of the various interpretations of homonymy, a charitable reconstruction of the name-and-definition-test should try to construe the *leukon* example of the non-standard case (iii) in close analogy to the more frequent case (ii)—and for this more frequent case it seemed reasonable to accept an account based on paronymy.

3. Non-Essentialist Readings of Being SAID OF

So far we have interpreted the name-and-definition-test as a way of making sure that whatever is SAID OF a substrate is actually meant to say *what* this substrate *is*, which, again, is a precondition for associating the SAID OF relation with essential predication. Indeed, this is the traditional interpretation and the interpretation defended by the majority of commentators; however, there are some serious challenges to this reading, both ancient and recent ones, that need to be addressed. In one way or the other, all these readings utilize seeming inconsistencies in Aristotle's use of the word *legesthai* or the verb-phrase *legesthai kata tinos* together with the corresponding verb *katēgoreisthai*. Indeed, the use of these words in the *Categories* is sometimes confusing, such that non-essentialist readings cannot be conclusively ruled out; on balance though, it seems that the traditional understanding of being SAID OF still provides the most consistent reading.

3.1 An Attempt to Codify Aristotle's Practice

In order to defend the traditional reading, it is crucial to concede that the terminological meaning of being SAID OF is unambiguously given *only* in cases when Aristotle uses the phrase *legesthai kata tinos* or *legesthai* with genitive, whereas other uses of the verb *legesthai* (for saying, calling, etc.) without the preposition *kata* or without genitive as well as occurrences of the verb *katēgoreisthai* (with or without the preposition *kata*, i.e., being predicated of) are not meant to reliably indicate the terminological use signifying a non-linguistic relation in the sense of being SAID OF. Especially the use of *katēgoreisthai* is vexed, since in ordinary, non-terminological usage it would be fully interchangeable with *legesthai kata tinos/legesthai tinos* and in some places in the *Categories* it actually seems to take

---

[20] Here is the full Greek formulation: τούτων γὰρ ὄνομα μόνον κοινόν, ὁ δὲ κατὰ τοὔνομα λόγος {τῆς οὐσίας} ἕτερος.

ESSENTIAL PREDICATION IN ARISTOTLE'S *CATEGORIES*   155

the place of *legesthai tinos*; however, if one takes *katēgoreisthai* as indicating the terminological relation of being SAID OF, all kinds of things could be SAID OF a substrate, many of which do not contribute to the what-is of this substrate. In order to defend a traditional reading, one has to assume that *katēgoreisthai* (or *katēgoreisthai tinos*) does not get introduced as an alternative rendering of *legesthai kata tinos* or *legesthai tinos*, but as a word that can correspond to both relations, being SAID OF and being IN, and is often used to signal the linguistic predication that corresponds to either of these two relations. Why *katēgoreisthai* is chosen to do this particular job is hard to tell, but if we suppose that the phrase *legesthai kata tinos* or *legesthai tinos* was already taken for its terminological use, the choice of *katēgoreisthai* for linguistic predications is not too outlandish. As a preliminary warrant for this suggested understanding of Aristotle's terminology I just want to refer to two relatively central passages from *Categories* 5:

[T2]   It is clear from what has been said that of the things that are said of a substrate (τῶν καθ᾿ ὑποκειμένου λεγομένων) both each thing's name and its definition are necessarily predicated of the substrate (κατηγορεῖσθαι τοῦ ὑποκειμένου). For example, human is said of a substrate (καθ᾿ ὑποκειμένου λέγεται), the particular human, and the name is also predicated (καὶ κατηγορεῖταί γε τοὔνομα), since you will be predicating human of the particular human (κατὰ τοῦ τινὸς ἀνθρώπου κατηγορήσεις), and also the definition of human will be predicated of the particular human (κατὰ τοῦ τινὸς ἀνθρώπου κατηγορηθήσεται), since the particular human is also a human. Thus both the name and the definition will be predicated of the substrate (κατὰ τοῦ ὑποκειμένου κατηγορηθήσεται).[21]

This passage is instructive for the transition from relations between beings or things (e.g., the relation of being SAID OF) to the corresponding predication. If X is SAID OF Y, we said, it is natural to assume that X and Y are beings and that the relation of being SAID OF is a relation between things or beings, but not between linguistic entities. Now, names and definitions are both linguistic entities if we take the definition to be the *definiens* or the defining clause. Names and definitions are attached to the entities they are the names and definitions of. Therefore, it is fully consistent that, when we move from the relation between things (e.g., that one is SAID OF the other) to names and definitions, the phrase that is used to signify the relations between things, *legesthai kata tinos*, is not repeated; rather Aristotle uses here *kategoreisthai* to refer to the linguistic predication or linguistic act of predication that corresponds to this relation. Consider the following sentence from [T2]: 'For example, human is said of a substrate (καθ᾿ ὑποκειμένου

---

[21]   *Cat.* 5, 2a19–27; translation based on Ackrill's.

156   CHRISTOF RAPP

λέγεται), the particular human, and the name is also predicated (καὶ κατηγορεῖταί γε τοὔνομα)…' This sentence would be tautological as long as we do not assume a clear-cut transition from beings to the words that we use to refer to these beings (i.e., either names or definitions); and it is, on our reading, precisely this transition that motivates the shift from *legesthai kata tinos* (being SAID OF) to *katēgoreisthai* (being predicated of).

[T3]   Further, it is because the primary substances are substrates for everything else that they are called substances most strictly. But as the primary substances stand to everything else, so the species and genera of the primary substances [i.e., the secondary substances] stand to all the rest: all the rest are predicated of these (κατὰ τούτων γὰρ πάντα τὰ λοιπὰ κατηγορεῖται). For if you will call (ἐρεῖς) the individual man knowledgeable-in-grammar (γραμματικὸν), then you will call (ἐρεῖς) both a man and an animal knowledgeable-in-grammar; and similarly in other cases.[22]

The passage claims that the secondary substances are the substrates for 'all the rest'; 'all the rest' clearly includes non-substantial predicates; and, indeed, the example mentioned is an example of a non-substantial attribute: namely, *grammatikos* (i.e., knowledgeable-in-grammar). These non-substantial things or predicates, he says, are predicated (*katēgoreitai*) of the secondary substances; this claim would make little sense, if *katēgoreisthai* were restricted to species- and genus-predicates that say *what* a thing *is*. Given that it elsewhere corresponds to the SAID OF relation (as in [T2] above) and given that in [T3] it cannot correspond to the SAID OF relation, it follows that it is used in a way that is *neutral* to the difference between the relations of being SAID OF and being IN something as a substrate. Aristotle also says here that when we *call* an individual human *grammatikos*, we will also *call* human and animal *grammatikos*, where the Greek word for 'call' is *ereis*, a future form of *legein*. This illustrates that the mere presence of the word *legein* or *legesthai* does not by itself indicate the relation of being SAID OF, as argued above, but that only the verbal phrase *legesthai kata tinos* or *legesthai tinos* is meant to do this job.

By and large, the *Categories* sticks to this convention. In many instances, I admit, it remains unclear or indeterminate whether *katēgoreisthai* refers to a relation between things in the world or between linguistic entities, presumably because it often does not seem to matter whether one speaks of the underlying non-linguistic (or 'metaphysical') relation or of the way in which this relation is mirrored in a linguistic predication.[23] Often, however, commentators treat *katēgoreisthai* with

---

[22]   *Cat.* 5, 2b37–3a6; translation based on Ackrill's.
[23]   Crivelli 2017, 532 gives a list of occurrences of *katēgoreisthai* that, in his view, express a relation obtaining between things in the world, not between linguistic entities. I admit that these cases do not clearly instantiate linguistic predication; however, I would insist that they are also not explicitly non-linguistic cases. Rather I would rate them as not clearly falling into one of these two classes.

or without *kata* just as a variant name for the relation usually referred to by *legesthai kata tinos* or *legesthai tinos*, presumably because they do not acknowledge its peculiar function in the transition from the relation between beings to the predicative relation between linguistic entities. The failure to acknowledge that *katēgoreisthai* can have a proper function in expressing linguistic predications and that as a linguistic predication it can correspond to both the being SAID OF and the being IN relation leads to, as it were, 'apostate' interpretations.

3.2 Andronicus' Challenge (with a Little Help from Stephen Menn)

An early report of such an apostate reading of SAID OF is given by Simplicius (*In Cat.* 54, 8–21 (Kalbfleisch)) who says that Andronicus (i.e., Andronicus of Rhodes, the famous editor of the Aristotelian oeuvre) and 'some others' said that not only secondary substances but also certain other things can be SAID OF[24] primary substances, as for example 'musical' or 'musician' (*mousikos*) is SAID OF Aristoxenus and 'Athenian' and 'philosopher' is SAID OF Socrates. It is clear that, if we allow for this possibility, the difference between being SAID OF and being IN would become slippery, for according to the traditional reading, Aristotle requires that what is IN a substrate is not SAID OF the same substrate. As a possible explanation for Andronicus' claim, Simplicius offers the linguistic criterion of whether we can or cannot say that a substrate *is* this thing: for example, we cannot say that Socrates *is* 'to walk' (*badizein*; i.e., we cannot say that Socrates is the activity of walking), but we could say that he *is* an Athenian or a philosopher. If this is indeed the rationale behind Andronicus' claim, everything that can be predicated by the use of the copula *is* would be SAID OF a substance, so that the connection between being SAID OF and answers to the question of *what* something *is* would vanish. Moraux tried to justify Andronicus' move by appealing to the idea of *sumbebēkota kath' hauta*: that is, attributes that are not part of the subject's essence, but are so closely connected with the essence—or this is Moraux's understanding—that the subject would cease to be what it is without these attributes.[25] This explanation seems to be quite far-fetched and it does not fit the given examples, for Socrates would certainly not cease to be what he is without being a philosopher or an Athenian (in spite of the patriotic commitment to Athens that he expresses in the *Crito*). Sharples quotes Moraux approvingly, but apparently tries to make more sense of his strategy by saying that 'Athenian philosopher' can

---

[24] Simplicius uses *katēgoreisthai kata*, but it is clear from the context that he is referring to being SAID OF.

[25] See Moraux 1973, 105: 'Auch Aristoteles hatte nämlich darauf hingewiesen, daß gewisse Eigenschaften, ohne dem Wesen eines Dinges zuzugehören, so eng von diesem Wesen abhängen, daß das Dinge aufhören würde, das zu sein, was es ist, wenn sie nicht mehr vorhanden wären.'

158   CHRISTOF RAPP

be seen as defining characteristics of Socrates (thus appealing to a sort of individual essence, it seems) in a way 'walking' cannot.[26]

Menn rejects this line of defence (rightly so, I think) altogether[27] and supplies a different justification for Andronicus' claim, which requires a non-technical use of 'being said of' and 'being predicated of'. In short, Menn's argument relies on the context we discussed in section 2 above (see [T1]). Of things that are IN a substrate, Aristotle says, in most cases neither the name nor the substrate is predicated of the substrate; however, it is possible to predicate, for example, 'knowledgeable-in-grammar' (*grammatikos*) of certain subjects. How is this possible? Well, because *grammatikos*, as opposed to *hē grammatikē* (the knowledge-of-grammar), is not IN a substrate. So Andronicus would have good reasons to interpret the *Categories* as saying that paronyms, such as *grammatikos*, can be said of a substrate, taking 'being said of' (*legesthai kata tinos*) in the usual, not in the technical sense (i.e., without aligning them to essential or quasi-essential predications). The same is true of the supposedly homonymous case of *leukon* (see section 2 above), for it refers to the inhering property of whiteness that is clearly not predicable, whereas the predicable concrete adjective is not IN its substrate and can hence be predicated of it.[28]

This is an understanding of the *Categories* Menn himself is sympathetic to, for Aristotle himself, he argues, says little about those paronymous terms and most notably does not mention them when he introduces the two relations of being IN and being SAID OF. From this perspective Andronicus could be used as a witness for a supposedly primordial reading of the *Categories* that predates the formation of the orthodox essentialist reading. However, even if Menn is right that this possibility is not strictly speaking ruled out by anything in the *Categories*, his suggestion would require taking *katēgoreisthai kata tinos* as not distinct from *legesthai kata tinos* or 'being said of', since passage [T1] is about things that can be predicated (*katēgoreisthai*) of certain substrates. Also, given that the examples that Simplicius reports do not seem to refer to random properties, but to more stable significations ('Athenian', 'philosopher' are indeed more stable signifiers;[29] and *mousikos* would also fall in this group, if we read it as 'musician'), Andronicus' remark could also, more easily and more prosaically, be motivated by passages in the *Categories* where people are called (*legetai*, *legomenos*) or given descriptions in accordance with their more permanent qualities ('the dark one', 'the irascible

---

[26]   Sharples 2010, 85.

[27]   Menn 2018, 15; see his n. 5 for a fuller documentation of related positions.

[28]   And what is more, if we think that homonymy, as opposed to paronymy, refers to two distinct entities, as we suggested above in section 2 (at least the ontological free-lunch option was not available to the homonymous interpretation), one might all the more be inclined to ask how the entity signified by the concrete adjective *leukon* might fit into the fourfold ontology if it is not IN the substrate. One might be tempted to answer—with Menn's Andronicus—that it is SAID OF it.

[29]   Chiaradonna, Rashed, and Sedley 2013, 170, highlight that these are topological and toponymic identifiers.

one'). Similarly, in *Categories* 10, Aristotle says 'the man is called (*legetai*) blind' (12a41). Observations like these might have given rise to interpretations along the lines of Moraux and Sharples. The point, however, is not to justify Andronicus' view by equating such quasi-sortal identifiers with essential predication (as Moraux and Sharples did); the point is rather that in the *Categories* Aristotle does as a matter of fact call people by designations deriving from their more permanent properties and that for this purpose he regularly uses cognates of *legesthai*.[30] Andronicus might have referred to this non-terminological use (on our reading, it is *obviously* non-terminological, because in none of these examples does Aristotle use the decisive formula *legesthai kata tinos*) or he might have been led into thinking by such examples that the range of things that can be SAID OF a substrate is actually broader than what has been suggested in *Categories* 2 (an assumption that is unwarranted by the given examples: see n. 32).

3.3 A Competing Attempt to Codify Aristotle's Practice

In a painstaking paper,[31] Paolo Crivelli challenges the traditional reading of being SAID OF by trying to show that in certain contexts 'being predicated of' (*katēgoreisthai tinos*) is contextually restricted to having exactly the same meaning as 'being SAID OF' (*legesthai kata tinos*). He then refers to passages from the *Postpraedicamenta*, where according to his account this contextual restriction is given and where Aristotle says that 'odd' and 'even' are predicated of numbers and 'good' and 'bad' are predicated of humans; since these attributes are not meant to be essential, the SAID OF relation (here allegedly being expressed by *katēgoreisthai*), Crivelli concludes, cannot be taken to indicate essential predication. Obviously, this would provide a serious challenge to all essentialist readings of the *Categories*.

---

[30] In *Categories* 8, the phenomenon of using 'the one-who-is-knowledgeable-in-grammar' as quasi-sortal in order to give a rather permanent characterization of a certain person seems to be peculiar to qualities and, more specifically, to certain stable qualities; for, in general, qualities are defined as 'that in virtue of which things are said to be qualified somehow (*poioi tines legontai*)', and the Greek phrase *poios tis legesthai* seems to suggest (not only that a certain quality-indicating adjective can be predicated of a subject, but more specifically) that someone is addressed or called in accordance with a certain quality: for example, as 'the one-who-is-knowledgeable-in-grammar' or 'the pale one'—instead of using, for example, proper names. According to Aristotle, this is only possible for relatively permanent qualities: for example, someone can be called 'the pale one' or 'the dark one' only if this qualification derives from a natural make-up or from a long-lasting disease or sunburn, but not if the pallor or darkness just derives from an easily dispersing affection, just as we would not call someone 'the red one' (or so Aristotle says), if his or her redness derived from a sudden momentary blushing (*Cat.* 8, 9b19–33). At least in these cases, it is obvious that the defining characteristic of qualities (i.e., that someone is called or addressed in virtue of this quality as being somehow qualified) does not boil down to ordinary predication, for there is no problem in saying of the momentarily blushing person that she is red, while it is not possible, according to Aristotle, to address her as 'the red one'.

[31] Crivelli 2017.

160 CHRISTOF RAPP

Crivelli's claim is based on a careful inventory and classification of all phrases by which the *Categories* usually refers to the fundamental relations that obtain between beings. One of the main results of this endeavour is that according to Crivelli the verb-phrase 'to be predicated of' (*katēgoreisthai kata* or *katēgoreisthai* with genitive) can be used—roughly speaking—in an exclusive and in an inclusive sense: namely, in an exclusive sense when it amounts to the same relation that is given when X is SAID OF Y, and in an inclusive sense when it comprises both the relation that is given when X is SAID OF Y and the relation that is given when X is IN Y. He thus objects to the widespread view that 'being predicated of' is automatically the same as 'being SAID OF'. He also formulates a rule for when the exclusive use comes into play: the meaning of 'to be predicated' (*katēgoreisthai*) becomes contextually restricted when it is employed in tandem with formulations indicating the relation of being IN a substrate.[32] He derives this rule from the discussion of one single passage in *Categories* 5 (2a24–b6). Next he turns to a troublesome passage in *Categories* 10 about opposites with and without intermediates (11b38–12a17), where Aristotle says that 'odd' and 'even' are *predicated of* (*katēgoreisthai kata*) numbers and 'bad' and 'good' are *predicated of* (*katēgoreisthai kata*) humans. Since in this passage being *predicated of* is distinguished from being IN, Crivelli wants to apply his general rule that, when *predicated of* is coupled with being IN, the meaning of *predicated of* is contextually restricted and amounts to being SAID OF.

In what follows I want to respond to Crivelli's argument in three steps. (1) Even if there are contextual restrictions to the meaning of *predicated of*, it is not warranted to assume that Aristotle always sticks to the same rules for using the restricted meanings; even if the two phrases 'being predicated of' and 'being IN' are coupled, he might use the first phrase in an unrestricted way. (I will refrain from commenting on the fact that the *Postpraedicamenta* is a far cry from the terminologically scrupulous passages from the beginning of the treatise that are the main basis for the terminological use of SAID OF.) (2) In order to assume that the neighbourhood of the phrase 'being IN' restricts the meaning of 'being predicated of', it is not enough to say that they are 'coupled'; the restriction only follows if it is the purpose of a passage to *contrast* 'being IN' with a distinct relation, the one of being SAID OF (which is indeed the case in Crivelli's key piece of evidence of *Cat.* 5, 2a24–b6). (3) In [T4] 'being in'[33] and 'being predicated of' are not contrasted; on the contrary, they are used in a parallel manner. The distinction between 'being IN' and 'being predicated of' is just not the issue here. In conclusion, there is no reason for assuming that when Aristotle says in [T4] that 'odd'

---

[32] Crivelli 2017, 353.
[33] I don't capitalize occurrences of 'in' in this particular passage, since I am not sure whether 'being in' or 'coming to be in' respectively in [T4] is used in the terminological sense at all, but, of course, I neither want to preclude this possibility.

ESSENTIAL PREDICATION IN ARISTOTLE'S *CATEGORIES*   161

and 'even' are predicated of numbers and 'bad' and 'good' predicated of humans, he would indicate that these are SAID OF the others. Since (1) and (2) are self-explanatory, I will focus on (3): that is, on Crivelli's treatment of [T4].

[T4]   (i) If contraries are such that it is necessary for one or the other of them to belong to the things they naturally come to be in or are predicated of (ἐν οἷς πέφυκε γίγνεσθαι ἢ ὧν κατηγορεῖται), there is nothing intermediate between them. (a) For example, sickness and health naturally occur (πέφυκε γίγνεσθαι) in animals' bodies and it is indeed necessary for one or the other to belong to an animal's body, either sickness or health; (b) again, odd and even are predicated of (κατηγορεῖται) numbers, and it is indeed necessary for one or the other to belong to a number, either odd or even. And between these there is certainly nothing intermediate—between sickness and health or odd and even. (ii) But if it is not necessary for one or the other to belong, there is something intermediate between them. (a) For example, black and white naturally occur (πέφυκε γίγνεσθαι) in bodies, but it is not necessary for one or the other of them to belong to a body (for not every body is either white or black); (b) again, bad and good (καὶ φαῦλον δὲ καὶ σπουδαῖον) are predicated (κατηγορεῖται) both of humans and of many other things, but it is not necessary for one or the other of them to belong to those things they are predicated of (κατηγορεῖται), for not all are either bad or good.[34]

The structure of this passage is straightforward: (i) There are contraries without intermediates; in this case it is necessary that one or the other of the contraries actually belong to the subject in which they naturally come to be or of which they are (naturally) predicated. (ii) There are contraries admitting of intermediates; here it is not the case that one or the other contrary necessarily belongs to the subject in which they naturally come to be or of which they are naturally predicated. For each group Aristotle gives two examples: (i.a) sickness and health, (i.b) odd and even, (ii.a) black and white, (ii.b) bad and good. The purpose of the passage is clear: it aims at distinguishing two kinds of contrary.

'Being in' is nowhere mentioned, but Aristotle speaks of the subjects 'in which (*en hois*)' these contraries naturally come to be (*gignesthai*). Crivelli is bound to argue that 'come to be in' amounts to 'to be IN', as the former describes the process that leads to the condition expressed by the latter.[35] I find this move only partially convincing, since, by the same token, we could turn each and every non-technical use of 'in' (most notably, mereological uses, e.g., 'the ulcer comes to be in the stomach') into the technical sense of 'being IN'. Also, given that the

---

[34] *Cat.* 10, 11b38–12a17; Ackrill's translation, with my numbering.
[35] See Crivelli 2017, 536.

162   CHRISTOF RAPP

terminological regimentation in *Categories* 2 was quite unequivocal in this respect, why should Aristotle modify this terminology at his convenience? Even if we grant this move, we should, however, bear in mind that not all cases of 'being IN' are the result of processes of 'coming to be in': some things might be IN their substrates without any process.

According to general Aristotelian doctrine, contraries belong to the same subjects, but cannot obtain of one and the same subject at the same time; different contraries require different kinds of subject that are 'receptive' (*dektikon*) of this particular kind of contraries. This relation between a given pair of contraries and their proper subjects can be expressed by phrases including the formulation 'by nature' (here: *pephuken*)—that is, by the nature of the receiving subject or by the nature of the contraries—and *pephuken* is regularly followed by *gignesthai* (to come to be), which is a standing idiom in Aristotelian language. Using this standard formulation for a common piece of Aristotelian doctrine, our present passage introduces subjects in which the contraries naturally come to be (ἐν οἷς πέφυκε γίγνεσθαι); as an alternative to 'in which they naturally come to be', he adds 'or of which they are predicated', which is a bit imprecise, because he must mean 'of which they are *naturally* predicated' in the sense explicated above. This alternative might have been added because it is less narrow than 'naturally coming to be'; when it comes to example (i.b), this generosity is an advantage, for 'odd' and 'even' do not, literally speaking, *come to be* in numbers, they are just predicated of them. From this perspective, 'coming to be in' and 'being predicated of' are not contrasted, but express two parallel ways of how the contraries belong to their subjects: 'in which they naturally come to be or, more generally speaking, of which they are naturally predicated'.

Now Crivelli is, of course, right to observe that in both parts, (i) and (ii), Aristotle gives a pair of contraries which 'naturally comes to be in' its subject—(i.a) and (ii.a)—and one pair of contraries that is 'predicated of' its subject—(i.b) and (ii.b). This is indeed an interesting observation; it could be used to say that the two cases (i) and (ii) are exemplified by two pairs of contraries representing two distinct relations. And in this sense, one could insist (and Crivelli would have to insist) that this is a context in which 'being predicated of' (in the sense of being SAID OF) is contrasted with 'being in' (in the sense of being IN something). However, it seems that (i.a) and (ii.a) on the one hand and (i.b) and (ii.b) on the other are not meant to contrast two distinct relations. We already pointed out for section (i) that the transition from (i.a) sickness and health that *come to be in* animals' bodies to (i.b) odd and even that *are predicated of* numbers could be triggered by the narrowness of the 'naturally come to be in'-phrase, since neither numbers nor their properties come to be. In addition, it would be odd to say (in analogy to sickness and health which are *in* animals' bodies) that 'odd' and 'even' are *in* numbers—with or without the technical sense of being IN something. If this (the narrowness of the 'come to be in'-rendering) is the reason for changing

ESSENTIAL PREDICATION IN ARISTOTLE'S *CATEGORIES*   163

to the 'being predicated of'-rendering when it comes to (i.b), the formulation 'being predicated of' would not be meant to exemplify the relation of being SAID OF, but would be a more appropriate way of attributing 'odd' and 'even' to numbers.

The transition from (ii.a) 'black' and 'white' that *come to be in* bodies to (ii.b) 'bad' and 'good' that *are predicated of* their substrates in section (ii) can be explained correspondingly. To begin with, if Aristotle intended the terminological sense of being IN, he should (and would?) not have used 'black' and 'white' without definite article in (ii.a). In *Categories* 5 (see the discussion in section 2 above) he used, after all, *to leukon*, '*the* white', when saying that the white is IN the body. In the adjacent chapter *Categories* 11, Aristotle is happy in a similar context to shift to the abstract nouns 'blackness' (*melania*) and 'whiteness' (*leukotēs*), with regard to which it would be more appropriate to say that they are IN the body in the terminological sense. This provides an additional reason for thinking that no terminological sense was intended. No terminological sense of being IN, no contextual restriction of 'to be predicated' (according to Crivelli's rule). More than that, 'bad' and 'good' are probably not the kinds of property that always *come to be* in their subjects by way of a process; at least in some kinds of subject they do not, so that the formulation 'in which they naturally come to be' would be inadequate for the wide range of heterogeneous subjects to which these predicates are applicable. On top of this, 'bad' and 'good' are applicable to a wide range of possible subjects: they have no proper subjects to which they 'naturally' belong or in which they 'naturally come to be'; the shift to an alternative formulation for attributing 'bad' and 'good' to a human being is inevitable for this simple reason;[36] accordingly, 'being predicated of' is used in the most neutral way. Again, if these are the reasons for the terminological shift between example (ii.a) and (ii.b), the purpose would be to make the point about contraries without intermediate as broad as possible and not to contrast the relation of being IN with the relation of being SAID OF.

At this point, one might object with regard to the particular example (ii.b) that, according to *Cat.* 11, 14a23–5, 'good' and 'bad' (this time *agathon* and *kakon*) are genera and that, as genera, they can be SAID OF their substrates in the terminological sense.[37] It is unclear, though, how this claim relates to the notorious problem of the trans-categorical character of good and bad. Also, it seems that, even if they *can* sometimes be taken as genera, they are not always genera; for clearly,

---

[36] 'Bad' and 'good' in *Categories* 10 translate the Greek words *phaulon* and *spoudaion*, which might have a narrower sense; most notably, *spoudaios* is one of Aristotle's favourite terms for a virtuous person, so that one might speculate about whether 'bad' and 'good' in this example are restricted to the moral sense of being bad or good. This would comply with the fact that they are predicated of a human being—however, and this speaks against a narrow moral sense of 'bad' and 'good', Aristotle adds in passing that they can be predicated of other things (καὶ κατ' ἄλλων) as well.

[37] I owe this objection to one of the anonymous readers.

164   CHRISTOF RAPP

neither of them is the genus of human being. And if, according to example (ii.b), *both* of them are attributed to human beings, they cannot be *genera* of human beings by the same token, for no subject belongs to contrary genera. This blocks the objection that the *Categories* 11 thesis about good and bad as genera could apply to the given example. If we consider, by contrast, cases in which either good or bad actually serves as the genus (*Topics* 4 repeatedly refers to pleasure or the pleasant as a possible example for something that is in the genus of good), we would get genuine examples of being SAID OF predications that indicate the essential genus of its subject; however, since in these cases 'good' is considered as part of the essence, we do not get the kind of example Crivelli is looking for: namely, non-essential predicates that are nevertheless SAID OF their subjects.

Even though sometimes the possibility of a consistent, terminological reading of *legesthai kata tinos* in the sense of being SAID OF a substrate seems to be hanging by a thread, the counterexamples offered by the 'apostate' readers do not compel us to give up the plausible idea that Aristotle at least intended a consistent terminological use and that this terminological use was meant to be connected with essential predication.

4. The *Categories'* Sortal Essentialism

The backbone of the *Categories'* essentialism is the distinction between the two relations of being IN and being SAID OF. In the preceding sections I tried to defend the distinctness of these two relations. Assuming now that they are indeed distinct and that the SAID OF relation is meant to capture the relation between an essence and what it is the essence of, what does the *Categories'* essentialism look like?

Throughout the *Categories*, Aristotle seems to presuppose that primary substances inevitably belong to certain secondary substances: that is, to a certain species and to the corresponding genera.[38] Since both the name and the definition of the secondary substances hold of the substrates they are SAID OF, the secondary substances signify what primary substances are. This is why a particular substance is called what it is called—for example, 'a particular human' or 'this human'—in accordance with what is SAID OF it. In the *Categories*, primary substances are always denoted like this: that is, by a sortal term and not, for example, by a proper name such as Socrates or Bucephalus (except in the *Postpraedicamenta*). In a similar vein, Aristotle insists that primary substances—and only primary substances—

---

[38] What he actually says is this: 'The species in which the things primarily called substances are (ἐν οἷς εἴδεσιν αἱ πρώτως οὐσίαι λεγόμεναι ὑπάρχουσιν), are called secondary substances, as also are the genera of these species' (*Cat.* 5, 2a14–16). Remarkably, he describes the relation between primary substances and their species by saying that the former 'are in', 'belong in', or 'are found in' (*huparchein en*) the latter. Clearly, this is not meant to be the IN of inherence. Here the preposition 'in' rather hints at the relation of being included in a class or being a member of a class.

ESSENTIAL PREDICATION IN ARISTOTLE'S *CATEGORIES*   165

signify a 'certain this' (*tode ti*), 'for the thing revealed is individual and numerically one' (*Cat.* 5, 3b10–13). Since primary substances are 'revealed', 'disclosed', or 'made obvious' (*dēloumenon*) by the secondary substances to which they belong, the point of saying that primary substances signify a 'certain this' seems to be that they are countable, individual objects exhibiting sortal determinacy. In this sense it seems to be essential to each primary substance that it belong to a secondary substance and thus that it be a member of a certain species (and its corresponding genera).[39]

If we want to look deeper into the relation between primary and secondary substances, we must start from the fact that the latter depend for their existence on the former, for the *Categories* defends what has been labelled 'Aristotelian realism': namely, the position that there are no non-instantiated universals: 'So if the primary substances did not exist it would be impossible for any of the other things to exist.'[40] It is a more challenging question whether, and if so how, primary substances depend on secondary ones:

[T5]   It is reasonable that, after the primary substances, their species and genera should be the only other things called secondary substances. For only they, of things predicated, reveal the primary substance ($\mu\acute{o}\nu\alpha$ $\gamma\grave{\alpha}\rho$ $\delta\eta\lambda o\hat{\iota}$ $\tau\grave{\eta}\nu$ $\pi\rho\acute{\omega}\tau\eta\nu$ $o\mathring{v}\sigma\acute{\iota}\alpha\nu$ $\tau\hat{\omega}\nu$ $\kappa\alpha\tau\eta\gamma o\rho o\nu\mu\acute{\epsilon}\nu\omega\nu$). For if one is to say of the particular human what he is, it will be appropriate to give ($o\mathring{\iota}\kappa\epsilon\acute{\iota}\omega s$ $\mathring{\alpha}\pi o\delta\acute{\omega}\sigma\epsilon\iota$) the species or the genus (though more informative ($\gamma\nu\omega\rho\iota\mu\acute{\omega}\tau\epsilon\rho o\nu$ $\pi o\iota\acute{\eta}\sigma\epsilon\iota$) to give human than animal).[41]

What does it mean to 'reveal' or 'disclose' a primary substance? Even though the term *dēloun* seems to appeal to the epistemic state of the one who has asked in the first place *what* a particular human *is* and to whom the primary substance is 'revealed', it is clear in our context that the success of 'revealing the primary substance' is not meant to be dependent on the knowledge actually possessed by one or another inquirer. Rather it seems that what we do when we 'reveal a primary substance' is to reveal a fact about it that exhibits it as an object of knowledge in general—a knowable object—regardless of the cognitive states of any individual inquirer. At the same time, saying that the secondary substance 'reveals' or

---

[39]   All this is not meant to imply that the *Categories*' essentialism would be restricted to substances. Clearly, there are essential predicates that can be SAID OF non-substantial entities. However, while the *Categories* has a good deal to say about the relation of primary and secondary substances, it does not expand on the what-it-is of accidental attributes; in particular, we do not really know what the definitions of accidental attributes look like. It therefore seems as if the *Categories* is committed to a (not only sortal) general term essentialism, even though it shows little interest in the non-sortal cases. The *Topics*, by contrast, explicitly develops an unrestricted general term essentialism and requires essences for virtually all subjects of discourse (which are, for the most part, general terms); correspondingly, the *Topics* does not share the *Categories*' emphasis on primary substances as ultimate substrates.

[40]   *Cat.* 5, 2b5–6; Ackrill's translation.

[41]   *Cat.* 5, 2b29–34; Ackrill's translation, slightly altered.

166 CHRISTOF RAPP

'discloses' the primary one does not amount to saying, or so it seems, that it *makes* the primary substance the kind of thing it is or that it *is the cause of its being* a member of this particular species. By contrast, this seems to be precisely the job of forms within the hylomorphic theory of Aristotle's *Metaphysics* (for forms, as opposed to universals such as species and genera, are causally involved in the physical world). There, forms and essences are supposed to do some significant causal-explanatory work: it is because of a certain form belonging to a portion of matter that there is a particular compound that is so-and-so specified and thus qualifies as a member of a certain kind (and all this, one might say, is connected with the *Metaphysics'* prevalent interest in principles and causes). For this reason, the provocatively sparse language with which the *Categories* describes the crucial role of secondary substances—that they 'reveal' the primary substances—might be deliberately chosen: they 'reveal', 'exhibit', 'disclose', or *explicate* a basic fact about primary substance—namely, that they instantiate a certain species—but they themselves do not ground this fact nor are they 'causes of being' of these primary substances, in the way in which forms are supposed to be 'causes of being' in the *Metaphysics*. In this sense, it seems that the job of the *Categories'* essentialism—though a genuine essentialism—is entirely different from that of the *Metaphysics'* essentialism; at any rate, it does not seem to be 'causal' or 'explanatory'[42] in the sense just described.

What should we make of this difference between the *Categories* and the *Metaphysics?* The two most promising options seem to be these. *Either* the *Categories* is just not interested in principles and causes, as the *Metaphysics* is, and thus deliberately refrains from going into the kinds of question that, in the *Metaphysics*, lead to the claims that essences are causes of being and that forms, being the essences of compound substances, are prior to these compound beings. *Or* the *Categories* just considers it a basic, unanalysable fact that primary substances instantiate certain general kinds, in disagreement with the *Metaphysics'* claim that the forms and essences explain how a particular must be constituted in order to qualify as a particular substance of a certain kind. Whichever reading we prefer, it is not at all strange to assume that the small, mostly classificatory treatise, *Categories*, defends a sort of essentialism—as long as we do not overload it with expectations taken from the *Metaphysics*.[43]

---

[42] In a different sense, Aristotle's essentialism is said to be 'explanatory' in that the essence is supposed to explain the per se-attributes of all members of a given species. In this sense (which is succinctly presented, e.g., in *DA* 1.1, 402b21–403a2) explanatory essentialism is the crucial idea underlying the demonstrations in the *Posterior Analytics*. Since the *Categories* does not introduce per se-attributes (nor *idia/propria*, i.e., peculiar attributes, which are sometimes thought to take the place of necessary, non-essential attributes), it is also not explicitly committed to *this* sort of explanatory essentialism (even though the *Categories* acknowledges that, e.g., numbers need to be either odd or even, and living bodies either healthy or sick, which comes close to the concept of necessary per se-attributes).

[43] For helpful comments I would like to thank Paolo Fait, Michail Peramatzis, Christopher Shields, and the anonymous readers.

Works Cited

Ackrill, J. L. 1963. *Aristotle* Categories *and* De Interpretatione. *Translated with Notes and Glossary.* Clarendon Aristotle Series. Clarendon Press.

Bodéüs, Richard. 2002. *Aristote: Catégories.* Les Belles Lettres.

Busse, Adolph. 1887. *Porphyrii in Aristotelis Categorias Commentarium.* Reimer.

Chiaradonna, Riccardo, Marwan Rashed, and David Sedley. 2013. 'A Rediscovered *Categories* Commentary', *Oxford Studies in Ancient Philosophy* 44, 129–94.

Crivelli, Paolo. 2017. 'Being-Said-Of in Aristotle's *Categories*', *Rivista di Filosofia Neo-Scolastica* 3, 531–56.

Kalbfleisch, Carolus (ed.). 1907. *Simplicii in Aristotelis Categorias Commentarium.* Reimer.

Mann, Wolfgang-Rainer. 2000. *The Discovery of Things: Aristotle's* Categories *and Their Context.* Princeton University Press.

Menn, Stephen. 1995. 'Metaphysics, Dialectic, and the *Categories*', *Revue de Métaphysique et de Morale* 100, 311–37.

Menn, Stephen. 2018. 'Andronicus and Boethus: Reflections on Michael Griffin's *Aristotle's* Categories *in the Early Roman Empire*', *Documenti e studi sulla tradizione filosofica medievale* 29, 13–44.

Minio-Paluello, Lorenzo. 1949. *Aristotelis Categoriae et Liber de Interpretatione.* Oxford Classical Texts. Clarendon Press.

Moraux, Paul. 1973. *Der Aristotelismus bei den Griechen* I. De Gruyter.

Sharples, Robert W. 2010. *Peripatetic Philosophy 200 BC to AD 200.* Cambridge University Press.

Shields, Christopher. 1999. Order in Multiplicity: Homonymy in the Philosophy of Aristotle. Oxford University Press.

Tolkiehn, Niels. 2020. *The Notions of Homonymy, Synonymy, Multivocity, and Pros Hen in Aristotle.* Doctoral thesis, LMU Munich.

8

Aristotle on How Essence Grounds Necessity

Michail Peramatzis

Introduction

Aristotle does not conceive necessity as primitive or basic. Rather, he maintains that necessary features of (types of) things are grounded in their essence.[1] Equivalently, propositions which ascribe necessary features to things are grounded in propositions about what essentially holds of those things.[2] Since he takes 'necessarily' as equivalent to 'not possibly not',[3] it seems that, in his view, modality quite generally is grounded in essence, while the converse is not the case. After sketching the main aspects of his view in section 1, I shall discuss whether and, if so, how Aristotle's essentialism can sustain this claim of asymmetry of essence over necessity. I shall argue that to underwrite this asymmetry we have to adopt a strong interpretation of his thesis that essence (the 'what-it-is') and cause (the 'why-it-is') are the same. While essence and cause are neither to be identified nor reduced to one another, they are the same or interdependent in that any essence intrinsically involves not only a thin, formal but also a robust, efficient, final, or material type of cause. Conversely, too, at least in the central cases an Aristotelian cause is sensitive to the nature of the relevant item caused (the *explanandum*) in that it determines (at least partly) that item's identity. I shall conclude by spelling out some of the implications of this interdependence view and by raising some important questions about it.

---

[1] In this sense, Aristotle is a 'non-modal' essentialist. Non-modal essentialism does not characterize essence on the basis of (modal) necessity. Rather, it normally takes essence as basic and uses it to set out necessity. A central example of a modern non-modal essentialist is Kit Fine; see his 1994a, 1994b, 1995a, 1995b.

[2] For present purposes, I shall use the verb 'to ground' and its cognates in a general and non-committal way to include, or not rule out, explaining, founding, underpinning, etc. What seems to unify such notions is the idea that something (the grounded item) obtains 'because of' or 'in virtue of' something else (the ground) whereas the converse is not the case. This idea can, I shall assume, be taken either propositionally or non-propositionally in the manner I just suggested.

[3] See, for example, *De Int.* 13, 22a20–2. Aristotle describes the implications among his modal notions at 22a14–31. Similarly, at *APr.* 1.13, 32a21–8, he maintains that 'impossible' and 'necessarily not' are the same or mutually entailed. See also *Met.* Δ.12, 1019b23–30: ἀδύνατον μὲν οὖ τὸ ἐναντίον ἐξ ἀνάγκης ἀληθές … δυνατόν, ὅταν μὴ ἀναγκαῖον ᾖ τὸ ἐναντίον ψεῦδος εἶναι.

Michail Peramatzis, *Aristotle on How Essence Grounds Necessity* In: *Aristotelian Metaphysics: Essays in Honour of David Charles*. Edited by: David Bronstein, Thomas Kjeller Johansen, and Michail Peramatzis, Oxford University Press.
© Oxford University Press 2024. DOI: 10.1093/oso/9780198908678.003.0008

1. Essence, Cause, Necessity, and Asymmetry: An Outline

I shall understand Aristotle's essentialism as consisting of the following four theses. Due to limitations of space, I shall assume that these theses could be accepted (at least roughly) by most interpreters.[4]

[A] **Necessity, Per Se, and Essence.** In *Posterior Analytics* 1.4–6 Aristotle argues that because demonstrative knowledge (*epistēmē*) is of necessities, demonstration proceeds from necessary principles or premises and proves necessary theorems or conclusions (1.4, 73a21–5). He goes on to clarify that demonstrative necessities hold of every case and 'in themselves' or per se (*kath' hauta*). Holding of every case seems to be equivalent to universality: demonstrative premises and conclusions are of the form '*every F is G*' (*APo.* 1.4, 73a28–34). Being in itself or per se, however, is a more interesting notion. It suggests that a predication holds good in virtue of a (type of) thing's own identity, nature, or essence: 'every *F* is *G* insofar as it is itself, i.e., *F*' or 'in virtue of itself, being *F*'. Indeed, in his discussion of specific types of holding per se, he understands this notion on the basis of what is essentially true (or true in virtue of a real definition; *APo.* 1.4, 73a34–b16; esp. 73a35–6: *en tō(i) logō(i) tō(i) legonti ti estin*; 38: *en tō(i) logō(i)...tō(i) ti esti dēlounti*; 73a35–6: *he ousia autōn*). Since holding 'in itself' is a major part of how he explicates demonstrative necessities, it follows that demonstrative necessities are based on real definition and ultimately on essential features.

[B] **Essential and Merely Necessary Per Se.** Aristotle distinguishes between per se features which are parts of an item's essence (mentioned in its real definition) and per se features which are 'in themselves' in that they obtain *in virtue of an item's essence* without being parts of that essence (*APo.* 1.4, 73b31–2). He offers the example of having a sum of interior angles equal to two right angles (= 2R). While this feature is a per se necessary attribute of every triangle, it is clearly not included in a triangle's essence. This distinction introduces a special category of necessary features, those which are per se but are not parts of a subject's essence. Aristotle sometimes calls them 'per se accidents' (*APo.* 1.6, 75a18–37; 1.7, 75a39–b2; 1.9, 76a4–9; 1.10, 76b3–22; *Met.* Δ.30, 1025a30–2). Such features are derived from a thing's essence (perhaps with the help of essential truths about other

---

[4] For example, see Charles 2000, 202–3, Barnes 1994, 120–2, Irwin 1980, 37–9; see also Irwin 1988, 118–20, 127–8, 529 n. 8, 530 n. 21. For a similar view, see Loux 1991, 72–5. White (1972–3) argues that it is a mistake to seek to understand Aristotelian essentialism on the basis of modal operators in the way Quine proceeds; similarly, Cohen 1978, 388. For a lucid discussion of Aristotle's essentialism and Quine's criticism, see Code 1976. Kung (1977, 362) argues that the centrepiece of Aristotle's essentialism is the claim that essential properties are explanatory, and offers cases of merely necessary properties which are not essential but without which their possessor would (or could) not exist. For a different view, see Wedin 1984, who sets out a 'standard' and a 'non-standard' version of Aristotelian essentialism but in both cases spells out essentialism in modal terms. Moreover, he focuses on essences of particular objects, not kinds. Lloyd (1981, 163) also doubts whether we can give an account of essence independently of necessity.

170 MICHAIL PERAMATZIS

relevant objects too) through Aristotelian explanatory demonstration. Using definitional truths about essences as first principles or premises, we can demonstrate that (for example) all triangles necessarily have 2R. Having 2R is a necessary per se feature which is not essential but is essence-based: for its belonging to every triangle obtains in virtue of a triangle's essence. It is precisely this 'in virtue of' claim that our explanatory demonstrations mirror.

[C] **Essence and Cause.** The language of 'in virtue of' just introduced implies that essence grounds necessity in a causal-explanatory manner. Aristotle argues that holding per se is to hold '*because* of itself' (*di' hauto*; *APo.* 1.4, 73b16–18; b25–32; 1.6, 74b26–32; 75a28–37). He consolidates the link between essence and cause in *Posterior Analytics* 2. He contends that knowing what something is (*ti estin*) is the same as knowing why something is the case (*dihoti*). In his syllogistic picture, this is understood as knowing what the middle term of an explanatory demonstration is (*APo.* 2.2, 89b38–90a1; 90a5–7; 2.8–10). This middle term picks out the cause of the relevant phenomenon. In the example of a lunar eclipse, the corresponding explanatory demonstration which constitutes knowledge of why something is the case runs as follows:

Light-loss of type L belongs to all screenings by the earth of type S.
Screening by the earth of type S belongs to the moon (in a certain position).
Light-loss of type L belongs to the moon (in a certain position).

Aristotle's claim that knowing why-it-is is the same as knowing what-it-is suggests that from this demonstration we can grasp the following scientific definition of a lunar eclipse:

Lunar eclipse $=_{def}$ light-loss of type L belonging to the moon (in a certain position) brought on by the earth's screening of type S.[5]

Similarly, the why-it-is for the example of thunder is captured by a demonstration such as the following:

Noise of type N belongs to every quenching of fire of type Q.
Quenching of fire of type Q belongs to every cloud of type C.
Noise of type N belongs to every cloud of type C.

Further, this demonstration contains the resources with which to grasp the explanatory definition of thunder:

---

[5] The symbol '$=_{def}$' denotes the relation of x's being (correctly) defined as y.

Thunder $=_{\text{def}}$ noise of type N belonging to clouds of type C brought on by quenching of fire of type Q.

A few important remarks are in order. First, it is clear from these examples that not all Aristotelian definitions are analytical or known a priori. Indeed, the important and interesting cases, such as those of lunar eclipse and thunder, suggest that to have a scientific, explanatory definition of a phenomenon we must engage in genuine scientific inquiry, such as astronomy or meteorology. For mere armchair theorizing could not provide us with causes such as the earth's screening the sun's light or fire's quenching in the clouds.

Second, while natural phenomena such as lunar eclipses and thunder have essences which ground merely necessary per se features, Aristotle takes natural phenomena (at least in the sublunary world) to be neither necessary nor eternal but 'for the most part' (*APo.* 1.8; 1.30). We may bracket this issue by supposing that while thunder (for example) does not exist necessarily, it involves a conditional type of necessity grounded in a corresponding sort of essential truth. Thus, it does not exist essentially or necessarily, yet if it exists, it essentially (and necessarily) is a certain type of noise in the clouds brought on by fire quenching. Further, if it exists, it necessarily has the feature of (for instance) occurring in noisy, dark-grey clouds (or something similar).

Third, Aristotle does not make only epistemic claims. Nor does he focus just on pragmatic or interest-based dependencies between explanatory/demonstrative and definitional knowledge. Rather, his epistemic claim that knowledge of why-it-is and knowledge of what-it-is are the same is underwritten by a claim of metaphysical sameness: the why-it-is, the cause of a phenomenon, is the same as the what-it-is, its essence (2.2, 90a14–15). It is precisely because cause and essence are the same that knowing the one is identified with knowing the other. This is strong evidence for the intimate link between essence and cause in Aristotle's essentialist picture.

Fourth, this link between essence and cause is neither extrinsic nor superficial. To use one of the examples just offered: Aristotle is not claiming that essence and cause are 'the same' in that the *definiens* of (for instance) thunder involves an essence-revealing part (the noise in the clouds) with a cause-specifying part (the fire's being quenched) accreted onto it. It is true that Aristotle fluctuates in specifying precisely what part of his formulae captures the essence. Sometimes he identifies the essence with what is described by the whole *definiens*-phrase, while at other times he associates it only with the causal part of the *definiens*-phrase, the correlate of the middle term (*APo.* 2.2, 90a15–22; 2.8, 93a21–9). In either case, however, it is clear that the whole *definiens*-phrase not only reveals the essence but also is causal in virtue of the middle term being present in it and referring to the cause. For, without the middle term, the *definiens*-phrase would not constitute a causal, scientific definition (*Met.* H.4, 1044b12–15). Rather, it would be

172 MICHAIL PERAMATZIS

a merely significatory definition, a semantic account that describes what the relevant names or name-like expressions signify: for example, 'thunder' signifies the same as 'a noise in the clouds' (*APo.* 2.10, 93b29–32). If this is correct, the whole essence (what is described by the whole *definiens*-phrase) is causal. While the dominant segment of the *definiens*-phrase, identified with the middle term, picks out the cause, the rest describes an *explanandum*, to be understood on the basis of that cause. In the case of thunder, for example, the quenching of fire is the dominant causal part of the essence, whereas noise belonging to the clouds is brought on by, and explained in terms of, it.

Fifth, in the cases discussed in *Posterior Analytics* 2.1–2 and 8–10, Aristotle seems to be applying his causal-explanatory model mainly to *explananda* and *definienda* that are types of process, such as thunder or lunar eclipse. In cases of this sort, the dominant causal part of the essence (or the cause described by the demonstrative middle term) seems to be identified with an efficient cause: the earth's screening the sun's light; the quenching of fire in the clouds. Apart from processes, he also offers some examples of substances, such as human or soul, and the mathematical case of a triangle but does not elaborate on how the causal-explanatory model of *Posterior Analytics* 2 applies to them (*APo.* 2.8, 93a23–4; 2.10, 93b29–32). However, in *Posterior Analytics* 2.11 he argues for the generalized claim that a demonstrative middle term refers to or reveals a cause (94a23–4). Furthermore, depending on the kind of *explanandum* or *definiendum* at issue, the cause picked out by the middle term can be any one among the four Aristotelian causes (94a20–4): some cases require an efficient, others a final, others a 'grounding' cause (the latter of which seems to be an abstract or analogical version of the material cause).

These causal resources are fully deployed in *Metaphysics* Z.17–H. After the fresh start of *Metaphysics* Z.17, Aristotle seeks to explicate substance as a principle and cause of a thing's being. He writes:

[T1]   It is clear, then, that one inquires into the cause; and this is the what-it-is-to-be [*to ti ēn einai*], to speak logically [*logikōs*], which in some cases is that for the sake of which the thing is [as it is], such as presumably in the case of a house or a bed, while in some cases it is that which first began the change; for the latter too is a cause.... For instance, the question may be 'why is this here a house?'[6] And the answer is 'because what being

---

[6] While this is not crucial, I read, with the α MSS οἷον οἰκία τοδὶ διὰ τί (instead of β's οἷον οἰκία ταδὶ διὰ τί) at 1041b5–6. The α reading seems parallel to the example regarding human: καὶ ἄνθρωπος τοδί [*sc.* διὰ τί] at b6–7. By contrast, the β reading eliminates this parallel. More importantly, it seems to be a theoretically committed reading, in which Aristotle clearly formulates the C-term in the plural to refer to the house's many material parts or elements. In the α reading we get two examples that are initially formulated in an innocuous way, with the singular τοδί, and then at b7 we have an improvement on this initial formulation: why does this body—a clear reference to matter—have this characteristic?

ARISTOTLE ON HOW ESSENCE GROUNDS NECESSITY   173

is for a house belongs to it'. Or it may be 'why is this thing here a human?'
or rather 'why does this body indeed have this feature?'[7] So what is inquired
into is the cause of matter (and this is the form)[8] by which the matter is
thus-and-so. And that is the substance. (*Met.* Z.17, 1041a27–30; b5–9)

Aristotle understands this argument as an extension of the causal-explanatory
model set out in *Posterior Analytics* 2. He explicitly refers to the process cases of
thunder and lunar eclipse (1041a15–16; 24–6). Here, however, he extends this
model to cases of substance-kinds, where we have explanatory demonstrations
such as the following:

Being arranged in a certain fashion belongs to being a human (the kind's essence).
Being a human belongs to this type of flesh, bones, etc.
Being arranged in a certain fashion belongs to this type of flesh, bones, etc.

If this is correct, the corresponding definition should run as follows:

Human $=_{def}$ living being constituted from this type of flesh, bones, etc. with a certain arrangement because of being a human.

It is clear that not only the explanatory demonstration but also the definition just
given are problematic as they stand. For, while the demonstrative middle term is
not the relevant kind as such (*human*) but the kind's essence (*being a human*), yet
it does not latch onto any deeper cause for each kind's being. More conspicuously,
the definition associated with this demonstration is blatantly and viciously circular. Aristotle, however, has an attractive answer to both challenges. He maintains

---

[7] I read 1041b6–7 as follows: ἤ [sc. διὰ τί] τὸ σῶμα τοῦτο [sc. ἐστίν] τοδὶ ἔχον. Here ἐστίν is understood as emphatic together with the predicative participle ἔχον ('indeed has'), presumably to emphasize that the existence of the substance-kind and the fact that the relevant matter has a certain
structure both obtain and are known to obtain. This presupposition made its first appearance at
1041a15–16 and 23–4 but is restated at 1041b4–5, just before our example. I follow the reading τοδὶ
ἔχον, where ἔχον follows the second sense of ἔχειν at Δ.23, 1023a11–13, in which the matter has a formal or structural feature; for this suggestion, see Frede-Patzig (1988), commentary on 1041b6–7. In
the alternative reading ὡδὶ ἔχον, stemming from Ps-Alexander and Bonitz, we can get this meaning
even more straightforwardly: 'why is this body in this state, structure, or arrangement?'

[8] At 1041b7–9 the MSS read ὥστε τὸ αἴτιον ζητεῖται τῆς ὕλης τοῦτο δ' ἐστὶ τὸ εἶδος ᾧ τί ἐστιν τοῦτο
δ' ἡ οὐσία. Several editors, including Jaeger, as well as Frede–Patzig, suspect that the phrase bracketed
by Ross, τοῦτο δ' ἐστὶ τὸ εἶδος, is an intrusion or a gloss. Frede–Patzig also argue that it interrupts
Aristotle's argument and breaks the link between primary substance as a cause and what it is the cause
of. I do not think that the phrase poses any serious problems. In fact, it is important for Aristotle to
establish the sameness between primary substance, essence/form, and cause. The anaphoric causal
dative hō(i) may be referring back not only to *aition* but also to *eidos* (or, perhaps more accurately, to
the relevant sort of *aition* as an *eidos*): this would be analogous to Plato's claim that the *eidos* F is the
cause 'because of which' or 'through which' any and every F is an F (or in virtue of which it has its
characteristic *pathē*); see *Meno* 72c7–8: ἕν γέ τι εἶδος ταὐτὸν ἅπασαι ἔχουσιν δι' ὃ εἰσὶν ἀρεταί;
Euthyphro 6d10–11:ἀλλ' ἐκεῖνο αὐτὸ τὸ εἶδος ᾧ πάντα τὰ ὅσια ὅσιά ἐστιν; compare 11a6–b5.

174   MICHAIL PERAMATZIS

that the bare formal cause—the what-it-is-to-be (1041a28: *to ti ēn einai*)—is only a first, abstract approximation to, or description of, the cause being sought after. If we move beyond this 'logical' manner of referring to the cause (a28: *hōs eipein logikōs*), we shall have to specify the essence or formal cause using weightier types of cause, the efficient or final cause, as the case may be, or perhaps even material (or material-grounding) causation (*APo.* 2.11, 94a24–36). To paraphrase Aristotle's words: 'this cause, which may, within the "logical" level of analysis, be referred to as the essence, is an efficient or final cause' depending on the kind of case at issue. This claim echoes the thesis advanced in *Posterior Analytics* 2 that what-it-is and why-it-is are the same.[9] Hence, the cause which is abstractly described as the essence is precisified by reference to real-world causes.[10] Conversely, too, however, efficient, final, or even material-grounding types of cause also function as identity-fixers of the relevant kind: for they are the basic or dominant referents of the kind's *definiens*-formula. Therefore, they too are inextricably dependent upon the notion of essence. This is a minimal implication of the sort of sameness thesis Aristotle seems to be endorsing. If this is correct, the middle term of the sample demonstration (being a human), also present in the corresponding definition, should be understood as a 'stand-in' for the relevant type of cause. In the present example, the causal part of the essence is identified with the final cause: being for the sake of realizing a certain sort of rational life or something similar. In the process cases of *Posterior Analytics* 2, the causal part of the essence is identified with the efficient cause.

Can we extend this causal-explanatory picture of essence to cover further, perhaps more recalcitrant examples? Let us discuss two possible cases. First, in mathematical essences we should expect the relevant cause to be material-grounding. In *Posterior Analytics* 2.11 Aristotle also includes, alongside efficient and final causation, what he calls the 'grounding' cause ('if certain items hold it is necessary for this to hold'; 94a21–2; 24–35). This seems to be an abstract version or an analogue of the material cause (hence, I am referring to it as the 'material-grounding cause'). It applies to cases that do not involve any change or perceptual matter, most prominently mathematical cases. His example of a grounding cause is taken from geometry. He seems to have two distinct ideas:

(a) Grounding causation seems to be the relation between the premises (principles) and the conclusion (theorem) of a mathematical proof, while a grounding cause seems to be identified with the premises of such a proof. It is important, however, to emphasize that the proof must be not only

---

[9] There are further passages in which Aristotle identifies the essence or the formal cause with an *aition*: e.g., *APo.* 2.11, 94a35–6; *Phys.* 2.7, 198a24–34; *DA* 2.4, 415b8–12; *GA* 1.1, 715a3–7; 2.1, 732a4; *Met.* H.4, 1044a33–b20.

[10] For a different interpretation of Aristotle's view of the relation between essence or form and causation (especially efficient causation), see Ferejohn 2013, 147–55.

deductively valid and sound but also *explanatory* of the truth it establishes. Similarly, the premises must be explanatory of the conclusion: they must show *why* the conclusion is the case.

(b) This point is related to the link between grounding and material causation: there seems to be a non-propositional notion of grounding causation and grounding cause. In this notion, derivative and/or more complex mathematical entities may be viewed as being grounded in more basic and/or simpler mathematical entities, some of which function in a quasi-material fashion, whereas others play the role of structuring, arranging, or generally enforming this type of mathematical matter. For example, a triangle may be considered as essentially consisting in a quasi-material two-dimensional extension being bounded by three straight lines. Notably, this is not a merely formal or logical essence, for it involves a type of matter and its very own form, not any isolated or free-floating form. In this view, the simpler or more basic, material and formal items would be the causes which explain the being (and features) of a more complex or derivative item. Accordingly, grounding causation would be the causal-explanatory relation between fundamental and derivative *explananda*.[11]

In our second recalcitrant case, the material-grounding cause could also be deployed for the essences of material elements, homoiomerous stuffs, or basic material substances. To be sure, such cases would also involve some sorts of structure, arrangement, configuration, or generally 'shape', roughly corresponding to the formal cause. The latter, however, ought to be understood not as merely definitional or quasi-logical. Rather, it is the form, structure, arrangement, or what have you, *of the material constituents* or *the matter* of the relevant item, not any sort of stand-alone form. Perhaps essences of this sort could also include even some features related to motion or change cognate with the efficient cause.[12] For instance, the essence of an Aristotelian element, such as earth, fire, air, or water,

---

[11] See Malink 2017 for an example of (a): he argues that demonstrative premises are material causes or elements of the conclusion. On the basis of *APo.* 2.11, 94a24–36, Paolo Fait (2019) argues for a view that is cognate with (b), in which geometrical demonstrations involve complex constructions that consist of simpler constructions: in the example of *APo.* 2.11, 94a27–34, we may think that a flat angle (adding up to two right angles) is a basic construction from which a more complex construction is made by drawing a perpendicular line to produce an angle that is half the flat angle (i.e., half of two right angles). For a different view of 'grounding' causation as discussed in *APo.* 2.11, see Stein 2020, who argues that this sort of causation is a type of determination by general features, such as the genus. Since Aristotle takes the genus to be analogous to matter, 'grounding' causation is merely analogous to material causation. I can remain neutral on the precise reading of this part of *Posterior Analytics* 2.11, for any notion of causation that is an abstract or even analogical version of the material cause would fit the bill.

[12] This strong link between material and efficient causation seems prominent in several important passages. For example, at *Phys.* 2.9, 200a30–2, the 'necessary', which typically refers to the matter, also includes the matter's motions (τὸ ἀναγκαῖον ἐν τοῖς φυσικοῖς τὸ ὡς ὕλη λεγόμενον καὶ αἱ κινήσεις αἱ ταύτης; compare 2.8, 198b10–16); see also *PA* 1.1, 640b4–16; *GA* 5.8, 789b2–15; *Met.* A.3, 984b5–11.

176   MICHAIL PERAMATZIS

would include items such as the hot, cold, dry, and wet (material features or stuffs?), together with their ratio or structure, as well as (perhaps) the relevant natural motions. Even our own chemical elements or compounds could be understood in a similar causal-explanatory essentialist fashion. For example, the essence of oxygen would be understood in terms of its constituent electrons, protons, neutrons, etc. together with their configuration in an atom's nucleus and electron cloud. Perhaps this essence would also include the nuclear forces binding the atom, as well as the motions of the particles resulting from such forces. A similar approach could be adopted for the case of a compound such as a water molecule: its essence would consist in the constituent atoms, hydrogen and oxygen, their 2–1 ratio, the type of their bond, and perhaps the motions associated with the polarity of their bond. In *Posterior Analytics* 2.12 Aristotle offers an example of a simple material substance, ice (95a16–21). The underlying essence of ice includes not only the constituent water and its solidified state but also the efficient cause that brings on solidification: the total lack of heat. If these considerations are correct, Aristotle's essentialist picture seems to have wide applicability and significant explanatory power.

In my comments on [T1] I pointed out that Aristotle's sameness thesis about essence and cause implies not only that an essence involves a causal part but also that a cause operates as an identity-fixer. That is to say, a cause, too, serves essence-related roles and so makes the items it is a cause of what they are. A clear formulation of this idea is found early on in the *Metaphysics*, in Aristotle's initial characterization of the four causes. In discussing the formal cause or essence (the 'what-it-is-to-be- something'), he remarks that, ultimately, all 'why?' or 'for what reason?' questions somehow refer back to the definition, which is obviously an account of the essence (A.3, 983a27–9: *anagetai gar to dia ti eis ton logon eskhaton*). In this context, in which he lists all four causes, this sort of remark would suggest that all causes are understood as carrying out essence-related tasks: for, in answering 'why?' questions, each in its distinctive mode, every cause (partly or fully) answers essence-seeking 'what is it?' questions.

It seems plausible to think that depending on the kind of *explanandum* or *definiendum* in question, its essence may be the same as an efficient, final, or even grounding-material cause. For instance, in cases of processes such as thunder or lunar eclipse, the essence is the relevant efficient cause. In cases of artefacts such as a house, it is the final cause of (for example) protecting humans and their belongings from adverse weather conditions. In mathematical cases such as a triangle, the essence presumably involves simpler geometrical items, such as lines, that function as formal delimiters of a triangle's quasi-material two-dimensional extension. This is analogous to the way in which a mathematical theorem (the conclusion of a mathematical proof) has as its grounding cause the constituents of the relevant proof: that is, the explanatory demonstrative premises (*APo.* 2.11, 94a24–35). This approach could defuse Alexander's worry (re-raised by

Bostock)[13] that not all causes invoke, let alone are identified with, the essence. For example, while the matter constituting a statue or the body constituting a human is a material cause, it is not part of, nor is it the same as, a statue's or a human's essence. Our present point suggests that, in Aristotle's view, essences and causes are sensitive to the relevant *definiendum* and/or *explanandum*. In some cases, such as the process case of thunder, the essence is the efficient cause; in others, such as a statue or a human, it is the final cause; finally, in some others, such as mathematicals, it is a quasi-material or grounding cause or, in the case of chemical elements and material stuffs, it is a straightforwardly material cause, in both cases together with the formal cause of the relevant type of matter.

The overall picture, at any rate, is one in which the basic notion of an essence is understood in terms of not only an essentialist concept which answers the 'what is it?' question but also a causal-explanatory notion which answers the 'why is it (as it is)?' question. An Aristotelian essence or identity-fixer is indissolubly a 'causal essence' or (equally) an 'essential cause'. It answers, therefore, both the 'what is it?' and the 'why is it (as it is)?' questions at the same time. Moreover, it answers the question of why something has its characteristic necessary features. In so doing, this causal-explanatory type of essence grounds necessities: that is, truths about a thing's necessary but non-essential features (such as per se accidents).

[D] **Asymmetry of Essence-Cause over Necessity**. Aristotle's causal-explanatory view of essence suggests that an essence, insofar as it is also a cause, grounds necessities, while the converse is not true. Aristotle insists on this asymmetry of essence over necessity in several important passages. In *Posterior Analytics* 1.13 he addresses the question of what makes a deduction explanatory and demonstrative, as opposed to merely a valid and sound deduction. He invites us to compare the following two deductions:

[I]   Being near belongs to all celestial bodies that do not twinkle.
      <u>Being a non-twinkling celestial body belongs to all planets.</u>
      Being near belongs to all planets.

[II] Non-twinkling belongs to all celestial bodies that are near.
      <u>Being a celestial body that is near belongs to all planets.</u>
      Non-twinkling belongs to all planets.[14]

While Aristotle's examples do not include any modal qualifiers, it is safe to assume that the conclusions inferred could be understood as necessary: for it seems correct to think that being near and non-twinkling necessarily belong to all

---

[13] Bostock 1994, 239–41.
[14] While Aristotle does not use any of his syllogistic quantifiers, I have presented [I] and [II] in Barbara.

178   MICHAIL PERAMATZIS

planets—at least in the sense of per se necessity also used in the mathematical example of having 2R. Aristotle notes that the deductive relation runs indifferently either from the planets' non-twinkling to their being near or from their being near to their non-twinkling (78a26–37). Both [I] and [II] are valid and sound: for (Aristotle assumes) being near and non-twinkling are (at least in the case of celestial bodies) counter-predicable (equivalently: the major premises are convertible; 78a26–30). Only [II], however, is an explanatory demonstration (a deduction or syllogism revealing the genuine 'why-it-is' (*dihoti*: 78a39–b4)): for its middle term, being near, latches onto the cause of non-twinkling for celestial bodies. It is because of being near that celestial bodies, and planets specifically, do not twinkle, while the converse does not hold good (78a37–8; b3–4). Indeed, in [I] it seems odd to think that the planets' non-twinkling could explain their being near. Hence, while [I] is valid and sound, it is a deduction or syllogism only of the 'that' or the fact (*hoti*: 78a36–7).[15] Being near, an essential feature of planets, is the cause of one of their necessary features, non-twinkling. It is, presumably, a part of a complex, efficient-cum-material essentialist cause which also includes the planets' material constitution, their opacity, their ability to reflect light, their motions, etc. This type of causal essence grounds the planets' necessary feature of non-twinkling but not conversely. To be sure, for this grounding to work, it is important also to employ causal-explanatory essentialist resources pertaining to items other than the planets: for instance, the sun, its emitting light; light and its ability to travel in interplanetary space; other celestial bodies, their motions and positions, etc.[16] The main point, however, is that the grounding basis involves such causal-explanatory essential truths which underwrite necessary truths about per se accidents such as the planets' non-twinkling. The fact that these essential truths describe relations of efficient (and perhaps also material) causation seems to secure their asymmetry over merely necessary (but non-essential) truths.

Aristotle insists on this idea of asymmetry in his account of teleology and hypothetical necessity in *Physics* 2.9. In this context the essence is identified with the form and the final cause in line with the causal-explanatory essentialist picture just outlined (200a34–5). While matter is hypothetically necessary for the essence, form, or final cause to obtain, yet it is not because of the matter that the essence, form, or final cause obtains. For example, if the essence or final cause of being a house is to exist (in a completed house), it is necessary that there exist certain types of bricks, stones, etc. (arranged in a certain way). However, it is because of the essence or final cause of being a house—being for the sake of protecting humans and their belongings from adverse weather conditions—that the matter is as it is: bricks, stones, etc. of certain types arranged in a covering

---

[15] See Koslicki 2012, 193–5, for a similar assessment of this example.
[16] Koslicki (2012, 201–6) argues convincingly for this point. McKirahan (1992, 111–21) and Ferejohn (2013, 115–18) differ from Koslicki (and from each other) on this issue.

structure (*Phys.* 2.9, 200a5–10; 200a33–4). Indeed, at 200a15–30, Aristotle likens such cases to the mathematical per se necessary (but non-essential) feature of having 2R, which holds of every triangle because of the nature of a straight line (and, presumably, of a triangle too, of parallel lines, of alternate angles, and so on), but not conversely. The same example and the claim about asymmetry recur in a celebrated passage at *De Anima* 1.1, 402b16–403a2. In that context, knowing the essence of a (type of) substance is to grasp the cause of certain necessary (but non-essential) features belonging to the substance. This claim echoes the epistemic and metaphysical interdependencies between essence and cause already set out in the *Posterior Analytics* and in *Metaphysics* Z.17. It also shows that the causal essences of (for example) straight lines, parallel lines, alternate angles, as well as triangles, ground necessary features such as the per se accident of triangles' having 2R.

2. How (if at all) Can Aristotle Secure the Asymmetry?

Aristotle's essentialism, if sound, has the resources with which to sustain the claim that essence grounds necessity but not conversely: for it invokes the concepts of cause and explanation. If an essence as such is a cause or an explanation of necessary (but non-essential) per se features, it is clear why *it* underwrites necessity, while the converse is not true: for essence is the cause of necessity, whereas necessity is not the cause of essence. The crucial question, then, is whether Aristotle's causal-explanatory essentialism is sound.

Aristotle's answer to this question, presumably, relies on the 'sameness' claim made in *Posterior Analytics* 2.1–2, 8–11, *Metaphysics* Z.17, and elsewhere: the middle term reveals the cause, while the cause and the what-it-is (or essence) are the same. But to make his view plausible, it is important to clarify and consolidate this 'sameness' claim. There seem to be at least five possible ways in which to spell it out:

(i) Stipulation. Aristotle simply defines essence in an artificial and idiosyncratic way as a cause. Instead of offering an essentialist view in which essence robustly grounds necessity, he just stipulates the meaning of 'essence' and so changes the topic.

(ii) Identity. Aristotle strictly identifies essence and cause without conferring priority on either. As it stands, this view seems a mere notational variant of (i). If, on the other hand, we drop its 'no priority' aspect, we end up with a generic version of either (iii) or (iv) below.

(iii) Reduction$_{(E \to C)}$. Aristotle reduces essence to cause. His view is not really essentialist but simply causal or explanatory, for what ultimately supports an essence's asymmetry over necessity is just its being an efficient,

180   MICHAIL PERAMATZIS

material-grounding, or final cause. Essence by itself does not inherently contain any robustly asymmetrical 'because'.

(iv) Reduction$_{(C \to E)}$. Aristotle reduces cause to essence. His use of efficient, material-grounding, or final causes is unimportant, for what underpins the asymmetry of essence over necessity is just its being that in virtue of which something is what it is. The notion of making something what it is (or being that in virtue of which something is what it is) is sufficient for the asymmetry in question. It does not need the contribution of any efficient, material-grounding, or final cause. It is just an additional, extrinsic fact that in some cases these types of cause may be, or are indeed, employed.

(v) Interdependence or Sameness without identity. Aristotle maintains that neither essence by itself nor cause by itself is independently specifiable. Nor is either of them sufficient to establish the asymmetry of essence over necessity. Rather, his essentialism invokes a distinctive 'causal essence' or 'essential cause', which achieves the grounding task. Perhaps, 'essence' and 'cause' are two 'modes of representation' of one single item. Each notion, however, carries out different theoretical and explanatory roles. If so, they should be deemed distinct from each other, if interdependent.

In what follows I shall argue directly in favour of (v), and so against (iii) and (iv). Indirectly, my arguments should also undermine (i) and (ii).

3. Can Essence without Cause, or Cause without Essence, Underwrite the Asymmetry?

In his *Aristotle on Meaning and Essence*, David Charles has argued extensively and convincingly in favour of a position that is congenial to my (v). In epistemic terms, he favours the so-called interdependence of the Aristotelian practices of explaining and defining. Moreover, he seems to think that this quasi-epistemic interdependence is sustained by the metaphysical thesis that essence and cause are co-determined.[17] In a more recent work co-authored with Stephen Williams, however, he sets out the co-determination of essence and cause in a way which suggests that essence by itself, without the assistance of any heavy-duty types of cause (such as efficient, material-grounding, or final cause), involves an explanatory asymmetry over necessity. This is roughly similar to claim (iv) introduced in section 2. In this more 'relaxed' view of the link between essence and cause, the efficient, material-grounding, or final cause *may* but *need not* be included in an

---

[17] For the interdependence of defining and explaining and the co-determination of essence and cause, see Charles 2000, mainly chs. 8 and 10; also his 2010.

essence. What is integral to an essence, by contrast, is the notion of explanation or the (generic) formal cause, which may but need not be fleshed out in terms of efficient, final, or even material-grounding causation. The relaxed view does not require that the essence of any and every type of object include efficient, final, or material-grounding causes. Correspondingly, it is not necessary that the definition of any and every object mention some or other among such causes.[18]

Charles and Williams have two main arguments in favour of this position. First, they hold that Aristotle's causal-explanatory picture advanced in the *Posterior Analytics* for types of process (such as thunder or eclipse) cannot be fully extended to mathematical entities or substance-kinds such as (for instance) biological kinds or chemical elements. In such cases, they maintain, essence works by itself as a ground for necessary (but non-essential) per se features. Moreover, it would be implausible to expect that apart from the essence there is also a type of cause in operation. Thus, for instance, the debunking of final causes and generally teleology in biological cases suggests that essence, by itself, without any final cause, should ground necessity. If so, Aristotle's insistence on the role of final causation in natural substance-kinds cannot be sustained in the light of modern biological theory. In the case of chemical elements, we may think that the essence of (for instance) hydrogen is specified in terms of its structure and atomic number, without any need to invoke any further, more substantive cause underlying its nature. In mathematical cases, we may conceive a natural number as being simply the successor of its predecessor, where the preceding number and the successor operation fully determine a number's nature, without any contribution by any heavy-duty cause. Alternatively, if we follow a more Aristotelian approach, a number would be simply a plurality of units. There is no place for any further cause in any mathematical entity's essence.

The second argument for the relaxed view is theoretical. Charles and Williams claim that the very notion of essence or nature can support its asymmetry over necessity. For, they contend, essence by itself involves the concept of being that because of which something is as it is, and has its characteristic necessary features, while the converse does not hold good. This idea is shared by Plato and Aristotle alike. Plato argues that the what-it-is or *ousia* of (for example) virtue, holiness, etc. is that because of, or through, which such items are what they are and have their affections or attributes (*Meno* 72c1–d1; *Euthyphro* 6d9–e2; 10e11: *dia to hosion einai*; 11a8: *pathos*; 9: *peponthe*; b3: *paskhei*; 11a8: *ousia*; 7: *to hosion hoti pot' estin*; b1: *hoti de on*). Aristotle, too, especially in *Metaphysics* A.3, seems to argue that all types of cause or explanation somehow refer back or are even reduced to essence or nature. For essence is by itself explanatory; after all, Aristotle himself maintains that it is a type of cause—the formal cause (*Met.* A.3, 983a26–9; compare *Phys.* 2.3, 194b16–23; 26–9).

---

[18] Williams and Charles 2013, 124–6.

182   MICHAIL PERAMATZIS

To address the relaxed view of essence and cause, it is important to emphasize, first, that our interpretation of Aristotle's claim that essence and cause are 'the same' should not saddle him with the idea that there are exactly four types of cause, no more or no fewer. Aristotle never maintains that he has proven that his four types of cause are the only possible answers to 'why?' questions.[19] The disagreement is over whether some or other type of cause (among the four, or even from some suitably expanded conception of causation) is necessarily present within every kind's essence or not. Second, and more importantly, we should not think that a type of cause that fails to account for the nature of specific kinds, or fails generally, ought to be retained in a dogmatic way. Rather, if any of Aristotle's types of cause fails, it should be discarded. At any rate, the criterion with which to decide whether a type of cause is successful or unsuccessful as part of a kind's essence is not speculative or a priori. It should be sensitive to scientific inquiry, progress, and established theory. However, rejecting a type of cause for specific cases, or even quite generally, does not entail that a corresponding essence should not include any cause at all. It is still possible—and indeed it may be necessary—to replace a failed type of cause with another: for instance, a final with an efficient and/or a material-grounding cause.

The case of biological essences is, admittedly, the most recalcitrant. Not even Aristotle himself, however, takes final causes as the only causal factors at work in this area. He also thinks that efficient and material causes are important, if not primary. Perhaps, in an updated version of his view, we could shift priorities and privilege non-teleological causes such as these. More ambitiously, it may be far from clear that the teleological picture is irredeemably debunked by modern biology. At least certain branches of modern biology and philosophy of biology seem to combine evolutionary theory with developmental views (the so-called 'evo-devo' approach). In this context the notion of organisms' development into more complete stages is cognate with Aristotle's view of generation.[20]

In less controversial cases, such as those of chemical elements, we can defend Aristotle's view that essence irreducibly involves some or other cause on the basis of some of the claims he makes in *Meteorologica* 4.12. Thus, he holds that lower-level kinds, such as elements or homoiomerous stuffs, have unclear and

---

[19] Most notably, in *Metaphysics* A.7, where he concludes the discussion of his predecessors regarding their grip on the notion of causation and the types of cause, he claims that no one among them has touched on any further type of cause over and above the four set out in his *Physics* (988a21–3); indeed, he closes the chapter by noting only that his discussion has offered some strong evidence (*marturein*) in favour of the doctrine of the four causes (988b16–18). He does not claim that he has proven that there are only four causes. In his introduction to this discussion, in *Metaphysics* A.3, he cautiously holds that his project will either help us discover some further type(s) of cause or make us more confident in—but presumably will not demonstrate—the correctness of the doctrine of the four causes (983b4–6: *mallon pisteusomen*).

[20] See Lennox 2017, 34 and 47–9. Gotthelf (2012, 367–9) argues that final causes are legitimate even in modern evolutionary biology. What evolutionary theory eschews, by contrast, is Aristotle's insistence on the primacy of final causes.

indeterminate natures (presumably, not just in an epistemic but also in a meta-physical sense) in respect of their function, *telos*, or generally final cause (389b29–30; 390a2–20). But this does not imply that they have no essence or nature at all, in the sense of a 'what-it-is'. Nor does it entail that their essence is cause-free. Rather, they have an essence that involves their material or quasi-material constituents plus the relevant structure, configuration, arrangement, shape, figure, etc. of these constituents, perhaps together with the natural motions they undergo or cause (a sort of efficient cause; *Phys.* 2.9, 200a30–2). Aristotle himself implies that in certain cases of natural beings or phenomena there are no final but only efficient and material-grounding causes. For example, while thunder and eclipse are natural phenomena, he does not even consider invoking final causes in their essence. Indeed, he seems implicitly to inveigh against views which introduce the final cause in such cases (*APo.* 2.11, 94a32–4; *Met.* H.4, 1044b12).

A similar picture seems to obtain in the case of mathematical essences. In fact, at *Met.* B.2, 996a21–33, Aristotle himself clearly maintains that efficient and final causes are absent from mathematical cases. At the same time, though, he seems to be deploying his model of material-grounding causation (*APo.* 2.11, 93b24–35). In this model the demonstrative premises of a mathematical proof entail that, and explain why, the relevant theorem holds good. Equivalently: the middle term picks out the feature in virtue of which the nexus described in the conclusion obtains. In this sense, the demonstrative principles are explanatory quasi-constituents of the demonstrated theorem.[21] Alternatively but consistently with this approach, Aristotle may use a quasi-material type of cause which is non-propositional: in it more complex mathematical *items* are grounded in more basic, less complex, or ultimately fundamental items. For instance, a natural number is made of its constituent units and is essentially just a plurality or collection of these units, with the unit being absolutely fundamental. Or a triangle consists of two-dimensional continuity or continuous extension (which indeed Aristotle suggests plays the role of intelligible matter)[22] bounded by three lines (or something similar), with points being the fundamental geometrical entities.[23] If

---

[21] For an excellent discussion of this idea, see Malink 2017.

[22] See *Met.* Z.11, 1036b8–13, where the implication seems to be that the correct definition of a triangle would be in terms of lines (bounding formal cause) and continuity (intelligible matter). The notion of mathematical, 'intelligible' matter has been introduced at *Met.* Z.10, 1036a9–12, and is taken up a few lines after the example of the triangle at Z.11, 1036b32–1037a5; it is also briefly mentioned at H.6, 1045a36–b2. For present purposes, I do not need to go into any of the controversial details about intelligible matter. My point is simply that even in mathematical cases there is a part of the essence that is a type of material cause, combined with its characteristic shape-like or formal cause.

[23] Similarly, at *Met.* B.5, 1002a4–8, Aristotle seems to imply that the order of priority mirrors the order from simpler to more complex items: unit, point, line, plane, solid. At Δ.3, 1014a26–35 and b8–9, he provides the examples of speech elements and syllables, the unit and numbers, and the point and geometrical figures. At M.2, 1076b16–24, in arguing against the separability of mathematical entities from perceptibles, he seems to affirm that items which are incomposite (or less complex: *ta asuntheta*) are prior to the composite (or more complex) items they bound (e.g., lines limit the

184 MICHAIL PERAMATZIS

this is correct, Aristotle conceives a mathematical essence not simply as a 'bare' what-it-is or a merely formal cause but as being underwritten by material-grounding causes plus their structure, configuration, arrangement, or other similar shape-like features. In the example of a natural number, while the units play the role of mathematical material causes, the relevant type of plurality is a mode of collecting these units, the counterpart to the formal cause. In the case of a triangle, two-dimensional continuous extension is the (intelligible) material cause, while the bounding lines are that extension's arranging or structuring formal cause. In all such cases, it is important to highlight a point already made in section 1: so understood, mathematical essences are not merely definitional, quasi-logical, or purely formal. For not only do they include a counterpart to the material-grounding cause; they also encode a formal cause that is the structure, arrangement, bounding, or plurality *of the relevant mathematical matter*, not any form that is separate from or prior to the material cause.

Let us turn to the second, theoretical argument in favour of the relaxed view of essence. Suppose that it is correct to think that a bare notion of essence—one devoid of any substantive types of cause—possesses intrinsically an asymmetric 'because' or 'in virtue of' aspect. Even so, it still seems fair to ask what, if anything, secures this asymmetry of a 'bare' essence over necessary features. In light of the following passage from *Topics* 6.4, I shall argue that the relaxed view would struggle to tackle this last question satisfactorily.

[T2]   But whether he has mentioned and defined its essence or not, should be examined as follows. First of all, see if he has failed to make the definition through items that are prior and more familiar [*mē dia proterōn kai gnōrimōterōn*]. For a definition is rendered in order to come to know the item stated, and we come to know things by taking not any random items, but such as are prior and more familiar, as is done in demonstrations [*kathaper en tais apodeixesin*] (for so it is with all teaching and learning); accordingly, it is clear that a man who does not define through items of this kind has not defined at all. Otherwise, there will be more than one definition of the same thing; for clearly he who defines through items that are prior and more familiar has framed a better definition, so that both will then be definitions of the same object. This sort of thing, however, does not seem to be so; for each entity there is a single essence [*hen esti to einai hoper estin*]; if, then, there are to be a number of definitions of the same thing, the object defined will be the same as the essences represented in each of the definitions; but these are not the same, inasmuch as the definitions are different. Clearly, then, anyone who has not defined a thing through items that are prior and more familiar has not defined it at all.

---

two-dimensional extension of triangles) and/or they constitute (e.g., units constitute the plurality a natural number consists in; *tōn sugkeimenōn*: b18–19).

The statement that a definition has not been made through more familiar items may be understood in two ways, either supposing that the items it consists of are without qualification less intelligible, or supposing that they are less intelligible to us [*haplōs agnōstoterōn ē hēmin agnōstoterōn*]; for either way is possible. Thus what is prior is more familiar unqualifiedly than the posterior, a point, for instance, more than a line, a line than a plane, and a plane than a solid; just as a unit is more intelligible than a number; for it is prior to and a principle of every number. Likewise, also, a letter is more familiar than a syllable. Whereas to us it sometimes happens that the converse is the case; for a solid falls under perception most of all, and a plane more than a line, and a line more than a point; for most people learn such things earlier; for any ordinary intelligence can grasp them, whereas the others require a precise and exceptional understanding.

Absolutely, then, it is better to try to come to know what is posterior through what is prior, inasmuch as such a way of procedure is more scientific [*epistēmonikōteron*]. Of course, in dealing with persons who cannot recognize things through items of that kind, it may perhaps be necessary to frame the account through items that are familiar to them. Among definitions of this kind are those of a point, a line, and a plane, all of which explain the prior by the posterior; for they say that a point is the limit of a line, a line of a plane, a plane of a solid. One must, however, not fail to observe that those who define in this way cannot show the essence of what they define, unless it so happens that the same thing is more familiar both to us and also without qualification...(*Topics* 6.4, 141a24–b25; Revised Oxford Translation with minor changes)[24]

This long passage introduces a further way in which to raise the asymmetry challenge against the relaxed view of essence: why are some definitions prior and more intelligible or familiar *only* to us but *not* unqualifiedly or (we might add) *not* by nature? While the relaxed view of essence would be hard-pressed to meet this challenge, Aristotle's essentialism (as I interpret it) could surmount it. For, to

---

[24] While the *Topics*, in general, is a treatise on dialectical argument, which largely remains neutral on metaphysical questions, we can safely draw on [T2] to shed light on Aristotle's views of scientific definition and essence. For [T2], in particular, seems serious about these views, mainly for the following three reasons: (1) Aristotle clearly prescribes a method with which to offer successful definitions that yields the same type of knowledge as that achieved within demonstrative sciences (141a29–30), one that is indeed more 'scientific' (141b15–17) than any alternative. (2) The crucial distinction of [T2], between defining in terms of items that are prior and more familiar (or more intelligible) *unqualifiedly* and defining in terms of items that are prior and more familiar *to us* (141b3–5), is basic for the *Posterior Analytics*: demonstrative principles ought to be prior to the conclusions to be proven (1.2, 71b19–23) not 'relative to us' but 'by nature' or 'unqualifiedly' (71b33–72a4; compare *Phys.* 1.1,184a16–18, and *Met.* Z.4, 1029b3–5). (3) The *Topics* invokes the *Posterior Analytics* to settle questions about scientific demonstration, explanation, and definition elsewhere too: e.g., 7.3, 153a7–15. The contexts of 6.4 and 7.3 suggest that when Aristotle is more serious about essence and definition, he may (temporarily) depart from the standard, merely formal or topic-neutral approach of the *Topics*.

underpin the ('unqualified' or 'by nature') primacy of the real essence over any putative alternative (only 'relative-to-us'), it would invoke some or other substantive type of cause. In [T2] Aristotle uses mathematical examples, one of the cases favoured by the relaxed view as indicating that essence by itself, without any weighty sort of cause, could ground the asymmetry over necessity. In these examples, however, it seems that essence is indeed supplemented with what appears to be an appropriate material-grounding cause, together with some specification of arrangement, structure, or some other similar shape-like feature that exemplifies the formal cause. For instance, the correct definitions should run as follows (141b5–9):

Line $=_{def}$ one-dimensional continuous extension bounded by points.
Plane $=_{def}$ two-dimensional continuous extension bounded by lines.
Solid $=_{def}$ three-dimensional continuous extension bounded by planes.
Natural number $=_{def}$ collection/plurality of units.
Syllable (morpheme?) $=_{def}$ letters/speech elements (phonemes?) arranged in a certain way.

In the three geometrical definitions, the items that are essentially and definitionally prior 'without qualification' (point, line, plane) are boundaries of the relevant continuous extension of the posterior items (line, plane, solid). While a boundary seems to be a real counterpart to a definer in a linguistic formula and so parallels the formal cause, continuity or extension plays the role of the (geometrical or intelligible) material cause. This idea is sketched in several places of the *Metaphysics* (Z.2, 1028b16–18; Z.10, 1036a9–12; Z.11, 1036b8–13; 1036b32–1037a5; H.6, 1045a36–b2; compare B.5, 1002a4–8; Δ.9, 1017b17–21). In the definition of a natural number, on the other hand, the arithmetical units are the material cause, while their collection or plurality is the correlate of the formal cause (see, e.g., *Met.* H.3, 1044a2–6). Similarly, in the syllable case, the speech elements are the analogues of matter, whereas their arrangement plays the role of the form (see, e.g., *Met.* B.3, 998a23–5; Δ.3, 1014a27–31; Z.10, 1035a9–17; Z.17, 1041b12–13; 16–17; 31–3).

By contrast, the incorrect definitions, which are nevertheless more intelligible and familiar 'to us' are the following (141b17–22):

Point $=_{def?}$ boundary of a line.
Line $=_{def?}$ boundary of a plane.
Plane $=_{def?}$ boundary of a solid.[25]

---

[25] The symbol '$=_{def?}$' stands for the relation of x's being (incorrectly) defined in terms of something definitionally posterior, if more familiar or intelligible to us.

Contrary to what such incorrect definitions may suggest, being a plane (for example) cannot be part of the essence of a line: for a plane's two-dimensional extension, its matter, is bounded by (a) line(s). The converse is just not the case. The primacy and asymmetry of the real essence—what is unqualifiedly or by nature prior, more familiar, and more intelligible—seems to be underpinned by the material-grounding cause together with its structurer, arranger, delimiter, or generally the formal cause. Let me spell out this argument.

In [T2] the question clearly is how to characterize real definitions, those which reveal the essence (141a24–5), in order to challenge dialectical opponents who have failed to offer such definitions. Indeed, Aristotle compares what is unqualifiedly prior and more intelligible in definition with what is unqualifiedly prior and better known in demonstration (141a28–31). This is another way to frame the thesis of interdependence between knowing definitions and knowing explanations (by demonstration), already familiar from *Posterior Analytics* 2. He rules out the possibility of there being more than one (correct) real definition of one and the same thing (141a35–b1). One may, of course, offer an incorrect putative real definition. Or one may offer a (correct or plausible) non-real definition: for example, an explication, a significatory account, or a semantic clarification of a term.

From 141b3 onwards Aristotle focuses on the distinction between unqualified and 'relative-to-us' intelligibility, familiarity, or knowability. It seems that what is unqualifiedly more intelligible, and so what determines a correct definition, mirrors what is prior by nature: point to line, line to plane, plane to solid; unit to the number 2, etc.; the constituent letters (or phonemes) to the relevant syllable (or morpheme); and so on. In the case of what is more intelligible only to us, by contrast, this order is reversed, as is clear from the examples given earlier. Such 'only-relative-to-us' definitions may be resting on what is perceptually, empirically, or pre-theoretically more accessible and intelligible to us or knowers like us (141b9–14). They may also be useful or even necessary as starting-points for teaching a science to beginners (b17–19). They are not, however, scientific (b15–17), nor do they reveal the essence (*ti ēn einai*; b22–4).

Essence-revealing, scientific definitions, by contrast, codify the natural order of priority of the items within a domain. A plane's essence, for example, consists in its continuous extension being bounded not by solids but by lines. More specifically, a plane is a figure (or a magnitude with a position) extending in two dimensions with lines as its delimiters. Indeed, it would be a case of putting the cart before the horse to suppose that solids define planes: for such a definition would entail that a solid somehow delimits a plane. But this would be nonsensical: planes bound the three-dimensional extension of solids, whereas solids could not bound the two-dimensional extension of planes. What underwrites such asymmetries, then, are the quasi-material constituents of mathematical entities together with their arrangement or formal cause: in our example, a plane's two-dimensional extension and its being bounded by lines. Similarly, in the case of a natural number, its essence consists in the material cause, its constituent units, plus their mode of collection. Neither a plane's nor a natural number's essence is devoid of a substantive type of cause. Rather, it inherently involves a material-grounding cause plus a formal cause. Crucially, the latter is not a pure or quasi-logical form but is intimately interwoven with the relevant material-grounding cause. This sort of causal order gives a straightforward response to the asymmetry challenge.

How, by contrast, is the relaxed view to address this challenge using just the 'bare', non-causal notion of essence? How is it to distinguish between what is unqualifiedly prior and more intelligible in definition and what is prior and more intelligible only-to-us? In fact, how is it to rule out definitions in which an essence or a part of it is defined in terms of a merely necessary per se feature? For the point made in [T2] on the basis of distinguishing between items that are definitionally and essentially prior without qualification and those that are prior only relative to us could be put equally well about essences and merely necessary features. We can define a plane in terms of a solid or a solid in terms of a plane. Both approaches yield true, indeed necessarily true statements, but only the definition of solid in terms of plane is correct and naturally prior. Similarly, it is true, indeed necessarily true, of all triangles, and triangles alone, that they have 2R, just as it is necessarily true that they are two-dimensionally extended figures bounded by three lines. Why is only the latter the correct and naturally prior, essence-specifying definition of a triangle? Indeed, why is it the definition that grounds the necessary truth that all triangles have 2R, whereas the converse does not hold good? In my view, Aristotle's answer is the same for both cases: a triangle's essence grounds its necessary features because it inherently involves the material cause (two-dimensional extension) together with that matter's bounding formal cause (the three lines), just as the correct definition of a solid involves its material cause (three-dimensional extension) delimited by the formal cause (planes).

It is worth noting that this challenge is particularly pressing as [T2] deploys mathematical examples. For the relaxed view deems such examples paradigmatic cases where essence does not involve any type of cause more robust than the purely formal cause. Without the idea that simpler geometrical entities delimit the (geometrical) matter of more complex or derivative geometrical entities, or that units are the basic (arithmetical) material causes collected together in the plurality that a natural number consists in, it seems hard to avoid the relativistic sort of pluralism about essence and definition Aristotle criticizes at 141b34–142a6. Thus, without the robust material-grounding and formal causes, we may end up with many different putative definitions and essences of the same thing for different people: for different things are more familiar to different people. More strikingly, we may reach many different putative definitions and essences of the same thing even for one and the same person: for one's cognitive resources change or improve over time, so that what one found less intelligible today one may find more intelligible tomorrow. In a more extreme view, where what is more intelligible to us is deemed unqualifiedly prior in definition, we may have to accept that a merely necessary feature, such as (for example) having 2R, is the 'real' essence of a triangle, which 'grounds' the essential feature of having two-dimensional extension or being limited by three lines. These unpalatable implications can be avoided in a systematic and elegant manner using Aristotle's view of a 'causal essence'. By contrast, they seem inescapable for the relaxed view, in which essence or formal cause may operate by itself, without any extra cause, especially in cases such as the mathematical examples just discussed.

This line of reasoning seems to support the dependence of essence on some substantive type of cause. What about the reverse direction? Here is an abstract argument for the dependence of cause upon essence. The example of the planets' being near and their non-twinkling provided in *Posterior Analytics* 1.13 (discussed in section 1) suggests that the sort of cause invoked in my version of Aristotle's essentialism is one which—together with the essence—will distinguish between a merely logical 'following from' and the causal-explanatory 'being demonstrated from' (*APo.* 1.2, 71b17–25). This distinction, though, cannot be drawn using just thin logical, inferential, or deductive resources: for an Aristotelian demonstration is not merely a different mode of deductive inference. Rather, it is (whereas a mere deduction or syllogism is not) sensitive to the subject-matter it pertains to: it is an explanatory demonstration because it takes into consideration the object it is about, and ultimately its essence. If this is correct, the cause picked out by a demonstration's middle term ought to reflect this subject-matter sensitivity. Not any old cause related to an object or kind will suffice. Rather, only the type of cause which fixes (at least partly) that object's or kind's identity will be relevant.

Let us consider specific cases using as a starting-point an analogy with Aristotle's discussion of the role of efficient causes in craft cases. Thus, at *Physics* 2.3, 195a32–5, his considered position is not that Polycleitus, the individual object as such—a Greek-Athenian, a human, or what have you—is the efficient cause of sculpting or the statue. Rather, he contends, Polycleitus *qua* a sculptor (or the sculptor *qua* sculptor) is the efficient cause of sculpting and/or produces the statue. Therefore, Polycleitus, *in virtue of* being sculptor—that is, *in virtue of* possessing the relevant craft and grasping the appropriate statue form—is sculpting and/or is producing the statue. Ultimately, the craft is the efficient cause (195a3–8). And the craft is the grasp of the essence, form, or *telos* of the relevant product, the statue.

Analogously, in the case of biological kinds such as human, the cause or *telos* of being a human is not any old item but that which makes humans what they are and explains their characteristic necessary features (*Phys.* 2.7, 198b8–9: *kai dihoti beltion houtōs, oukh haplōs, alla to pros tēn hekastou ousian*; 2.8, 199a30–2). Thus, the relevant *telos*, say being for the sake of realizing a certain type of rational life,

190   MICHAIL PERAMATZIS

determines the structure, shape, or arrangement of the bodily parts constituting a human: for instance, it fixes the type of shape human hands have so that they sustain the kind's tool-wielding capacities (presumably, a subsidiary *telos* linked with human rational activity). In a teleological case taken from a craft, the cause of a house integral to its essence is the final cause which fixes the sort of covering shape that belongs to bricks, stones, and other types of house-buildable materials. It could not be a cause that does not discriminate between such a covering shape and the shape had by a square top face covering a geometrical cube.

In the process cases discussed in *Posterior Analytics* 2, the cause within the thunder's essence is not any old efficient cause, nor even any old fire quenching, but that which determines the nature of the relevant types of noise and clouds and explains why that kind of noise belongs to clouds in such a state. It would be odd if a candidate efficient cause for this phenomenon could not sharply differentiate between the noise characteristic of thunder and that caused by an aeroplane jet-engine hidden in grey clouds. Indeed, that Aristotle is intending the sort of efficient cause that is sensitive to, and the determinant of, the nature of the relevant noise is implied by his use of the phrase 'some sort of *F*' in *Posterior Analytics* 2.8–10 (93a21–4: *psophos tis*; *sterēsis tis*; *zō(i)on ti*).[26]

It is not surprising that our modern conception of causation may be less than sensitive to this type of dependency of cause on essence. Our standard construal of the language of causation may narrow our focus on just Humean causes, particular items (events, objects participating in such events, etc.) such as this billiard ball hitting another billiard ball and setting it in motion, or this rock breaking this window, etc. Aristotelian essences and the causes inherent in them, however, are not such items. Nor are they essences and causes *of* such items. In *Metaphysics* Z.15 Aristotle argues that no particular—not even an eternal particular—can be properly defined or have an essence. First, a perishable particular may pass away and so cease to be what our putative definition states it is: for, in that case, the particular would not be at all as it would go out of existence (1039b27–1040a7). In the case of imperishable particulars, any putative description could, in principle, be satisfied by another particular 'popping into' existence. Second, on the assumption that the particular may change some of its intrinsic properties, it could cease to satisfy the initial characterization. For instance, the sun may be defined as the only celestial body that revolves around the earth in a specific celestial sphere; or as the only celestial body that is 'hidden' during night. But the sun may suddenly interrupt its motion or appear during night. Or another celestial body may come into being which revolves in the same sphere or is

---

[26] Accordingly, at *APo*. 2.10, 94a7–9, in his example of a definition which is the conclusion of a demonstration of the what-it-is, he omits the *tis*: for, presumably, given that the middle term of the demonstration picks out the correct efficient cause, the nature of the thunder's noise is fixed: it is *that type* of noise in the clouds (*psophos en nephesi*), not simply *some sort of noise* (*psophos tis*) in the clouds.

hidden by night (1040a27–b2). These points suggest that the types of cause which are intimately linked with essence are definitory of a kind's nature. They are not particular or individual Humean causes. Rather, they are identity-fixers for kinds and their members, where the latter are taken to be essentially members of the respective kind.[27]

Furthermore, the sort of cause at issue is not something which simply obtains always. Nor is it just necessarily co-occurring with, or necessarily holding good of, the relevant kind of object. Its underlying modal force is stronger than such cases if indeed it is the kind's essence, nature, or identity-fixer. In an important example provided in *Posterior Analytics* 1.5, while every triangle is necessarily either scalene or isosceles or equilateral, a proof that uses this necessity as a basic premise and yields the theorem that every triangle has 2R would not be an explanatory demonstration (74a25–32). For it would not mirror the causal essence of a triangle, that in virtue of which having 2R necessarily holds of every triangle. A proper explanatory demonstration would employ the cause which is the nature of the unified single kind triangle, as opposed to a fragmented or 'episodic' disjunctive necessary feature such as being either scalene or isosceles or equilateral. As Aristotle puts it, such a merely necessary feature does not reveal what the triangle is as such (or in virtue of itself) or as a kind (74a30: *ou hē(i) trigōnon*; 31: *kat' eidos ou pan*).

The general picture I am adumbrating reflects Aristotle's interest in what he calls 'per se' causes: those in virtue of which the item caused (or *explanandum*) is as it is (*Phys.* 2.3, 195a5–7: *ou kata sumbebēkos…ou kath' heteron ti all' hē(i) andrias*; 195a32–b21; 2.5, 196b23–9: *oikias kath' hauto men aition*; 197a5–6; 12–15; 32–5). Indeed, at *Physics* 2.7, 198a24–7, Aristotle himself identifies certain substantive types of cause (efficient and final) with the essence or formal cause (*to ti esti*): while the efficient cause is the same as the essence in kind, the final cause and the essence are one in number. In light of these considerations, it seems fair to conclude that the cause, too, depends on the essence, just as the essence depends on the cause. If this is correct, what grounds the asymmetry of essence over necessity is precisely this intimate and insoluble interdependence, which gives rise to the distinctive concept of a 'causal essence' or 'essential cause'.

Conclusion

Aristotle's essentialism, as I interpret it, consists in the idea that essence grounds necessity in that it intrinsically involves a substantive type of cause. In virtue of

---

[27] I agree with the argument advanced by Williams and Charles 2013, 133–9, for the claim that, necessarily, if something is a member of a substance-kind, *K*, then it is necessarily a member of *K*. They also argue that it is necessary that a kind *K* has the essence it has iff it is a *K* (128–31).

this sort of cause, it possesses a robust asymmetric 'because' aspect. In the other direction, too, the relation of such a cause to essence is not extrinsic or chancy. Rather, it is a cause that is object-sensitive: an identity-fixer. So understood, Aristotle's claim that essence and cause are 'the same' entails that the essence–cause bond is so intimate that there cannot be any cases of essence which do not inherently include some weighty (not merely formal) type of cause. Nor can there be any genuine cases of cause which are accidental. Rather, a cause, too, should be an (at least partial) determinant of the relevant kind's nature. This essentialist position, then, conceives the essence–cause relation as interdependence or as sameness without identity. Moreover, it avoids reducing essence to cause, or conversely.

One may ask, at this juncture, why this position does not just identify essence and cause. Similarly, why not simply reduce essence to cause, or cause to essence, if the two are so intimately interwoven? There are philosophical as well as exegetical reasons to resist this stronger, identity view. It seems plausible to think that an item, x, taken as an essence discharges different theoretical and explanatory roles from x taken as a cause. Leibniz's Law, if it applies in the present context, would entail that there is a (hyperintensional?) difference between being an essence and being a cause. If so, the identity view proves unattractive. This is so despite the fact that being an essence and being a cause are necessarily equivalent, interdependent, or the same (without being identical).

It may be helpful to compare the interdependence view with some claims made in *Posterior Analytics* 1.8 and 2.8–10 about the relation between an explanatory demonstration and a scientific (causal) definition (2.10, 93b39: *horos logos ho dēlōn dia ti estin*). For example, the definition of thunder is the same or 'such as' the demonstration pertaining to thunder. But the two differ in position, arrangement, or mode in which they are said (1.8, 75b31–2; 2.10, 94a1–2; 94a3; a6–7). The explanatory demonstration is a demonstrative syllogism with premises and conclusion: noise belongs to fire quenching; fire quenching belongs to the clouds; therefore, noise belongs to the clouds. On the other hand, the causal definition consists of the same terms as the demonstration but is arranged as a continuous account specifying thunder's 'causal essence': noise in the clouds brought on by fire quenching. The claim that such demonstrations and definitions are 'the same but said in different ways' seems to be an epistemic counterpart to my interdependence thesis: our knowledge (or practices) of demonstration and definition are the same without being identical. Analogously, on the metaphysical, real-world side, essence and cause are interdependent or the same (without being identical): for they differ in the theoretical and explanatory roles they discharge. Perhaps this difference is merely notional or theoretical. But this seems unproblematic: after all, essentialism invokes highly abstract or theoretical considerations to devise philosophical explanations of things' natures and necessary features. At the same time, though, Aristotelian essentialism is anchored in scientifically discoverable specific essences and substantive types of cause.

A different sort of question is whether insisting on the presence of a cause in the essence of any and every type of object (and conversely) is a form of dogmatism or an a priori fixation. We may frame this question as arising from a dialectical impasse. An opponent to my interdependence view—perhaps a thinker who is sympathetic to Charles' and Williams' relaxed view—will insist that the notion of essence by itself involves an 'in virtue of' and so can sustain the asymmetry over necessity. My view disagrees and suggests that essence by itself is not sufficient but depends on causes (and conversely) to underpin that asymmetry. Have we reached a point where the discussion turns into a merely scholastic quibble? I don't think so. The question is whether and (if so) how the 'essence-alone' or 'essence-without-cause' view can tackle the asymmetry challenge raised in section 3. And this challenge cannot be met by simply insisting that essence by itself—without efficient, final, or material-grounding causes—is causal. Nor can it be addressed by simply distinguishing between real and non-real essence or definition, or between what is unqualifiedly prior and more intelligible in definition versus what is prior and more intelligible 'only-relative-to-us'. For, as argued earlier, these distinctions are shaky and vacuous unless they are underwritten by more weighty types of cause such as Aristotle's efficient, final, or material-grounding cause.

It is worth pointing out that the absence of a specific type of cause does not entail the complete absence of any and every type of cause from (a) particular case(s) of essence. If so, it does not warrant the 'essence alone' view. Aristotle himself admits that different cases call for different types of cause (*APo.* 2.11, 94a20–b26; *Met.* Z.17, 1041a28–32). He also holds that certain cases completely lack specific types of cause: for example, mathematical essences do not involve any efficient or final causes (*Met.* B.2, 996a21–b1). Moreover, in some cases, such as natural beings and phenomena, he maintains that all four types of cause are operative but one among them occupies a privileged position of primacy (*Phys.* 2.2, 194a15–b8; 2.7, 198a21–4; *DA* 1.1, 403a25–b19). His view, then, is not that some cases involve only the formal cause or 'essence alone'. Rather, he advances the attractive thesis that there are appropriate (substantive but not merely formal) types of cause for each *explanandum, definiendum*, or field of inquiry.

It is not detached metaphysical speculation but actual scientific inquiry, at any rate, which reveals what, if any, the relevant type of cause is. Indeed, in some cases, scientific investigation will show that there is no cause at all: for example, there are no causes for non-existents such as a goat-stag (*APo.* 2.7, 92b5–8). Further, in other cases it will discover that there is not a single kind of entity or phenomenon but several. For instance, while there is a common generic term 'magnanimity', there may be (at least) two distinct types of character-trait lumped together under this term: intolerance of insult and indifference to fortune (assuming that there is no state of character that genuinely unifies these two features; *APo.* 2.13, 97b13–25). Hence, Aristotle's view of how inquiry determines what types of cause are appropriate to specific essences is analogous to the idea that the best scientific method is devised by reference to the subject-matter's nature. For instance, just as the method of scientific experimentation would be inapposite in mathematics, similarly final and efficient causes are inappropriate for, and so absent from, mathematical essences. Material-grounding causes, however, together with the structure or arrangement of the relevant mathematical matter, are integral to such cases. These considerations are compatible with the idea that there may be some non-scientific definition even of a non-existent (*APo.* 2.10, 93b29–32; 2.7, 92b28–30). Similarly, there may be a single, pre-scientific definition of a term which lumps together several disparate phenomena: for example, an abstract or generic account of 'magnanimity', say 'greatness of soul', that encompasses schematically or artificially both intolerance of insult and indifference to fortune. Such a 'nominal' or 'semantic essence' would, presumably, be a priori graspable as a term's signification, or as the correct linguistic usage and practice, or what have you. It would not, however, involve any cause, explanation, or real essence.

My view of Aristotelian essentialism invites (at least) two further questions. In what follows I shall simply formulate these questions without tackling them in any detail. First, what is the relation between Aristotle's essentialism, as I understand it, and his modal syllogistic? If a causal essence or essential cause grounds necessity (and generally modality), can it also underwrite the truth of deductions with apodeictic and problematic premises and conclusions?[28] There is also a related exegetical question: why does Aristotle, in the *Posterior Analytics*, argue that scientific demonstrations consist of necessary premises and conclusions but systematically offer examples which are simply assertoric, or at least lack modal copula modifiers? Is this practice a symptom of the casual manner in which he usually provides examples or does it rest on some more significant point?

The second question is whether and (if so) how the present essentialist view would ground 'generic' or 'logical' necessities. Examples of generic or logical necessities include features such as not being both *F* and not *F* (*APo.* 1.11, 77a10–21); being either *F* or not *F* (77a22–3); being self-identical (*Met.* Z.17, 1041a16–20); or even a conclusion's necessarily following from some premises (*APr.* 1.1, 24b19–20). Such features belong necessarily to any and every kind of object regardless of its specific essence.[29] Can the present essentialist view ground such necessities? Suppose for the sake of the argument that Aristotle's defence of the Principles of Non-Contradiction (PNC) and of the Excluded Middle (PEM)

---

[28] In my view Aristotelian modalities should be understood as copula modifiers; see Patterson 1995, Charles 2000, 383–6, Malink 2006, 96–7, 106–16, Malink, 2013, 27 n. 10.

[29] The case of syllogistic following is difficult. Its necessity holds of any and every object irrespective of its essence in the sense that necessarily following from some syllogistic premises is independent of the specific content of a syllogism's terms. This is so provided that the terms are used in a uniform and non-homonymous way (see the conditions of *hen kai to hauto* and *mē homōnumon* at *APo.* 1.11, 77a5–9; compare *APr.* 1.23, 41a11–13, 1.28, 44b38–45a1).

in *Metaphysics* Γ may provide a form of grounding for generic or logical necessities. In particular, his arguments for the impossibility of coherently denying PNC may be taken as grounds for the fact that features such as not being both *F* and not *F* hold necessarily of any and every object: for PNC holds necessarily of any and every object in this way. At crucial junctures in his defence of PNC, however, Aristotle invokes the notion of essence—albeit in an innocuous, pre-theoretical, and non-partisan form (*Met.* Γ.4, 1006a28–34; 1007a20–7; 1007a25–33; also Γ.7, 1012a12–15, where essence is invoked in the defence of PEM).[30] If so, the argument would go, essence is pivotal in grounding even generic or logical necessities insofar as it is central in underpinning PNC (or at least in showing that PNC cannot be meaningfully denied).

Does this work, however, and if so, how? There are at least three different types of approach one may adopt:

(i) In a sceptical or pessimistic vein, it may be thought that generic or logical necessities are topic-neutral, whereas essence is topic-sensitive. If so, essence does not fit the bill as a ground for such necessities. Aristotle may be invoking some form of essentialism in *Metaphysics* Γ, but he is plainly wrong. What grounds the necessities at issue are the primary logical principles by themselves: PNC, PEM, the claim made at *Metaphysics* Z.17, 1041a18–19, that each thing is indivisible from (or the same as) itself, etc.[31]

(ii) It may be suggested that essence does play a role in grounding generic or logical necessities but only in the form of the abstract concept of the essence of some or other entity.

(iii) An optimistic or bolder view would maintain not only that essence is crucial for grounding such necessities, but also that this grounding is achieved by essences of determinate kinds of entity. For, to be the (determinable) essence of some or other entity is always to be a (determinate) essence of some specific (type of) entity.

Even in the more optimistic views, (ii) and (iii), however, it is important to clarify the notion of essence that contributes to grounding the necessities in question. Is it the causal-explanatory type of essence which relies on specific types of

---

[30] Code 1986, 346, Politis 2004, 150–3.

[31] Approach (i) may be missing the point of Aristotle's view: for (i) fails to distinguish between topic-neutral and reality-independent considerations. Aristotle does seem to think that the generality of PNC or PEM and of his discussion of such principles is topic-neutral: for example, he invokes dialectical methods of inquiry (e.g., his elenctic proof: 1006a11–18) or a non-partisan notion of essence. However, he does not think that this type of generality is independent of the structure of reality: metaphysics, which includes the inquiry into the logical principles, is the study of being *qua* being. Moreover, PNC and PEM are principles of all beings insofar as they exist. I owe this point to an anonymous OUP reader.

cause (favoured in the present argument)? Or is it an essence which is causal only in the thin, minimal sense of formal causation, unaided by any robust efficient, final, or material-grounding causes?

My present purpose is simply to raise these important questions. To offer a fuller picture of the Aristotelian causal-explanatory essentialism I am proposing, it would be necessary to treat these and other related questions in appropriate detail. I shall postpone this task for a separate, future study.[32]

Works Cited

Barnes, Jonathan (ed.). 1984. *The Complete Works of Aristotle*. Revised Oxford Translation. 2 vols. Princeton University Press.

Barnes, Jonathan. 1994. *Aristotle* Posterior Analytics. *Translated with a Commentary*. 2nd edition. Clarendon Aristotle Series. Clarendon Press.

Bostock, David. 1994. *Aristotle* Metaphysics *Books Z and H. Translated with a Commentary*. Clarendon Aristotle Series. Clarendon Press.

Charles, David. 2000. *Aristotle on Meaning and Essence*. Clarendon Press.

Charles, David. 2010. 'Definition and Explanation in the *Posterior Analytics* and *Metaphysics*', in *Definition in Greek Philosophy* (ed. D. Charles). Oxford University Press, 286–328.

Code, Alan. 1976. 'Aristotle's Response to Quine's Objections to Modal Logic', *Journal of Philosophical Logic* 5 (2), 159–86.

Code, Alan. 1986. 'Aristotle's Investigation of a Basic Logical Principle: Which Science Investigates the Principle of Non-contradiction?', *Canadian Journal of Philosophy* 16 (3), 341–58.

Cohen, S. M. 1978. 'Essentialism in Aristotle', *Review of Metaphysics* 31 (3), 387–405.

Fait, Paolo. 2019. 'Material Cause and Syllogistic Necessity in *Posterior Analytics* II 11', *Manuscrito* 42 (4), 282–322.

Ferejohn, Michael. 2013. *Formal Causes: Definition, Explanation, and Primacy in Socratic and Aristotelian Thought*. Oxford University Press.

Fine, Kit. 1994a. 'Essence and Modality', in *Philosophical Perspectives, 8: Logic and Language* (ed. J. Tomberlin). Ridgeview Publishing, 1–16.

Fine, Kit. 1994b. 'Senses of Essence', in *Modality, Morality, and Belief: Essays in Honour of Ruth Barcan Marcus* (ed. W. Sinnott-Armstrong). Cambridge University Press, 53–73.

---

[32] It is a great pleasure and honour to be editing and contributing to the present volume. David Charles' supervision of my D.Phil. thesis in 2002–6 and our subsequent discussions, collaborations, and friendly chats changed my intellectual outlook and shaped my approach to philosophy. I am deeply indebted to him and thank him for all he has done for me. Earlier versions of this chapter have been presented at the Universities of Campinas, Rio de Janeiro, Helsinki, UNAM, Oxford, and Stanford. I thank the participants for their questions, and especially Landon Hobbs and Emily Katz for their detailed written comments.

Fine, Kit. 1995a. 'Ontological Dependence', *Proceedings of the Aristotelian Society* 95, 269–90.

Fine, Kit. 1995b. 'The Logic of Essence', *Journal of Philosophical Logic* 24, 241–73.

Frede, Michael and Günther Patzig. 1988. *Aristoteles 'Metaphysik Z': Text, Übersetzung und Kommentar*. 2 vols. C. H. Beck.

Gotthelf, Allan. 2012. *Teleology, First Principles, and Scientific Method in Aristotle's Biology*. Oxford University Press.

Irwin, T. H. 1980. 'The Metaphysical and Psychological Basis of Aristotle's Ethics', in *Essays on Aristotle's Ethics* (ed. A. O. Rorty). University of California Press, 35–53.

Irwin, T. H. 1988. *Aristotle's First Principles*. Clarendon Press.

Koslicki, Kathrin. 2012. 'Essence, Necessity, and Explanation', in *Contemporary Aristotelian Metaphysics* (ed. T. E. Tahko). Cambridge University Press, 187–206.

Kung, Joan. 1977. 'Aristotle on Essence and Explanation', *Philosophical Studies* 31 (6), 361–83.

Lennox, James G. 2017. 'An Aristotelian Philosophy of Biology: Form, Function and Development', *Acta Philosophica* 26 (1), 33–51.

Lloyd, A. C. 1981. 'Necessity and Essence in the *Posterior Analytics*', *Aristotle on Science: The Posterior Analytics*. Proceedings of the Eight Symposium Aristotelicum. Antenore, 157–71.

Loux, Michael J. 1991. *Primary Ousia: An Essay on Aristotle's* Metaphysics *Z and* H. Cornell University Press.

McKirahan, Richard. 1992. *Principles and Proofs: Aristotle's Theory of Demonstrative Science*. Princeton University Press.

Malink, Marko. 2006. 'A Reconstruction of Aristotle's Modal Logic', *History and Philosophy of Logic* 27, 95–141.

Malink, Marko. 2013. *Aristotle's Modal Syllogistic*. Harvard University Press.

Malink, Marko. 2017. 'Aristotle on Principles as Elements', *Oxford Studies in Ancient Philosophy* 53, 163–214.

Patterson, Richard. 1995. *Aristotle's Modal Logic: Essence and Entailment in the Organon*. Cambridge University Press.

Politis, Vasilis. 2004. *Routledge Philosophy Guidebook to Aristotle and the* Metaphysics. Routledge.

Stein, Nathaniel. 2020. 'The Supposed Material Cause in *Posterior Analytics* 2.11', *Phronesis* 66 (1), 27–51.

Wedin, Michael V. 1984. 'Singular Statements and Essentialism in Aristotle', *Canadian Journal of Philosophy* 14 (Supplementary Volume 10: *New Essays on Aristotle*, ed. F. J. Pelletier and J. King-Farlow), 67–88.

White, Nicholas P. 1972–3. 'Origins of Aristotle's Essentialism', *Review of Metaphysics* 26, 57–85.

Williams, S. G. and David Charles. 2013. 'Essence, Modality and the Master Craftsman', in *Aristotle on Method and Metaphysics* (ed. E. Feser). Palgrave Macmillan, 121–45.

PART III
FORM, MATTER, AND TELEOLOGY

9

Predicative Hylomorphism
in *Metaphysics* Z

Mary Louise Gill

Introduction

In *Metaphysics* Z Aristotle analyses the relation between matter and form using what I call *predicative hylomorphism*. I contend that *Metaphysics* Z.1–16 are aporetic: these chapters set out various criteria for substantiality and in so doing reveal that nothing can jointly satisfy all the criteria and so succeed as primary substance. Aristotle's treatment of matter as a subject and as a continuant through change undermines the substantiality of even Aristotle's most promising candidate, substantial form. My chapter ends by gesturing towards a second attempt to solve the problem of substance in Z.17 and H.1–5, and finally towards a third and more satisfactory way to solve the problem in H.6 and Θ, a scheme using a different conception of matter and its relation to form.

1. Criteria for Substantiality in Z.1: Thisness and Separation

Aristotle's metaphysics, which he calls wisdom, first philosophy, the science of being *qua* being, and—in reference to its highest objects—theology, differs in structure from the special sciences, including natural philosophy. The special sciences carve off a genus of being and examine being *qua* numerable (arithmetic) or *qua* changeable (natural philosophy) or *qua* living (biology), and restrict their investigation to a single genus—number, change, life. Each science seeks the causes and principles in its own generic domain and assumes principles whose definition extends beyond that domain.[1] First philosophy examines being itself simply as being. Since being is not a genus (*APo.* 2.7, 92b14; *Met.* B.3, 998b22) but divides immediately into the categories—substance, quantity, quality, place, and so

---

[1] Aristotle claims that the extreme and middle terms of a demonstrative syllogism must all come from the same genus: *APo.* 1.7, 75b10–11; see also 1.9, 76a8–9 and 1.28, 87a38–9. I am grateful to Heike Sefrin-Weis (2002) for helping me understand the key difference between the structure of first philosophy and the special sciences.

Mary Louise Gill, *Predicative Hylomorphism in* Metaphysics Z In: *Aristotelian Metaphysics: Essays in Honour of David Charles*. Edited by: David Bronstein, Thomas Kjeller Johansen, and Michail Peramatzis, Oxford University Press.
© Oxford University Press 2024. DOI: 10.1093/oso/9780198908678.003.0009

202   MARY LOUISE GILL

on—first philosophy has a different structure from the special sciences and involves dependency relations focused on a core notion of being: substantial being (*ousia*) (*Met.* Γ.2).[2] The *Metaphysics*, though it explores all being *qua* being and its principles and causes, particularly studies the primary sort of being and seeks the causes and principles of substance.

Metaphysics Z.1 asserts at the start that being is said in many ways and refers to the chapter on being in Aristotle's philosophical lexicon, *Metaphysics* Δ.7, which distinguishes four modes of being: accidental being, being as truth, sorts of categorial being, and potential and actual being (see also *Met.* E.2, 1026a33–b2). Book E treats accidental being and being as truth and then sets them aside in the search for the causes and principles of being *qua* being (E.4, 1028a2–4). Z and H focus on categorial being with an emphasis on substance, the primary sort of categorial being, and ask: what is primary substance and on what grounds is it primary? Both books ask and answer the question from the perspective of the categories, a scheme laid out in the *Categories*, though *Metaphysics* H maps potentiality and actuality onto predicative hylomorphism. H.6 and Θ continue the same project—the investigation of substance—but from the perspective of potential and actual being and use a different model of hylomorphism.

After stating in Z.1 that being is said in many ways, Aristotle mentions the first category, not as *ousia*, but as *to ti esti kai tode ti* ('the what is it and this something'). Since the *ti esti* question seeks to spell out what a thing is and can be asked of entities in all the categories (*Top.* 1.9), and indeed of the highest categorial genera and of being itself (Z.1, 1028a36–b7), the expression in the initial characterization suggests that Aristotle is seeking something that satisfies both descriptions, *ti esti* and *tode ti*, but with emphasis on the second.

Etymologically, *tode* can serve as a neuter demonstrative pronoun or adjective, and *ti* can serve as a neuter indefinite pronoun or adjective. So either term could be the subject and the other an adjective modifying it.[3] On one interpretation *tode ti* is modelled on such phrases as *anthrōpos tis*, 'a certain human', with *tode* corresponding to *anthrōpos*, *ti* to *tis*. Aristotle speaks in the *Categories* of *ho tis anthrōpos*, the particular human, and characterizes it as indivisible (*atomos*) and one in number (*hen arithmō(i)*) (*Cat.* 2, 1b3–9).[4] In *Categories* 5 he reserves the

---

[2] Owen (1960) labelled the dependency relation 'focal meaning'; Shields (1999) relabelled the relation 'core-dependent homonymy'. The second label has the advantage of emphasizing that the notion is primarily ontological, not linguistic.

[3] On this topic, see Frede and Patzig 1988, vol. ii 15.

[4] Outside the *Categories* and other works in the *Organon* particular substances are analysed into matter and form. I am persuaded by Frede ([1978] 1987) that *atomos*, at least in the *Categories*, applies to entities that are not divisible into more specific items of the same sort, items Frede calls 'subjective parts' (52–4). Note that individuals in non-substance categories, such as the particular white, are also captured by the expressions *ta atoma* and *hen arithmō(i)* (1a6–9). Such entities are at the bottom of their own division tree but depend for their existence on particular substances as their subjects.

PREDICATIVE HYLOMORPHISM IN *METAPHYSICS Z*   203

expression *tode ti* for individuals in the first category (3b10–23), as distinct from all non-substances and the species and genera of substance. On this construal the phrase may be limited to particulars in the first category. The phrase also admits another interpretation. On the alternative construal, *tode* has demonstrative force pointing to something, and *ti* specifies what that thing is: *ti* indicates an object's identifying feature. In *Metaphysics* Z.3 Aristotle uses the expression *ti* ('something') on its own to specify some definite being in the category of substance, as distinct from *poson* ('so much') in reference to something in the category of quantity, and other categorial features (1029a20–1, a24–5).[5] So construed, the phrase need not specify a particular thing, though of course it can. We speak of 'this horse' and can pick out an individual or a certain breed, such as Arabian. On some occasions Aristotle contrasts *tode ti* as something definite with *toionde* ('such') as something indefinite, especially a genus (Z.13, 1039a1–3). On this construal the definiteness of the designated object is paramount.

Some scholars have called attention to an apparent tension between *ti esti* and *tode ti*, because in the *Categories* Aristotle uses *ti esti* especially in connection with species and genera in the category of substance, such as human being and animal, entities he there calls secondary substances, since both answer the question 'what is it?' asked of a particular human being, the species answering the question more specifically than the genus (2b7–22). G. E. L. Owen spoke of Aristotle as introducing a 'pincer movement' in Z, with *ti esti* pressing the search for substance towards something general and *tode ti* towards something particular.[6] A leading puzzle in book B to be resolved in the *Metaphysics* is precisely the question whether the first principles of first philosophy are universal or particular. Aristotle claims that, if a first principle is a universal, it is not a *tode ti* but a *toionde* ('such'). On the other hand, if first principles are particulars (*ta kath' hekasta*), they fail to be knowable, for knowledge of anything is universal (B.6, 1003a5–17). Evidently, he hopes to resolve this puzzle about the status of substance in the central books of the *Metaphysics*.[7]

The *Categories* defends one main criterion for substantiality—subjecthood— and attaches the label *tode ti* to an ultimate subject, such as a particular human or a particular horse. These individual substances are the ultimate *subjects* (*hupokeimena*) to which other entities belong—species, genera and differentiae that classify them, and non-substantial properties, such as qualities and quantities, that characterize them. Remove the individual objects, and everything else is removed

---

[5] Aristotle sometimes uses τόδε for the same purpose (e.g., *Met.* Z.7, 1032a14–15, H.6, 1045b1–2). So perhaps he would welcome either interpretation of *tode ti*, as long as one component specifies a feature and the other points to a subject possessing that feature.

[6] Owen 1978. See also Ross 1953, vol. ii 159–60, Burnyeat et al. 1979, 1. Frede and Patzig (1988, vol. ii 11–15), on the other hand, argue that already in the first sentence of Z Aristotle refers to his target primary substance—individual substantial form—from two perspectives.

[7] Reeve (2000, 12–17) calls this the 'Primacy Dilemma' and takes Aristotle's metaphysics and epistemology to be chiefly engaged in solving it.

204   MARY LOUISE GILL

as well (*Cat.* 2a34–b6).[8] Because they are ultimate subjects, concrete physical objects are *existentially* prior to their kinds, differentiae, and non-substance properties.

One claim in the *Categories*, also highlighting the role of an individual substance as the subject of properties, must be modified in light of Aristotle's analysis of change in *Physics* 1. He says in the *Categories* that it seems most distinctive of substance that something the same and numerically one is receptive of contraries: for instance, a particular human, who is at one time pale, comes to be at another time dark (*Cat.* 5, 4a10–21). In *Physics* 1 Aristotle argues that change requires three principles—a pair of opposites, such as pale and dark in the category of quality, and a substance such as a particular human as subject, at first pale and later dark. The subject persists intact while the human ceases to be pale and comes to be dark. The *Categories*' claim adequately captures three sorts of non-substance change: change of quality (alteration), change of quantity (growth and diminution), and change of place (locomotion). In all three cases a particular substance persists through the replacement of a pair of non-substance properties, either qualities, quantities, or places.

There is, however, a fourth sort of coming-to-be, the emergence of a new substance, and here a particular substance results from the change and so cannot be what persists through it. To accommodate substantial generation and destruction, Aristotle introduces form and matter: in substantial generation, form replaces its privation, and matter persists through the generation.

And so, when Aristotle returns to the question about primary substance in the *Metaphysics*, particular physical objects are not—at least not straightforwardly—primary, given their composition from matter and form. If we ask, 'what is the ultimate subject?', the hylomorphic complex is the subject for the kinds that classify it and for the properties that characterize it, but within the complex, matter is the subject for form, and so might have a better claim to be an ultimate subject than the hylomorphic compound it constitutes. Moreover, now when we ask, 'what is it?' of a particular human, the answer need not be the species or genus,

---

[8] An editor of this volume objects that we cannot properly secure asymmetry with the modal-existential view (priority in existence) because individual objects will be removed if other properties are removed. Peramatzis (2011, 12–13) offers an alternative notion of ontological priority, which he calls Priority in Being (PIB), according to which A is ontologically prior to B, if and only if A can be what it is independently of B being what it is, but the converse is not true. In the passage I cite, however, Aristotle appears to ignore PIB when he argues that everything else—including the species and genus of primary substance—depends on primary substance as its subject. To be sure, Aristotle says that secondary substances answer the question 'what is it?' asked of an individual substance (2b29–3a6), but he does not highlight the consequent priority in being of secondary substances to primary substances. PIB may come into play in the dependence of non-substances on substances, even in the *Categories*: see my discussion of the various modes of separation and priority below, pp. 205–7. Aristotle's failure to consider the essential dependence of primary substances on secondary substances is a shortcoming of his position in the *Categories*, rectified by his account of *kath' hauto* predication in *APo*. 1.4, to be discussed below in section 2.

called secondary substances in the *Categories*. If I point to a hunk of iron and ask 'what is it?', you might answer 'iron'. In *Physics* 2.1 Aristotle argues that both the form and the matter are natures of a sort, but form has a better claim than matter to be the nature of a natural thing, since nature is the inner source of the thing's proper motion and rest. In *De Anima* and the biological works, he identifies the nature of a living organism as its soul. So the soul might best answer the question asked of an individual living organism, 'what is it?'.

In Z.3 Aristotle calls both the hylomorphic compound and its form *tode ti* while withholding the label from an ultimate subject all of whose features belong to it accidentally. The main lesson: a *tode ti* is something with some definite feature in its own right (*kath' hauto*, 1029a20–30). Whether thisness demands particularity as well as definiteness remains an open question. If substantial form—such as the human soul—is a *tode ti*, must it be particular to Socrates alone? Or can it be definite because it is not divisible into more specific souls (and thus *atomos*), yet nonetheless be repeatable across the human species? The end of Z.8 states that substantial forms are not further divisible but repeatable:

> The whole thing—the form of such a kind (*to toionde eidos*) in these flesh and bones—is Callias and Socrates; and they are different on account of their matter (for it is different), but the same in form (*tō(i) eidei*), for the form is indivisible (*atomon gar to eidos*).[9] (1034a5–8)

This passage indicates that substantial forms can apply to multiple members of the same species, and yet be definite because not divisible into more specific forms.[10] If this passage represents Aristotle's considered view, then *tode ti* can pick out both particular substances and their repeatable but indivisible substantial form.

By coupling *tode ti* with *ti esti* Aristotle indicates that he is asking of a *tode ti*, say a particular human being, 'what is it?'. And the answer will specify something general and repeatable, even if the question is asked about a particular. The initial definite article tying the two expressions into one compound expression—*to ti esti kai tode ti*—reminds us that first philosophy seeks to understand the *being* of the things that are and in the first place something that is both *ti esti* and *tode ti*.

The remainder of Z.1 argues that, while both substances and non-substances are beings, substance is prior to non-substances in various ways, since they depend on it, whereas it does not depend in a comparable way on them. After

---

[9] Translations are my own.
[10] Frede and Patzig (1988, vol. i 87 and vol. ii 146–8) would dispute my claim. They translate *eidos* in its first occurrence as 'Form' and take it to pick out the form of the species, and in its second and third occurrences as 'Spezies'. This passage poses a problem for their view that Aristotle is committed to individual forms, unique to one sensible substance.

206 MARY LOUISE GILL

asking whether walking and being healthy and sitting are beings, Aristotle explains why we might ask the question:

> For none of them is naturally by itself (*kath' hauto*) or able to be separate (*chōrizesthai*) from substance, but rather, if in fact [they are beings], the walking thing, and the sitting thing, and the healthy thing are among the beings. These are evidently more beings [than walking, being healthy, and sitting], because there is some definite subject (*ti to hupokeimenon... hōrismenon*) for them, and this is the substance (*hē ousia*) and the particular (*to kath' hekaston*). (Z.1, 1028a22–7)

Qualities, such as being healthy, and changes, such as walking, depend for their existence on something else, some definite subject that is healthy or walking; and that subject, Aristotle says in Z.1, is the substance and the particular. In this passage he appeals to a further criterion of substantiality, which non-substances fail to satisfy: separation. He will use the expression in various ways in his later discussion, but here he appears to state a criterion already articulated in the *Categories*, albeit not in terms of separation. As we have already observed, entities in non-substance categories depend on substance as their subject and cannot exist without it. And within the category of substance, secondary substances—the species and genera of particular substances—are said of primary substances as their subject. So primary substance—something indivisible and one in number—is the subject of everything else. In *Physics* 1.2 he speaks of separation in the relevant sense: 'None of the other things is separate (*chōriston*) besides substance: for all of them are said of substance as their subject' (185a31–2).

I have already mentioned that Aristotle attributes thisness to both material composites and their form while withholding it from an ultimate bare subject in Z.3. There Aristotle rejects a bare subject as substance on grounds of separation, as well as thisness, and credits the composite and its form as satisfying both conditions (1029a26–30). In *Metaphysics* H.1, when he returns to the subject criterion and again mentions matter, form, and the compound as three sorts of subject, he claims that form is a *tode ti* and separate in account (*tō(i) logō(i) chōriston*), while the compound is simply separate (*chōriston haplōs*) (1042a26–31). Evidently there is more than one way to be separate. Eventually he will differentiate substances from other things, including artefacts, on grounds that they are causally separate from other things, because genuine substances are responsible for their own motion, whereas artefacts and other things depend in performing their function on some external source of motion (e.g., an axe, in order to chop, depends on someone to wield the axe). The notion of causal dependence and independence is already implicit in Z.1 in the phrase *kath' hauto*, a phrase we shall discuss more fully in the next section. In Z.3 Aristotle argues that a bare subject is nothing *kath' hauto*—not something (*ti*), or so much (*poson*), or anything else. All of its features belong to it accidentally (*kata sumbebēkos*) (1029a20–6). Indeed, no non-substance being is *kath' hauto*, claims Aristotle in Z.1: all non-substances depend on substance. That this dependence is causal will become more evident as we proceed. At this stage of the argument, it remains an open question whether a primary substance can be separate in account/logically without also being simply and causally separate, or whether genuine substances must be separate in all the ways articulated. I believe that Aristotle can ultimately answer this question in *Metaphysics* Θ: a primary substance is separate in all three ways.

Aristotle claims in Z.1 that substance is prior to other things in three ways: in account, in knowledge, and in time. The label 'priority in time' is odd in light of the characterization he goes on to give, but the notion spelled out is precisely the one he has just articulated in terms of separation. He says: 'None of the other things predicated is separate (*chōriston*), but this alone' (1028a33–4). Other things depend on substance as their subject; substance is existentially prior to them. Priority in knowledge tracks logical priority but adds something more: Aristotle claims that we know each of the categories when we know what it is. Non-substances cannot exist without belonging to a substance as their subject, and moreover they must be defined with reference to something in the category of substance (1028a34–6). As indicated, even in the *Categories* (2, 1a24–8) there is something at some level of generality in the category of substance with reference to which a non-substance is defined. For example, health is defined with reference to living thing, since health depends on living things to exist and to be what it is, and only living things can be healthy or sick; justice is defined with reference to human being, since justice cannot exist without rational beings who live in a community, and only humans can be just or unjust.[11] So substance is logically prior to non-substances and therefore also epistemically prior. At the same time, epistemic priority appears to point towards a further criterion, causal priority: to know what something is, we must be able to explain it, and to do that we appeal to causes.[12] Z.1 has thus set out two main criteria for substantiality—thisness and separation. Aristotle has also gestured towards definability and causal priority as further criteria or as ways of being separate. He appeals to thisness and separation explicitly in excluding a bare subject as substance in Z.3. Definability and causal primacy become central in Z.4–6 in the investigation of essence.

Before we turn to the essence criterion in Z.4–6, we should examine Aristotle's use of the phrase *kath' hauto* ('by itself', 'because of itself'), a key phrase in his treatment of essence but with more than one use. The preposition *kata* with the

---

[11] See Frede [1978] 1987. Note the importance of determining the generic level of the dependence, a point Aristotle emphasizes in *APo.* 1.5.

[12] Aristotle makes a distinction on several occasions between what is more knowable to us and what is more knowable by nature. Perceptible things are more knowable to us, so Aristotle often starts with them in an investigation, but he aims to reveal and make knowable things more knowable by nature, which are universal and causally explanatory. See 1029b3–12; see also *APo.* 1.2, 71b33–72a5.

208 MARY LOUISE GILL

accusative often has causal force: X is what it is *by* or *because of* something—either because of itself (*kath' hauto*) or because of something else (*kat' allo*).

2. Modes of Predication and *kath' hauto* Being

Posterior Analytics 1.4 spells out two modes of *kath' hauto* predication which structure the special sciences, and distinguishes accidental predication from both (73a34–b5).

(1) P belongs to S *kath' hauto* in one way (call it *kath' hauto*$_1$), if and only if P belongs to S, S cannot exist without P, and P must be mentioned in the account of what S is.

Aristotle gives two examples: line belongs *kath' hauto*$_1$ to triangle, and point to line. A triangle is defined as a two-dimensional figure limited by three lines, and a line is defined as a length limited by two points. The number of lines will be among the features that differentiate a triangle from other two-dimensional figures, such as a square. The genus of triangles—plane figure—also belongs to a triangle and other two-dimensional figures *kath' hauto*$_1$. An example from biology: both animal and biped belong *kath' hauto*$_1$ to the species human and to individual members of the species. In *Metaphysics* Δ.18, Aristotle discusses the various ways the phrase *kath' hauto* is used and says: 'In one way what is present in the what it is (*en tō(i) ti esti*): e.g., Callias is *kath' hauton* animal; for animal is present in his account, since Callias is a certain animal' (1022a27–9). Let us call features that belong to a subject *kath' hauto*$_1$ *essential* features of the subject—they are features a subject must have to exist and be what it is.

Posterior Analytics 1.4 then distinguishes a second type of *kath' hauto* predication:

(2) P belongs to S *kath' hauto* in a second way (call it *kath' hauto*$_2$), if and only if P belongs to S, P cannot exist without S, and S must be mentioned in the account of what P is.

Both odd and prime belong to number *kath' hauto*$_2$. Their existence and definition depend on number as their subject. Similarly, biped belongs to animal *kath' hauto*$_2$. Call odd and prime and biped *special* features of the subject to which they belong. They cannot exist or be what they are without the subject. Note that odd and prime are mere *pathē* ('affections') of number, because a number need not be odd or prime. At the same time, besides being their subject, number is also the genus that marks off a scientific domain to which they belong and so, not only do they belong to number *kath' hauto*$_2$, but it belongs to them *kath' hauto*$_1$—number is mentioned in the account of what odd and prime are. Likewise, biped is a *pathos* of animal, but animal is a defining feature of biped and so belongs to it *kath' hauto$_1$*.

Different from both (1) and (2) is:

(3) P belongs to S accidentally (*kata sumbebēkos*), if and only if P belongs to S, but neither is S defined as what it is with reference to P, nor is P defined as what it is with reference to S.

Aristotle's favourite example of accidental predication is *white human*. There is something general in the category of substance to which whiteness belongs *kath' hauto$_2$*—namely, body (*Cat.* 2, 1a27–9), and more precisely the surface of a body (*Met.* Δ.18, 1022a29–31)—but there is no definitional connection between white and human, since humans can be other colours, and colours can belong to the surface of other bodies.

Posterior Analytics 1.4 marks off a further key use of *kath' hauto* (73b5–8):

(4) P is precisely what S is (*estin hoper estin*) (call it *kath' hauto$_3$*), if and only if P belongs to S both *kath' hauto$_1$* and *kath' hauto$_2$*.

Aristotle illustrates failures of *kath' hauto$_3$* with two examples: the walking thing, being some different thing (*heteron ti on*), is walking; and similarly, the white thing. By contrast, he says: 'substance (*hē d' ousia*) and what signifies *tode ti*, not being something different, is precisely what it is' (*hē d' ousia kai hosa tode ti semainei ouch heteron ti onta estin hoper estin*) (73b7–8). Aristotle's initial examples display a failure of *kath' hauto$_3$* because they are something different *kath' hauto$_2$*. Recall a passage quoted above from *Metaphysics* Z.1: walking and being healthy and sitting are not *kath' hauto* but depend on something else that is walking or healthy or sitting. They depend on some definite subject, and that is the substance and the particular (1028a22–7). For example, they depend on a particular human being who is walking or healthy or sitting. As Aristotle states the point in *Metaphysics* Z.1, such entities fail to be separate on purely *existential* grounds: their existence depends on some definite substance as their subject. Existential dependence is not yet *kath' hauto$_2$*, *logical* dependence. It is not because walking belongs to a human being that something is a walking thing, since other sorts of animal walk besides humans. There is some general kind, which a human being is *kath' hauto$_1$*, in virtue of which a walking thing is a walking thing—namely, a footed or terrestrial thing—and walking depends on that general kind *kath' hauto$_2$*. Whatever succeeds as an *ousia* and *tode ti* should be what it is without being something else *kath' hauto$_1$* or *kath' hauto$_2$*. Thus *kath' hauto$_3$* is the limiting case of *kath' hauto$_1$* and *kath' hauto$_2$*. Aristotle gives some examples of *kath' hauto$_3$* in *Metaphysics* Δ.18. Having claimed that *kath' hauto* is said in many ways, he announces: 'In one way the essence (*to ti ēn einai*) for each thing is [that thing] *kath' hauto*, e.g., Callias is *kath' hauton* Callias and the essence of Callias' (1022a25–7). I aim to show that this notion captures the primary things Aristotle discusses in connection with the essence and causal criteria in Z.4–6.

3. The Project of Z.1–16

Aristotle ends Z.1 by stating that all his philosophical predecessors inquired into the question, what is being? (*ti to on*), a question which—given the dependence of other things on substance—comes down first to the question: what is *ousia*, the primary sort of being? While his predecessors answered the question in various ways, they shared an interest in determining what being of that sort is (1028b2–7). Z.2 then canvasses various candidates for substance—things most people agree on, such as animals and plants and their parts, the elements earth, water, air, and fire, and things composed of them, and the sun, moon, and stars; and then candidates advocated by various philosophers, such as the limits of bodies, Platonic forms, and numbers. Aristotle raises the question whether these should all count as substances or only some of them, or other things, and he asks whether there is a separate substance or not, apart from the perceptible things. But the first question is: what is substance? (1028b32).

Z.3 says at the start that substance is said in at least four ways and lists: essence, universal, genus, and subject. Scholars debate what this list amounts to.[13] Is he asking: for what reason do the entities listed in the previous chapter have a claim to be substance? Because they are subjects, essences, universals, genera? Or is he asking: what is the substance *of* the various candidates canvassed in the previous chapter? In the chapter on substance in Δ.8, Aristotle enumerates a list similar to the one in Z.2 and gives reasons why various candidates are substances. Elements and animals and their parts are substances because they are not said of a subject but other things are said of them (1017b10–14). He also considers the constituent of those subjects which is the cause of their being: for instance, the soul of a living thing (1017b14–16). In addition, he lists those constituent parts of such things that define and signify their thisness, whose elimination would eliminate the whole; he mentions that some people say that eliminating a plane eliminates a body, and eliminating a point eliminates a line (1017b17–21). Recall that *Posterior Analytics* 1.4 uses the example of point belonging to line as an instance of *kath' hauto*$_1$ (73a34–7): point is part of the essence of line. In Δ.8 he goes on to speak of the essence (*to ti ēn einai*), whose account is a definition, and he calls this the substance *of* each thing. He sums up his survey in the following statement:

---

[13] For a helpful discussion, see Devereux 2003.

It follows, then, that substance is said in two ways, both the ultimate subject, which is not further said of anything else; and whatever, being a *tode ti*, is also separate (*chōriston*), and such is the shape of each thing and the form. (1017b23–6)

We should presumably understand the list in Z.3 in a similar way. Aristotle is listing reasons why items in Z.2 have a claim to be substance. The genus and universal are not explicitly mentioned in Δ.8, but they could be cited as reasons why some of the candidates in Z.2 are regarded as substances. Aristotle associates Platonic forms with universals and genera (H.1, 1042a13–16) and says in Z.13 that some people regard the universal especially as a cause and principle (1038b6–8). He will argue that no universal is a substance in Z.13–16.

The list in Z.3 serves as a sort of table of contents for Z.3–16. Z.3 examines subjecthood, Z.4–11 examine essence, and Z.13 goes back to the table of contents and claims to have discussed essence and subject, and then turns to the universal, which Aristotle rejects. The genus gets no separate treatment, but the summary of Z in H.1 suggests that the genus was rejected along with the universal (1042a21–2).

4. Essence Criterion in Z.4–6

In tackling essence, Aristotle says in Z.4 that he will approach his topic *logikōs* ('logically', 1029b13), a phrase he sometimes contrasts with *phusikōs* ('physically'). He uses the term again in Z.17, where he asks, 'Why are these bricks and stones a house?' It is evident, he says, that one seeks the cause, and adds: 'It is evident that this is the essence, to speak *logikōs*, which is in some cases the final cause—what something is for the sake of—and in others the first mover' (1041a27–32). In Λ.1 he speaks of the early natural philosophers, who sought the principles and elements and causes of particulars, such as fire and earth, rather than what they share in common, body; and contrasts them with the Platonists, who regard universals as substances, 'because genera are universals, which they say are principles and causes, because they seek *logikōs*' (1069a25–30). The reference to the Platonists and their judgement that universals and genera, not particulars, are substances points towards the search for definitions by division especially in Plato's late dialogues.

Scholars have noticed that *Metaphysics* Z.4–6 avoid mentioning matter and form and that Aristotle restricts himself to terminology used in the logical works that constitute the *Organon*, including the *Categories* and *Posterior Analytics*, such as 'substance', *tode ti*, 'essence', 'definition', 'subject', 'predicate', 'genus', 'species', 'universal', 'particular', and the categories.[14] Whatever the motive for resisting talk

---

[14] Burnyeat 2001, 8.

212   MARY LOUISE GILL

of matter and form and not showing his hand in Z.4–6 as to what satisfies the essence criterion on Aristotle's own view, these chapters clearly emphasize the close relationship between essence and definition.[15] Z.5 ends with the claim: 'It is clear that definition (*horismos*) is the account of the essence, and that the essence belongs either to substances alone or especially and primarily and simply' (1031a11–14). As the point has been aptly put: 'essence is the ontological correlate of the definiens in a definition'.[16]

In *Metaphysics* Z.4 Aristotle marks off the essence (*to ti ēn einai*) of something as what that thing is *kath' hauto*$_1$ (1029b13–22).[17] The essence, he says, is precisely what something is. When one thing is said of another (*allo kat' allou legetai*), it is not precisely this something (*ouk estin hoper tode ti*) (1030a3–6). Put another way, there is an essence of those things whose account is a definition. Not just any account is a definition—the *Iliad* in twenty-four books is an account but not a definition. A definition is an account of something primary. Such things, he repeats, are not specified by predicating one thing of another: an essence will belong only to the species of a genus and to those alone (1030a6–13).

Aristotle makes his point a bit differently in Z.6, and the difference is significant. Whereas Z.4 uses the preposition *kata* with the genitive and denies that anything spelled out by predicating one thing *of another* (*kat' allou*) is a *tode ti* and substance, Z.6 uses the same preposition with the accusative, meaning *by* or *because of another* (*kat' allo*). After discussing the Platonic forms of Goodness and Beauty and Being and Oneness as candidate primary things, which are one and the same as their essence, he says:

So it is necessary that the Good and the essence of Good are one and Beauty and the essence of Beauty, and all things said not because of another (*mē kat' allo*) but because of themselves (*kath' hauta*) and primary. (1031b11–14)

And later in the same chapter, after raising worries about Platonic Forms and the infinite regress that results if a Form is what it is because of something other than itself, he concludes:

---

[15] Loux 1991, Code 1997, and Burnyeat 2001 argue in different ways that in these chapters Aristotle presents the framework for a theory of substance which is neutral between competing theories, especially his own and Plato's. I have rejected that interpretation (which Burnyeat calls 'the two levels') in Gill 2005 and argue that these chapters focus, not merely on substance, but on categorial being more generally.

[16] Code 1984, 15.

[17] I take the difficult passage, 1029b15–22, about white surface to exclude from a thing's essence what it is *kath' hauto*$_2$. Whiteness, a quality, is defined with reference to surface (Δ.18, 1022a16–17), itself abstracted from body, something in the category of substance (*Cat.* 2, 1a27–8). In Gill 1989 I identified the essence in Z.4 as form, taking the chapter to build on Z.3. Burnyeat (2001, 4–6) took me and others to task for assuming the identification of form and essence in Z.4–6. Although in Gill 2005 I reject Burnyeat's hypothesis of non-linearity (that each new beginning in Z.3, Z.4, Z.13, and Z.17 argues independently for the conclusion that primary substance is substantial form, without relying on conclusions of previous sections), Burnyeat is right to stress that Aristotle avoids appealing to matter and form in Z.4–6.

Therefore it is clear that, in the case of primary things and things said *kath'* *hauta*, each thing and its essence are the same and one. (1032a4–6).

Scholars have debated precisely what sort of oneness and sameness Aristotle is talking about.[18] In my view Aristotle's discussion of *kath' hauto* in *Posterior Analytics* 1.4 enables us fairly easily to understand what he is saying. A primary thing is something whose being is exhausted by what it is *kath' hauto*$_1$—by 'exhausted' I mean the predicate contains all and only what the subject is *kath' hauto*—and so the subject and its essence are one and the same, identical. In terms of Aristotle's distinctions in *Posterior Analytics* 1.4, the subject is precisely what it is *kath' hauto*$_3$. It is what it is *by* or *because of itself* and itself alone.[19]

At the end of Z.6 Aristotle tantalizingly suggests that Socrates might satisfy the essence criterion (1032a6–11), or at least that one might answer the sophistical objection about Socrates based on his argument that primary things and things said *kath' hauto* are the same as their essence. But Socrates does not succeed as a primary thing according to Aristotle's hylomorphism in *Metaphysics* Z, only on the revised version in Θ.[20]

5. The Snubness Analogy and Predicative Hylomorphism

Z.5 states a series of puzzles about things whose account is 'from addition' (*ek prostheseōs*), things like the property snubness, whose account is specified as 'this in that' (*tode en tō(i)de*). Snubness is defined as 'concavity in a nose'. Snubness—a property and not a matter–form composite—does not contain matter but its account must mention the bodily part in which it must be realized.

Snubness nicely exemplifies the first three sorts of predication marked off in the *Posterior Analytics*. Concavity belongs to snubness *kath' hauto*$_1$—as an *essential* property—because snubness must be concave to exist at all, and concavity must be mentioned in the account of what snubness is. Snubness belongs to the nose *kath' hauto*$_2$—as a *special* property—because snubness can exist only in noses, and nose must also be mentioned in the account of what snubness is.[21] Finally,

---

[18] There is a vast literature on Z.6. See, e.g., Code 1985, Dahl 1997, and recently Meister 2021.

[19] Philosophers tend to baulk, especially in discussing self-predication in Plato, at the strangeness to our ears of claims such as 'justice is just', and especially statements such as 'humanity is human', and want to read the 'is' as an 'is' of identity, not essential predication. But once we make clear that we are talking about the *being* of things—the content abstracted from enmattered particulars—it is not odd to predicate justice of justice, and humanity of humanity. In the case of a primary thing, its *being* is one and the same as its *essence*, what it is *kath' hauto*$_1$.

[20] Scholars cite Z.11, 1037a5–10, for Aristotle's response to the sophistical objection at the end of Z.6: Socrates' soul is the same as its essence, but Socrates the hylomorphic compound is not. This is a disappointing answer, and I suggest that Aristotle intends it to be a disappointing and provisional answer. It certainly does not measure up to the example from Δ.18, that Callias is *kath' hauton* Callias and the essence of Callias.

[21] The nose also belongs to snubness *kath' hauto*$_1$, as its genus, the domain studied by rhinology.

214 MARY LOUISE GILL

concavity belongs to the nose as an *accidental* property, if a nose happens to have that shape, because a nose can be what it is without being concave, and concavity can be what it is without belonging to a nose (e.g., bandiness, another property, is concavity in the legs: *SE* 31, 181b35–182a6).[22]

In *Metaphysics* E.1 Aristotle claims that some things resemble concavity and are definable without reference to perceptible matter, whereas others resemble snubness and require such a reference. Things resembling snubness include living organisms and their parts—nose, eye, face, flesh, bone, and animal as a whole; leaf, root, bark, and plant as a whole. He explains that the defining formula of all of these involves change, and so always involves matter (1025b30–1026a6).[23] In light of the snubness analogy, we should expect that material composites match snubness in involving the three types of predication: (1) form belongs to the composite *kath' hauto*$_1$, as an essential property; (2) the being of the composite—what the composite is—belongs to the matter *kath' hauto*$_2$, as a special property;[24] and (3) form belongs to matter accidentally.

---

[22] Charles (2021, ch. 2) appeals to the snubness analogy to make sense of Aristotle's hylomorphism but interprets the analogy differently from me. He takes snubness to be especially analogous to substantial form, which he regards as 'enmattered' or 'matter-involving' or *impure*, whereas I take the analogy to apply to the hylomorphic compound and regard substantial form as *pure* (analogous to concavity in the snubness analogy). He agrees that snubness belongs to the nose *kath' hauto*$_2$ (40 n. 18) and that nasality does not entail concavity (since some noses are aquiline) (82 n. 85) and that concavity does not entail nasality (47), since concavity can occur in other sorts of surface. I am uncertain whether he would agree that snubness entails concavity—that is, that concavity belongs to snubness *kath' hauto*$_1$—but I suspect that he would disagree, since he agrees (47 n. 12) with Peramatzis' (2011, 122–32) interpretation of the passage in *SE* 31. Although the passage claims that concavity reveals the same thing in common in the case of the snub and the bandy (181b32–4), Peramatzis thinks that being concave when applied to different objects is already permeated, in its very nature, by the material attributes integral to snubness or bandiness (126–7). An editor of this volume told me that concavity cannot be the essence of snubness, because concavity is an abstract, geometrical feature, whereas snubness is something material, concrete, perceptible, and changeable. My reply: changeability and so on are thanks to the nose to which snubness belongs *kath' hauto*$_2$ as a special property. Snubness is *impure*—and 'nasal concavity' gives a full account of what it is (i.e., the *being* of snubness)—but the being of snubness includes more than its essence. Let me stress that all non-substances are impure (as Aristotle claims in Z.1) because they must be defined with reference to something in the category of substance. Substantial form is not a non-substance property: it belongs in the category of substance. We should therefore be wary of regarding substantial form as impure, like a quality.

[23] Peramatzis (2011, 99–110) puts weight on Aristotle's claim immediately following this passage, where Aristotle says: 'and hence it belongs to the natural philosopher to study some soul too, as much of it as is not without matter' (1026a5–6). Peramatzis construes this claim to extend the snubness analogy to substantial form itself. But the claim could simply indicate that the natural philosopher needs to study those parts of the soul associated with particular bodily parts: for example, nutritive soul is realized in the digestive and reproductive organs, and perceptive soul in the sense organs. Intellect, which is not directly associated with any material part, might be a topic beyond the scope of natural philosophy, though I would argue that it, too, must be studied by the natural philosopher, since some of our material parts—for example, two feet and hands—are as they are because of our intellect. I discuss this topic in Gill, forthcoming. Thanks to Samuel Meister for pressing me to think harder about the text in E.1.

[24] Loux (1991, 140) objects to the idea of predicating a composite of its matter as logically 'grotesque', but the oddity is reduced once we recognize that what is predicated of the matter is the *being* of the composite: the being of the composite is the content mentioned in a full answer to the question, 'what is it?'. There is a fair amount of evidence that such predication is part of Aristotle's predicative model of

Z.4–6 avoid mentioning matter and form, though we have noted that Z.5 speaks at length about snubness, which Aristotle compares to material composites in E.1 and Z.11. Such entities can only be properly specified by mentioning the name or account of the subject to which the entity necessarily belongs (Z.5, 1030b23–8). Similarly, the account of the hylomorphic compound must mention its matter as well as its form.

Aristotle turns to material composites and their generation explicitly in Z.7–9. These chapters, which seem reminiscent of his natural philosophy, have often been taken to be a later addition to *Metaphysics* Z, though even scholars who regard them as a later addition agree that Aristotle added them himself.[25] Whether they were part of the original design or added later, Aristotle had good reasons to include them, given the architectonic of Z. Back-references to Z.8 in Z.15 (1039b20–7) and H.3 (1043b16–18) indicate that Aristotle takes Z.7–9 to have shown that substantial form is not generated.

These chapters argue that anything generated contains matter which pre-exists the compound and persists as a component of it.[26] Z.7 insists in conclusion that the persisting matter must be mentioned in the account of the generated compound:[27]

> Therefore, as is said, something cannot come to be if nothing pre-existed. It is then evident that some part will exist; for matter is a part, since this [matter] is present in and comes to be [the product]. But is it also one of the things [mentioned] in the account? We speak in both ways about what brazen circles are (*tous chalkous kuklous ti eisi*), mentioning both the matter that it is bronze, and the form that it is such a shape, and this [shape] is the kind (*genos*) in which it [the brazen circle] is first placed. Certainly the brazen circle includes matter in its account. (1032b30–1033a5)

---

hylomorphism. See *Met.* Z.3, 1029a23–4 and Z.17, 1041a23–7. Compare Devereux 2003: whereas Devereux regards this sort of predication as the 'new view' in Z.3 and Z.17 improving on what he argues is Aristotle's earlier view in H, I regard it as part of the predicative model articulated in *APo.* 1.4 that Aristotle ultimately rejects for hylomorphic compounds.

[25] Burnyeat (2001, 29–38) discusses in detail why he takes Z.7–9 to be a later insertion by Aristotle.

[26] Compare Aristotle's frequent characterization of matter as 'that from which (*ex hou*) something is generated, being present in it (*enuparchontos*), as the bronze of the statue and the silver of the bowl' (*Phys.* 2.3, 194b23–6; see also *Met.* Δ.4, 1014b17–18, b26–35).

[27] Peramatzis (2011, 41) regards this passage as evidence that matter must be part of the *form* of the composite and so as evidence for impure forms. Given that just earlier in the chapter Aristotle said 'by substance without matter I mean the essence' (1032b14), Peramatzis distinguishes between matter involved in the form (in the later passage) from bits of matter in the earlier passage. Malink 2013 (348, 350–1) has a helpful discussion of this part of Peramatzis' view. Charles' (2021, 61) view is similar to Peramatizis' in this respect. He speaks of matter *as principle* (involved in the form) and matter *as matter*. I should think that we could ask of matter as matter 'what is it?' and reply, for example, 'earth' or 'bronze, consisting of some ratio of copper to tin'. The distinction between matter as principle and matter as matter seems problematic, especially in Z.7–8, where Aristotle is arguing that anything generated contains matter which pre-exists its generation.

216 MARY LOUISE GILL

In Z.8 Aristotle argues that a producer generates a product by causing the form to be in the matter. The form is not generated, because if it were, it too would be a compound, with matter as a constituent of it (1033b3–8). Only the hylomorphic compound is generated. Aristotle extends his claim about the brazen sphere in Z.7 to natural individuals and their kinds in Z.8:

> The whole this, Callias or Socrates, is like this brazen sphere, and human being and animal like brazen sphere generally. (1033b24–6)

These conclusions prepare the ground for an important claim in Z.10:

> Human being and horse and the things that apply in this way to particulars, but universally, are not substance but a certain compound from this formula and this matter taken universally. (1035b27–30)

The species of living organisms are universal composites whose account mentions both form and matter. For example, the species human is human soul in flesh and bones (1037a5–10). As snubness does not contain matter but is defined with reference to the material part in which it must be realized, so the substantial species does not contain matter, but its account must mention the sort of matter that constitutes the thing and persists when it perishes. Thus Z.7–9 show that form is not generated and so does not involve matter, at least not on grounds of being generated. The question remains whether substantial form resembles snubness on some other ground. Z.10–11, as I read them, argue that form is definable without reference to matter. If I am right, substantial form will satisfy the Z.6 criterion and be separate in account.

6. Hylomorphism in *Metaphysics* Z.11

To understand Aristotle's hylomorphism in the section on essence, let us start with his summary of conclusions at the end of Z.11. I translate the first half of the summary:

> What, then, the essence is and how it is itself by itself (*auto kath' hauto*), has been said generally for every case, and why in some cases the account of the essence includes the parts of the thing defined, while in other cases not; and that in the account of substance the parts as matter are not included, for they are not parts of that substance but of the compound substance. And of this [compound substance] there is in a way an account, and [in a way] not; for there is no account with the matter (for it is indefinite), but in accordance with the primary substance there is, for example, of human being the account of the soul. For the substance is the indwelling form, from which and the matter the compound is called substance. (1037a21–30)

PREDICATIVE HYLOMORPHISM IN *METAPHYSICS Z*   217

For many readers (including me) this passage comes as a shock. How can it be that the compound has no account that mentions the matter?[28] In the previous section I quoted texts from Z.7, Z.8, and Z.10 in which Aristotle says that the matter is mentioned in the account of the compound. Later in this section we shall consider the much-discussed Socrates the Younger passage earlier in Z.11, which adds to the evidence. The argument of Z.4–11 has prepared us to hear that substantial form alone is strictly definable and that the compound has an account but not a strict definition, since a full answer to the question 'what is it?' must mention the matter as well as the form: the compound is *this in that*. The summary states, as expected, that definition is of the form alone, and that the account of the form omits the matter. But the passage goes on to say that the hylomorphic compound has an account in a way because of (*kata* + accusative) its primary substance—for instance, of human being an account of its soul—but no account with its matter, because it is indefinite (*aoriston*).

The summary is the main evidence Michael Frede relied on to urge that in the Socrates the Younger passage Aristotle argues that, not only are forms definable without reference to matter, but so are sensible substances.[29] Since that passage appears to conflict with the summary, Frede undertook to reinterpret the Socrates the Younger passage. We begin with the context.

Z.11 opens by saying, in reflection on the discussion about various sorts of parts in Z.10, that one might reasonably be puzzled about which parts are parts of the form, and which not but part of the hylomorphic compound, and he says that if the answer is not clear, it is not possible to define each thing. He then considers three puzzles, the first (1036a29–b7) concerning substantial form, which he resolves by means of a thought experiment either to show that the form is definable without reference to matter or (as some scholars argue) to raise a question to be resolved in the third puzzle.[30] The second passage (1036b7–20) considers mathematical objects and argues that Platonists and others go too far in removing matter, such as points and continuity, and so end up unable to differentiate things that are evidently different: for instance, the number two and a line (which is twoness in length). At the end of the second puzzle passage, Aristotle says:

> So, then, we have said that the situation concerning definitions has some difficulty, and for what reason. Hence, too, to reduce all things in this way and do away with matter is useless labour; for some things perhaps are *this in that* (*tod' en tō(i)d'*) or *these things in that state* (*hōdi tadi echonta*). (1036b21–4)

---

[28] Gill 1989, 136–8 and n. 60.   [29] Frede 1990.
[30] I take the passage in the first way (Gill 1989, 131–3). Peramatzis (2011, 55–9) agrees that this passage concerns substantial form, but (93) regards it as raising a question to be resolved in the Socrates the Younger passage.

218   MARY LOUISE GILL

Evidently Aristotle rejects the extreme view of the Platonists as going too far in removing what he calls 'intelligible' matter, including points, lines, and extension. Such parts must be mentioned to distinguish geometrical objects from numbers.

But then he goes on in a third puzzle to discuss a comparison the Platonist Socrates the Younger used to make between human being and circle, a comparison Aristotle says leads away from the truth:

> And the comparison about animal which Socrates the Younger used to state, is not sound; for it leads away from the truth, and makes one think that it is possible for the human being to exist without its parts, just like the circle without the bronze. But the case is not similar. For animal is something perceptible,[31] and cannot be defined without motion, hence not without the parts being in some state (*oud' aneu tōn merōn echontōn pōs*). For a hand in not every state is part of the human being, but one able to perform its function, therefore one that is ensouled; if it is not ensouled it is not a part. (1036b24–32)

This passage focuses on a hylomorphic compound. Whereas the first passage was discussing the substance of circle (*tēs tou kuklou ousias*, 1036a33) and the form of human (*to tou anthrōpou eidos*, 1036b3), here Aristotle speaks, not of the form, but of something perceptible, with material parts, something that can be characterized in two ways, either as *this in that* (*tod' en tō(i)d'*) or as *these things in that state* (*hōdi tadi echonta*) (1036a23–4). He used the first phrase, 'this in that', in Z.5 in connection with properties such as snubness, whose account must mention the subject to which snubness belongs *kath' hauto₂*: snubness is concavity *in a nose*.[32] Hylomorphic compounds, too, are *this* (form) *in that* (matter): for instance, soul in flesh and bones. The second phrase, 'these things in that state', focuses on the relevant subject: matter disposed in such and such a way. The passage goes on to deny that parts in just any state are parts of the animal—a hand is part of a human being only if it is able to perform its function (1036b28–32). A dead hand is not a genuine hand, but a hand 'in name only', as he sometimes says.[33] A genuine hand must be properly hooked up to the organism's soul.

---

[31] I reject Frede and Patzig's (1988) proposed emendation of *aisthēton* (perceptible) to *aisthētikon* (perceptive) in their translation: there is no MS support for their proposal and the text makes excellent sense as it is.

[32] Neither Charles nor Peramatzis discusses Z.5 in any detail. Why does Aristotle say in Z.5 (compare the summary in Z.11, 1037a29–33) that snubness in a nose is *concavity in a nose in a nose* (1030b28–1031a1)? The duplication makes sense if we realize that Aristotle is talking about one sort of matter, which must be mentioned in an account of the property snubness and mentioned again when we speak of an actual nose with that property. The nose must be mentioned twice. The puzzles in Z.5 should perhaps caution us not to extend the snubness analogy to substantial forms, lest an account of the hylomorphic compound require mentioning the matter twice.

[33] E.g., Z.10, 1035b24–5; *Meteor*. 4.12, 389b31–390a1, 390a10–13.

The subject in the appropriate state to perform its function is the matter that constitutes the organism and survives when it dies. Functional matter is destroyed when the animal dies, but on the predicative model of hylomorphism in *Metaphysics* Z, matter at the next level down persists. As Aristotle states more than once in Z.10, a human being perishes into flesh and bones (1035a17–22, a31–4).[34] These material parts have a definite nature in their own right, independent of the form of the complex, and so can survive as what they are when the organism's form is removed. For things with functional matter, the proximate matter occupies the next lower rung of material analysis, described in the first half of Θ.7 as matter sufficiently worked up to be turned into the product without further transformations of it (1049a8–11). For example, bronze, but not earth, is the proximate matter of a sphere. Earth must first be transformed into stuff of sufficient complexity to serve as the proper or proximate matter of a sphere. In the case of living organisms, the proper matter is stuff that can survive the destruction of an organism—stuff Aristotle calls in H.4 the *proper* (*oikeia/idia*) matter and sometimes the *proximate* (*eschatē*) matter.[35] The functional capacities belong to this matter *accidentally*. The functional matter is therefore determined in two ways—as the organism itself is due to its proper matter—with reference to the form and with reference to the proper matter, as *this in that* or *these things in that state* (1036b23–4).[36]

---

[34] In contrast with *Met. Z*, *GA* 2.1, 734b24–31, treats flesh as a functional part which loses its identity when separated from the living body. Compare *Meteor.* 4.12, 390a14–15. To show that the matter is functional all the way down, even including vital heat, Aristotle needs the alternative model of hylomorphism he presents in H.6 and Θ.

[35] Scholars frequently identify the *proximate* matter with the functional matter and contrast it with the *remote* matter (see, e.g., Irwin 1988, ch. 11 §131; ch. 12 §§135, 138–9). This identification seems to me misleading. If a thing has functional matter, the proper or proximate matter is, in my view, one level below the functional matter. At that level of hylomorphic analysis, a thing with functional matter is comparable to a bronze sphere, which lacks functional matter.

[36] Peramatzis (2011, 91–102) and Charles (2021, 53–4) take the Socrates the Younger passage to concern substantial forms, which they regard as matter-involving. I have profited from reading Malink's (2013, 343–8) discussion of Peramatzis' interpretation of the passage. Charles puts considerable weight on the two phrases, *tod' en tō(i)d'* and *hōdi tadi echonta*, and takes both to refer to substantial form. Returning to the analogy with snubness, Charles claims that Aristotle is indifferent whether I say 'nasal concavity' or 'concave nasality' (54 n. 33). Either component can serve as the indefinite determinable and the other as the determinant. Caston's (2009) 'Commentary on Charles' (2009) helpfully clarifies these issues. I take it that both Charles and Peramatzis are motivated by a desire to save the hylomorphic complex as substance in the face of the Z.6 essence criterion and the summary at the end of Z.11 claiming that the account of the compound specifies the form and not the matter. If the form itself is matter-involving, such claims might seem unproblematic. There is a worry, however. The substantial form, conceived as impure, is arguably defined with reference to two distinct and independent items—comparable to nose and concavity—and therefore those more fundamental items should be prior to what is defined with reference to both (compare n. 22 above). The form will be defined *kat' allo* and not *kath' hauto* (Z.6, 1031b13–14). Charles (2009, 2021, 51–3) argues that substantial form is inextricably matter-involving, an idea I find hard to grasp: even non-substances, which depend for what they are on something in the category of substance, can be analysed into two distinct components—something more general in their own category, and a substance at some level of generality, on whose being and existence the non-substance depends. Though I share the desire to save the hylomorphic complex, I do not think impure forms are the answer. For a thorough discussion of the debate about pure and impure forms in Z.10–11 and a different solution, see Meister 2020.

220   MARY LOUISE GILL

We now return to Aristotle's claim in the summary that the compound has an account in one way—an account of its indwelling form—and in another way not. He explains: 'for there is no account with the matter (for it is indefinite)' (1037a27). How should we understand matter's indefiniteness? Consider the continuation of the summary in Z.11. Here Aristotle compares the indwelling form to concavity and then returns to snub nose and snubness:

> For example, concavity—for from this and the nose are snub nose and snubness (for the nose will be present twice in these). In the compound substance, e.g., in snub nose or Callias, the matter too is present. (1037a30–3)

The hylomorphic compound not only resembles snubness—concavity in a nose— but more importantly concavity in a nose (a property) in some particular nose, which has, in addition to functional capacities determined by the form of the animal whose nose it is, also dispositional properties belonging to its material parts—the nose consists of soft, squeezable flesh; hard, breakable nasal bridge. Moreover, a particular snub nose, though it retains its concave shape (unless subjected to the scalpel), has other non-substance properties that change from moment to moment: it is paler now, darker later, in the house of Agathon now, in the Agora later, suffering from sniffles and allergies now, healthy later, and so on. The nose and the concrete hylomorphic compound whose nose it is are indefinite because their matter varies over time, and that variability cannot be captured in a stable account. A full account of the compound would be like a film, different from frame to frame, from moment to moment. Or to use Aristotle's own favourite example, such an account would be like the *Iliad* in twenty-four books. He explicitly denies that such accounts are definitions (Z.4, 1030a7–9, H.6, 1045a12–14).

I have given an account of the indefiniteness of matter, but why does Aristotle claim in the summary that the hylomorphic compound has an account in terms of its form alone, of human being an account of the soul? He adds: 'for substance is the indwelling form, from which and the matter the compound is called substance' (1037a29–30). Not only does the claim that an account of the compound mentions only the form conflict with the passages from Z.7, Z.8, Z.10, discussed in section 5, and with the Socrates the Younger passage discussed in this section, it also conflicts with the final part of the summary itself. After mentioning concavity, snubness, and snub nose (quoted above), Aristotle continues:

> [We have said] also that the substance and each thing is in some cases the same, as in the case of primary substances, e.g., concavity and the being of concavity, if it is primary (I mean by primary what is not said by being one thing in another and in a subject as matter), while those things that are as matter or combined with matter, are not the same, nor if they are one accidentally, e.g., Socrates and the musical thing; for these are the same accidentally. (1037a33–b7)

Aristotle thus ends his summary by reminding us of the Z.6 thesis, that primary things are the same as their essence, whereas others are not. Things the same as their essence are not said by being one thing in another (*mē legetai tō(i) allo en allō(i)*), and in a subject as matter (*kai hupokeimenō(i) hōs hulē(i)*). Things combined with matter are not the same as their essence. Whereas a primary thing is the same as its essence, as required by the essence criterion in Z.6, the compound is not the same, because its being includes its matter as well as its form. As Aristotle puts the point plainly in H.3, 'soul is the same as the essence of soul, whereas human being is not the same as the essence of human being' (1043b2–4).[37]

The claim in the summary of Z.11, that the hylomorphic complex has an account in terms of its form alone, can only be a sort of booby prize, since it is not supported by Aristotle's argument in Z. Either that, or the claim is aspirational. Once Aristotle revises his conception of matter and its relation to form in H.6 and Θ, the hylomorphic complex will be definable with reference to its form alone. But he needs a different model of hylomorphism to get there.

In Z.4–11 Aristotle has argued that substantial form satisfies the essence criterion, whereas the hylomorphic compound—whether particular or universal— does not. Many scholars regard the conclusion at the end of Z.11 as Aristotle's final conclusion. And yet Z.11 is not the end of the story, and what follows calls into question the status of substantial form.

7. Problems for Substantial Form

In Z.13–16 Aristotle argues—primarily against the Platonists—that no universal is a substance. There is an obvious problem, as many have noticed: definitions are of universals (Z.10, 1035b34, Z.11, 1036a28–29); form is repeatable and therefore satisfies the definition of a universal—something predicated of more than one thing (Z.13, 1038b11–12, Z.16, 1040b25–6; see also *De Int.* 7, 17a38–b1). One might therefore conclude immediately that substantial form is not substance. Some scholars have undertaken to show that Aristotle's substantial forms do not fit his notion of a universal in Z.13. To be sure, Z.13 does especially target genera for disqualification, kinds predicable of more than one species (not to mention of more than one individual), and he labels a universal as an indefinite 'such' (*toionde*), not a definite *tode ti* (1039a1–2). As we have seen, in Z and elsewhere Aristotle applies the label *tode ti* to substantial form, as well as the particular

---

[37] Charles (2021, 90–1 and n. 99) has attributed to me (1989) the view that the compound has two essences, one corresponding to its form, the other to its form-matter being. That is not my view: I distinguish between the being of something (the full answer to the question, 'what is it?', whose answer mentions what it is both *kath' hauto*₁ and *kath' hauto*₂) and its essence, which specifies only what it is *kath' hauto*₁. For primary things, the being and essence are one and the same. In Z the compound is not a primary thing.

222   MARY LOUISE GILL

hylomorphic compound. Other scholars have argued that Z.13 demonstrates Aristotle's commitment to individual forms.

According to Z.13–16, substantial forms are repeatable—including forms with a single instance, such as the sun—because there could be another instance with all the same properties (Z.15, 1040a27–b4). Although substantial forms are different from generic universals, in my view neither of the main interpretive strategies proposed can save substantial form from all the objections to the universal in Z.13–16.[38] There is one serious objection that undermines substantial forms along with the indefinite kinds he has chiefly in view. Aristotle claims that substance is not predicated of a subject:

> That which is not predicated of a subject is said to be substance, but the universal is always predicated of some subject. (1038b15–16)

Substantial form, too, is predicated of a subject, since it is predicated of matter and of the compound whose form it is. And that is so, whether form is a universal or a particular, with only one bearer.

Some commentators urge that the objection does not apply to substantial form because form is not predicated of the composite (contrary to my understanding of *kath' hauto* predication and its application to hylomorphic compounds in sections 2, 5, and 6 of this chapter). They insist that, although form is predicated of matter, matter is not a proper subject. This response is not convincing: at the beginning of Z.13 Aristotle mentions that he has already discussed two ways to be a subject, either as a *tode ti*, as an animal is the subject of its properties, or as the matter for the actuality (1038b3–6). Matter may fail to be a *tode ti*, but as matter it is evidently a sort of subject. If form is predicated of matter as a subject, Aristotle's objection that a universal is always predicated of a subject tells against substantial form as well. Substantial form depends on matter for its existence, even if it can be defined apart from matter. Aristotle has a good reason, when he returns to subjecthood in H.1, to identify form as merely separate in account. Only the hylomorphic compound is said to be simply separate (1042a28–31).

This conclusion is reinforced by another objection Aristotle makes against the Platonists in Z.13: 'Further, substance will be present in Socrates, so that it is the substance of two things' (1038b29–30). I have argued that proper matter—the matter at one level down from the functional matter, to which functional capacities belong as a subject—is definite and distinct from the form of the compound whose matter it is. This matter persists when the compound ceases to exist. And so, whether substantial form belongs only to proper matter (accidentally) or also to the compound (*kath' hauto*$_1$), form fails to be simply separate: it depends on distinct matter as a subject for its realization. If, at some level of

---

[38] I have discussed Z.13 in detail in Gill 2001.

hylomorphic analysis, form belongs to matter accidentally, form belongs to a distinct subject and is therefore the substance of two things—itself (as argued in Z.6) and of an individual such as Socrates whose being is determined by his proper matter as well as his form.[39]

And now it becomes doubtful that substantial form even satisfies the main objection raised against the universal in Z.13, the so-called *Idion* Argument, that substance is proper (*idios*) to each thing and does not belong to something else, whereas the universal is common to more than one thing (1038b9–15). If the essence of Socrates is proper to itself and to Socrates, then Socrates' essence belongs to at least two things—itself and Socrates. Substantial form may be separate in account from other things, as required by the essence criterion in Z.6, but because its existence depends on something else whose being is distinct from its essence, the essence fails to be proper to only one thing.

By the end of Z.16 the aporia about substance has been fully stated. Nothing succeeds as primary substance: not an ultimate bare subject, which is neither a *tode ti* nor separate (Z.3); not the hylomorphic compound, including ordinary Aristotelian matter, because the being of the compound is not the same as its essence (Z.4–11); and not substantial form, because it depends on a distinct subject for its realization (Z.13–16). Doubtless one could try to finesse these results: for instance, downgrade subjecthood and simple separation as criteria for substantiality so that substantial form wins by satisfying the other criteria. Or argue that form is the cause of substantial being, the substance *of* the hylomorphic compound but not predicated of the matter that constitutes that compound or of the compound itself.[40]

8. Solving the Problem of Substance

Aristotle has in my view a better and more satisfying solution to the problem of substance. Perhaps ironically, saving substantial form depends on saving the hylomorphic compound at the same time. To save the compound he must confront the troublesome conception of matter responsible for the unhappy results in Z.3–16. Aristotle makes two more attempts to solve the problem of substance in the central books of the *Metaphysics*, one in Z.17 and spelled out in more detail in H.1–5, the other in H.6 and developed in Θ.

Z.17 makes a fresh start and argues that we must explain why one thing belongs to another (*dia ti allo allō(i) tini huparchei*, 1041a11) or *ti kata tinos* ('one thing predicated of another', 1041a23). For example, why are these bricks and stones a house? Put another way: why does being a house belong to these bricks and

---

[39] Compare Z.16, 1040b23–4: 'Substance belongs to nothing except itself and that which has it, of which it is substance.'

[40] See Witt 1989, ch. 4.

stones? (1041a26–7). Aristotle's answer: because of the form—substance as form is the first cause of being (*touto gar aition proton tou einai*, 1041b28).[41] In this second attempt to solve the problem of substance, Aristotle continues to treat the matter as something definite and distinct in being from the form, something whose potentiality to be the product is grounded in its actual being as the matter that it is—for example, bricks and stones are actually bricks and stones and potentially a house (H.2, 1043a14–19). Moreover, he clearly speaks of the thing predicated of the matter as substantial form (characterized as *energeia*) (H.2, 1043a4–7). And so, in my view, the second approach faces the same obstacles as the first.

Aristotle's solution comes instead in his third approach to the problem of substance, from the perspective of potential and actual being. The solution demands a reassessment of proper or proximate matter in H.6 and Θ.7 as *indefinite* and *potential*.[42] The matter from which a compound is generated is *transformed* into the functional parts, leaving mere traces of its former self as dispositional properties of those functional parts. Matter that constitutes a hylomorphic complex is an indefinite determinable which form differentiates into some definite thing. On this conception Aristotle can embrace functional matter all the way down to the elements—material whose being is exhausted by the form of the complex it constitutes.

On the reconceived model of hylomorphism, Aristotle can finally make good on his claim in the summary of Z.11 that the compound is definable in terms of its form alone, as well as his claim in Δ.18 that Callias is *kath' hauton* Callias and the essence of Callias (1022a25–7). He can also answer the sophistical objection about Socrates at the end of Z.6, 1032a6–10. Living organisms satisfy the essence criterion in Z.6, because their being is exhausted by their essence. They are also *tode ti* and simply separate, as well as separate in account from everything else. They are, moreover, causally separate because they are responsible for their own natural behaviour. Such individuals claim priority over other things in all the ways enumerated in Z.1 and elaborated in Θ.8. I call Aristotle's reconception of matter and its relation to form *genus-differentia hylomorphism*.[43,44]

---

[41] For a compelling analysis of Z.17, see Pfeiffer 2021.

[42] This indefiniteness is different from that mentioned in the summary in Z.11. Matter in Z was quite definite in its nature but indefinite because of its many changing properties.

[43] I discuss Aristotle's genus-differentia model of hylomorphism in Gill 2010 on Z.12 and H.6 and in Gill 2021 on *Met.* Θ.

[44] I dedicate this chapter to my friend and colleague David Charles. David is a model for all of us in ancient philosophy both for his groundbreaking work on Aristotle's natural philosophy, metaphysics, and ethics, work deeply informed by contemporary treatments of the same philosophical issues, and for his collaborative approach to these topics. I have profited enormously from our ongoing discussions about hylomorphism, and his work has been a vital stimulus for this chapter. I am very grateful to the editors of this volume for their penetrating comments on an earlier version, and to Samuel Meister and Fei-Ting Chen for valuable comments on the penultimate draft.

Works Cited

Burnyeat, Myles. 2001. *A Map of* Metaphysics *Zeta*. Mathesis.

Burnyeat, Myles, et al. 1979. *Notes on Zeta*. Faculty of Philosophy, University of Oxford.

Caston, Victor. 2009. 'Commentary on Charles', *Proceedings of the Boston Area Colloquium in Ancient Philosophy* 24, 30–49.

Charles, David. 2009. 'Aristotle's Psychological Theory', *Proceedings of the Boston Area Colloquium in Ancient Philosophy* 24, 1–29.

Charles, David. 2021. *The Undivided Self: Aristotle and the 'Mind–Body Problem'*. Oxford University Press.

Code, Alan. 1984. 'The Aporematic Approach to Primary Being in *Metaphysics Z*', *Canadian Journal of Philosophy* 14 (Supplementary Volume 10: *New Essays on Aristotle*, ed. F. J. Pelletier and J. King-Farlow), 1–20.

Code, Alan. 1985. 'On the Origins of Some Aristotelian Theses about Predication', in *How Things Are* (ed. J. Bogen and J. E. McGuire). Reidel, 101–31.

Code, Alan. 1997. 'Aristotle's Metaphysics as a Science of Principles', *Revue Internationale de Philosophie* 201, 357–78.

Dahl, Norman. 1997. 'Two Kinds of Essence in Aristotle: A Pale Man Is Not the Same as His Essence', *Philosophical Review* 106, 233–65.

Devereux, Daniel. 2003. 'The Relationship between Books Zeta and Eta of Aristotle's *Metaphysics*', *Oxford Studies in Ancient Philosophy* 25, 159–211.

Frede, Michael. 1987. 'Individuals in Aristotle', in Michael Frede, *Essays in Ancient Philosophy*. University of Minnesota Press, 40–71. (English translation by Wolfgang Mann.) (Originally published as 'Individuen bei Aristoteles', *Antike und Abendland* 24 (1978), 16–39.)

Frede, Michael. 1990. 'The Definition of Sensible Substances in *Metaphysics Z*', in *Biologie, logique et métaphysique chez Aristote* (ed. D. Devereux and P. Pellegrin). Éditions du CNRS, 113–29.

Frede, Michael and Günther Patzig. 1988. *Aristoteles 'Metaphysik Z': Text, Übersetzung und Kommentar*. 2 vols. C. H. Beck.

Gill, Mary Louise. 1989. *Aristotle on Substance: The Paradox of Unity*. Princeton University Press.

Gill, Mary Louise. 2001. 'Aristotle's Attack on Universals', *Oxford Studies in Ancient Philosophy* 20, 235–60.

Gill, Mary Louise. 2005. 'Myles Burnyeat's *Map of Metaphysics Zeta*', *Philosophical Quarterly* 55, 114–21.

Gill, Mary Louise. 2010. 'Unity of Definition in *Metaphysics* H.6 and Z.12', in *Being, Nature, and Life in Aristotle* (ed. J. G. Lennox and R. Bolton). Cambridge University Press, 98–121.

Gill, Mary Louise. 2021. 'Aristotle's Hylomorphism Reconceived', *Proceedings of the Aristotelian Society* 121 (2), 183–201.

Gill, Mary Louise. Forthcoming. 'Mind's Place in Aristotle's Science of Nature: The Evidence of *Parts of Animals* I.1', in *Aristotle's Parts of Animals: A Critical Guide* (ed. Sophia Connell). Cambridge University Press.

Irwin, T. H. 1988. *Aristotle's First Principles*. Clarendon Press.

Loux, Michael J. 1991. *Primary Ousia: An Essay on Aristotle's* Metaphysics Z *and* H. Cornell University Press.

Malink, Marko. 2013. 'Essence and Being: A Discussion of Michail Peramatzis, *Priority in Aristotle's Metaphysics*', *Oxford Studies in Ancient Philosophy* 45, 341–62.

Meister, Samuel. 2020. 'Aristotle on the Purity of Forms in *Metaphysics* Z.10–11', *Ergo* 7, 1–33.

Meister, Samuel. 2021. 'Aristotle on the Relation between Substance and Essence', *Ancient Philosophy* 41, 477–94.

Owen, G. E. L. 1960. 'Logic and Metaphysics in Some Earlier Works of Aristotle', in *Aristotle and Plato in the Mid-Fourth Century*. Proceedings of the Symposium Aristotelicum (ed. I. Düring and G. E. L. Owen). Elanders Roktryckeri, 163–90. (Reprinted in Owen 1986, 180–99.)

Owen, G. E. L. 1978. 'Particular and General', *Proceedings of the Aristotelian Society* 72, 1–21. (Reprinted in Owen 1986, 279–94.)

Owen, G. E. L. 1986. *Logic, Science, and Dialectic: Collected Papers in Greek Philosophy* (ed. M. Nussbaum). Cornell University Press.

Peramatzis, Michail. 2011. *Priority in Aristotle's Metaphysics*. Oxford University Press.

Pfeiffer, Christian. 2021. 'What Is Matter in Aristotle's Hylomorphism?', *Ancient Philosophy Today: Dialogoi* 3 (2), 148–71.

Reeve, C. D. C. 2000. *Substantial Knowledge: Aristotle's Metaphysics*. Hackett.

Ross, W. D. 1953. *Aristotle's* Metaphysics. *A Revised Text with Introduction and Commentary*. 2 vols. Clarendon Press.

Sefrin-Weis, Heike. 2002. *Homogeneity in Aristotle's Metaphysics*. Ph.D. dissertation, University of Pittsburgh.

Shields, Christopher. 1999. *Order in Multiplicity: Homonymy in the Philosophy of Aristotle*. Clarendon Press.

Witt, Charlotte. 1989. *Substance and Essence in Aristotle: An Interpretation of* Metaphysics VII–IX. Cornell University Press.

10

Aristotelian Matter and 'the Underlier'

Lindsay Judson

As friends and colleagues, David Charles and I have talked about Aristotle for four decades—about method in ancient philosophy, about action and desire, form and matter, per se causation, teleology in biology and in the heavens, definition, nature, first philosophy, thought, perception, and the relation of the psychological and the physical. These conversations have been for me a privilege and a great pleasure, and it is an equal pleasure to write this chapter in David's honour.

In a series of masterly articles on *Physics* 1.7, *On Generation and Corruption* 1.3, and *Metaphysics* Θ.7–8,[1] Charles has developed a wide-ranging and compelling account of Aristotelian matter—or, as I shall argue, nearly compelling: as Aristotle says, 'though we love both our friends and the truth, it is only right to love the truth more'.[2] In particular, I shall examine Charles' philosophically sophisticated and powerfully defended interpretation of what it is that Aristotle takes to persist through the process in which a natural substance such as a human being or an oak tree comes into being. I shall focus principally on Charles' interpretation of *to hupokeimenon* ('what underlies', or 'the underlier') as Aristotle introduces it in his account of the principles of natural things in *Physics* 1. I shall consider two related questions about the underlier, and shall suggest different answers to these questions from the ones which Charles proposes. The first is, what is the status of the claim that *to hupokeimenon* persists through the change? Is this claim, as Charles holds, definitional of *to hupokeimenon*, or is the underlier defined independently of this? The second concerns the underlier, potentiality, and explanatory bedrock. In the case of the substantial generation and development of an *F*, is the persistence of what is potentially an *F* always grounded in some other matter, or, as Charles maintains, is the sameness of what is potentially an *F* throughout the change the explanatory bedrock for the unity of the generation in question? In neither case do I pretend to show that Charles' view is incorrect, but at most to suggest that one can—as I do—agree with a great deal of his account of Aristotelian matter and nonetheless think that some important alternatives are still open.

---

[1] See especially Charles 1994, 2000, 2004, 2010, and 2018.
[2] ἀμφοῖν ὄντοιν φίλοιν ὅσιον προτιμᾶν τὴν ἀλήθειαν... (*NE* 1.6, 1096a16–17).

Lindsay Judson, *Aristotelian Matter and 'the Underlier'* In: *Aristotelian Metaphysics: Essays in Honour of David Charles.*
Edited by: David Bronstein, Thomas Kjeller Johansen, and Michail Peramatzis, Oxford University Press.
© Oxford University Press 2024. DOI: 10.1093/oso/9780198908678.003.0010

228   LINDSAY JUDSON

How do these question about 'what underlies' relate to Aristotelian matter? Charles and I agree that, for Aristotle, 'matter' can be understood in two distinct, albeit closely related, ways—matter understood as a principle and matter understood as what is material—and that in *Physics* 1 Aristotle's concern is with matter understood in the first way, as a principle.[3] Briefly, to be a principle of natural substances is to be one of the items in terms of which such substances are to be properly understood.[4] Charles and I agree that while one can without qualification speak of a thing's material constituents as its matter, this is a different usage from that involved when one speaks of matter as one of its principles. My two questions are, in effect, about how matter understood as material, or as constituents, relates to matter understood as a principle. Either these constituents have no direct part to play in matter as a principle (Charles' view), or they do, but only in virtue of their having the potentiality to take on or to sustain the substance's fully developed form. To anticipate a later illustration, the difference is analogous either to that between an individual holder of the office of President of the USA and *being President of the USA*, or to that between an individual human being— Barack Obama, say—and an individual holder of the office of President of the USA. I shall return to the first case when I discuss Charles' view; in the second case, there were many things which Barack Obama did or was able to do only in virtue of holding that office; likewise, even while President he did or was able to do many things to which holding that office was irrelevant. Terminology aside, however, nothing in this discussion relies on accepting this duality in Aristotle's use of the term 'matter'.

In *Physics* 1 Aristotle investigates the principles of things which are by nature,[5] and arrives at three such principles: form, privation, and *to hupokeimenon*. In chapter 7 he offers some general considerations in favour of the need for a third principle in addition to form and privation. His basic idea is that every changing thing is in some sense a *compound*: one 'ingredient' of the compound—a privation—disappears in the change and is replaced by something new—the 'form'—but the other 'ingredient' does not disappear:

[T1]   From what has been said it is clear that everything that comes to be is always a composite: there is something that comes to be and something that comes to be that <thing which comes to be>. There are two types of

---

[3] Charles 2000, 100–1. Anyone who denies this distinction will be (in one way or another) much more fundamentally in disagreement with Charles than I am.

[4] This leaves much unsaid. (i) Principles are primarily ontological: items on which other things depend in some fundamental way—my expression 'are to be properly understood' gestures at the idea that here epistemology is supposed to track ontology. (ii) If form and matter are principles, are they schematic, so that lions and tortoises, say, have without qualification exactly these same two principles, or is it that their principles are really more concrete—say, lion-form/matter and tortoise-form/ matter? For discussion of this question see Judson 2019a, 136–9.

[5] See Kelsey 2008, esp. 203–7, Judson 2018, 135–6 and 141, Charles 2018, 194–6.

the latter: either that which underlies or what is opposed <to that which comes to be>. I say that the uneducated is opposed and human underlies; and shapelessness and formlessness and lack of order are opposed and bronze or stone or gold is what underlies. (190b10–17)[6]

In Aristotle's example of a human being who becomes educated, we can identify the changing thing as a compound of human being + uneducated; what results from the change is (same) human being + educated. Involved in the change there is a privation (the absence of educatedness), a form (educatedness), and something which is the subject, first of the privation and subsequently of the form. It is important to note that *both* the subject of the privation *and* the compound of the subject and the privation can be said to be 'what comes to be'—this means the thing which comes to be *F*, or in other words, the subject of the change. Aristotle talks first as if the underlying thing is the *compound*, the uneducated human being:

[T2] one can grasp in all cases of things that come to be... that something must always underlie (i.e., that which is in the process of coming to be), and that this,[7] even if it is one in number, is not one in form (by 'in form' I mean 'in account'). For being a human being is not the same as being uneducated. And the one remains, the other does not. (190a13–18)[8]

But as we have seen in [T1], he says 'I mean that... the human being underlies... bronze or stone or gold is what underlies' (190b14–17): that is, what underlies is the *subject* of the privation. This seems likely to be his view of what the underlier primarily is, for at least two reasons. First, *to hupokeimenon* is Aristotle's standard term elsewhere for the subject of predication, so it is more likely to be chosen as the term which primarily denotes the subject of the privation than for the compound of subject and privation (even if his idea of a subject here is not precisely that of a subject of predication). Second, Aristotle is seeking the *principles* involved in change and in natural, changing substances; form, privation,

---

[6] ὥστε δῆλον ἐκ τῶν εἰρημένων ὅτι τὸ γιγνόμενον ἅπαν ἀεὶ συνθετόν ἐστι, καὶ ἔστι μέν τι γιγνόμενον, ἔστι δέ τι ὃ τοῦτο γίγνεται, καὶ τοῦτο διττόν· ἢ γὰρ τὸ ὑποκείμενον ἢ τὸ ἀντικείμενον. λέγω δὲ ἀντικεῖσθαι μὲν τὸ ἄμουσον, ὑποκεῖσθαι δὲ τὸν ἄνθρωπον, καὶ τὴν μὲν ἀσχημοσύνην καὶ τὴν ἀμορφίαν καὶ τὴν ἀταξίαν τὸ ἀντικείμενον, τὸν δὲ χαλκὸν ἢ τὸν λίθον ἢ τὸν χρυσὸν τὸ ὑποκείμενον. Translations of *Phys.* 1.7 are from Charles' translation (ed. D. Quarantotto and L. Judson) in Quarantotto 2018, 258–61 (with one modification in [T5] and [T6]). We use angular brackets to indicate words we take to be implied by the text (where this is potentially controversial) and square brackets to indicate explanations of the text. Other translations are my own.

[7] Charles takes 'this' to refer to 'that which is in the process of coming to be' rather than to 'something which underlies'; but this does not affect the present point, which is that 'what underlies' is identified here with 'that which is in the process of coming to be' and is characterized as the compound item.

[8] ἐξ ἁπάντων τῶν γιγνομένων τοῦτο ἔστι λαβεῖν, ἐάν τις ἐπιβλέψῃ ὥσπερ λέγομεν, ὅτι δεῖ τι ἀεὶ ὑποκεῖσθαι τὸ γιγνόμενον, καὶ τοῦτο εἰ καὶ ἀριθμῷ ἐστιν ἕν, ἀλλ' εἴδει γε οὐχ ἕν· τὸ γὰρ εἴδει λέγω καὶ λόγῳ ταὐτόν· οὐ γὰρ ταὐτὸν τὸ ἀνθρώπῳ καὶ τὸ ἀμούσῳ εἶναι. καὶ τὸ μὲν ὑπομένει, τὸ δ' οὐχ ὑπομένει.

230 LINDSAY JUDSON

and subject are obviously more basic than form, privation, and the compound of privation and subject. To summarize: Aristotle holds that, in addition to the form and its absence, in every change there is something which 'underlies'. This is the subject of the privation (the human being in his example)—though we should bear in mind that Aristotle is also willing to use 'what underlies' to refer to the compound of the subject and the privation (that is, in the example, the uneducated human being). By the end of *Physics* 1 form, privation, and what underlies have been re-characterized as form, privation, and matter: although it is unclear exactly how Aristotle takes himself to be able to do this,[9] the question about the nature of the underlier is nonetheless plausibly a question—or principally a question—about the nature of matter as a principle.

Charles argues that, not only is the underlier the subject of the original privation, but it is also what persists through the change; and he argues that for Aristotle, the underlier persists through the change even in the case of substantial generation.[10] I agree with these claims, and shall first offer some defence of them; I shall then ask what *defines* the underlier, and take issue with Charles' view that what underlies is not characterized independently of its role as what persists through the change. Discussion of this will lead, finally, to the question of explanatory bedrock.

We start with 190a21–31:

[T3]   The expression 'this comes to be from that' (as opposed to the expression 'this comes to be that') is more used in the case of what does not remain, as when we say that what is educated comes to be from what is uneducated but not that it [i.e. the educated] comes to be from human. Nonetheless we do also sometimes speak in a similar way [i.e. using the 'this comes to be from that...' way] about what remains, saying that from bronze a statue comes to be, not the bronze comes to be a statue. However, we do speak in both ways in the case of something opposed that does not remain: we say both that this comes to be from that and this comes to be that. And so we talk of something educated coming from something which is not educated and of something which is not educated coming to be something which is educated. This is why we speak in a similar way about what is put together. For we say that both: from an uneducated human and the uneducated human comes to be educated.[11]

---

[9] For discussion, see Bostock 1982, Charles 2018, Lennox 2018, Judson 2019a, prologue to ch. 2, §4. For a very different view of Aristotle's strategy, see Kelsey 2008. Apart from the anticipatory remarks in *Phys.* 1.4 (187a18 and 19), the term ὕλη does not appear in Aristotle's discussion until towards the end of ch. 7 (190b9, 190b25, [191a10]), and the explicit identification with what underlies is not made until ch. 9 (192a31–2; compare 192a3–6).

[10] See Charles 2018, esp. 179–82 and 185–93.

[11] τὸ δ' ἔκ τινος γίγνεσθαί τι, καὶ μὴ τόδε γίγνεσθαί τι, μᾶλλον μὲν λέγεται ἐπὶ τῶν μὴ ὑπομενόντων, οἷον ἐξ ἀμούσου μουσικὸν γίγνεσθαι, ἐξ ἀνθρώπου δὲ οὔ· οὐ μὴν ἀλλὰ καὶ ἐπὶ τῶν ὑπομενόντων ἐνίοτε λέγεται ὡσαύτως· ἐκ γὰρ χαλκοῦ ἀνδριάντα γίγνεσθαί φαμεν, οὐ τὸν χαλκὸν ἀνδριάντα. τὸ μέντοι ἐκ τοῦ

ARISTOTELIAN MATTER AND 'THE UNDERLIER'   231

There are two important points to note about Aristotle's example of the uneducated human being becoming educated. First, in this case the underlying thing certainly persists through the change: this raises the question whether this is a necessary—or even a defining—feature of 'what underlies', or whether there are cases in which Aristotle thinks that the subject of the original privation does not persist through the change. Second, the underlying thing in this example is a human being—an Aristotelian substance, a hylomorphic compound—and the acquired form is a non-essential property of that substance; how can Aristotle derive his conclusion that the third principle, what underlies, is *matter*?

The question of whether, in Aristotle's view, the subject of the privation persists through the change in every case arises most sharply in connection with substantial generation: at least at first view, this is precisely *not* a case of something persisting and acquiring a new form, but rather of a new substance coming into existence. It is over this question that there is most interpretative controversy. Aristotle has been seen as holding that in substantial generation nothing persists,[12] as holding that something—that is, something other than the substance—persists,[13] and as failing to see the problem clearly enough to present any explicit doctrine.[14] Yet Aristotle seems quite explicit: at 190a9–13 he says that in *every* change something underlies, and that the underlying thing persists:

[T4]   Of the things that come to be, in cases we describe as involving simples,[15] in one case something comes to be by remaining, in the other by not remaining. For the human remains when coming to be an educated human and is an educated human but that which is not educated and the uneducated remains neither without qualification nor in a composite form.[16]

– and, as we saw, he says it again in [T2]. In the face of these claims, why have some commentators taken Aristotle to draw back from this in the case of substantial generation? In short, because in this case they struggle to see how anything does persist through this sort of change. They often point to another key text. It is evident in all *other* cases, Aristotle says at 190a33–4, that something underlies,

---

ἀντικειμένου καὶ μὴ ὑπομένοντος ἀμφοτέρως λέγεται, καὶ ἐκ τοῦδε τόδε καὶ τόδε τόδε· καὶ γὰρ ἐξ ἀμούσου καὶ ὁ ἄμουσος γίγνεται μουσικός. διὸ καὶ ἐπὶ τοῦ συγκειμένου ὡσαύτως· καὶ γὰρ ἐξ ἀμούσου ἀνθρώπου καὶ ὁ ἄμουσος ἄνθρωπος γίγνεσθαι λέγεται μουσικός.

[12] Jones 1974, Frey 2007, esp. 167–70 and 190–7.

[13] Code 1976, Freeland 1987, Gill 1989, ch. 3, Charles 2018.   [14] Charlton 1970, 74–8.

[15] 'By a simple I mean when the human and what is not educated is what is coming to be. What comes to be and what is coming to be are compounded when we say that the not educated human comes to be an educated human' (190a1–5: ἁπλοῦν μὲν οὖν λέγω τὸ γιγνόμενον τὸν ἄνθρωπον καὶ τὸ μὴ μουσικόν, καὶ ὃ γίγνεται ἁπλοῦν, τὸ μουσικόν· συγκείμενον δὲ καὶ ὃ γίγνεται καὶ τὸ γιγνόμενον, ὅταν τὸν μὴ μουσικὸν ἄνθρωπον φῶμεν γίγνεσθαι μουσικὸν ἄνθρωπον).

[16] τῶν δὲ γιγνομένων ὡς τὰ ἁπλᾶ λέγομεν γίγνεσθαι, τὸ μὲν ὑπομένον γίγνεται τὸ δ᾿ οὐχ ὑπομένον· ὁ μὲν γὰρ ἄνθρωπος ὑπομένει μουσικὸς γιγνόμενος ἄνθρωπος καὶ ἔστι, τὸ δὲ μὴ μουσικὸν καὶ τὸ ἄμουσον οὔτε ἁπλῶς οὔτε συντεθειμένον ὑπομένει.

[T5] but that even substances, and whatever things simply are, come to be from something underlying will be evident to one who looks closely. For always there is something that underlies, from which the thing generated comes to be: as in the case of plants and animals coming to be from seed. (190b1–5)[17]

The apparent focus of this remark on the idea that there is in these cases something pre-existing which can be called the subject of the change is sometimes taken to signal a retreat on Aristotle's part from the claim that 'what underlies' in these cases *persists* through the generation. And commentators rightly point out that the 'seed'—construed as, say, an acorn—does not persist through the generation and development of the animal or plant—the oak tree.[18]

There are at least three reasons to resist this interpretation. (i) Aristotle will have gone back on his earlier claims in [T2] and [T4]. (ii) He will exhibit some confusion over the characterization of 'what underlies' as between the (mere) starting-point of the change and its persisting subject. (iii) As Charles points out,

> If Aristotle were to surrender his original thesis that what underlies remains throughout the coming to be, he would have no grounds for his next major claim: that every object that comes to be is complex (190b11–12). If he merely claims that each case of coming to be has a starting-point, he cannot rule out the possibility that what results from such a process is a simple (non-complex) object.[19]

On the other hand, to defend the view that there is an underlier in the case of substantial generation, Aristotle points to the fact that such generations come to be 'from seed'. We thus seem to face a dilemma: we have to say that Aristotle has either a good argument for the wrong claim (that there is a starting-point for substantial generation), or a hopeless argument for the right one (the persistence claim). The best solution is to take Aristotle to be arguing for the persistence claim, but to construe his appeal to 'seed' as a less direct way of indicating that there is a persisting underlier. One way to do this is Charles' way: as we shall see, he thinks that the acorn (say) is a stage or phase of the underlier, regarded as itself an item of a quite different ontological kind, and 'the phrase "the seed", so understood, is used to give a contingent way to fix the reference of the term "the underlier", not to define what it is to be an underlier'.[20] I have some doubts about this interpretation, as we shall see: here is an alternative view. The term 'seed' has so far been taken to indicate a *particular object*, such as an acorn. But Aristotle could

---

[17] ὅτι δὲ καὶ αἱ οὐσίαι καὶ ὅσα [ἄλλα] ἁπλῶς ὄντα ἐξ ὑποκειμένου τινὸς γίγνεται, ἐπισκοποῦντι γένοιτο ἂν φανερόν. ἀεὶ γὰρ ἔστι ὃ ὑπόκειται, ἐξ οὗ τὸ γιγνόμενον, οἷον τὰ φυτὰ καὶ τὰ ζῷα ἐκ σπέρματος. Charles translates ἐκ σπέρματος as 'from a seed': I prefer the equally possible, but more neutral, 'from seed', for reasons which will become clear below.
[18] A point well made by Freeland (1987, 392).   [19] 2018, 189.   [20] 2018, 188 n. 11.

ARISTOTELIAN MATTER AND 'THE UNDERLIER'   233

have in mind *something about* the acorn—something which underlies *it*—which might persist.[21] As I noted earlier, Aristotle is prepared to use the term 'what underlies' for the *compound* of the subject and the privation as well as for the subject itself.[22] If we take this to be his usage here, the fact that the seed—regarded as the compound of the subject and the absence of the relevant form—does not persist would be on a par with the fact that the uneducated human being does not persist; mentioning the seed is simply a way of drawing our attention to *its* persisting 'subject'. This interpretation requires, of course, that Aristotle can identify a subject within the seed (thought of as a compound—e.g., the acorn) which does persist through the generation, and I shall return to this idea later.[23]

Note that neither here nor anywhere else does Aristotle explain *why* he thinks that in every change something persists.[24] The most likely reason is that he took it as self-evident that without something persisting we would not have a case of genuine *change* at all, but only of the replacement of one entity by another. If so, he will have to avoid thinking of what stays the same through the change as simply a feature or property of the object; for otherwise he would not have shown that the supposed change was not the mere replacement of an $[F + not\text{-}G]$ entity by a new $[F + G]$ one.

What is the underlier, thought of as a principle of natural substances? Notice that it seems very hard to see how Aristotle could say that it is the thing's *substantial form*—despite form's popularity as the candidate for the bearer of diachronic identity (in some Aristotelian exegesis[25] and more especially in contemporary neo-Aristotelian metaphysics[26]): what is needed here is something which persists

---

[21] Compare Freeland 1987, 398–404 (discussed in n. 36 below).

[22] At 190a14–18: see [T2] above.

[23] Another issue which may motivate doubts about persistence here concerns animal generation. If Aristotle does think that something persists through the change in this case, it is the material provided by the mother that does so, not the seed provided by the father (see *Met.* H.4, 1044a32–5 and *GA* 2.4, 738a33–b4, 738b20–7, 740b18–25). But Aristotle is also prepared to describe the material provided by the mother as 'seed': see *GA* 1.2, 716a4–13, 1.20, 728a26–7; Gill 1989, 228–9, Connell 2016, 101–7, Carraro 2017, 283–4. Once again there might be something about this maternal seed which persists. I shall argue below that what is at issue is the *constituents* of the seed (however 'seed' is properly to be construed in Aristotle's remarks).

[24] Unless his response to Parmenides, which I shall discuss later, constitutes such an explanation. See n. 42 below.

[25] See, e.g., Furth 1978, Frede 1985.

[26] See, e.g., Fine 1999, Johnston 2006, Koslicki 2008, part four, Koslicki 2018. For some discussion, see Skrzypek 2017, esp. §VI, and Peramatzis 2019. These contemporary views have their origin in Locke's *Essay*: 'We must therefore consider wherein an Oak differs from a Mass of Matter, and that seems to me to be in this; that the one is only the Cohesion of Particles of Matter any how united, the other such a disposition of them as constitutes the parts of an Oak; and such an Organization of those parts, as is fit to receive, and distribute nourishment, so as to continue, and frame the Wood, Bark, and Leaves, *etc*, of an Oak, in which consists the vegetable Life. That being then one Plant, which has such an Organization of Parts in one coherent Body, partaking of one Common Life, it continues to be the same Plant, as long as it partakes of the same Life, though that Life be communicated to new Particles of Matter vitally united to the living Plant, in a like continued Organization, conformable to that sort of Plants' (*Essay Concerning Human Understanding* II.XXVII.4 [1982, 330–1]).

234 LINDSAY JUDSON

during the *acquisition* of the relevant substantial form (though, as we shall see, it may persist after that acquisition as well). How the subsequent persistence of this item relates to the persistence of the substantial form of the mature organism is an issue which I shall not pursue here.

Charles rightly says that in *Physics* 1 Aristotle is to some extent keeping his options open,[27] but nonetheless Charles' distinctive theory emerges in his discussion of 1.7: it is developed further in relation to Aristotle's accounts of potentiality in *Metaphysics* Θ.7–8 and of elemental transformation in *On Generation and Corruption* 1.3. In relation to *Physics* 1.7, Charles' account is principally based on two arguments. The first is that in saying 'and the one remains, the other does not' at 190a17–18 ([T2]), Aristotle is clearly not introducing the claim that the underlier persists through the change as 'an independent thesis, that what underlies in fact remains (or survives) through the coming to be'.[28] Charles infers that the underlier is therefore *defined as* what remains or survives, rather than as the starting-point or the subject of the change. The second argument appeals to the passage at 190b3–10 (this overlaps with [T5]):

[T6] For always there is something which underlies, from which the thing generated comes to be: as in the case of plants and animals coming to be from seed.[29] Some of the things that come to be in the unqualified way come to be by some change of shape (as a statue),[30] others by addition (as things that grow bigger), others by subtraction (as Hermes from the stone), others by composition (as a house), others by alteration (as things change in accordance with their matter). It is evident that all things that come to be in this way come to be from what underlies.[31]

Charles writes:

These comments are not, it seems, designed merely to support the truism that there is, in all these cases of coming to be, an origin from which the change starts. Instead they suggest that there is some one thing (that which underlies) present from the beginning which survives throughout the change in some modified way (either by being added to/changed in shape/growing etc.). It appears that the thing in question remains from the beginning, albeit changed, for example, in shape, quality, size or material features. What remains need not

---

[27] Charles 2018, 191; see also 181.   [28] Charles 2018, 180.   [29] See n. 17 above.
[30] Aristotle is thinking of the casting of a bronze statute; the carving of a statue from stone or marble is the Hermes example.
[31] ἀεὶ γὰρ ἔστι ὃ ὑπόκειται, ἐξ οὗ τὸ γιγνόμενον, οἷον τὰ φυτὰ καὶ τὰ ζῷα ἐκ σπέρματος. γίγνεται δὲ τὰ γιγνόμενα ἁπλῶς τὰ μὲν μετασχηματίσει, οἷον ἀνδριάς, τὰ δὲ προσθέσει, οἷον τὰ αὐξανόμενα, τὰ δ' ἀφαιρέσει, οἷον ἐκ τοῦ λίθου ὁ Ἑρμῆς, τὰ δὲ συνθέσει, οἷον οἰκία, τὰ δ' ἀλλοιώσει, οἷον τὰ τρεπόμενα κατὰ τὴν ὕλην. πάντα δὲ τὰ οὕτω γιγνόμενα φανερὸν ὅτι ἐξ ὑποκειμένων γίγνεται.

(indeed, will not) be a seed: it may come to lose the shape, size and many of the qualities of the seed. [Charles' footnote: The phrase 'the seed', so understood, is used to give a contingent way to fix the reference of the term 'the underlier', not to define what it is to be an underlier.] It is enough that that which underlies (which is at various times a seed, a sapling etc.) remains the same. (2018, 188)

His argument seems to be that since (in Aristotle's view) there must be something which persists as the same thing throughout a substantial change, and since (apparently) no material entity does stay the same, this persisting continuant must be a *logical or abstract entity*. To make this more concrete, since all (substantial) changes involve the replacement of one sort of entity by another, and then by another (the seed, the shoot, the sapling, etc.), what remains must be some single enduring thing which can be each of these in turn:

In Aristotle's example of a plant, that which underlies will be the same (in number) throughout the whole process of its coming to be, even though it is first a seed, next a sapling, etc. That which underlies, while remaining the same entity, will change in certain respects as the process develops. In any particular case, there will be a particular underlier of this general type: one thing which underlies change and remains the same, even though at differing times it may be different things: first an embryo, next a child, then an adult etc. All such particular underliers will be instances of one general type of thing: the underlier, with its own distinctive general nature....In Aristotle's terminology, that which underlies may differ 'in being' at different times (first being a seed, then being a sapling) while remaining the same....[Charles' footnote: Compare the following case: a person on his (or her) way to becoming fifty may remain the same person throughout even though she (or he) was initially a foetus, then a child, then an adolescent....While what underlies the process of becoming fifty remains from the outset when it was a foetus, it does not remain as a foetus throughout!][32]

Thus the underlier (in the case of substantial generation, at any rate) is a logical or abstract entity—a non-material entity whose nature we grasp through the notion of a *role*. To modify an example of Charles', 'The President of the USA is the Commander in Chief'[33] is plausibly made true (whatever account one might give of its semantics), by something to do with the role of being President of the USA; by contrast, 'The President of the USA is a Democrat' is made true by something to do with the person who occupies the role, not by the role itself. In the case of the underlier, the role is *persisting through the change*. It also emerges that in Charles' view, this entity does not perish when the substantial generation is

---

[32] Charles 2018, 186–7; see also 188 and 198.   [33] Charles 2004, 154.

complete, but persists through the mature life of the substance as well: 'first an embryo, next a child, then an adult etc.'[34] We may compare with this the idea that behind a statement such as 'The President of the USA has been the head of the government of America for over 200 years' is a logical or abstract entity, *what fulfils the role of being the President of the USA*, which has persisted throughout this period and has at different times been George Washington, Abraham Lincoln, Theodore Roosevelt, Barack Obama, and so on.

It is an important consequence that if Charles' argument is correct, the persistence of this non-material entity is the explanatory bedrock of the change in question being a unified change with the same subject throughout. No further account can be given of what it is in virtue of which the developmental changes we see form a *single* process of the coming to be of a single substance—no further account, that is, beyond the entities produced at each stage of the development being phases of the same (logical or abstract) entity. We have reached explanatory bedrock. This is because Charles' argument commits him to the view that (for Aristotle) nothing else stays the same; so the sameness and persistence of this entity as the subject of the change is not explained by the sameness and persistence of something else.

These two arguments are powerful ones, but I think that they can be resisted. I shall defend an alternative view, that what underlies is introduced independently of its role of persistence, on the basis of the idea of the subject of the change.

As regards Charles' first argument, I agree that Aristotle does not regard the persistence of what underlies as an independent fact in the sense of its being the subject of empirical discovery—something which could just as easily have turned out to be otherwise. But this is compatible with his taking it to be, not a matter of the definition of the underlier, but a deep truth about *genuine change*. It is in virtue of the underlier's fulfilling the role of what persists that the change is indeed a change as Aristotle understands it, and not a mere Russellian one, or the mere replacement of one entity by another. If this is correct, the definition or essence of the underlier could be *being the subject of the change* rather than *being what persists through it*.

As regards his second argument, I wish to offer some defence of the view that something *else* persists through the change: namely (as a first approximation), the thing's matter understood as its (relevant) constituents. On this view the underlier, both as the subject of the change and as what persists, is these constituents, properly understood, and thus they are the 'matter as a principle' of a substance. If this is right, the underlier is the thing which (whatever it is) fulfils the role of persisting throughout the change, not the logical entity defined in terms of the role itself. While the acorn, say, clearly does not persist as the oak tree develops,

---

[34] The claim that the potentiality for being an F remains even after the F has fully come to be is persuasively developed in Charles 2010.

this does not immediately rule out that what persists is the *constituents* of the acorn: indeed, I think it is actually quite hard to read the passage to which Charles appeals in [T5] (190b3–5) in the way he does:

> For always there is something that underlies, from which the thing generated comes to be: as in the case of plants and animals coming to be from seed.

The point of the passage (Charles and I agree) is to show, or at least to affirm, that even in cases of substantial generation something persists. If 'seed' in 'from (a) seed' refers to an individual stage of the underlier, such as an acorn (as Charles takes it to do), it is very odd that Aristotle chooses to introduce the thing which remains by mentioning something quite different which clearly does *not* remain. If, instead, 'seed' refers to the compound of the constituent matter and the relevant privation (which is my view: see above), then Aristotle is indeed introducing the idea of the constituent matter, which is thus already in the frame as the underlier and as what remains.[35]

Nonetheless, the view that the constituents of the acorn persist through the change may well seem quite unpromising, and perhaps little better than the view that the acorn persists: surely the constituents of the acorn need not be found anywhere in the mature oak tree, and if they are to be found there, they play an insignificant role in its constitution.[36] Defending my view in the face of this obvious truth raises complex issues, to which I cannot do justice here—and perhaps insuperable difficulties! All I can do here is to outline what I think is the best position available to Aristotle: this is what I shall call a *majoritarian and ancestral view* of persistence. As a first step, consider the production of a statue made by removing quite small parts of a marble block. We might be inclined both to the

---

[35] Gill (1989, 106–8) thinks that the seed is only a stage in the generation of the animal or plant, and that the underlier in question is actually the ultimate matter from which the seed is generated, which she takes to be 'earth or some assortment of elements' (107): this underlier 'remains present in the product [the mature animal or plant] but acquires an additional form' (107). While I agree with Gill that Aristotle is concerned with the constituents of the seed rather than the seed considered as an object, there are a number of difficulties with her particular view. (i) In [T5]/[T6] Aristotle specifies the seed as what the generation is from, and not as a mere stage in the generation. (ii) Earth (or an assortment of the elements) seems too remote a form of constituent to be what is properly speaking potentially the animal or plant (see *Met.* Θ.7). (iii) Even if the earthy component of the seed does persist into the mature animal, it seems, both quantitatively and ontologically, too insignificant an item to do the 'heavy lifting' of being (a) what guarantees the unity of the change by being what persists through it and (b) the proper subject of the 'additional [i.e., the substantial] form'.

[36] Freeland also thinks that it is something about the seed which persists through the development of the organism—in the case of animals, the blood of which the *katamenia* is composed (1987, 398–402). She then considers the problem that the mature animal is not made of blood, and concedes that while blood is the key basis (in Aristotle's view) for the development of bones and flesh, 'perhaps it is too much to expect the same strict identity in these more complex cases as can be found for the far simpler bronze statue' (401). But Aristotle does need a positive account of the persistence of this blood as what underlies, beyond its biological importance in the animal's development. For a detailed discussion of the role of this blood, see Schriefl unpublished.

238   LINDSAY JUDSON

view that the marble in the original block has *not* persisted through the change—since some of it has been removed—and to the view that it has. This latter inclination might be based on the point that all the matter in the statue was in the original block, but this point will not, I think, do for Aristotle here. For one thing, it threatens to restrict the subject of the change to the relevant proper part of the block's constituents. But suppose that a builder has a pile of 1,001 identical bricks when the house needs any 1,000 of them: the potential for being the house would appear to have belonged, all along, to whichever 1,000 bricks the builder ends up happening to choose. And for another thing, all natural generations (Aristotle's principal target) are cases in which material is *added* as the plant or animal grows. So it is better to suppose that *all* of the marble in the original block is the subject of the change, and that it persists because a *majority of it* does.[37] There are no doubt further complexities to be taken into account here that go beyond bare majoritarianism, when the original constituents are not homogeneous: perhaps the persistence of (a majority of) some constituents is more important than the persistence of others; but I shall not pursue this issue further here. This *survival* of marble (thought of as a constituent) seems plausibly enough to meet the 'mere replacement' worry: enough, that is, for the case to be a genuine change, and not one in which one entity (the original marble + the privation) is merely replaced by another (the surviving marble + the form). There does not need to be a further persisting entity to secure this result. It is true that we may have different views of *identity* here. On one side is Hume's trenchant stance:

> Suppose any mass of matter, of which the parts are contiguous and connected, to be plac'd before us; 'tis plain we must attribute a perfect identity to this mass, provided all the parts continue uninterruptedly and invariably the same, whatever motion or change of place we may observe either in the whole or in any of the parts. But supposing some very *small* or *inconsiderable* part to be added to the mass, or to be subtracted from it; tho' this absolutely destroys the identity of the whole, strictly speaking; yet as we seldom think so accurately, we scruple not to pronounce a mass of matter the same, where we find so trivial an alteration. (*A Treatise of Human Nature* I.4.6 [2007, 167])

---

[37] Why not say that it persists because a majority *of the matter of the statue* was in the original block? (I owe this suggestion to Ellen Judson.) This would have the advantage of dealing straightforwardly with the case in which the statue is made by removing most of the original block. The problem with this move is that plants or animals which grow from seed will not count as new animals/plants, but merely as persisting parts of the parent. (What then about the statue made by removing most of the original? Here I think we should appeal to Θ.7's account of the conditions under which X is properly potentially an F, as persuasively interpreted by Charles: X is properly potentially an F when the changes needed to make it an actual F require the operation of the relevant nature or art (2010, 171–83). If the original block is much too big, its initial reduction in size does not require the sculptor's art (even if it is carried out by the sculptor herself): the block is, properly, potentially the very small statue only when further reductions require the sculptor's art.)

On the other hand is the more relaxed view which Hume brands as an error 'strictly speaking', that the large rock in my garden is indeed the same rock as the one which was there last week despite the abrasion of some molecules thanks to the recent heavy rains. If we take this more relaxed view, we shall have to accept the indexing of some of the rock's properties to times, to avoid falling foul of Leibniz's Law—and it has to be conceded that some will not find that move attractive.[38] As the quotation from Hume reminds us, we also need to allow that the *addition* of constituents not in the original item does not undermine the persistence claim.[39]

Even on what I have called the more relaxed view of identity, further complexity is required for Aristotle's account of persistence. As the oak tree develops, fewer and fewer of the constituents of the original acorn may remain—indeed, at some point *none* may remain—and many other constituents external to the acorn have been added. What Aristotle needs is an ancestral relationship, analogous to the one sometimes suggested to rescue Locke's account of personal identity from Reid's famous 'brave officer' objection.[40] On this view, the constituents of X—the developing oak tree—persist from t_1 to t_n if there are successive times $t_1, t_2, t_3, \ldots t_n$ such that the majority of the constituents of X at t_1 are constituents of X at t_2, the majority of the constituents of X at t_2 are constituents of X at t_3, and so on up to X at t_n. No doubt much more needs to be said (and I shall briefly address one issue at the end), but I think it is plausible that we do think of the persistence of constituents in natural generations in something like this way. Note that it seems to be a consequence of a view of this kind that we should say that in the case of the ship of Theseus, the *repaired* ship is the ship of Theseus, and not the reassembled ship.[41] I hasten to say that I do not think that this is any sort of argument in favour of the view I am suggesting; but I shall return to the ship of Theseus later.

---

[38] The issues here are analogous to those faced by similar responses to McTaggart's argument against the existence of the A-series ordering of time.

[39] It is tempting, as a first approximation, to suggest a majoritarian account of this too, requiring that a majority of the developed item's constituents were constituents of the original item; I shall touch on a related issue at the end, but exploring this more fully goes beyond the scope of this chapter.

[40] 'Suppose a brave officer to have been flogged when a boy at school, for robbing an orchard, to have taken a standard from the enemy in his first campaign, and to have been made a general in advanced life: Suppose also, which must be admitted to be possible, that when he took the standard, he was conscious of his having been flogged at school, and that when made a general he was conscious of his taking the standard, but had absolutely lost the consciousness of his flogging. These things being supposed, it follows, from Mr LOCKE's doctrine, that he who was flogged at school is the same person who took the standard, and that he who took the standard is the same person who was made a general. When it follows, if there be any truth in logic, that the general is the same person with him who was flogged at school. But the general's consciousness does not reach so far back as his flogging, therefore, according to Mr LOCKE's doctrine, he is not the person who was flogged. Therefore the general is, and at the same time is not the same person as him who was flogged at school.' *Essays on the Intellectual Powers of Man*, essay three, ch. 6 (2002, 276). This form of defence of Locke originates in Grice 1941.

[41] I am grateful to Ellen Judson for suggesting that I think about this question.

240   LINDSAY JUDSON

Why suppose that this is Aristotle's view—that what underlies is to be under-stood as the subject of the substantial change, rather than as the logical entity whose essence is to persist through that change? I first offer three pieces of textual evidence from *Physics* 1 and one from outside the *Physics*, and then some philo-sophical considerations relating to the issue of explanatory bedrock.

(i) As we have seen in looking at [T1–6], Aristotle's focus throughout the dis-cussion in *Physics* 1.7 is much more on the underlier as the starting-point of the change: he begins with the compound of subject and privation, and the point that the subject *persists*, once made, is not pursued, except to relate it to what the change is said to be *from* (190a21–31: [T3]). Again, as we have seen, when he argues that something underlies even in the problematic case of substantial gen-eration in [T5–6], he is content to point out that there is an antecedent item. So, although Aristotle is firmly committed to the persistence of what underlies, the notion of the antecedent or starting-point of the change seems to be primary.

(ii) This is confirmed, I think, by Aristotle's response to Parmenides in *Physics* 1.8. The general form of Parmenides' argument against the reality of change was dilemmatic: any given change is either from what is, or from what is not; but (for reasons that are now perhaps not fully recoverable) neither of these alternatives is coherent. Although his account of how to disarm Parmenides' challenge is obscure, it does not focus on persistence through the change, but on the status of the starting-point of change. Aristotle's reply is based on the idea that in charac-terizing the possible starting-points of change, Parmenides construed 'what is' and 'what is not' too restrictively. He construed 'what is not' as equivalent to 'nothing': thus change from what is not would be *ex nihilo*. And he construed 'what is' as 'what is F [where being F is the property supposedly acquired in the change]': thus 'change from what is' would in fact involve no change at all. Aristotle argues that the starting-point of the change can in fact be described both as what is and as what is not without either of these damaging implications. That his interest is with the starting-point of the change is also shown by the fact that he refers to another way to show Parmenides' error, in terms of actuality and potentiality. We are given a clear account of this in *Metaphysics* Λ.2 (1069b18–20): X comes to be F from *what is not* in the sense that it is from an antecedent which is not actually F; but it comes to be from *what is* in that it is from an antecedent which is potentially F.[42]

---

[42] Interpreters (e.g., Waterlow 1982, ch. 3, Gill 1989, ch. 3) often take Aristotle's understanding of the problem here to be as follows. If change to (say) red is from what is red, it looks as if everything has stayed the same; if it is from what is not-red, there is still no *change*, but only the passing away of one entity (the not-red thing) and the emergence of a new one (the red thing)—and this sort of gen-esis *ex nihilo* is impossible. Aristotle's solution, on this interpretation, is to seek a characteristic middle way through the dilemma. His principles of change enable him to show, first, that change does involve something passing away and something else coming to be—so the world is *different* after a change has occurred—and, second, that change involves something *persisting*—so change is not the mere

(iii) At 191a7–13 Aristotle says that the 'underlying nature' must be grasped by analogy:

[T7] The underlying nature is knowable by analogy. For as bronze stands to a statue or wood to a bed or the matter—that is, what is shapeless before it takes on shape—stands to what is shaped, so the underlying nature stands to the substance, which is a this such [i.e. an informed object] and what is. This then is one principle, although it is not one in the way a this such is one nor does it exist in the way a this such exists. (191a7–13).[43]

Aristotle is talking here, I think, of the 'nature' which underlies a *substance*, and not of what underlies in general. If the 'underlying nature' is Charles' logical or abstract entity, it is unclear why it can only be grasped by analogy: for the essence of this entity is fixed by its role as what persists through substantial change, and that role seems to be the same in all cases.[44]

(iv) One might add the evidence of *Metaphysics* Λ.4.[45] Here Aristotle again appeals to analogy in connection with matter as a principle,[46] but his primary concern is with the analogical sameness of principles in and across different categories, and Aristotle might hold that Charlesian logical subjects in different categories are at most analogically the same. But Λ.4 is also concerned with the sameness and difference of principles (including matter) *within* a category, and gives as examples to illustrate Aristotle's view, that they are both the same and different, visible surface, air, body, and bricks:[47] these are specific items which play the relevant role, not abstract entities.

I turn, finally, to some philosophical considerations relating to the issue of explanatory bedrock. On the basis of other texts (and especially *Metaphysics* Θ.7–8), Charles thinks that more can be said about what persists: namely, that it is what is

---

replacement of one entity by another. Change does involve the replacement of a privation by a form. But neither the privation nor the form is a self-standing entity: they have a subject, and this persists through the change. As we saw above, Aristotle probably does rely on this argument at another point in his theory, as the basis of his belief that in every change something persists. But I do not think it is the response he gives to Parmenides in *Phys.* 1.8. For a full discussion of Aristotle's response to Parmenides, see Clarke 2015.

[43] ἡ δὲ ὑποκειμένη φύσις ἐπιστητὴ κατ' ἀναλογίαν. ὡς γὰρ πρὸς ἀνδριάντα χαλκὸς ἢ πρὸς κλίνην ξύλον ἢ πρὸς τῶν ἄλλων τι τῶν ἐχόντων μορφὴν [ἡ ὕλη καὶ] τὸ ἄμορφον ἔχει πρὶν λαβεῖν τὴν μορφήν, οὕτως αὕτη πρὸς οὐσίαν ἔχει καὶ τὸ τόδε τι καὶ τὸ ὄν. μία μὲν οὖν ἀρχὴ αὕτη, οὐχ οὕτω μία οὖσα οὐδὲ οὕτως ὂν ὡς τὸ τόδε τι.

[44] For a discussion of Aristotle's concept of analogy, see Judson 2019a, 135–6.

[45] It might be objected (i) that what Aristotle says while doing first philosophy is of doubtful relevance to his second-philosophical account in the *Physics*, or (ii) that in any case the account of matter in Λ is quite different from that in *Phys.* 1. Charles 2000 argues for (ii) (see, e.g., 95 n. 7), but I am unpersuaded (see Judson 2019a, 82–6). As regards (i), it is worth noting that Λ.2 clearly relies on a direct recap of material from *Phys.* 1, and would not be easily intelligible to anyone who had not read that. More generally, we should resist the (admittedly widespread) idea that first and second philosophy do not have a common interest in the principles of natural substances: see Judson 2019b and 2023.

[46] A point made by an anonymous reader.   [47] Λ.4 1070b19–21, 28–9.

242 LINDSAY JUDSON

potentially an *F* (where '*F*' denotes the substantial form in question). As I mentioned above, he argues convincingly that 'what persists' in substantial generation—for example, what is potentially a house or an oak tree—does not perish when the generation is complete, but endures through the mature life of the substance:

> [I]n theoretically more developed contexts, Aristotle uses phrases such as 'that which is potentially a…house' to characterise what is present throughout the process of the coming to be of a house (1049a8–11). That which is potentially a house is present when nothing needs to be added or changed for the process of house-building to get under way. This characterisation [of what is potentially a house] is consistent with the initial object being re-moulded (and changed) in the process of house-building, provided that there remains (at each step of the process) some one thing which is potentially a house.…While what is potentially an oak was initially a seed, as growth continues it will be (as time goes by) a stripling, a half-grown tree etc. Indeed, as we shall soon see, what is potentially an oak may remain after the process of coming to be is completed (in the grown tree which fully realises the potential to be an oak).[48]

I shall not discuss the Θ texts here, except to say that it seems to me to be compatible with Charles' arguments about those chapters that what Aristotle has in mind as 'what has the potential for being an *F*' is the constituent matter (properly understood);[49] I want to focus on the fact that Charles is committed to 'what is potentially an *F*' being the explanatory bedrock. As I have said, the persistence of this entity, its character as a continuant, is not underwritten by or grounded in the persistence of the thing's constituents. This is because, for Charles, although the potentiality to be an *F* is, at any moment, realized in some matter—thought of as the developing thing's constituents at that moment[50]—this matter does not persist, or does not persist in the right way to count as persisting through the change.[51] If it did, Charles would lose his argument for the need for the logical or abstract entity as what persists. This is reflected in his view that the seed (and likewise the sapling) is a stage or phase of the persisting thing. This view is also hinted at in the footnote at the end of the passage quoted on p. 235 above:

---

[48] Charles 2018, 190.

[49] I will briefly register my views on these texts, but cannot argue for these views here. (i) In relation to *Met.* Θ.7–8, Aristotle may not be asserting that what matter (namely, as a principle) essentially is, is the potentiality for being an *F*, but rather that it is what has the potentiality for being an *F*. Note that Charles says that the underlier is needed to guide and constrain the process (2018, 191–2); but this does not require that the potentiality itself be the primary continuant through the generation rather than the matter which has the potentiality. (ii) For reasons analogous to those given below, I think that the explanatory bedrock in the case of elemental transformation (discussed in Charles 2004) needs to be one level down—in this case to the physical extension of the portion of the element from which the transformation starts. For further discussion of elemental transformation, see Bostock 1995 and 2001, Broadie 2004, Krizan 2013.

[50] See Charles 2018, 190 n. 14.   [51] See pp. 234–6 above.

Compare the following case: a person on his (or her) way to becoming fifty may remain the same person throughout even though she (or he) was initially a foetus, then a child, then an adolescent.... While what underlies the process of becoming fifty remains from the outset when it was a foetus, it does not remain as a foetus throughout!

Now Charles may not intend to say that 'same person' is the explanatory bedrock in the case of personal identity, but may instead intend merely to illustrate how a persisting thing may have different stages or phases. I shall in any case leave the question of diachronic personal identity on one side, and look at two other types of case to illustrate the way in which one might worry that the sameness of the potentiality to be an F is not sufficiently robust to explain what is continuous throughout a change if it is not itself grounded in the persistence of some material item—that it is an unsatisfactory place, in other words, at which to locate explanatory bedrock. These cases will not involve questions of Lockean consciousness of self; and they will be everyday cases—partly because this would be Aristotle's way of doing things, and partly to avoid issues about the relevance or irrelevance of extreme or science-fiction cases.[52]

Before I talk about these, however, I shall return to the question of the ship of Theseus. If we adopt Charles' way of thinking of things, the question takes on the air of the Cheshire Cat's smile. The repaired ship *is* Theseus's ship if, and only if, it possesses numerically the same potentiality for being a ship that Theseus's original ship possessed; but exactly the same can be said for the reassembled ship. There is simply nothing else that can be adduced—for example, by consideration of the two ships' constituents—as a determinant of which of these (if either) is the case. There are three obvious reactions to this: the first is to regard it as a problem for Charles' view; the second is to regard it as an *advantage* of his view, since taking constituents into account is what seems to lead to difficulty or even paradox here; the third is to say that artefacts are metaphysically unreliable—and in an Aristotelian context, at any rate, this is quite a tempting move, since although they are his go-to source for illustrations of metaphysical points, he does not regard them as paradigm substances.[53]

My two more positive types of case involve butterflies, and roses, vines, and other plants. Aristotle knows about the stages in the development of butterflies (as he knows about the development of other insects such as bees and wasps):

[T8] Butterflies come to be from caterpillars, which live on green-leaved plants.... At first they are smaller than a grain of millet, then they grow into small larvae; then in three days they are [or: grow into] small caterpillars; after

---

[52] See (in relation to personal identity) Parfit 1971 and Wilkes 1988.
[53] This view is most explicit at *Met.* H.3, 1043b18–23.

244   LINDSAY JUDSON

this, having grown further, they become motionless and change their shape, and are called chrysalises. They have a hard covering and move if this is touched.... They have no mouth or other visible [namely, organic] parts. After a short while the covering bursts open and from them fly the winged animals we call butterflies. (*HA* 5.19, 551a13–24)[54]

Should we regard these various processes as parts of the unified development of a single being, or as a series of separate developments of distinct beings? If we think that the persistence of constituents (as I characterized it earlier) underpins substantial generation, then we have ontological resources (whether or not we have the corresponding epistemological resources) for dealing with this question. If we suppose that this is the substantial generation of a single entity, we will be supposing that there is the appropriate sort of persistence of material constituents throughout the process as a whole; if there turned out not to be, we would change our view. Charles' Aristotle, by contrast, seems simply free to choose—or simply unable to choose—as he has no ontological resources for answering the question.

What about roses and other plants? If we graft a cutting of plant A onto the stock of plant B, what should we say about the resulting growth? If we take a cutting of a plant and plant it separately, and it grows successfully, is it part of numerically the same plant as the original?[55] What should we say if we dig up most of a shrub and plant it somewhere else? We might well, for instance, wish to say that in the last case the transplanted shrub is numerically the same plant; that in the second case we have a new plant much in the way that a plant which grows from seed is a new plant; and that in the first case—the case of grafting—plant A survives to a degree in a new hybrid plant. These may or may not be the right answers, and nothing hinges on whether they are. My point is that the idea that the bedrock for persistence through substantial generation is what is potentially a plant of the given kind would mean that there is no basis for correctness or incorrectness in these answers; whereas if it is the plant's matter (understood in something like the way I have outlined), there is, plausibly, such a basis. We will no

---

[54] γίνονται δ᾽ αἱ μὲν καλούμεναι ψυχαὶ ἐκ τῶν καμπῶν, αἳ γίνονται ἐπὶ τῶν φύλλων τῶν χλωρῶν..., πρῶτον μὲν ἔλαττον κέγχρου, εἶτα μικροὶ σκώληκες αὐξανόμενοι, ἔπειτα ἐν τρισὶν ἡμέραις κάμπαι μικραί· μετὰ δὲ ταῦτα αὐξηθεῖσαι ἀκινητίζουσι, καὶ μεταβάλλουσι τὴν μορφήν, καὶ καλοῦνται χρυσαλλίδες, καὶ σκληρὸν ἔχουσι τὸ κέλυφος, ἁπτομένου δὲ κινοῦνται...οὔτε στόμα ἔχουσαι οὔτ᾽ ἄλλο τῶν μορίων διάδηλον οὐδέν. χρόνου δ᾽ οὐ πολλοῦ διελθόντος περιρρήγνυται τὸ κέλυφος, καὶ ἐκπέτεται ἐξ αὐτῶν πτερωτὰ ζῷα, ἃς καλοῦμεν ψυχάς. Note that Aristotle's language here is (probably deliberately) somewhat non-committal about the ontological fine print. In *GA* 3.9 he talks of the 'threefold genesis' involving larva, pupa ('egg'), and the final form of the insect (I owe this reference to Sophia Connell).

[55] Aristotle seems to have written a treatise on plants (a work in two books is mentioned in ancient lists of his writings), but we do not have it. He refers to material on plant development in 'the work on plants' at *HA* 5.1, 539a20–1; this is either to that treatise or (conceivably) to work in progress by his pupil Theophrastus, a work which does survive. Theophrastus discusses propagating plants from cuttings (lilies and roses: *Research into Plants* II.2.1; trees II.1 and 5), and apparently mentions grafting at II.1.4.

doubt get to explanatory bedrock sooner or later, but in this case I think that there is a philosophical advantage to getting there later.

This chapter is itself more of an acorn or a sapling than an oak tree, but I hope that it has at least some potentiality to be the basis for an alternative view of what persists in Aristotelian generation.[56]

Works Cited

Bostock, David. 1982. 'Aristotle on the Principles of Change in *Physics* I', in *Language and Logos: Studies in Ancient Philosophy Presented to G. E. L. Owen* (ed. M. Schofield and M. Nussbaum). Cambridge University Press, 179–96. (Reprinted in Bostock 2006, 1–18.)

Bostock, David. 1995. 'Aristotle on the Transmutation of Elements in *De generatione et corruptione* 1.1–4', *Oxford Studies in Ancient Philosophy* 6, 255–70. (Reprinted in Bostock 2006, 19–29.)

Bostock, David. 2001. 'Aristotle's Theory of Matter', in *Aristotle and Contemporary Science* II (ed. D. Sfendoni-Mentzou, J. Hattiangadi, and D. M. Johnson). Peter Lang, 3–22. (Reprinted in Bostock 2006, 30–47.)

Bostock, David. 2006. *Space, Time, Matter, and Form: Essays on Aristotle's* Physics. Oxford University Press.

Broadie, Sarah. 2004. '*On Generation and Corruption* I.4: Distinguishing Alteration–Substantial Change, Elemental Change, and First Matter in *GC*', in de Haas and Mansfeld 2004, 123–50.

Carraro, Nicola. 2017. 'Aristotle's Embryology and Ackrill's Problem', *Phronesis* 62, 274–304.

Charles, David. 1994. 'Matter and Form: Unity, Persistence, and Identity', in *Unity, Identity, and Explanation in Aristotle's* Metaphysics (ed. T. Scaltsas, D. Charles, and M. L. Gill). Clarendon Press, 75–105.

Charles, David. 2000. '*Metaphysics* Λ 2: Matter and Change', in *Aristotle's* Metaphysics Lambda: *Symposium Aristotelicum* (ed. M. Frede and D. Charles). Clarendon Press, 80–110.

Charles, David. 2004. 'Simple Genesis and Prime Matter', in de Haas and Mansfeld 2004, 151–69.

---

[56] After I wrote this chapter, I read Anna Schrief's excellent unpublished paper 'The Persistence of Aristotelian Matter and the Generation of Animals', which argues for a very different interpretation of what persists in generation. An earlier version of this chapter was presented at a work in progress seminar at New York University: I am grateful to the audience there, and especially to Bridget Brasher, David Konstan, Daniel Kranzelbinder, and Christian Pfeiffer. I am also grateful to two anonymous readers, the editors of this volume, Sophia Connell, and Ellen Judson for comments on particular points.

Charles, David. 2010. '*Metaphysics* Θ.7 and 8: Some Issues Concerning Actuality and Potentiality', in *Being, Nature, and Life in Aristotle: Essays in Honour of Allan Gotthelf* (ed. J. G. Lennox and R. Bolton). Cambridge University Press, 168–97.

Charles, David. 2018. '*Physics* I.7', in Quarantotto 2018, 178–205.

Charlton, W. 1970. *Aristotle* Physics *Books I, II. Translated with Introduction and Notes*. Clarendon Aristotle Series. Clarendon Press.

Clarke, Timothy. 2015. 'Aristotle and the Ancient Puzzle about Coming to Be', *Oxford Studies in Ancient Philosophy* 49, 129–50.

Code, Alan. 1976. 'The Persistence of Aristotelian Matter', *Philosophical Studies* 29, 357–67.

Connell, Sophia M. 2016. *Aristotle on Female Animals: A Study of the* Generation of Animals. Cambridge University Press.

de Haas, Frans and Jaap Mansfeld (ed.). 2004. *Aristotle's* On Generation and Corruption, *Book I: Symposium Aristotelicum*. Clarendon Press.

Fine, Kit. 1999. 'Things and Their Parts', *Midwest Studies in Philosophy* 23, 61–74.

Frede, Michael. 1985. 'Substance in Aristotle's *Metaphysics*', in *Aristotle on Nature and Living Things: Philosophical and Historical Studies* (ed. A. Gotthelf). Mathesis Publications and Bristol Classical Press, 17–26.

Freeland, Cynthia. 1987. 'Aristotle on Bodies, Matter, and Potentiality', in *Philosophical Issues in Aristotle's Biology* (ed. A. Gotthelf and J. G. Lennox). Cambridge University Press, 392–407.

Frey, Christopher. 2007. 'Organic Unity and the Matter of Man', *Oxford Studies in Ancient Philosophy* 32, 167–204.

Furth, Montgomery. 1978. 'Transtemporal Stability in Aristotelean Substances', *Journal of Philosophy* 75, 624–46.

Gill, Mary Louise. 1989. *Aristotle on Substance: The Paradox of Unity*. Princeton University Press.

Grice, H. P. 1941. 'Personal Identity', *Mind* 50, 330–50.

Hume, David. 2007. *A Treatise of Human Nature* (ed. D. F. Norton and M. J. Norton). Oxford University Press.

Johnston, Mark. 2006. 'Hylomorphism', *Journal of Philosophy* 103, 652–98.

Jones, Barrington. 1974. 'Aristotle's Introduction of Matter', *Philosophical Review* 83, 474–500.

Judson, Lindsay. 2018. '*Physics* I.5', in Quarantotto 2018, 130–53.

Judson, Lindsay. 2019a. *Aristotle* Metaphysics *Book Λ. Translated with an Introduction and Commentary*. Clarendon Aristotle Series. Clarendon Press.

Judson, Lindsay. 2019b. 'Aristotle and Crossing the Boundaries between the Sciences', *Archiv für Geschichte der Philosophie* 101, 177–204.

Judson, Lindsay. 2023. 'What Is Aristotle's Metaphysics About?', *Phronesis* 68, 169–92.

Kelsey, Sean. 2008. 'The Place of I 7 in the Argument of *Physics* I', *Phronesis* 53, 180–208.

Koslicki, Kathrin. 2008. *The Structure of Objects*. Oxford University Press.

Koslicki, Kathrin. 2018. *Form, Matter, Substance*. Oxford University Press.

Krizan, Mary. 2013. 'Elemental Structure and the Transformation of the Elements in *On Generation and Corruption* 2.4', *Oxford Studies in Ancient Philosophy* 45, 195–224.

Lennox, James G. 2018. '*Physics* I.9', in Quarantotto 2018, 226–45.

Locke, John. 1982. *An Essay Concerning Human Understanding* (ed. P. H. Nidditch). Oxford University Press.

Parfit, Derek. 1971. 'Personal Identity', *Philosophical Review* 80, 3–27.

Peramatzis, Michail. 2019. 'Review of Kathrin Koslicki, *Form, Matter, Substance*', *Mind* 129, 235–45.

Quarantotto, Diana (ed.). 2018. *Aristotle's* Physics *I: A Systematic Exploration*. Cambridge University Press.

Reid, Thomas. 2002. *Essays on the Intellectual Powers of Man* (ed. D. R. Brookes and K. Haakonssen). Edinburgh University Press.

Schriefl, Anna. Unpublished. 'The Persistence of Aristotelian Matter and the Generation of Animals'.

Skrzypek, Jeremy. 2017. 'Three Concerns for Structural Hylomorphism', *Analytic Philosophy* 58, 360–408.

Waterlow (Broadie), Sarah. 1982. *Nature, Change, and Agency in Aristotle's* Physics: *A Philosophical Study*. Clarendon Press.

Wilkes, Kathleen V. 1988. *Real People: Personal Identity without Thought Experiments*. Clarendon Press.

11

Matter-Involving Form and Hypothetical Necessity in Aristotle's *De Anima*

T. K. Johansen

1. The Text

The starting-point for our discussion is the passage from the first chapter of the *De Anima* where Aristotle lays out his strategy for how to account for psychological affections. The passage is programmatic for the rest of his psychology in so as far as it falls under natural philosophy. The key message is that psychological affections are to be studied as belonging to body, and not in the way a mathematician will study mathematical properties as separate from body:

[T1]   If this is so, it is clear that the accounts are accounts in matter. Consequently, definitions will be of this sort, for example, 'being angry is a sort of motion of a body of such a sort, or of a part or capacity of a body, brought about by this for the sake of that.' And for these reasons, a consideration of the soul, either all souls or of this sort of soul, is already in the province of the natural scientist. The natural scientist and the dialectician would define each of these affections differently, for example, what anger is. The dialectician will define it as desire for retaliation, or something of this sort, while the natural scientist will define it as boiling of the blood and heat around the heart. Of these, one describes the matter and the other the form and the account. For this is the account of the thing, but it is necessary that it be in matter of this sort if it is to exist. It is just as if the account of a house is of this sort—that it is a shelter capable of guarding against destruction by wind, rain, and heat: one will say that it is stones and bricks and timber and another will say that it is the form in these things, for the sake of which these things are. So who among them is the natural scientist? Is it the one who knows about the matter but is ignorant of the account? Or the one who knows only about the account? Or is the natural scientist rather the one concerned with what comes from both of these? In that case, who is each of the other two? Or is no one concerned with the inseparable affections of matter in so far as they are not separable? But the natural

---

T. K. Johansen, *Matter-Involving Form and Hypothetical Necessity in Aristotle's* De Anima In: *Aristotelian Metaphysics: Essays in Honour of David Charles.* Edited by: David Bronstein, Thomas Kjeller Johansen, and Michail Peramatzis, Oxford University Press. © Oxford University Press 2024. DOI: 10.1093/oso/9780198908678.003.0011

scientist is concerned with all those things which are the functions and affections of this sort of body and of this sort of matter. Someone else deals with things not of this sort, perhaps some of them concern some craftsman or other, for example, a carpenter or a doctor; but among affections which are not separable, some, in so far as they are not affections of this sort of body and are from abstraction, concern the mathematician, and others, the separate ones, the first philosopher. But it is necessary to return to the point where our discussion began. We were saying, then, that the affections of the soul are in this way inseparable from the natural matter of animals, at any rate in so far as they are of the sorts which are present as anger and fear are, and are unlike line and surface. (403a25–b19; Shields' translation)[1]

Psychological affections, says [T1], are enmattered accounts or forms. *Logos* often takes the place of form, consistently with Aristotle's view that the form is what we define (see, e.g., *DA* 2.2, 414a9–14). Aristotle distinguishes between three characters: one who studies just the matter, the 'materialist', another who studies just the form, the 'dialectician', and a third, 'the natural scientist' (or 'natural philosopher', Greek *phusikos*), who studies both. It is agreed by all that Aristotle wants to say that a full natural scientific account of the soul's affections will involve both an account of the form and an account of the matter. But there are at least three different possible views about how the form will relate to the matter in these definitions, which I shall refer to here as Readings A, B, and C.

Reading A says that the account of the natural scientist simply combines the matter and the form as studied by his two rivals. Both the materialist and the dialectician give correct accounts of their objects of study, as far as they go. It is just that neither account on its own captures the entire phenomenon, since this is a complex of form-and-matter. To use Aristotle's favoured example of the snub, concavity in the nose: the dialectician studies concavity, the materialist the nose; but neither studies, as the natural scientist ought to, concavity in the nose.[2]

---

[1] At 403b16–19 Shields adopts the Greek text of W. D. Ross. Charles (2021, 18), rejecting Ross' addition of *hoia* (such as) at b18, translates: 'We have said that the affections of the soul are inseparable from the physical matter of living beings in the way in which anger and fear are inseparable and not in the way in which line and plane.' One difference between the two is that Charles' reading does not, in the manner of Ross' text, open the door for psychological affections that might not be inseparable from the body in the way anger and fear are. On either reading, however, the contrast between mathematical and the psychological affections in question here is clear.

[2] A is the reading which Victor Caston favours in his reply to Charles: 'Moderate hylomorphism only claims that the psychological state as a whole is inseparable (in both ways) from its formal and material components. Nothing follows about the inseparability of the components, either from the psychological state as a whole or from each other. In the abstract, each might be separable in existence: a material state like boiling blood might be found apart from anger or the desire for retaliation, just as the desire for retaliation might be found apart from anger or from boiling blood, as "a dish best served cold," in more mature and less hot-headed people. And these components might well be separable in thought, as Aristotle's own discussion suggests. Each of the partial definitions he considers

The materialist's and the dialectician's vice is that of incompleteness, the natural scientist's virtue that of completeness.

Reading B is the interpretation of David Charles.[3] He takes the form itself to be essentially enmattered. The 'snub' is not just a shape, concavity; it is essentially a shape in a certain kind of matter, 'concavity-in-the-nose'. To define the form as if it were simply a shape is to treat the psychological affections as a mathematical form: an attribute that can be defined without reference to any particular matter, even if it requires some matter in order to exist. The formal account of anger requires a specification of the matter in order to determine which form it is. So anger is a desire for retaliation as realized in boiling of the blood. Without this reference to matter the desire for retaliation is insufficiently distinguished from other psychological states, such as the desire for retaliation of the elderly embittered person, who lacks the heat characteristic of the angry. The way the identity of the form is underdetermined without reference to matter is mirrored by the way matter requires form for its determination. The wood is determined as a certain kind of wood by the form of a chair or a bed; similarly, the flesh may be different as employed in touch or in taste. On Reading B, the vice of the materialist and the dialectician is not just the incompleteness of their individual accounts but also their joint inadequacy. For the natural scientist both the account of the form and of the matter will be inextricably connected.

Readings A and B may appear to be the only options. However, it is possible to discern a third way, a Reading C. This reading accepts Charles' key point that there is a difference between natural and mathematical form. The natural scientist differs from the dialectician not just in that he studies form and matter, but in that the form he studies is conceived differently from mathematical form. It is a form that is such as to be enmattered in a particular way, 'natural form' as one may call it. The mathematical form in contrast has no implications for any particular material realization. When asked how the natural form implies a certain matter, Reading C may answer that the natural form *hypothetically necessitates* a certain kind of matter. The reason in turn why natural form, unlike mathematical form, hypothetically necessitates a certain kind of matter is that natural form is *functional*. The difference between Reading B and Reading C is that while Reading B requires that the definition of natural form *explicitly* mention matter, it suffices on Reading C that the definition of the natural form provide information that entails, given certain basic assumptions about the world, the presence of a certain kind of matter.

---

contains just one component, and while he thinks that this is the wrong way to understand the psychological state as a whole, nothing indicates that these other definitions have inaccurately characterized the components. Aristotle's objection is not that their definitions are wrong as far as they go, but that they do not go far enough. They are incomplete: one proponent "ignores" the form, while the other is "concerned with the form exclusively" (403b6–7). All the true natural philosopher has to do is bring the two together.' Caston 2008, 36.

[3] Proposed in Charles 2008 and now developed in book form in Charles 2021.

MATTER-INVOLVING FORM AND HYPOTHETICAL NECESSITY IN *DE ANIMA*   251

The difference between Reading B and Reading C relates to an ambiguity in the basic claim that the definition of the formal aspect 'essentially involves' a material change. It is one thing for the formal definition to involve the material change by explicitly mentioning it, as per Reading B; it is another for the formal definition to involve the material change as a consequence. It is the latter relationship we often find in demonstrations between an object's essence and certain other necessary attributes. So one may demonstrate that a human being is able to learn mathematics given the definition of human being as rational, but one would not mention mathematical potential as part of the definition of human being. One can say then that such necessary attributes are involved by the thing's essence but are not involved in its essence. Similarly, Reading C says that a certain bodily state necessarily follows from a certain psychological state, given the essence of the psychological state, but nonetheless the bodily state is not mentioned in its definition.

So far, I have given a sketch of the three readings. Let's return now to [T1] to note some features that might be taken to support one or other of the three readings.

Reading A may point to the fairly clear structure of Aristotle's argument in [T1]: there are three characters, one studies form, the second matter, the third form plus matter. Readings B and C meanwhile seem to insert qualifications on the form so that the form studied by the natural scientist is not the form as studied by the dialectician: it is the matter-involving natural form and not the mathematical one. Readings B and C will thus have to argue that the initial schematic distinction between the three characters is revised when Aristotle moves to distinguish affections that cannot be separated in account from those that can. Reading A will maintain that Aristotle is here simply referring to the psychological affection understood as the compound: of course, *this* affection cannot be separated from the matter since matter is a constituent part of it.[4] The defender of the other two readings will respond that Aristotle must be referring to the form, not the compound, when he says 'the natural scientist is concerned with all those things which are the functions and affections of this sort of body and of this sort of matter' (403b11–12). For clearly Aristotle is referring to the form that the mathematician

---

[4] See Charles 2008, 6–7: '[Aristotle's] conclusion is spelled out more fully in his next remarks: being angry is a given type of process, the boiling of the blood around the heart, for the sake of revenge (403a31). But how precisely is Aristotle's conclusion to be understood? It could be interpreted in two ways. It might mean that anger is essentially a compound made up of two distinct processes, or process descriptions, one purely psychological, desire for revenge, and one purely physical, the boiling of the blood, where, e.g., the latter necessitates the presence of the former. In this account, the relevant type of desire for revenge would be separable in thought, and abstractable, from the physical process involved. So understood, anger would be a compound like the bronze circle, defined as a mathematical form combined with matter. Even though anger as composed from these two elements is inseparable in thought from, and not abstractable from, the physical process involved, it can be defined in terms of a purely psychological and a purely physical component. Alternatively, Aristotle's conclusion might mean the relevant type of desire is inseparable in thought from, and not abstractable from, the boiling of the blood. So understood, the type of desire for revenge which defines anger is a-boiling-of-the-blood-type of desire for revenge. In this model, anger is essentially enmattered because its form is essentially enmattered: it is the very form it is because it is enmattered in this type of physical process.'

252   T. K. JOHANSEN

studies when he says that it is separable from matter in account, so when Aristotle contrasts the mathematician with the natural scientist he must also mean to refer to the *form* that the natural scientist studies and studies as inseparable in account from its matter. So the point is about the difference between two kinds of form and their relationship to matter. But this is what Readings B and C want to say when they contrast natural form with mathematical form.

Second, that Aristotle calls the person who just mentions the form a 'dialectician' may indicate a criticism in itself of how this person studies form. For only a few lines back Aristotle criticized definitions that do not allow us to explain derived properties as 'dialectical and vacuous'.[5] If form is prior to matter and is such as to explain matter, we may say that a definition of the form that does not allow us to derive the sort of matter that realizes it is 'vacuous'. But this may count as a criticism of Reading A, since Reading A treats the form itself along the lines of concave, a mathematical form, which does not in itself tell us anything about the matter. In contrast, both Readings B and C may claim support from this point, since they take the form essentially to involve matter. Reading B will say that it is by mentioning the matter in the definition of the form that the natural scientist is able to demonstrate material features on the basis of this definition. Reading C will say that this is too strong: the dialectical account is contrasted only with an account of the form that allows us to know *what follows from it*. In other words, Aristotle requires of the definition of the form that one should be able to demonstrate from it other features of that which has the form. But that does not require that the features to be demonstrated are themselves contained in the definition of the form; only that the material features can be demonstrated on the basis of the definition and certain other premises about the world. Reading C thus takes the material features specified in the account of matter to be such that they can be demonstrated through the definition of the form, though the definition of the form does not itself mention those material features.

Third, [T1] says that 'it is necessary for such a formula (*logos*) to be in this kind of matter': a form that is of this kind must have a specific kind of matter. This is what one on Readings B and C would refer to as a 'natural' form. Reading B would take the matter to be necessary as a part of the definition of the form: we need to refer to boiling of the blood to understand which kind of desire for revenge is in question. Reading C, meanwhile, would take the necessity to be hypothetical. The matter is not part of the definition itself but follows from the definition of the form because it shows the form to be a certain kind of *function* which requires matter for its realization. Reading A, of course, will acknowledge the hypothetical necessity that obtains between form and matter, but as the form of the compound can be

---

[5] 'For the starting-point of every demonstration is what a thing is, so that those formulas which do not lead us to ascertain the properties of a substance, or at least to know of them in a ready sort of way, will clearly and in every case be dialectical and vacuous' (402b25–403a2; Shields' translation). On this point, see further Charles 2021, 23.

MATTER-INVOLVING FORM AND HYPOTHETICAL NECESSITY IN *DE ANIMA*   253

defined independently of the matter—Reading A favours the view of form which Michail Peramatzis and Charles call 'purism'[6]—the matter is contingent from the point of view of the definition of the form itself. Supporting hypothetical necessity is not a constraint on the definition of the form itself, as it is for Reading C.

2. Mathematical vs. Natural Form

So much by way of clarifying the basic difference between the three readings. In order to decide between them, it helps to bring in some other Aristotelian texts with close bearing on [T1]. So the key distinction between those mathematical-style affections that can be studied as separable and those physical affections that cannot seems to be the one familiar from book 2 of the *Physics*. This is how Aristotle explains the difference there:

[T2]   Now the mathematician, though he too treats of these things, nevertheless does not treat of them as the limits of a natural body, nor does he consider the attributes as the attributes of such bodies. That is why he separates them; for in thought they are separable from motion, and it makes no difference, nor does any falsity result, if they are separated. The holders of the theory of Forms do the same, though they are not aware of it; for they separate the natural attributes, which are less separable than those of mathematics. This becomes plain if one tries to state in each of the two cases the definitions of the things and of their attributes. 'Odd' and 'even', 'straight' and 'curved', and likewise 'number', 'line', and 'figure', do not involve motion, not so 'flesh' and 'bone' and 'man'—these are defined like 'snub nose', not like 'curved'... (*Phys.* 2.2, 193b30–194a7; Hardie and Gaye's translation in Barnes 1984)

We learnt from [T1] that mathematical attributes can be separated in thought from body without loss of explanatory power. The attributes of natural bodies as natural cannot be so studied. In [T2] Aristotle specifies the aspect of *motion* as the basis of inseparability: the reason why natural forms cannot be studied in separation from bodies is that natural form involves motion. Since it is motion that makes the form inseparable in account from matter, the implication must be that it is motion that requires matter. The link to saying that the natural form is a function seems clear: where functions are such that they involve a motion of some sort,[7] they will also involve a body of the sort to undergo this motion. For

---

[6] Peramatzis 2015, a terminology followed in Charles 2021.
[7] Of course, we may think also of mathematical functions, so it is not every function as such that involves motion in its subject. When I talk of 'functional' in the following I shall be concerned with functions that involve motion or change in or by the subject.

example, to use the example of [T1], a house is a covering of people and property of a certain sort, resistant to wind and rain. The function is such that it requires a certain material realization, because the function involves a kind of change (and rest) that can only be realized by a certain kind of matter, matter that is durable, impenetrable to rain and wind, insulating, etc.[8]

Imagine in contrast an attempt to specify the form of a house mathematically. So, one might outline the form of a house geometrically:

Here there is nothing to indicate that the shape must be composed of any specific sort of matter. Nothing about the geometrical attributes indicates ability to initiate, withstand, or undergo any sort of change. The geometrical determination of the form is neutral as to any particular material realization. It is separable in account from matter.

3. Hypothetical Necessity and Instrumentality

The claim of Reading C then is that a natural form *by hypothetical necessity* entails a specific material realization. Somebody might challenge this claim by saying that all that hypothetical necessity as such establishes is dependency on some necessary conditions. There is an indeterminate number of factors that can be said to be necessary for the construction of a house. Hypothetical necessity itself, it seems, is insufficient to single out those preconditions that concern the material *cause*.

So we might say both:

(i) If there is going to be a house, the law of gravity has to obtain.
(ii) If there is going to be a house, there have to building materials of such and such a kind.

One might agree that it is possible to conceive of hypothetical necessity such that it does not distinguish between (i) and (ii). However, it seems clear that Aristotle understands hypothetical necessity not in the context of merely necessary or

---

[8] Charles (2021), in contrast, understands the final cause of a house to be insufficient to determine the specific choice of materials, as a part of his argument for the form's requiring explicit mention of matter: 'Nor is it obvious why coverings (defined independently of matter) made to protect belongings need be made of stones and timber. There can, after all, be house-shaped tents, caves, igloos, or even tree awnings, which (as was suggested in Chapter 1) can serve this purpose as effectively. Houses are defined as specific kinds of material (e.g. wooden) coverings' (66).

MATTER-INVOLVING FORM AND HYPOTHETICAL NECESSITY IN *DE ANIMA*   255

sufficient conditions, but in the context of a certain causal theory. The item referred to in the protasis is a final cause, identified with the form and function of a house. The item or items referred to in the apodosis is a contributing cause: for example, if there is to be the final cause or function of the house, necessarily there have to be such and such building materials. What is hypothetically necessary is then considered from the point of view of what specifically contributes to this final cause. The notion of hypothetical necessity is embedded in that of final causality or teleology. There are final causes and contributory causes, and the latter are hypothetically necessary for the former.[9] This is then a much stronger notion than a mere necessary condition: it is the relationship between an end and a specific causal means to that end.

One way to bring out this point is to show passages where Aristotle talks about the hypothetically necessary as *instrumental*. Aristotle thinks that it is a general fact about final causes that they require instruments. So in the discussion of sexual differentiation in the *Generation of Animals* he says that 'Instruments (*organa*) are needed for all functioning (*ergasia*) and since the bodily parts are the tools that serve the faculties, it follows that certain parts must exist for the union and production of offspring' (*GA* 1.2, 716a24–7; Platt's translation in Barnes 1984).

It is clear that the notion of an instrument is much more specific than that of a (mere) necessary condition. Not only are tools geared to specific kinds of jobs, but they are often themselves manufactured for the purpose of this job. In such cases their own nature is dependent on the function they serve. This is not to say that what is hypothetically necessitated might not have other causes, or might not exist even if not hypothetically necessitated; but it is to say that it as hypothetically necessitated has characteristics that are at least in part caused by the end it serves.[10]

Parts of Animals 1.1 offers a clear example of hypothetical necessity joined with instrumentality:

[T3]   For we say nourishment is something necessary according to neither of these two sorts of necessity, but because it is not possible to be without it. And this is, as it were, necessity from hypothesis; for just as, since the axe must split, it is a necessity that it be hard, and if hard, then made of bronze or iron, so too since the body is an instrument (for each of the parts is for the sake of something and likewise also the whole), it is therefore a necessity that it be of such a character and constituted from such things, if that is to be. (642a8–14; Lennox's translation)

---

[9] A thought he inherits from Plato. See further Johansen 2020.
[10] As Cooper 2009, 157–9 shows, there are clear instances of materially necessary processes which are also employed for ends and so count as also hypothetically necessary.

256   T. K. JOHANSEN

An axe is an instrument with a certain function that determines its composition by hypothetical necessity. It is because the axe has this function, splitting, that it requires a certain material composition. In the same manner the animal's body is an instrument by which the animal realizes its functions. The *Parts of Animals* is based on the psychology of the *De Anima* on this point. So in *De Anima* 2.2 Aristotle presents the general view of the living body as instrumental in relation to the soul, and again in *De Anima* 2.4, at 415b18–20, he accounts for the soul as the final cause of the instrumental body. When Aristotle explains that the soul is the form and final cause of the body, he turns to hypothetical necessity to articulate how the soul so understood determines the body, naturally so since the body is an instrument for the functions by which the animal realizes its goals.

4. 'Making the Matter Clear'

Let us return to the question of how the soul–body relationship (so understood) is reflected in the definition of the form. In *Metaphysics* Z.10–11 Aristotle reflects on the role of matter in relation to the definition of substance. Aristotle here considers when, and when not, we should take the matter to be part of the definition of the substance. His general position is that the matter would enter into the account of particulars only. However, only an account of the universal, not the particular, is a proper definition. In the case of the universal, the substance defined will be the form alone.[11] In Z.10 he argues that the parts of the definition are prior to the whole in those cases where the definition is just of the form, as it is when we define the substance as such. He uses the example of the soul of animals:

[T4]   Now since the soul of animals (for this is the substance of the animate) is the substance that is in accord with the account and is the form and the essence of such-and-such a body (certainly each part if it is to be defined correctly, will not be defined without its function, which it could not have without perception), it follows that the parts of this are prior, either all or some, to the compound animal, and similarly, then, to each particular animal, whereas the body and its parts will be posterior, and what is divided into these as into matter is not the substance but the compound. (1036a14–21; Reeve's translation)

---

[11] This is in line with Aristotle's account of the soul in *DA* 2.4 as the substance and *logos* of the living being.

MATTER-INVOLVING FORM AND HYPOTHETICAL NECESSITY IN *DE ANIMA*   257

Aristotle's view here is that we can and should define the parts of the soul which is the form and essence of the body prior to accounting both for the whole soul and for the compound of soul and body. In Z.11 he proceeds to clarify which parts of the definition are parts as form and which not. Clearly here one possibility is that some kinds of matter are part of the definition of the form, since it is of the essence of that thing to have a certain kind of matter. To assess this possibility, he then distinguishes various kinds of case. There is first the case of the bronze circle. Since the same circle can be found in different kinds of material, clearly the circle cannot have any of these kinds of matter as part of its definition. Next is the case of human. The relationship between the form of human and the bodily parts appears to be different from the first case, since this form is always found in these bodily parts. However, Aristotle seems to allow that it nonetheless might be possible—perhaps in account—to separate the form from the matter in the human case.[12] Yet this is only one side of competing intuitions. Aristotle is clearly worried that an exclusive focus on the form can lead to the Platonic view that the substance simply is the form without regard for the matter. He then returns to this 'puzzle' to say:

[T5]   It has been stated, then, that there is a puzzle where definitions are concerned, and what its cause is. And that is why to lead all things back to Forms in this way and to subtract the matter is beside the point. For some things are presumably a this in this, or these things in this state. And the comparison in the case of animal that Socrates the younger used to make is not correct. For it leads away from the truth and makes us suppose that the human can exist without the parts, as the circle can without the bronze. But the case is not similar. For the animal is presumably something capable of perceiving, and it is not possible to define it without movement, nor, therefore, without the parts being in a certain state. For a hand in any and every state is not a part of the human, but one that is capable of fulfilling its function, and so is animate, and if not animate is not a part. (1036b21–32; Reeve's translation)

If one approached 'animal' in the same way as 'circle', one might get the impression that it too can be defined without reference to matter.[13] However, the correct definition of animal will make it clear that it is capable of perceiving,[14] and so is

---

[12] This is the option that he uses as a premise for his next line of reasoning (1036b5ff.).

[13] A suggestion that does not seem so farfetched in light of the mathematical definition of soul in Plato's *Timaeus* 35b–36d.

[14] Reading *aisthētikon*, 'capable of perceiving', with Frede/Patzig and Reeve. The manuscripts have *aisthēton*, 'capable of being perceived', but this makes little sense of the argument in terms of the animal body's proper function. See Frede and Patzig 1988, 210–11. For a contrasting reading, defending the MS reading, see Peramatzis 2011, appendix 1. (See also Gill in Chapter 9 of this volume.) Even if one reads *aisthēton*, however, the point will clearly rely on a conception of the animal's essentially being such as to undergo change.

258   T. K. JOHANSEN

such as to undergo movement or change (*kinēsis*), and therefore also such as to have certain material parts.[15] Notice here the parallel with *Physics* 2.2, [T2]: mathematical form can be studied in abstraction from body; the form of natural bodies cannot because the form is a function that involves change.

But why does Aristotle at the end of [T5] bring up the point that the body cannot be determined without the psychic capacities: for example, a hand without its motive function? Is his main point not that *the soul* cannot be defined without bringing in movement and bodily parts? A plausible reason, I think, is that Aristotle thinks that the two points are two sides of the same coin. If we defined the soul in the mathematical manner, then a bodily part possessing such a 'mathematical' soul would not necessarily differ from a dead body part or a drawing of a body part, which could have the same 'mathematical' characteristics. If you define the soul functionally, it is clear that it will not be realized without certain bodily parts, or as he says in [T5], 'without the parts being in a certain state'. And this is the viewpoint from which we talk about the bodily parts as functional. For example, we talk about the eye as essentially an instrument of vision (*DA* 2.1, 412b19–22). So an eye without vision is an eye only 'homonymously', an eye in name only. Aristotle's point in [T5] is then to say that the functional account of the soul naturally joins up with the way we talk about the body parts as instrumental, and so is supported by this view of the body.

To have the ability to undergo change requires matter, since change is the fulfilment of a potentiality.[16] To have the ability to undergo a specific form of change, like perception, requires a specific sort of matter, the sort of matter that can be changed by perceptible qualities. Having, even more specifically, the ability to see requires having matter that can be changed by colours. Pointing to perception

---

[15] Michael Frede comments on [T5] that 'it is clear that all Aristotle is saying so far is that, unlike circles, human beings ought not to be defined in such a way as to create the impression that they could exist without the material parts they have or perhaps even without material parts altogether.... We can, e.g., define a human being as, among other things, capable of perception, more specifically capable of sight, hearing, taste, smell and touch. For defining a human being in this way we explicitly only refer to its form, or rather to parts of its form. But we do this in such a way as to make it perfectly clear that a human being cannot exist without material parts. For the ability to touch, e.g., does presuppose material parts. And such a definition not only makes it clear that human beings have to have material parts, it also makes it clear that human beings have to have material parts of a certain kind, perhaps even in some sense that they have to have the material parts they have. For how could something be capable of sight without having an eye or eyes? Thus it seems that we could define a human being solely in terms of its form without giving the mistaken impression that human beings could exist without the material parts they have or even without material parts altogether' (Frede 1990, 120). Frede's analysis does not explicate what it means to give an account of the form 'that makes it clear' that a human being must have certain material parts. Certainly, he wants to exclude that the definition explicitly mentions the matter, since his main point is that the definition is of the form alone. So Reading B is off the table. On the other hand, Frede also seems to reject the 'purity' aspect of Reading A, since the formal definition does give information somehow about the specific matter that something answering to the formal definition must have.

[16] E.g., 'there is no motion without a natural body' (*DC* 1.9, 279a15–16). Motion (*kinēsis*) is the actuality of the potential *qua* potential (*Phys.* 3.1, 201b5–6) and potentiality is aligned with matter (*DA* 2.1, 412a9).

MATTER-INVOLVING FORM AND HYPOTHETICAL NECESSITY IN *DE ANIMA* 259

then opens an explanatory path to material parts. I speak of a 'path' here because the definition of the soul need not *explicitly* mention those bodily parts, as long as it mentions a change, such as the ability to perceive, which in turn will eventually require us to mention matter. This information suffices for us to know that the soul is realized in a body since the ability to move in a certain way is in Aristotle's physics always a property of a certain matter. This is also all that is required to avoid the mistake of the young Socrates: the idea that the soul could exist on its own, like a Platonic Form.

5. Hypothetical Necessity 'in the Definition'

We need to be clearer about both why certain forms involve matter and what is the manner of the involvement. Reading C, I have suggested, can answer these questions by reference to hypothetical necessity. Consider now the closing passage of *Physics* 2.9:

[T6] Perhaps the necessary is also in the definition. For if one defines the operation of sawing as being a certain kind of dividing, then this cannot come about unless the saw has teeth of a certain kind; and these cannot be unless it is of iron. For in the definition too there are some parts that are, as it were, its matter. (200a32–b9; Hardie and Gaye's translation, slightly altered)

Significantly, [T6] makes reference to the matter in the definition as 'the necessary'. It is clear from the example Aristotle gives here that he has in mind what is hypothetically necessary, as in the similar case of the axe in [T3]. If the matter is in the definition of the form as the hypothetically necessary, it is natural to take this to mean that the form hypothetically necessitates the matter. Again, in parallel with the *Parts of Animals*, we understand why the form necessitates the matter, because it is a certain function, here a kind of dividing.

Now Aristotle said previously in *Physics* 2.9 that 'the necessary is in the matter but that for the sake of which is in the definition (*logos*)' (200a14–15).[17] This was when he identified the matter in natural beings as necessary for the end. The end was not necessary but the matter was necessary given the end, hypothetically necessary. So it made sense to say that the necessary was on the side of the matter. What is striking is that Aristotle now refers to the 'necessary' in the *definition*. On Reading C, I have suggested, is not hard to see the ground for the shift: if the definition shows what this function is, and this could not be realized without this matter, then there is a sense in which one by giving the

---

[17] ἐν γὰρ τῇ ὕλῃ τὸ ἀναγκαῖον, τὸ δ'οὗ ἕνεκα ἐν τῷ λόγῳ.

260   T. K. JOHANSEN

definition already specifies that which necessitates the matter. So the necessary matter is in a sense already given by giving the function. This is the key claim of Reading C.

In reply, Reading B may emphasize the final line in [T6] ('For in the definition too there are some parts that are, as it were (*hōs*), its matter') and say that this means that the matter must be mentioned explicitly in the definition. Reading C, in turn, will stress 'as it were', as one could translate *hōs*. The qualification may be taken to distance Aristotle from the claim that the definition must explicitly mention the matter.

Simplicius' comment on [T6] supports the point:

> [Aristotle] has said that the definition and the account are the starting-point and the cause of the matter, which represented necessity even among causes, since even matter is included in many definitions, sometimes in potentiality in the definition of the form, as he himself suggests, and sometimes in actuality as in the compound. It is, then, clear in the former case that the definition will no longer be the starting-point and cause of the matter by including it in itself, which is why he adds 'perhaps necessity is in the account too'. (*On Aristotle Physics* 392.6–393.14; Fleet's translation (1997))

There are two ways of including the matter in the account, one in potentiality, the other in actuality. Including it in actuality is to offer a compound account like the account of anger in *De Anima* 1.1, 'anger is a desire for revenge accompanied by a boiling of the blood around the heart'. This is the full natural philosophical account. But another, where the matter is included potentially, is to give an account of the form which will 'show up alongside' (*sunanaphainō*) the matter. So Simplicius says, 'If one were to define a saw and say "A saw is a tool for cutting timber or stone in a certain way, being fitted with teeth of a particular kind", it will be apparent at the same time that the teeth need to be made of iron' (393.3–5; Fleet's translation). The mention of 'iron' lies outside of the definition of the form proper (here within double quotes), but the definition of the form makes it apparent because of the way in which the form has been specified as a function. This seems to be the potential presence of the matter that Simplicius refers to.

Simplicius takes teeth of a certain kind to be part of the formal specification of sawing. It is the iron that represents the matter here. Alternatively, we can take the definition of the form simply to be that of a certain kind of dividing. In that case both the hypothetical necessity of the saw's being made of certain teeth and the hypothetical necessity of the teeth's being made of iron follow as a consequence of the definition of the function itself. But in either case the basic point remains that one need not mention the matter, the iron, explicitly for it to be present potentially in the definition of the form, in a way that will be made clear and actual if

MATTER-INVOLVING FORM AND HYPOTHETICAL NECESSITY IN *DE ANIMA* 261

one specifies the matter in a distinct account, as in the full natural philosophical account.

Reading B may reply that teeth do count as matter and are exactly required to offset sawing from other kinds of cutting: sawing is a kind of dividing that takes place with teeth. The other material conditions, iron, we can leave outside of the definition of the form. Yet this is not how Aristotle formulates the relationship between sawing and teeth. Rather he says in [T6] 'if one defines the operation of sawing as being a certain kind of dividing, then this cannot come about unless the saw has teeth <u>of a certain kind</u>' (my underlining).[18] That is, the presence of certain teeth follows by hypothetical necessity from the conception of sawing as a particular kind of dividing. It is not the presence of a certain kind of teeth that makes sawing a particular kind of dividing, as Reading B would have it. Perhaps it is hard to define a saw without reference to teeth (sawing seems essentially distinguished from other kinds of cutting, e.g., with a knife, by the use of teeth). But it seems non-problematic to define a saw without reference to teeth of a *certain kind.*[19] So *Merriam-Webster* defines a saw as 'a hand or power tool or a machine used to cut hard material (such as wood, metal, or bone) and equipped usually with a toothed blade or disk'. Mentioning a toothed blade is not itself to mention certain kinds of teeth, and specifically it is not to mention teeth made of a certain kind of matter. Yet we understand that when a toothed blade is 'used to cut hard material', then it must itself have certain material properties, hardness, rigidity, sharpness, the combination of which properties in turn prescribes a certain kind of matter, iron. Or so Reading C would have it.

---

[18] Cooper (2009) observes that 'hypothetical necessities are conditions sine qua non for ends (*Phys.* 2.9, 200a5–6, *PA* 1.1, 641b8), which is to say that they are things not already included in the end in view but rather things that are needed as external means to its realization' (152). On this conception, one could not accommodate the matter as hypothetically necessary yet also part of the definition of the form, which as we have seen is also the functional end in living beings and artefacts. Put differently, it seems that Reading B cannot properly acknowledge the hypothetical necessitation of matter by form. One possible response to this objection may lie in Charles' suggestion that the material side is the further details of matter beyond those that enter into the essential determination of the form. However, this would clearly not apply to Aristotle's example of the hypothetical necessitation of the teeth or the iron of the saw.

[19] Contrast Charles 2021, 77 n. 76: 'Aristotle does not attempt to define the specific type of dividing wood that saws do in the purist style (without explicit reference in the definition to some type of metal, such as iron), and then to show that their form (defined as what is capable of dividing wood in this way) requires or "hypothetically necessitates" the presence of iron. To do so would have been a major undertaking. He would have needed to show what it is about the capacity (defined in the purist way) that requires the presence of iron rather than bronze. Enmattered capacities, by contrast (such as the material capacity to divide wood with hard metallic teeth), clearly require the presence of iron rather than bronze. Claims of hypothetical necessity are, in the impurist account, grounded in the definition of the type of form at issue. However, purist interpreters cannot simply insist that, for Aristotle, the relevant pure forms "hypothetically necessitate" the presence of some matter. They need to show how, in his account, pure forms actually require the presence of specific types of matter.'

6. Hypothetical Necessity and Definitional Dependence

Reading C, as I have developed it, takes the matter to be hypothetically necessitated by the form. But I have also said that there is a definitional and so a conceptual connection between form and matter. How, if at all, are these two points compatible? Let us start with Aristotle's point in [T5] that a function such as perception involves change or motion, and this involves matter. The connection between change and matter clearly obtains at a very general conceptual level for Aristotle. So the account in *Physics* 3.1 says that change is the fulfilment of a potentiality as such, and Aristotle aligns matter with potentiality in various places.[20] Yet these are conceptual relationships that are determinable in various categories in more specific ways. So qualitative change will be the activity of a specific kind of matter capable of receiving qualities, and the matter involved can in turn be further determined according to the kind of quality in question.

Hypothetical necessity may be mediated by such conceptual relationships. So to say that vision requires transparent matter, specifically water, or that sawing requires teeth made of a certain matter, specifically iron, is to offer a determination of how the conceptual relationship between change and matter works out in a specific case within a specific category of change. There is no question here but that we require experience to find out which matter does the job. The conceptual connection between function and matter here does not imply that truths about the material realization of a function can be determined a priori. Yet when we find that it is iron that serves the job of sawing or transparent liquid the job of seeing, we also see that the specific matter is necessary for sawing or seeing given what sawing or seeing is: that is, how these functions are defined.

On Reading B, it makes little sense to involve hypothetical necessity in the definition of the form. Concavity-of-the-nose is one property, not a relationship between two properties, one necessitating another.[21] Reading A, meanwhile, may want to claim that the formal definition hypothetically necessitates the material definition: for example, that only boiling of the blood around the heart can realize a desire for revenge. But unless the formal definition makes it clear what would support the necessitation, the danger is that this relationship appears as merely contingent. And so we are left in the position of the functionalist. On Reading C, in contrast, we can see why it must be this matter that realizes the form, given the sort of form it is, not simply because of the explicit information the formal definition offers us, but because of the conceptual connections this information establishes to other basic facts about the world. To reason on the basis of hypothetical

---

[20] E.g., *Met.* Θ.8, 1050a15.
[21] In this sense I agree with Cooper 2009 that we do not find hypothetical necessity within the definition of the essence; compare n. 18 above.

necessity is to match the items in our experience with the conceptual requirements of the formal definition.

7. Further Objections to Reading C

The central claim of Reading C is that form is function and as such hypothetically necessitates a certain material realization. But Reading B may object that as long as the matter is not explicitly mentioned in the definition of the form, the connection to the matter will depend on external factors and not be per se. If it is not a definitional truth about the form that it comes with this kind of matter, then we may imagine scenarios where the form is realized in some other matter. But then the form as such will not necessitate this matter. While Reading C insists that the matter is necessary given the function, the suspicion here may be that such hypothetical necessity is based on contingent facts about this world which could be otherwise under other circumstances. We can see this in the example of the saw. Cutting in the manner of the saw requires certain hard and flexible materials. In Aristotle's age perhaps only iron could have done the job; but today's saws can be made out of a range of synthetic materials. This example seems to put the form of the saw in the same relationship to its matter that we saw in the case of the circle made of bronze. But that is the view Reading B would rightly criticize as purist.

A related objection would have it that Reading C collapses into a sort of functionalism. By failing to mention the matter in the definition of the form, Reading C treats the function as something that can be specified 'independently' of any particular material realization. We seem, in other words, to understand the relationship between function and matter in the manner of modern functionalists, when they take the functional description of the mental to be 'topic neutral': that is, neutral as to the sort of entity that might satisfy the description, and therefore as 'multiply realizable'.[22]

The objections can be answered from the perspective of either matter or form. From the perspective of matter, we should note that Aristotle's conception of matter such as iron is itself functional: iron is as iron does.[23] The key point is then not

---

[22] Charles 2021, 41 n. 39 raises, *inter alia*, this objection: '[Johansen's] approach requires Aristotle to hold that the relevant purely psychological ingredient (such as the desire for revenge) requires the presence of a specific kind of material process (such as boiling of the blood) because of the nature of the psychological ingredient itself. That is: one must have reason to think (in his account) that this psychological ingredient, so understood, can only be present in matter so organized (see *De Anima* A.3, 407b16 for his statement of this requirement). This is clearly a non-trivial task. Why cannot the desire for revenge be found in the aged, or Maupassant's cool, calculator, without any boiling blood at all? Or, as Putnam once suggested, realized in "soul stuff"? It is far from clear that the task Johansen envisages can be successfully accomplished. Nor is there evidence in *De Anima* A.1 to suggest that Aristotle himself undertook it or thought it could be done.'

[23] See *Meteor.* 4.12, 390a7–16. Charles 2021, 79–84 makes the same point arguing against the purist view of matter.

264   T. K. JOHANSEN

that this material should be iron *rather than* some synthetic material, say, but that the matter has those functional properties that allow it to realize the function of sawing. The functional conception of matter follows naturally from its role in hypothetical necessity: given the function of the form, this matter is selected as instrumental in performing this function. So we specify the matter from the point of view of those properties that are necessary for the realization of the function. And those properties of matter are themselves functional. Talk of multiple realizability relies on picking out the matter by properties other than those that make them necessary for this function. But in the context of final causal explanation, such talk is beside the point. This a point any of the three readings, A, B, and C, could in principle make, as it is a point about the definitional priority of form over matter. However, it is a point more naturally made on Readings B and C, since these are both concerned to show the specification of matter is already involved in the specification of the form, explicitly on Reading B, implicitly on Reading C. It is easier to see how on these characterizations of the form the matter is suited to a particular form.

From the viewpoint of form, the objection misrepresents the nature of an Aristotelian function. An Aristotelian function is also a final cause. So, for example, the psychic functions are the final causes of the body (see *DA* 2.4, 416a18–21). As such, the functions determine specific bodily parts, processes, or materials as their end. This point reflects the difference between a functional and a mathematical form: the functional form is such as to determine a specific bodily arrangement. In contrast, a function understood in the manner of philosophers like Putnam is exclusively determined by input and output relations without prejudice to its material realization. Similarly, Aristotle's mathematical form one might say is 'topic neutral' as to its material realization. Reading C answers the objection then by saying that the modern functionalist conception of function would place function on the wrong side of Aristotle's distinction between mathematical and natural form.[24]

It is tempting to think that once a functional definition of the form has been given without explicit mention of the matter, then whatever ties this form to a particular material realization is just a question of the contingent physical facts that obtain in this world. Perhaps the function is always realized by this matter in this world at this point, but in another world or at another time, other material features would do the job. But for Aristotle the connection between function and material realization is not contingent. The function necessitates the material features in a way that clearly reflects *conceptual* connections. So as Aristotle said in [T5], 'For the animal is presumably something capable of perception, and it is not possible to define it without movement, nor, therefore, without the parts being in

---

[24] For an insightful analysis, assimilating the functionalist with the mathematical soul, see Langton 2000.

MATTER-INVOLVING FORM AND HYPOTHETICAL NECESSITY IN *DE ANIMA* 265

a certain state.' Here the thought was that since perception is a change, we refer to change in the definition of animal, but the definition of change will involve reference to matter, since every change is the realization of a material potentiality. The point is not, then, that the definition of animal soul explicitly mentions matter, but that there is a conceptual path that goes from form, via change and potentiality, to matter. For this reason, it seems appropriate to say that there is also conceptual connection between form and matter. These conceptual connections are articulated at the level of the science in question: it is a question of the basic principles of Aristotelian physics that certain forms, natural forms, necessitate matter, while it will be a question of individual disciplines of natural science to work out in the light of experience which material structures are necessitated by which natural forms.

A proponent of Reading B will fail to be impressed by this stipulation of conceptual connections if it is of so general a nature that nothing specific, or only something insufficiently specific, can be inferred about the matter. To Reading B, Reading C resembles a functionalist who would say that a mental function must have *some* material realization, insofar as it a function, but beyond that the material realization is left (too) open. Charles is similarly concerned to show how only Reading B can close the explanatory gap between the particular form and the specific material realization: why should the form of anger be realized specifically in boiling of the blood round the heart? Reading B answers: because the material realization is part of what determines this kind of desire for revenge as anger. But here Reading B may underestimate Reading C's resources. For while it is true to say that a natural function simply described as a function implies no more than the presence of some change and some matter, the more specific the function entertained, the more specific the change and the matter implied. So a passive change will involve matter that can undergo change; a qualitative change, such as perception, will involve matter that can undergo qualitative change; and a change in colour, such as vision, will require matter that can undergo a change in colour, such as the transparent. Add further functional constraints to the transparent (e.g., containability)[25] and the only suitable matter left in Aristotle's physics is the actual matter of the eye, water. Observing the appropriate levels of specification of the function will ensure the appropriate specificity of the changes and the matter involved, down to the level of the actual matter. The impression that Reading C's account of form underdetermines the necessitation of matter arises only if one approaches the form as a function at too general or abstract a level.

Reading C may turn the tables on Reading B at this point: it is because Reading B's notion of form is not itself sufficiently rich to determine matter that it needs to insert the matter into the definition of the form. Charles' key example of snub

---

[25] The other option would be air, which is transparent, but less useful than water for the eye because it is difficult to contain; see *De Sensu* 2, 438a15–16, *PA* 2.10, 656b2.

266   T. K. JOHANSEN

here is just a concavity in a certain matter, but the formal side of this form (if the expression be allowed) seems, while unique to the nose, to remain the same as the one that the purist would maintain, although the purist would then add a distinct material account to give the full account of snubness. What could 'snub' mean, after all, other than this shape in a nose? But unique realization does not itself imply any internal difference in the shape or form. Reading B's definition of form appears to be a projection of the full natural philosophical account Simplicius mentioned, form + matter, unto the form itself. On Reading C, meanwhile, we distinguish the functional form from the mathematical form more thoroughly: because the form is functional, we do not need to add the matter into the form explicitly to make it different from the purely mathematical form.

8. The Snub, Partly Snubbed

Reading B might argue that it is simply working with Aristotle's example, the snub, while Reading C fails to appreciate Aristotle's parallel between snub and natural form. If the form is 'snub' and 'snub' means 'concavity of nose', then Charles must be right that the definition of the form involves an explicit mention of the matter, corresponding to 'nose'. A key text here is *On Sophistical Refutations* 31:

[T7]   In the case of the predicates through which something is revealed we should say the following, i.e., that what is revealed is not the same [when the predicate is used] separately by itself and [when it is used] as part of an account (*logos*). For the concave reveals the same thing commonly when used of the snub and of the bandy, whereas nothing prevents it from signifying different things when added to the nose and when added to the legs; for in the former case it signifies the snub, while in the latter it signifies the bandy, and it makes no difference to say snub-nose or concave-nose. Further, we should not allow the phrase to be in direct cases; for it is false. For the snub is not a concave nose but something of a nose, i.e. an affection of nose, so that there is nothing absurd if the snub nose is a nose that has the concavity of nose. (181b35–182a6; Peramatzis' translation in 2011, 123)

The main point is that snub is an affection, concavity *of* the nose. If snubness had been a substance, a nose characterized by concavity, there would have been a problem with mentioning 'nose' twice. But as snubness is an affection, concavity *of* the nose, there is no problem with saying that something is a snub nose. For this is a nose characterized by concavity of the nose (not a nose which is a nose concave nose). The qualification 'of a nose' (genitive) avoids then the repetition of 'nose' (in the nominative). This is the key point since it is one that answers the sophistical strategy of making the opponent babble by saying the same thing several times over. Leading up to this point, Aristotle argues that there are certain terms that are relative and therefore acquire a specific meaning in relation to their relatum. 'Knowledge' is one such term, where knowledge of health has a specific meaning relative to health. 'Concavity' is another such term, which means something else applied to noses and legs, snubness and bandiness, respectively. He then says that 'it makes no difference to say snub-nose or concave-nose'. Here his point must be that, since 'snub' already implies 'concave', it is unproblematic to add it to 'nose'. There would only be a problem if 'snub' added 'nose' (nominative) as part of its meaning in a way that would involving babbling. But it doesn't since (as we saw) 'snub' means 'concavity of nose (genitive)' rather than 'concave nose'.

Charles takes [T7] to show that '"Snubness" signifies a distinctive type of feature, nasal-concavity, which cannot be defined as a combination of concavity (defined independently of the nose) and the nose.'[26] Now while snubness here does indicate a particular kind of concavity, specific to noses, it is important that 'snub' is also substitutable with 'concave' in the context 'snub nose': it makes no difference, as Aristotle says, which you use. If the matter-involvement of *form* was at issue, it is hard to see how snub nose can equally be expressed by concave nose. Sure, the concavity is specific to the nose, but this is achieved by the combination of the terms 'concave' plus 'nose' rather than by one of the terms. After all, Aristotle's point is not that 'concave' is ambiguous in the contexts of snub noses and bandy legs, but rather that it is a general term that acquires specific significance in relation to a relatum. If then you specify the relatum, there is no problem with using 'concave' in both cases. The underlying thought is the commonsensical one, I take it, that both bandy legs and concave nose can have the same shape, the same concavity. However, we have specific words for that shape in those two contexts.[27] Just as in the case of knowledge, where there is a shared sense in which medicine and horticulture both count as knowledge, there is a general notion of concavity that applies to both cases, with snub only used in the specific case of noses. While snubness is defined as concavity in noses, it is still concavity of a general kind we can identify also in bandiness.[28]

---

[26] Charles 2021, 47.

[27] Contrast Charles 2021, 48 n. 15: 'One can, as Aristotle notes, describe both snub noses and bandy legs as concave (S.E. 181b36f.). Just don't think, he adds, that "snubness" is composed of this common element added to the nose or that "snubness" is decomposable into this common element and something else. The way in which concavity is combined with the nose to form "snubness" signifies a distinct type of concavity which is not decomposable in that way. If it were, concavity would, contrary to his hypothesis, signify the very same thing in snubness and in bandiness.'

[28] Contrast again Charles 2021, 49: 'while one well-defined common feature, or nature (being spherical), is used to define both bronze and wax spheres, there is no such common feature, or nature (being concave), used in the definition of snubness or bandiness', with his n. 19, 'this is not, of course, to deny that concavity can be understood as an independent feature found in many objects, including snub noses. It is simply to claim that snubness itself is not to be defined in terms of a combination of that independent common feature and noses.'

268   T. K. JOHANSEN

I have already given a reason to limit the way in which the snub example is supposed to carry over to the natural case: the snub itself seems to be analysable into concavity and nose in a way that leaves the formal element like the mathematical case, or so I have argued. The example in a sense only shifts the problem of distinguishing mathematical and natural form one step back. The corresponding side of this issue is the non-functional specification of the matter. Aristotle is concerned that the matter will only homonymously be said to be this matter—for example, this hand—if it does not possess the functional form. But the snub understood as concavity in the nose does not give a functional specification of the nose, any more than bronze in spherical bronze is functionally determined by the form. The purpose of the snub analogy is to identify a sort of form that is always found in a specific sort of matter. But beyond that, the example of 'snub' clearly has its limitations as an analogy for natural form.[29]

9. Conclusion: The Three Readings and Inextricability

With Reading B Charles offers us the prospect of an exciting philosophical development: viewing mental processes as *inextricably* psycho-physical, we are liberated from the problem of finding the right relation between the psychological and the physical as two different kinds of event, the problem that has dominated post-Cartesian philosophy of mind. Reading A offers little succour here, since it presents the psychological and the physical as two kinds of event separable in account, even if one in number. The question remains on Reading A why this type of psychological event should be realized together with this kind of physical event. Reading C does not offer the strong anti-Cartesian payoff of Reading B, as the psychological is not also defined explicitly in terms of the physical. Yet Reading C may more modestly insist that as long as the definition of the form gives a final cause that hypothetically necessitates the matter as the required instrument for this function, there is no significant residual question about why such a form is realized in such a matter. The form understood in the proper functional way necessitates that the function must also be realized in a certain kind of matter. While inextricability is then not, as on Charles' reading, advertised in the formal definition itself, it still seems a consequence of it.[30]

---

[29] For further worries about Reading B's use of the 'snub', see Corcilius 2023.

[30] From his serving as my Ph.D. examiner at Cambridge to my time at Oxford, David stood out by his kindness and support. That he is also a model of philosophical acumen and scholarly originality goes without saying. It is an honour to be part of this volume celebrating his work.

Works Cited

Barnes, Jonathan (ed.). 1984. *The Complete Works of Aristotle*. Revised Oxford Translation. 2 vols. Princeton University Press.

Caston, Victor. 2008. 'Commentary on Charles', *Proceedings of the Boston Area Colloquium in Ancient Philosophy* 24, 30–49.

Charles, David. 2008. 'Aristotle's Psychological Theory', *Proceedings of the Boston Area Colloquium in Ancient Philosophy* 24, 1–29.

Charles, David. 2021. *The Undivided Self: Aristotle and the 'Mind–Body Problem'*. Oxford University Press.

Cooper, John M. 2009. 'Hypothetical Necessity', in *Knowledge, Nature, and the Good: Essays on Ancient Philosophy*. Princeton University Press, 130–47.

Corcilius, Klaus. 2023. '*The Undivided Self: Aristotle and the "Mind–Body Problem"*', by David Charles', *Mind* 132, 303–313.

Fleet, Barrie. 1997. *Simplicius On Aristotle Physics 2*. Bloomsbury.

Frede, Michael. 1990. 'The Definition of Sensible Substances in *Metaphysics Z*', in *Biologie, logique et métaphysique chez Aristote* (ed. D. Devereux and P. Pellegrin). Éditions du CNRS, 113–29.

Frede, Michael and Günther Patzig. 1988. *Aristoteles 'Metaphysik Z': Text, Übersetzung und Kommentar*. 2 vols. C. H. Beck.

Johansen, T. K. 2012. *The Powers of Aristotle's Soul*. Oxford University Press.

Johansen, T. K. 2020. 'From Craft to Nature: The Emergence of Natural Teleology', in *The Cambridge Companion to Ancient Science* (ed. L. Taub). Cambridge University Press, 102–20.

Langton, Rae. 2000. 'The Musical, the Magical, and the Mathematical Soul', in *The History of the Mind–Body Problem* (ed. T. Crane and S. Patterson). Routledge, 13–33.

Lennox, James G. 2001. *Aristotle On the Parts of Animals I–IV. Translated with a Commentary*. Clarendon Aristotle Series. Clarendon Press.

Peramatzis, Michail. 2011. *Priority in Aristotle's Metaphysics*. Oxford University Press.

Peramatzis, Michail. 2015. 'What Is Form in Aristotle's Hylomorphism?', *History of Philosophy Quarterly* 32, 195–216.

Reeve, C. D. C. 2016. *Aristotle Metaphysics. Translation with Introduction and Notes*. Hackett.

Shields, Christopher. 2016. *Aristotle De Anima. Translated with an Introduction and Commentary*. Clarendon Aristotle Series. Clarendon Press.

12

Life, Agency, and Value

James G. Lennox

Introduction

Over the course of his career, David Charles has visited and revisited the topic of the relationship between beings and processes that are goal-oriented and normativity—in Aristotle, certainly, but also in reality. Going back as far as *Aristotle's Philosophy of Action* in 1984, he stated:

> [W]hat is distinctive of Aristotle's treatment of psychological states such as desire and rationality is that they are essentially defined as aiming at the good or well-being. (Charles 1984, 231)

In the footnote to this statement he cites a long list of passages from *Parts of Animals* and *Generation of Animals*.

In this chapter I shall take as my starting-point a recent revisitation to this territory, David's contribution to *The Oxford Handbook to Aristotle*, considered against the background of a longstanding disagreement between David Charles and Allan Gotthelf over, to borrow from the title of a paper of Gotthelf's that addresses this issue directly, 'the place of the good in Aristotle's teleology'.[1] I will close by considering their discussion in light of recent defences, among philosophers of biology, of the necessity of the use of normative concepts[2] associated with goal-directed agency in order to properly characterize the activities of all living things. In light of our review of Charles and Gotthelf on Aristotle's teleology, these recent discussions will have an unmistakable flavour of déjà vu.

---

[1] Gotthelf 1989, 113–39 (reprinted in Gotthelf 2012, 45–66). All references to Allan Gotthelf's papers, unless otherwise noted, will be to the reprinted versions in Gotthelf 2012.

[2] For reasons that will become clear in section 5, I am using 'normative' in a very broad sense here: by a 'normative concept' I mean one which refers to something's value as judged by a wide range of standards, be they biological, economic, ethical, or aesthetic. In fact, part of my purpose in this chapter is to identify a specific standard of value implicit in David Charles' analysis of teleology. For a valuable categorization of types of normativity discussed in contemporary philosophy, see Christensen 2012 (discussed in section 5 of this chapter).

James G. Lennox, *Life, Agency, and Value* In: *Aristotelian Metaphysics: Essays in Honour of David Charles.*
Edited by: David Bronstein, Thomas Kjeller Johansen, and Michail Peramatzis, Oxford University Press.
© Oxford University Press 2024. DOI: 10.1093/oso/9780198908678.003.0012

1. Teleological Causation

I begin by laying out what I take to be the core of the argument in 'Teleological Causation', David Charles' contribution to *The Oxford Handbook of Aristotle*.[3] My ultimate goal will be to point to a crucial, but implicit, premise in the argument, one which lies behind the aforementioned disagreement and, as we will see, lies equally behind current defences of the legitimacy and importance of normative concepts in contemporary biology. That implicit premise has to do with the value of life. Charles' paper stresses that for Aristotle, scientific explanations are *causal* explanations, so that if one is to understand Aristotle on teleological explanation, one must come to grips with his thesis that the ends of natural processes are *causes*. In other words, we need to answer the question 'What is a cause for Aristotle?' in such a way that a *telos* is one kind of cause.[4]

Charles helpfully specifies three requirements that Aristotle insists must be met for genuine cases of teleological causation:

[i] the presence of goals *tied to the needs* or *desires* of organisms or agents which are required if they are to live or live well[5]

[ii] agents or organisms essentially defined in terms of *sensitivity* to such goals

[iii] capacities present (in *appropriately unified* natures) for the sake of actions [or processes?] directed toward such goals. (Charles 2012, 243)

Though he takes it that genuine teleological causation so defined may well coexist with genuine efficient causation (another view we find as far back as 1984), the truth of teleological causal claims is not dependent on the truth of some concomitant efficient causal claim.

In this discussion I want to focus on two questions this view raises: (a) what is the nature of this *goal-sensitivity* of agents and organisms? and (b) what is the relationship between *life* and *goodness*?

This second question is not raised explicitly by the above listed requirements,[6] but when, later in the paper, Charles characterizes his own view, it is in terms of sensitivity, not merely to *goals*, but to *goodness*. The goodness of goals is absolutely

---

[3] Charles 2012.

[4] Another aim of Charles' paper, which I do not address, is to answer the question of the *scope* of teleological causation: that is, are ends among the causes of *all* natural processes or only some; and is it only *processes* that are subject to teleological causation, or are other things as well, such as the parts of animals and plants or the products they make (spiders' webs, birds' nests, beavers' dams)?

[5] The paper consistently makes use of the disjunction, 'needs or desires': I take the intent of this disjunction to reflect the fact that Aristotle appeals to teleology in explaining both reason-based actions (of agents) and sub-rational processes such as the activities performed by organs (e.g., the lungs or gills) or the development of an embryo (organisms). The problems this raises for understanding his teleology has again been on Charles' radar for a long time: see Charles 1984, 1988, 1991.

[6] Though it is implicit in the phrase 'to live or live well'.

272   JAMES G. LENNOX

central to Charles' understanding of teleology. This reveals what I believe is a deep commitment running through Charles' work on Aristotle's teleology, but a commitment that is often left implicit: a commitment to *the value of life*—or, put somewhat differently, a commitment to life as an ultimate or final good.

We see this commitment at play, for example, in 'Aristotle on Hypothetical Necessity and Irreducibility' published in 1988. Using the phototropism of plants as his example, Charles comments:

> Talk of goals picks out certain features of the outcome as significant and discards others as inessential because they are not directly *connected with the survival of the organism....* [I]t is only when one is aware that they grow in this way *because it is good for them* to do so that one grasps why it is so. (1988, 38; emphasis added)

Notice the move from the first italicized phrase to the second. The *significant* features picked out by teleological language are those features of the 'outcome' that contribute to the *survival*—that is, the continued life—of an organism, but these are assumed, without further argument, to be features that are present because they are *good* for the organism. Their significance consists in their contribution to the life of the organism, and to make such a contribution is to do what is good for the organism. Is there any space, into which a wedge can be driven, between 'contributing to life' and 'doing what is good' here? As we will see, Allan Gotthelf insists that there is. Before turning to that question, however, I will work through Charles' defence of what he refers to as the *basis* of Aristotle's teleology in 'Aristotle on Teleology', in order to support my claims that this is (a) typically an *implicit* assumption and (b) one to which Charles remains steadfastly committed.

2. What Is a Teleological Cause?

In section [2] of his paper, which is subtitled 'Goals and the Good', Charles begins (2012, 228–9) with a widely shared reading of Aristotle's typically unexplained distinction between two ways of being 'that for the sake of which'[7] as a way into exploring the nature of the causation involved in teleology:

a. the beneficiary of an action (designated by a dative pronoun)

b. that for the sake of which an action/process is performed/takes place (designated by a genitive pronoun).[8]

---

[7] Referred to at *DA* 2.4, 415b3–4, 415b21–2; *Met.* Λ.7, 1072b3–4; and *Phys.* 2.2, 194a35–7 (where he attributes the distinction to *De Philosophia*). Charles uses the example cited by Aristotle when he first introduces the final cause in the *Physics* as his paradigmatic case: someone takes a walk after dinner for the sake of their health, but for their own sake *qua* beneficiary of the walk (compare *Phys.* 2.3, 194b32–5, discussed in section 3, below).

[8] As is common to most of his work on teleology, throughout this paper Charles formulates his points so that goal-directed *actions* are distinct from, yet analysable in a parallel way to, *natural processes* and *functions*.

Charles sees this distinction as allowing for three cases of apparently teleological actions, only the first two of which are genuine.

(i) Actions for the sake of X that benefit the agent who performs the actions.

(ii) Actions for the sake of X that benefit someone/thing other than the agent who performs them.

(iii) Actions that benefit someone or something but do not occur for the sake of what/whom is benefited.[9]

This allows for genuine cases of teleological causation independent of specifying the beneficiary of the action. What is critical is that the action (or process, or function) occurs *because* it brings about the goal.

Charles summarizes the view of genuine teleology that emerges by stating that what is explained occurs '*because* it leads to the goal, the good in question' (2012, 229). I note the substitution of 'the good in question' for 'the goal' here: this is a common substitution in Charles' writing on teleology—indeed, a few lines later goals are characterized as 'what is *good for an agent* to bring about *given its nature*' (2012, 229). The relationship of the agent to such goals is spelled out in two independent ways:

[i] 'The agent has a *self-directed* desire/need to bring G about'
[ii] 'The agent's life will *go better/well* if G occurs'.

Up to this point, the focus is on processes and actions as the explananda, and on explaining why they occur. In genuine cases of teleological causation, they occur *because* they bring about some goal, taken to be good in some way, though not necessarily good for the agent. A goal is not just a reliable outcome of a process—rather it is *some good that agents desire or organisms need to bring about*, because given their natures, their lives will go well, or at least go better, if the goal is achieved.[10] These *desires or needs* are, in a way that has yet to be spelled out, '*self-directed*'. The goal makes a 'contribution to the life' of the agent or organism, and is a goal *because* of that contribution—where 'contribution' is understood as making the lives of agents or organisms go well or better. Once again, then, the tight connection between goals and goodness is the goal's contribution to life: something is a *telos* for an organism to the extent that it contributes positively to the organism's life.

---

[9] It may be significant that the starting-point of Charles' analysis is 'actions', but I am going to assume for the purposes of this discussion that the machinery developed in the context of teleological agency is intended to transfer to goal-directed processes generally.

[10] Greg Salmieri pointed out to me that, since desires can be for things that *appear*, but are not objectively, good, the actions of agents may well be directed towards goals that do not actually contribute to their lives going better or well.

3. Goals, Goodness, and Life

The question to which Charles turns next is the scope question: what sorts of thing are (legitimately) explained teleologically? He takes the example Aristotle uses to introduce the 'cause for the sake of which' in *Physics* 2.3, walking for the sake of health, as his paradigm. In discussing this example there is a good deal of stress on this walking being done *in just the way required* to bring about health. Why this stress? We might get at the answer by asking a different question: what is the contrast class? One contrast might be with coincidental outcomes that have the appearance of being purposeful—such outcomes are, after all, a central concern of Aristotle's in his consideration of chance as a cause in *Physics* 2.5–6,[11] and they are a key feature of the way Aristotle characterizes the opponent of teleology in *Physics* 2.8.[12] Charles might be walking aimlessly, or under compulsion, or for a reason unrelated to concerns about health, and improve his health nevertheless. In that case, achieving health was in no way responsible for the walking that took place, even though the walking produced health. There was no 'self-directed desire' *for that end*, though there may have been other self-directed desires in play that happened to bring that end about.

Charles next expands the range of examples, first to the teeth of saws (see the juxtaposition of these two examples at *Phys.* 2.9, 200b1–8), and then to the teeth of organisms (see *Phys.* 2.8, 198b24–31):

> What is teleologically caused is *the development of teeth in ways, times, and places which are beneficial for the organism in question.*... [O]ne may explain, in terms of material and efficient causes why sharp teeth come to be (at a given time) and why flat teeth come to be in certain animals (at the same time) and then observe that such teeth are indeed useful....But one will lack a cause of their coming to be in just those ways, times and positions that are useful for the animal....It will be an accident that sharp and flat teeth come to be in ways, times and places that are useful for the organism. (2012, 231; emphasis in original)

He summarizes the position being attributed to Aristotle to this point in the following two points:

(A) The cause is a goal that is good for some agent (given its nature) to bring about.

(B) The effect is the coming to be of certain features/processes in ways which contribute to achieving the goal.

---

[11] See 196b21–4, b33–6, 197a5–8.   [12] See 198b21–9, 199b13–26.

Again, the goodness of the goal is explicated as 'life will be sustained or go better if the goal is achieved'. Contrasting a living thing with a rolling stone that comes to a stop at a certain point, Charles notes that 'it is not good *for the stone* (given its nature) that it stops where it does. Its life (or existence) does not go better because it stops at this point rather than any other' (2012, 232). What is clearly implied, here and elsewhere, is that evaluative language is linked conceptually to what *sustains* life or causes life to go *better*. Highlighting this commitment to a tight connection between life and value has helped me to understand a longstanding disagreement between two friends, David Charles and Allan Gotthelf. The disagreement concerns, as I noted earlier, the relationship between teleology and the good in Aristotle's philosophy.

4. Sensitivity to Goodness

The next two sections of Charles' 'Teleological Causation' are a defence of his 'Sensitivity to Goodness' model of Aristotelian teleology in comparison to what he terms the 'Goal-directed Efficient Cause' model. He considers Allan Gotthelf's 'irreducible potential for form' account of Aristotle's teleology as an example of the latter.[13] This, I think, is incorrect—but in looking at Charles' reasons for so characterizing Gotthelf's account, we will be able to come to grips with what I think is the critical issue in this neck of the philosophical woods: put ontologically, what is the connection between life and value?[14]

As Charles understands it, Gotthelf's model reduces to the view that there is an irreducible capacity for form which is 'non-valuational'—that is, aimed not at the good as such, but at form[15]—and that being so, two things follow:

1. That capacity is an efficient cause.
2. If genuinely teleological, then that capacity must be caused by the goal, and therefore it is the end that explains the capacity, not the opposite.

I think it can be shown that, on the view Gotthelf defended, the efficient cause operates as it does *only because of its goal*. On this point, he and Charles agree. Let me flesh out Gotthelf's argument in order to make this clear.

Gotthelf insisted that, while it was clear that for Aristotle the goals at which organic development and activity aim are good, that fact about them was

---

[13] See, in particular, Charles 2012, 260, n. 21.

[14] On this issue, Allan Gotthelf was clearly influenced by Ayn Rand's views: see Rand 1964, 6–11; Gotthelf 2011, 33–46 and Wright 2011, 3–32 in Gotthelf and Lennox 2011; and for this connection explored within the context of biological teleology, Binswanger 1990, esp. chs. V, VI, and XI.

[15] Or informed being—which of these one takes to be the goal is important, but raises issues outside the scope of this chapter.

derivative from the fact that these goals constitute or contribute to the form and actuality of living things. The life (or soul, or form) of the organism serves as the standard by which parts, processes, and activities are judged as good—they are good insofar as they are *contributing to* or *constitutive of* that life. As he put it in the conclusion of the essay to which I just referred:

> [F]or Aristotle the goodness of something, at least in biological contexts, is regularly its capacity to contribute to the continued life (*to zēn*) of the organism which has or performs or undergoes that something, where the notion of what it is to live does not itself rest on a prior notion of the good.... I suggest that Aristotle's notion of goodness is rather itself defined in terms of the notions of actuality and end (and that Aristotle's theory here is not circular). (Gotthelf 2012, 48–9)

What arguments and evidence lie behind this view?

I begin with Gotthelf's reaction to my attempt to come to grips with the problem of reconciling Aristotle's account of spontaneity in the *Physics* with his account of spontaneous generation in the *Generation of Animals*.[16] It was his view that what I had dubbed the Formal Replication Model of Aristotle's teleological account of generation[17] confused efficient causality with final causality.[18] What was needed, he wrote, was an explanation of 'how it [the form] is responsible *as end*', and for his own attempt to satisfy that need, he referred his readers to the postscript to 'Aristotle's Conception of Final Causality'.[19] In that postscript, Gotthelf reminds us of the wider philosophical view in which Aristotle's teleology is embedded: all explanation is by reference to natures and potentials, and teleological explanations make reference to a potential that is irreducibly for a complex end (Gotthelf 2012, 31).

But this reference, given the position it was invoked to counter, raises the following question: is this irreducible potential for form not a special sort of efficient cause? Admittedly, not a material level, *elemental* efficient cause—rather, an efficient cause derived from, and sometimes identified with, the parental form, a capacity of the nutritive soul. It is this core claim of Gotthelf's position that lies behind Charles listing Gotthelf among the proponents of the 'Goal-directed Efficient Cause' model of Aristotelian teleology.[20]

---

[16] Lennox 1982, 219–38 (reprinted in Lennox 2001, 229–49).

[17] The idea that for genuine teleology, the *telos* had to be one in form with the efficient cause of the process leading to that *telos*.

[18] This concern is most clearly presented in n. 5 of 'Teleology and Spontaneous Generation in Aristotle: A Discussion', in Gotthelf 2012, 144.

[19] The original paper was published in 1976 in the *Review of Metaphysics*. Because there had been a number of published responses to that paper, he added a lengthy postscript reacting to those published responses when it was reprinted in Gotthelf and Lennox 1987, 204–42. (It was again reprinted in Gotthelf 2012, 3–44.)

[20] See Charles 2012, 235–8, esp. n. 20 and n. 21.

LIFE, AGENCY, AND VALUE   277

But let's read on, for the postscript from which I quoted earlier does not end there. Gotthelf insists that the primary motivating question with respect to teleology is 'why the fact that something A, is necessary for some end B, should explain the presence of A, and how, thus, B would be *responsible* for A' (Gotthelf 2012, 31). How can the outcome be responsible for some antecedent thing that was necessary for that outcome? The first thing to notice is that it is *this* question that Gotthelf views as central: how is *the end responsible* for antecedent changes leading to it? He insists that this question can be answered without appealing to the goodness of the end. The initial step in Gotthelf's answer is this: 'the identity of a nature or potential is given in part by its object or end (i.e., by what it is irreducibly *for*), so we have to ask what the object or end is in each case' (2012, 31). The identity of the potential for form is specified (at least in part) by the 'object' or end towards which it is directed. This sounds like a view that prioritizes the final cause over the efficient, as, given his criticism of the Formal Replication Model, one would expect.

Yet one might still ask, given the many passages in which the male semen is said to have the potential it does in virtue of the nature or form or soul of the semen's *donor*, why is the identity of the potential for form not given primarily by its 'whence': that is, the *prior* actuality?

Gotthelf, certainly in part due to conversations with David Charles, was sensitive to this worry—he goes on to insist that the fact that the identity of the irreducible potential is given by the end 'makes the explanation teleological, because it puts into the explanans an irreducible reference to an outcome for which the explanandum is antecedently necessary'. Teleological explanations, he insists, are 'legitimated by the fact that the outcomes are the result of actualizations of potentials that are *in fact* [my emphasis] for (and *thus* whose descriptions make inescapable reference to) complex living forms as such' (Gotthelf 2012, 31).

But this seems in the end to be subject to a related but different concern: yes, the description of the potential makes an inescapable reference to complex living forms—but why could that not be to the form of the parent? Take the following passage in *Metaphysics* Z.8:

> And speaking generally, nature is both that from which and that according to which; for that which comes to be, e.g., a plant or an animal, has a nature; and that by which is *the nature spoken of according to the form*, the nature of what is like-in-form to that which comes to be (but in another); for a human being reproduces a human being. (1032a22–5)[21]

---

[21] All translations are my own. See also *GA* 2.1, 734b34–735a5; 2.4, 740b35–741a3; *PA* 1.1, 640a22–7.

278   JAMES G. LENNOX

In this passage from the *Metaphysics*, and in a number of similar ones throughout the corpus, the formal nature that is governing the developmental process is identified with *that by which*—form is playing the role, to use Charles' phrase, of goal-directed *efficient* cause. Indeed, on those many occasions when Aristotle says 'for (*gar*) a human being generates a human being', the *gar* seems to point to the fact that it is the *prior* actuality, as the efficient cause of generation, that accounts for the form of the end product.

Gotthelf is not done yet, however! His next move is to remind the reader that Aristotle's concept of an *aitia* is not to be confused with the understanding of causation that has been dominant since the early modern period. There are, he says, 'two conditions [that] will have to be satisfied' in order that the irreducible potential for form account of teleological explanation be successful:

1. B, the end, must 'in some objective way' be responsible for A, the fact to be explained.
2. The fact that the potential (*dunamis*) for B is being realized will have to be a basic fact (i.e., not reducible to something more basic) (Gotthelf 2012, 31–2).

He admits to not having a worked out general view about what an *aitia* is for Aristotle, but takes it that the English expression 'being responsible for' captures much of it.

The next step is the critical, but also problematic, one:

[For Aristotle] when an (irreducible) potential for some end is being realized, that end is responsible for the process leading up to it as that which the process is (irreducibly) for. *That is to say, the end is a sort of intentional object of the process, much as the object of a desire (or perhaps intention) is the object of the action aimed at satisfying that desire.* The end has a real status as aim, and was the end of the process even if the process failed to reach that end. Objects that perform such real functions clearly deserve the label '*aitia*', according to Aristotle. (Gotthelf 2012, 32; emphasis added)

He goes on to suggest that any adequate account of 'being responsible for' must be able to explain why it is 'appropriate to view such *objects (of potentials; of desires or intentions)* as actually *responsible* for their effects' (2012, 32).

This is a definite step beyond the position articulated so far, and a definite step in the direction of the view being defended by David Charles in 'Teleological Causation'. If the end is 'a sort of intentional object',[22] such that objects of

---

[22] And notice the position is *not* that it is analogous to, or like, an intentional object.

LIFE, AGENCY, AND VALUE   279

potentials, desires, and intentions can be spoken of in one breath, so to speak, then the realized form that is the *telos* of the process leading to it is quite different from, and is playing a causal role independent of, the formal nature that *initiated* the process.[23] And, as if responding to any suggestion that this is a 'goal-directed efficient cause' view, Gotthelf adds, in parentheses:

> (This is not a demand to collapse the final into the efficient cause. It is the potential [or its bearer *qua* bearer of that potential] which is the efficient cause, while the final cause is the object of the potential, what, as we say, it is 'for', and this distinction must be maintained.) (Gotthelf 2012, 32)

The danger here, of course, is that it may be hard to see how to distinguish this view from another take on Aristotle's teleology that Gotthelf explicitly rejected, which he labelled the 'immaterial agency' view, according to which 'Aristotle understands natural teleology fundamentally on an analogy to human purposeful action, in a way that implies that the developing embryo is (or embodies) some sort of conscious or quasi-conscious agent…guiding its development to maturity' (Gotthelf 2012, 26). A view that considers the goal to be 'a sort of intentional object', akin to an object of desire, would seem to skate pretty near to one that claims a quasi-conscious agent is guiding the development of the embryo to maturity. Nevertheless, he quite explicitly denies this:

> The notion of an irreducible potential for form supplies the proper content to the awareness that, for Aristotle, organic development is actually direct*ive*, without implying (as the 'immaterial agency' interpretation does) that it is direct*ed*; and it identifies the ontological basis of the awareness that the existence and stages of development can be understood only in terms of its end—by establishing that the *identity* of the development is its being *irreducibly* a development to that end, irreducibly the actualization of a potential for form (Gotthelf 2012, 28; emphasis in original).[24]

He concludes this defence of his view as genuinely a final causal view with an interesting and provocative suggestion: ultimately, the defence of such a view will

---

[23] Stated this way, the view presupposes that both the relevant source of change and the relevant *telos* are the formal natures of parent and offspring, respectively. An alternative view, suggested to me by Michail Peramatzis, would be to suppose it is the parent and offspring as material/formal compounds that are the relevant efficient and final causes. Whether this alternative is compatible with passages such as *Met.* Z.8, 1032a22–5 (quoted earlier) depends on one's understanding of the relationship between matter and form in natural substances. The view Gotthelf is articulating, in any case, is one in which the relevant efficient cause is a *dunamis* for *form*, though of course the outcome will be an informed compound.

[24] As we will see in section 5 of this chapter, the question of whether this way of understanding biological teleology can avoid making reference to something akin to what Gotthelf terms 'immaterial agency' is a chief concern of recent defences of teleology that are Aristotelian in spirit.

280 JAMES G. LENNOX

depend on ascribing 'a sort of ontological individualism' (2012, 32) to Aristotle, according to which

> the basic fact about the living world is the existence of living organisms with the capacity to produce other individuals like themselves. According to this view, other facts at this level of generality which might be thought to ground teleological explanation (e.g., the permanence of species, or the pervasive seeking of the good),[25] are to be seen as consequences of the existence of self-sustaining, reproducing individuals. Some such view is defended by David Balme in Balme 1987c,[26] and at least suggested by the arguments in Lennox 1985a and 1987b.[27] If such a view can be made out, as I firmly believe it can, then the fundamental analysis of teleological explanation will in fact be one in terms of irreducible potentials. (2012, 32–3)

Only recently, as I've been working intensely on the argument of *De Anima* 2.4, have I begun to see what Gotthelf might have been getting at here, and I'd like to sketch out a view like the one he might have had in mind in this passage. Before doing so, however, it will be helpful to see what David Charles says about the teleology in *De Anima* 2.4 in section [3] of 'Teleological Causation'.

After reviewing various troublesome passages in *De Caelo* and *Generation and Corruption* discussing the eternality and cyclic patterns to be found in the movements of the heavenly bodies and sublunary elemental transformations, where Charles argues that appeals to teleology are best seen as attempts to offer 'reasonable accounts' or at least to remove a sense of paradox from apparently puzzling phenomena, he turns to Aristotle's comments about the phenomena of animal and plant reproduction. It will be helpful to have the key passage from *De Anima* 2.4 before us:

> So, first we must speak about nutrition and reproduction. This is both the first and the most common capacity of the soul, in virtue of which living belongs to all living things, a capacity whose functions are reproducing and making use of nutrients; *for* most natural among the functions for living things, as many as are complete and not deformed or spontaneously generated, is the production of another like itself, animal an animal, plant a plant, in order that it may partake, as far as possible, in the always and the divine; for all [perfect living things] strive for this and do whatever they do in accordance with nature for the sake of

---

[25] I am reasonably certain that Gotthelf is referring, respectively, to the views defended in Cooper 1985, 1987 and the views of David Charles currently under discussion.

[26] The reference is to 'Teleology and Necessity' in Gotthelf and Lennox 1987, 275–85.

[27] The references are to 'Are Aristotelian Species Eternal?' in Gotthelf 1985, 67–94 (reprinted in Lennox 2001, 131–59) and 'Kinds, Forms of Kinds, and the More and the Less in Aristotle's Biology', in Gotthelf and Lennox 1987, 339–59 (reprinted in Lennox 2001, 160–81).

LIFE, AGENCY, AND VALUE   281

this. (But that for the sake of which is double, the *of* which and the *for* which.)
Now since they are unable to partake of the always and the divine continuously,
each one partakes in so far as possible, some more and some less, and it remains
not itself but like itself, not one in number but one in form. (415a22–b7)[28]

Charles' discussion of this passage begins by acknowledging that, unlike Aristotle's
discussion of the cyclic transformations of the elements, here he 'is connecting
reproduction with the needs, desires, and capacities of the unified organisms in
question. Given their natures, it is good for them to reproduce in the way they do'
(Charles 2012, 249).

But he raises a very serious concern about the alleged connection:

It is by no means obvious that individual animals, let alone plants, have a desire
(or need) for the eternal and divine (or even for being part of a species which is
eternal). Did Aristotle think that, appearances notwithstanding, they literally
did, perhaps following Diotima's 'prophetic' remarks in the *Symposium* that all
mortal nature seeks as far as possible to be immortal (207D2)? (2012, 249)

He sees a possible way of avoiding this 'platonizing' interpretation:

[I]n *DA* 415b4ff., Aristotle may simply mean that the individual plant or animal
aims at the eternal only to the extent of aiming at producing another like itself.
(2012, 249)

There is indeed a way of reading this passage that avoids reading it as an echo of
the *Symposium*; but before offering that reading, a couple of preliminary points
are in order. First, there is no direct reference to the good in this passage. One
may think that a reference to 'desire' (*oregetai*) and the 'divine' (*tou theiou*) implies
such a reference—I will have more to say about this momentarily. But the claims
that are *directly* made here are these. (I've interspersed occasional questions
I think Aristotle is addressing.)

[i] The nutritive soul is the primary soul capacity, that which is responsible
for life.

[28] ὥστε πρῶτον περὶ τροφῆς καὶ γεννήσεως λεκτέον· ἡ γὰρ θρεπτικὴ ψυχὴ καὶ τοῖς ἄλλοις ὑπάρχει,
καὶ πρώτη καὶ κοινοτάτη δύναμίς ἐστι ψυχῆς, καθ' ἣν ὑπάρχει τὸ ζῆν ἅπασιν, ἧς ἐστιν ἔργα γεννῆσαι καὶ
τροφῇ χρῆσθαι. φυσικώτατον γὰρ τῶν ἔργων τοῖς ζῶσιν, ὅσα τέλεια καὶ μὴ πηρώματα ἢ τὴν γένεσιν
αὐτομάτην ἔχει, τὸ ποιῆσαι ἕτερον οἷον αὐτό, ζῷον μὲν ζῷον, φυτὸν δὲ φυτόν, ἵνα τοῦ ἀεὶ καὶ τοῦ θείου
μετέχωσιν ᾗ δύνανται· πάντα γὰρ ἐκείνου ὀρέγεται, καὶ ἐκείνου ἕνεκα πράττει ὅσα πράττει κατὰ φύσιν.
(τὸ δ' οὗ ἕνεκα διττόν, τὸ μὲν οὗ, τὸ δὲ ᾧ). ἐπεὶ οὖν κοινωνεῖν ἀδυνατεῖ τοῦ ἀεὶ καὶ τοῦ θείου τῇ συνεχείᾳ,
διὰ τὸ μηδὲν ἐνδέχεσθαι τῶν φθαρτῶν ταὐτὸ καὶ ἓν ἀριθμῷ διαμένειν, ᾗ δύναται μετέχειν ἕκαστον,
κοινωνεῖ ταύτῃ, τὸ μὲν μᾶλλον τὸ δ' ἧττον, καὶ διαμένει οὐκ αὐτὸ ἀλλ' οἷον αὐτό, ἀριθμῷ μὲν οὐχ ἕν,
εἴδει δ' ἕν.

282 JAMES G. LENNOX

[ii] That capacity is expressed in two functions, nutrition *and* reproduction.

[Why also reproduction?]

[iii] Because (*γάρ*) the most natural function for a complete organism is to replicate: to produce another like itself (τὸ ποιῆσαι ἕτερον οἷον αὐτό).

[Why do they replicate?][29]

[iv] In order that they may, as far as possible, 'participate in the always and the divine' (τοῦ ἀεὶ καὶ τοῦ θείου μετέχωσιν).

[v] All complete living things do *as many things as they do in accordance with their nature* for the sake of this (πάντα γὰρ ἐκείνου ὀρέγεται, καὶ ἐκείνου ἕνεκα πράττει ὅσα πράττει κατὰ φύσιν); since no perishable being can share in the always and divine by remaining continuously one and the same being, it does so in the way that is possible for it.

[And what is that way?]

[vi] It can persist in form, by producing another being like itself.

The language of 'for the sake of' only appears once in this passage, in point [v]; and the reference of *ekeinou* in *ekeinou heneka* is most naturally taken to be 'participating in the always and the divine'. Producing another being like oneself is the *means* to achieving that goal, not the goal. And immediately after saying this, we find the gnomic expression with which Charles starts in 'Teleological Causation': that for the sake of which is double, the *of* which and the *for* which.[30] In this case, the goal, the 'of which', is *continuous being*.[31] The key to seeing this is to consider why Aristotle repeatedly asserts that reproduction is a function of the *nutritive* soul. This theme is not only developed in *De Anima* 2.4; it is also a key element in his theory of generation:

For the matter by which it grows and from which it is first constituted is the same, so too the producing capacity is the same. *Therefore if this is the nutritive soul it is also the reproductive soul* (εἰ οὖν αὕτη ἐστὶν ἡ θρεπτικὴ ψυχή, αὕτη ἐστὶ καὶ γεννῶσα) and this is the nature of each thing, present within all plants and animals. But the other parts of the soul, while present in some animals are absent in others. (*GA* 2.4, 740b25–741a3)

---

[29] And why 'most natural'? To attempt to answer that question would takes us too far afield.

[30] This phrase is repeated at 415b20–1, and commentators have sometimes suggested this might be a copyist's error. However, it is possible that the repetition is intentional: in the second occurrence, it follows a claim about the body being like an instrument for the soul. Following a suggestion of Jessica Gelber's, if one takes the dative pronoun instrumentally, this is a case of the soul being the 'instrumental end', what the body is instrumentally for; while in the passage we are discussing, it is an intrinsic end that is aimed at. See Gelber 2018.

[31] This suggestion is defended in Coates and Lennox 2020.

LIFE, AGENCY, AND VALUE   283

The goal of the nutritive and generative capacity is one and the same: *persistent being*. During an individual animal's life, this goal is achieved by all the activities that support the animal's being. And when Aristotle says 'for all [perfect living things] strive for this and do *whatever* they do in accordance with nature for the sake of this', I believe the scope of 'whatever they do in accordance with nature'[32] should be understood quite broadly. With the possible exception of certain human beings, whether we focus on their perceptual activities, their (closely connected) locomotive activities, their behaviour related to reproduction,[33] or their actual feeding activities, the goal is preservation of life, of (living) being. As Aristotle says later in the chapter, after distinguishing the growth promoting capability from that of nutrition:

> For the ensouled thing preserves its being and exists so long as it is nourished; and it is capable of generating not the very thing that is nourished, but rather something like what is nourished, since its being already is, and nothing reproduces its very self, but preserves it. (*DA* 2.4, 416b14–18)

And the metaphysical backing for this claim is to be found earlier in the chapter, during Aristotle's claim that the soul is a cause of the ensouled being in three of the four senses of cause:

> For in all cases the essential being (ἡ οὐσία) is the cause of being (αἴτιον τοῦ εἶναι), and in the case of living things to be is to live, and the soul is the cause and principle of this. (*DA* 2.4, 415b12–14)[34]

Charles sees a different message being sent by a well-known passage near the beginning of *Generation of Animals* 2.1: namely, that the goal of reproducing is, not the individual's persistent being, but the eternity of the species (Charles 2012, 249). I want to suggest that that passage is sending the same message as *De Anima* 2.4.[35] Here are the key lines:

> And since soul is better than body, and the ensouled than what lacks soul because of the soul, and being than non-being and living than non-living—for these reasons there is a generation of animals. For since the nature of such a kind

---

[32] The following passage in the *Politics* sheds some light on the meaning of *kata phusin*: 'the union of female and male for the sake of generation…is not out of deliberation, but just as in the other animals and plants the longing to leave behind another such as oneself is natural' (*Pol.* 1.2, 1252a26–34). This longing is not deliberative, but built into the nature of male and female organisms.

[33] Here I am thinking not only of copulation but of the scope of activity covered by *HA* 5–6, 9 and (as Balme 1991, 56 n. b stresses) how many of the activities discussed in *HA* 7–8 are also related to reproduction: mating, nest building, incubating, the rearing of young, and so on.

[34] Τὸ γὰρ αἴτιον τοῦ εἶναι πᾶσιν ἡ οὐσία, τὸ δὲ ζῆν τοῖς ζῴοι τὸ εἶναί ἐστιν, αἰτία δὲ καὶ ἀρχὴ τούτου ἡ ψυχή.

[35] The case for this is made in Lennox 1985.

284   JAMES G. LENNOX

cannot be eternal, that which comes into being is eternal in the way that is possible for it. Now it is not possible [for it to be eternal] in number (for the substance of existing things is in the particular, and if it were such it would be eternal) but it is possible in form—for which reason there is always a *genos* of human beings, animals and plants. (731b29–732a2)[36]

As I argued in my 1985 paper, the way to understand *genos* in this passage, given the context, is in accordance with the very first meaning specified in *Metaphysics* Δ.28: 'a continuous generation of things which have the same form ... for example, we say "as long as the human *genos* exists", which means "as long as the generation of human beings continues" ' (1024a29–31). This is not a specification of the goal of generation. The goal of generation is eternal being in the way possible for a perishable being, being one in form with what is generated. And as a *consequence* (διό) of animals and plants striving for the goal, there is always a continuous generation of things with the same form.

How, then, did Gotthelf see this as providing further grounds for his understanding of Aristotle's teleology? As far as I can tell, there is no further exploration of this question in his published work, but I think I now see what he had in mind. There is a natural drive, in all living things, towards self-maintenance, towards being in full actuality—in sexually reproducing organisms, that drive also manifests itself in producing something one in form with the producer. That is the basis of Aristotle's teleology: whatever contributes to this goal is good, but the goal is specified independently of the good.

Gotthelf was on board, then, with ends as genuine causes of natural processes, though he resisted the idea that what made ends genuinely causal was a 'goodness' to which natural processes were in some way 'sensitive'. But what about that striving, that natural drive, for being? Is *that* the expression of a sensitivity for goodness? It is to this question I now turn.

5. Organisms *qua* Organisms as Agents

Charles' 'Teleological Causation' closes by pointing to 'two areas in which Aristotle's account ... is philosophically controversial' (2012, 254).[37] In this final section of

---

[36] βέλτιον δὲ ψυχὴ μὲν σώματος, τὸ δ' ἔμψυχον τοῦ ἀψύχου διὰ τὴν ψυχὴν καὶ τὸ εἶναι τοῦ μὴ εἶναι καὶ τὸ ζῆν τοῦ μὴ ζῆν διὰ ταύτας τὰς αἰτίας

γένεσις ζῴων ἐστίν· ἐπεὶ γὰρ ἀδύνατος ἡ φύσις τοῦ τοιούτου γένους ἀΐδιος εἶναι, καθ' ὃν ἐνδέχεται τρόπον, κατὰ τοῦτόν ἐστιν ἀΐδιον τὸ γιγνόμενον.

ἀριθμῷ μὲν οὖν ἀδύνατον—ἡ γὰρ οὐσία τῶν ὄντων ἐν τῷ καθ' ἕκαστον· τοιοῦτον δ' εἴπερ ἦν, ἀΐδιον ἂν ἦν· εἴδει δ' ἐνδέχεται. διὸ γένος ἀεὶ ἀνθρώπων καὶ ζῴων

ἐστὶ καὶ φυτῶν.

[37] The other area of concern Charles discusses, which I do not consider directly here, is whether teleological causation is otiose even in the case of agents with reasons and desires.

the chapter, I will look at what Charles takes to be the more controversial of these two areas—whether the parts, processes and activities of natural organisms are best explained by teleology of the Aristotelian sort—and I will also discuss some recent literature in the philosophy of biology that offers a positive answer to that question and at the same time suggests a resolution of the impasse I've outlined between Charles and Gotthelf. In essence, the solution comes down to arguing that the concept of *agency*, and with it a related cluster of normative concepts, should be (and in practice is) extended to all living things. Before outlining the view, I begin with Charles' concern.

> While the rational agent or craftsman may see certain goals as good and select them because they are good, plants (at least) cannot be sensitive in this way to what is good for them. (Charles 2012, 254–5)

After briefly sketching a Darwinian, adaptationist answer to the question of how organisms came to be organized in ways that are good for them, he notes that if that answer is satisfactory, 'Aristotle's account will not give the best explanation of these phenomena and should be rejected' (2012, 255).

On Charles' view, 'sensitivity to the goodness of the goal' is what grounds genuine teleological causation, so that if Aristotle does not have an account of why it is that organisms have such sensitivity, his view is vulnerable to Darwinian attack. The key to the worry here is that there seems to be no sensitivity to goodness account of teleology unless there are agents that can *see goals as good*. In its absence, the best Aristotle can do is to insist that it is a fundamental fact about living things that they are so organized as to be self-maintaining and/or form-maintaining. Once the Darwinian solution comes along, we should no longer rest content with Aristotle's teleology.

However, since the 1970s (at least) there have been a number of distinct (though related) challenges to the Darwinian synthesis—some explicitly indebted to Aristotle. The challenge on which I am going to focus would seem to resolve at least the most central concern expressed by Charles at the close of his paper. Charles' persistent disjunction of 'desires or needs' suggests to me that he would look sympathetically on the resolution to be discussed.

The challenge we are concerned with rests in part on an analysis of the use of certain concepts that are broadly speaking 'normative', and in part on questioning certain reductive presuppositions implicit in the Darwinian framework. For, despite its pervasive stress on adaptation and 'advantageous traits', there is an equally pervasive insistence that there is no longer a place for teleology or value concepts in biology.[38]

---

[38] For an introduction to this issue, and how contentious it can be, see the exchange between Lennox and Ghiselin in Lennox 1993, Ghiselin 1994, and Lennox 1994.

286   JAMES G. LENNOX

The key conceptual innovation in the proposed resolution is 'value significance', a concept I borrow from Binswanger 1992. But to prepare the ground for its introduction, I begin with a recent paper by Wayne Christensen entitled 'Natural Sources of Normativity'.[39] The paper begins by providing a useful categorization of types of norm and normativity, after which it introduces and characterizes 'autonomous systems': a system is autonomous if it 'tends to generate the conditions for its persistence, and if it has infrastructure that contributes to this self-maintenance' (Christensen 2012, 106). The sort of 'infrastructure' he has in mind is some relatively stable structure that shapes the system-maintaining processes, such as a cell membrane (2012, 106). The key feature of such systems on which I want to focus is that they are *self-maintaining*: that is, they persist *because of their own activities.*

In explicating this idea of an autonomous system, Christensen provides a description of cardiac arrest:

If the heart stops beating then there will be a cascade of failures as physiological processes that depend on fluid transport cease to function, leading to the death of the organism. The dysfunction here is systemic—a property of the pattern of network dependencies—and as such not attributable to the heart in isolation. (2012, 106)

In this description, terms like 'failure' and 'dysfunction' play a central role: but note that these concepts gain traction in this context because they pick out processes that 'lead to the death of the organism'. That is, it is not so much the *systemic* character of these physiological changes that gives rise to the feeling of the appropriateness of the normative language, but the fact that these changes are *life-threatening*, the *opposite* of self-maintaining activity. That is to say, it is the fact that organisms constantly face the alternative of life and death that gives rise to the applicability of these concepts.[40]

The next move in Christensen's argument is towards ascribing *agency* to any truly autonomous system, though it again appears that there is an assumption in the background that the goal of all this self-regulation and self-perpetuation is to remain alive, and that the normative perspective is legitimate for that reason. In the next phase of Christensen's argument, he comes close to recognizing this. He notes that the organic systems on which he is focused are organized so as to be 'self-perpetuating', and as if it followed directly from that fact, he writes:

---

[39] Christensen 2012, 104–12.
[40] For a clear discussion of the way in which the fact that living things continuously face this alternative underwrites the application of normative concepts to them, see Gotthelf 2011, 33–46 and Lennox 1995, 499–511.

Thus, the use of evaluative concepts is not simply an imaginative projection, it is required to properly characterize the causal structure of these kinds of systems. Moreover, in many cases the infrastructure possessed by these systems is regulative: it repairs, avoids, seeks, etc. In a limited but significant way living systems are doing their own evaluation, which is a persuasive reason for treating them as having a genuinely normative perspective. (Christensen 2012, 107)

Two key claims need to be underlined here: (i) evaluative concepts are *required* in order to capture the causal structure of such systems and (ii) the evaluative concepts are applicable in virtue of the fact that living systems are 'doing their own evaluation' and have 'a normative perspective'. Both of these claims are problematic, and problematic in just the way that gave rise to the concern raised by David Charles that I discussed earlier: true agency seems to require that the agent acts to achieve goals because they are cognized as of value; but the physiological activities of internal organs, cells, or plants are not acting in self-maintaining ways because of an awareness that doing so is good for them (Charles 2012, 254–5). That is, this remark of Christensen's begs the question: whether biological systems without such awareness can be properly goal-directed is precisely the question under consideration. The move Christensen wants to make is to treat the normativity normally restricted in its application to rational agents pursuing values as grounded in a more 'fundamental' form of normativity:

> With regard to origins, the basic idea is to treat personhood as just a particular kind of agency, and more specifically as a cognitively sophisticated form of agency that has evolved from more basic non-cognitive forms of agency. (Christensen 2012, 108)

In support of this, he points to the fact that there are often both psychological and biological responses to the same normatively charged (i.e., life-threatening) situations. Food that is toxic can be responded to negatively either by prudent behaviour based on knowledge of its harmful effects or by involuntarily vomiting. (2012, 108) Christensen concludes that

> without an account of valuational normativity we are left with an incomplete understanding of key [biological] phenomena like regulation and adaptive plasticity. Conversely, approaches that ground normativity in high-level features of human agency, such as personhood or purposes, also leave us with an incomplete and somewhat mysterious picture. The structures and capacities that support high level agency are themselves, arguably, constrained by broader forms of functional normativity. (2012, 112)

Christensen's argument, then, is that a proper characterization of organisms as autonomous systems requires normative concepts and a thick concept of

288   JAMES G. LENNOX

goal-directed agency. But at key points in the argument it appears that what is doing the heavy lifting is the idea that, to use the lingo of systems biology, organisms are 'far from equilibrium' systems: that is, systems that must be constantly active in appropriate ways to remain alive. Moreover, and for this next point I turn to two other authors, given the unstable and constantly changing nature of their environments, acting appropriately (i.e., in life-maintaining ways) is radically dependent on being sensitive to changes in critical environmental variables. This issue is central to a paper of James Barham's entitled 'Normativity, Agency and Life'[41] and to a recent book by Denis Walsh entitled *Organisms, Agency and Evolution*.[42] I begin with the latter.

In chapter 10 of Walsh's book he defends the view that organisms, even organisms as simple as slime moulds or bacteria, are 'purposive systems, agents of a sort' (Walsh 2015, 208). Evolution at the population level, he has argued in previous chapters, is 'a consequence of individual organisms' purposeful engagement with their conditions of existence in the struggle for life' (2015, 208), language purposively lifted from *On the Origin of Species* to show that, though contemporary evolutionary biologists might bridle at this claim, Charles Darwin certain would not. The view Walsh has defended up to this point is 'tantamount to saying that organisms are agents of evolutionary change' (2015, 209), and he criticizes the modern Evolutionary Synthesis for treating adaptation as something that happens to organisms, ignoring 'the way that organisms participate in—indeed enact—the process of evolution' (2015, 209). To cash out this notion of organisms as agents, he imports James J. Gibson's concept of affordances, developed as part of Gibson's ecological account of perception,[43] into evolutionary theory in order to emphasize that agency is an ecological phenomenon—it is 'the capacity of a system…to attain its goal by responding to its affordances *as* affordances' (Walsh 2015, 210), where an affordance is 'either an opportunity for, or an impediment to, the attainment of a goal' (2015, 211). Walsh insists that natural agency of this sort is 'metaphysically unproblematic, certainly no more problematic than natural purpose' (2015, 211).

I suspect Walsh had his tongue in his cheek as he typed those words, for the obvious response from one not already disposed to his way of thinking is, 'Yes, and no less'. For we are face to face with the same issue left on the table with Christensen: what does it mean to respond to affordances *as* affordances? Is this Walsh's version of having some sort of 'sensitivity to goodness'? I suspect so: the idea is that bacteria are responsive in just the right ways and at just the right times to just those changes in their environment that are either life enhancing or life threatening…for bacteria! That is, they are 'attuned' to what counts as good or bad for bacteria. And the same is true of every organism: their actions are determined

---

[41] Barham 2012.   [42] Walsh 2015.   [43] Gibson 1979, esp. 127–43.

by a highly selective awareness of their environment. What changes matter to a *spider* are very different from those that matter to a *honey-bee*, and life or death for each of them is dependent on them acting appropriately in the face of those changes.

What is needed at this point is a careful discussion of the relationship between agency, normativity, and life—which, conveniently, is the subject on offer in a recent paper by James Barham entitled 'Agency, Normativity, and Life'! As with Christensen, Barham begins by distinguishing a number of distinct categories of normativity,[44] and argues that what he refers to as 'instrumental normativity' is fundamental. His first step is to characterize a broad, generic category of norms:

> What all of these normative claims have in common is the prescription or proscription of an action, considered as a means to attaining an end. In this respect we can see that norms are instrumental in character. They seem to be essentially involved with furthering the actualization of ends by specifying means conducive to such actualization. (Barham 2012, 93)

Barham then identifies a network of concepts linking this broad notion of normativity to agency: purpose, value, well-being, need, and 'being a reason for action' (2012, 93). After considering and rejecting two extreme views, one which argues for the non-existence of norms as objective features of the world and the 'naïve naturalism' of Hornsby that grants them a place in nature only by restricting them to rational beings, Barham zeroes in on what he refers to as 'elementary normative concepts'. These concepts, which include 'purpose', 'need', and 'well-being', are, he argues, constituents in a complex concept of normative agency, and are 'properly ascribable to organisms as such' (2012, 96). What Walsh highlights about an organism's behaviour by means of the notion of 'affordance', Barham captures by saying that organisms with needs partition their environment into valenced categories (2012, 97). Biological functions, he argues, are in part defined by their role in satisfying specific life-preserving needs of specific organisms. He considers two candidates for a 'normative state of affairs' that are logically prior to this concept of need: life and well-being.[45] The justification for these claims derives from two sources, each of which can be challenged on methodological grounds: he notes that ordinary language sanctions claims such as 'water is good for plants', 'plants need water', 'some plants turn their leaves toward the sun in order to capture more light...which is the reason why some plants turn their leaves toward

---

[44] Although the categorization is quite different, and on the whole less well delineated than Christensen's.

[45] There is really no argument for this restriction: he simply cites Richard Kraut's 2007 book *What is Good and Why: The Ethics of Well-Being*. Barham also permits substituting 'survival and reproduction' for 'life', a substitution which opens up a very large can of worms, given that reproductive behaviour often comes at the cost of survival for the reproducing animal.

290   JAMES G. LENNOX

the sun'. 'So much', he says, 'is, or ought to be, tolerably obvious' (2012, 98). It is tolerably obvious that people do talk this way—it is not tolerably obvious to many biologists and philosophers that this is the best way to describe the physiology of plants, bacteria, or livers. To deal with this sort of objection, the next section of Barham's paper describes in some detail research on bacterial chemotaxis, noting how bacteria act in just the ways that are needed to maintain themselves as living beings:

> All this makes it seem natural to say that swimming toward the food is something that the bacterium does, not something that happens to it. In short, bacteria act. (Barham 2012, 99)

His argument at this point makes close contact with Walsh's—citing (as Walsh does) the work of Kirschner and Gerhart,[46] Barham notes that

> the capacity for flexible and purposive behavior is the key to the 'robustness', or stability, of the cell, and ultimately all living things. (2012, 99)

In this closing section of his paper, Barham has reviewed the many prominent philosophers of action who defend extending the language of purpose, volition, and agency to animals that respond with flexibility and selectivity to circumstances,[47] but who refuse to extend it to 'organisms as such'. The detailed discussion of bacterial behaviour is in the interests of arguing that there is no good reason not to do so. A common theme running through all of these discussions is either the necessity or advisability of seeing organisms *qua* organisms as agents, in some sense aware of the actions that are needed in constantly varying circumstances to achieve what is beneficial and avoid what is harmful—sensitive to what is good according to the standard of its own life. And with that, we return to the central theme of the David Charles paper with which we began.

In doing so, I wish to highlight a feature of Charles' discussions of Aristotle's teleology that might pass unnoticed, but which is suggestive of a persistent concern about the legitimacy of applying the network of concepts associated with agency—both teleological concepts like purpose, ends, and goals, and normative concepts such as valuable, beneficial, harmful, and advantageous: his repeated distinction between *desires*, associated with rational agency, and *needs*, associated with organisms more broadly. To pick one instance more or less at random:

---

[46] Kirschner and Gerhart 2005.
[47] He quotes in particular from Railton 2009 on 'fluent (but non-deliberative) agency', Steward 2009 and Korsgaard 2009 on animals as authors of their own actions, Glock 2009 and Boyle and Lavin 2010 on scientific explanations of animal behaviour that appeal to desires, intentions, goals, and purposes, and Hurley 2003 on non-conceptual animals acting for reasons.

LIFE, AGENCY, AND VALUE   291

[Aristotle's account of teleological causation] requires (or so I have argued) the presence of (i) goals, tied to the *desires and needs* of *an agent or organism* which are required if it is to live (or live well); (ii) *agents and organisms* essentially defined in terms of sensitivity to such goals; and (iii) capacities present (in appropriately unified natures) for the sake of actions directed towards such goals. (Charles 2012, 243; emphasis added)

Running through the recent literature on agency and normativity I have been discussing is an insistence on the legitimacy of applying the language of teleological explanation and of norms to organisms *qua* organisms. One way of reading this literature is as attempting to avoid the disjunctive partitioning of the domain of goal-directed beings into agents or organisms by arguing that all organisms, simply in virtue of being organisms, *are* agents. But we have seen that in doing so each of the authors we have looked at, whether via the concept of an affordance (Walsh), a 'valenced partitioning' of the environment (Barham), or 'doing their own evaluating' (Christensen), are raising the same issues over which Gotthelf and Charles so productively disagreed: must we ascribe something like a 'sensitivity to goodness' to organisms in order to make the application of this language to organisms, simply as organisms, appropriate? And in any case, how are we to understand the connection between the goals for the sake of which living things act and the value attributed to these goals?

Conclusion

What is needed, it seems, is a concept that captures just those features *shared* by the desires of conscious, deliberating agents and the needs that are fulfilled by the robust and context-sensitive nature of *all* living activity. Harry Binswanger[48] coined the term 'value significance' to capture those features of an organism's environment which are properly described as useful, beneficial, advantageous, or needed in order to sustain its life. He introduces this notion in a way that resonates with Charles' concerns:

In vegetative action, though the absence of consciousness precludes the existence of emotions and evaluations, there is nonetheless something that plays a role similar to that played by desires in the case of purposeful action: *needs*. (Binswanger 1990, 58)

He goes on to note that 'need' belongs to a family of concepts (including 'benefit', 'harm', 'value', and 'advantage') that identify 'the value significance of things for the agent' (Binswanger 1990, 59). Notice that 'agent', here, has been broadened in

---

[48] Binswanger 1990. For a briefer presentation of the key ideas, see Binswanger 1992.

292 JAMES G. LENNOX

its reference to include the phototropism of plants, a broadening we have seen defended by Christensen, Walsh, and Barham.

As Binswanger summarizes this idea:

> The organism's life is the implicit ultimate value by reference to which the value-significance of all other states is determined. (Binswanger 1990, 61)

The goals of organic activity can have value *significance* based on what the organism needs to maintain and further its life and what it needs to do to achieve those goals, independently of whether it desires them or otherwise cognizes them *as* valuable or beneficial. Features of an organism's environment have such significance only relative to the needs of living things: the existence of lactose is neither good nor bad, independent of organisms that derive energy by means of locating, ingesting, and digesting it. The network of concepts on which Walsh, Christensen, and Barham are focused only have meaning in the precarious world of living things, a world in which the alternative of life or death is always present and continued life demands constantly adjusting organic activity in response to a constantly changing, potentially hostile, environment.

In Charles' final characterization of Aristotle's account of teleological causation, the desires and needs of an agent or organism must be for goals that are required if the agent or organism is to live (or live well): that is, they must have value significance. Viewed in this light, the philosophical investigations of the nature of life found in Aristotle's *De Anima* and their scientific mobilization in his animal inquiries are as relevant today as they ever have been. And it is our good fortune to have the decades-long study of Aristotle's teleology in the writings of David Charles to illuminate those investigations.[49]

Works Cited

Balme, D. M. 1987. 'Teleology and Necessity', in Gotthelf and Lennox 1987, 275–85.

Balme, D. M. 1991. *Aristotle: History of Animals, Books VII–X*. Loeb Classical Library. Harvard University Press.

---

[49] Thanks to Jessica Gelber, Michail Peramatzis, and Greg Salmieri for helpful comments on an earlier draft of this chapter, and to the editors for the invitation to contribute to this volume honouring David Charles. I was first introduced to David by Allan Gotthelf in 1985 at a conference in Cambridge organized by Allan and Geoffrey Lloyd, and it seemed fitting that my contribution engage with a productive dialogue between them on a topic of profound importance to all of us. I have had so many valuable interactions with David Charles over the last three decades that it is hard to single out one occasion—but if forced to, I would identify Trinity term 1994, when David invited Allan and me to co-teach a graduate seminar at Oxford with him on 'Philosophical Issues in Aristotle's Biology'. This was one of the most pleasurable teaching experiences of my life; and as has always been the case, I learned an immense amount from David during that seminar, both about the issues under discussion and even more about philosophical method.

Barham, James. 2012. 'Normativity, Agency, and Life', *Studies in History and Philosophy of Biological and Biomedical Sciences* 43 (1), 92–103.

Binswanger, Harry. 1990. *The Biological Basis of Teleological Concepts.* The Ayn Rand Institute Press.

Binswanger, Harry. 1992. 'Life-Based Teleology and the Foundations of Ethics', *The Monist* 75 (1), 84–103.

Boyle, Matthew and Lavin, Douglas (2010). Goodness and desire. In Sergio Tenenbaum (ed.), *Desire, Practical Reason, and the Good.* Oxford University Press. pp. 161–201.

Charles, David. 1984. *Aristotle's Philosophy of Action.* Duckworth.

Charles, David. 1988. 'Hypothetical Necessity and Irreducibility', *Pacific Philosophical Quarterly* 69, 1–53.

Charles, David. 1991. 'Teleological Causation in the *Physics*', in Judson 1991, 101–28.

Charles, David. 2012. 'Teleological Causation', in Shields 2012, 227–66.

Christensen, Wayne. 2012. 'Natural Sources of Normativity', *Studies in History and Philosophy of the Biological and Biomedical Sciences* 43, 104–12.

Coates, Cameron and James G. Lennox. 2020. 'Aristotle on the Unity of the Nutritive and Reproductive Functions', *Phronesis* 65 (4), 414–66.

Cooper, John M. 1985. 'Hypothetical Necessity', in Gotthelf 1985, 151–68.

Cooper, John M. 1987. 'Hypothetical Necessity and Natural Teleology', in Gotthelf and Lennox 1987, 243–74.

Gelber, Jessica. 2018. 'Two Ways of Being for an End', *Phronesis* 63, 64–86.

Ghiselin, Michael T. 1994. 'Darwin's Language May Seem Teleological, but His Thinking Is Another Matter', *Biology and Philosophy* 9, 489–92.

Gibson, J. J. 1979. *The Ecological Approach to Visual Perception.* Houghton Mifflin.

Glock, Hans-Johann. 2009. 'Can Animals Act for Reasons?', *Inquiry* 52, 232–54.

Gotthelf, Allan (ed.). 1985. *Aristotle on Nature and Living Things: Philosophical and Historical Studies.* Mathesis Publications and Bristol Classical Studies.

Gotthelf, Allan. 1989. 'The Place of the Good in Aristotle's Teleology', *Proceedings of the Boston Area Colloquium in Ancient Philosophy* 4, 113–39. (Reprinted in Gotthelf 2012, 45–66.)

Gotthelf, Allan. 2011. 'The Choice to Value', in Gotthelf and Lennox 2011, 33–46.

Gotthelf, Allan. 2012. *Teleology, First Principles, and Scientific Method in Aristotle's Biology.* Oxford University Press.

Gotthelf, Allan and James G. Lennox (eds.). 1987. *Philosophical Issues in Aristotle's Biology.* Cambridge University Press.

Gotthelf, Allan and James G. Lennox (eds.). 2011. *Metaethics, Egoism, and Virtue: Studies in Ayn Rand's Normative Theory.* University of Pittsburgh Press.

Hurley, Susan. 2003. 'Animal Action in the Space of Reasons', *Mind and Language* 18, 231–56.

294 JAMES G. LENNOX

Judson, Lindsay (ed.). 1991. *Aristotle's Physics: A Collection of Critical Essays*. Clarendon Press.

Kirschner, Marc W. and John C. Gerhart. 2005. *The Plausibility of Life: Resolving Darwin's Dilemma*. Yale University Press.

Korsgaard, Christine M. 2009. *Self-Constitution: Agency, Identity, and Integrity*. Oxford University Press.

Kraut, Richard. 2007. *What Is Good and Why: The Ethics of Well-Being*. Harvard University Press.

Lennox, James G. 1982. 'Teleology, Chance, and Aristotle's Theory of Spontaneous Generation', *Journal of the History of Philosophy* 20, 219–38. (Reprinted in Lennox 2001, 229–49.)

Lennox, James G. 1985. 'Are Aristotelian Species Eternal?' in Gotthelf 1985, 67–94. (Reprinted in Lennox 2001, 131–59.)

Lennox, James G. 1987. 'Kinds, Forms of Kinds, and the More and the Less in Aristotle's Biology', in Gotthelf and Lennox 1987, 339–59. (Reprinted in Lennox 2001, 160–81.)

Lennox, James G. 1993. 'Darwin *Was* a Teleologist', *Biology and Philosophy* 8, 408–21.

Lennox, James G. 1994. 'Teleology by Another Name: A Reply to Ghiselin', *Biology and Philosophy* 9, 493–5.

Lennox, James G. 1995. 'Health as an Objective Value', *Journal of Medicine and Philosophy* 20, 499–511.

Lennox, James G. 2001. *Aristotle's Philosophy of Biology: Studies in the Origins of Life Science*. Cambridge University Press.

Railton, Peter. 2009. 'Practical Competence and Fluent Agency', in Sobel and Wall 2009, 81–115.

Rand, Ayn. 1964. 'The Objectivist Ethics', in Ayn Rand, *The Virtue of Selfishness: A New Concept of Egoism*. New American Library, 1–34.

Shields, Christopher (ed.). 2012. *The Oxford Handbook of Aristotle*. Oxford University Press.

Sobel, David and Steven Wall (eds.). 2009. *Reasons for Action*. Cambridge University Press.

Steward, Helen. 2009. 'Animal Agency', *Inquiry* 52, 217–31.

Walsh, Denis M. 2015. *Organisms, Agency, and Evolution*. Cambridge University Press.

Wright, Darryl. 2011. 'Reasoning about Ends: Life as a Value in Ayn Rand's Ethics', in Gotthelf and Lennox 2011, 3–32.

PART IV
MODALITY, CHANGE, AND SPACE

13
Reflections on Aristotle's Modal Ontology

Kei Chiba

Introduction

In this chapter I shall investigate Aristotle's two newly coined technical ontological terms, *entelecheia* ('completeness') and *energeia* ('at-workness'), and their connections with three traditional terms he inherited: *dunamis* ('potentiality'), *ergon* ('work'), and *logos* ('account').[1] On my reading, Aristotle uses his two new concepts, *entelecheia* and *energeia*, to make his ontology subtler and more comprehensive than his predecessors' traditional combinations of *ergon* and *dunamis*. I shall clarify Aristotle's conceptions of *dunamis*, *ergon*, and *logos* at the same time as I clarify *entelecheia* and *energeia*, so that we may understand the roles of these novel words within a newly interpreted traditional framework. I shall call Aristotle's ontological investigation, conducted in terms of completeness, at-workness, and potentiality, his 'modal ontology'.

In section 1, I outline the roles of completeness, at-workness, and potentiality as modes of being in Aristotle's general ontology. In section 2, I provide an overview of Aristotle's key modal terms, focusing on their core meanings and uses in texts such as *De Anima* and *Metaphysics*. In section 3, I switch focus and consider Aristotle's investigative strategies in the central books of the *Metaphysics* through the lens of what I call the *logos* and *ergon* initiatives. These are distinct but complementary methods of analysis, and both play a role in Aristotle's ontological investigations in the *Metaphysics*, in particular his modal ontological investigations of completeness, at-workness, and potentiality—or so I shall argue. Finally, in section 4, I apply the methodological distinction between *logos* and *ergon* to Aristotle's account of the soul in *De Anima*, arguing that the concept of completeness mediates between these two perspectives.

The guiding thought throughout my discussion is that Aristotle uses the term 'completeness' (*entelecheia*) to establish the fundamental connection between a thing's form or substance as what is defined (*logos*) and as what is at work (*ergon*). In short, *entelecheia* is the link between *logos* and *ergon*. I disagree with

---

[1] While I have retained standard English translations of *dunamis*, *ergon*, and *logos*, I have opted for non-standard translations of *entelecheia* and *energeia*. I shall explain and justify these translations below.

Kei Chiba, *Reflections on Aristotle's Modal Ontology* In: *Aristotelian Metaphysics: Essays in Honour of David Charles*.
Edited by: David Bronstein, Thomas Kjeller Johansen, and Michail Peramatzis, Oxford University Press.
© Oxford University Press 2024. DOI: 10.1093/oso/ 9780198908678.003.0013

298   KEI CHIBA

interpretations that conflate *energeia* with *entelecheia*[2] and that understand Aristotle's modal otology solely in terms of capacities and their realizations or actualizations or activities.[3] On my reading, *energeia* and *entelecheia* are best understood as distinct modes of being with distinct roles in Aristotle's modal ontology.

1. Three Modes of Being: 'The Elements of the Thing that Is *Qua* Being'

I shall first outline the roles of the three modal terms ('completeness', 'at-workness', and 'potentiality') in Aristotle's general ontology, his study of being '*qua* being'. The phrase '*qua* being' indicates the thoroughness of his inquiry and its distinctive perspective: everything is 'referred back to' or 'hung upon' 'one thing and some single nature' or 'the primary and simple being' called 'substance' (*Met.* Γ.2, 1003a33, b5–7, 16–7, 1004a25–6, H.1, 1028a30–1).[4] Thus Aristotle's general ontology has a *pros hen* ('focused to one') structure. In his general ontology, Aristotle studies 'the elements of the thing that is *qua* being (*ta stoicheia tou ontos hē(i) on*)' and 'the things that belong to the thing itself that is *qua* being (*ta huparchonta autō(i) hē(i) on*)' (Γ.1, 1003a30, Γ.2, 1005a14, E.1, 1026a29–32). Among these elements, he counts not only 'the genera (categories) of entities (*ta genē tōn ontōn*)' such as substance and its attributes but also their three modes or ways of being: completeness (*entelecheia*), potentiality (*dunamis*), and at-workness (*energeia*) (Δ.11, 1019a4–7, Θ.1, 1045b32–4).

The three 'elements' that 'belong to the thing itself that is *qua* being' are its constituents, not as its immanent *nature* (*phusis*)—that is, form and matter—but as its ways or modes of *being*. The latter are sometimes called *tropoi*, as when Aristotle asks 'whether the elements are in potentiality or some other *mode* (*tropon*)' and says 'another *mode* is that we can say the same things according to the potentiality and according to the at-workness'.[5] He aims to explain *what* a substance is and *how* it is at work in his study of the modes of being *qua* being.

Aristotle's study of all entities, including 'separate and unmovable things' *qua* being, paves the way for a science of being (E.1,1026a16). While the distinct special sciences such as geometry are 'based on a presupposition' (*ex hupotheseōs*) about what is 'contrariety' or 'a perfect thing (*teleion*)' or 'being' or 'one' or 'same'

---

[2] See, e.g., Beere 2009, 218. Both *entelecheia* and *energeia* are translated as *actus* in *S. Thomae Aquinatis In Duodecim Libros Metaphysicorum Aristotelis Expositio*, L.IX,I.i, p. 423 (Marietti Editori, Italy 1971).

[3] See, e.g., Kosman 1984. The origin of the traditional 'potentiality–actuality' dichotomy can be traced back to the first Latin translation of the *Metaphysics* by William of Moerbeke.

[4] Translations are my own. I use square brackets to indicate my explanations or expansions of the text.

[5] *Met.* B.6, 1002b33, *Phys.* 1.8, 191b27–9, see also *Met.* A.9,992b18-20, *DA.*2.5,417b26.

REFLECTIONS ON ARISTOTLE'S MODAL ONTOLOGY   299

or 'other', 'there is one science to contemplate the thing that is *qua* being and the things that belong to the thing itself that is *qua* being' (Γ.5, 1005a11–4). Accounts of these general terms are given by reference to the modes of being of the relevant entities. The modal definition of 'a perfect thing', for example, is that 'outside of which it is impossible to grasp any potential thing' (I.4, 1055a11).

Aristotle uses his three terms—'potentiality', 'at-workness', and 'completeness'—in offering solutions to problems arising from his predecessors' ontological theories. Against Eleatic monism, the claim that 'the same thing cannot be one and many', he suggests that 'one thing is both in *potentiality* and in *completeness*' and so 'the *same* thing can be and not be the *contrariety* at the same time in *potentiality*, but not in *completeness*' (*Phys.* 1.2, 186a2–3, *Met.* Γ.5, 1009a34–6). He also uses these terms to criticize the Heraclitean flux theory, the Anaxagorean mixture theory, Protagorean relativism, and Plato's Third Man Argument.[6] His modal ontology offers a comprehensive understanding of general terms such as 'being', 'becoming', 'non-being', 'one', 'sameness', and 'substance' as well as 'account' (*logos*) and 'work' (*ergon*).

2. Introduction to Aristotle's Modal Terms

2.1 Entelecheia

Some linguistic points are important for a proper understanding of Aristotle's wide-ranging study of being. His new terms *entelecheia* and *energeia* are composed of words in current usage, such as *entelōs* ('*en*' + '*telos*') + *echein* + *ia* and *en* + *ergon* + *eia*. This enables readers to grasp their lexical meanings as the basis for Aristotle's further investigations in his modal ontology. *Entelecheia* only occurs in the singular feminine substantive expression and never in any plural form nor in its verbal expression in its approximately 140 occurrences (according to TLG).[7]

Because its verbal stem *entelōs* + *echein* signifies 'to be completely', and because it is based on the idiom *houtōs* + *echein* ('to be so', the adverb of manner) and is accompanied by a suffix ('-*ia*') indicating abstractness, I shall translate the word *entelecheia* as 'completeness'.[8]

Aristotle explains what *entelecheia* means in the context of defining what the soul is in *De Anima* 2.1. This modal concept is suitable for capturing a non-sensible

---

[6] See *GC* 1.3, 317b23–6, *Met.* Γ.4, 1007b25–9, Z.4, 1030a25–6, Z.13, 1039a3–6.

[7] The only exception seems to be *De Anima* 2.1, 413a6-7, but perhaps *entelecheias* could be construed as a genitive singular.

[8] Themistius endorses the reading of *entelōs* + *echein* signifying 'to be completely'. See Themistius, *In de Anima* 39.15–25 (Heinze). See also Smyth 1956, 840 and 1709b: '*kalōs echein* be well (*bene se habere*)'. The mode of being of abstractness and generality of *logos* (form) can be captured by the singular noun *entelecheia* (completeness) *qua* being rather than 'fulfilment' and 'completion', which are *ergon* words involving process towards the goal.

300 KEI CHIBA

entity in itself such as a soul, which is not accessible to direct sense-perception. The basic ontological significance of the term *entelecheia* is explained by reference to unity and being. Aristotle says: 'Since "one" and "to be" are said in more than one way, the completeness is the *one* and *to be* principally (*to kuriōs*)' (412b9). Aristotle employs the term 'principal(ly)' (*kurios*) to indicate the soul's supremacy over the body, as he says that 'what unites the [four] elements is the most governing entity (*kuriōtaton d'ekeino sunechon*)' (*DA* 1.5, 410b11–2). Following the basic sense of the noun *kurios*, which means the governor or lord, I shall understand *kuriōs* in the sense of 'principally': that is, 'in the governing manner' (see, e.g., *Met.* Δ.12, 1020a4, *NE* 3.1, 1110a6).

In *Metaphysics* Λ, Aristotle investigates the first cause, which is dominant over all things that are. While he points to such causes as 'matter, form, privation, and mover' which are 'analogically' applied as 'the *same* causes' of all things, Aristotle points to another route that linearly traces back to the first cause. He says that 'the causes of substances are as the causes of all things in the following way: when the causes are removed, all things are removed. Furthermore, the first cause is in virtue of completeness (*to prōton entelecheia(i)*)' (Λ.5,1071a33–6). Here 'completeness' signifies the governing mode of being one with respect to the first cause of all things that are. Thus the 'completeness' of a thing specifies and governs the unity and the being of other relevant subordinate things. Thus I understand 'completeness' as the abbreviation of 'to be completely one in the governing mode'.

In *De Anima* 2.1, Aristotle introduces completeness in order to connect the definition (*logos*) of the soul with its work (*ergon*):

> While the matter is potentiality, the form is completeness. This [form] is said in two ways, either as 'knowledge' is said or as 'to contemplate' is said.... This [completeness] is said in two ways (*dichōs*), either as [*logos*] 'knowledge' (*hē epistēmē*) is said or as [*ergon*] 'to contemplate' (*to theōrein*) is said. Therefore, it is evident that the soul is as knowledge. For there is both sleeping and waking in virtue of [*logos*] the soul [*ergon*] to belong (*tō(i) huparchein tēn psuchēn*), but waking has analogy with 'to contemplate' and sleeping with 'to have [the knowledge] and not to be at work'. The knowledge of the same thing is prior in terms of generation. Therefore, the soul is the first completeness of a natural body having life in potentiality (412a9–11, 22–8).

Aristotle's expression 'said in two ways' does not mean that there are two senses of 'completeness'. Rather, it means that completeness is found in two contexts: in the pursuit of the modal definition of soul and in the pursuit of observing its work. The role of completeness in connecting *logos* and *ergon* is illustrated by two parallel examples: 'knowledge' and 'to contemplate'. 'Knowledge' comes *first* 'in terms of generation'.

REFLECTIONS ON ARISTOTLE'S MODAL ONTOLOGY   301

Aristotle identifies the soul as 'the *first* completeness' with the *logos* such as 'knowledge', which is propositional in character: say, '$E = mc^2$'. A causal relation of *logos* and *ergon* is stated here as 'in virtue of the soul to belong there is sleeping and waking' (412a24). Just as the knowledge that $E=mc^2$ is expressed by an account 'in virtue of which we know (*hō(i) epistametha)*', the soul is a substance as a *logos* 'in virtue of which we live (*hō(i) zōmen*) and perceive and think' (2.2,414a4-5, a12).

The modal turn of this causal formulation is characterized by employing the technical phrase 'being in virtue of completeness' such that 'the person who is contemplating here and now (*ēdē*) is being in virtue of completeness (*entelecheia(i) ōn*) and is contemplating this *A* in the governing manner (*kuriōs*)' (2.5, 417a28–9). This present participle construction (*entelecheia(i) ōn*) indicates that Cathy, who is being in virtue of completeness as *having* the knowledge, say, $E = mc^2$ or as *being* the knower of the *logos* which is to be completely one in the governing mode such that nothing more is required to contemplate it, is now contemplating $E = mc^2$ at her own discretion. In this way, the construction shows that completeness connects the person to whom the *logos* (knowledge) belongs and the same person at work (*ergon*) contemplating.

Therefore, the parallel locution of causal and modal relations suggests that '*entelecheia*' is contrived in order to capture how substances, either agents or patients, are at work either *simpliciter* or incompletely from the perspective of general ontology.

2.2 Dunamis

In *De Anima* 2.4, Aristotle says that 'the completeness is an account (*logos*) of the thing being in potentiality' (415b14–5). He means that the form as the first completeness is an account that determines the being and identity of a potential thing. I shall translate the term *dunamis* as 'potentiality' following the longstanding tradition and take this to cover both ordinary and technical usages, such as power, ability, possibility, and disposition (see *Met.* Θ.1).

Dunamis has a *positive* use in Aristotle's ontology, because it is governed by completeness. Without appeal to completeness, a potentiality cannot be made definite: 'a thing being in virtue of potentiality (*to dunamei on*) and not in virtue of completeness is indefinite' (Γ.4, 1007b28). A natural principle, 'the matter', should be taken to be 'in potentiality…according to its acquired disposition (*kat' hexin*) and its form' rather than according to its privation (H.5, 1044b32–4; see b36). My employment of the traditional translation 'potentiality' is not limited to conveying the presence of some latent, yet to be developed, passive capacity or ability. It also indicates the acquired *positive* disposition of a power, a *hexis*, which implies both *having* the relevant potentiality here and now and 'being able to be at work' at any time (Θ.8, 1049b13).

302   KEI CHIBA

2.3 *Energeia*

The term *energeia* is formed in the same way as *entelecheia*: the suffix '*-ia*' or '*-eia*', which is added to the verbal stem ('*energ-*'), signifies abstractness. Unlike *entelecheia*, however, the noun *energeia* is often used in its plural form according to the number of corresponding potentialities (in the same way as its component '*ergon*' has the plural '*erga*') and is expressed in its verbal forms such as *energein* (being at work). Its plural form depends linguistically on the number of potentialities manifested in the traditional framework of *ergon* (Δ.15, 1021a14–16, Λ.6, 1071b23). Based on the literal composition of *energeia* ('*en*' + '*ergon*' + '*eia*'), Aristotle characterizes his distinctive use of this term when he writes: 'the *energeia* is being definite (*hōrismenē*) of a thing that is definite (*hōrismenou*), being some *this* of some *this*' (M.10, 1087a18–20). Here *energeia* is the mode of being at work that is grasped by observation here and now as something definite together with the reference to 'this'.

Another important linguistic feature is that the verbal form *energein* is never found in the passive voice in Aristotle's works. In addition, in the Aristotelian corpus there is no case where *energein* is accompanied by a direct object. This linguistic observation leads me to translate it by the general expression 'being at work' (compare Heidegger's 'am Werk sein') and to translate the noun *energeia* as 'at-workness'. Some justification for these translations is found in Aristotle's remark: 'to begin with, let us say that there is no difference between being affected or moved and being at work (*tou paschein kai tou kineisthai kai tou energein*)' (*DA* 2.5, 417a14–6). The active verb (*energein*) can be explained by the passive verbs (*paschein*, which is passive in sense if not in voice, and *kineisthai*) without changing the truth value, insofar as the active agent and patient are to be in contact. Aristotle says that 'everything is affected and moved by what is able to produce and by the thing being at work' (417a17–8).

Assuming that that my translations 'being at work' and 'at-workness' are correct, the range to which the new word *energeia* is applied covers anything that is at work taken generally or taken particularly. Its particular definite work is observable directly or indirectly because the relevant form is at work by being built into its matter. Aristotle generally says about a definite at-workness of the agent that 'the mover will always transmit (*oisetai*) a form, either a "this" or such or so much, which, when it moves, will be the principle and cause of the movement, e.g., the human in virtue of completeness begets a human from what is potentially human' (*Phys.* 3.2, 202a9–12). Also, it is said that 'the form of human always appears (*phainetai*) in flesh and bones and such parts' (*Met.* Z.11, 1036b3).

Indeed, the term *energeia* is designed to cover not only all general active and passive verb terms, such as 'learning' and 'seeing', but also 'being' and 'becoming'. Whether or not something has a potentiality is readily detected by observing the relevant object at work here and now. If its being at work is detectable by sense-perception, movement will be possible for it. Thus Aristotle says: 'I mean, for instance, if a thing is capable of sitting and is allowed to sit, there will be nothing impossible, if sitting belongs to it' (Θ.3, 1047a26–8). This also applies to 'being' and 'becoming'. Aristotle notes that 'it is possible for a thing to be capable of being something [F] and not being [F at work] (*dunaton men ti einai mē einai de*), and capable of not being [F] and yet being [F at work]' (1047a20–2; see also a29: 'either to be or to become (*ē einai ē gignesthai*)').

2.4 *Kinēsis* vs. *Energeia Simplicter*

Aristotle distinguishes between two kinds of potentiality and correspondingly two kinds of at-workness in *De Anima* 3.7: 'While movement (*kinēsis*) is an at-workness (*energeia*) of that which is incomplete (*atelēs*), the at-workness (*energeia*) *simpliciter* of that which has been completed (*tetelesmenou*) is different' (431a6–7). Accordingly, Aristotle identifies two potentiality/at-workness (*dunamis/energeia*) pairs. Aristotle needed a new technical noun, *entelecheia*, to distinguish between them (as he says, 'completeness separates (*chōrizei*)', *Met.* Z.13,1039a7). The one pair is the incomplete continuous *energeia*: that is, movement (*kinēsis*) based on 'the potentiality according to movement (*dunamis kata kinēsin*)'. The other pair is the *energeia simpliciter* based on the completed potentiality that is gained at the goal of movement. In order to discern the *energeia simpliciter*, the tense test is useful, according to which both the present and perfect tenses are successfully applied, so that she 'is living' and at the same time she 'has lived' (Θ.6,1048b27).

I shall describe 'the potentiality according to movement' as an 'incomplete' and 'passive potentiality (*hē tou pathein dunamis*)', which involves three items: (1) the efficient cause as the agent; (2) the patient to which the movement belongs; and (3) their contact (Θ.1, 1046a2, a11, b2).

Aristotle characterizes the passive potentiality in change: 'this [potentiality] is (3) the beginning of change in (2) the patient itself by (1) another thing or by (2) itself regarded as (1) another' (Θ.1, 1046 a11–3, '(1) a doctor cures ((2)=(1)) himself' *Phys.* 2.8, 199b31). Therefore, this potentiality is 'the *definite* kind (*tēs hōrismenēs*)' in time and space because of its observable contact. I shall call this the 'triadic structure of movement'.

By contrast, I shall call a completed potentiality 'a stand-by potentiality', being ready to be at work. The stand-by potentiality, which is capable of moving and remaining at rest, is defined as follows: 'the primary potential thing is said to be capable because it is able to be at work (*tō(i) endechesthai energēsai dunaton esti to prōtōs dunaton*)' (*Met.*Θ.8, 1049b13). This state, 'able to be at work' or 'being allowed to be at work', is one in which the agent is ready to be at-work: 'he has the potential to contemplate, whenever he wishes, if nothing external hinders' (*DA.*2.5, 417a27–b8). That is why 'the at-workness *simpliciter*' requires the agent

304   KEI CHIBA

who is being in virtue of completeness as *having* the form and thus holds the standby-potentiality.

2.5 *Ergon*

Aristotle points to these two kinds of *energeia* in explicating the traditional term *ergon*. He notes that *ergon* 'is said in two ways', pointing to an act/result ambiguity (*EE* 2.1, 1219a13). *Ergon* is said to be either 'the employment (*chrēsis*)' (e.g., seeing) or 'something else besides the employment' (e.g., a new-born baby, a house). Aristotle disambiguates these two uses of the word by making the ordinary word 'employment' (or 'exercise', 'use') more explicit and more precise. These two uses have in common their connection with the goal or end. When focusing on its role as a goal, he applies the expression *energeia simpliciter* to 'employment' alone and distinguishes this from the *product* achieved at the end of the movement (*kinēsis*): that is, the *work* (*Met.* Θ.8, 1050a24–8). In this way, traditional terms such as 'work' (*ergon*) and 'goal' (*telos*) are clarified through Aristotle's new modal terms.

2.6 Final Remarks

Aristotle's three basic modal terms share a common characteristic. When they are accompanied by the present participle of the verb 'to be' (*ōn, ousa, on*), they invariably take the form of the singular dative noun (dative of means: 'in virtue of~' or '~lly'): *entelecheia(i), energeia(i), dunamei*. Each singular dative noun is also accompanied by prepositions such as *hupo* ('by') and *ek* ('from') so as to convey the contact of agent and patient and its ordered at-workness: for examples, 'by the thing being in virtue of completeness' and 'from the thing in virtue of being at work'. These combinations of the present participle of the verb 'to be' and the dative singular noun systematically exhibit a definite at-workness either taken universally or taken particularly 'here and now' (*ēdē*) and exhibit the completeness shared by the agent and the patient with regard to their unity under a general modal system within the analysis of being.[9]

For example, the generation of an artefact (e.g., the building of a house) is analysed by a combination of modal terms: 'when what is buildable [e.g., stone and wood], insofar as we call it such [i.e., buildable], is in virtue of completeness (*entelecheia(i) ē(i)*), it is being built, and that is building' (*Phys.* 3.1, 201a16–8). Stone and wood are identified as 'buildable' by reference to the relevant completeness as the mode of being of the form (i.e., 'a thought in completeness (*apo*

---

[9] See *Met.* Θ.3, 1047b2, Θ.7, 1049a5, Θ.8, 1049b24, *Phys.* 3.1, 201a9–b22, 4.9, 217a23, *DA* 2.5, 417 a18, a29, b4, b12–3, 3.7, 431a4, *GC* 1.5, 320b19, *PA* 2.1, 647a8, *GA* 2.1, 734a30, b21.

dianoias entelecheia(i))' which is the blueprint of the house grasped by the builder) (*Met.* Θ.7, 1049a5). Without the concept of completeness, Aristotle would have lacked the resources to identify any potential thing (e.g., buildable) or its being at work (e.g., building) in terms of its account or range of operations. If the act of building succeeds, the house will be completed in virtue of the blueprint: that is, its *logos*, which governs the materials and their movement over time. Of the house Aristotle says: 'while matter is earth and stone, the form is the *logos*' (*Met.* B.2, 996b6–7; see also *PA* 1.1, 640a31–2). Insofar as the goal of the building and the agent as the efficient cause share the same *logos*, they must both be in virtue of completeness *qua* being. Aristotle says: 'there must be the completeness of both [of the agent and the patient]' (*Phys.* 3.3, 202a15).

'Completeness' is, therefore, used to describe *both* the efficient cause that transmits some form to the patient as that 'from which (*aph' hou*)' *and* the goal as that 'towards which (*eph' ho*)'.[10] The completeness at issue governs the order of generation and corruption by showing the mode of being one principally *qua* being that into which something comes (*eis entelecheian ion erchetai*) and that out of which something passes (*apelthontes ek tēs entelecheias*) (*DC* 4.3, 311a5, *Met.* Z.10, 1036a6). Thus things according to nature and art are analysed in modal terms as something definite. The agent and patient exemplify completeness with regard to their unity and being in terms of the account of what each of them is and of how each is at work here and now.

3. *Logos* and *Ergon* Initiatives: Central Books of the *Metaphysics*

The universe does not consist solely of random works, but is, in its totality, a dynamic ordered system. Aristotle says that 'nature is the cause of order for everything (*aitia pasin taxeōs*). But there is no *logos* in the relation of the infinite to the infinite, whereas every order is a *logos*' (*Phys.* 8.1, 252a12–4). Each *pragma* ('thing') is understood in terms of a *logos* and an *ergon* as a natural phenomenon in the world. The same applies to the soul's cognitive works and intentional actions. Aristotle expresses the relevant complementariness by using conjunctive phrases such as 'by *logos* and by *ergon*' and 'not only in *logos*, but also in *ergon*'. He suggests that both approaches are in mutual 'agreement', 'witness', and even 'harmonize' when they are successful.[11] Throughout he keeps both approaches in mind.

When describing particular agents as efficient causes, Aristotle points to two of the soul's cognitive faculties: discursive thought (*dianoia*), which operates under

---

[10] See *Met.* Z.8, 1033b32, Z.9, 1034b2, b16–19, Δ.17, 1022a4–9, *Phys.* 3.2, 202a9, *DA* 2.4, 415b8–15; see also *Phys.* 2.1, 193b12, *PA* 1.1, 640a25.

[11] See, e.g., *DA* 1.5, 409b15, *GA* 1.21, 729b22, *Met.* Λ.7, 1072a22, M.9, 1086a9, *NE* 10.1, 1172b3–8.

the guidance of a normative way of speaking ('how one should speak (*pōs dei legein*)' and 'how one should define (*pōs dei horizesthai*)') and sense-perception (*aisthēsis*) (*Met.* E.1, 1026a4, Z.4 1030a27; see also K.7, 1064a21, *Top.* 8.1, 155b3). These faculties offer different ways in which the soul can access the world. He notes: 'while universals are prior according to the account (*kata ton logon*), particulars are prior according to sense-perception (*kata tēn aisthēsin*)' (*Met.* E.1, 1018b31–4; see also *APo.* 1.31, 87b28–88a17, *Phys.* 1.5, 189a7).

I shall call the soul's grasp through discursive thought aimed at definition its '*logos* initiative' and the soul's access through the direct observation of the efficient cause here and now its '*ergon* initiative'. Priority in account and priority in sense-perception, respectively, give the basis for each of these initiatives. They cooperate to comprehend the relevant thing that is in its being one and at work. Aristotle uses these two routes in combination by taking the initiative of one or the other to indicate the connection between the world's two constituents (*logos* and *ergon*) and the soul's two cognitive faculties (universal definition and particular observation).

Within the framework of his *pros hen* structure, Aristotle investigates questions such as 'what a *pragma* is' (*ti esti*) by offering a modal account of its unity, and he investigates 'how a *pragma* is [at work]' (*pōs echei* (*esti*)) by observing its being at work. The efficient cause is grasped by observing the contact between the mover and its patient at a specific place and time, such as '*whence* (*hothen*) the first movement belongs to each thing' and 'when (*hotan*) it is set in movement' (*Met.* Γ.3, 1014b18, *DA* 2.8, 419b35). Grasping the *logos* is one thing, grasping its *ergon*, or how it works, is another. Aristotle says that 'we must inquire how one should speak about each thing but still more how a thing is (*pōs echei*)' (*Met.* Z.4, 1030a27–8). He also adds that 'we must not fail to notice *how* the essence and its *logos* are [at work] (*pōs esti*), as inquiring without this is no better than doing nothing' (E.1, 1025b28–30; see also A.9, 992b18–20, Z.11, 1037a21–2, H.2, 1043a26–7, Λ.7, 1072a34).

3.1 *Logos* Initiative: Inquiry into the Form from the Essence

In the central books of the *Metaphysics*, Aristotle investigates what substance is and how it is at work as the cause of unity of a thing. Aristotle develops a comprehensive ontology as the product of the complementary and cooperative approaches of the *logos* and *ergon* initiatives by explaining the natures and roles of the three modal notions (potentiality, at-workness, completeness) and their relations.

In *Metaphysics* Z, Aristotle begins his investigation of substance as essence in a *logikōs* (formal argumentative) fashion (Z.4–6). He follows the Eleatic tradition, which is based on the principle of non-contradiction.[12] Aristotle explains essence

---

[12] See *Top.* 7.3, 153a12, 8.1, 155b3, *Met.* Γ.3, 1005b8–19, E.1, 1026a4, Z.4, 1030a27, Z.17, 1041a6–7. See also *antilogikos* (enemy of *logos*) in Plato's *Sophist* 232b, with *Top.* 1.12, 105a19, *SE* 34, 183a30, b10, and *Met.* K.7, 1064a21.

REFLECTIONS ON ARISTOTLE'S MODAL ONTOLOGY   307

as follows: 'we will say that the essence of each thing is that which is said according to itself. For to be you is not to be musical. For you are not musical according
to yourself' (*Met.* Z.4, 1029b13–5). His *logikōs* approach does not yield claims
about the natural world but can distinguish the substance 'to be you' from attributes such as 'being musical' by discerning the criterion for a subject such as 'you'
that is not predicated of other things. It also makes ontological claims about being
one and about the existence of the single essence required for anything to be one:
'to be precisely what something is (*to einai hoper estin*) is single for each of the
things that are' (*Top.* 6.4, 141a24, a35–7; see also 141b25, 142a7, *Met.* Γ.4,
1007b25–9). In his 'discussions about definition' in the *Metaphysics*, he asks 'why
is the thing whose account we call a definition, one?' (Z.12, 1037b11). His *logikōs*
pursuit is a preparatory step designed to assist the soul in its subsequent
observation-based cognitive endeavours.

At the end of *Metaphysics* Z.3, Aristotle states that his goal is to grasp 'the most
perplexing' (1029a34) substance: that is, the 'form'. Subsequently, in Z.4, the
'essence', as 'more knowable to each person', having 'little or nothing of being', is
the starting-point of the inquiry into substance (Z.4, 1029b2, b8–10).[13] This
remark is characteristic of the *logos* initiative: 'the what it was to be F' (*to ti ēn
einai*, also translated 'essence') is originally 'what Socrates sought for' in his 'what
is F (e.g., virtue)?' question and is 'the thing itself' that is stated in a successful
definition as its answer (see *Top.* 1.9, 103b35–4a2, *NE* 7.3, 1147b14). As Aristotle
says, 'speaking in a *logikōs* fashion, this [the cause] is the essence' (*Met.* Z.17,
1041a28). Essence is a *logikōs* concept, a place-holder to be filled with an entity,
such as the form, which satisfies the conditions on definition set by how one
should define.

A logical inquiry is the first step in the soul's cognitive access to the natural
order. Aristotle says that 'it is effective to proceed to the more knowable. For
learning proceeds in this way through that which is less knowable by nature [i.e.,
essence] to that which is more knowable [i.e., form]' (Z.4, 1029b3–5). Examples
of the 'less knowable by nature' but 'more knowable to us' are 'what a name signifies' and 'what the item said is (*ti to legomenon esti*)': that is, the literal sense of the
term that can be understood without referring to the world (*APo.* 1.1, 71a13, 2.10,
93b30).[14] Grasping the 'essence' as 'what is capable of being defined' also belongs
to this stage (*Met.* Z.4, 1029b13–5, *Top.* 1.5, 102a1–2). Aristotle says that 'one
must start from that which is barely knowable [by nature] but is knowable to

---

[13] I follow Bekker in keeping 1029b3–12 in *Metaphysics* Z.4. I disagree with Bonitz (followed by
Jaeger and Ross) who transposed these lines to the end of Z.3. The effect of Bonitz's transposition is to
make *sensible substance* the referent of the phrases 'that which is more knowable to each person' and
'that which has little or nothing of being'. When we keep the lines in Z.4, the referent of these phrases
is *essence* (*to ti ēn einai*). Bonitz is puzzled: 'Concerning the essence, it is in the least degree (*minime*)
that its nature is indeed first and nearest [for us], but it is the most remote and hidden for us' (1849,
303). Bonitz did not grasp the significance of the *logikōs* approach to essence initiated in Z.4.
[14] See Charles 2000, 1–2, 78–95.

308   KEI CHIBA

oneself [i.e., essence, e.g., "to be you"], and then attempt to come to know what is wholly knowable [i.e., form]' (*Met.* Z.4, 1029b7–10). If our inquiry is successful, 'what is wholly knowable [by nature]' will become 'knowable to oneself'. We will then have knowledge of the 'form' as the causally basic substance in the 'sensible things' at issue (1029a34).

3.2 'How One Should Define'

In *Metaphysics* Z.10–17, Aristotle is engaged in investigating 'how one should define' the composite substance (*Met.* E.1, 1026a4). In Z.10 he argues that the account (*logos*) of substance as form is embedded in the matter in terms of its work (*ergon*). In addition, the at-workness (*energeia*) of the form is invariably built into the account. This interlocking of *logos* and *ergon* is indispensable if we are to gain both a causal and a modal definition in which the effects (the works) are unified by a causally basic substance: a being in virtue of completeness (*entelecheia*). Aristotle says: 'since the soul of living things (for this is the substance *of* an ensouled thing (*emphsuchou*)) is their substance according to the *logos* and the form and the essence of a body of a certain kind, each part [e.g., sight], if it is defined well (*ean horizētai kalōs*), is not defined without its work (*ergou*) [e.g., seeing], and its work will not belong to [the animal] without sense-perception' (1035b14–8). In terms of *ergon*, the phrase '*of* an ensouled thing' indicates that the soul is the substance *of* a living body here and now (an *ergon* concept), where 'of' is a genitive of belonging. The soul's *ergon* is discovered inductively as the body's being alive. This feature is to be built into the relevant definitional account, 'if it is defined well'.

Aristotle distinguishes knowledge through definition from knowledge by observation. He says:

> To be a soul [i.e., its essence] is the same as the soul. But, when we come to the unified whole (*sunholon*) here and now (*ēdē*), e.g., to *this* circle, one of the particular circles, whether sensible or intelligible (I mean by intelligible circles the mathematical, and by sensible circles those of bronze and of wood), of these there is no definition, but they are known by the operation of intellect (*noēsis*) or sense-perception. (Z.10,1036a1–7)[15]

Here we find an example of the *ergon* initiative: a particular bronze circle is perceived here and now rather than defined. But when Aristotle says that 'even if all circles that had ever been seen were of bronze, the bronze would be nonetheless no part of the form', he shows that, in his view, the *logos* of substance as the form

---

[15] See also 1036b1, Z.15, 1040a2–3, *DA* 3.4, 429a10–18, b5–9, 3.5, 430a19, 3.6, 431a1.

REFLECTIONS ON ARISTOTLE'S MODAL ONTOLOGY 309

(e.g., soul) is non-sensible and so must be grasped as the form on the basis of an account that involves the causally basic unifying element of the substance (Z.11, 1036b1–2).

Aristotle's ontological project is to grasp 'the *logos*' 'of essence' or 'of substance' and to show how the form as a *logos* belongs to the matter if it is at work here and now. This is a supplementary way to grasp non-sensible things. When he says '*logos* of substance' and '*logos* of essence', Aristotle always takes it to be the form.[16] This is because the account of 'what a thing is' is primarily applied to substance, which is taken to be the cause of 'being' (Z.17, 1041a32; see his *ergon* turn 'another starting-point': Z.17,1041a6–8).

Aristotle's final unified account allows us to gain access to the non-sensible entity, the form. The account (*logos*), as a linguistic expression, is divisible but points to some indivisible part of the thing (*adiaireton, atomon*) in terms of its *ergon* here and now.[17] He argues that the best account captures what a thing is in a general way, using universal terms under the guidance of 'how one should define'.

Aristotle offers causal and modal definitions in which the causally basic or modally governing part constitutes 'the *logos* of substance'. He says:

In the *logos* of substance, there will not be such parts as matter, for the matter is not a part of that substance but of the composite, but there is in some sense a *logos* of the composite but there is not in another. There is no *logos* of a thing accompanied by matter (for it is indefinite), but there is according to the first substance [i.e., form]: thus, for example, the *logos* of the soul is an account of human. For the substance is the inherent form (*to eidos to enon*), and on the basis of this and the matter the composite is called a substance. (Z.11, 1037a24–30)

This implies that the *best* account can separate the form (the governing part) from the composite's material parts. While the composite is being at work here and now as a definite thing, the matter is in itself indefinite.

3.3 *Ergon* Initiative: Observation-Based Inductive Argument

Observation-based inquiry is an independent cognitive source, though it cooperates with the *logos* initiative. It is clear from inductive observation that things are at work in movement and in order. Insofar as induction yields some universal statement through reasoning, this is carried out by discursive thought on the basis of observation. This investigation is conducted *phusikōs* ('naturally') in

---

[16] See *Met.* B.3, 998b12, Δ.2, 1013a27, Z.4,1029b20, b25, Z.5,1031a12, Z.9, 1034b8, Z.11, 1037a23, a24, *GA* 1.1, 715a5, 2.1, 731b19.

[17] See *Phys.* 1.2, 185b8, *Met.* H.3, 1043b35.

accordance with the following assumptions: 'we must take it for granted that the things that are by nature are, either all or some of them, in movement, which is indeed made plain by induction' (*Phys.* 1.2, 185a12–4).[18] One can gain 'sufficient conviction', as part of the *ergon* initiative, through 'induction' concerning the orderliness of the world (*APo.* 2.3, 90b13).

Aristotle notes a shortcoming in the Academy's inductive definitions in terms of genus and differentia: there is no unified connection between, for example, mortal, footed, two-footed, wingless animal. In a division-based defining phrase, one can always ask 'why is this one, but not many: animal *and* biped?' (*Met.* Z.12, 1037b13–4). On this basis, 'a unity can be made out of any set of attributes' (1037b24). Aristotle continues: 'but surely all elements in the definition must be one; for the definition is some single account and a *logos* of substance, so that there must be an account being itself of some one thing. For substance means a "one" and "some this"' (1037b24–7). Therefore, his task is to build pieces of inductive information into his new theory of definition as the causally unified account of substance.

In *Metaphysics* H, Aristotle seeks to answer the question of 'what a sensible substance is' by engaging in an inductive inquiry into the 'shape (*morphē*)' of a thing being at work here and now (H.2, 1043a26). The 'what a thing is' is identified observationally by referring to various shapes and affections proper to sensible things, such as 'hardness and softness, density and rarity, dryness and wetness' (1042b22). For instance, the answer to the question 'what is still weather?' is 'smoothness of sea', where the substratum is the sea (as the matter) and 'the at-workness and the shape is the smoothness' (1043a24–6). The reason why Aristotle cannot use 'form' at this point is that the smoothness of the sea can be identified by referring to the relevant *shape* here and now. Thus his new task is to build this information of *shape* into the causal account of *form*.

3.4 The Efficient Cause as the Bearer of the *Logos* and the *Ergon*

While Aristotle discusses inductive definition in *Metaphysics* Z.17–H.6, the agent as the efficient cause plays a crucial role in connecting the *logos* and the *ergon*. In H.6, Aristotle offers the efficient cause as an answer to the question 'What is the cause of being one (*ti aition tou hen einai*)?' (1045a8). This cause brings about the at-workness based on the potential thing. Aristotle then confirms his realism about *logos*: 'the definition is an account that is one…by being of one thing' (1045a12–4). The unity of definition must be based on the unity of a thing being at work.

---

[18] See also *Phys.* 1.7, 191a21, *Phys.* 8.1, 251a6, *DA* 2.5, 417b23, *GA* 2.3, 737a16, *Met.* A.9, 992b14, Z.4, 1030a27.

REFLECTIONS ON ARISTOTLE'S MODAL ONTOLOGY   311

Aristotle examines the views of his predecessors who have offered various accounts of the unity of a thing. He explains their failed attempts in terms of his own system (H.6, 1045b16–23). In Aristotle's view, his predecessors' conceptual resources, such as 'communion', 'composition', and 'connection', are put forward as middle or causally basic terms to link and unify two items (1045b7–16). But these unifying elements are not internally built into the *explananda*. Their definition of 'knowledge' will be something like 'the unity of soul and knowing because of their communion'. In Aristotle's view, by contrast, knowledge is a *logos in virtue of which* the person is now at work in actively knowing. Since the agent to whom the *logos* belongs is a being in virtue of completeness, he/she has authority with regard to his/her contemplation and its potentiality. Aristotle's predecessors failed to grasp the internal link between the items to be connected. As a result, they sought an account 'unifying' the completeness and potentiality in terms of a further account. They were looking for a further mediator to unify two items that they themselves had distinguished. In criticizing their attempts, Aristotle offers his own solution by introducing the efficient cause as something that has a hold of the *logos* and transfers it to the patient. This is how, in this case, Aristotle connects his *logos* and *ergon* perspectives in his ontological project by focusing on the efficient cause.

3.5 New Modal Analyses as Solutions to the Predecessors' Ontological Difficulties: *Metaphysics* Θ

In *Metaphysics* Θ as a whole, Aristotle seeks to 'determine' his three modal terms and their interrelations.[19] In this analysis, he specifies two kinds of *dunamis* and the relevant *energeia* by appealing to *entelecheia* ('potentiality according to movement' in chapters 1–5 and stand-by potentiality in chapters 6–10; Θ.6, 1048a26–8).[20] I shall now investigate the role of *entelecheia* in connecting *logos* and *ergon* in this book, while considering the definition of movement in *Physics* 3.1 and 5.1.

Here is Aristotle's synopsis of *Metaphysics* Θ in chapter 1:

Since (*epei*) 'being' is said, ... [*logos* initiative] according to potentiality and completeness (*kata dunamin kai entelecheian*) and (*kai*) [*ergon* initiative] according to the work (*kata to ergon*), we will determine (*diorisōmen*) also about potentiality and completeness, and first potentiality in the strictest sense [i.e., potentiality

---

[19] See *Met.* Θ.1, 1045b34, 1046a3, a5, Θ.5, 1048a2, a20, Θ.6, 1048a26, 1048b5, Θ.7, 1048b37, Θ.8, 1050b31.
[20] Commentators fail to grasp the completed stand-by potentiality in a precise way. For example, Frede, when discussing the conceptions of *dunamis* in *Metaphysics* Θ.1–5 and 6–10, respectively, accuses Aristotle of being 'unclear, disorganized', noting that 'important commentators...have accused Aristotle of being himself confused' (1994, 176). See also Makin 2006, xxiii.

312   KEI CHIBA

for movement, chapters 1–5], which is, however, not particularly useful for our present purpose. For potentiality and at-workness (*hē dunamis kai hē energeia*) extend beyond the cases that are said merely according to movement (*kata kinēsin*). But after having discussed this potentiality, we will reveal, in the specifications of the at-workness, other [useful] kinds [e.g., stand-by potentiality] too. (1045b32–46a4)

In his synopsis, Aristotle's immediate task of marking out his three modal terms presupposes, as the causal conjunct 'since'(*epei*) suggests, the results of his investigations in *Metaphysics* Z and H. By deploying his modal terms Aristotle confirms that there are two approaches to accessing 'being' (*to on*): the *logos* initiative ('according to potentiality and completeness'), which reveals 'what a thing *is*' universally, and the *ergon* initiative ('according to the work'), which reveals 'how a thing *is* at work'. While these two approaches are connected by a conjunction (*kai*), which shows their complementarity, the preposition 'according to' (*kata*), which is employed twice, indicates the two different points of access according to which 'being' is said.

Aristotle introduces the concept of at-workness in his criticism of the Megarians in *Metaphysics* Θ.3. They denied the difference between potentiality and at-workness without developing a plausible theory of their own. In their view, it is only while Socrates is seeing that he has the potentiality to see. Otherwise, this potentiality does not exist. When he opens his eyes again, he regains it. If this were the case, 'the same people will be blind many times in the day'. These views, as Aristotle says, 'do away with movement and becoming' (1047a9–14). Aristotle's solution is to treat some kind of not-being-F (say, not-seeing) as a preparatory stage—that is, as a stand-by potentiality—for F's being at work (1047a32–b2). He suggests that insofar as anything whose relevant potentiality is at work (F-ing) is perceived, one can confirm that this is 'not impossible' (1047a24–6).

Aristotle differs from the Eleatics in not 'assigning being moved (*to kineisthai*) to non-being' (1047a33). Instead, he asserts that the operation of *energeia* is internally governed by *entelecheia*. He says that 'the name *energeia*, being put together (*suntithemenē*) in reference to *entelecheia*, has extended chiefly from movements to other things' (1047a30–1).

As the term *entelecheia* did not exist before Aristotle, his predecessors lacked the linguistic and ontological resources to distinguish between, on the one hand, movement and incomplete potentiality and, on the other hand, complete at-workness and stand-by potentiality. As a result, they understood being at work in terms only of the category of becoming and movement. Plato, using the traditional pair *dunamis–ergon*, followed Heraclitus' flux doctrine and explained becoming and movement by appealing to the triadic structure in which an agent and a patient and their contact (*suniontōn*) are observed here and now. What happens in the phenomenal world is identified by observation-based

REFLECTIONS ON ARISTOTLE'S MODAL ONTOLOGY   313

measurement.[21] While Aristotle assigned to *entelecheia* the task of distinguishing *dunamis* from *energeia*, he also distinguished complete at-workness from movement by introducing a stand-by potentiality of the agent.

While his predecessors' treatment of movement in terms of difference or inequality or not-being was partial and one-sided, Aristotle thinks that his modal definition of *kinēsis* is 'said well': 'movement' is 'the completeness of the potential thing *qua* such potential' (*Phys.* 3.1, 201a10, 201b16–7). While a movement is a composite entity made up of completeness and potentiality involving the mode of being of form in terms of the account, it is a *continuous* incomplete entity because it excludes the goal; this is expressed by the phrase '*qua* such [incomplete passive] potential'.

There are four kinds of movement according to this modal definition, insofar as it involves four kinds of *form* captured by the completeness: substantial, qualitative, quantitative, and locative (3.1, 201a12–5). The movement is said to be 'indivisible in terms of time' because of its continuity, so that it is characterized not as 'becoming white (*ginetai leukon*)', which is 'named after' the result of change, but as 'whitening (*leukansis*)' (*Met.* Δ.6, 1016a4, *Phys.* 5.1, 224b7, 15). Since the results of a change, such as a shape or a colour, are perceived, the movement must be assisted and supplemented by the observation-based 'change' that is characterized as the perception of a difference between two *nows*: while 'every movement is some kind of change (*metabolē tis*)', 'we *see* (*horōmen*) in each that the change proceeds from a contrary to a contrary or to something intermediate' (5.1, 225a34, *DC.* 4.3, 310a24–6). Therefore, the movement only belongs to a group of changes that are 'from subject to subject' as something intermediate among four combinations of change between 'subject' and 'non-being' (*Phys.* 5.1, 224b35–225a7).

By maintaining its identity, substance does not undergo any change as the subject of its attributive changes. The invisible work of the *logos* of substance can be verified by observing various attributive changes such as a process of cell divisions of the fertilized egg. We can observe the generation of a substance as a change in such a way that a baby is born at t1 who was a non-being some time ago at t0. Therefore, there are four kinds of movement in terms of account, insofar as there is a form of substance. Also, we can say that 'there are three kinds of movement', insofar as a continuous and incomplete entity *qua* being is observed within the framework of change (5.1, 225b7; see *GC* I.3, *Met.* Γ.3, 1009a32–6). In this way, two initiatives require different words and locutions, according to their characteristics as an account and a work, so as to be cooperative.

Since Aristotle is confident that he has solved a problem inherited from the Eleatics and the Heracliteans by clearly grasping movement in terms of a modal account and its verification by observing the relevant change, he could find a firm

---

[21] See *Sophist* 248b–c; see also 218c, 219d, 235a, 263a, 252a, *Theaetetus* 153a, 156a, *Timaeus* 46e, 48d.

314   KEI CHIBA

standpoint on the basis of which he can solve other ontological problems by introducing the modal concepts.

In *Metaphysics. Θ.6*, Aristotle seeks to articulate the relation between *energeia* and *dunamis*. He says, 'we will determine what *energeia* is. For at the same time it will also become clear what is the potential' (1048a25–7). Aristotle invokes the *ergon* initiative and holds that 'it becomes evident what we would like to say about *particular things* by induction, and we should not [merely] seek for a defining-phrase of everything but also seek in virtue of *seeing* the analogical item *together* (*sun-horan*)' (1048a35–b1). His analogy is grasped by considering a variety of cases: *having* sight with closed eyes and *seeing, having* knowledge without *contemplating* it, *having* the art of building as the capacity to build (*to oikodomikon*) and *building* (1048a37–b2, Θ.8, 1050a28, *DA* 2.1, 412a25).

These analogical grasps depend on their agents being at work living. Thus 'a person who sleeps' is perceived as analogous to a person having sight without seeing (1048b1). While sleeping is as much a life activity as being at work living, a person asleep can be treated as possessing the relevant stand-by potentiality for waking. As we saw, the stand-by potentiality is the completed potentiality which belongs to the agent holding its relevant *logos*. Aristotle analogically grasps the second context of completeness which is illustrated as 'to contemplate' in contrast with 'knowledge'. Anything being at work as *energeia simpliciter* such as contemplating and seeing is the context in which completeness is detected and verified, because it does not suffer from any incompleteness of movement.

By giving the example of teaching in *Metaphysics* Θ.8, Aristotle illustrates a case in which the second context of completeness is found from the perspective of the mover. A teacher who is teaching is regarded as a being in virtue of completeness because the teacher has the knowledge in the governing mode in terms of its being one and thus does not undergo any change from ignorance to knowledge, while the patient, who is a pupil, undergoes a movement in the process of learning. He says that 'teachers think they have achieved the goal (*to telos apodedōkenai*) when they have exhibited the pupil at work, and the nature [is at work] in this way too' (1050a17–9).

Aristotle characterizes this case as involving 'things in which the goal is a movement' (1050a18). This case is taken to be similar to the ordered works of nature in general, as an agent transmitting the form to a womb in the reproductive mechanism.

Aristotle offers a reason for this claim: 'for the *ergon* ('work') is *telos* ('a goal'); but the *energeia* ('at-workness') is the *ergon*, therefore the name *energeia* is said according to the *ergon* and stretches together in reference to (*sunteinei pros*) *entelecheia*' (1050a21–3). This passage shows how the term *ergon* together with *telos* can be clarified through his new modal terms. There are two kinds of *energeia*, which connect his two uses of *ergon* on the basis of the notion of *telos* involved in the completeness. One kind of *ergon* is grasped from the agent's perspective who is engaged in *energeia simpliciter* and the other kind is grasped as an end product towards which a movement is directed.

Energeia is always 'put together' and 'stretched together' in reference to *entelecheia*, where the at-workness and completeness stretch together in terms of *ergon* over time. *To be one in the governing mode* can be detected and confirmed in an *energeia* as a goal from the agent's perspective who is being in virtue of completeness and is at work, say, teaching the knowledge as an *energeia simpliciter*. In order to discern this, it is useful to apply a tense test; 'a man sees and simultaneously has seen' (Θ.6, 1048b23).

4. *Logos, Ergon,* and *Entelecheia* in Aristotle's Account of Soul

Aristotle emphasizes his realist commitments about *logos* as a nature by appealing to the complementarity between the *logos* concerning what a thing *is* universally and the *ergon* concerning how a thing *is* at work. While the form is 'separate [from matter] in terms of *logos* alone' in its definition, it is at work through its relevant matter (see *DA* 2.2, 413b14, *Met.* H.2, 1042a29). In terms of *ergon*, the form is not separate from the matter. As Aristotle says: 'In all instances of coming-to-be, the matter is non-separate (*achōriston*), being numerically identical and one, though not one in terms of account' (*GC* 1.5, 320b12–4). When the matter loses the potentiality to maintain the form, the unified whole (*sunholon*) is dissolved (*luetai*) (1.10, 328a27). The form itself as a *logos*, however, does not suffer from the process of extinction. In the case of a human, severing the soul from the body in terms of *ergon* brings about its death: 'the ensouled body (*emphsuchon*) is distinguished from the soulless body in virtue of living (*tō(i) zēn*)' (*DA* 2.2, 413a21). Dead or alive is confirmed by observation.

In *De Anima* 2.1, the apparent tension between separability of soul in terms of account and its non-separateness in terms of *ergon* is resolved by introducing the concept of completeness. He achieves this result by sorting out and connecting two contexts in which *entelecheia* is found: in his definition of what the soul is and on the basis of an analogical grasp of how it is at work (412a5, 413a9).

As a first step, Aristotle prepares for a modal definition of the soul by referring to the causal role of 'substance as the form', which is separated from the body in terms of account: 'it is necessary for the soul to be the substance as form of a natural body *having* life in potentiality' (412a27–8), where '*having* life' taken universally is built into the account of a natural body in potentiality with respect to living here and now.

Given that this is primarily applied to the nutritive soul as the principle of life, the next step is to carry out the organic interpretation of the natural body so as to gain 'a commonest (*koinotatos*) account' of the soul including its 'perceptive' and 'intellectual' parts (412a5). Thus, his comprehensive modal definition is that 'the

316 KEI CHIBA

soul is the first completeness of a natural body having life in potentiality. This sort of body may be organic' (412a27–8; see 2.4, 416a4–6). The soul is picked out as 'the first completeness' when separated from 'the natural body' in terms of an *account* (although it is an important issue whether the soul 'is separate in terms of *account* alone' or has some part separate 'in terms of place' too: 2.2, 413b15).

An analogical understanding of organs is stated 'according to their functions (*ergois*)': for example, 'the root is analogous to the mouth' (2.1, 412b3). Organs are governed by their bearer: this is the living thing that is being in virtue of completeness such that the at-workness of the organ is ready at any time as the stand-by potentiality. Given the link afforded by his idea of 'completeness', 'it is unnecessary to seek if the soul and body are one' (412b6). Insofar as the composite is at work living for a certain duration of time, this is because it is being in virtue of completeness: to be one in the governing mode. Soul's being at work is confirmed both by its *logos* and by observing its sensible work (*ergon*; see *Met.* Z.10, 1035b13, H.2, 1042b10).

Since 'it has now been said universally what the soul is', the third step in the account is aimed at overcoming the problem of homonymy in applying the word 'soul' to both the living and the dead body (*DA*.2.1, 412b10). By taking a counterfactual example of an artefact (an axe) Aristotle argues that there is no homonymy in the case of artefacts. There is no internal relationship between the artefact and its essence, because its essence 'to be axe' is imposed from outside on its matter by its maker and user. Even if one removes the substance of the axe, 'it is now an axe [after all]' (412b15).

On the other hand, if the soul of Socrates were severed from his body in terms of *ergon*, he wouldn't be called by the same name 'except homonymously' (412b11). What remains should be called a 'corpse' (*Met.* H.5, 1044b36). By considering this homonymy principle, Aristotle concludes that the soul must be described as holding an internal relation with its body such that 'the soul is the essence and the account *of* a natural body of such a [organic] sort *having* in itself the principle of movement and rest' (*DA*.2.1, 412b16–7).

Aristotle overcomes the homonymous understanding of 'soul' by making an *ergon* turn: 'Then we must grasp the part of the body in relation to the whole *living* (*zōntos*) body' (412b22–3). On the presupposition that the nutritive soul is basic and is being at work by making the whole body alive, any part of soul is grasped here and now by its *energeia*. This is the only way to avoid homonymy and to make the analogical grasp of the soul's various works inevitable.

4.1 The Bearer of the Soul and Its Parts Being At-Work

Aristotle goes on to discuss how the 'soul' as the object of definition is the same soul that is particularly at work by appealing to the completeness of *logos* that governs the soul's at-workness with respect to its goal. He first allocates living things analogically into *energeia* and *dunamis*. Aristotle claims that 'it is not the body that has lost the soul, but the one *having* (*echon*) it that is in [stand-by] potentiality so as to live (*hōste zēn*)' (412b22–6). The immediate connection between 'having the soul' and 'living' is expressed by the resultant conjunctive (*hōste zēn*: 'so as to live'), if nothing external hinders (see 'simultaneously': *Met.* Z.10, 1035b25). *Having* the basic soul does not guarantee that the relevant body is simultaneously *living*, because something external such as a natural disaster or murder may prevent it from living at this very moment. Therefore, it is legitimate to allocate the natural body '*having* life' and '*having* the soul' in a stand-by potentiality to live. Thus 'having soul' in contrast with 'living', which is just the matter of observation, is allocated to the potentiality in terms of the account.

Aristotle confirms that the second context of completeness is found through the analogical analyses of parts of body and the whole body: 'consequently, on the one hand, just as the cutting and the seeing are, the waking is also completeness *in this way* (*houtō*); on the other hand, just as the sight and the [stand-by] potentiality of the instrument [tooth] are, the soul is [completeness]. But the body is the thing being in virtue of potentiality' (*DA* 2.1, 412b28–413a2). The parallelism between part and whole is expressed by 'just as … in this way'. The phrase 'in this way' indicates a way of mediation by 'the whole living body (*zōntos*)', with respect to which its part is taken to be potentiality in the sense that having the *logos* of tooth itself does not guarantee its being at work (412b23). In the same way, the whole living body in virtue of its nutritive soul being at work is taken to be stand-by potentiality with respect to its being at work of waking, just as having knowledge without contemplating. In this way the second context of completeness is analogically confirmed for a certain period of time, during which the *energeia simpliciter* is observed.

4.2 Final Remarks on the *Logos* and *Ergon* Initiatives

We have discussed how *logos* and *ergon* cooperate by making clear how *logos* involves its relevant works and how the works that are observed are built into the definition. The efficient cause, which is being in virtue of completeness, transmits the form as a *logos* to the patient by making the patient move towards the goal. It is for the sake of this goal that the patient, together with its movement towards a goal, is governed over time in terms of *ergon* and defined in terms of *logos*.

On the basis of his realism about *logos* as a nature (*phusis*), Aristotle employs different but related terms depending on which initiative he is following, sometimes speaking of non-sensible form and 'the for the sake of which', which are revealed in definitions, while elsewhere using inductive observations that reveal how the shape is at work and how the goal is achieved. Thus the relevant works must be built into the unified accounts of the non-sensible entities. 'The most difficult entity'—that is, form—is investigated by these two routes (*Met.* Z.3,1029a34).

These two groups of terms are closely interrelated and mutually complementary but are not synonyms. Thus within the *logos* initiative, 'form' (*eidos*) as 'the substance according to the account' corresponds to, and complements, 'shape' (*morphē*), as 'the substance being at-work (*tēn hōs energeian ousian*)' within the *ergon* initiative (and vice versa; Z.10, 1035b15, H.2, 1042b10). Since both form and shape are referred to by one linguistic expression ('this'), the name 'Socrates' signifies both the composite and his soul, insofar as he is living (Z.11, 1037a7–8; see also H.3, 1043b2–4). When 'form' and 'shape' are juxtaposed by the conjunction 'and', form and shape complement each other.[22]

Likewise, 'in the things of which there is some goal (*telos*), what precedes and what succeeds are done for the sake of that [goal] (*toutou heneka*)', while ' "the for the sake of which (*to hou heneka*)" is in the account' in virtue of which the goal of an *ergon*, say, building is realized here and now (*Phys.* 2.8, 199a8, 2.9, 200a14, 32–4). Insofar as the goal and the agent as the efficient cause share the same *logos*, they must both be in virtue of completeness.

Conclusion

Aristotle's modal ontology offers a comprehensive understanding of things that are and are becoming *qua* being. Within the *logos* initiative, the pair *dunamis* and *entelecheia* corresponds to, and complements, the pair *dunamis* and *energeia* within the *ergon* initiative (and vice versa). While potentiality and completeness are components of the modal definition of entities such as soul and movement, potentiality and at-workness are the components of particular things at work here and now when seen from the *ergon* perspective.

Works Cited

Beere, Jonathan. 2009. *Doing and Being: An Interpretation of Aristotle's* Metaphysics Theta. Oxford University Press.

Bonitz, Hermann. 1849 (1992). *Commentarius in Aristotelis Metaphysicam*. Georg Olms Verlag.

Charles, David. 2000. *Aristotle on Meaning and Essence*. Clarendon Press.

Frede, Michael. 1994. 'Aristotle's Notion of Potentiality in *Metaphysics* Θ', in *Unity, Identity, and Explanation in Aristotle's* Metaphysics (ed. T. Scaltsas, D. Charles, and M. L. Gill). Clarendon Press, 173–94.

---

[22] See, e.g., *GC* 2.9, 335b7, *DA* 2.1, 412a8, *Phys.* 2.1, 193a30, *GA* 2.1, 734a33, *Met.* H.1, 1042a28.

Heinze, Richard. 1899. *Themistii in Aristotelia Libros de Anima Paraphrasis*. Reimer.

Kosman, L. A. 1984. 'Substance, Being, and *Energeia*', *Oxford Studies in Ancient Philosophy* 2, 121–49.

Makin, S. 2006. *Aristotle Metaphysics Book* Θ. Translated with an introduction and commentary. Clarendon Press.

Smyth, Hebert Weir. 1956. *Greek Grammar*. Revised by Gordon M. Messing. Harvard University Press.

14

How Aristotle Understands Change

A Reading of *Physics* 3.1–3

Frank A. Lewis

Introduction

In the first three chapters of *Physics* 3, Aristotle continues the project begun in *Physics* 2 of explicating notions fundamental to work in natural philosophy. In book 2, he explains what it takes to be a *natural* object (as opposed to an artefact), and the different kinds of *causes* (*aitiai*) best suited to our understanding of objects of this kind. The first sentence of book 3 recalls this background, and lists a range of topics—the nature of change itself, the infinite (since change is continuous), place, void, and time—central to a world of changing natural objects. Work on these topics, begun in book 3, is completed in book 4; and each 'requires treatment in advance' (*skepteon prokheirisamenois*, is 'preliminary to further inquiry'; Hussey's translation), for the consideration of special features (*tōn idiōn*) is subsequent to that of what is common (*tōn koinōn*), 200b22–5.

The discussion of *kinēsis*—'change', as I will call it (n. 1 below)—begins in 3.1, where Aristotle sets out the different capacities, active and passive, constitutive of change—'what is capable of producing change and what is capable of being changed' (*to kinētikon te kai kinēton*, 200b31, see also 202a26–7)—and the *entelecheia* (the 'actuality'? 'actualization'?) of each.[1] The reference to potentiality and actuality in these lines signals a significant elaboration of the notion familiar from the *Categories* and *Physics* 1. In these latter texts, Aristotle contrasts an earlier state of an underlying subject characterized by one contrary, and a later state of that same subject characterized by a different contrary: a man now unaware that P, now knowing full-well

---

[1] Aristotle's *kinēsis*, sometimes his term for just motion in place, in these chapters has a wider meaning and is standardly translated 'change' (as in my title and in the main text above), but can also bear the translation, 'process', or even (to avoid prejudicing the extension of the term) '*change*', as in Charles 2015. Meanwhile, Aristotle's term *entelecheia* is rendered in some accounts by 'actuality', in others, by 'actualization' or even 'actualizing'. Later in these chapters, Aristotle himself switches to the term *energeia*, usually translated 'activity'. The difficulties in establishing a firm reading of these terms in the present context are discussed in Kostman 1987 and Anagnostopoulos 2010. Another term that requires attention is Aristotle's *dunamis*, variably 'power' or 'potentiality' (Code 2003), where the latter term supplies the adverbial use, 'potentially', that the former lacks, and which Aristotle's frequent dative, *dunamei*, requires.

Frank A. Lewis, *How Aristotle Understands Change: A Reading of* Physics *3.1–3* In: *Aristotelian Metaphysics: Essays in Honour of David Charles.* Edited by: David Bronstein, Thomas Kjeller Johansen, and Michail Peramatzis, Oxford University Press.
© Oxford University Press 2024. DOI: 10.1093/oso/9780198908678.003.0014

HOW ARISTOTLE UNDERSTANDS CHANGE   321

that P (say), where canonically at least the change is due to the action of an efficient cause in the person of the teacher. As understood in *Physics* 3, by contrast, the change in a thing from one state to another is no less than *the joint manifestation of two matching powers or potentialities*—as when the teacher has the active power to teach the learner that P, the learner has the passive power to learn from the teacher that P, and the two powers are jointly manifested as the learner comes to know that P.

In other respects, Aristotle's approach in these chapters is traditional in form, if not in content. From the very beginning, the debt to the *Organon* is to the fore. As elsewhere, the theory of categories underpins the four modes of change he takes as his target in these chapters. At the same time, as in *Physics* 1 and 2, and in accordance with his renewed warnings in *Phys.* 3.1, 200b22–5, the discussion in all three chapters employs modes of reasoning typical of dialectic: in *Phys.* 3.1, at 200b28–32, a reference to the notion from the *Categories* of 'relatives that reciprocate', which play a major role in the argument of *Physics* 3.3;[2] and *reductio* arguments using rules of inference from the *Topics* and *Posterior Analytics*, designed to explain, albeit tangentially, the use of *qua*-expressions in the account of change (change is 'the actuality of that which potentially is, *qua* such'; 201a10–11); in *Physics* 3.2, a review of previous reputable opinions on change; and in *Physics* 3.3, a constellation of puzzles of varying force, collected under the title, *aporia logikē*,[3] and arranged in the form of a dilemma.

The puzzles, together with their resolution, in part by means of an argument by analogy,[4] are used first to settle the 'puzzling' but evident point that the activities that jointly comprise a change are located in what is being acted on, rather than in what is acting on it: for example, the activity of the teacher is located, not in him, but in the learner. Because this account assumes the analysis of change in terms of the activities of agent and patient, Aristotle will eventually migrate (in two obscure and contested lines at 202b20–1) from the location of a change to his announced topic, which is the analysis of change itself.

In pursuit of these conclusions, Aristotle adapts Heraclitus's example of the road up and the road down, and adds the road between the two destinations, to form one side of an analogy, on the second side of which appear the activities of the teacher and of the learner and the change that is the learner's coming to know a certain item of knowledge. As a first step in the analogy, we suppose that just as the road up to Thebes is paired with the road down to Athens (say), so a given episode of the teacher's teaching the learner that P is paired with the learner's learning from [being taught by] the teacher that P. The pairing is aided by the fact that 'heading up' and

---

[2] See n. 39 and surrounding main text, with sections 3.7 and 3.5.

[3] *aporia logikē*: 'a dialectical difficulty', Revised Oxford Translation, see n. 24 below. For helpful discussion of Aristotle's term *logikos* and cognates, see Burnyeat 2001, 19–25.

[4] Analogy is another procedure with roots in the *Organon*; see *Top.* 1.7, 108a7–12, 5.8, 138b24, with n. 40 below. The example of the road up and the road down is as old as Heraclitus DK B60. In Aristotle's hands, Heraclitus's roads sometimes become the road to Athens and the road to Thebes: the shift may be an insider's joke—Athens is, of course, a coastal city, while Thebes is some 700 feet above mean sea level.

322   FRANK A. LEWIS

'heading down' and the activities of teaching and learning are 'relatives that reciprocate': on this view, the road up exists just in case the corresponding road down also
exists; and the teacher teaches this student that P just in case the student also learns
that P from the teacher.[5] It is also important that, contrary to many readings,
Aristotle does not take a 'projectivist' view of Heraclitus's roads, reflecting only different ways of talking or thinking about a thing, without there being any difference
between individuals in the real order. With no restrictions on how one thinks of the
roads, the example cannot illustrate the structuring that both sides of Aristotle's
analogy require, both internally and across its two sides. Contrary to projectivist
accounts, on the view adopted here the roads example involves relations of
sameness—strict sameness in some cases, less-than-strict sameness in others—
among real entities. In particular, in accidental compound theory (ACT), the road
up—that is to say, R + up—is *accidentally the same* as the underlying road, R, and R +
down too is accidentally the same as R; and because each singly is accidentally the
same [no asterisk] as the underlying road, R, it follows that the two roads, R + up
and R + down, are *accidentally the same** as each other.[6] The different sameness
relations help give structure to the one side of Aristotle's analogy. They also help
promote the account of change on the other side of the analogy, where the teacher's
power or capacity to teach the student that P and the student's power or capacity to
learn that P from the teacher are both directed at the same goal: namely, the change
as the student newly comes to know that P. In the end, the various relations among
the roads are not fully replicated on the second side of his analogy, where the full
story about change is centred around the role of teleology, already signalled in
Physics 3.2. The powers to teach and to learn are *for* the *energeiai* that together constitute the target change. On this view, the teleological character of the powers to
teach and to learn gives structure to the second side of Aristotle's analogy, matching
the use of ACT to yield the arrangement of the three roads on the first side.

Finally, Aristotle's is a 'two-constituent' analysis of change, in which the activities of teaching and learning combine in the change that is the learner's coming
to know what he is being taught.

Aristotle's writing in these chapters is typically dense, but also quite carefully
structured, and my reading follows the order of his account.

1. *Physics* 3.1: An Initial Account

Aristotle begins his account of change with the distinction between being potentially and being actually,[7] which applies across the board, within all the categories.

---

[5] For relatives that reciprocate, see n. 2 above.
[6] I discuss the different relations of so-called accidental sameness in more detail in the introduction to section 3 and in section 3.5.
[7] *To men entelecheia(i) monon* [= the unchangeable, Ross 1936, 535], *to de dunamei kai entelecheia(i)*,
200b26–7, see also 201a9–10.

HOW ARISTOTLE UNDERSTANDS CHANGE   323

But the larger list of categories is kept in the background, and just four categories line up with four basic kinds of change. Each of the four chosen categories yields pairs of polar contraries present in things: in the category of substance, the form vs. the privation; in quality, white vs. black; in quantity, complete vs. incomplete; and in place, above vs. below, light vs. heavy. These four basic modes of change are swept together in the general account of change in terms of the distinction between potentiality and actuality:

> The actuality of that which potentially is (*hē tou dunamei ontos entelecheia*), *qua* such, is change. (201a10–11. Translations are my own, unless otherwise noted. I use angular brackets to indicate words I take to be implied by the text and square brackets to indicate explanations of the text.)

Aristotle will know that this bare statement can hardly pose as a *definition* of change, with the terms 'potentially' and 'actuality' left undefined (or at the least not agreed),[8] not to mention the obscurity of the attached '*qua*' locution. He goes on immediately to offer help on both fronts.

Aristotle tackles first the intent of a10–11 as a whole—not, however, with definitions of its constituent terms, but by expanding the circle of terms in play.[9] He unpacks a10–11 in terms of the four basic modes of change already noted:

> The actuality of what can change in quality (*tou... alloiōtou*), *qua* changeable in quality, is qualitative change (*alloiōsis*);
>
> the actuality of what can grow or decline, *qua* capable of growing or declining, is growth or decline;
>
> the actuality of what can come to be or can perish, *qua* capable of coming to be or perishing, is coming to be or perishing;
>
> the actuality of what can move in place, *qua* capable of moving in place, is movement in place (locomotion). (201a11–15)

And by way of yet further explanation, he adds some examples: the buildable and its being built ('the process of building', Hussey), learning, healing, and more.

The review of both the various modes of change and the concrete examples may help a10–11 pass as a definition after all, given the effort to make the defining terms there 'agreed', even though they are not themselves defined. (For the claim that he has defined change, see the closing summary at *Phys.* 3.3, 202b23–9, and Kostman 1987, 11.)

---

[8] *Top.* 6.4, 142a33–b6, 9, 147b12–20; see also Plato, *Meno*, 75c ff.

[9] Coope 2009, Charles 2015, and for a similar case in the *Metaphysics*, Peramatzis 2010, 166–8, and Lewis 2013, 73–4. As Charles points out, 'widening the circle' can be an appropriate answer to circularity objections sometimes levelled against Aristotle's views.

324 FRANK A. LEWIS

Later, at 201a27, Aristotle repeats his account of change at a10–11, and goes on to explain his use of '*qua*' expressions in his account:

> The actuality of what is potentially—whenever being in actuality it is operating not *qua* itself, but *qua* changeable (*hotan entelecheia(i) on energēi oukh hēi auto all' hēi kinēton*)—is change (*kinēsis*). I mean '*qua*' thus: the bronze is potentially a statue, but yet it is not the actuality of bronze *qua* bronze that is change. For it is not the same thing to be bronze and to be potentially something. (201a27–32; after Hussey's translation)

For example, suppose a given parcel of bronze is potentially a statue. Then whenever that very potentiality in the bronze is being exercised—when the bronze is acting not *qua* itself, bronze, but *qua* its potentiality for being a statue[10]—*that* is change. Against this, suppose that there is no distinction such as the *qua* clause is intended to capture. Thus,

1	1. being potentially a statue = being potentially bronze	(Assumption)
1	2. being a statue = being bronze	(Taking equals from equals in 1)
3	3. the bronze is potentially a statue	(Assumption)
1, 3	4. the bronze is potentially bronze	(Putting equals for equals in 3)
1, 3	5. the actuality of the bronze, *qua* bronze, is change	(from 4, by Aristotle's definition of change)
3	6. being potentially a statue ≠ being potentially bronze	(*Reductio ad impossibile* in 5)

According to 5, change is present when the bronze realizes its potential for being bronze. The negation of 1 in 6 follows by *reductio ad impossibile*, given only the assumption in 3 that the bronze is potentially a statue, the definition of change as the actuality of the potential *qua* potential (201b4), and the misapplication of that definition in 5. Meanwhile, the larger moral, as predicted, is that being an underlying subject (e.g., bronze) is not the same as that subject's being potentially something.[11,12]

---

[10] 'its potentiality for being a statue'—see n. 13 below.

[11] As to the roots of the argument in the *Organon*, for *reductio ad impossibile*, see *APr.* 1.23, 41a21ff., 1.44, 50a19–28 (the example of health and disease appears here as well as in *Physics* 3.1), with 1.29 and 2.11–14. For the rule that taking equals from equals leaves equals, and its counterpart for adding equals to equals, see *Top.* 7.2, 152b10–16.

[12] Aristotle adds that the point is clear in the case of contraries. He begins with much the same moves as in the primary argument. In brief: being potentially healthy ≠ being potentially sick—were it otherwise, then (taking equals from equals) being healthy would = being sick. 'But', Aristotle concludes, 'the underlying subject, that which is healthy and that which is diseased, be it moisture or blood, is one and the same' (201b2–3; Hussey's translation). In line with this, say that Archimedes + healthy ≠ Archimedes + diseased; but that Archimedes is one and the same throughout. So it is not the case that being healthy = being sick, and so also is not the case that being potentially healthy = being

HOW ARISTOTLE UNDERSTANDS CHANGE   325

The route from the proof of the previous paragraph to an explanation of Aristotle's use of '*qua*' is not obvious. At the least, in the example of the bronze the expression serves to steer us away from one single *occurrent* property of the subject— the fact about the bronze that it is bronze. Arguably, we are directed instead to a *non-occurrent* property: namely, the potentiality in the bronze for the property that will be occurrent once the change has taken place.[13]

As to the subject's occurrent properties before the change gets under way, Aristotle's argument from contraries suggests that they will include a property contrary to the property that results from the change.[14] So, for example, while presently healthy, I have the potential for being sick, which is realized when I later am sick. But there is a need for caution. My illness fulfils the initial potential, only providing the later illness and the initial potential *match*. My potential for having a headache, for example, is not fulfilled by my contracting a cold. In a given change, then, the initial potential and the final actuality must both be *for the same outcome*. The potentiality is for being a statue, or for being sick; and these very outcomes constitute the corresponding actuality. So to the question 'does the *qua* clause modify the potential or the actuality?' the answer is: (in a way) both.[15]

In the closing section of the chapter beginning at 201b5, Aristotle pronounces himself satisfied with his account of change and, perhaps unexpectedly, adds a comment about the *duration* of change and the corresponding actuality: the one occurs whenever—and neither later nor sooner than—the other does. His purpose is to reinforce the correct construal of the phrase, 'the actuality (*energeia*) of the buildable (say), *qua* buildable', and the like in different examples of the account of change.[16] The difficulty is that the *energeia* (the 'realization') of the buildable *qua* buildable may be (in our terms) *either* the different stages in the structure's

---

potentially sick. This in turn clears the way for the correct application of Aristotle's proposed definition of change.

[13] Regarding the nature of the *dunamis* involved in Aristotle's account of change, many (but not all) interpretations fall into one of two camps: on the one side, it is the *dunamis* in the bronze for *becoming* a statue, on the other, the potentiality for *being* a statue. (For discussion of the different uses of *dunamis* in these two claims, see Code 2003.) On the first, 'process' view, defended in Penner 1970, Kostman 1987, and most recently, Charles 2015, Aristotle explains change in terms of the potential for the very process that is change. On the second, 'actuality' view in Kosman 1969 and (perhaps) the majority of later writers, the change is the process by which the potentiality for the end-product is realized. I do not try to adjudicate between these views here, but for consistency's sake and (I hope) without prejudice, I adopt the language of the second.

[14] The role of contraries in the different kinds of change is to the fore also in the summary at *GC* 1.4, 319b31–320a2, where the apparatus of *dunamis* and *energeia* distinctive of the treatment in *Physics* 3 does not appear.

[15] Scholars assign the *qua*-clause variously to modify the potentiality or the actuality: Aristotle himself appears to attach the clause indifferently to each, 201a10–11, 16–17, 27–8. For help in avoiding some of the complexities some of his commentators have found in Aristotle's *qua*-clause, see Anagnostopoulos 2010, n. 27 and throughout, especially his ##2(d) and 3(c).

[16] 'The *energeia* of the buildable, *qua* buildable, is *the act of building* (*oikodomēsis*)', b9–10, see also 201a16–18 (where the earlier term, *entelecheia*, appears). At b10–11, Aristotle suggests that the problem is a simple ambiguity in the term *energeia*, but the modal, 'build*able*', is also open to different interpretations.

326   FRANK A. LEWIS

being built—the *process*—or the resulting structure—the *product*. Which of these readings is meant is settled by noting that any change *runs concurrently* with the corresponding *energeia*. This condition is satisfied by *energeia* as process, which runs step by step with the change, but not at all by *energeia* understood as the product. The structure or product properly speaking exists only when it is 'built out'—when there is no more building to be done.

Aristotle's remarks to this point constitute his account of change, which he buttresses, first, in *Physics* 3.2, by way of comparisons with the views of his predecessors on the same subject; and second, in *Physics* 3.3, with an extensive puzzle against which to test his account. The result will also be to fill in some details in the initial account.

2. *Physics* 3.2: Connecting with the Tradition

In *Physics* 3.2, Aristotle sets his own views outlined in *Physics* 3.1 against the troubles his predecessors found in characterizing change. Much of the difficulty lies in the peculiar nature of change as what appears to be an *energeia*, but an *energeia* that is *incomplete*, because the corresponding *potential* (*to dunaton*) is incomplete. Speculatively, the *qua*-clause that appears in Aristotle's account of change[17] invites attention to the *respect* in which the potential is incomplete. Aristotle addresses precisely how it is incomplete a few lines later at 202a9–12 with the reference to the form which the agent 'carries' into the change, and which is 'the principle of, and responsible for, the change (*archē kai aition tēs kinēseōs*)'.[18] He connects the transmission of form with the point that what produces change (in the ordinary case) makes *contact* with what it changes, with the result that it is itself *reciprocally changed*. The transmission of form is also Aristotle's guarantee that the potentiality in a given change is *incomplete* and in this way *for* the very actuality that is the result of the change.[19]

---

[17] Repeated at 202a5–6, 'to operate on this [the changeable], *qua* such [namely, changeable], is just what it is to produce change'.

[18] Charles 2015 connects the incompleteness of change with the 'imperfective paradox', according to which a thing as it changes has *not yet* achieved the target form. Aristotle himself explains that changes, *kinēseis*, housebuilding (say), or walking from A to B, are incomplete because the end—the finished house, arriving at B—is *not yet* achieved so long as the change is taking place, in contrast to *energeiai*, 'activities', which are complete and, once begun, are ongoing with no goal yet to be realized, *Met.* Θ.6, 1048b28–35. In the former case, the target form is present, only when the change is (satisfactorily) over, *GC* 1.7, 324b13–18; see also *DA* 2.5, 417a16, 3.7, 431a6–7, and *NE* 10.4, 1174a19–b5. For incompleteness, see also n. 54 below and Hussey 1983, xiv.

[19] On the account offered in the main text and in section 1 above, in Aristotle's '*qua*-so-and-so', the 'so-and-so' is a place-holder for the relevant feature the potentiality for which is constitutive of the particular change in question. Arguably, Aristotle's list of the different modes of change and concrete examples at 201a11–19 (section 1 above) indicates how the different *qua*-clauses zero in on the feature that is the *terminus ad quem* of the change in question. In this same vein, Polycleitus accidentally (*kata sumbebēkos*) sculpts—Polycleitus is the sculptor, and properly speaking—flagging the capacity

3. *Physics* 3. 3: The 'Logical Puzzle', Some Solutions, and the Analogy

Aristotle's opening remarks in the final chapter, *Physics* 3.3, in the account of change set up the puzzle that drives the remainder of the chapter save for the summaries at the end. He begins with a point that is both puzzling and (he says) clear (202a13–14): the change is *located in the thing liable to be changed*, on the grounds that the change is the actuality of what is liable to be changed at the hands of what is capable of bringing about the change.[20] Arguably, he thinks that the location of the change is settled, if we can settle the location of the active and passive actualities that together make it up. Little argument is needed to show that the location of the actuality of what is liable to be changed is in the very object liable to be changed; and if the change is made up of the realizations of the appropriate active and passive potentialities together, presumably both realizations, and with them the change itself, are located in the same place: namely, in the thing that is undergoing the change.

At 202a15–21, Aristotle goes on to support this conclusion with an analogy with the road that runs uphill to Thebes, the road downhill to Athens, and the road between the two cities. He introduces his analogy by unpacking what it means for that which can produce change (*to kinētikon*) to have an actuality. Both what can produce change and what is liable to be changed have an actuality; what can produce change is so thanks to its *capacity* to do so (*tō(i) dunasthai*), and it in fact produces change thanks to its *activity* (*tō(i) energein*); and it *brings about activity* (*energētikon*) on the part of what can be made to change. In short,

> the activity of both [= of what can bring about change and of what can be made to so change] is <u>in the same way</u> one (*homoiōs mia hē amphoin energeia*, a18), <u>just as</u> (*hōsper*) one to two and two to one are the same interval,[21] and also the uphill and the downhill, for these are one even though their definition is not one. (202a18–20)

Aristotle's *homoiōs...*, *hōsper...* constitutes his direct statement of the analogy he develops later in the chapter. In the case of the roads, a single road R runs between Thebes and Athens, while R + up is the road to Thebes and R + down is the road to Athens. I represent the latter two roads as accidental compounds: for further

---

responsible for the product—the sculptor built the statue, *Phys.* 2.3, 195a32–b12. Or again, the doctor builds a house not *qua* doctor (and not *qua* amateur painter or *qua* family man) but *qua* housebuilder—the art of housebuilding, or the relevant form, is the true, non-accidental cause of his actions, *Phys.* 1.8, 191b4–10. For Polycleitus and the doctor, see Lewis 1991, ch. 9, #3, and for the application to the account of change, Anagnostopoulos 2010, 46, 50, and throughout.

[20] *entelecheia gar esti toutou* [= *tō(i) kinētō(i)*, a14] *hupo tou kinētikou*, 202a14; see also b26–7.

[21] For the examples of one to two and two to one, see Marmodoro 2014, 58, with her n. 65.

328   FRANK A. LEWIS

examples, consider pale Socrates (= Socrates + pale), or Socrates in the market-place (= Socrates + in the marketplace).[22] Now, Socrates is accidentally the same as Socrates + pale, while Socrates is also accidentally the same as Socrates in the marketplace; accordingly (thanks to the role of Socrates as shared 'root' entity in the two compounds), Socrates + pale and Socrates + in the marketplace are *accidentally the same** as each other. On this basis, the two roads, R + up and R + down, too are (accidentally) the same* *as each other*, 'even though their definition is not one', in that they share the identical underlying road, R, and the location of R and that of both remaining roads is the same.

Similarly, Aristotle claims (202a18 above), the activity of what can bring about change and the activity of what can be so changed are one (*homoiōs mia hē amphoin energeia*); if so, and if the actuality of what is liable to be changed is located in the patient, then arguably the two actualities, active and passive alike, are located in the same place, in the patient.[23] And if the change is made up of just these two, then the change itself is located in the patient—in the thing liable to be changed—as claimed in the opening lines of *Physics* 3.3.

The results collected here—that the two activities are in a certain way the same, and located together in the patient—are major topics in the complex puzzle that follows. It is noteworthy, however, that the demonstration that the two activities, and hence the change, are alike present in the patient presupposes that we already know the constitution of the change from the two activities. In later lines of *Physics* 3.3, Aristotle has in mind a further application of his analogy, in addition to the location of the activities that constitute a change, to address the very constitution of the change from those same ingredients.

3.1 The 'Logical Puzzle'

From here on, the entirety of *Physics* 3.3 save for a closing summary is taken up with what Aristotle calls a 'logical puzzle' (*aporian logikēn*, 202a21–2).[24] The puzzle takes its start from the puzzling point from the opening lines of the chapter

---

[22] The '+' notation is borrowed from accidental compound theory (ACT), where it indicates the compound of one entity with another; associations that the notation may have in other contexts should be disregarded. For accidental compounds and ACT, see n. 44 below and surrounding main text in section 3.5.

[23] To modern eyes the inference may seem to be an application of Leibniz's Law, but Aristotle is clear that the two activities 'are one but not the same in being', 202a20 (for why this variety of sameness is too weak to validate 'putting equals for equals', see 202b10–16 with *SE* 24, 179a26–b7, and n. 31 with surrounding main text and (ii′) with n. 47 below). The activities may, however, be (in a way) the same as each other, as the two roads, R + up and R + down, are (in a different way) the same in virtue of their common 'root' entity, R (see the previous paragraph in the main text). I say more about the different kinds of sameness at work here in section 3.5.

[24] Aristotle's term 'logical' here is in tune with the generally 'dialectical' tone of these chapters; n. 3 above.

HOW ARISTOTLE UNDERSTANDS CHANGE   329

and its aftermath noted above: the location of a given change in the thing that is being acted on, and various issues of sameness between what brings about the change and what is being changed. The different parts of the puzzle lead to a variety of negative conclusions not all of which are in the end compelling; but putting them to rest allows Aristotle to suggest some positive conclusions—not the least of which in the cryptic lines at 202b19–22 arguably concerns the prior question of the composition of a change from matching active and passive actualities.

Aristotle begins (202a22–4) by connecting a divide in the notion of an actuality (*energeia*) with similar divides in a wider range of terms. There must, it seems, be an actuality both for what is capable of acting and for what is capable of being acted on (*tou poiētikou kai tou pathētikou*); the one is an acting-on (*poiēsis*) and the other a being-acted-on-by (*pathēsis*); while the 'work and end-point' (*ergon de kai telos*) of the one is an action (*poiēma*) and of the other a passion (*pathos*). Finally, (a25), we come to the starting-point of the puzzle proper: both of these— the acting-on and the being-acted-on-by—will count as changes (*kinēseis*).[25]

The ensuing puzzle comprises one large dilemma about change and changes; one side leads to a second dilemma, while the other side presses two coordinate objections. The larger dilemma: are the changes noted (the *poiēsis* and the *pathēsis* from a23–4) different—*two* distinct changes?—or just *one*? If they are *two*—the smaller dilemma—are they distributed the first in the agent the second in the patient, or are both present in just one of these? There are difficulties on either choice. And if instead they are *one*, two coordinate objections await.

3.2 The Difficulties Aristotle Sees

As to the difficulties Aristotle sees: if the *poiēsis* and the *pathēsis*—the acting-on and the being-acted-on-by—are both changes (*epei oun amphō kinēseis*, 202a25), and these are *two* changes, the acting-on *distributed* in the agent, the being-acted-on-by in the patient, then the change (*hē kinēsis*) will belong also to what brings about the change.[26] It then follows that either everything that moves another is

---

[25] Aristotle's use of the term *kinēsis*, 'change', for these two—by earlier standards, both activities constitutive of a change—is anomalous; see n. 26 below.

[26] Aristotle introduces his first two puzzles at 202a25 with the hypothesis that the activities constitutive of a given change are themselves changes, and writes indifferently of *changes* (202a25) and of *activities*; the hypothesis is suddenly dropped at a36. He does not explain how, having analysed the constituent activities in a given change as themselves changes, he is not obliged to analyse these changes too in terms of yet further activities, and so on ad nauseam. The official view in these chapters is that activities are the exercise of the active and passive potentials in the agent and patient and (not themselves changes, but) jointly constitutive of change, as on the more generally favoured reading of 202b20–1, cited as (iii´) in section 3.6 and discussed in the final paragraphs of this chapter. Aristotle is clear at *DA* 2.5, 417b8–9, that the exercise of the builder's active potential to build is not a change in the builder; similarly, then, for the teacher and the exercise of his active potential to teach the learner. Aristotle reverts to counting activities rather than changes at 202a36.

330   FRANK A. LEWIS

itself moved, or a change is present in something without that thing's moving. If, on the other hand, there are two changes and these are *not* distributed, but found solely in one place, presumably in the thing that is acted on (202a31–6),[27] other difficulties arise. How can the activity of the teacher not be found in him, but elsewhere, in the learner? And it is impossible that there should be two qualitative changes ('alterations') on the part of a single thing headed towards a single form.

Alternatively, we may think that there is just *one* activity (a36–b5).[28] But in this case, how can there be one and the same activity (*tēn autēn kai mian energeian*) of two things that are different in form? And if (a) teaching and learning (*hē didaxis* and *hē mathēsis*), acting-on and being-acted-on-by (*poiēsis* and *pathēsis*), are the same (*to auto*), so that (b) to teach and to learn (*to didaskein* and *to manthanein*), to act and to be acted on by (*to poiein, to paskhein*), too are the same[29]—will it not follow that the teacher learns, and that the one who acts is acted on?

3.3 Aristotle's Solutions

It is not Aristotle's view that these difficulties stand, and in the paragraph at 202b5–22, he sets about unravelling most of them. First (taking up the option that the activities are *two*, but *in the same thing*, namely [Aristotle assumes] in the patient, so that the activity of the teacher is to be found not in the teacher, but in the learner), we have, first, the nice point that the activity of the teacher *can* after all be in the learner, because the operation of teaching 'is *on* something, and not cut off, but is of this on this' (202b5–8).

(Aristotle does not respond to the remaining option, that the activities are again *two*, but *distributed* between agent and patient—so if it is a seat of change, does the agent itself change, or not?—perhaps because in the ordinary case, a mover will always itself be reciprocally moved, as already noted at *Phys.* 3.2, 202a3–9.)

Alternatively, we might suppose that the activities are *one*[30]—how then can there be one activity of two capacities that are themselves different in form? Aristotle's response addresses the use of 'one' or 'same': nothing prevents it that two capacities have one and the same actuality (*mian duoin tēn autēn einai*,

---

[27] See Ross 1936, 540, on 202a25–7 for Aristotle's omission of the alternative that acting and being acted on are both to be found in the agent.

[28] As the sequel will show, the single activity hypothesis collapses almost immediately in favour of the idea that there is in a way one activity (a weaker form of sameness), but in another way two (they are not the same in being).

[29] Aristotle almost immediately at 202b16–22 walks back the suggestion from b2–4 that (b) in the main text follows from (a). The sense in which the teacher's activity of teaching and the learner's activity of learning are the same comes under scrutiny at b19–22: they are not 'strictly the same'. (In fact, they are in a weaker sense the same, in that the two jointly constitute the change that is the learner's coming to know that P.) The sense of 'same' in general is under challenge in section 3.3, n. 32 below. For *didaxis* vs. *didaskein*, see further below.

[30] For qualifications to the dichotomy between one/two activities, see n. 28 above.

HOW ARISTOTLE UNDERSTANDS CHANGE   331

202b8–9; see earlier at a18), provided we do not mean that the first capacity is *the same in being* as the second—else in manifesting the capacity to teach, the teacher would simultaneously learn. Rather, the capacities are the same in the way that what potentially is is related to what is in actuality, 202b9–10: a reference to Aristotle's earlier explanation, which he repeats shortly below at b13–14, in terms of the road up and the road down and the weaker notions of sameness that apply there.[31]

The appeal to different notions of sameness in this last answer serves Aristotle well in his response to the further objection, that on the option (again) that the activities are one, it follows, putting equals for equals, that the teacher learns. The inference fails, 202b10–16, because acting-on and being-acted-on-by are one, not in the way that raiment and clothing are one (the reference is to *Top.* 1.7, 103a25–7), where the being of the two is the same, but rather in the way that the road from Athens to Thebes is the same as that from Thebes to Athens: while there is just one road between the two cities, the road leading (uphill) to Thebes is in only a weak sense the same as the road (downhill) to Athens, so that a principle of 'putting equals for equals' does not apply.[32]

The immediate sequel too (202b16–19) features only a weaker form of sameness, which falls short of sameness in being. Even if the teaching is the same as the learning (*hē didaxis, hē mathēsis*)—even if the token acts are (in a certain way) the same,[33] given their relation to the single change that is the learner's

---

[31] The reference to potentiality and actuality (*hōs huparkhei to dunamei on pros to energoun*, b9–10) recalls the language at the beginning of the chapter (in particular, *kinētikon... tō(i) dunasthai, kinoun tō(i) energein*, 202a16–17), and Aristotle's mention there of the example of the road up and the road down, 202a18–21, which he returns to explicitly at b13–14 (with an acknowledgement of his earlier account, b14). For the reference to potentiality and actuality, see also Marmodoro 2007, 228–30, and the quite different views in Hussey, 1983, 72. As I understand Aristotle, the principles that govern the relation between the road up and the road down and those governing potentiality and actuality are quite different—but (he seems to say, 202b9–10) it is in common to both that the sameness in each pair is not sameness in being, but only a weaker form of sameness. Now, R + up and R + down are accidentally the same* as each other, in virtue of the fact that they are each accidentally the same [no asterisk] as the same underlying road, R (see the introduction to this section, and section 3.5). As to potentiality and actuality: earlier at a15–20, Aristotle mentions the two roads to illustrate the relation, not (i) between potentiality and actuality—a power vs. its manifestation—as at b9–10, but (ii) between 'what can bring about change and what can be so changed'—an active power vs. its passive partner, or agent vs. patient with their respective active and passive powers. The same facts fill out the cases slightly differently. In (i), the first item is (weakly) the same as the second, in that the first is *for*, and is manifested in, the second. In (ii), the items on the two sides of the contrast are (weakly) the same in that they are each *for*, and are jointly manifested in, the same ongoing change. For details, see section 3.7.

[32] 202b14–16, see also *SE* 24, 179a26–b7, with n. 23 above. Aristotle frequently contrasts sameness in being, or sameness in account, with a weaker form of sameness; the label of accidental sameness appears less frequently (and not at all in *Physics* 3.1–3), but see, for example, *Top.* 1.7, 103a29–31, *Met.* Γ.9, 1017b27, Z.6, 1031a22–3, and Z.11, 1037b5–7.

[33] The example of the roads is relevant here. The roads R + up and R + down are accidentally the same* as each other, given that they are each accidentally the same [no asterisk] as the underlying road, R; see the introduction to section 3, and section 3.5. These relations have a counterpart in the different logic appropriate for powers and their manifestations: thus, the act of learning and the act of

332 FRANK A. LEWIS

coming to know that P—<it does not follow that> also 'to learn' <is the same as> 'to teach' (*to manthanein, to didaskein*).[34] Similarly, even if there is a single interval between things distant from each other, <it does not follow that> to extend from the first to the second and < to extend> from the second to the first are one and the same [= the same in being] (202a18–20). And in general, in the single change that is the learner's coming to know that P, neither teaching nor learning, nor acting-on nor being-acted-on-by, are the same in the strict sense (*to auto kuriōs*). By contrast, Aristotle appears to imply, teaching and learning each belong to *strictly the same thing*.[35] But as to teaching and learning themselves, 'to be the *energeia* of this *in* this, and of that *by* that are different in definition' (*heteron tōi logōi*); 202b21–2. I suppose that Aristotle has in mind token activities of teaching and learning, so that on a given occasion we have, located in a given learner,

Teaching. The (present) realizing[36] of this given teacher's active potential to teach this given learner that P[37]

(this is 'the activity of this [= of the active potential on the part of the given teacher] *in* that' [in the patient, the given learner]); and in the learner again,

Learning. The (present) realizing of this given learner's passive potential to learn from (be taught by) this teacher that P

(this is 'the activity of this [of the passive potential in the learner] *due to* that [the activity of the active potential in the teacher]'). While the potentials for teaching and for learning belong to different persons, the activities themselves are lodged together at the same time in the same place: namely, in the passive partner, the learner. Aristotle is crystal clear that the episodes of teaching and learning are '*not strictly the same*', or are '*different in account*'; yet they are *in another way one*,

---

teaching are accidentally the same* as each other, given that they are manifested jointly in the ongoing change that is the learner's coming to know the relevant subject-matter.

[34] The lines at 202b16-17 are especially difficult. For the distinction between teaching and learning on the one side, and 'to teach' and 'to learn' on the other, see Hussey 1983, 69, and Ross 1936, 647, on *Phys.* 6.4, 235a16. And *pace* Charles 2015, 198, I suppose that, as in the parallel passage at 202a18-20 cited in the main text immediately below, the sameness is still not sameness in being.

[35] This last claim, at 202b21, is almost impossibly epigrammatic; I give it closer attention in section 3.8.

[36] 'Realization' may seem more obvious English, but (like Aristotle's *energeia*) it is process–product ambiguous, as 'realizing' is not; Penner 1970. The preferred term, 'realizing', is intended to suggest that the teaching is ongoing—but in a change, not yet finished.

[37] *hen de en amphoin to theōrēma* ('in both cases [= teaching and learning], the object of study is one'), Themistius *In Phys* 78.18, 22–3 (Schenkl). As always in what follows, the teaching and the learning are with respect to one and the same subject-matter, which I abbreviate as 'knowledge that P'. See also Marmodoro 2007, n. 7.

HOW ARISTOTLE UNDERSTANDS CHANGE 333

corresponding to the way in which in Aristotle's analogy the road to Athens and the road to Thebes too are one.[38]

The token activities of teaching and learning are connected in yet another way. Our way of stating the token activities, that Aristotle currently teaches Alexander (say), and that Alexander currently learns from Aristotle, is convenient, but it is not Aristotle's. For Aristotle, teaching and learning are relatives that 'reciprocate' (*ta pros ti pros antistrephonta*, *Cat.* 7, see also *Phys.* 3.1, 200b28–32): the teacher is teacher of the learner, and the learner is learner from the teacher (and the topic taught and learned is one and the same, n. 37 above). Equally, if instead a relative 'is given as related to some chance thing' (*pros to tukhon*, *Cat.* 7, 7a24)—that the teacher is teacher of the man (say), or of Alexander—reciprocity fails. For Alexander may no longer learn: he may no longer have the potential to learn, or he may no longer be exercising it. So the causal connections highlighted by introducing the causally relevant entities—the teacher, the learner—are lost. Similarly, the housebuilder builds the house, but my next-door neighbour does not; the two are accidentally the same, but not identical, and only the first has the potential to build a house.[39]

3.4 The Analogy between the Roads on One Side and Teaching and Learning on the Other

Given the complexities surrounding the different sameness claims in Aristotle's text, it may be worth stating dogmatically here what I take to be the main thrust of his argument. In the body of *Physics* 3.3, Aristotle is busy assembling materials for an argument by analogy, first signalled at 202a18–20 (see the introduction to this section above).[40] It is apparent immediately that his notion of analogy is not ours, in which one thing is compared with another. Rather, one set of items and the relations among them are compared to a second set of items among which the same (or roughly similar) relations obtain; see (under the title, *homoiotēs*) *Top.* 1.17, 108a7–12, and 5.8, 138b24 (referring to 5.7, 136b33–137a7). For an analogy to succeed, the items and the relations among them on the one side of the analogy

---

[38] 202a18–21 in the introduction to section 3, 202b10–14 = (ii′) in section 3.6, and 202b17–19 = (i) in section 3.5. The examples assume that both powers or potentials, active and passive alike, are located in the same place, in the learner, but this does not seem to be the point that the repeated references to the roads example suggest. For more discussion, see section 3.8.

[39] For relatives that reciprocate, see *Phys.* 3.1, 200b28–32, and *Cat.* 7 and 10, 11b24–32, with section 3.7. For the causal point, see the Polycleitus/sculptor example, *Phys.* 2.3, 195a32–b3, 5, 196b25–9, with Lewis 1991 and n. 19 above.

[40] Other examples include Plato's analogy of the sun in the *Republic*, and in Aristotle, his account 'by analogy' of the 'underlying nature' in *Phys.* 1.7, 191a7–12, and of the relation of *energeia* to *dunamis*, *Met.* Θ.6, 1048a35–b9, where arguably the analogy begins with a variety of *energeiai* (with the example, housebuilding) that answers to the notion of *kinēsis* under study in *Physics* 3.1–3.

334   FRANK A. LEWIS

must line up appropriately with the items and relations on the other. For more light on the analogy, I offer two versions, the first, a bare bones account, which conceals some mismatches between the two sides, and a fleshed-out version, which does not:

Aristotle's Analogy: The Skeleton

R + up and	the teacher's power to teach the student that P and
R + down	the student's power to learn from the teacher that P
------------------------ ::	---
the underlying road R	the student's coming to know that P

The Fleshed-Out Version

The way in which R + up and R + down are the same as each other	the way in which the teacher's power to teach the student that P and the student's power to learn from the teacher that P are the same as each other
----------------------------- ::	---
the (different) way in which R + up and R + down are each the same as the very same thing: namely, the underlying road, R	the way in which the manifestation of the teacher's power to teach the student that P and of the student's power to learn from the teacher that P are each constituents in (and jointly constitute) the very same thing: namely, the student's coming to know that P

Despite the heuristic value of the example of the roads, the logic governing the two sides of the analogy is not altogether the same. The arrangement of the three roads corresponds neatly to the procedures of ACT, which organizes the different kinds of road in line with different notions of 'accidental sameness', in contrast to 'sameness in the strict sense'.[41] But the arrangement among teaching, learning, and the change that is the learner's coming to know that P, is due only in part to ACT, but more importantly, to quite different principles surrounding the nature of *powers*—the power to teach, the power to learn, and their manifestations as the student comes to know that P. The differences in the organization of its two sides by themselves need not be a defect in the analogy, whose purpose after all is to use cases we understand to illuminate cases we do not. All the same, we are owed an explanation of the new principles that govern the teaching and learning and change on the second side of the analogy,

---

[41] R + up and R + down are each accidentally the same as the identical underlying road, R, so that they are (accidentally) the same* as each other; see the introduction to section 3, and section 3.5 below.

HOW ARISTOTLE UNDERSTANDS CHANGE   335

corresponding to the way ACT organizes the examples on the first.[42] The details are our topic in the pages that follow.

3.5 Sameness and the Roads Example on the One Side of Aristotle's Analogy

Accounts of the road example and the companion case of teaching and learning often take the 'projectivist' or 'constructivist' line, that the distinction between the different roads (as also between teaching and learning) is an *intensional* one, reflecting different ways of talking or thinking about one and the same thing, without there being any difference between individuals in the real order.[43] Contrary to these accounts, on the view adopted here the roads example involves relations of sameness—strict sameness in some cases, less-than-strict sameness in others—among real entities, much in the way that musical Socrates and the masked one are real entities that are accidentally the same as some underlying substance, Socrates, Coriscus, and the like.[44]

For more about the varieties of sameness that fall short of sameness in being or in definition, we turn to ACT and the relevant notions of accidental sameness there. Socrates is pale, for example, just in case there exists the accidental compound, Socrates + pale, and Socrates is in the marketplace just in case the compound, Socrates + in the marketplace, exists. Pale Socrates and Socrates in the marketplace are each 'compounds by way of other categories.'[45] We say that Socrates is *accidentally the same* as Socrates + pale when and only when Socrates is pale; and Socrates is *accidentally the same* as Socrates + in the marketplace when and only when Socrates is in the marketplace.

At the same time, when Socrates is both pale and in the marketplace, Socrates + pale and Socrates + in the marketplace are each *accidentally the same* [no asterisk] as Socrates, as before; and, hence, they are also *accidentally the same** as each

---

[42] I take it that Aristotle can use his analogy not only to establish the *location* of a given change but also, with the appropriate accommodations, to support the analysis of its *constitution*: for example, the change that is the student's coming to know that P is constituted by the joint *energeiai* of the teacher's power to teach that P and the learner's to learn that P; see section 3.8.

[43] A classic statement of the 'projectivist' view is in Sellars 1967, 73–124. Other proponents of the view include Ross 1936, 362 and 540–1 on 202a21 and b9–10; Hardie and Gaye, Notes to the Oxford Translation; Waterlow 1982, 180–2; hesitantly, perhaps, in Hussey 1983, 70–1; Burnyeat 2008, 224; Coope 2009 (where 'perspectival' talk is explicit; see her n. 5); Beere 2009, 57 n. 42; and Charles 2015, 198–9. Similar views are expressed in Joachim 1922, 105 on *GC* 1.3, 319b3–4, and for discussion of the contrary view adopted in the main text above, see Lewis 1994, 256–7. The wider history of the projectivist view is surveyed nicely in Marmodoro 2007, 207, 220 with n. 20, where she too rejects the projectivist view criticized here, although her view sees no room for 'any familiar type of the Aristotelian ontology' (2007, 222), contrary to the resort to ACT which I find in *Physics* 3.3 in the next paragraph in the main text.

[44] For these and other examples, see Lewis 1991, ch. 3, with n. 22 above.

[45] *Met.* Z.4, 1029b22–7, see also M.2, 1077b4–9. For the '+' notation, see n. 22 above.

336   FRANK A. LEWIS

other. Accidental sameness* is defined in terms of plain accidental sameness [no asterisk]:

x is accidentally the same* as *y* if and only if (i) *x* and *y* are both accidental compounds, and (ii) for some *z*, *x* and *y* are both accidentally the same as *z*. (= (D3) from Lewis 1991, 106)

Less formally, z is the 'root entity' to the two compounds:

The pale <thing> and the musical <thing> are <accidentally> the same <*> because they [= pallor, musicality] are accidents of the same thing. (*Met.* Δ.9, 1017b27–8)

Accordingly, the road down to Athens and the road up to Thebes are accidentally the same* as each other. As before, one and the same underlying road, R, between the two cities is the 'root' entity in common to the two compounds, R + up and R + down.

Aristotle is helped by a further point about the destinations of the two roads. The directions, headed up, and headed down, are 'relatives that reciprocate' (n. 39 and surrounding main text above): there can be no road with the property of being headed up, unless there exists the corresponding road headed down, and vice versa. The same result holds in ACT: R + up exists, if and only if there exists the corresponding road, R + down.

Similarly, as we will see, the ability to teach that P on the part of the teacher can be manifested, if and only if simultaneously the capacity to learn that P is manifested on the part of the student. That is, the act of teaching and the act of learning too are relatives that reciprocate.[46] (But the corresponding *powers* to teach or to learn do not reciprocate: the ability to teach can exist without there being a student with the ability to learn, and no doubt vice versa.)

We can now state Aristotle's claims about the different sameness relations among the three roads:

(i) The road to Athens is the same as [= accidentally the same* as] the road to Thebes. 202b13–14, 17–19 (the contrary relation is denied in (ii) below, and compare with (i´) in section 3.6 below).

(ii) The road to Athens and that to Thebes are 'not strictly the same' or are 'different in account'. 202b13–19 (see also a18–20, and compare with (ii´) below).

(iii) The road between Athens and Thebes is one and the same (by implication at 202b17–18; and arguably parallel to (iii´) below).

---

[46] At the same time, arguably, the two powers are united also in that they are jointly manifested in the acts of teaching and learning, and thereby in the ongoing change that is the student's coming to know that P; see section 3.7.

HOW ARISTOTLE UNDERSTANDS CHANGE   337

(i), (ii), and (iii) together express the different sameness relations around which the collection of roads in Aristotle's analogy are structured, as in section 3.4 above. As before, the road up to Thebes and the road down to Athens are *accidentally the same** as each other; and simultaneously—to expand (iii)—both roads are accidentally the same [no asterisk] as *one and the same* underlying road between the two cities.

3.6 Sameness and Teaching and Learning on the Other Side of the Analogy

As with the different roads, various relations of sameness do or do not hold among teaching (the [token] realizing of this teacher's active potential to teach that learner that P), learning (the [simultaneous and token] realizing of that learner's potential to learn from [be taught by] this teacher that P), and some third entity to which these [= the teaching and learning] 'belong', *hōi huparkhei tauta*, 202b21 above:

(i′) Teaching and learning are in a certain way the same (202b10–14, and compare with (i) in section 3.5 above).

(ii′) Teaching and learning are *not* 'strictly the same' (*to auto kuriōs*), or are 'different in account' (b10–20, 21–2, contrast with (i′) and compare with (ii) above).[47]

(iii′) 'That to which these [= teaching and learning, the acting-on and the being-acted-on-by] belong (*hōi tauta huparkhei*, 'in which these are present'; Hussey), the change (*hē kinēsis*), <that is strictly the same>' (b20–1, compare (iii) above).[48]

Different sameness relations and their *relata* are in evidence in (i′) through (iii′)—the weaker kind of sameness in (i′) and perhaps also in (ii′), and the strict sameness set to one side in (ii′) but by implication (*alla*, b20) asserted in (iii′). So-called strict sameness—sameness in being, or in account—is familiar here and in other Aristotelian texts, but its application in (iii′) is a matter for further discussion below. And a further caveat: unlike the version of accidental sameness on the roads side of

---

[47] In the text, following (iii′), Aristotle adds, (iv′). 'For to be the activity of this *in* that [the activity of the active power] and <to be> the activity of this *due to* that [the activity of the passive power] are different in account', b21–2 (discussed in section 3.3 above), which is meant to buttress (ii′).

[48] Different options exist for the grammatical antecedents to Aristotle's *tauta*: all four items, teaching and learning, acting-on and being-acted-on-by, or just the active partners in each pair, the teaching and the acting [-on], as in Charles 2015. It is also unclear whether Aristotle means to refer to the combination of teaching and learning, or to each constituent in the change, teaching and learning, separately (the 'distributive' use of *tauta*). I will argue that the latter reading is in order here: the act of teaching that P by the teacher and the act of learning that P on the part of the student are each alike directed at (and jointly constitute) *one and the same* change: namely, the student's coming to know that P.

338   FRANK A. LEWIS

the analogy, features of the version here are not due to ACT, but will have some other source. The differences between the two sides of the analogy are our next topic.

3.7 The Different Organizing Principles on the Two Sides of the Analogy

We begin with the nature of Aristotle's examples. Aristotle pairs the case of teaching and learning with that of the road up and the road down precisely to persuade us of something that, in the ordinary case, seems out of the question. The two accidents, being pale and being in the marketplace, for example, may or may not be jointly lodged in one and the same subject. They are 'jointly lodged', as when pale Socrates enters the marketplace (say); but it is hardly the case that anyone who enters the marketplace is pale, or that a person is pale only when in the marketplace. By contrast with these perhaps more familiar cases, a road will not have the property of being headed uphill in one direction, without simultaneously having the property of being headed downhill in the other. Similarly with the two activities, teaching and learning: on Aristotle's view, neither will go on without the other (the case of the autodidact will be like that of the doctor who heals himself, *Phys.* 1.7, 191b23–7). As noted above, Aristotle's analogy is helped by its use of 'relatives with correlatives that reciprocate'—the teacher, the learner; the road up, the road down—as examples.[49] In his analysis, as the road up to Thebes is paired with the road down to Athens, so a given episode of the teacher's teaching the learner that P is paired with the learner's learning from [being taught by] the teacher that P. The pairing sets the stage for the further step in the analogy, in which Aristotle uses the relation between the roads R + up and R + down vis-à-vis the underlying road, R, on the one side of the analogy, to illustrate the relation between the active and passive powers of teaching and learning on the one side vis-à-vis their manifestation in the change which is the student's coming to know that P on the other side.[50] In this way, it may not be overreach to say that the device of 'relatives that reciprocate' works equally well on both sides of his analogy to allow Aristotle to reach his conclusion about the analysis of change.

But these correspondences between the two sides of Aristotle's analogy can in other ways seem not only elusive but also approximate. To begin with, on what passes for the 'familiar' side in the analogy, where we expect help in grasping the complexities of the second side, Aristotle leaves us to gather support from other texts (largely the *Organon* and *Metaphysics* Δ) for the details of ACT on which his account of the roads rests. At the same time, much of the reasoning in terms of

---

[49] I discuss relatives that reciprocate in the final paragraph of section 3.3.
[50] For the point, see the 'Fleshed-Out Version' of the two sides of Aristotle's analogy in section 3.5.

HOW ARISTOTLE UNDERSTANDS CHANGE   339

ACT does not apply to the analysis of change on the other side of the analogy: for example, the change is not a constituent in teaching and learning (as R is in R + up and R + down), rather, the latter are constituents in the change. So the organizing principles from ACT that lead to the underlying road do not always have a counterpart in the case of change.

Happily, organizing principles for change from altogether outside ACT are ready to hand. In the first place, the manifestations or *energeiai* of teaching and learning are alike constituents in, indeed *exhaustively constitute*, the change, so that (providing that 'nothing external hinders')[51] *nothing more need happen* for the change to take (or to have taken) place. Above all, second, Aristotle can back up claims about the constitution of a given change by appeal to essentially *teleological* considerations. It is *the very nature* of the powers to teach and to learn that they are *for* the manifestations or *energeiai* that together constitute the target change.[52] It is worth emphasizing that because the powers to teach and to learn are active and passive, respectively, for them to be jointly manifested in the acts of teaching and learning just is for them to be manifested in the ongoing change that is the student's coming to know that P. On this view, the teleological character of the powers to teach and to learn, which have the student's coming to know as their goal, gives structure to the second side of Aristotle's analogy, matching the use of ACT to yield the arrangement of the three roads on the first side.

Mention of powers and their manifestations can seem ubiquitous in *Physics* 3.1–3. From the very beginning, Aristotle defines change in terms of powers and their manifestations (*Phys.* 3.1, 201a10–11, reproduced in the first paragraph of section 1 above). The corollary, that a power is *for* its manifestation, is summarized in the final sentence of *Phys.* 3.2, 202a9–12, from the point of view of the agent, who will bring one version or another of form (*eidos ti*), whether for a this, a such, or a so much, which will be the principle and cause of the change (*arkhē kai aition tēs kinēseōs*)—as when a man *in actuality* makes a human being out of what is *potentially* a human being. The topic of powers and their *energeiai* also bobs in and out of the discussion of the puzzles in the first half of *Physics* 3.3, and Aristotle returns to the topic in the very last lines of the chapter. The discussion in all three chapters also lays the foundation for solving the difficulties that people have found with the idea that change is incomplete (*Phys.* 3.2, 201b27–202a3).[53] Aristotle returns to the incompleteness of change in *Metaphysics* Θ.6. As here, a *kinēsis* is an activity *directed at* some end; but the *kinēsis* itself is *atelē*, 1048b29,

---

[51] As often in Aristotle; see, e.g., *Phys.* 8.1, 251b1–3, 8.4, 255a28–256a3, and *DC* 4.3, 311a8–13, and in the same vein, Heil 2004, 235–6, 201–2.

[52] To adapt a phrase from a different context in Heil 2004, 235–6, the powers are 'intrinsically "projectile"', so that each 'is *for* a particular kind of manifestation <in company> with a particular disposition partner'.

[53] For incompleteness and the 'imperfective paradox', see Charles 2015 and n. 18 above.

340 FRANK A. LEWIS

30, or not *teleia*, b21–2. Otherwise put, the *kinēsis* itself is *incomplete*: the end is not contained in the *kinēsis* (b20–1), which on the contrary ceases once the end is achieved.

Finally, the mingling of topics in the analogy, ACT (largely) on one side, teleology on the other, need not compromise the analogy, if its purpose is to persuade us, by reference to a familiar example of the roads (as old as Heraclitus), of the existence and nature of other cases that may be less well understood.

3.8 The Lesson of Aristotle's Great Analogy in *Physics* 3.3

Despite the body of theory at the close of the previous section, questions remain about textual details in Aristotle analogy, particularly the problematic (iii´), repeated here:

> (iii´) <that?> to which these (*tauta*)[54] [= the teaching, the learning, the acting-on and the being-acted-on-by] belong (*hōi tauta huparkhei*, 'in which these are present'; Hussey), the change (*hē kinēsis*), <that is strictly the same> (*Phys.* 3.3, 202b20–1).

In previous sections, I have followed what is perhaps the simplest view, which gets its plausibility from the immediate context of (iii´). In (ii´) and again in (iv´) (n. 47 above), Aristotle insists, elaborating on (i´), that teaching and learning are *not strictly the same* (as each other). By contrast, he seems to suggest, these 'belong' to *one and the same thing*, the *kinēsis*, the change, in just the way that corresponding to the two roads, R + up and R + down, there is a single road, R, between the higher and lower destinations.

The result is in line with what is perhaps the more generally favoured reading of (iii´):

> A. The (concurrent) realizings of the teacher's active potential to teach the learner that P and of the learner's passive potential to learn from the teacher that P together constitute *one and the same thing*, the change as the learner comes to know that P. (The change is *completed* once the teacher has successfully passed on to the learner the knowledge that P.)

The reading assures us of symmetry between the active and passive contributions of teacher and learner: they each belong equally to one and the same change as its constituents.

---

[54] See n. 48 above.

HOW ARISTOTLE UNDERSTANDS CHANGE 341

A second perhaps less common reading, by contrast, indicates asymmetry,[55] and identifies the change with the passive contribution of the learner. As a first approximation:

B. The change in which are present the (concurrent) realizings of the teacher's active potential to teach the learner that P and of the learner's passive potential to learn from the teacher that P *is one and the same thing as* the realizing of the learner's passive potential to learn from the teacher that P.

Early in these chapters, Aristotle seems to suggest the 'one constituent', asymmetric view of change on display in B; the 'two constituent' symmetric view in A, on the other hand, may be his considered view in *Physics* 3.3.

But B is subject to an immediate objection. How can Aristotle simultaneously list both the acting-on and the being-acted-on-by as ingredients in the change, yet also say that the change is one and the same as *just one* of these—while the active constituent has simply dropped away? If there is asymmetry, it is not systematically enforced in Aristotle's exposition. Arguably, his *hē tou dunamei ontos entelecheia*, 201a10–11, does not distinguish between active and passive; but the added *hēi kineton* at a27–9 singles out the passive *dunamis*; see also 202a7–9, text as in Ross.[56] But the 'general' (*haplōs*) statement at 202b26–7 explicitly gives both sides.[57] More than this, the repeated references in all three chapters to the agent in a change can easily seem to make room for the active potential in the agent, with its realization (which Aristotle argues takes place in the patient) not far behind.

Meanwhile, one line of defence of the apparently asymmetric, 'single potential' view in B may have an unwanted deflationary effect. So, for example, the problematic reading B is represented as follows in Hussey's 1983, 71:

The change, in which these things are present, i.e. of which it is true that it is an acting-upon and a being-acted-upon, is the same as the being-acted-upon.

---

[55] For the 'strange asymmetry' sometimes found in Aristotle's analysis, see Hussey 1983, 71, and n. 57 below.

[56] The lines b26–8, which Hussey excludes, are perhaps 'clumsy', as he says, but they accurately restate and then expand the formula for *alloiōsis* and the rest at 3.1, 201a9–19.

[57] For both kinds of *dunamis*, active as well as passive, see *Metaphysics* Γ.12 and Θ.1, where the bias in favour of the passive *dunamis* is again in evidence. Symmetry is defended in Coope 2009, 285–7, while Anagnostopoulos 2010, 60–1, explicitly endorses the 'passive *dunamis* only' view of change that leaves no room for symmetry. Arguments for asymmetry are given earlier by David Charles 1984, 14, amplifying the reading in Hussey 1983; for critical discussion, see Marmodoro 2007, n. 25. In his 2015, Charles suggests that Aristotle is tempted by both choices offered in the puzzle at 202a21–8 and may not feel the need to decide between readings A and B above. As Charles sees it, on one view, teaching and learning are not strictly identical: strictly, there are two *changes, not one. A different solution straightforwardly rejects symmetry; instead, the passive activity at work in a given *change is 'strictly identical with' the *change, while the active activity is the same as the *change in some weaker sense, possibly even as in the 'perspectival' view in Charles 1984 and earlier in Ross 1936 and others; see n. 43 above.

342   FRANK A. LEWIS

Similarly, Hussey offers the following counterpart to A:

> But that in which these things are present, i.e. that of which it is true that it is both an acting-on and a being-acted-upon, is the change.

Altogether, Hussey's 'i.e. that *of which it is true that...*' provides us with *three ways of thinking* of a given change indifferently as what is a being-acted-on-by (as in B); or as what is an acting-on; or as both together.[58] The result is to disable B as a statement of a distinctively 'single (passive) *dunamis*' view of change, while staying one remove away from the subject-matter of natural philosophy in favour of a 'projectivist' view of the kind described in n. 43 and surrounding main text above. As before, a projectivist view of the three roads abandons hope of finding any real structure among the roads, regimented in the way that ACT makes possible, and reflected in the teleological structure inherent in the powers to teach and to learn on the other side of the Aristotle's analogy.

Two further readings of (iii′) address not the constitution of change, but the *location* of various of the constituents involved; the first is unproblematically asymmetric:

C. The (concurrent) realizings of the teacher's active potential to teach the learner that P and of the learner's passive potential to learn from the teacher that P are *located in one and the same thing*, the learner.

Questions about location first appear as the first difficulty Aristotle sees among the puzzles early in *Physics* 3.3 at 202a25–7 (see also *Phys.* 3.1, 201a36–b3). The reading in C opts for the solution that both activities, of teaching as well as of learning, are located in a single person, namely, the learner.

In C above, Aristotle describes where to place the *realizing* of active and passive potentials. The *so far unrealized potentials* in D below are given a very different account:

D. The unrealized active potential of the teacher to teach the learner that P and the unrealized passive potential of the learner to learn from the teacher that P are *distributed between the learner and the teacher*—the passive potential in the former and the active potential in the latter.

The distribution of unrealized active and passive potentials in D is symmetric, and only indirectly relevant to the location of the same potentials once they are being realized in the ongoing change; I include D in order to emphasize the contrast with C.

---

[58] The same might be said of Ross's '[t]he movement *which is describable as* both'; Ross 1936, 362 (my emphasis).

As to the authenticity or otherwise of these different readings of (iii'): A and B each find support separately in the text, but both together cannot be Aristotle's finished view. By contrast, C and D are incontrovertibly his view throughout. The task of sorting through these four as readings of Aristotle's (iii') is made harder by the fact that at different times he seems to hold that each is true. All the same, I take it that the analysis of change is Aristotle's final target, as in the 'two constituent' analysis registered in reading A, where symmetry is on full display, exactly as the road example suggests.[59]

Works Cited

Anagnostopoulos, Andreas. 2010. 'Change in Aristotle's *Physics* 3', *Oxford Studies in Ancient Philosophy* 39, 33–79.

Barnes, Jonathan (ed.). 1984. *The Complete Works of Aristotle*. Revised Oxford Translation. 2 vols. Princeton University Press.

Beere, Jonathan. 2009. *Doing and Being: An Interpretation of Aristotle's* Metaphysics *Theta*. Oxford University Press.

Burnyeat, Myles. 2001. *A Map of* Metaphysics *Zeta*. Mathesis.

Burnyeat, Myles. 2008. '*Kinēsis* vs *Energeia*: A Much-Read Passage In (but Not Of) Aristotle's *Metaphysics*', *Oxford Studies in Ancient Philosophy* 34, 219–92.

Charles, David. 1984. *Aristotle's Philosophy of Action*. Duckworth.

Charles, David. 2015. 'Aristotle's Processes', in *Aristotle's* Physics*: A Critical Guide* (ed. M. Leunissen). Cambridge University Press, 186–205.

Code, Alan. 2003. 'Change, Power and Potentialities in Aristotle', in *Desire, Identity, and Existence: Essays in Honor of T.M. Penner* (ed. N. Reshotko). Academic Printing and Publishing, 251–71.

Coope, Ursula. 2009. 'Change and Its Relation to Potentiality and Actuality', in *A Companion to Aristotle* (ed. G. Anagnostopoulos). Wiley-Blackwell, 277–91.

Hardie, R. P. and R. K. Gaye. 1930. *The Works of Aristotle, Translated into English, under the Editorship of W.D. Ross. Vol. II: Physica*. Clarendon Press.

Heil, John. 2004. *Philosophy of Mind*. 2nd edition. Routledge.

Hussey, Edward. 1983. *Aristotle* Physics *Books III and IV. Translated with Introduction and Notes*. Clarendon Aristotle Series. Clarendon Press.

Joachim, Harold H. 1922. *Aristotle on Coming-To-Be and Passing-Away* (De Generatione et Corruptione)*: A Revised Text with Introduction and Commentary*. Clarendon Press.

---

[59] My debt to David Charles for his years of friendship, personal as well as professional, reaches back many years, and I am delighted to have the opportunity to acknowledge it here. I am grateful also to the editors of this volume for helpful comments on an earlier draft.

344   FRANK A. LEWIS

Kosman, L. A. 1969. 'Aristotle's Definition of Motion', *Phronesis* 14, 40–62.

Kostman, James. 1987. 'Aristotle's Definition of Change', *History of Philosophy Quarterly* 4 (1), 3–16.

Lewis, Frank A. 1991. *Substance and Predication in Aristotle*. Cambridge University Press.

Lewis, Frank A. 1994. 'Aristotle on the Relation between a Thing and Its Matter', in *Unity, Identity, and Explanation in Aristotle's* Metaphysics (ed. T. Scaltsas, D. Charles, and M. L. Gill). Clarendon Press, 247–77.

Lewis, Frank A 2013. *How Aristotle Gets by in Metaphysics Zeta*. Oxford University Press.

Marmodoro, Anna. 2007. 'The Union of Cause and Effect in Aristotle: *Physics* 3.3', *Oxford Studies in Ancient Philosophy* 32, 205–32.

Marmodoro, Anna. 2014. *Aristotle on Perceiving Objects*. Oxford University Press.

Penner, Terry. 1970. 'Verbs and the Identity of Actions: A Philosophical Exercise in the Interpretation of Aristotle', in *Ryle: A Collection of Critical Essays* (ed. O. P. Wood and G. Pitcher). Anchor Books, 393–460.

Peramatzis, Michail. 2010. 'Essence and Per Se Predication in Aristotle's *Metaphysics* Z.4', *Oxford Studies in Ancient Philosophy* 39, 121–82.

Ross, W. D. 1936. *Aristotle* Physics. *A Revised Text with Introduction and Commentary*. Clarendon Press.

Schenkl, Henricus (ed.). 1900. *Themistii in Aristotelis Physica Paraphrasis*. Reimer.

Sellars, Wilfred. 1967. *Philosophical Perspectives*, Springfield, Illinois.

Waterlow (Broadie), Sarah. 1982. *Nature, Change, and Agency in Aristotle's* Physics: *A Philosophical Study*. Clarendon Press.

15

Aristotle: Processes and Continuants

Ursula Coope

Introduction

What type of entity is an Aristotelian *kinēsis*? David Charles has argued that a *kinēsis* corresponds more closely to what we would call a 'process' than to what we would call an 'event'. In defending this view, Charles makes two important claims about *kinēsis*: first, that a *kinēsis* has 'modal depth'[1] and second, that a *kinēsis* is the kind of entity that can have contrary properties at different times.

To say that a *kinēsis* has 'modal depth' is to say that it could have developed differently from the way it in fact did develop. If it in fact reached its end, it could instead have been interrupted before doing so; if it was in fact interrupted, it could instead have gone on to reach its end.[2] For instance, an acorn that *was becoming an oak tree* might not survive long enough finally to become an oak tree: its growth into a mature tree might (or might not) be interrupted. The travellers walking to Larissa might fail to reach their destination: their journey to Larissa might (or might not) be cut short or be diverted from its course. Events (at least as understood in the Davidsonian tradition) do not, in this sense, have modal depth. An event that lasted for a longer time would be a different event.

Charles' second claim is that Aristotelian *kinēseis* 'have different properties at different times: some are initially slow then fast' (2015, 186). A journey to Larissa can start out quickly and then get slower as the travellers become tired. A process of learning might speed up as the learners become more proficient. Charles claims that in such cases the *kinēseis* are '(non-derivatively) the subjects of these properties at different times'.[3] When Charles says that a change is *non-derivatively* the subject of these incompatible properties at different times, he means that its being

---

[1] I take the term from Charles 2017. For a similar idea, see Steward 2013.

[2] Charles (2015, 186) says that some changes 'are interrupted, failing to reach their goal: these could have continued longer'. This is most obviously a possibility for the kinds of process that are goal-directed. Aristotle's account suggests he thinks of a process as a progression towards a certain goal or end. But it is not clear that everything we would classify as a movement counts as end-directed in this sense. For instance, *aimless strolling around* seems to be a movement, but does not seem to be directed towards any particular end. In this chapter, I leave to one side the questions of what Aristotle should say about movements of this kind, and of whether they too have modal depth.

[3] Charles 2015, 186. He goes on to say that such changes are the kind of entities that 'last through time and move through space'.

Ursula Coope, *Aristotle: Processes and Continuants* In: *Aristotelian Metaphysics: Essays in Honour of David Charles.*
Edited by: David Bronstein, Thomas Kjeller Johansen, and Michail Peramatzis, Oxford University Press.
© Oxford University Press 2024. DOI: 10.1093/oso/9780198908678.003.0015

346   URSULA COOPE

the subject of these properties at different times is not simply derived from the fact that it has two different temporal parts, one of which is the subject of one property and the other of which is the subject of the other. An event, by contrast, is not the kind of entity that can be said, non-derivatively, to be first slow and then later fast. If an event is first slow and then fast, then this can only be in virtue of its having earlier parts that are slow and later parts that are fast. As Charles says:

> There is not one event which itself was (underivatively) initially slow and is now fast. An event (as understood in the philosophical literature) may have parts which are slow and quick. But the event itself does not itself (underivatively) possess these different properties at different times. It is quick and slow in virtue of having parts that are quick and slow.[4]

Both these claims imply that a *kinēsis* is in certain important respects like an enduring substance. An enduring substance has modal depth: Socrates could have died earlier, or he could have escaped from prison and lived longer. And an enduring substance can have incompatible properties at different times (and can do so non-derivatively, i.e., not merely in virtue of having temporal parts that have incompatible properties): Socrates can be first ignorant and then knowledgeable, and this is not, for Aristotle, a matter of his having one temporal part that is ignorant and another temporal part that is knowledgeable.[5]

However, Aristotle's writings provide clear indications that a *kinēsis* is importantly different from an enduring substance. He holds that a *kinēsis* has temporal parts.[6] At *Physics* 6.1–2 he argues that divisions in a particular movement must correspond to divisions in the time taken by the movement and also to divisions in the path covered by the movement. For instance, a movement over the path ABC must have parts corresponding to the parts of the path AB and BC. These will be temporal parts of the movement: in the movement from A to C along the path ABC, the part which is a movement over AB is temporally prior to the part which is a movement over BC. Elsewhere, Aristotle says that a *kinēsis*, like time, is 'always other and other' ($a\grave{\iota}\epsilon\grave{\iota}$ ἄλλη καὶ ἄλλη, *Phys.* 4.11, 219b9–10; all translations are my own). In his discussion of the infinite, he contrasts this way of being (being 'always different and different', $\dot{a}\epsilon\acute{\iota}\ldots\acute{\epsilon}\tau\epsilon\rho o\nu$ καὶ ἕτερον) with the way of being of a substance, such as a human or a house (*Phys.* 3.6, 206a30–4). Moreover, Aristotle

---

[4] Charles 2017.

[5] Of course, certain modern philosophers have argued that for a substance to change is for its temporal parts to possess incompatible properties: if I sit down, I change in virtue of the fact that one temporal part of me is standing and another part of me is sitting (see, e.g., Lewis 1986, 203–4). But I am here interested in the relation between *kinēsis* and enduring substance *as enduring substance is understood by Aristotle* (and, I would say, as it is understood in ordinary thought).

[6] Rosen (2015, 209–10) points out that this tells against the view that Aristotle regards a *kinēsis* as a continuant: that is, as 'something that endures through time in much the way that substances are naturally thought to do'.

ARISTOTLE: PROCESSES AND CONTINUANTS   347

tells us (both in the *Physics* and in the *Categories*) that a *kinēsis* cannot itself be the subject of change: only a substance can be such as to undergo change by taking on contrary properties at different times.[7]

Charles' claims about the ontological status of *kinēsis*, when considered alongside these remarks of Aristotle's, prompt two questions. First, if a *kinēsis* is not the kind of entity that is able to undergo change, then can Aristotle really hold that one and the same *kinēsis* is (non-derivatively) the subject of contrary properties at different times? Second, if a *kinēsis* is composed of temporal parts, then how can a *kinēsis* have modal depth: how can it be the kind of thing that could have been interrupted but wasn't?

In what follows, I shall argue that Aristotle's works suggest two different views on the ontological status of *kinēsis*, and that there is some reason to think that he changed his mind about this. The *Categories* and *Physics* 5–6 present a view on which a *kinēsis* is not the kind of thing that can (non-derivatively) have contrary properties at different times. I shall argue that this view also implies that a *kinēsis* is not the kind of entity that could have modal depth. However, elsewhere in the *Physics*, Aristotle suggests a different view of *kinēsis*, a view that is compatible both with the claim that a *kinēsis* can (non-derivatively) have contrary properties at different times and also with the claim that a *kinēsis* has modal depth. On this second view, a *kinēsis* is still importantly different from an enduring substance. Unlike a substance, a *kinēsis* has temporal parts; for a *kinēsis* to be is for one of its parts to be after another. Nevertheless, on this second view, a *kinēsis* is in some ways like a continuant. This is because it has a kind of unity that allows it (non-derivatively) to have contrary properties at different times and to have (what we have been calling) 'modal depth'.

If my interpretation is right, this second account opens up an interesting possibility. It allows for a category of entity that is neither quite like an enduring substance nor quite like an event. Such an entity is not, like a substance, present as a whole at each moment at which it exists, but nor is it related to its temporal parts in the way an event is usually taken to be related to its temporal parts. In recent philosophy, Helen Steward has argued that processes are entities of this kind, and that they raise important questions about what it is to be a 'continuant'.[8] If I am right, then Aristotle's second account is very close to Steward's.

---

[7] In *Phys.* 5.2, he says explicitly that a *kinēsis* cannot be the subject of change. In *Cat.* 5, he argues that only a substance can be the subject of change (and hence, by implication, that a *kinēsis* cannot be the subject of change). I discuss these passages in section 1, below. Charles (2017) acknowledges this point, when he says that *kinēseis* are 'not things that change but are the changings themselves'. But this leaves us with the question: if *the changing itself* is not a *thing that changes*, then in what sense is the changing an entity that develops in different ways through time, being at first quick and then slow? Charles (2015) describes *kinēseis* as 'a distinctive type of continuant...unfoldings or processes (changings), with different properties at different times' (204).

[8] See especially Steward 2013 and 2015. As will be clear in what follows, my own thinking on these matters has been much influenced by Steward's.

348   URSULA COOPE

1. The Claim that a *Kinēsis* Cannot Be the Subject of Change: *Categories* 5 and *Physics* 5.2

In *Categories* 5, Aristotle lays out his account of substance, and explains why primary substances are prior to all other entities. In the course of this account, he claims: 'it seems to be most distinctive of substance that what is numerically one and the same is receptive of contraries' (μάλιστα δὲ ἴδιον τῆς οὐσίας δοκεῖ εἶναι τὸ ταὐτὸν καὶ ἓν ἀριθμῷ ὂν τῶν ἐναντίων εἶναι δεκτικόν, 4a10–11). One and the same individual human, he says, can be pale at one time then dark at another. Aristotle goes on to emphasize that nothing other than a substance can receive contraries in this way. For example, numerically one and the same colour cannot be dark and light, and 'nor can numerically one and the same action be good and bad' (οὐδὲ ἡ αὐτὴ πρᾶξις καὶ μία τῷ ἀριθμῷ οὐκ ἔσται φαύλη καὶ σπουδαία, 4a14–16). The reference to action (*praxis*) is important for our purposes, since Aristotle, at least in some texts, claims that an action is a type of *kinēsis*.[9]

What exactly does Aristotle mean by this claim that nothing other than a substance can remain numerically one and the same while receiving contraries? We can get clearer about this by considering his response to a potential counterexample. He allows that numerically one and the same belief or statement can be true at one time and false at another. For example, the statement 'Socrates is sleeping' might be true at one time and false at another. This is a potential counterexample to Aristotle's view, since statements and beliefs are not substances. Aristotle's response is to claim that it is not really true in such a case that *the statement* (or belief) receives contraries. When a statement goes from being true to being false, this is because something else receives contraries. When the statement 'Socrates is sleeping' goes from being true to being false, this is because *Socrates* has undergone a change (from sleeping to being awake). The statement has not itself undergone a change, and hence (Aristotle goes on to say) it has not 'received contraries' (4b10–13). By contrast, he explains, 'a substance is said to be receptive of contraries in virtue of it itself receiving contraries' (ἡ δέ γε οὐσία τῷ αὐτὴν τὰ ἐναντία δέχεσθαι, τούτῳ δεκτικὴ τῶν ἐναντίων λέγεται, 4b13–14).

This response is interesting because it suggests a strategy Aristotle might employ in dealing with other potential counterexamples. For instance, a certain colour could be fashionable at one time and unfashionable at another, but presumably Aristotle would say that this is a change in our preferences (and hence in us) rather than in the colour and hence that the colour itself has not received

---

[9] Charles (2017) claims that for Aristotle an action is a *kinēsis*. This claim needs some qualification. Aristotle does say this at *EE* 2.3, 1220b28–30, but elsewhere his position is less clear. Aristotle's remarks in *Met.* Θ (1048b18–35) suggest that he is prepared to count as actions (*praxeis*) not only *kinēseis* but also the kinds of *energeiai* that he distinguishes from *kinēseis*. Indeed, at least in this passage, he seems to imply that *kinēseis* are not fully, or strictly speaking, actions: 'these are not cases of action, or at any rate of complete action' (οὐκ ἔστι ταῦτα πρᾶξις ἢ οὐ τελεία γε, 1048b21–2).

ARISTOTLE: PROCESSES AND CONTINUANTS 349

contraries. One might wonder, then, whether Aristotle could say something similar about the fact that a certain *kinēsis* can be quicker at one time and then slower at another. Could Aristotle say that when a *kinēsis* gets slower, what receives contraries is not the *kinēsis* itself, but rather the subject of the *kinēsis*? For instance, could he maintain that when John's running goes from being quick to being slow, the subject that has received contraries is *John*, not *John's running*? The trouble here is that it is hard to see any way of specifying the relevant contraries without presupposing that the change itself also receives contraries. What, for instance, are the contraries that John receives when his running gets slower? It is not enough to say that he is first *quick* then *slow*, because he might be the subject of some other change that is speeding up (as his running slows down, his rate of speaking might speed up). The sense in which he receives contraries as his running gets slower seems to be that he is first *running* more quickly and then *running* more slowly. But that suggests that he receives contraries just because his *running* receives contraries (being first quick and then slow).[10]

This leaves us wondering how Aristotle might justify his claim that entities other than substances cannot (in the relevant sense) receive contraries. In *Physics* 5.2, Aristotle repeats the claim that a *kinēsis* cannot be the subject of *kinēsis*. But his remarks there do not shed much light on how he would defend this claim. The context in *Physics* 5.2 is a more general argument that there cannot be a *kinēsis* of a *kinēsis*. He spells out two things someone might mean by the claim that there is a *kinēsis* of a *kinēsis*. First, someone might mean that a *kinēsis* is itself the subject of another *kinēsis*. Second, someone might mean that a *kinēsis* is the starting-point of another *kinēsis*. He argues that, on either understanding, *kinēsis* of *kinēsis* is impossible. Most of his argument focuses on the second way of understanding '*kinēsis* of *kinēsis*', but it is the first that is more relevant for us. All he says in relation to this is the following: 'Can it be that in this way also *kinēsis* heats up or gets cold or changes place or increases or decreases? This is impossible, for change (*metabolē*) is not one of the things that is a subject' (ἆρά γε οὕτω καὶ ἡ κίνησις ἢ θερμαίνεται ἢ ψύχεται ἢ τόπον ἀλλάττει ἢ αὐξάνεται ἢ φθίνει; τοῦτο δὲ ἀδύνατον· οὐ γὰρ τῶν ὑποκειμένων τι ἡ μεταβολή, 225b18–21).

By itself, this is not much of an explanation. In the previous chapter, Aristotle has distinguished between *kinēsis* and change (*metabolē*). Any *kinēsis* is also a change (*metabolē*) (225a34), but there are certain kinds of change (*metabolē*) that do not count as *kinēsis*. The termini of a *kinēsis* must be contraries or intermediates. Hence, generation and destruction are changes but not *kinēseis*.[11] When

---

[10] This is not, of course, a conclusive argument in favour of the view that the subject here must be the running. As Oliver Primavesi has pointed out to me, Aristotle could reply that the contrary properties in question are *being quick in respect of running* and *being slow in respect of running*, and that it is the substance (John) that receives first one and then the other of these contrary properties.

[11] Similarly, Aristotle says in *Phys.* 5.5 that a change to a goal but without any specified starting-point counts as a *metabolē* but not a *kinēsis* (229b10–11).

350   URSULA COOPE

Aristotle says that a change (*metabolē*) is not a subject, he is, then, simply telling us that nothing in the larger class to which *kinēsis* belongs is a subject. But this gets us no further forward. He provides no defence of this claim that a change (*metabolē*) is not a subject, and this claim seems no more secure than the original claim it was meant to justify: the claim that one *kinēsis* cannot be the subject of another *kinēsis*.

2. The Relation between a *Kinēsis* and Its Parts in *Physics* 5–6

What justifies Aristotle's confidence, in *Physics* 5, that a *kinēsis* cannot itself be a subject of change? I shall suggest that this claim follows from his more general views, in *Physics* 5–6, about the relation between a *kinēsis* and its parts.

In *Physics* 5.4, in his account of regularity and irregularity, Aristotle makes some remarks that shed light on the question of what it is for a *kinēsis* to be first quick and then slow. He is interested in the notion of regularity here because he is explaining what it is for a *kinēsis* to be a unity. Something that is irregular (*anōmalos*), he says, is divided and hence lacks a certain kind of unity (228b16–18). One way for a *kinēsis* to be irregular is for it to have an irregular path: for instance, a movement along a path that has an angle in it will be irregular in this sense. The path is irregular iff the parts of this path cannot be superimposed on each other.[12] Another way for a *kinēsis* to be irregular is for it not to be at a constant speed: for instance, it might be first quick and then slow (228b27–8). Why does such a *kinēsis* count as irregular? Aristotle doesn't tell us explicitly, but he goes on to claim that a *kinēsis* only counts as regular if its parts can be superimposed (*epharmottein*) on each other (229a6). This suggests that a *kinēsis* that is first quick and then slow fails to be regular because it has temporal parts that cannot be superimposed on one another: some of these parts are quick and others are slow. For our purposes, the important point is that Aristotle is quite happy to allow here that a certain token change might be first quick and then slow.[13] What he insists is that such a change will be irregular. Moreover, it will be irregular because its temporal parts have contrary properties: some of them are quick and others are slow.

Now it would be possible to accept this account of regularity while also claiming that an irregular *kinēsis* of this kind is itself (non-derivatively) a subject of

---

[12] Aristotle says irregular magnitudes are those 'of which any chance part will not fit onto another chance part' (ὧν μὴ ἐφαρμόττει τὸ τυχὸν ἐπὶ τὸ τυχὸν μέρος, 228b24–5). Examples of regular magnitudes are straight or circular paths (228b20–1). (Aristotle seems to treat 'going in a circle' as if that amounted to going in the same direction.) Examples of irregular magnitudes are helixes or paths with a bend in them (228b23–4).

[13] Such a *kinēsis* still counts as continuous, but it is not regular. The reason such a *kinēsis* can still count as continuous is that quickness and slowness are not differentiae that distinguish between different species of *kinēsis* (228b26–229a2). Because of this, quick locomotion followed by slow locomotion can make up one continuous (though irregular) *kinēsis*. By contrast, an alteration followed by a locomotion would not make up one continuous *kinēsis*, since alteration and locomotion are different species of movement.

change when it goes from being quick to being slow. To defend such a view, one would have to argue that the fact that the *kinēsis* is first quick and then slow is not simply derived from the fact that it has some temporal parts that are quick and others that are slow. That is, one would have to argue that the *kinēsis* as a whole is, in important ways, explanatorily prior to its temporal parts, and that because of this, even though the *kinēsis* has temporal parts, the fact that the whole *kinēsis* has contrary properties at different times is not simply derived from explanatorily prior facts about the properties of those temporal parts.

As I say, this is the line one might pursue if one wanted to defend the claim that a *kinēsis* is (non-derivatively) the subject of change. But we know that Aristotle himself, in *Physics* 5, does *not* want to defend this claim. As we have seen, just two chapters earlier, in 5.2, he has argued that a *kinēsis* cannot be a subject of change. We can assume, then, that in 5.4, when he allows that a single *kinēsis* can be first quick and then slow, he is not taking this to show that the *kinēsis* itself can undergo a change from being quick to being slow.

What view of the relation between a *kinēsis* and its temporal parts would allow Aristotle to grant that a certain kind of irregular *kinēsis* could be first quick and then slow, while also insisting that it is impossible for a *kinēsis* to be (non-derivatively) the subject of contrary properties at different times, and hence that it is impossible for a *kinēsis* to be itself the subject of change? We can make sense of this, I suggest, if we take Aristotle to be assuming not merely that a *kinēsis* has temporal parts, but also, crucially, that the temporary properties of a *kinēsis* are simply derived from the properties of its temporal parts. On this view, the *kinēsis* itself is only in a derivative sense the subject of these contrary properties. The *kinēsis* is first quick and then slow just in virtue of the fact that one (temporal) part of it is quick and another (temporal) part of it is slow.

This view about the way in which a *kinēsis* is related to its temporal parts is also suggested more generally by Aristotle's approach, in *Physics* 5.4, to questions about the unity of *kinēsis*. He attempts to derive an account of the unity of a single *kinēsis* from facts about the relations between the sub-*kinēseis* that are its parts. Thus, he proceeds by asking what it is for one *kinēsis* to be unified *with another*.[14] He argues that two particular token *kinēseis* will make up one unified *kinēsis* iff (i) they have the same subject, (ii) they are of the same type (e.g., they are both loco-motions) and are continuous in the sense that the end of one is the beginning of the next (e.g., one is a movement from A to B and the next is a movement from B to C), and (iii) they are not separated from each other by an interval of time in which the subject is at rest.[15] He then adds that this single *kinēsis* will be more

---

[14] For this point, see Rosen 2015, 210–12.
[15] *Phys.* 5.4, 227b20–228a3 and 228a20–228b11. In these sections of 5.4, Aristotle is discussing what it is for a token *kinēsis* to be 'one without qualification (*haplōs*)': that is, to be one 'in essence and in number' (227b21–2).

352   URSULA COOPE

unified if it is regular: for instance, if the two *kinēseis* of which it is composed are both along a path pointing in the same direction and are both at the same speed (5.4, 228b15–29a3).

Throughout *Physics* 5 and 6, Aristotle assumes that the temporal parts of a *kinēsis* are themselves *kinēseis* in their own right, each with its own end.[16] There is no suggestion here that the parts are in any way derivative from the whole. Instead, as we have seen, a single *kinēsis* counts as a unity just in virtue of explanatorily prior facts about the relations between the *kinēseis* that are its temporal parts. Given these views, it is not surprising that Aristotle assumes that if a *kinēsis* has contrary properties at different times, then this must be just because one temporal part of it has one of these properties and another part has the other property. This, I suggest, explains Aristotle's claim, in *Physics* 5.2, that a *kinēsis* cannot itself be the subject of a change.

This view of the relation between a *kinēsis* and its temporal parts also bears on the question of whether a *kinēsis* has modal depth. If the features of a *kinēsis* are derived from features of its temporal parts, then it is natural to conclude that it necessarily has just the temporal parts that it in fact has. On such a view, it is hard to make sense of the idea that one and the same *kinēsis* could have been interrupted earlier, and hence could have stopped at some point other than the point at which it did in fact stop.

The *Physics* 5–6 account also poses a further difficulty for the notion of interruption. To make sense of a change's being interrupted, we need to be able to allow for the possibility of a changing thing progressing towards a certain goal but failing to reach that goal. On the *Physics* 5–6 account, the moving thing completes infinitely many movements, each with its own end-point. Every point through which it moves is thus a point towards which it was progressing.[17] There is thus no one goal that the moving thing is aiming for, more than any of the others. On such an account, it is hard to see how the 'final goal', the goal the whole change is directed towards, can be picked out as anything other than the goal that is followed by absence of change.[18] If so, then whatever state the changing thing is in when it stops changing will count as the state towards which the change was progressing. This leaves Aristotle with no way of allowing for the possibility that the change was progressing towards some goal that it failed to reach.

I want to claim, though, that there are good reasons for Aristotle to reject an account that has these consequences. First, if a *kinēsis* cannot be the subject of a

---

[16] See, for instance, *Phys.* 6.6, 237a25–8, where Aristotle says that since every change takes time and time is infinitely divisible, in half the time the changing thing will have completed another change, and again in half of this, another, and so on ad infinitum. See also *Phys.* 6.6, 237a33–4, where Aristotle says that when a changing thing moves over a spatially extended path, it changes to (*eis*) each of the infinitely many points at which that path can be divided.

[17] See again *Phys.* 6.6, 237a33–4.   [18] On this, see Waterlow 1982, 135–6 and 145–6.

kinēsis, this makes it difficult to explain acceleration and deceleration.[19] Of course, as we have seen, there is something Aristotle can say in response to this: he can insist that in such cases, some parts of the *kinēsis* are fast and other parts of it are slow. However, it is not clear that he would be able to explain *continuous* acceleration in this way (at least, not unless he was prepared to introduce an actual infinity of parts). Second, there are also good reasons for Aristotle to reject an account that implies that a *kinēsis* lacks modal depth. If a *kinēsis* lacks modal depth, then there will be difficulties in making sense of Aristotle's views on teleology. Aristotle's teleological account of natural developments implies that a *kinēsis* can be a progression towards some definite end: for example, a plant's growth is its progression towards maturity. But it is hard to make sense of this, unless one allows for a distinction between the end-point that is in fact reached by a changing thing and the goal towards which the changing thing was progressing. To allow for this distinction, we need to be able to say that one and the same *kinēsis* might have been interrupted before reaching its goal; the changing thing would still have counted as progressing towards that goal, even if it had not in fact reached it. In what follows, I shall ask whether Aristotle's remarks about *kinēsis* elsewhere in the *Physics* suggest any solution to these difficulties.

3. How Far Does Aristotle Revise This Account of *Kinēsis* Elsewhere in the *Physics*?

In *Physics* 5–6, Aristotle makes two important claims about the way in which a *kinēsis* is related to its parts:

(i) A *kinēsis* has temporal parts, and it persists through time in virtue of one of these occurring after another.

(ii) These parts are changes in their own right, with their own ends, and they are, in an important sense, explanatorily prior to the whole *kinēsis*. In particular, the unity and the regularity of the whole *kinēsis* must be explained in terms of the relations between these parts.

I have argued that these two claims, taken together, yield a view on which a *kinēsis* cannot either have modal depth or be something that itself undergoes change. In this section, I ask whether Aristotle's remarks elsewhere in the *Physics* also commit him to accepting these two claims. I shall argue that, although he consistently maintains (i), his discussion of the unity of *kinēsis* in *Physics* 8 implies a rejection of (ii).

---

[19] Bostock (1991, 205) objects that 'the somewhat astounding claim [in *Phys.* 5] that there is *no* kind of change of change—for example, a change cannot increase or decrease' leads Aristotle to deny any subject-matter to the study of acceleration and deceleration.

Aristotle remains committed, throughout the *Physics*, to the view that a *kinēsis* has temporal parts. He holds that these parts stand in a relation of structural isomorphism both to the parts of the path of that *kinēsis* and also to the parts of the time taken by the *kinēsis*. This point is clear, for instance, in his discussion of time (4.11, 219a10–14), where the continuity of time is derived from that of *kinēsis* and the continuity of *kinēsis* is derived from the continuity of magnitude.[20]

Moreover, his account of the infinite in *Physics* 3 implies that the way in which a *kinēsis* continues through time is fundamentally different from the way in which a substance continues through time. When he wants to explain the sense in which the infinite 'is', he draws a distinction between the way in which a substance has being and the way in which a contest or a day has being. A day or a contest has being in virtue of 'always another and another coming to be' (τῷ ἀεὶ ἄλλο καὶ ἄλλο γίγνεσθαι, 206a22). As Aristotle puts it a little later, the being (εἶναι) of such things is not like that of a substance that has come to be (οὐχ ὡς οὐσία τις γέγονεν, 206a32). Instead, they have their being 'always in generation or destruction, limited, but always different and different' (ἀεὶ ἐν γενέσει ἢ φθορᾷ, πεπερασμένον, ἀλλ᾽ ἀεί γε ἕτερον καὶ ἕτερον, 206a32–3). I take it that the point here is that a contest or a day is not present all at once, in the way that a statue is. Rather, it has its being in the successive being of one part after another.[21] A contest is a kind of *kinēsis* (and, as Cooper points out, although a day is not itself a *kinēsis*, Aristotle holds that the being of a day depends on the *kinēsis* of the sun).[22] Aristotle's remarks here seem, then, to imply that the being of a *kinēsis* is a kind of successive being: its parts are not all present at once.

This impression is confirmed by Aristotle's closing remarks about the infinite. Aristotle holds that the possibility of there being an infinite *kinēsis* rests on the fact that the parts of a *kinēsis* do not persist. As he says, 'time and *kinēsis* are infinite…since the thing that is taken does not remain' (ὁ δὲ χρόνος καὶ ἡ κίνησις ἄπειρά ἐστι…οὐχ ὑπομένοντος τοῦ λαμβανομένου, 3.8, 208a20–1). It is just because time and *kinēsis* have their being in becoming that time or *kinēsis* can be infinite in extent. By contrast, a spatial magnitude cannot be infinite in extent, because its parts are all present at once (as, for instance, the spatial parts of a statue are all present at once).

In these discussions, then, Aristotle continues to accept claim (i): a *kinēsis* has temporal parts and these parts cannot all be present at once while the *kinēsis* is going on. What about claim (ii), the claim about the explanatory priority of these parts? In *Physics* 8, Aristotle defends a view that implies the rejection of this claim. He argues that a *kinēsis* is, in a sense to be explained, prior to its parts.

---

[20] I take it that he is making essentially the same point at *Phys.* 3.7, 207b21–5, where he says that a movement is called infinite in virtue of the magnitude the moving thing covers, and that the time (of the movement) is called infinite because of the movement. Given his view that no spatial magnitude is infinite in extent, 'infinite' here must mean 'infinitely divisible'.

[21] For interpretations of this, see Coope 2012 and Cooper 2016.   [22] Cooper 2016, 198.

In *Physics* 8.8, Aristotle argues that no single, continuous *kinēsis* can have parts that are themselves *kinēseis*. Any proper part of a *kinēsis* must have the same end as the whole *kinēsis*. Since it does not have its own end, such a part cannot itself be a *kinēsis*.[23] This argument forms a crucial part of his defence of the claim that the only possible single, eternal *kinēsis* is a circular movement. If a single *kinēsis* cannot be made up of sub-*kinēseis*, then there could not be a single eternal back-and-forth change, alternating between a change towards one contrary and a change towards the opposite contrary (and similarly, there could not be a single eternal back-and-forth movement along a straight line, from A to B to A to B...).[24]

Moreover, this argument provides Aristotle with a new response to Zeno's dichotomy puzzle: the puzzle arising from the claim that, in order to complete any movement, the moving thing would need first to have completed infinitely many other movements (a movement over half the distance, a movement over quarter of the distance, and so on). In *Physics* 6.2, 233a21–31, Aristotle's response was to say that this poses no threat to the possibility of movement, since time and movement are subject to the same divisions. In completing any one movement, a moving thing must indeed complete infinitely many others, but this infinite task can be accomplished in a finite amount of time, since a finite amount of time itself has infinitely many subdivisions, each corresponding to one of the movements to be completed. In *Physics* 8.8, 263a11–23, Aristotle argues that this solution is inadequate. The puzzle raised by Zeno's dichotomy is not merely a puzzle about how infinitely many movements could be completed *in a finite period of time*, it is a puzzle about how an infinite series could ever be completed *at all*.

In *Physics* 8.8, Aristotle claims that when the moving thing moves continuously from A to B, it does not complete movements from A to *any* of the points along the path from A to B. The only way in which the moving thing could complete a movement to some mid-point M (on the path from A to B) would be by

---

[23] Rosen (2015, 214) argues that in *Phys.* 8.8 Aristotle allows that the proper parts of a *kinēsis* can be *kinēseis* provided that they are 'the same in kind' as the whole *kinēsis*. However, I think Aristotle's account of *kinēsis* rules out the possibility of there being a *kinēsis* that has no end (*telos*) of its own. Rosen bases his view on 264a5–6, where Aristotle clarifies his claim that a *kinēsis* must be preceded by a period of rest, with the words 'I mean those [*kinēseis*] that are different in kind, and not if something is a part of the whole' (λέγω δ'ὅσαι ἕτεραι τῷ εἴδει, καὶ μὴ εἴ τι μόριόν ἐστιν τῆς ὅλης). But these lines don't *commit* Aristotle to the view that a part of the whole *kinēsis* is itself a *kinēsis*. He is ruling out a possible misunderstanding of his view. He warns us not to argue as follows: (i) a *kinēsis* is preceded by rest; (ii) any part of a *kinēsis* is itself a *kinēsis*; so (iii) any part of a *kinēsis* is preceded by rest. Rosen takes Aristotle to be accepting (ii) and introducing a restriction on (i): the claim that a *kinēsis* must be preceded by rest only applies to a subset of *kinēseis*: namely, those that are not parts of (and the same in kind as) some longer continuous *kinēsis*. But an alternative would be to take Aristotle simply to be clarifying what he means here by '*kinēsis*': in speaking of '*kinēseis*' here, I'm referring to those items that are different in kind, not to items that are parts of a longer *kinēsis*. This would leave it open whether or not he himself accepts claim (ii), the claim that the items that are parts of some longer *kinēsis* are themselves *kinēseis*.

[24] For discussion of this argument, see Cohoe 2018.

356   URSULA COOPE

coming to a halt at M. But if the moving thing were to do that, it would not move continuously from A to B, but instead would complete two movements, separated by a period of rest: first a movement from A to the mid-point M and then (after a period of rest) another movement from M to B. If the moving thing does not stop at M, then M cannot function as the end of one movement and the start of another (262a22–5; 262b5–6). If the moving thing moves continuously, without stopping at M, then the point M is merely a potential division in the movement: it is a point at which the movement could be divided, but it is not itself the end of any sub-movement.

This implies that the parts of a continuous *kinēsis* have a derivative ontological status.[25] They are not *kinēseis* in their own right with their own ends. Instead, they are definitionally posterior to the whole *kinēsis* of which they are parts. The first half of a single, continuous movement to B can only be defined in terms of its relation to the whole movement towards B. The 'whole movement' is the movement that would occur in the absence of interruption. Its parts are 'definitionally posterior' in the sense that they are defined in terms of their contribution to the progress of that movement.

A single *kinēsis* is defined in terms of the goal the moving thing is progressing towards. At any time when the *kinēsis* is occurring, the moving thing is progressing towards that same goal.[26] As Aristotle says, 'for everything that is moving continuously, if it is not interrupted by anything, it was being carried also earlier to that to which it went by locomotion, for example if it went to B, it was also being carried to B, and not just when it was near, but immediately when it began to be moved. For why now rather than earlier?' (ἅπαν γὰρ τὸ κινούμενον συνεχῶς, ἂν ὑπὸ μηδενὸς ἐκκρούηται, εἰς ὅπερ ἦλθεν κατὰ τὴν φοράν, εἰς τοῦτο καὶ ἐφέρετο πρότερον, οἷον εἰ ἐπὶ τὸ Β ἦλθε, καὶ ἐφέρετο ἐπὶ τὸ Β, καὶ οὐχ ὅτε πλησίον ἦν, ἀλλ' εὐθὺς ὡς ἤρξατο κινεῖσθαι· τί γὰρ μᾶλλον νῦν ἢ πρότερον, 264a9–13). As we have seen, Aristotle claims that any mid-points in such a movement are merely potential divisions in the movement, and that a division that is merely potential cannot function as the end of one sub-movement and the beginning of another. This implies that, during the movement, the moving thing is not moving towards any

---

[25] See Rosen 2021 and Coope 2012 and 2005, 10–13 for different answers to the question of whether Aristotle allows that there can be an infinite plurality of entities that have this derivative status. What matters for my argument here, however, is a point on which Rosen and I agree: *whatever temporal parts there are* within a continuous change must be (in the sense described) definitionally posterior to the whole change (where the 'whole change' is the change that would occur, if there were no interruption).

[26] Certain examples of human action raise difficulties for this view. I might start off on the way to visit a friend, and then change my mind and decide, since I'm close to the shops, to buy some milk instead. How many processes are there in a case of this kind? Since there is a spatiotemporally continuous stretch of walking, it is tempting to say that there is one process of walking that changes from being *a walk to visit a friend* to being *a walk to the shops*. It is not clear how Aristotle can make sense of this, given what he says in *Phys.* 8.8. I'm grateful to an anonymous OUP reader for raising this difficulty.

such intermediate ends. What the moving thing is doing during the first half of its movement is *moving towards the end-point B*, and not *moving towards some mid-point M*. This is true even if the movement is interrupted and so the moving thing never in fact ends up at B. As Aristotle makes clear in the above passage, the end-point that the moving thing is progressing towards is the end-point it will eventually reach *if not interrupted* (ἂν ὑπὸ μηδενὸς ἐκκρούηται, 264a10).

4. Dependent Parts, Modal Depth, and Subjecthood

What does this account imply about whether a *kinēsis* has modal depth or about whether a *kinēsis* can itself be the subject of a *kinēsis*? I shall first argue that the account given in *Physics* 8, unlike that in *Physics* 5–6, allows for the possibility that a *kinēsis* has modal depth. I shall then ask whether this account also allows for the possibility of a *kinēsis* being the subject of a change.

It is quite clear that Aristotle himself holds that a finite *kinēsis* is the kind of thing that might or might not be interrupted. As we saw above, in specifying the end-point of a *kinēsis* he says that it is the point the moving thing will reach if not interrupted (264a10). In that sense, then, he holds that a finite *kinēsis* has modal depth: a finite *kinēsis* that is interrupted is such that it might have gone on for longer and have reached its goal; a finite *kinēsis* that is not interrupted is such that it might have been interrupted, and so might have stopped earlier and failed to reach its goal. Our question, though, is not whether Aristotle is committed to this view, but rather whether he is entitled to this view, given his overall account of *kinēsis* in *Physics* 3–4 and 8. If a *kinēsis* is something whose temporal parts are not all present at once and is in that respect *not* like a persisting substance, can it also be the kind of entity that might have lasted for more or less time than it in fact did?

If the identity of a *kinēsis* simply depended on its having just the temporal parts it in fact had, then a *kinēsis* would not be the kind of thing that might or might not be interrupted before it was over. The *kinēsis* that resulted from interruption would be a different *kinēsis* from the one that would have occurred had there been no interruption. However, as we have seen, Aristotle's arguments in *Physics* 8.8 imply that a *kinēsis* is, in an important sense, prior to its temporal parts. Although these temporal parts are not 'all present together' and so the being of the *kinēsis* depends upon 'another and another' part coming to be, these parts are themselves definitionally dependent on the *kinēsis* as a whole: they are essentially parts of an ongoing process towards some final end. If a movement towards B is interrupted at an intermediate point M, the movement that has occurred is not a movement towards M, but rather a half-movement towards B. The moving thing, in such a case, was never travelling towards M, but rather towards the end-point B. Although the *movement towards B* cannot exist as a whole at any moment (given that it has temporal parts), what the moving thing is doing at any moment of this movement is *moving towards B*, not moving towards some intermediate point M. This allows for an account on which the identity of a *kinēsis* does not depend on its having the temporal parts it in fact has. If the moving thing had been interrupted before reaching B, the movement that would then have occurred would still have been defined in terms of the end-point B. It would have been an interrupted *kinēsis towards B*, not some other *kinēsis* towards an intermediate endpoint. Thus, the *kinēsis* towards B is such that *it*—that very *kinēsis*—either could have been interrupted and hence have stopped earlier, or (if it *was* interrupted) could have gone on for longer and stopped at B. To say this just is to say that the *kinēsis* has modal depth.

I have argued that Aristotle's account of *kinēsis* in *Physics* 8 allows a *kinēsis* to have modal depth. On this account, a finite *kinēsis* is the kind of entity that could have been interrupted, and hence could have lasted for less time than it in fact did.[27] Can this account also allow for the possibility that a *kinēsis* might itself be the subject of a *kinēsis*? This is less obvious. Aristotle himself never indicates an intention to revise his claim in *Categories* 5 and *Physics* 5.2 that a *kinēsis* cannot be a subject of change.[28]

However, I want to suggest that (whether or not he himself recognized this), the account he presents in *Physics* 8 at least removes one obstacle to maintaining that a *kinēsis* can be the subject of a *kinēsis*. If a *kinēsis* is prior to its temporal parts (in the sense explained above), there is no longer the same reason for insisting that what is true of the *kinēsis* at different times must be true in virtue of facts about the temporal parts of that *kinēsis*. Thus, there is no longer the same reason for insisting that if the *kinēsis* is first quick and then slow, this must be solely in virtue of the fact that one part of it is quick and another part of it is slow. Even if it is true to say that the first part of the *kinēsis* is quick and the second part slow, this truth might itself depend upon facts about the *whole developing kinēsis*. For instance, if the movement towards B is quick at t_1 and slow at t_2 (and hence the earlier temporal parts of this movement are quicker than the later ones), this could be because at both t_1 and t_2 the moving thing is engaged in doing the same thing, *moving towards B*, and it is doing this first quickly and then slowly. What is *going on* at each of these times cannot be understood without reference to the progress of the *kinēsis* as a whole: progress towards the end that will eventually be reached, if there is no interruption.

---

[27] An eternal *kinēsis* cannot be interrupted, but that is just because there is nothing that could interfere with it.

[28] Bostock (1991, 205) argues that the view that a *kinēsis* cannot be a subject of change conflicts with Aristotle's claim in *Phys.* 4 that 'change is ... the subject of which time is predicated'. Although (as I have said) I agree that Aristotle has good reason to revise his *Phys.* 5.2 view about the subjecthood of *kinēsis*, I don't agree that Aristotle's remarks in *Phys.* 4 about the relation between time and change themselves provide such a reason. That's because I don't take him to be saying, in *Phys.* 4.10–14, that change is a subject of which time is predicated. See Coope 2005, esp. 31 n. 1, 42–3.

This doesn't, of course, quite settle the matter. In *Physics* 3.1, Aristotle defines a *kinēsis* as 'the fulfilment of what is potentially, *qua* such' (201a10–11). 'What is potentially' here is the subject that is changing (e.g., the bronze that is becoming a statue). If Aristotle were to allow that a *kinēsis* could itself be the subject of a *kinēsis*, he would have to be prepared to describe a *kinēsis* as 'what is potentially'. Depending on our interpretation of *Physics* 3.1, he would need to describe deceleration either as 'the fulfilment of what is potentially slow, *qua* such' or as 'the fulfilment of what is potentially decelerating, *qua* such',[29] where 'what is potentially slow/decelerating' picks out the underlying *kinēsis* that goes from being quick to slow. Aristotle never indicates a willingness to describe deceleration in this way. Whether or not it even makes sense to do so is a difficult question that depends partly on how exactly this *Physics* 3.1 definition is to be understood. What I have tried to show in this chapter is that the question is not settled either by the fact that Aristotle denies the subjecthood of *kinēsis* in *Physics* 5 and in the *Categories* or by the fact that he consistently regards a *kinēsis* as having temporal parts. If a *kinēsis* is definitionally prior to its temporal parts, then this opens up the possibility that the *kinēsis* itself could be subject to change.

Conclusion

If the interpretation I have sketched is right, then the account of *kinēsis* in *Physics* 8 differs importantly from that in *Physics* 5–6. Moreover, there is reason to regard the *Physics* 8 account as an improvement: it allows Aristotle to make sense of the idea that a *kinēsis* is the kind of entity that can be interrupted, and also opens up the possibility that a *kinēsis* might be the kind of entity that (non-derivatively) has incompatible properties at different times. On this account, a *kinēsis* is in important ways both different from and similar to an enduring substance. It differs from an enduring substance in that it has temporal parts: it has its 'being in generation' (206a32–3) and is always 'other and other' (219b9–10). It is like an enduring substance in that it has modal depth (it could have lasted for less time than it did), and also in that it is the kind of entity that can (non-derivatively) have incompatible properties at different times (it can go from being slower to being quicker).[30]

---

[29] The first suggestion follows the interpretation of Kosman 1969, Waterlow 1982, and Coope 2009. The second follows the suggestion developed by Heinaman 1994 and Charles 1984.

[30] It is thus very close to the account of process defended by Steward (2013, 807). She argues that processes are 'entities which are potentially rather robust with respect to their temporal parts—they can be conceived of as the very same tokens even shorn of many of their actual constituent temporal parts, and hence as existing in possible worlds where they are interrupted and do not run to completion. But they still do have temporal parts: they are perdurants not endurants.'

Of course, to show that the *Physics* 8 account really is an improvement, one would need to argue that there can, in fact, be an entity that combines these features. This is beyond what I attempt to do in this chapter. Instead, I have argued that we can find, in Aristotle's *Physics*, two views of the ontology of *kinēsis*, and that these two views differ in a philosophically interesting way. They differ in the account they give of the relation between a *kinēsis* and its temporal parts. Because of this, they suggest different answers to the question of whether a *kinēsis* is the kind of entity that has modal depth, and I have argued that they may perhaps also suggest different answers to the question of whether a *kinēsis* is the kind of entity that could itself be a subject of change.

Works Cited

Bostock, David. 1991. 'Aristotle on Continuity in *Physics* VI', in *Aristotle's* Physics: *A Collection of Essays* (ed. L. Judson). Clarendon Press, 179–212. (Reprinted in David Bostock, *Space, Time, Matter, and Form: Essays on Aristotle's* Physics. Oxford University Press (2006), 158–88.)

Charles, David. 1984. *Aristotle's Philosophy of Action*. Duckworth.

Charles, David. 2015. 'Aristotle's Processes', in Leunissen 2015, 186–205.

Charles, David. 2017. 'Aristotle on Agency', in *The Oxford Handbook of Topics in Philosophy*. Online edition, Oxford Academic. https://doi.org/10.1093/oxfordhb/9780199935314.013.6

Cohoe, Caleb. 2018. 'Why Continuous Motions Cannot Be Composed of Submotions: Aristotle on Change, Rest, and Actual and Potential Middles', *Apeiron* 51 (1), 37–71.

Coope, Ursula. 2005. *Time for Aristotle:* Physics *IV.10–14*. Clarendon Press.

Coope, Ursula. 2009. 'Change and Its Relation to Potentiality and Actuality', in *A Companion to Aristotle* (ed. G. Anagnostopoulos). Wiley-Blackwell, 277–91.

Coope, Ursula. 2012. 'Aristotle on the Infinite', in *Oxford Handbook of Aristotle* (ed. C. Shields). Oxford University Press, 267–86.

Cooper, John M. 2016. 'Aristotelian Infinites', *Oxford Studies in Ancient Philosophy* 51, 161–206.

Heinaman, Robert. 1994. 'Is Aristotle's Definition of Change Circular?', *Apeiron* 27, 25–37.

Kosman, L. A. 1969. 'Aristotle's Definition of Motion', *Phronesis* 14, 40–62.

Leunissen, Mariska (ed.). 2015. *Aristotle's* Physics: *A Critical Guide*. Cambridge University Press.

Lewis, David. 1986. *On the Plurality of Worlds*. Blackwell.

Rosen, Jacob. 2015. '*Physics* V–VI versus VIII: Unity of Change and Disunity in the *Physics*', in Leunissen 2015, 206–24.

Rosen, Jacob. 2021. 'Aristotle's Actual Infinities', *Oxford Studies in Ancient Philosophy* 59, 133–85.

Steward, Helen. 2013. 'Processes, Continuants, and Individuals', *Mind* 122, 781–812.

Steward, Helen. 2015. 'What Is a Continuant?', *Aristotelian Society Supplementary Volume* 89, 109–23.

Waterlow (Broadie), Sarah. 1982. *Nature, Change, and Agency in Aristotle's* Physics: *A Philosophical Study*. Clarendon Press.

16

Why Is Space Discontinuous?

De Lineis Insecabilibus 968b5–22

Vassilis Karasmanis

A metaphysical problem raised in antiquity was that of the continuity of space, and, following the order of Aristotle's discussion in the *Physics* (219a10–13), of motion and time.[1] *De Lineis Insecabilibus*, a short pseudo-Aristotelian treatise, was written to refute the theory of 'indivisible lines' in which lines (and therefore space) are not continuous magnitudes but constituted from small discrete line-atoms. The work starts with the exposition of five arguments presented by supporters of this theory and continues with their refutation, thereby refuting the whole theory. The treatise was probably written by one of Aristotle's immediate followers. Aristotle, in his *Physics* (206a17), refers to some people who hold this theory, saying that 'it is not difficult to refute the theory of indivisible lines'. Therefore, it seems probable—as Heath suggests (1949, 255)—that Aristotle assigned this task to one of his students.

We do not have clear evidence about the identity of this student of Aristotle's. Some people believe that the author could be Theophrastus or Strato,[2] the two immediate successors of Aristotle in the Lyceum, but this remains conjectural. The fact that the author was a follower of Aristotle is evident from the text. In his refutation of the second argument, he denies the existence of 'separate' Forms. His explanation of Zeno's argument is Aristotelian in spirit, and his conception of motion at 970bff. reflects Aristotelian theses about motion and the continuous, as set out in *Physics* 6.2. Further, it seems that his objections to the theory of indivisible lines at 969a19–35 rely on Aristotle's *De Caelo* 299a5–6.[3]

A first question about the theory of indivisible lines is who its proponents are. It is certain that the author does not refer to Democritus but to some contemporary or contemporaries of his own. Unlike Democritus, the advocates of the theory of indivisible lines held that not only matter[4] but also space, geometrical entities, time, and

---

[1] A first version of this chapter was published in Greek, in *ΝΕΥΣΙΣ* 17 (2008), 80–93.

[2] See Joachim 1908, introduction. Recently John Dillon (2003, 113) supported the case of Theophrastus.

[3] For this topic, see Timpanaro Cardini 1970, 28–9.

[4] That the atomism of Democritus is not geometrical, see Furley 1987, 128–30, Baldes 1978, 1–12, Taylor 1999, 183–4, Timpanaro Cardini 1970, 11–15.

Vassilis Karasmanis, *Why Is Space Discontinuous?* De Lineis Insecabilibus *968b5–22* In: *Aristotelian Metaphysics: Essays in Honour of David Charles*. Edited by: David Bronstein, Thomas Kjeller Johansen, and Michail Peramatzis, Oxford University Press. © Oxford University Press 2024. DOI: 10.1093/oso/9780198908678.003.0016

WHY IS SPACE DISCONTINUOUS?   363

motion are discontinuous. Modern scholars believe the advocates of this theory were Xenocrates (the second successor of Plato in the Academy) and his followers.[5]

As we have said, the author of the treatise opens with five arguments advanced by the supporters of indivisible lines and then tries to refute them. The first is a general argument that refers to quantities of any kind. The second refers to Platonic Forms, the third to the discontinuity of matter, and the fourth to the discontinuity of physical space, time, and motion. The fifth argument, which I shall examine here, aims to prove that geometrical objects (lines and planes) are not continuous but constituted from small indivisible parts, thereby undermining the whole science of geometry. This argument is the most interesting, ingenious, and difficult to refute. In my view, this argument was misunderstood not only by our treatise's Aristotelian author but also by modern scholars.

The text of the treatise is problematic and corrupt in many places, especially in the exposition of the fifth argument. The medieval scribe of codex Urbinas 44 (W^a) writes in the margin: 'very wrong original text; let no one accuse me; I write what I see'.[6] My first task is to establish which text is to be preferred and how it should be translated. Second, I shall examine the logical formulation of the argument, which ends with a paradox. I shall try to show its importance and consider plausible ways to escape the paradox on the basis of the Aristotelian theory of the infinite and the continuous. In my discussion of the text, I shall mainly follow, with some changes, the new edition of Harlfinger,[7] as well as the reading of Timpanaro Cardini.

***

[968b5] Ἔτι καὶ ἐξ ὧν αὐτοὶ οἱ ἐν τοῖς μαθήμασι
λέγουσιν, εἴη ἄν τις ἄτομος γραμμή, ὡς φασίν, εἰ σύμμε-
τροί εἰσιν αἱ τῷ αὐτῷ μέτρῳ μετρούμεναι· ὅσαι δ' εἰσὶ σύμμετροι, πᾶσαί εἰσι μετρούμεναι. Εἴη γὰρ ἄν τι μῆκος, ᾧ
πᾶσαι μετρηθήσονται. Τοῦτο δ' ἀνάγκη ἀδιαίρετον εἶναι. Εἰ

[b10] γὰρ διαιρετόν, καὶ τὰ μέρη μέτρου τινὸς ἔσται. Σύμμετρα
γὰρ τῷ ὅλῳ. ὥστε μέρους τινὸς εἶναι διπλασίαν τὴν ἡμί-
σειαν <γραμμήν>· ἐπεὶ δὲ τοῦτ' ἀδύνατον, <ἀδιαίρετον> ἄν εἴη μέτρον.
ὡσαύτως δὲ καὶ αἱ μετρούμεναι ἅπαξ ὑπ' αὐτοῦ, ὥσπερ
πᾶσαι αἱ ἐκ τοῦ μέτρου σύνθετοι γραμμαί, ἐξ ἀμερῶν σύγ-

---

[5] See Timpanaro Cardini 1970, 17–19, Krämer 1971, Exkurs: *Die 'Physik' des Xenokrates*, Isnardi Parente 1979, 193–4, Dillon 2003, 113. In his comments on the first book of Euclid's *Elements* (Friedlein 1873, 279) and referring to proposition 10 (finding the mid-point of a segment), Proclus says that 'one could use this problem to refute the doctrine of Xenocrates that posits indivisible lines'. Indeed, if geometrical space is composed of quanta, it is not certain whether a segment can be divided into two equal parts—a problem for the foundations of geometry. This is also a main point against the theory of 'indivisible lines' raised by our treatise's author.

[6] See Timpanaro Cardini 1970, 19.

[7] Harlfinger 1971. The first modern edition of the treatise was by Bekker (1831), followed by the edition of Apelt (1888), who took note of Hayduck's remarks (see Timpanaro Cardini 1970, 19–20).

364 VASSILIS KARASMANIS

[b15] κεινται. Τὸ δ' αὐτὸ συμβήσεται κἂν τοῖς ἐπιπέδοις· πάντα
γὰρ τὰ ἀπὸ τῶν ῥητῶν γραμμῶν σύμμετρα ἀλλήλοις, ὥστε
ἔσται τὸ μέτρον αὐτῶν ἀμερές. ἀλλὰ μὴν εἴ τι τμηθήσεται
μέτρον τινὰ τεταγμένην καὶ ὡρισμένην γραμμήν, οὐκ ἔσται
οὔτε ῥητὴ οὔτ' ἄλογος οὔτε τῶν ἄλλων οὐδεμία, ὧν δὴ νῦν

[b20] εἴρηται, οἷον ἀποτομὴ <ἢ ἡ> ἐκ δυοῖν ὀνομάτοιν· ἀλλὰ
καθ' αὑτὰς μὲν οὐδέ τινας ἕξουσι φύσεις, πρὸς ἀλλήλας δὲ
ἔσονται ῥηταί καὶ ἄλογοι.

(b5) Again, according to what is said by those engaged in mathematics, there must be some indivisible line, as they say, if commensurable <lines> are those that are measured by the same unit of measurement.

(b7) Those that are commensurable are all measured <by a common measure>. This is because there must be some length by which they are all measured. And this <length> necessarily is indivisible.

(b10) For, if it were divisible, the parts of some unit of measurement would also be so [i.e., measured by a common unit of measurement].[8] This is because they will be commensurable to the whole. Thus the half <line> of some part will be double [of the part]. And because this is impossible, the unit of measurement must be indivisible.

(b13) Again, just as the lines that are compounded of the unit, so also the lines that the unit measures once, will consist of units without parts.

(b15) And the same thing will be true in the case of plane <figures>. For all made of rational lines are commensurable with each other, so that their unit of measurement will also be without parts.

(b17) But if <it were possible> that some such a unit be dissected along any prescribed and determinate line, that <line> will be neither rational nor irrational, nor any of the others of which have now (or recently) been said [i.e., by mathematicians], such as the 'apotome' or the 'of two terms'. But in themselves they [the lines at which the unit might be divided] will have no nature of their own at all; though they will be rational and irrational in relation to each other.

***

I shall offer some comments on the text and the translation.

1. To whom does the phrase ὡς φασίν in line b6 refer and what do they say? Those who 'say' must be either mathematicians or followers of the theory of

---

[8] I use angular brackets for material I take to be implied by the text and square brackets for my explanations of the text.

WHY IS SPACE DISCONTINUOUS? 365

indivisible lines. If what they say is 'there are indivisible lines', they cannot be ordinary mathematicians, since the latter do not support this theory but rather that of the continuum of lines.[9] So, Timpanaro Cardini (1970, 51) holds that they are the followers of the theory of indivisible lines and that what they say is described in this passage's argument. While this reading is possible, I do not find it compelling. The text implies that those who $\phi a\sigma i\nu$ must be the same as those who 'speak in the mathematical sciences' ($\dot{\epsilon}\nu$ $\tau o\hat{\iota}s$ $\mu a\theta\dot{\eta}\mu a\sigma\iota$ $\lambda\dot{\epsilon}\gamma o\upsilon\sigma\iota\nu$) because it is unlikely that there is an abrupt change of subject without explicitly naming the new subject. Further, what immediately follows is a definition of commensurable lines as formulated by mathematicians. In my view, in the phrase '$\dot{\omega}s$ $\phi a\sigma i\nu$' what is 'said' is the definition of commensurable lines and those who 'say' it are mathematicians. But the essence of the argument does not depend on this issue.

2. At b7–8 codices (except N) write: '$\ddot{o}\sigma a\iota$ δ' $\epsilon\dot{\iota}\sigma\dot{\iota}$ $\sigma\dot{\upsilon}\mu\mu\epsilon\tau\rho o\iota$, $\pi\hat{a}\sigma a\dot{\iota}$ $\epsilon\dot{\iota}\sigma\iota$ $\mu\epsilon\tau\rho o\dot{\upsilon}\mu\epsilon\nu a\iota$. Bekker and Joachim (in his translation) follow this reading. However, this leads to a repetition of the definition of commensurable lines of the previous sentence. Because of this difficulty, Apelt, Cardini, Krämer, and Harlfinger follow codex N which writes '$\ddot{o}\sigma a\iota$ δ' $\epsilon\dot{\iota}\sigma\dot{\iota}$ $\mu\epsilon\tau\rho o\dot{\upsilon}\mu\epsilon\nu a\iota$, $\pi\hat{a}\sigma a\dot{\iota}$ $\epsilon\dot{\iota}\sigma\iota$ $\sigma\dot{\upsilon}\mu\mu\epsilon\tau\rho o\iota$, which is the converse of the definition. However, this proposition does not seem to be used as a premise in the argument, as opposed to the proposition found in all codices except N. We should, in my view, keep the reading of the majority of the codices for the following reasons. First, this proposition is not identical with the definition of commensurable lines in the previous line. The point is that within a broader class of lines, the lines that are commensurable are measured. While this proposition is directly derived from the definition, it is not identical with it. Second, to infer the conclusion 'there must be some length by which they are all measured' (b8–9), we need the reading of the codices rather than its converse. The reason why the same sentence seems to be repeated within two lines of text is the following: in lines b6–7 ($\epsilon\ddot{\iota}\eta\ldots\mu\epsilon\tau\rho o\dot{\upsilon}\mu\epsilon\nu a\iota$), we have the enunciation[10] of the problem, which consists of what is given (the definition of commensurable lines) and the demonstrandum. At this point the proof begins: its first premise is our proposition. This explains why the same proposition is repeated.

3. At b11 the text is corrupt and codices disagree. As we see from the apparatus criticus of Harlfinger's edition, the word '$\delta\iota\pi\lambda a\sigma i a\nu$' is also written as '$\delta\iota\pi\lambda a\sigma i a$' and '$\delta\iota\pi\lambda\dot{a}\sigma\iota o\nu$'. Codex W[a] writes '$\epsilon\hat{\iota}\nu a\iota$' instead of '$\epsilon\ddot{\iota}\eta$' and codex Z[a] writes '$\tau\hat{\eta}s$

---

[9] Hett (1936, 419) accepts that the mathematicians are the proponents of the argument. He translates: 'The next argument, as we are told, is used by the mathematicians to prove that the indivisible line must exist.'

[10] According to Proclus (*In Eucl.* 203.16–18, 5–7 (Friedlein)), 'the most essential parts of a problem or a theorem, and those which are always present, are enunciation, proof, and conclusion;... of these the enunciation ($\pi\rho\dot{o}\tau a\sigma\iota s$) states what is given and what is being sought from it, for a perfect enunciation consists of both these parts.'

366 VASSILIS KARASMANIS

$\dot{\eta}\mu\acute{\iota}\sigma\upsilon\sigma$' instead of '$\tau\dot{\eta}\nu$ $\dot{\eta}\mu\acute{\iota}\sigma\epsilon\iota\alpha\nu$'. Further, it has been proposed that, instead of '$\mu\acute{\epsilon}\rho\sigma\upsilon\varsigma$' we should read '$\mu\acute{\epsilon}\tau\rho\sigma\upsilon$' or '$\mu\acute{\epsilon}\tau\rho\sigma\nu$' or '$\mu\epsilon\tau\rho\epsilon\hat{\iota}\nu$' and introduce '$\ddot{\alpha}\nu$' before '$\epsilon\ddot{\iota}\eta$'. Indeed, many readings have been proposed. Joachim[11] reads '$\ddot{\omega}\sigma\tau\epsilon$ $\mu\acute{\epsilon}\rho\sigma\upsilon\varsigma$ $\tau\iota\nu\dot{\sigma}\varsigma$ <$\ddot{\alpha}\nu$> $\epsilon\ddot{\iota}\eta$ $\delta\iota\pi\lambda\alpha\sigma\acute{\iota}\omega\nu$, $\tau\hat{\eta}\varsigma$ $\dot{\eta}\mu\iota\sigma\epsilon\acute{\iota}\alpha\varsigma$' and translates 'the unit of measurement would turn out to be twice one of its parts, viz. twice its half'. But in this way, as he himself admits, '$\tau\hat{\eta}\varsigma$ $\dot{\eta}\mu\iota\sigma\epsilon\acute{\iota}\alpha\varsigma$' does not add anything to the meaning, since it is only explanatory of '$\mu\acute{\epsilon}\rho\sigma\upsilon\varsigma$ $\tau\iota\nu\dot{\sigma}\varsigma$'. Further, in this view, there is nothing absurd. We are simply told that if the measure is something that cannot be seen as a multiple, it cannot be divided. The reading of Timpanaro Cardini, Harlfinger, and Hett[12] ($\ddot{\omega}\sigma\tau\epsilon$ $\mu\acute{\epsilon}\rho\sigma\upsilon\varsigma$ $\tau\iota\nu\dot{\sigma}\varsigma$ $\epsilon\ddot{\iota}\eta$ $\delta\iota\pi\lambda\alpha\sigma\acute{\iota}\alpha\nu$ $\tau\dot{\eta}\nu$ $\dot{\eta}\mu\acute{\iota}\sigma\epsilon\iota\alpha\nu$) seems to be plausible because it reveals the absurdity with which the argument concludes and is closer to the codices. However, the problem for this reading is that the '$\epsilon\ddot{\iota}\eta$' needs a subject in the nominative not the accusative. Further, Hett (1936, 419) and Timpanaro Cardini (1970, 51) offer different translations of the text they both accept. Hett translates 'so that the measurement of each part would be double its half' and Timpanaro Cardini 'so that half of some measure would be equivalent to its double'. Both authors have as subject of the proposition the word '$\mu\acute{\epsilon}\tau\rho\sigma\nu$' (measure), which does not occur in the text but, in their view, is implied. However, according to their translations, the words '$\delta\iota\pi\lambda\alpha\sigma\acute{\iota}\alpha\nu$' and '$\dot{\eta}\mu\acute{\iota}\sigma\epsilon\iota\alpha\nu$' should be in the neuter not feminine, because they refer to '$\mu\acute{\epsilon}\tau\rho\sigma\nu$'. But no codices contain such a reading.

With these problems in mind, I propose the following reconstruction of the text: '$\ddot{\omega}\sigma\tau\epsilon$ $\mu\acute{\epsilon}\rho\sigma\upsilon\varsigma$ $\tau\iota\nu\dot{\sigma}\varsigma$ $\epsilon\hat{\iota}\nu\alpha\iota$ $\delta\iota\pi\lambda\alpha\sigma\acute{\iota}\alpha\nu$ $\tau\dot{\eta}\nu$ $\dot{\eta}\mu\acute{\iota}\sigma\epsilon\iota\alpha\nu$ <$\gamma\rho\alpha\mu\mu\acute{\eta}\nu$>'. On this reading we should translate 'thus the half <line> of some part will be double (of the part)'. That is, one half of some part (which is the measure, because the measure measures all the commensurable lines, hence it is a part) will be a multiple (double) of it. At the same time, because the part is part of the measure, the measure will be a multiple of the part. So the measure is both a multiple and a sub-multiple (half and double) of the part—which is absurd. In this way, we reach a paradoxical result.[13]

4. In lines b19–20 codices have '$\ddot{\omega}\nu$ $\delta\dot{\eta}$ $\nu\hat{\upsilon}\nu$ $\epsilon\ddot{\iota}\rho\eta\tau\alpha\iota$' (N writes '$\nu\hat{\upsilon}\nu$ $\delta\dot{\eta}$'). This reading, which Bekker keeps, seems at first sight to be meaningless. No other line has been mentioned so far apart from rational ($\dot{\rho}\eta\tau\dot{\eta}$) or irrational ($\ddot{\alpha}\lambda\sigma\gamma\sigma\varsigma$). Apelt[14] proposed the correction '$\ddot{\omega}\nu$ $\delta\upsilon\nu\acute{\alpha}\mu\epsilon\iota\varsigma$ $\dot{\rho}\eta\tau\alpha\acute{\iota}$', which most subsequent editors and scholars accept. This reading not only makes sense but is also directly related to the '*apotome*' and the '*of two terms*', two kinds of incommensurable line.

---

[11] See comment and translation at 968b11.

[12] Bekker follows the same reading with the difference that he prefers '$\delta\iota\pi\lambda\alpha\sigma\acute{\iota}\alpha$' instead of '$\delta\iota\pi\lambda\alpha\sigma\acute{\iota}\alpha\nu$'.

[13] At b12 Hayduck adds the word '$\dot{\alpha}\delta\iota\alpha\acute{\iota}\rho\epsilon\tau\sigma\nu$', which Hett, Timpanaro Cardini, and Harlfinger accept. With the addition of this word the conclusion becomes simpler and more direct. But even without this addition we can reach the same result, translating the conclusion as follows: 'there should be <such a> measure', i.e., an indivisible line (compare b6, $\epsilon\ddot{\iota}\eta$ $\ddot{\alpha}\nu$ $\tau\iota\varsigma$ $\ddot{\alpha}\tau\sigma\mu\sigma\varsigma$ $\gamma\rho\alpha\mu\mu\acute{\eta}$).

[14] See Joachim 1908, comment on lines b19–21.

WHY IS SPACE DISCONTINUOUS? 367

However, there is a serious problem with this reading, which Apelt himself did not see and which has remained largely unnoticed.[15] According to Euclid, the '*apotome*' and the '*of two terms*' (or *binomial*—διώνυμος) are not incommensurable lines of which the squares are commensurable, but are irrationals (ἄλογοι).[16] Hett, who follows Apelt's reading translates as follows: 'will neither be rational nor irrational, nor will belong to any of the categories to which rational functions[17] belong as "apotome" or "of two terms"' (1936, 421). According to Apelt, and all who follow his reading, we have three kinds of line: the rational, the irrational, and those that have rational squares, examples of which are the 'apotome' and the 'of two terms' (or binomial). But, as just pointed out, the 'apotome' and the 'of two terms' are not lines that have rational squares, but are irrationals. Further, this reading makes the supporter of the indivisible lines (or at least his Aristotelian rival) ignorant of the mathematical terminology of the theory of incommensurables current in his time. Apelt takes the word 'ῥητή' to mean 'σύμμετρος' (commensurable) and the expression 'δυνάμει ῥητή' (which does not occur in Euclid) to mean 'δυνάμει σύμμετρος'. For these reasons, Apelt's emendation should not be accepted. Timpanaro Cardini (1970, 79) refers to Hirsch and Schramm who observed that the 'apotome' and the 'of two terms' are irrational lines and, on this ground, rejected Apelt's emendation.[18] Nevertheless, she keeps Apelt's reading, adding the words 'αἱ σύνθετοι'. According to her reading, a 'δυνάμει ῥητή' line is not an 'apotome' or an 'of two terms', but the parts of this line are an 'apotome' or an 'of two terms'. However, the codices offer no evidence for her addition. Nor does her reading overcome the disadvantage of making the author's terminology different from that of Euclid. Hirsch[19] accepted the correction of Wilamowitz, 'ὧν νῦν διήρηνται', which, however, is not convincing: it presupposes a taxonomy of lines which did not exist in ancient mathematics.

I propose that we keep the reading of the codices 'ὧν δὴ νῦν εἴρηται', provided that the 'εἴρηται' is not taken to refer to things that have already been said by the

[15] Joachim (1908, comment on lines b19–21) expresses some reservations, but because he does not have any alternative proposal, he accepts Apelt's reading.

[16] Euclid, *Elements* X, propositions 36 and 73. According to Euclid's terminology (*Elements* X, def. 2), straight lines that are commensurable in square (δυνάμει σύμμετροι) are the incommensurable lines of which the squares are commensurable (e.g., square roots, in modern terminology). Lines that are commensurable and commensurable in square are called 'rational' (ῥηταί). Incommensurable lines that are not rational are called 'irrational' (ἄλογοι—see def. X, 3). A great part of book X of the *Elements* deals with lines that are commensurable in square. Binomial lines are defined in proposition X 36 as follows: 'if two rational straight lines, commensurable in square only, be added together, the whole is irrational and is called binomial'. Apotome is defined in proposition X 73: 'if from a rational straight line there be subtracted a rational straight line, commensurable with the whole in square only, the remainder is irrational; and let it be called an apotome'. Therefore, both binomial and apotome are special cases of irrational lines, each with its own special name.

[17] The term 'rational function' is unfortunate. Hett presumably means 'commensurable squares'.

[18] Heath (1949, 256) also makes this observation.

[19] See Timpanaro Cardini 1970, 80. Schramm (see Timpanaro Cardini 1970, 80) changes 'δυνάμεις' of Apelt to 'δυνάμει'. But this does not solve any problem.

368   VASSILIS KARASMANIS

author, but to the kinds of line of which the mathematicians just referred to spoke, especially since the theory of incommensurables—and, indeed, even more complex kinds of incommensurable line such as 'apotome' and 'of two terms'—were a novelty in Aristotle's time. So, I translate: 'of which have now (or recently) been said [i.e., by mathematicians]'. This reading and translation make sense. For, according to the mathematicians, straight lines are either rational ($\dot{\rho}\eta\tau\alpha\acute{\iota}$) or irrational ($\ddot{\alpha}\lambda o\gamma o\iota$; see above, n. 16). Rational lines include commensurable lines, which can be measured, and lines that are commensurable in square ($\delta\upsilon\nu\acute{\alpha}\mu\epsilon\iota$ $\sigma\acute{\upsilon}\mu\mu\epsilon\tau\rho o\iota$): while the latter are incommensurable, their squares are commensurable. Irrational lines are not measured, whether as lines or as squares. However, there are two specific cases of irrational lines which we can treat in certain ways, because they are the sum or difference of two rational lines that are only commensurable in square. Each of these cases of lines has its own special name: 'apotome' and 'of two terms'. So understood, the defender of 'indivisible lines', as presented by our author, will say that the line in which the measure will be divided would be neither rational nor irrational nor any of these specific cases of irrationals, which have their own names (i.e., 'apotome' and 'of two terms') and have been discovered recently by mathematicians. In this reading and translation, the codices can be retained and the text becomes intelligible. Further, so understood, the defender of 'indivisible lines', who advances the argument, uses the terms '$\dot{\rho}\eta\tau\dot{\eta}$' and '$\ddot{\alpha}\lambda o\gamma o s$' with their proper mathematical meaning.

***

We can conclude, on this basis, that the proponents of 'indivisible lines' were well acquainted with the mathematics of their time. Their definition of commensurable lines is the same as that of Euclid.[20] In the third argument, which refers to planes, they rightly speak of commensurable planes that are made of rational (b16), not commensurable, lines. As in Euclid, the word '$\dot{\alpha}\pi\acute{o}$' (b16) governs the genitive to denote the plane (square) that is formed from a straight line. Also, they rightly say at b19 '$o\ddot{\upsilon}\tau\epsilon$ $\dot{\rho}\eta\tau\dot{\eta}$ $o\ddot{\upsilon}\tau'$ $\ddot{\alpha}\lambda o\gamma o s$' and not '$o\ddot{\upsilon}\tau\epsilon$ $\sigma\acute{\upsilon}\mu\mu\epsilon\tau\rho o s$ $o\ddot{\upsilon}\tau'$ $\ddot{\alpha}\lambda o\gamma o s$': for commensurable planes (squares) are constructed from rational lines, while incommensurable planes are constructed from irrational lines. As we have seen, the terms 'apotomē' and 'of two terms' are technical mathematical terms in Euclid. Moreover, the overall structure of the argument follows the model of a mathematical demonstration. The advocate of the theory of indivisible lines starts with the enunciation of the problem, stating what is given and what ought to be demonstrated (b6–9). We then have a demonstration in the form of a *reductio ad absurdum* (b9–12), and finally we get the conclusion (b12). After the end of this

---

[20] See *Elements X* def. 1: '$\Sigma\acute{\upsilon}\mu\mu\epsilon\tau\rho\alpha$ $\mu\epsilon\gamma\acute{\epsilon}\theta\eta$ $\lambda\acute{\epsilon}\gamma\epsilon\tau\alpha\iota$ $\tau\grave{\alpha}$ $\tau\hat{\wp}$ $\alpha\dot{\upsilon}\tau\hat{\wp}$ $\mu\acute{\epsilon}\tau\rho\wp$ $\mu\epsilon\tau\rho o\acute{\upsilon}\mu\epsilon\nu\alpha$'.

WHY IS SPACE DISCONTINUOUS? 369

argument, two other cases are examined, one for unit lines (b13–15) and one for planes (b15–22).

In his criticism of this argument, the Aristotelian author (969b6–10) claims that it is sophistical because it relies on the hypothesis that all lines are commensurable, something that contradicts the principles of mathematics. He claims (b12–14) that the line of reasoning of the supporters of the 'indivisible lines' is ridiculous, 'since, whilst professing that they are going to demonstrate their thesis in accordance with the opinions of the mathematicians, and by premises drawn from the mathematicians' own statements, they lapse into an argument which is a mere piece of contentious and sophistical dialectic—and a feeble piece of sophistry too' (Joachim's translation). If he intends to suggest that the advocates of the 'indivisible lines' do not know mathematics, the Aristotelian author is wrong. In analysing the argument, I shall argue, against our Aristotelian author and most modern scholars, that it is not based on the uncritical and 'anti-mathematical' assumption that all lines are commensurable.[21] The argument has been misinterpreted: it is more interesting and more difficult to rebut than has been generally recognized.

***

There are three different arguments in our text. The first (968b5–12), which is the most important, aims to prove that there are indivisible lines. The second (b13–15), a direct consequence of the first, says that the unit lines are also indivisible. The third (b15–22) extends the proof to planes and proves that there are indivisible planes.

1. The First Argument (968b5–12)

The first argument starts with the enunciation ($\pi\rho\acute{o}\tau\alpha\sigma\iota\varsigma$) of the problem, divided into what is given and what is sought.

Enunciation (b6–7): If indivisible lines are those that are measured by the same unit of measurement (what is given), there is some indivisible line (what is sought).

Demonstration (b7–12): The demonstration contains two sub-arguments.

---

[21] See Joachim 1908, comment on b8–9, Timpanaro Cardini 1970, 26, 78, Dillon 2003, 114 n. 77, Isnardi Parente 1979, 198–9, Krämer 1971, 354–5. Heath, in his comments on the mathematical passages of this treatise (1949, 255–7), ignores this argument, presumably because he follows the opinion of the Aristotelian author. Both Joachim and Timpanaro Cardini think that the author of the treatise probably does not present correctly the argument of the supporters of 'indivisible lines'. Krämer takes the overall aim of the proponent of the argument (Xenocrates) to be ontological rather than mathematical.

(A)   P1 (b7–8): Commensurable lines are measured <by a common measure>.[22]
      P2: <Let us take the class of all commensurable lines.>[23]

C1(b8–9): There must be some length by which they are all measured.

After showing that there is a common measure for all commensurable lines, the second step is to show that this measure is indivisible (b9). This is the task of the second sub-argument.

(B)   This argument follows the pattern of a *reductio ad absurdum*.
      P3: <Let us take the common measure.>[24]
      P4 (b9–10): (Assume, for *reductio*, that) the common measure is bisected.
      P5 (b10–11): The parts (e.g., the halves) of the measure will be commensurate with the whole measure.[25]

C2 (b10): The parts of the measure are measured (by the measure).[26]

C3: <The measure of all commensurable lines measures also its parts.>

C4 (b11–12): Therefore, the half of a part is double of it.[27]
But this is impossible[28] (b12), therefore:
C5 (b12): The (common) measure is indivisible.

As already said, the Aristotelian author considers the argument to be sophistical because it posits—unlike mathematical science—that all lines are commensurable and therefore there is no incommensurability.[29] However, as we have seen

---

[22] P1 is a direct conclusion from the definition of commensurate lines, which is the given in the enunciation. It says that if we have a multitude of lines, the ones that are commensurate have a common unit of measurement.

[23] P2 is not explicit in the text. It is a simple implicit premise necessary to draw the conclusion. It is important to note that from P1 and P2 we cannot conclude that the Platonic supporter of the indivisible lines accepts that all lines are commensurate. Simply, from a broad class of lines, he takes only those that are commensurable among them. Obviously, there are other lines incommensurable to them.

[24] We could formulate premises P2 and P3 as follows: 'X is the class of all commensurable lines' and 'Y is the common measure', but since the argument is mathematical, I opt for mathematical formulations.

[25] Therefore, they also belong to the class of commensurable lines.

[26] That is, since the parts belong to the class of commensurable lines, they are also measured by the common unit of measurement.

[27] Since the part (of the unit of measurement) is measured by the unit of measurement, it will be the double of the unit of measurement.

[28] Because conclusion C4 is self-contradictory. In this sense, we have arrived at a paradox.

[29] Of course, the conclusion of the argument—that there are indivisible lines—contradicts the principle of continuity in geometry. Proclus (*In Eucl.* 277.25–278.12 (Friedlein)) says that some people considered that proposition I 10 of the *Elements* ('to bisect a given segment') 'assumes in advance as a hypothesis that a line does not consist of indivisible parts' and so secures the continuity and infinite

WHY IS SPACE DISCONTINUOUS? 371

from the formulation of the argument, this is not the case. The argument does not posit a priori that all lines are commensurable but simply takes the class of all commensurate lines (see n. 20). The text does not say 'all lines are commensurable and therefore measured' but only that 'those that are commensurable are measured'. So it does not rule out the existence of incommensurable lines.[30] Moreover, the argument does not even assume a single indivisible measure of all lines. The demonstrandum is that 'there will be some indivisible line' (b6), not that 'there will be one and only one'. There may well be other indivisible lines incommensurable with that of the argument. Let us examine this point more cautiously.

The process of taking a class of commensurable straight lines is, according to Euclid's definition X, 3, to take a straight line ($\tau\hat{\eta}$ $\pi\rho o\tau\epsilon\theta\epsilon\iota\sigma\eta$ $\epsilon\vartheta\theta\epsilon\iota\alpha$) and call it commensurate or rational. It is in relation to this line that we will call all other lines commensurable, rational, or irrational. So if, for example, we take all the lines that are commensurate with a square's diagonal, they will be incommensurable with the square's sides, just as the square's diagonal is. Hence, by the same argument, they will have a common measure that will be incommensurable with the previous common measure. In this way we can have many classes of lines, where the lines belonging to the same class are commensurate with each other, but the lines of different classes are incommensurable. If, according to this argument, each such class of lines has an indivisible (atomic) measure, it is possible to have several indivisible lines incommensurable with each other. Consistently with this, we may say that all lines are always commensurate with some others. Commensurability is not a property but a relation. So, the diagonal, d, of a square is incommensurable with the side, a, but commensurable with its double $2d$. Hence, the argument seems to be more interesting than the Aristotelian author thinks.[31]

---

divisibility of lines. Indeed, proposition I 10 does not prove the existence of the mid-point (something that is presupposed) but finds it. In Euclid, continuity is not secured by some axiom. Perhaps the first postulate ('from any point to any point we can draw a straight line') may play the role of an axiom of continuity together with the definition of a point. But if a point is what is indivisible or 'what does not have parts' (*Elements* def. I, 1), then we have two possibilities: (A) The point is indivisible and without magnitude. (B) The point is indivisible, having magnitude, and, therefore, is identical with an indivisible line. But I think that this latter case is ruled out by definition I, 3 (the extremities of a line are points) together with the definition of line (I, 2) as 'breadthless length'. A 'point' that has magnitude is not a point but a line. A point is an extremity (or a dissection) of a line that does not have magnitude. It seems then that the first three definitions of the *Elements*, together with the first postulate, secure geometrical continuity.

[30] I formulated the above interpretation of the argument in early 1995, when we discussed *On Indivisible Lines* in my graduate seminar. In August 1998, I presented this analysis of the argument in a conference on Ancient Mathematics, organized by David Fowler in France. Later on, I realized that Michael White (1992, 225–30) had proposed a similar interpretation.

[31] As we said, the writer of the treatise has misunderstood the argument, saying that it presupposes that all lines are commensurable (969b6–10). In his examination of the argument, the author adds that 'it is contradictory that every line becomes commensurable and that there is a common measure of all commensurable lines' (969b10–12). This statement is rather odd. I find Joachim's explanation

372 VASSILIS KARASMANIS

2. The Second Argument (968b13–15)

The second argument (968b13–15) is a direct consequence of the first and may well be omitted. What the Platonic defender of 'indivisible lines' tells us is that as all lines constituted from the measure consist of indivisibles, so too will the lines be counted only once by the measure (i.e., the measure itself). The fact that the measure is indivisible (or atomic) has been proven in the previous argument. His point is that if all the commensurate lines of the previous argument are of the form $k\,n$ (where k is a natural number and n the atomic measure), then $1n\,(=n)$ is an atom.

3. The Third Argument (968b15–22)

The third argument extends the previous argument from lines to planes (from one dimension to two). It is divided into two somewhat independent shorter arguments.

The first (b15–17) runs as follows: if we take all the squares formed by rational lines, then all of them will be commensurable and therefore, by exactly the same reasoning as in the previous argument, they will have a common measure, which will be indivisible. The comments we made on the first argument apply to this one too. But it is worth making two further observations. First, the Platonic defender of indivisible lines rightly says 'τὰ ἀπὸ τῶν ῥητῶν γραμμῶν' (b16) and not 'τὰ ἀπὸ τῶν συμμέτρων γραμμῶν' because, as we have seen (n. 16 b), the squares of rational incommensurable lines are commensurable. Here too we can see that he has good knowledge of his contemporary mathematics. Second, in this passage he does not take all the planes to be commensurable, only those that are formed from rational lines (and are, therefore, commensurable). This corroborates our interpretation of the first argument, but also our thesis that the Aristotelian author misunderstood the argument as saying that all lines are commensurable and have one single, unique measure.

The second short argument (b17–22) is far more difficult to interpret. It follows the method of *reductio ad absurdum* and says the following: Let us suppose that we can divide the common plane-measure 'along any prescribed and determinate

---

(comment on the passage, see also Timpanaro Cardini 1970, 85) the most satisfactory and in the spirit of our author. That is, if all lines are commensurable in a weak sense (i.e., commensurable with some others), this does not mean that *all* lines are commensurable in a strong sense (i.e., that all lines are commensurable with each other). In this way, if the advocate of 'indivisible lines' maintains that (a) all lines are commensurable in a weak sense and (b) there is a single and unique common measure of all of them, then he is inconsistent. For if (a) is true, (b) is false. If, on the other hand, 'commensurable' is used in a strong sense, then (b) is true but it contradicts the principles of geometry.

WHY IS SPACE DISCONTINUOUS? 373

line'.[32] The resulting line will be neither rational nor irrational, nor any other, such as the *apotome*. Moreover, lines of this sort (i.e., segments of the measure) do not have their own nature: 'there will be both rational and irrational among them'. The argument is elliptical since apart from the assumption that it is possible to divide the measure, all the other premises are missing.[33] Is it possible to find the premises that lead to such strong conclusions? I will suggest an interpretation that fits the bill.

The argument ends with three conclusions: (1) The line that divides the measure will be neither rational nor irrational nor of any other kind. (2) Lines of this sort will not have any nature of their own. (3) These lines will be between them both rational and irrational. The distinction made in (1) is exhaustive. Each geometric line should belong to one of these groups. There is no geometric line that is neither rational nor irrational nor anything else. Such a 'line' will not be a line in the geometric sense. Conclusion (3) is equally paradoxical. Given a line of a certain sort, any other line is either rational or irrational with respect to it. No line can be both. Conclusion (2) tells us that these lines do not have their own nature. This may mean either that these lines do not have their own properties or that they do not have the nature of geometrical lines. But either way we reach the same conclusion. Lines that do not have their own nature are not geometrical in nature.

If conclusion (2) follows validly, then obviously conclusions (1) and (3) also follow validly. So the basic conclusion is (2) and has to do with the nature of the line. But premises referring to the nature of a line should invoke the definition of a line. It is likely, therefore, that the missing premise is a definition of a line. The definition of a line given by Euclid (I, 2) as 'breadthless length' does not seem to help in this particular case. But there is another, older definition that considers the line as a 'limit of a plane'.[34] It is likely that the Platonic advocate of the argument had in mind this Platonic definition of the line. Based on this definition, the line that is supposed to intersect the measure (square) is not a 'limit of a plane' since the minimum plane is the measure and is therefore not a geometrical line. Therefore, this line does not have a geometrical nature or the properties of geometrical lines. In this way, all the other paradoxical conclusions follow.

***

---

[32] In the case of planes, we can consider the measure as one very small square.

[33] Joachim (1908, comment on the passage) recognizes that the argument follows the method of *reductio ad absurdum*, but his interpretation is not clear as it simply paraphrases the point made in the text. He claims that the line in which the measure is to be divided is not a geometrical line and therefore, by its nature, does not have any quality. However, this position is not explained. I find the interpretation of Timpanaro Cardini (1970, 80) incomprehensible. She talks about the measure as if it were a line rather than a square and thinks the line will have relative but not absolute qualities. But she gives no explanation of how she arrives at these conclusions. White (1992) and Krämer (1971) do not deal with this argument at all.

[34] See Aristotle *Top.* 141b5–15, *Cat.* 5a2–6, *Met.* 1060b14–17. This definition seems to belong to the Platonic tradition, as we see from its similarity to Plato's definition of shape in the *Meno* (76a). For these definitions, see Karasmanis 1990, 128–9 and n. 33.

374 VASSILIS KARASMANIS

4. Assessment of the Arguments

The first argument is the most important, while the first part of the third argument follows the same reasoning as the first argument. It is worth examining the first argument in more detail. First, it is by no means certain that ancient mathematicians accepted infinite collections of things like 'the class of all commensurable lines'. In cases where they speak of infinity, they usually conceive it as a process in which in a series (or plurality) of numbers, sizes, shapes, etc. it is always possible to find a smaller or larger one, etc. For example, in *Elements* X, 3, Euclid finds the greatest common measure of two commensurable lines; in proposition X, 4, he extends his finding across three magnitudes; finally, in the conclusion of X, 4, he writes: 'in the same way we will receive the greatest common measures of more magnitudes'. Euclid claims that 'for any number of commensurable magnitudes we can find the greatest common measure'. He does not say whether there is a greatest common measure in an infinite set of magnitudes or whether it can be found. However, if we leave this reservation on one side and accept, like the author of our argument, that it is possible to have infinite collections of lines, we can see commensurability in two ways: either as a binary relation between magnitudes, resembling the relation of equality or similarity,[35] or as a property of a set of magnitudes. If we see commensurability as a binary relation, then given the infinite set of all commensurable lines $(X_1, X_2, \ldots X_i, \ldots)$, for each pair X_i, X_j we will always have a common measure (1). But this is not to say that for all the pairs X_i, X_j there will be one and the same common measure (2).[36] But it is the latter proposition (2) that is needed for the argument. This is not a consequence of (1). Although P1 holds for a finite number of magnitudes, we cannot say that it holds for an infinite multitude. Therefore, it is not certain that we have a common measure and, hence, conclusion C1 is not validly drawn.

However, it may be that the proponent of the argument, as well as Euclid, accepted commensurability not as a binary relation but as a property of a collection of lines. Indeed, the definition of commensurable lines at the beginning of the argument does not speak of pairs but of a collection of lines. Similarly, Euclid

---

[35] The relation of commensurability, as well as those of equality and similarity, is reflexive, symmetrical, and transitive.

[36] White (1992, 228) formulates the same problem as follows: Let [x] be the equivalence class of all commensurable lines with X. Then,

> (1) For all magnitudes Y and Z ϵ [X], there is a magnitude W ϵ [X] such that Y and Z are each integral multiples of W.

The argument requires the following claim:

> (2) There is a magnitude W ϵ [X] such that, for all magnitudes Y and Z ϵ [X], Y and Z are integral multiples of W.

But (1) does not imply (2), as our argument suggests. Such an implication, says White, causes the logical error of the illegitimate quantifier-shift.

WHY IS SPACE DISCONTINUOUS? 375

in definition X, 1 of commensurable magnitudes does not refer to pairs, but accepts commensurability as applying to a collection of magnitudes.[37] Therefore, if we accept (a) that we can have infinite sets of lines and (b) that commensurability is a property of a set of lines, premise P1 will be true and the reasoning leading to conclusion C1 will be valid.

We have seen that the supporter of 'indivisible lines' thinks that the paradox to which his argument leads is due to the continuum hypothesis and so concludes that we have to accept indivisible lines. On the other hand, if we accept the discontinuity of space, the whole science of geometry—at least as we know it—collapses. For, as we already mentioned above (n. 5), allowing 'indivisible lines' entails that there will be many cases in which it will be impossible to find the middle point of a line or to have two lines intersect at any point. But is there any way for an Aristotelian (such as our author) to respond to the argument just presented and refute the theory of indivisible lines? Such a refutation is possible even though our author does not attempt it. First, he could argue that, according to the Aristotelian theory of infinity, infinity is only potential and never actual.[38] In this way he would directly deny premise P2 which claims that it is possible actually to have at our disposal an infinite collection of lines. Perhaps, such a refutation of the argument is implied by Aristotle when he says that 'it has been stated that magnitude is not in actual operation infinite; but it is infinite in division—it is not hard to refute indivisible lines—so that it remains for the infinite to be potentially' (*Phys.* 206a16–19). Further, even if the Aristotelian author allowed his opponent to have infinite collections, he could refute the argument as follows. Let's say that we actually have the set of all the incommensurable lines and let these lines have a common measure. We can easily find the common measure of two commensurable lines (*Elements*, prop. X, 3). Similarly, we can find the greatest common measure of three lines (X, 4) or as many as we wish (corollary of X, 4). But if our lines are infinite, the process of finding the common measure will be infinite and endless.[39] So, even if we accept the infinite set of commensurable lines and the existence of a common measure of them, the common measure can never be found. Therefore, premise P3[40] is false, the argument collapses, and the principle of continuity is preserved. Thus, following the Aristotelian discussion of the infinite

---

[37] But in def. X, 3, Euclid calls straight lines commensurable, incommensurable, rational, and irrational with respect to 'an assigned straight line'.

[38] See *Phys.* 204a20–2: 'besides, it is manifest that is not possible for the infinite to exist as something in actual operation and as a substance and principle' (translation from Hussey 1983). Aristotle examines the infinite in *Phys.* 3.4–7, esp. ch. 6.

[39] According to Aristotle, the infinite is only potential and obtains as a process without end; see *Phys.* 206a27–9: 'in general, the infinite is in virtue of one thing's constantly being taken after another—each thing taken is finite, but it is always one followed by another' (translation from Hussey 1983).

[40] 'Suppose we have the common measure.' This does not occur in the text, but is implied in P4 (b9–10).

376 VASSILIS KARASMANIS

as we find it in *Physics* 3.6, we can easily refute the argument of the proponent of indivisible lines. In this way, we can not only save geometry from great problems but also accept all kinds of continuous magnitudes (such as time, motion, etc.).[41]

Works Cited

Baldes, Richard W. 1978. '"Divisibility" and "Division" in Democritus', *Apeiron* 12, 1–12.

Dillon, John. 2003. *The Heirs of Plato: A Study of the Old Academy (347–274 BC)*. Oxford University Press.

Friedlein, Gottfried. 1873. *Procli Diadochi In Primum Euclidis Elementorum Librum Commentarii*. Lipsiae.

Furley, David. 1987. *The Greek Cosmologists*: Volume 1, *The Formation of the Atomic Theory and Its Early Critics*. Cambridge University Press.

Harlfinger, D. 1971. *Die Textgeschichte der Pseudo-Aristotelischen Schrift ΠΕΡΙ ΑΤΟΜΩΝ ΓΡΑΜΜΩΝ*. Hakkert.

Heath, Thomas. 1949. *Mathematics in Aristotle*. Oxford University Press.

Hett, W. S. 1936. *Aristotle, Minor Works*. Loeb Classical Library. Harvard University Press.

Hussey, Edward. 1983. *Aristotle* Physics *Books III and IV. Translated with Introduction and Notes*. Clarendon Aristotle Series. Clarendon Press.

Isnardi Parente, Margherita. 1979. *Studi sul Academia Platonica Antica*. Olschki.

Joachim, Harold H. 1908. *De Lineis Insecabilibus*. Oxford University Press.

Karasmanis, Vassilis. 1990. 'The Hypotheses of Mathematics in Plato's *Republic* and His Contribution to the Axiomatization of Geometry', in *Greek Studies in the Philosophy and History of Science* (ed. P. Nicolacopoulos). Kluwer, 121–36.

Krämer, Hans Joachim. 1971. *Platonismus und Hellenistische Philosophie*. De Gruyter.

Taylor, C. C. W. 1999. 'The Atomists', in *The Cambridge Companion to Early Greek Philosophy* (ed. A. A. Long). Cambridge University Press, 181–204.

Timpanaro Cardini, Maria. 1970. *Pseudo-Aristotele: De lineis insecabilibus*. Instituto Editoriale Cisalpino.

White, Michael. 1992. *The Continuous and the Discrete*. Oxford University Press.

---

[41] I very much thank David Charles, Michail Peramatzis, and Pantazis Tselemanis for their useful comments on the chapter.

Index Locorum

ALEXANDER OF APHRODISIAS / PSEUDO-
    ALEXANDER OF APHRODISIAS
On Aristotle's Metaphysics
  162.6–10 42
  435.5–14 36
  542.12–543.26 31
  554.2–5 36, 38
  554.22–33 34
  555.6–10 42
  561.33 33

ANTISTHENES
  14.8 38 (Caizzi)
  53.8 38 (Prince)

ARISTOTLE
Categories
  1 1a6–9 202
  2 1a20 144
     1a24–9 122, 124, 126, 141, 146, 148,
       207, 209, 212
     1b1–9 120, 129, 148, 202
  3 1b10–15 148
  4 1b25–7 144
  5 2a14–16 164
     2a19–b6 123, 132, 146, 148, 160,
       165, 204
     2a34–b6 [A, Ch. 6] 127
     2a27–34 [T1, Ch. 7] 146, 149, 158
     2a19–27 [T2, Ch. 7] 146, 155, 156
     2b7–22 132, 203
     2b29–3a6 204
     2b37–3a6 [T3, Ch. 7] 156
     2b29–34 [T5, Ch. 7] 165
     3a12ff. 124
     3a16 151
     3a17–21 146, 148
     3b10–13 120, 165, 203
     3b10–18 [B, Ch. 6] 129–30
     4a10–22 [F, Ch. 6] 129, 140; 204, 348
     4b10–14 348
  6 5a2–6 373
  7 6b28–30 122
     7a24 333
     8b13–15 122
  8 9b19–33 159

     10a3ff. 150
     10a27–b11 150
     10b19 144
     10b21 144
  10 11b24–32 333
     11b38–12a17 [T4, Ch.7] 160, 161
     12a41 159
  11 14a7–9 131
     14a16–19 148
     14a23–5 163
De Interpretatione
  7 17a38–b1 221
     17a39–b1 [C, Ch. 6] 130
  12 22a14–31 168
Prior Analytics
  1.1 24b19–20 194
  1.4 26a2 18
  1.13 32a21–8 168
  1.23 41a11–13 194
     41a21ff. 324
  1.28 44b38–45a1 194
  1.44 50a19–28 324
Posterior Analytics
  1.1 71a13 307
  1.2 71b17–25 185, 189
     71b33–72a5 185, 207
  1.3 72b5–15 40, 42, 45
     72b16–18 45
  1.4 73a21–5 169
     73a28–34 169
     73a34–7 169, 208, 209, 210
     73b16–8 170
     73b25–32 169, 170
  1.5 74a25–32 191
  1.6 74b26–32 170
     75a18–37 169, 170
  1.7 75a39–b2 169
     75b10–1 201
  1.8 75b31–2 192
  1.9 76a4–9 169, 201
  1.10 76b3–22 169
  1.11–2 77a5–9 125, 194
     77a10–21 194
     77a22–3 194
  1.13 78a26–38 178
     78a39–b4 178

378 INDEX LOCORUM

ARISTOTLE (*cont.*)
1.28 87a38–9 201
1.31 87b28–88a17 [D (87b28–32),
      Ch.6] 130; 306
2.2 89b38–90a1 170
      90a5–7 170
      90a14–22 171
2.3 90b13 310
2.6 92a27–33 6
2.7 92b5–8 193
      92b14 201
      92b28–30 193
2.8 93a21–9 4, 171, 172, 190
2.10 93b29–32 172, 183, 194, 307
      93b39 192
      94a1–2 192
      94a3 192
      94a6–7 192
      94a7–9 190
2.11 94a20–b26 172, 174, 175, 176,
      183, 193
2.12 95a16–21 176
2.13 96a20–3 [T1, Ch. 1] 4, 8
      96a24–32 [T2, Ch. 1] 10–11, 13,
      14, 18, 26
      96a32–b1 [T3, Ch. 1] 4, 11, 12, 18, 23
      96b6 4, 12
      96b25–35 5, 14, 16
      96b35–97a6 [T4, Ch. 1] 14
      97a14–22 12, 14, 24
      97a23–6 [T5, Ch. 1] 17, 20,
      22, 23, 26
      97a26–8 17
      97a28–34 [T6, Ch. 1] 17–18,
      19, 20, 21
      97a35–7 14
      97a35–b6 24
      97b13–25 6, 193

Topics
1.5 102a1–2 307
1.7 103a19–23 141
      103a25–7 331
      103a29–31 331
1.8 103b12–16 11
1.9 103b35–104a2 307
1.11 104b20–1 36
1.12 105a19 306
1.17 108a7–12 321, 333
2.2 110a4–9 41
4.6 128a20–9 7
5.6 136b33–137a7 333
5.8 138b24 321, 333
6.1 139a26–7 149
6.3 140a27–32 8, 11

6.4 141a24–b25 [T2, Ch. 8] 184–8;
      307, 373
      141b34–142a6 188
      142a7 307
      142a33–b6 323
      142b9 323
6.6 144b12–30 8
6.7 146a33–5 41
6.9 147b12–20 323
6.14 152b10–16 324
7.3 153a7–15 185, 306
7.5 154a31–2 31
      155b3 306

Sophistical Refutations
24 179a26–b7 73, 328, 331
31 181b32–4 214
      181b35–182a6 214; [T7, Ch. 11]
      266, 267
34 183a30 306
      183b10 306

Physics
1.1 184a16–18 185
1.2 185a12–14 310
      185a31–2 206
      185b8 309
      186a2–3 299
1.4 187a18 230
      187a19 230
1.5 189a7 306
1.7 190a1–5 231
      190a9–13 [T4, Ch. 10] 231–2
      190a13–18 [T2, Ch. 10] 229, 231–4
      190a21–31 [T3, Ch.10] 230, 240
      190a33–4 231
      190b1–5 [T5, Ch. 10] 229, 232, 234,
      237, 240
      190b3–10 [T6, Ch. 10] 229, 230,
      234, 237
      190b10–7 [T1, Ch. 10] 228–9,
      232, 240
      190b25 230
      191a7–13 [T7, Ch. 10] 230, 241; 333
      191a21 310
1.8 191b4–10 327
      191b23–7 338
      191b27–9 298
1.9 192a3–6 230
2.1 192a31–2 230
      193a30 318
      193b12 305
2.2 193b30–194a7 [T2, Ch. 11] 253, 258
      194a15–b8 193
      194a35–7 272
2.3 194b16–23 181

INDEX LOCORUM 379

194b23–6 215
194b26 64
194b26–9 181
2.4 194b32–5 272
195a3–8 189, 191
195a32–b21 189, 191, 327, 333
2.5 196b21–9 191, 274, 333
196b33–6 274
197a5–8 191, 274
197a12–15 191
197a32–5 191
2.7 198a21–4 193
198a24–34 174, 191
198b8–9 189
2.8 198b10–6 175
198b21–31 274
199a8 318
199a30–2 189
199b13–26 274
199b31 303
2.9 200a5–10 179, 261
200a14–15 259, 318
200a15–30 179
200a30–2 175, 183
200a32–b9 178, 179; [T6, Ch. 11]
259–61; 274, 318
3.1 200b22–5 320, 321
200b26–7 322
200b28–32 320–3
201a9–b22 258, 304, 313, 321–6,
339, 341, 359
201a36–b5 329, 330, 342
3.2 201b27–202a3 339
202a3–9 305, 326, 330, 341
202a9–12 302, 326, 339
3.3 202a13–14 327
202a15 305
202a15–21 327–8, 331–3, 335–6
202a21–8 329–30, 341, 342
202a31–6 330
202b2–4 330
202b5–22 321, 328–33, 335–7, 340
202b23–9 320, 323, 327, 341
3.5 204a20–2 375
3.6 206a16–19 362, 375
206a22 354
206a27–9 375
206a30–4 346, 354, 359
3.7 207b21–5 354
3.8 208a20–1 354
4.9 217a23 304
4.11 219a10–14 354, 362
219b9–10 346, 359
5.1 224b7 313

224b15 313
224b35–225a7 313
225a34 313, 349
225b7 313
5.4 227b18–228a3 349, 351
228a20–228b11 351
228b15–229a3 350, 352
229a6 350
5.5 229b10–1 349
6.2 233a21–31 355
6.6 237a25–8 352
237a33–4 352
8.1 251a6 310
251b1–3 339
252a12–14 305
8.4 255a28–256a3 339
8.8 262a22–5 356
262b5–6 356
263a11–23 355
264a9–13 356, 357
264a25–6 355

De Caelo
1.9 279a6–11 136
279a15–16 258
3.1 299a5–6 362
4.3 310a24–6 313
311a5 305
311a8–13 339

On Generation and Corruption
1.3 317b23–6 299
319b3–4 3 35
1.4 319b31–320a2 325
1.5 320b12–14 315
320b19 304
1.7 324b13–18 326
1.10 328a27 315
2.9 335b7 318

Meteorology
4.12 389b29–30 183
389b31–390a1 218
390a2–24 133, 183, 218, 219, 263

De Anima
1.1 402b16–403a2 166, 179, 252
403a24–b19 xxiv, 193;
[T1, Ch. 11] 248–54
1.3 407b16 263
1.5 409b15 305
410b11–12 300
2.1 412a5 315
412a8 318
412a9 258
412a9–11 300
412a22–8 300–1, 314–16
412b3 316

380 INDEX LOCORUM

ARISTOTLE (*cont.*)

	412b6 316
	412b9 300
	412b10 316
	412b11 316
	412b15 316
	412b16–17 316
	412b19–22 258
	412b22–6 316, 317
	412b28–413a2 317
	413a6–7 299
	413a9 315
2.2	413a21 315
	413b14 315
	413b15 316
	414a4–5 301
	414a9–14 249, 301
2.4	415a22–b7 272, 280–1
	415b8–15 174, 283, 301, 305
	415b18–20 256
	415b20–1 282
	415b21–2 272
	416a4–6 316
	416a18–21 264
	416b14–18 283
2.5	417a14–16 302, 326
	417a17–18 302, 304
	417a27–b8 301, 303–4
	417b8–9 329
	417b12–13 304
	417b23 310
	417b26 298
2.8	419b35 306
3.4	429a10–18 308
	429b5–9 308
3.6	430a19 308
3.7	431a1 308
	431a4 304
	431a6–7 303, 326

De Sensu

2 438a15–16 265	

History of Animals

5.1	539a20–1 244
5.19	551a13–24 [T8, Ch. 10] 243–4

Parts of Animals

1.1	639a23–30 [E, Ch. 6] 137
	640a22–7 277, 305
	640a31–2 305
	640b4–16 175
	641b8 261
	642a8–14 [T3, Ch. 11] 255, 259
1.3	643b9–16 9
1.4	644a14–24 53

2.1	647a8 304
2.10	656b2 265

Generation of Animals

1.1	715a3–7 174, 309
1.2	716a4–13 233
	716a24–7 233, 255
1.21	729b22 305
2.1	731b19 309
	731b29–732a2 283–4
	732a4 174
	734a30 304
	734a33 318
	734b21 304
	734b24–31 219
	734b34–735a5 277
2.3	737a16 310
2.4	738a33–b4 233
	738b20–7 233
	740b18–25 233
	740b25–741a3 277, 282
5.8	789b2–15 175

De Lineis Insecabilibus

	968b5–22 362–72, 375
	969a19–35 362
	969b6–10 371
	969b10–12 371
	970bff. 362

Metaphysics

A.3	983a26–9 176, 181
	983b4–11 175, 182
A.7	988a21–3 182
	988b16–18 182
A.9	992b14 310
	992b18–20 298, 306
α.2	994b16–23 41, 42
B.1	995a12–13 39
B.2	996a21–b1 183, 193
	996b6–7 305
B.3	998a23–5 186
	998b12 309
	998b22 201
B.5	1002a4–8 183, 186
B.6	1002b33 298
	1003a5–17 203
Γ.1	1003a30 298
Γ.2	1003a33ff 62, 298
	1003b5–7 298
	1003b16–17 298
	1004a25–6 298
	1005a11–14 299
	1005a14 298
Γ.3	1005b2–5 39
	1005b8–19 306

Γ.4	1006a5–9 39			1030a3–6 212
	1006a11–18 195			1030a6–13 31, 212, 220
	1006a28–34 195			1030a25–6 299
	1007a20–33 195			1030a27 306, 310
	1007b25–9 299, 301, 307			1030a27–8 306
Γ.5	1009a32–6 299, 313			1030b5–7 31
Γ.7	1012a12–15 195			1030b23–8 215
Δ.2	1013a24–b2 63, 309			1030b28–1031a1 218
	1013b9–11 45			1031a11–14 31, 212, 309
Δ.3	1014a26–35 36, 183, 186		Z.6	1031a22–3 331
	1014b8–9 183			1031b11–14 212, 219
Δ.4	1014b18 306			1031b23–5 152
Δ.6	1016a4 313			1032a4–6 213
Δ.8–9	1017b10–14 210			1032a6–11 213, 224
	1017b14–16 210		Z.7	1032a14–15 203
	1017b17–21 186, 210			1032a22–5 277, 279
	1017b23–30 145, 211, 331, 336			1032b1–2 8
Δ.11	1018b31–4 306			1032b14 215
	1019a4–7 298			1032b30–1033a5 215
Δ.12	1019b23–30 168, 309		Z.8	1033a24–b19 33, 216
	1020a4 300			1033b24–6 216
Δ.15	1021a14–16 302			1033b32 305
Δ.17	1022a4–9 305			1034a5–8 205
	1022a16–17 212		Z.9	1034b2 305
	1022a25–7 210, 224			1034b8 309
	1022a27–9 208			1034b16–19 305
	1022a29–31 209		Z.10	1035a9–17 186
Δ.23	1023a11–13 173			1035a17–22 219
Δ.28	1024a29–31 284			1035a31–4 219
	1024b8–9 32			1035b13 316
Δ.29	1024b29–1025a1 36–7			1035b14–18 308
Δ.30	1025a30–2 169			1035b15 318
E.1	1025b28–30 306			1035b24–5 218
	1025b30–1026a6 214, 306, 308			1035b25 317
	1026a5–6 214			1035b27–30 216
	1026a16 298			1035b34 221
	1026a29–32 298			1036a1–7 305, 308
E.2	1026a33–b2 202			1036a9–12 183, 186
E.4	1028a2–4 202			1036a14–21 [T4, Ch. 11] 256, 258
Z.1	1028a22–7 206, 209			1036a23–4 217
	1028a30–1 298		Z.11	1036a28–9 221
	1028a33–4 207			1036a29–b7 217–18, 257, 302, 308–9
	1028a34–6 207			1036b7–20 217
	1028a36–b7 202, 210			1036b8–13 183, 186
Z.2	1028b16–18 186			1036b21–32 217–19; [T5, Ch. 11]
	1028b32 210			257–8, 262, 264
Z.3	1029a20–30 203, 205–7, 215			1036b32–1037a5 183, 186
	1029a34 307–8, 318			1037a5–10 213, 216, 318
Z.4	1029b2 307			1037a21–33 216, 218, 220, 306, 309
	1029b3–12 185, 207, 307–8			1037a33–b7 220, 331
	1029b13 211		Z.12	1037b8–9 22
	1029b13–22 212, 307, 309			1037b11 307
Z.5	1029b22–7 335			1037b13–14 310

382 INDEX LOCORUM

ARISTOTLE (*cont.*)
 1037b24 310
 1037b24–7 310
 1037b27–9 22
 1038a5–9 32
 1038a9–35 9, 16, 22
Z.13 1038b3–6 222
 1038b6–8 211
 1038b9–15 221, 223
 1038b15–16 222
 1038b29–30 222
 1039a1–3 203, 221
 1039a3–6 299
 1039a7 303
 1039a17–19 35
Z.14 1039a24–6 33
 1039a26 33
 1039a30–2 33
Z.15 1039b20–7 215
 1039b27–1040a7 190
 1040a2–3 308
 1040a18 33
 1040a27–b4 191, 222
Z.16 1040b23–4 223
 1040b25–6 221
Z.17 1041a6–8 306, 309
 1041a11 223
 1041a15–16 173
 1041a16–20 194, 195
 1041a23 223
 1041a23–6 35
 1041a23–7 173, 215, 224
 1041a27–b9 [T1, Ch. 8]
  172–4, 176, 193; 211, 307, 309
 1041b11–35 xxv, 31–2, 186, 215, 224
H.1 1042a13–21 31, 211
 1042a21–2 211
 1042a22–4 35
 1042a26–31 206, 222, 315, 318
H.2 1042b10 316, 318
 1042b22 310
 1043a4–7 35, 224
 1043a7–12 35
 1043a14–19 224
 1043a24–6 310
 1043a26 310
 1043a26–7 306
H.3 1043b2–4 221, 318
 1043b4–14 31–2, 34, 45
 1043b14–23 33, 215, 243
 1043b23–32 30–1, 33–8, 42–5
 1043b32–1044a11 xxv, 35, 42,
  186, 309
H.4 1044a32–b20 171, 174, 183, 233

H.5 1044b32–4 301
 1044b36 301, 316
H.6 1045a8 310
 1045a12–14 220, 310
 1045a23–5 33
 1045a36–b2 183, 186, 203
 1045b7–16 311
 1045b16–23 311
Θ.1 1045b32–1046a4 298, 303,
  311–2
 1046a5 311
 1046a11 303
 1046a11–13 303
Θ.2 1046b2 303
Θ.3 1047a9–14 312
 1047a20–2 303
 1047a24–6 312
 1047a26–8 303
 1047a29 303
 1047a30–1 312
 1047a32–b2 304, 312
Θ.5 1048a2 311
 1048a20 311
Θ.6 1048a25–8 311, 314
 1048a35–b9 314, 333
 1048b18–35 303, 315, 326, 339,
  340, 348
Θ.7 1048b37 311
 1049a5 304, 305
 1049a8–11 219, 242
Θ.8 1049b13 301, 303
 1049b24 304
 1050a15 262
 1050a17–19 314
 1050a21–3 xxv, 314
 1050a24–8 304
 1050a28 314
 1050b2–3 xxv
 1050b31 311
I.4 1055a11 299
I.8 1057b37–1058a2 32
 1058a23–4 32
K.2 1060b14–17 373
K.7 1064a21 306
Λ.1 1069a25–30 211
Λ.2 1069b18–20 240
Λ.4 1070b5–6 45
 1070b7–8 35
 1070b19–21 241
 1070b28–9 241
Λ.5 1071a33–6 300
Λ.6 1071b23 302
Λ.7 1072a22 305
 1072a34 306

INDEX LOCORUM   383

	1072b3–4 272
Λ.8	1074a31–5 136
	1074a35–6 136
	1074a36–7 136
M.2	1076b16–24 183–4
	1077b4–9 335
M.9	1086a9 305
M.10	1087a18–21 131, 302
N.3	1091a7–8 38
N.5	1092a19–20 139

Nicomachean Ethics
1.6   1096a16–7 227
3.1   1110a6 300
7.3   1147b14 307
10.1 1172b3–8 305
10.4 1174a19–b5 326

Eudemian Ethics
2.1   1219a13 304
2.3   1220b28–30 348

Politics
1.2   1252a26–34 283

DESCARTES
Meditationes de prima philosophia
2nd Meditation 43

DIOGENES LAERTIUS
De vitis
6.3, 1–2 31
6.40, 5–9 3

EUCLID
Elements
I.1 371
I.2 371, 373
I.10 370–1
X.1 368
X.2 367
X.3 367, 371, 374–5
X.4 374–5
X.36 367
X.73 367

HERACLITUS
DK B60 321

HUME
A Treatise of Human Nature
I.4.6 238

LOCKE
An Essay Concerning Human Understanding
II.XXVII.4 233
III. X.28–9 59

PLATO
Cratylus
387a1–9 101
Euthyphro
6d9–e2 173, 181
10e11 181
11a6–b5 173, 181
Meno
72c1–d1 173, 181
75c ff. 323
76a 373
Phaedrus
265c8–266c1 98–9
265e3 101
266a3 100
274c5–275c4 111
Philebus
15d4–6 108
16b5–c3 109
16c5–17a5 102–3
17b3–d3 110–1, 113–15, 117
17d3–6 117
18c7–d2 113
18b6 115
18b6–d2 111
57e6–59d6 115
Sophist
218c 313
219d 313
221a7–c3 104–5
232b 306
235a 313
248b–c 313
251a 147
252a 313
263a 313
263a2–3 38
Statesman
266e4–7 8
Symposium
207d2 281
Theaetetus
153a 313
156a 313
201e1–202b5 35
Timaeus
35b–36d 257
46e 313
48d 313

PORPHYRY
On Aristotle's Categories
113.24 152

384   INDEX LOCORUM

PROCLUS
On Euclid's Elements
277.25–278.12 370

SEXTUS EMPIRICUS
Outlines of Pyrrhonism
2.207 43

SIMPLICIUS
On Aristotle's Categories
37.18–21 152
54.8–21 157
On Aristotle's Physics
392.6–393.14 260
393.3–5 260

THEMISTIUS
On Aristotle's On the Soul
39.15–25 299
On Aristotle's Physics
78.18, 22–3 332

THEOPHRASTUS
Research into Plants
II.1 244
II.1.4 244
II.2.1 244

THOMAS AQUINAS
On Aristotle's Metaphysics
L.IX.I.i 298

General Index

accidental compounds 322, 327
accidental compound theory ('ACT') 322, 335–6, 338–40, 342
Ackrill, J. L. 121–2
actuality, 'at-workness', 'being at-work' (*energeia*) 302, 316–18
agency 270, 273–4, 279, 285–92
Alexander of Aphrodisias 176
analogy 52–5
    road up, road down 321–2, 331, 336–8
Andronicus of Rhodes 158–60
anger 248–50, 260, 265
anti-realism 85, 87, 90, 91–2
Antisthenes
    denial of falsehood 36 (*See also* definition)
Apelt, O. 365, 367
Augustine 82–4, 85–6
Austin, J. L. 62, 120

Barham, J. 289–92
Barlen, K. 37
Binswanger, H. 286, 291–2
Bonitz, H. 36–8
Bostock, D. 38, 177
Burnyeat, M. F. 30, 37, 44

Cajetan, T. 62–3, 66
Cardini, T. 363, 365, 367
Caston, V. 249
causes 8–9, 13, 63–6, 68–9, 166, 170–84, 186–96 (*see also* essence)
    efficient 65, 321, 339
change, motion, movement (*kinēsis*) 175–6, 183, 201, 204, 214, 220, 227–38, 240–4, 253, 258, 262, 303–4, 320–43, 345–60, 362–3
    and potentiality/actuality 320, 323–6
    as *metabolē* 313
    as 'process' 345
    continuant in 201, 235, 242, 347
    subject of 348–51, 358
    temporal parts of 346–7, 350–4, 357–60
Charles, D.
    and Oxford 79–81, 120
    on action 121
    on change (*kinēsis*) as process 345–8
    on craftsmen in Wittgenstein and Aristotle 81–94

on division and definition 5–6
on essence and causation 3, 180–1
on essence and unity 6, 27, 56
on form as enmattered 250–3, 263–8
on scientific inquiry 58
on teleology 270–85, 290–2
on 'what underlies' 227–8, 230–7, 241–4
Christensen, W. 286–9, 291–2
classification 104–9, 115–17, 144–5, 160
    (*see also* division)
completeness (*entelecheia*) 297–301, 311–18
composition 43–5
concept-mastery 87–92
conceptual analysis 51–60
continuity 354, 362–3, 376 (*see also* discontinuity)
craft or expertise (*technē*)/craftsmen 82, 90–3, 105, 109–17
Crivelli, P. 159–62

Darwin, C. 286, 288
Davidson, D. 345
definition 64, 169–74, 184–9, 192–4, 250–3, 256–7, 259–66, 268 (*see also* causes, essence, and *logos*)
    and infinite regress 38–43
    in Aristotle 3–27
    in Antisthenes 29–45
dialectic 99, 102, 143, 321
differentia 5–10, 12–19, 21–7, 23–6, 30, 32–6, 42–5, 133–4, 224, 310 (*see also* division, and species and genera)
discontinuity 363, 375
division 4–5, 7–10 (*see also* classification, definition, differentia and genus/species)
    and entailment 17–21
    'carving nature at the joints' 27, 97, 99–102, 116–17
    exhaustive 14–17
    'Promethean' method in Plato 102–9, subsumptive 22–3
Dummett, M. 85

Eddington, A. 68–9
essence 6–7, 12–13, 21–2, 145–6, 166, 168–96, 207, 209–13, 216, 221, 223–4 (*see also* division, definition, and unity)
    of language 82–3

386 GENERAL INDEX

essentialism 144, 164–6 (*see also* essence and predication)
Euclid 367–8, 371, 373–4
expertise (*see* craft)
explanation 6, 68, 179–81, 194, 276–80, 285

final causation 191, 211, 254–6, 264, 268
(*see also* teleology)
focality 55–6, 62–4, 66–8
form/matter 31–6, 166, 201, 204–6, 211–25
(*see also* causes, composition, and matter)
Frede, M. 121–2, 126, 217, 258
Frege, G. 73

genus/species 5, 7, 18–21, 32–3
generation 227, 230–5, 237, 240, 242, 244–5
geometry 174, 298, 363, 375
goal (*telos*) 313–15, 317–18 (*see also* final causation and teleology)
Gibson, J. 288
Goodman, N. 117
Gotthelf, A. 275–80, 285, 291

Hart, H. 62
Heath, T. 362
Heraclitus 312, 322, 340
homonymy 57–60
Hume, D. 238
Hussey, E. 341–2
hylomorphism 221–4 (*see also* composition and form/matter)
'predicative' 201–2, 213–21

identity
loose and strict 72–6
incommensurability 366–8, 370–2, 375
individuals
non-substance 124, 128, 129–32, 135
inextricability thesis 268
infinity 39–42, 45, 353, 374, 375
instrumentality 254–5 (*see also* final causation)

knowledge 62–3
Kostman, J. 323

language-learning 82–4, 87
Leibniz's Law 50, 73, 192, 239
lines 362–76
indivisible (atomic) 362–5, 367–72, 375–6
Locke, J. 59–60
logos (account) 300–1, 305, 308–10 (*see also* definition)
and *ergon* (work) 310–15, 317–18

magnitudes 187, 354, 362, 374–6
mathematical form 248–53, 258, 264, 266, 268
matter 227–8, 231, 234, 236–8, 241–2, 244
(*see also* form/matter)
meaning 85–6
Menn, S. 33, 157–8
modality 168, 194 (*see also* actuality, completeness, necessity, potentiality)

natural philosophy 201, 215, 248, 320
necessity 168–71, 177–81, 191, 193–4
hypothetical 253–6, 259–64
normativity 270, 286–91

oneness 300, 305–7, 310, 314
organisms 284–92
Owen, G. E. L. 62, 121

Parmenides 240
Pears, D. 81
particular 120–1, 130–1, 137–9 (*see also* individual and universal)
Plato 8, 312
Academy of 43, 131
method of division 132, 211
on classification 97–117
theory of forms 125
'third man' argument 299
potentiality, power (*dunamis*) 227–8, 234, 240, 242–3, 298–304, 311–17
active vs passive 321–2, 334
predication
'being in (a subject)' 121, 124, 128, 146–9, 155–8, 160–4
'said of (a subject)' 123–5, 127–32, 134–5, 140–1, 145–9, 153–66
essential 144, 164–6
per se (*kath' hauto*) 169, 208, 213–14, 222, *see also* definition and essence
presumption 74–6
priority 179, 187, 207, 224
definitional 264
explanatory 354
properties 125–6

Quine, W. v. O. 80, 84

realism 97–8, 115–16

sameness 321–2, 329–38
accidental 334–7
self-maintenance 284, 286
Shields, C. 57, 63–6

Sider, T. 97–8
Simplicius 153, 260, 266
snub 220, 249–50, 253, 265–8
soul 248–9, 256–9, 265, 308–9, 315–18
space 362–3, 375, 376
Stebbing, S. 68–9
Steward, H. 347
Substance (*ousia*) 121, 176, 179, 201–7, 227,
    231, 236, 241–2, 313, 316
  enduring 346–8, 354, 357, 359
  in the *Categories* 123–5, 128–32, 135, 140–1,
    144–6, 148, 153, 164–6
  in the *Metaphysics* 172–3, 209–12, 216–18,
    220–4, 298, 306–10
supervenience 66

teleology 271–84 (*see also* causes, final
    causation, instrumentality)
  and efficient causation 275–9
  and goodness 271–7, 281, 284–90

and the divine 280–2
and the eternal 281, 283–4
Theseus, ship of 74, 239, 243

unity (*see* essence)
  in object of definition 6–7, 9
universal 121, 126, 130–2, 139 (*see also* particular)

vagueness 74–6

Walsh, D. 288–92
Ward, J. 64
'what underlies' (*to hupokeimenon*) 227–36, 240–3
Wiggins, D. 49, 72
Williams, S. G. 181
Wittgenstein, L. 81–8

Xenocrates 363

Zeno of Elea 355, 362